The U.S. Justice System

The U.S. Justice System

WITHDRAWN

AN ENCYCLOPEDIA

VOLUME THREE

Steven Harmon Wilson, Editor

 ABC-CLIO

Santa Barbara, California • Denver, Colorado • Oxford, England

Copyright 2012 by ABC-CLIO, LLC.

Library of Congress Cataloging-in-Publication Data

The U.S. justice system : an encyclopedia / [edited by] Steven Harmon Wilson.
    p. cm.
Includes bibliographical references and index.
ISBN 978-1-59884-304-0 (hardback) – ISBN 978-1-59884-305-7 (ebook)
1. Justice, Administration of—United States—Encyclopedias. 2. Law—United
States—Encyclopedias. I. Wilson, Steven Harmon, 1964–
KF8700.A68U7 2012
349.7303—dc23   2011041731

ISBN: 978-1-59884-304-0
EISBN: 978-1-59884-305-7

16 15 14 13 12   1 2 3 4 5

This book is also available on the World Wide Web as an eBook.
Visit www.abc-clio.com for details.

ABC-CLIO, LLC
130 Cremona Drive, P.O. Box 1911
Santa Barbara, California 93116-1911

This book is printed on acid-free paper ∞
Manufactured in the United States of America

Contents

Volume One

Preface, ix
Acknowledgments, xi

Introduction, 1

Chapter 1: Law and Constitution in Early America, 7

Chapter 2: The Structure and Function of the Federal Government, 39

Chapter 3: The Federal Judiciary, 73

Chapter 4: The State Judiciary, 113

Chapter 5: Judicial Procedure, Power, and Policy in America, 149

Chapter 6: Administrative Law, Bureaucracies, and
Regulatory Enforcement, 191

Chapter 7: The Civil Justice System and Civil Procedure in the
United States, 225

Chapter 8: Public Law Litigation and Public Interest Law in the
United States, 267

Chapter 9: The Criminal Justice System in the United States, 299

Chapter 10: Criminal Procedure in the United States, 341

Volume Two

List of A–Z Entries, vii

Entries: People, Groups, Cases, and Constitutional and Legal Principles, 389

Volume Three

List of Documents, vii

Documents, 745

Glossary of Common Legal Terms, 1209
General Bibliography, 1225
Editor and Contributors, 1231
Index, 1235

List of Documents

1. Magna Carta, 1215, 745

2. The Libel Case of John Peter Zenger, 1735, 755

3. Articles of Confederation, 1777, 762

4. An Act for the Gradual Abolition of Slavery, March 1, 1780, 770

5. Virginia Statute for Religious Freedom, 1786, 775

6. Article III of the Constitution of the United States of America, 1787, 777

7. Judiciary Act, 1789, 789

8. Alien and Sedition Acts, 1798, 797

9. Judiciary Act, 1801, 799

10. Judiciary Act, 1802, 815

11. *Marbury v. Madison,* 1803, 825

12. Establishment of the Seventh Circuit, 1807, 832

13. Establishment of the Eighth and Ninth Circuits, 1837, 834

14. Declaration of Sentiments, 1848, 837

15. New York Married Woman's Property Act, 1848, 839

16. Compromise of 1850, 840

17. Fugitive Slave Act, 1850, 842

18. Establishment of the Circuit Court for California, 1855, 847

19. Homestead Act, 1862, 850

20. Abraham Lincoln's Emancipation Proclamation, 1863, 852

21. Establishment of the Tenth Circuit, 1863, 854

22. Black Codes of Mississippi, 1865, 856

23. Civil Rights Act, 1866, 859

24. Reorganization of the Judicial Circuits, 1866, 861

25. The Judiciary Act of 1869 (Circuit Judges Act), 862

26. *Minor v. Happersett,* 1872, 864

27. Civil Rights Act [Excerpt], 1875, 866

28. The Jurisdiction and Removal Act of 1875, 868

29. Chinese Exclusion Act, 1882, 873

30. Dawes Act, 1887, 877

31. Interstate Commerce Act, 1887, 882

32. Sherman Antitrust Act, 1890, 887

33. Establishment of the U.S. Circuit Courts of Appeals (Evarts Act, 1891), 889

34. *Plessy v. Ferguson,* 1896, 894

35. *Lone Wolf v. Hitchcock,* 1903, 903

36. *Lochner v. New York,* 1905, 907

37. *Muller v. Oregon,* 1908, 912

38. The Judicial Code of 1911 [Excerpt], 916

39. Establishment of the Conference of Senior Circuit Judges, 1922, 918

40. The Judges' Bill, 1925, 923

41. Establishment of the Tenth Judicial Circuit, 1929, 933

42. Fireside Chat on Reorganization of the Judiciary, 1937, 936

43. Senate Judiciary Committee, Adverse Report on Roosevelt's Proposed Reorganization of the Federal Judiciary, 1937, 946

44. Establishment of the Administrative Office of the U.S. Courts, 1939, 947

45. Franklin D. Roosevelt: Executive Order 8802, 1941, 952

46. Executive Order 9066, 1942, 954

47. *Hirabayashi v. United States,* 1943, 955

48. *Korematsu v. United States,* 1944, 968

49. Harry Truman: Executive Order 9981, 1948, 972

50. *Brown v. Board of Education,* 1954, 973

51. *Brown v. Board of Education,* 1955, 977

52. Executive Order 10730, 1957, 980

53. Equal Pay Act, 1963, 982

54. Civil Rights Act, 1964, 984

55. *Griswold v. Connecticut,* 1965, 1021

56. Voting Rights Act, 1965, 1025

57. Establishment of the the Federal Judicial Center, 1967, 1032

58. Federal Magistrates Act, 1968, 1042

59. *Roe v. Wade,* 1973, 1058

60. "The Notion of a Living Constitution" by William H. Rehnquist, 1976, 1063

61. Establishment of the U.S. Bankruptcy Courts [Excerpt], 1978, 1075

62. Establishment of the Eleventh Judicial Circuit, 1980, 1101

63. Establishment of the Federal Circuit, 1982, 1104

64. Defense of Marriage Act, 1996, 1109

65. *Romer v. Evans,* 1996, 1111

66. *Bush v. Gore,* 2000, 1119

67. Federal Courts Improvement Act, 2000, 1127

68. An Act Relating to Civil Unions, 2000, 1145

69. USA PATRIOT Act, 2001, 1173

Documents

1. Magna Carta, 1215

Introduction

Few, if any, documents have been as important to the development of the English and American constitutions as the Magna Carta, or Great Charter. By a show of force, English barons obtained King John's signature on the document at a field called Runnymede on June 15, 1215. The Magna Carta, divided into 63 chapters, affirmed not only that the king was subject to the law but also that the law superseded the king's whim. Although King John had the document annulled shortly thereafter, it was reaffirmed after his death in October 1216 by the vice regents for King Henry III, who were anxious to have the support of the barons. The Magna Carta was reissued and reconfirmed many times in the years that followed. One of the beauties of the original document was that its language could accommodate developing notions of justice, and over time such ideas as parliamentary representation and trial by jury were incorporated into the provisions of the Magna Carta.

Primary Source

JOHN, by the grace of God King of England, Lord of Ireland, Duke of Normandy and Aquitaine, and Count of Anjou, to his archbishops, bishops, abbots, earls, barons, justices, foresters, sheriffs, stewards, servants, and to all his officials and loyal subjects, Greeting.

KNOW THAT BEFORE GOD, for the health of our soul and those of our ancestors and heirs, to the honour of God, the exaltation of the holy Church, and the better ordering of our kingdom, at the advice of our reverend fathers Stephen, archbishop of Canterbury, primate of all England, and cardinal of the holy Roman Church, Henry archbishop of Dublin, William bishop of London, Peter bishop of Winchester, Jocelin bishop of Bath and Glastonbury, Hugh bishop of Lincoln, Walter Bishop of Worcester, William bishop of Coventry, Benedict bishop of Rochester, Master Pandulf subdeacon and member of the papal household, Brother Aymeric master of the knighthood of the Temple in England, William Marshal earl of Pembroke, William earl of Salisbury, William earl of Warren, William earl of Arundel,

Alan de Galloway constable of Scotland, Warin Fitz Gerald, Peter Fitz Herbert, Hubert de Burgh seneschal of Poitou, Hugh de Neville, Matthew Fitz Herbert, Thomas Basset, Alan Basset, Philip Daubeny, Robert de Roppeley, John Marshal, John Fitz Hugh, and other loyal subjects:

(1) FIRST, THAT WE HAVE GRANTED TO GOD, and by this present charter have confirmed for us and our heirs in perpetuity, that the English Church shall be free, and shall have its rights undiminished, and its liberties unimpaired. That we wish this so to be observed, appears from the fact that of our own free will, before the outbreak of the present dispute between us and our barons, we granted and confirmed by charter the freedom of the Church's elections—a right reckoned to be of the greatest necessity and importance to it—and caused this to be confirmed by Pope Innocent III. This freedom we shall observe ourselves, and desire to be observed in good faith by our heirs in perpetuity.

TO ALL FREE MEN OF OUR KINGDOM we have also granted, for us and our heirs for ever, all the liberties written out below, to have and to keep for them and their heirs, of us and our heirs:

(2) If any earl, baron, or other person that holds lands directly of the Crown, for military service, shall die, and at his death his heir shall be of full age and owe a "relief", the heir shall have his inheritance on payment of the ancient scale of "relief". That is to say, the heir or heirs of an earl shall pay £100 for the entire earl's barony, the heir or heirs of a knight l00s. at most for the entire knight's "fee", and any man that owes less shall pay less, in accordance with the ancient usage of "fees".

(3) But if the heir of such a person is under age and a ward, when he comes of age he shall have his inheritance without "relief" or fine.

(4) The guardian of the land of an heir who is under age shall take from it only reasonable revenues, customary dues, and feudal services. He shall do this without destruction or damage to men or property. If we have given the guardianship of the land to a sheriff, or to any person answerable to us for the revenues, and he commits destruction or damage, we will exact compensation from him, and the land shall be entrusted to two worthy and prudent men of the same "fee", who shall be answerable to us for the revenues, or to the person to whom we have assigned them. If we have given or sold to anyone the guardianship of such land, and he causes destruction or damage, he shall lose the guardianship of it, and it shall be handed over to two worthy and prudent men of the same "fee", who shall be similarly answerable to us.

(5) For so long as a guardian has guardianship of such land, he shall maintain the houses, parks, fish preserves, ponds, mills, and everything else pertaining to it, from the revenues of the land itself. When the heir comes of age, he shall restore the whole land to him, stocked with plough teams and such implements of husbandry as the season demands and the revenues from the land can reasonably bear.

(6) Heirs may be given in marriage, but not to someone of lower social standing. Before a marriage takes place, it shall be made known to the heir's next-of-kin.

(7) At her husband's death, a widow may have her marriage portion and inheritance at once and without trouble. She shall pay nothing for her dower, marriage portion, or any inheritance that she and her husband held jointly on the day of his death. She may remain in her husband's house for forty days after his death, and within this period her dower shall be assigned to her.

(8) No widow shall be compelled to marry, so long as she wishes to remain without a husband. But she must give security that she will not marry without royal consent, if she holds her lands of the Crown, or without the consent of whatever other lord she may hold them of.

(9) Neither we nor our officials will seize any land or rent in payment of a debt, so long as the debtor has movable goods sufficient to discharge the debt. A debtor's sureties shall not be distrained upon so long as the debtor himself can discharge his debt. If, for lack of means, the debtor is unable to discharge his debt, his sureties shall be answerable for it. If they so desire, they may have the debtor's lands and rents until they have received satisfaction for the debt that they paid for him, unless the debtor can show that he has settled his obligations to them.

(10) If anyone who has borrowed a sum of money from Jews dies before the debt has been repaid, his heir shall pay no interest on the debt for so long as he remains under age, irrespective of whom he holds his lands. If such a debt falls into the hands of the Crown, it will take nothing except the principal sum specified in the bond.

(11) If a man dies owing money to Jews, his wife may have her dower and pay nothing towards the debt from it. If he leaves children that are under age, their needs may also be provided for on a scale appropriate to the size of his holding of lands. The debt is to be paid out of the residue, reserving the service due to his feudal lords. Debts owed to persons other than Jews are to be dealt with similarly.

(12) No "scutage" or "aid" may be levied in our kingdom without its general consent, unless it is for the ransom of our person, to make our eldest son a knight, and

(once) to marry our eldest daughter. For these purposes only a reasonable "aid" may be levied. "Aids" from the city of London are to be treated similarly.

(13) The city of London shall enjoy all its ancient liberties and free customs, both by land and by water. We also will and grant that all other cities, boroughs, towns, and ports shall enjoy all their liberties and free customs.

(14) To obtain the general consent of the realm for the assessment of an "aid"—except in the three cases specified above—or a "scutage", we will cause the archbishops, bishops, abbots, earls, and greater barons to be summoned individually by letter. To those who hold lands directly of us we will cause a general summons to be issued, through the sheriffs and other officials, to come together on a fixed day (of which at least forty days notice shall be given) and at a fixed place. In all letters of summons, the cause of the summons will be stated. When a summons has been issued, the business appointed for the day shall go forward in accordance with the resolution of those present, even if not all those who were summoned have appeared.

(15) In future we will allow no one to levy an "aid" from his free men, except to ransom his person, to make his eldest son a knight, and (once) to marry his eldest daughter. For these purposes only a reasonable "aid" may be levied.

(16) No man shall be forced to perform more service for a knight's "fee", or other free holding of land, than is due from it.

(17) Ordinary lawsuits shall not follow the royal court around, but shall be held in a fixed place.

(18) Inquests of novel disseisin, mort d'ancestor, and darrein presentment shall be taken only in their proper county court. We ourselves, or in our absence abroad our chief justice, will send two justices to each county four times a year, and these justices, with four knights of the county elected by the county itself, shall hold the assizes in the county court, on the day and in the place where the court meets.

(19) If any assizes cannot be taken on the day of the county court, as many knights and freeholders shall afterwards remain behind, of those who have attended the court, as will suffice for the administration of justice, having regard to the volume of business to be done.

(20) For a trivial offence, a free man shall be fined only in proportion to the degree of his offence, and for a serious offence correspondingly, but not so heavily as to deprive him of his livelihood. In the same way, a merchant shall be spared his mer-

chandise, and a husbandman the implements of his husbandry, if they fall upon the mercy of a royal court. None of these fines shall be imposed except by the assessment on oath of reputable men of the neighbourhood.

(21) Earls and barons shall be fined only by their equals, and in proportion to the gravity of their offence.

(22) A fine imposed upon the lay property of a clerk in holy orders shall be assessed upon the same principles, without reference to the value of his ecclesiastical benefice.

(23) No town or person shall be forced to build bridges over rivers except those with an ancient obligation to do so.

(24) No sheriff, constable, coroners, or other royal officials are to hold lawsuits that should be held by the royal justices.

(25) Every county, hundred, wapentake, and tithing shall remain at its ancient rent, without increase, except the royal demesne manors.

(26) If at the death of a man who holds a lay "fee" of the Crown, a sheriff or royal official produces royal letters patent of summons for a debt due to the Crown, it shall be lawful for them to seize and list movable goods found in the lay "fee" of the dead man to the value of the debt, as assessed by worthy men. Nothing shall be removed until the whole debt is paid, when the residue shall be given over to the executors to carry out the dead man's will. If no debt is due to the Crown, all the movable goods shall be regarded as the property of the dead man, except the reasonable shares of his wife and children.

(27) If a free man dies intestate, his movable goods are to be distributed by his next-of-kin and friends, under the supervision of the Church. The rights of his debtors are to be preserved.

(28) No constable or other royal official shall take corn or other movable goods from any man without immediate payment, unless the seller voluntarily offers postponement of this.

(29) No constable may compel a knight to pay money for castle-guard if the knight is willing to undertake the guard in person, or with reasonable excuse to supply some other fit man to do it. A knight taken or sent on military service shall be excused from castle-guard for the period of this service.

(30) No sheriff, royal official, or other person shall take horses or carts for transport from any free man, without his consent.

(31) Neither we nor any royal official will take wood for our castle, or for any other purpose, without the consent of the owner.

(32) We will not keep the lands of people convicted of felony in our hand for longer than a year and a day, after which they shall be returned to the lords of the "fees" concerned.

(33) All fish-weirs shall be removed from the Thames, the Medway, and throughout the whole of England, except on the sea coast.

(34) The writ called precipe shall not in future be issued to anyone in respect of any holding of land, if a free man could thereby be deprived of the right of trial in his own lord's court.

(35) There shall be standard measures of wine, ale, and corn (the London quarter), throughout the kingdom. There shall also be a standard width of dyed cloth, russett, and haberject, namely two ells within the selvedges. Weights are to be standardised similarly.

(36) In future nothing shall be paid or accepted for the issue of a writ of inquisition of life or limbs. It shall be given gratis, and not refused.

(37) If a man holds land of the Crown by "fee-farm", "socage", or "burgage", and also holds land of someone else for knight's service, we will not have guardianship of his heir, nor of the land that belongs to the other person's "fee", by virtue of the "fee-farm", "socage", or "burgage", unless the "fee-farm" owes knight's service. We will not have the guardianship of a man's heir, or of land that he holds of someone else, by reason of any small property that he may hold of the Crown for a service of knives, arrows, or the like.

(38) In future no official shall place a man on trial upon his own unsupported statement, without producing credible witnesses to the truth of it.

(39) No free man shall be seized or imprisoned, or stripped of his rights or possessions, or outlawed or exiled, or deprived of his standing in any other way, nor will we proceed with force against him, or send others to do so, except by the lawful judgement of his equals or by the law of the land.

(40) To no one will we sell, to no one deny or delay right or justice.

(41) All merchants may enter or leave England unharmed and without fear, and may stay or travel within it, by land or water, for purposes of trade, free from all illegal exactions, in accordance with ancient and lawful customs. This, however, does not apply in time of war to merchants from a country that is at war with us. Any such merchants found in our country at the outbreak of war shall be detained without injury to their persons or property, until we or our chief justice have discovered how our own merchants are being treated in the country at war with us. If our own merchants are safe they shall be safe too.

(42) In future it shall be lawful for any man to leave and return to our kingdom unharmed and without fear, by land or water, preserving his allegiance to us, except in time of war, for some short period, for the common benefit of the realm. People that have been imprisoned or outlawed in accordance with the law of the land, people from a country that is at war with us, and merchants—who shall be dealt with as stated above—are excepted from this provision.

(43) If a man holds lands of any "escheat" such as the "honour" of Wallingford, Nottingham, Boulogne, Lancaster, or of other "escheats" in our hand that are baronies, at his death his heir shall give us only the "relief" and service that he would have made to the baron, had the barony been in the baron's hand. We will hold the "escheat" in the same manner as the baron held it.

(44) People who live outside the forest need not in future appear before the royal justices of the forest in answer to general summonses, unless they are actually involved in proceedings or are sureties for someone who has been seized for a forest offence.

(45) We will appoint as justices, constables, sheriffs, or other officials, only men that know the law of the realm and are minded to keep it well.

(46) All barons who have founded abbeys, and have charters of English kings or ancient tenure as evidence of this, may have guardianship of them when there is no abbot, as is their due.

(47) All forests that have been created in our reign shall at once be disafforested. River-banks that have been enclosed in our reign shall be treated similarly.

(48) All evil customs relating to forests and warrens, foresters, warreners, sheriffs and their servants, or river-banks and their wardens, are at once to be investigated in every county by twelve sworn knights of the county, and within forty days of their enquiry the evil customs are to be abolished completely and irrevocably. But we, or our chief justice if we are not in England, are first to be informed.

(49) We will at once return all hostages and charters delivered up to us by Englishmen as security for peace or for loyal service.

(50) We will remove completely from their offices the kinsmen of Gerard de Athée, and in future they shall hold no offices in England. The people in question are Engelard de Cigogné, Peter, Guy, and Andrew de Chanceaux, Guy de Cigogné, Geoffrey de Martigny and his brothers, Philip Marc and his brothers, with Geoffrey his nephew, and all their followers.

(51) As soon as peace is restored, we will remove from the kingdom all the foreign knights, bowmen, their attendants, and the mercenaries that have come to it, to its harm, with horses and arms.

(52) To any man whom we have deprived or dispossessed of lands, castles, liberties, or rights, without the lawful judgement of his equals, we will at once restore these. In cases of dispute the matter shall be resolved by the judgement of the twenty-five barons referred to below in the clause for securing the peace (Section 61). In cases, however, where a man was deprived or dispossessed of something without the lawful judgement of his equals by our father King Henry or our brother King Richard, and it remains in our hands or is held by others under our warranty, we shall have respite for the period commonly allowed to Crusaders, unless a lawsuit had been begun, or an enquiry had been made at our order, before we took the Cross as a Crusader. On our return from the Crusade, or if we abandon it, we will at once render justice in full.

(53) We shall have similar respite in rendering justice in connexion with forests that are to be disafforested, or to remain forests, when these were first aforested by our father Henry or our brother Richard; with the guardianship of lands in another person's "fee", when we have hitherto had this by virtue of a "fee" held of us for knight's service by a third party; and with abbeys founded in another person's "fee", in which the lord of the "fee" claims to own a right. On our return from the Crusade, or if we abandon it, we will at once do full justice to complaints about these matters.

(54) No one shall be arrested or imprisoned on the appeal of a woman for the death of any person except her husband.

(55) All fines that have been given to us unjustly and against the law of the land, and all fines that we have exacted unjustly, shall be entirely remitted or the matter decided by a majority judgement of the twenty-five barons referred to below in the clause for securing the peace (Section 61) together with Stephen, archbishop of Canterbury, if he can be present, and such others as he wishes to bring with him. If

the archbishop cannot be present, proceedings shall continue without him, provided that if any of the twenty-five barons has been involved in a similar suit himself, his judgement shall be set aside, and someone else chosen and sworn in his place, as a substitute for the single occasion, by the rest of the twenty-five.

(56) If we have deprived or dispossessed any Welshmen of lands, liberties, or anything else in England or in Wales, without the lawful judgement of their equals, these are at once to be returned to them. A dispute on this point shall be determined in the Marches by the judgement of equals. English law shall apply to holdings of land in England, Welsh law to those in Wales, and the law of the Marches to those in the Marches. The Welsh shall treat us and ours in the same way.

(57) In cases where a Welshman was deprived or dispossessed of anything, without the lawful judgement of his equals, by our father King Henry or our brother King Richard, and it remains in our hands or is held by others under our warranty, we shall have respite for the period commonly allowed to Crusaders, unless a lawsuit had been begun, or an enquiry had been made at our order, before we took the Cross as a Crusader. But on our return from the Crusade, or if we abandon it, we will at once do full justice according to the laws of Wales and the said regions.

(58) We will at once return the son of Llywelyn, all Welsh hostages, and the charters delivered to us as security for the peace.

(59) With regard to the return of the sisters and hostages of Alexander, king of Scotland, his liberties and his rights, we will treat him in the same way as our other barons of England, unless it appears from the charters that we hold from his father William, formerly king of Scotland, that he should be treated otherwise. This matter shall be resolved by the judgement of his equals in our court.

(60) All these customs and liberties that we have granted shall be observed in our kingdom in so far as concerns our own relations with our subjects. Let all men of our kingdom, whether clergy or laymen, observe them similarly in their relations with their own men.

(61) SINCE WE HAVE GRANTED ALL THESE THINGS for God, for the better ordering of our kingdom, and to allay the discord that has arisen between us and our barons, and since we desire that they shall be enjoyed in their entirety, with lasting strength, for ever, we give and grant to the barons the following security:

The barons shall elect twenty-five of their number to keep, and cause to be observed with all their might, the peace and liberties granted and confirmed to them by this charter.

If we, our chief justice, our officials, or any of our servants offend in any respect against any man, or transgress any of the articles of the peace or of this security, and the offence is made known to four of the said twenty-five barons, they shall come to us—or in our absence from the kingdom to the chief justice—to declare it and claim immediate redress. If we, or in our absence abroad the chief justice, make no redress within forty days, reckoning from the day on which the offence was declared to us or to him, the four barons shall refer the matter to the rest of the twenty-five barons, who may distrain upon and assail us in every way possible, with the support of the whole community of the land, by seizing our castles, lands, possessions, or anything else saving only our own person and those of the queen and our children, until they have secured such redress as they have determined upon. Having secured the redress, they may then resume their normal obedience to us.

Any man who so desires may take an oath to obey the commands of the twenty-five barons for the achievement of these ends, and to join with them in assailing us to the utmost of his power. We give public and free permission to take this oath to any man who so desires, and at no time will we prohibit any man from taking it. Indeed, we will compel any of our subjects who are unwilling to take it to swear it at our command.

If one of the twenty-five barons dies or leaves the country, or is prevented in any other way from discharging his duties, the rest of them shall choose another baron in his place, at their discretion, who shall be duly sworn in as they were.

In the event of disagreement among the twenty-five barons on any matter referred to them for decision, the verdict of the majority present shall have the same validity as a unanimous verdict of the whole twenty-five, whether these were all present or some of those summoned were unwilling or unable to appear.

The twenty-five barons shall swear to obey all the above articles faithfully, and shall cause them to be obeyed by others to the best of their power.

We will not seek to procure from anyone, either by our own efforts or those of a third party, anything by which any part of these concessions or liberties might be revoked or diminished. Should such a thing be procured, it shall be null and void and we will at no time make use of it, either ourselves or through a third party.

(62) We have remitted and pardoned fully to all men any ill-will, hurt, or grudges that have arisen between us and our subjects, whether clergy or laymen, since the beginning of the dispute. We have in addition remitted fully, and for our own part have also pardoned, to all clergy and laymen any offences committed as a result of

the said dispute between Easter in the sixteenth year of our reign (i.e. 1215) and the restoration of peace.

In addition we have caused letters patent to be made for the barons, bearing witness to this security and to the concessions set out above, over the seals of Stephen archbishop of Canterbury, Henry archbishop of Dublin, the other bishops named above, and Master Pandulf.

(63) IT IS ACCORDINGLY OUR WISH AND COMMAND that the English Church shall be free, and that men in our kingdom shall have and keep all these liberties, rights, and concessions, well and peaceably in their fulness and entirety for them and their heirs, of us and our heirs, in all things and all places for ever.

Both we and the barons have sworn that all this shall be observed in good faith and without deceit. Witness the abovementioned people and many others.

Given by our hand in the meadow that is called Runnymede, between Windsor and Staines, on the fifteenth day of June in the seventeenth year of our reign (i.e. 1215: the new regnal year began on 28 May).

Source: "Magna Carta" (New Haven, CT: Yale University, Avalon Project, 1996; http:// avalon.law.yale.edu/medieval/magframe.asp)

2. The Libel Case of John Peter Zenger, 1735

Introduction

John Peter Zenger, the immigrant printer of the *New York Weekly Journal*, became a symbol of the cause of freedom of the press when he was arrested for publishing articles critical of New York's royal governor, William Cosby. The free press enshrined in the U.S. Constitution lay years in the future. Criticizing the government in print was against the law in colonial America and thus automatically considered libelous. Governor Cosby was greedy and corrupt. His political enemies persuaded Zenger, who needed new business, to start a newspaper and publish opposition views. Zenger had nothing to do with the opinions expressed in his paper; however, New York authorities arrested him in November 1734 and set his bail so high that he remained in prison until his August 1735 trial. Cosby disbarred Zenger's local defense attorneys, so Andrew Hamilton of Philadelphia volunteered to defend him. In the trial proceedings excerpted here, Hamilton wins Zenger's acquittal by arguing that a statement is not libelous if it is known to be true. He also instructs the jurors to defy the judge and make their own decision on whether the words in question were actually libelous. The *Journal* article reprinted here accuses Cosby of being a French sympathizer and allowing French visitors to acquire valuable military intelligence.

Primary Source

[. . .]

Mr. Hamilton. I thank your Honour. Then Gentlemen of the Jury, it is to you we must now appeal, for Witnesses, to the Truth of the Facts we have offered, and are denied the Liberty to prove; and let it not seem strange, that I apply my self to you in this Manner, I am warranted so to do both by Law and Reason. The Law supposes you to be summoned, *out of the Neighbourhood where the Fact is alledged to be committed*; and the Reason of your being taken out of the Neighbourhood is, *because you are supposed to have the best Knowledge of the Fact that is to be tried*. And were you to find a Verdict against my Client, you must take upon you to say, the Papers referred to in the Information, and which we acknowledge we printed and published, are *false, scandalous and seditious*; but of this I can have no Apprehension. You are citizens of *New York*, you are really what the Law supposes you to be, *honest and lawful Men*; and according to my Brief, the Facts which we offer to prove were not committed in a Corner; they are notoriously known to be true; and therefore in your Justice lies our Safety. And as we are denied the Liberty of giving Evidence, to prove the Truth of what we have published, I will beg Leave to lay it down as a standing Rule in such Cases: *That the suppressing of Evidence ought always to be taken for the strongest Evidence*; and I hope it will have that Weight with you. But since we are not admitted to examine our Witnesses, I will endeavour to shorten the Dispute with Mr. Attorney, and to that End, I desire he would favour us with some Standard Definition of a Libel, by which it may be certainly known, whether a Writing be a Libel, yea or not.

Mr. Attorney. The Books, I think, have given a very full Definition of a Libel; they say it is *in a strict Sense taken for a malicious Defamation, expressed either in Printing or Writing, and tending either to blacken the Memory of one who is dead, or the Reputation of one who is alive, and expose him to publick Hatred, Contempt or Ridicule. But it is said, That in a larger Sense the Notion of a Libel may be applied to any Defamation whatsoever, empressed either by Signs or Pictures, as by fixing up a Gallows against a Man's Door, or by painting him in a shameful and igmoninious Manner. And since the chief Cause for which the Law so severely punishes all Offences of this Nature, is the direct Tendency of them to a Breach of Publick Peace, by provoking the Parties injured, their Friends and Families to Acts of Revenge, which it would be impossible to restrain by the severest Laws, were there no Redress from Publick Justice for Injuries of this kind, which of all others are most sensibly felt; and since the plain Meaning of such Scandal as is expressed by Signs or Pictures, is as obvious to common Sense, and as easily understood by every common Capacity, and altogether as provoking as that which is expressed by Writing or Printing, why should it not be equally criminal? And from the same Ground it seemeth also clearly to follow, That such Scandal as is expressed in a scoffing and ironical Manner, makes a Writing as properly a Libel, as that which is expressed in direct Terms; as where a Writing, in a taunting Manner reckoning up several Acts of publick charity done by one, says* You will not play the Jew, nor the Hypocrite, *and so goes on in a Strain of Ridicule to insinuate, that what he did was owing his Vain-Glory; or where a Writing, pretending to recommend to one the Characters of several great men for his Imitation, instead of taking Notice of what they are generally esteemed famous for, pitched on such Qualities only which their Enemies charge them with the Want of, as by proposing such a one to be imitated for his Courage, who is known to be a great Statesman, but no Soldier, and another to be imitated for his Learning, who is known to be a great General, but no Scholar, &c. which Kind of Writing is as well understood to mean only to upbraid the Parties with the Want of these Qualities, as if it had directly and expressly done so.*

Mr. Hamilton. Ay, Mr Attorney; but what certain Standard Rule have the Books laid down, by which we can certainly know, whether the Words or the Signs are malicious? Whether they are defamatory? Whether they tend to the Breach of the Peace, and are sufficient Ground to provoke, a Man, his Family, or Friends to Acts of Revenge, especially those of the *ironical* sort words? And what Rule have you to know when I write *ironically*? I think it would be hard, when I say, *such a Man is a very worthy honest Gentleman, and of fine Understanding,* that therefore I meant *he was a Knave or a Fool.*

Mr. Attorney. I think the Books are very full; it is said in I *Hawk. p.* 193 just now read, *That such Scandal as is expressed in a scoffing and ironical Manner, makes a Writing as properly a Libel, as that which is expressed direct Terms; as where a Writing, in a taunting Manner says, reckoning up several Acts of Charity done by one, says,* You will not play the Jew or Hypocrite, *and so goes on to insinuate, that what he did was owing to his Vain-Glory &c. Which Kind of Writing is as well understood to mean only to upbraid the Parties with the Want of these Qualities, as if it had directly and expressly done so.* I think nothing can be plainer or more full that these Words.

Mr. Hamilton. I agree the Words are very plain, and I shall not scruple to allow (when we are agreed that the Words are *false and scandalous, and were spoken in an ironical and scoffing Manner, &c.*) that they are really *libellous*; but here still occurs the Uncertainty, which makes the Difficulty to know, what Words are *scandalous* and what are not; for you say, they may be *scandalous, true or false*; besides, how shall we know whether the Words were spoke in a *scoffing and ironical manner* or seriously? Or how can you know, whether the Man did not think as he wrote? For by your rule, if he did, it is no *Irony*, and consequently no *Libel*. But under Favour, Mr. Attorney, I think the same Book, and the same Section will shew us the only Rule by which all these things are to be known. The Words are these; *which Kind of Writing is as well UNDERSTOOD to mean only to upbraid the Parties with the Want of these Qualities, as if they had directly and expressly done so.* Here it is plain, the words are *scandalous, scoffing and ironical*, only as they are UNDERSTOOD. I know no rule laid down in the Books but his, I mean, as the Words are *understood*.

Mr. Ch. Just. That is certain. All Words are libellous or not, as they are *understood*. Those who are to judge of the Words, must judge whether they are *scandalous* or *ironical, tend to the Breach of the Peace*, or are *seditious*: There can be no Doubt of it.

Mr. Hamilton. I thank Your Honour; I am glad to find the Court of this Opinion. Then it follows that those twelve Men must Understand the Words in the Information to be *scandalous*, that is to say *false*; for I think it is not pretended they are of the *ironical* Sort; and when they understand the Words to be so, they will say we are guilty of publishing a *false Libel*, and not otherwise.

Mr. Ch. Just. No, Mr. *Hamilton*; the Jury may find that *Zenger* printed and published those papers, and leave it to the Court to judge whether they are libellous; you know this is very common; it is in the Nature of special Verdict, where the Jury leave the matter of Law to the Court.

Mr. Hamilton. I know, may it please Your Honour, the Jury may do so; but I do likewise know, they may do otherwise. I know they have the Right beyond all Dispute, to determine both the Law and the Fact, and where they do not doubt of the Law, they ought to do so. This of leaving it to the Judgment of the Court, *whether the Words are libellous or not*, in Effect renders Juries useless (to say no worse) in many Cases; but this I shall have Occasion to speak to by and by; and I will with the Court's Leave proceed to examine the Inconveniencies that must inevitably rise from the Doctrines Mr. Attorney has laid down; and I observe, in support of this Prosecution, he has frequently repeated the Words taken from the Case of *Libel, famous,* in *5 Co.* This is indeed the leading Case, and to which almost all the other Cases upon the Subject of Libels do refer; and I must insist upon saying, That according as this Case seems to be understood by the Court and Mr. Attorney, it is not Law at this Day: for tho' I own it to be base and unworthy to scandalize any Man, yet I think it is even villainous to scandalize a Person of publick Character, and I will go so far into Mr. Attorney's Doctrine as to agree, that if the Faults, Mistakes, nay even the Vices of such a Person be private and personal, and don't affect the Peace of the publick, or the Liberty or Property of our Neighbour, it is unmanly and unmannerly to expose them either by Word or Writing. But when a Ruler of a People brings his personal Failings, but much more his Vices, into his Administration, and the People find themselves affected by them, either in their Liberties or Properties, that will alter the Case mightily, and all the high Things that are said in Favour of Rulers, and of Dignities, and upon the side of Power, will not be able to stop People's Mouths when they feel themselves oppressed, I mean in a free government. It is true in Times past it was a Crime to speak Truth, and in that terrible Court of Star Chamber, many worthy and brave Men suffered for so doing; and yet even in that Court, and in those bad Times, a great and good Man durst say, what I hope will not be take amiss of me to say in this place, *to wit, The Practice of Informations for Libels is a Sword in the Hands of a wicked King, and an arrand Coward, to cut down and destroy the innocent; the one cannot, because of his high Station, and the other dares not, because of his Want of Courage, revenge himself in another Manner.*

Mr. Attorney. Pray Mr. *Hamilton*, have a Care what you say, don't go too far neither, I don't like those Liberties.

[. . .]

Mr. Hamilton. I hope to be pardon'd Sir for my Zeal upon this Occasion; it is an old and wise Caution. *That when our Neighbour's House is on Fire, we ought to take Care of our own.* For tho' Blessed be God, I live in a Government where Liberty is well understood, and freely enjoyed; yet Experience has shewn us all (I'm sure it has to me) that a bad Precedent in one Government, is soon set up for an Authority in another; and therefore I cannot but think it mine, and every Honest Man's duty, that (while we pay all due Obedience to Men in Authority) we ought at the same Time to be upon our Guard against Power, wherever we apprehend it may affect ourselves or our Fellow-Subjects.

I am truly very unequal to such an Undertaking on many Accounts. And you see I labour under the Weight of many Years, and am born down with great Infirmities of Body; yet Old and Weak as I am, I should think it my duty if required, to go to the utmost Part of the Land, where my Service cou'd be of any Use in assisting to quence the Flame of Prosecutions upon Informations, set on Foot by the Government, to deprive a People of the Right of Remonstrating, (and complaining too) of the arbitrary Attempts of Men in Power. Men who injure and oppress the People under their Administration, provoke them to cry out and complain; and then make that very Complaint the Foundation for new Oppressions and Prosecutions. I wish I could say there were no Instances of this Kind. But to conclude; the Question before the Court and you Gentlemen of the Jury, is not so small nor private Concern, it is not the Cause of a poor Printer, nor of *New-York* alone, which you are not trying: No! It may in its Consequence, affect every Freeman that lives under a British Government on the main of *America*. It is the best Cause. It is the Cause of Liberty; and I make no Doubt but your upright Conduct, this Day, will not only entitle you to the Love and Esteem of your Fellow-Citizens; but every Man who prefers Freedom to a Life of Slavery will bless and honour You, as Men who have baffled the Attempt of Tyranny; and by an impartial and uncorrupt Verdict, have laid a noble Foundation for securing to ourselves, our Posterity, and our Neighbours, That, to which Nature and the Laws of our Country have given us a Right,—The Liberty—both of exposing and opposing arbitrary Power (in these Parts of the World, at least) by speaking and writing Truth.

Mr. Ch. Just. Gentlemen of the Jury. The great Pains Mr. *Hamilton* has taken to shew how little Regard Juries ought to pay to the Opinion of the Judges; and his insisting so much upon the Conduct of some Judges in Tryals of this kind; is done no doubt, with a Design that you should take but very little Notice of what I might say upon this Occasion. I shall therefore only observe to you that as the Facts or Words in the Information are confessed, the only thing that can come in Question before you is, whether the Words as set forth in the Information made a Libel. And that is a Matter of Law, no doubt, and which you may leave to the Court. But I shall trouble you no further with any Thing more of my own, but read to you the Words of a learned and upright Judge in a Case of the like Nature.

'To say that corrupt Officers are appointed to administer Affairs, is certainly a Reflection on the Government. If People should not be called to account for possessing the People with an ill Opinion of the Government, no Government can subsist. For it is very necessary for all Governments that the People should have a good opinion it. And nothing can be worse to any Government, than to endeavour to procure Animosities; as to the Management of it, this has been always look'd upon as a Crime, and no Government can be safe without it be punished.'

'Now you are to consider, whether these Words I have read to you, do not tend to beget an ill Opinion of the Administration of the Government? To tell us, that those that are employed know nothing of the matter, and those that do know are not employed. Men are not adapted to Offices, but Offices to Men, out of a particular Regard to their Interest, and not to their Fitness for the Places; this is the Purport of these Papers.'

Mr. Hamilton. I humbly beg your Honours Pardon: I am very much misapprehended, if you suppose what I said was so designed.

Sir, you know I made an Apology for the Freedom I found my self under a Necessity of using upon this Occasion. I said, there was Nothing personal designed; it arose from the nature of our Defence.

The Jury withdrew, and in a small Time returned, and being asked by the Clerk whether they were agreed on their Verdict, and whether *John Peter Zenger* was guilty of Printing and Publishing the Libels in the Information mentioned? They answered by *Thomas Hunt*, their Foreman, *Not Guilty*. Upon which there were three Huzzas in the Hall which was crowded with People, and the next Day I was discharged from my Imprisonment.

New York Weekly Journal 12-17-1733

It is agreed on all Hands, that a Fool may ask more Questions than a wise Man can answer, or perhaps will answer if he could; but notwithstanding that, I would be glad to be satisfied in the following Points of Speculation that the above Affidavits afford. And it will be no great Puzile to a wise man to answer with a *Yea*, or a *Nay*, which is the most that will be required in most of those Questions.

Q. 1. It is prudent in the French governours not to suffer an Englishman to view their Fortificatoins, sound their harbours, tarry in their country to discover their Strength?

Q. 2. It is prudent in an English Governour to suffer a French man to view our Fortifications, sound our harbours? &c.

Q. 3. If the above Affidavits be true, had the French a bad Harvest in Canada? Or do they want Provisions?

Q. 4. Was the Letter from the Governour of Louisburg to our Governour true?

Q. 5. Might not our Governour as easily have discovered the falsehood of it as any body else; if he would?

Q. 6. Ought he not to have endeavored to do it?

Q. 7. Did our governour endeavour to do it?

Q. 8. Was it not known to the greatest Part of the town, before the Sloop Le Caesar left New-York, that the French in the Sloop Le Caesar had founded and taken the Land-Marks from without Sandyhook up to New-York? Had taken the View of the Town?

Had been in the Fort?

Q. 9. Might not the governour have known the same Thing, if he would?

Q. 10. Is there not great Probability that he did know it?

Q. 11. Was it for our Benefit or that of the French these soundings and Landmarks were taken, and View made?

Q. 12. Could we not, by seizing their Papers, and confining their Persons, have prevented them in great Measure from making use of the Discoveries they made?

Q. 13. Ought they not to have been so prevented?

Q. 14. Was it prudent to suffer them to pass through Hellgate, and also to discover that Way of Access to us?

Q. 15. If a French Governour had suffered an English Sloop and company to do what a French sloop and Company has done here, would he not have deserved to be _____?

Q. 16. Since it appears by the Affidavits, there was no such scarcity of provisions as by the letter from the Governour of Louisburgh to our Governour, since the conduct of the French to the English that happen to go to Canada, shews they think it necessary to keep us ignorant of their State and Condition as much as they can. Since the Sounding our harbours, viewing our Fortifications, and the honourable Treatment they have received here (the reverse of what we receive in Canada) has let them into a perfect Knowledge of our State and Condition. And since their Voyage must appear to any Man of the least Penetration to have been made with an Intent to make that Discovery, and only with that Intent. Whether it would not be reasonable in us to provide as well and as soon as we can for our Defence?

Q. 17. Whether that can be done any way so well and effectually as by calling the Assembly very together?

Q. 18. If this be not done, and any dangerous consequences follow after so full Warning, Who is Blameable?

> *Source:* Rutherfurd, Livingston. *John Peter Zenger, His Press, His Trial and A Bibliography of Zenger Imprints.* New York: Dodd, Mead & Company, 1904

3. Articles of Confederation, 1777

Introduction

Written primarily by John Dickinson of Pennsylvania, the Articles of Confederation called for a loose organization of states with a weak central authority. The Second Continental Congress adopted the Articles on November 15, 1777, and forwarded the new constitution to the states, from which it required unanimous approval. The Articles of Confederation did not go into effect until March 1, 1781, when Maryland finally granted its approval. A number of defects in the Articles became apparent almost immediately, as the national government proved extremely ineffective due to its limited powers. Legislators made several attempts to rectify the problems associated with the Articles, but by September 1786 such men as Alexander Hamilton were calling for a massive government reform effort. At a special convention held for this purpose in Philadelphia beginning in July 1787 reformers decided to replace the Articles altogether with a new constitution, which is the current U.S. Constitution.

Primary Source

To all to whom these Presents shall come, we, the undersigned, Delegates of the States affixed to our Names, send greeting: Whereas the Delegates of the United States of America in Congress assembled, did on the fifteenth day of November, in the year of our Lord one thousand seven hundred and seventy seven, and in the second year of the Independence of America, agree to certain articles of Confederation and perpetual Union between the states of New Hampshire, Massachusetts-bay, Rhode Island and Providence Plantations, Connecticut, New York, New Jersey, Pennsylvania, Delaware, Maryland, Virginia, North Carolina, South Carolina, and Georgia, in the words following, viz. Articles of Confederation and perpetual Union between the States of New Hampshire, Massachusetts-bay, Rhode Island and Providence Plantations, Connecticut, New York, New Jersey, Pennsylvania, Delaware, Maryland, Virginia, North Carolina, South Carolina, and Georgia.

Article I. The stile of this confederacy shall be, "The United States of America."

Article II. Each State retains its sovereignty, freedom, and independence, and every power, jurisdiction, and right, which is not by this confederation, expressly delegated to the United States, in Congress assembled.

Article III. The said States hereby severally enter into a firm league of friendship with each other, for their common defence, the security of their liberties, and their mutual and general welfare, binding themselves to assist each other against all force offered to, or attacks made upon them, or any of them, on account of religion, sovereignty, trade, or any other pretence whatever.

Article IV. The better to secure and perpetuate mutual friendship and intercourse among the people of the different States in this union, the free inhabitants of each of these States, paupers, vagabonds, and fugitives from justice excepted, shall be entitled to all privileges and immunities of free citizens in the several States; and the people of each State shall have free ingress and regress to and from any other

State, and shall enjoy therein all the privileges of trade and commerce, subject to the same duties, impositions, and restrictions, as the inhabitants thereof respectively; provided that such restrictions shall not extend so far as to prevent the removal of property imported into any State, to any other State, of which the owner is an inhabitant; provided also that no imposition, duties, or restriction, shall be laid by any State on the property of the United States, or either of them.

If any person guilty of, or charged with, treason, felony, or other high misdemeanor in any State, shall flee from justice, and be found in any of the United States, he shall, upon demand of the governor or executive power of the State from which he fled, be delivered up, and removed to the State having jurisdiction of his offence.

Full faith and credit shall be given, in each of these States, to the records, acts, and judicial proceedings of the courts and magistrates of every other State.

Article V. For the more convenient management of the general interests of the United States, delegates shall be annually appointed in such manner as the legislature of each State shall direct, to meet in Congress on the first Monday in November, in every year, with a power reserved to each State to recall its delegates, or any of them, at any time within the year, and to send others in their stead for the remainder of the year.

No State shall be represented in Congress by less than two, nor by more than Seven Members; and no person shall be capable of being delegate for more than three years, in any term of Six years; nor shall any person, being a delegate, be capable of holding any office under the United States, for which he, or another for his benefit, receives any salary, fees, or emolument of any kind.

Each State shall maintain its own delegates in a meeting of the States, and while they act as members of the committee of the States.

In determining questions in the United States in Congress assembled, each State shall have one vote.

Freedom of speech and debate in Congress shall not be impeached or questioned in any Court or place out of Congress; and the members of Congress shall be protected in their persons from arrests and imprisonments during the time of their going to and from, and attendance on, Congress, except for treason, felony or breach of the peace.

Article VI. No State, without the consent of the United States, in Congress assembled, shall send any embassy to, or receive any embassy from, or enter into any conference, agreement, alliance, or treaty, with any king, prince or State; nor shall any person holding any office of profit or trust under the United States, or any of them, accept of any present, emolument, office, or title of any kind whatever, from any king, prince, or foreign State; nor shall the United States, in congress assembled, or any of them, grant any title of nobility.

No two or more States shall enter into any treaty, confederation, or alliance whatever, between them, without the consent of the United States, in Congress assembled, specifying accurately the purposes for which the same is to be entered into, and how long it shall continue.

No State shall lay any imposts or duties, which may interfere with any stipulations in treaties, entered into by the United States, in congress assembled, with any king, prince, or State, in pursuance of any treaties already proposed by congress to the courts of France and Spain.

No vessels of war shall be kept up in time of peace, by any State, except such number only as shall be deemed necessary by the United States, in congress assembled, for the defence of such State, or its trade; nor shall any body of forces be kept up, by any State, in time of peace, except such number only as, in the judgment of the United States, in congress assembled, shall be deemed requisite to garrison the forts necessary for the defence of such State; but every State shall always keep up a well-regulated and disciplined militia, sufficiently armed and accounted, and shall provide and constantly have ready for use, in public stores, a due number of field-pieces and tents, and a proper quantity of arms, ammunition, and camp equipage.

No State shall engage in any war without the consent of the United States, in congress assembled, unless such State be actually invaded by enemies, or shall have received certain advice of a resolution being formed by some nation of Indians to invade such State, and the danger is so imminent as not to admit of a delay till the United States, in congress assembled, can be consulted; nor shall any State grant commissions to any ships or vessels of war, nor letters of marque or reprisal, except it be after a declaration of war by the United States, in congress assembled, and then only against the kingdom or State, and the subjects thereof, against which war has been so declared, and under such regulations as shall be established by the United States, in congress assembled, unless such State be infested by pirates, in which case vessels of war may be fitted out for that occasion, and kept so long as the danger shall continue, or until the United States, in congress assembled, shall determine otherwise.

Article VII. When land forces are raised by any State, for the common defence, all officers of or under the rank of colonel, shall be appointed by the legislature of each State respectively by whom such forces shall be raised, or in such manner as such State shall direct, and all vacancies shall be filled up by the State which first made appointment.

Article VIII. All charges of war, and all other expenses that shall be incurred for the common defence or general welfare, and allowed by the United States, in congress assembled, shall be defrayed out of a common treasury, which shall be supplied by the several States, in proportion to the value of all land within each State, granted to, or surveyed for, any person, as such land and the buildings and improvements thereon shall be estimated, according to such mode as the United States, in congress assembled, shall, from time to time, direct and appoint. The taxes for paying that proportion shall be laid and levied by the authority and direction of the legislatures of the several States, within the time agreed upon by the United States, in congress assembled.

Article IX. The United States, in congress assembled, shall have the sole and exclusive right and power of determining on peace and war, except in the cases mentioned in the sixth Article, of sending and receiving ambassadors; entering into treaties and alliances, provided that no treaty of commerce shall be made, whereby the legislative power of the respective States shall be restrained from imposing such imposts and duties on foreigners, as their own people are subjected to, or from prohibiting the exportation or importation of any species of goods or commodities whatsoever; of establishing rules for deciding, in all cases, what captures on land or water shall be legal, and in what manner prizes taken by land or naval forces in the service of the United States, shall be divided or appropriated; of granting letters of marque and reprisal in times of peace; appointing courts for the trial of piracies and felonies committed on the high seas; and establishing courts; for receiving and determining finally appeals in all cases of captures; provided that no member of congress shall be appointed a judge of any of the said courts.

The United States, in congress assembled, shall also be the last resort on appeal, in all disputes and differences now subsisting, or that hereafter may arise between two or more States concerning boundary, jurisdiction, or any other cause whatever; which authority shall always be exercised in the manner following. Whenever the legislative or executive authority, or lawful agent of any State in controversy with another, shall present a petition to congress, stating the matter in question, and praying for a hearing, notice thereof shall be given, by order of congress, to the legislative or executive authority of the other State in controversy, and a day assigned for the appearance of the parties by their lawful agents, who shall then be directed to appoint, by joint consent, commissioners or judges to constitute a court for hearing and determining the matter in question: but if they cannot agree, congress shall name three persons out of each of the United States, and from the list of such persons each party shall alternately strike out one, the petitioners beginning, until the number shall be reduced to thirteen; and from that number not less than seven, nor more than nine names, as congress shall direct, shall, in the presence of congress, be drawn out by lot, and the persons whose names shall be so drawn, or any five of them, shall be commissioners or judges, to hear and finally determine the controversy, so always as a major part of the judges, who shall hear the cause, shall agree in the determination: and if either party shall neglect to attend at the day appointed, without showing reasons which congress shall judge sufficient, or being present, shall refuse to strike, the congress shall proceed to nominate three persons out of each State, and the secretary of congress shall strike in behalf of such party absent or refusing; and the judgment and sentence of the court, to be appointed in the manner before prescribed, shall be final and conclusive; and if any of the parties shall refuse to submit to the authority of such court, or to appear or defend their claim or cause, the court shall nevertheless proceed to pronounce sentence, or judgment, which shall in like manner be final and decisive; the judgment or sentence and other proceedings being in either case transmitted to congress, and lodged among the acts of congress, for the security of the parties concerned: provided that every commissioner, before he sits in judgment, shall take an oath to be administered by one of the judges of the Supreme or Superior court of the State where the cause shall be tried, "well and truly to hear and determine the matter in question, according to the best of his judgment, without favour, affection, or hope of reward": Provided, also, that no State shall be deprived of territory for the benefit of the United States.

All controversies concerning the private right of soil claimed under different grants of two or more States, whose jurisdictions as they may respect such lands, and the States which passed such grants are adjusted, the said grants or either of them being at the same time claimed to have originated antecedent to such settlement of jurisdiction, shall, on the petition of either party to the congress of the United States, be finally determined, as near as may be, in the same manner as is before prescribed for deciding disputes respecting territorial jurisdiction between different States.

The United States, in congress assembled, shall also have the sole and exclusive right and power of regulating the alloy and value of coin struck by their own authority, or by that of the respective States fixing the standard of weights and measures throughout the United States; regulating the trade and managing all affairs with the Indians, not members of any of the States; provided that the legislative right of any State, within its own limits, be not infringed or violated; establishing and regulating post-offices from one State to another, throughout all the United States, and exacting such postage on the papers passing through the same, as may be requisite to defray the expenses of the said office; appointing all officers of the land forces in the service of the United States, excepting regimental officers; appointing all the officers of the naval forces, and commissioning all officers whatever in the service of the United States; making rules for the government and regulation of the said land and naval forces, and directing their operations.

The United States, in congress assembled, shall have authority to appoint a committee, to sit in the recess of congress, to be denominated, "A Committee of the States," and to consist of one delegate from each State; and to appoint such other committees and civil officers as may be necessary for managing the general affairs of the United States under their direction; to appoint one of their number to preside; provided that no person be allowed to serve in the office of president more than one year in any term of three years; to ascertain the necessary sums of money to be raised for the service of the United States, and to appropriate and apply the same for defraying the public expenses; to borrow money or emit bills on the credit of the United States, transmitting every half year to the respective States an account of the sums of money so borrowed or emitted; to build and equip a navy; to agree upon the number of land forces, and to make requisitions from each State for its quota, in proportion to the number of white inhabitants in such State, which requisition shall be binding; and thereupon the Legislature of each State shall appoint the regimental officers, raise the men, and clothe, arm, and equip them, in a soldier-like manner, at the expense of the United States; and the officers and men so clothed, armed, and equipped, shall march to the place appointed, and within the time agreed on by the United States, in congress assembled; but if the United States, in congress assembled, shall, on consideration of circumstances, judge proper that any State should not raise men, or should raise a smaller number than its quota, and that any other State should raise a greater number of men than the quota thereof, such extra number shall be raised, officered, clothed, armed, and equipped in the same manner as the quota of such State, unless the Legislature of such State shall judge that such extra number cannot be safely spared out of the same, in which case they shall raise, officer, clothe, arm, and equip, as many of such extra number as they judge can be safely spared. And the officers and men so clothed, armed, and equipped, shall march to the place appointed, and within the time agreed on by the United States in congress assembled.

The United States, in congress assembled, shall never engage in a war, nor grant letters of marque and reprisal in time of peace, nor enter into any treaties or alliances, nor coin money, nor regulate the value thereof nor ascertain the sums and expenses necessary for the defence and welfare of the United States, or any of them, nor emit bills, nor borrow money on the credit of the United States, nor appropriate money, nor agree upon the number of vessels of war to be built or purchased, or the number of land or sea forces to be raised, nor appoint a commander in chief of the army or navy, unless nine States assent to the same, nor shall a question on any other point, except for adjourning from day to day, be determined, unless by the votes of a majority of the United States in congress assembled.

The congress of the United States shall have power to adjourn to any time within the year, and to any place within the United States, so that no period of adjournment be for a longer duration than the space of six months, and shall publish the journal of their proceedings monthly, except such parts thereof relating to treaties, alliances, or military operations, as in their judgment require secrecy; and the yeas and nays of the delegates of each State, on any question, shall be entered on the journal, when it is desired by any delegate; and the delegates of a State, or any of them, at his or their request, shall be furnished with a transcript of the said journal, except such parts as are above excepted, to lay before the legislatures of the several States.

Article X. The committee of the States, or any nine of them, shall be authorized to execute, in the recess of congress, such of the powers of congress as the United States, in congress assembled, by the consent of nine States, shall, from time to time, think expedient to vest them with; provided that no power be delegated to the said committee, for the exercise of which, by the articles of confederation, the voice of nine States, in the congress of the United States assembled, is requisite.

Article XI. Canada acceding to this confederation, and joining in the measures of the United States, shall be admitted into, and entitled to all the advantages of this union: but no other colony shall be admitted into the same, unless such admission be agreed to by nine States.

Article XII. All bills of credit emitted, monies borrowed, and debts contracted by or under the authority of congress, before the assembling of the United States, in pursuance of the present confederation, shall be deemed and considered as a charge against the United States, for payment and satisfaction whereof the said United States and the public faith are hereby solemnly pledged.

Article XIII. Every State shall abide by the determinations of the United States, in congress assembled, on all questions which by this confederation are submitted to them. And the articles of this confederation shall be inviolably observed by every State, and the Union shall be perpetual; nor shall any alteration at any time hereafter be made in any of them, unless such alteration be agreed to in a congress of the United States, and be afterwards confirmed by the legislatures of every State.

And Whereas it hath pleased the Great Governor of the World to incline the hearts of the legislatures we respectively represent in congress, to approve of, and to authorize us to ratify the said articles of confederation and perpetual union, Know Ye, that we, the undersigned delegates, by virtue of the power and authority to us given for that purpose, do, by these presents, in the name and in behalf of our respective constituents, fully and entirely ratify and confirm each and every of the said articles of confederation and perpetual union, and all and singular the matters and things therein contained. And we do further solemnly plight and engage the faith of our respective constituents, that they shall abide by the determinations of the United States, in congress assembled, on all questions which by the said confederation are submitted to them; and that the articles thereof shall be inviolably observed by the States we respectively represent, and that the Union shall be perpetual. In witness whereof, we have hereunto set our hands, in Congress. Done at Philadelphia, in the State of Pennsylvania, the ninth day of July, in the year of our Lord one thousand seven hundred and seventy eight, and in the third year of the Independence of America.

Source: National Archives

4. An Act for the Gradual Abolition of Slavery, March 1, 1780

Introduction

An Act for the Gradual Abolition of Slavery, passed by the Pennsylvania legislature on March 1, 1780, did not free any slave immediately (indeed, those enslaved in Pennsylvania before the 1780 law went into effect remained enslaved for life), but the statute prohibited further importation of slaves into the state. The Act also required Pennsylvania slaveholders to register their slaves annually and established that the future children of Pennsylvania's slaves would be born free. The 1780 Act was the first attempt by a state government in the United States to bring about the end of slavery, and it became a model for freeing slaves through legislation in other Northern states in succeeding years.

Primary Source

When we contemplate our Abhorence of that Condition to which the Arms and Tyranny of Great Britain were exerted to reduce us, when we look back on the Variety of Dangers to which we have been exposed, and how miraculously our Wants in many Instances have been supplied and our Deliverances wrought, when even Hope and human fortitude have become unequal to the Conflict; we are unavoidably led to a serious and grateful Sense of the manifold Blessings which we have undeservedly received from the hand of that Being from whom every good and perfect Gift cometh. Impressed with these Ideas we conceive that it is our duty, and we rejoice that it is in our Power, to extend a Portion of that freedom to others, which hath been extended to us; and a Release from that State of Thraldom, to which we ourselves were tyrannically doomed, and from which we have now every Prospect of being delivered. It is not for us to enquire, why, in the Creation of Mankind, the Inhabitants of the several parts of the Earth, were distinguished by a difference in Feature or Complexion. It is sufficient to know that all are the Work of an Almighty Hand. We find in the distribution of the human Species, that the most fertile, as well as the most barren parts of the Earth are inhabited by Men of Complexions different from ours and from each other, from whence we may reasonably as well as religiously infer, that he, who placed them in their various Situations, hath extended equally his Care and Protection to all, and that it becometh not us to counteract his Mercies.

We esteem a peculiar Blessing granted to us, that we are enabled this Day to add one more Step to universal Civilization by removing as much as possible the Sorrows of those, who have lived in undeserved Bondage, and from which by the assumed Authority of the Kings of Britain, no effectual legal Relief could be obtained. Weaned by a long Course of Experience from those narrow Prejudices and Partialities we had imbibed, we find our Hearts enlarged with Kindness and Benevolence towards Men of all Conditions and Nations; and we conceive ourselves at this particular Period extraordinarily called upon by the Blessings which we have received, to manifest the Sincerity of our Profession and to give a substantial Proof of our Gratitude.

And whereas, the Condition of those Persons who have heretofore been denominated Negroe and Mulatto Slaves, has been attended with Circumstances which not only deprived them of the common Blessings that they were by Nature entitled to, but has cast them into the deepest Afflictions by an unnatural Separation and Sale of Husband and Wife from each other, and from their Children; an Injury the greatness of which can only be conceived, by supposing that we were in the same unhappy Case. In Justice therefore to Persons so unhappily circumstanced and who, having no Prospect before them whereon they may rest their Sorrows and their hopes have no reasonable Inducement to render that Service to Society, which they otherwise might; and also in grateful Commemoration of our own happy Deliverance, from that State of unconditional Submission, to which we were doomed by the Tyranny of Britain.

Be it enacted and it is hereby enacted by the Representatives of the Freemen of the Commonwealth of Pennsylvania in General Assembly met and by the Authority of the same, That all Persons, as well Negroes, and Mulattos, as others, who shall be born within this State, from and after the Passing of this Act, shall not be deemed and considered as Servants for Life or Slaves; and that all Servitude for Life or Slavery of Children in Consequence of the Slavery of their Mothers, in the Case of all

Children born within this State from and after the passing of this Act as aforesaid, shall be, and hereby is, utterly taken away, extinguished and for ever abolished.

Provided always and be it further enacted by the Authority aforesaid, That every Negroe and Mulatto Child born within this State after the passing of this Act as aforesaid, who would in Case this Act had not been made, have been born a Servant for Years or life or a Slave, shall be deemed to be and shall be, by Virtue of this Act the Servant of such person or his or her Assigns, who would in such Case have been entitled to the Service of such Child until such Child shall attain unto the Age of twenty eight Years, in the manner and on the Conditions whereon Servants bound by Indenture for four Years are or may be retained and holden; and shall be liable to like Correction and punishment, and intitled to like Relief in case he or she be evilly treated by his or her master or Mistress; and to like Freedom dues and other Privileges as Servants bound by Indenture for Four Years are or may be intitled unless the Person to whom the Service of any such Child Shall belong, shall abandon his or her Claim to the same, in which Case the Overseers of the Poor of the City Township or District, respectively where such Child shall be so abandoned, shall by Indenture bind out every Child so abandoned as an Apprentice for a Time not exceeding the Age herein before limited for the Service of such Children.

And be it further enacted by the Authority aforesaid, That every Person who is or shall be the Owner of any Negroe or Mulatto Slave or Servant for life or till the Age of thirty one Years, now within this State, or his lawful Attorney shall on or before the said first day of November next, deliver or cause to be delivered in Writing to the Clerk of the Peace of the County or to the Clerk of the Court of Record of the City of Philadelphia, in which he or she shall respectively inhabit, the Name and Sirname and Occupation or Profession of such Owner, and the Name of the County and Township District or Ward where he or she resideth, and also the Name and Names of any such Slave and Slaves and Servant and Servants for Life or till the Age of thirty one Years together with their Ages and Sexes severally and respectively set forth and annexed, by such Person owned or statedly employed, and then being within this State in order to ascertain and distinguish the Slaves and Servants for Life and Years till the Age of thirty one Years within this State who shall be such on the said first day of November next, from all other persons, which particulars shall by said Clerk of the Sessions and Clerk of said City Court be entered in Books to be provided for that Purpose by the said Clerks; and that no Negroe or Mulatto now within this State shall from and after the said first day of November by deemed a slave or Servant for life or till the Age of thirty one Years unless his or her name shall be entered as aforesaid on such Record except such Negroe and Mulatto Slaves and Servants as are hereinafter excepted; the said Clerk to be entitled to a fee of Two Dollars for each Slave or Servant so entered as aforesaid, from the Treasurer of the County to be allowed to him in his Accounts.

Provided always, That any Person in whom the Ownership or Right to the Service of any Negro or Mulatto shall be vested at the passing of this Act, other than such as are herein before excepted, his or her Heirs, Executors, Administrators and Assigns, and all and every of them severally Shall be liable to the Overseers of the Poor of the City, Township or District to which any such Negroe or Mulatto shall become chargeable, for such necessary Expence, with Costs of Suit thereon, as such Overseers may be put to through the Neglect of the Owner, Master or Mistress of such Negroe or Mulatto, notwithstanding the Name and other descriptions of such Negroe or Mulatto shall not be entered and recorded as aforesaid; unless his or her Master or Owner shall before such Slave or Servant attain his or her twenty eighth Year execute and record in the proper County, a deed or Instrument securing to such Slave or Servant his or her Freedom. And be it further enacted by the Authority aforesaid, That the Offences and Crimes of Negroes and Mulattos as well as Slaves and Servants and Freemen, shall be enquired of, adjudged, corrected and punished in like manner as the Offences and Crimes of the other Inhabitants of this State are and shall be enquired of adjudged, corrected and punished, and not otherwise except that a Slave shall not be admitted to bear Witness agaist [sic] a Freeman.

And be it further enacted by the Authority aforesaid That in all Cases wherein Sentence of Death shall be pronounced against a Slave, the Jury before whom he or she shall be tried shall appraise and declare the Value of such Slave, and in Case Such Sentence be executed, the Court shall make an Order on the State Treasurer payable to the Owner for the same and for the Costs of Prosecution, but in Case of a Remission or Mitigation for the Costs only.

And be it further enacted by the Authority aforesaid That the Reward for taking up runaway and absconding Negroe and Mulatto Slaves and Servants and the Penalties for enticing away, dealing with, or harbouring, concealing or employing Negroe and Mulatto Slaves and Servants shall be the same, and shall be recovered in like manner, as in Case of Servants bound for Four Years.

And be it further enacted by the Authority aforesaid, That no Man or Woman of any Nation or Colour, except the Negroes or Mulattoes who shall be registered as aforesaid shall at any time hereafter be deemed, adjudged or holden, within the Territories of this Commonwealth, as Slaves or Servants for Life, but as freemen and Freewomen; and except the domestic Slaves attending upon Delegates in Congress from the other American States, foreign Ministers and Consuls, and persons passing through or sojourning in this State, and not becoming resident therein; and Seamen employed in Ships, not belonging to any Inhabitant of this State nor employed in any Ship owned by any such Inhabitant, Provided such domestic Slaves be not aliened or sold to any Inhabitant, nor (except in the Case of Members of Congress, foreign Ministers and Consuls) retained in this State longer than six Months.

Provided always and be it further enacted by the Authority aforesaid, That this Act nor any thing in it contained shall not give any Relief or Shelter to any absconding or Runaway Negroe or Mulatto Slave or Servant, who has absented himself or shall absent himself from his or her Owner, Master or Mistress, residing in any other State or Country, but such Owner, Master or Mistress, shall have like Right and Aid to demand, claim and take away his Slave or Servant, as he might have had in Case this Act had not been made. And that all Negroe and Mulatto Slaves, now owned, and heretofore resident in this State, who have absented themselves, or been clandestinely carried away, or who may be employed abroad as Seamen, and have not returned or been brought back to their Owners, Masters or Mistresses, before the passing of this Act may within five Years be registered as effectually, as is ordered by this Act concerning those who are now within the State, on producing such Slave, before any two Justices of the Peace, and satisfying the said Justices by due Proof, of the former Residence, absconding, taking away, or Absence of such Slave as aforesaid; who thereupon shall direct and order the said Slave to be entered on the Record as aforesaid.

And Whereas Attempts may be made to evade this Act, by introducing into this State, Negroes and Mulattos, bound by Covenant to serve for long and unreasonable Terms of Years, if the same be not prevented.

Be it therefore enacted by the Authority aforesaid, That no Covenant of personal Servitude or Apprenticeship whatsoever shall be valid or binding on a Negroe or Mulatto for a longer Time than Seven Years; unless such Servant or Apprentice were at the Commencement of such Servitude or Apprenticeship under the Age of Twenty one Years; in which Case such Negroe or Mulatto may be holden as a Servant or Apprentice respectively, according to the Covenant, as the Case shall be, until he or she shall attain the Age of twenty eight Years but no longer.

And be it further enacted by the Authority aforesaid, That an Act of Assembly of the Province of Pennsylvania passed in the Year one thousand seven hundred and five, intitled "An Act for the Trial of Negroes;" and another Act of Assembly of the said Province passed in the Year one thousand seven hundred and twenty five intitled "An Act for the better regulating of Negroes in this Province;" and another Act of Assembly of the said Province passed in the Year one thousand seven hundred and sixty one intitled "An Act for laying a Duty on Negroe and Mulatto Slaves imported into this Province" and also another Act of Assembly of the said Province, passed in the Year one thousand seven hundred and seventy three, intitled "An Act for making perpetual An Act for laying a duty on Negroe and Mulatto Slaves imported into this Province and for laying an additional Duty on said Slaves;" shall be and are hereby repealed annulled and made void.

John Bayard, Speaker

Enacted into a Law at Philadelphia on Wednesday the first day of March, Anno Domini One thousand seven hundred Eighty
Thomas Paine, Clerk of the General Assembly

Source: An Act for the Gradual Abolition of Slavery, March 1, 1780. Record Group 26: Records of the Department of State, Engrossed Laws

5. Virginia Statute for Religious Freedom, 1786

Introduction

Thomas Jefferson served as governor of Virginia from 1779 to 1781 and worked—with mixed results—to bring about a number of changes in Virginia law, including reform of inheritance laws and public education. One of Jefferson's most notable legislative achievements was the Statute for Religious Freedom, which he introduced in 1779. Freedom of religion and freedom of conscience were ideas that had taken root in American soil from the earliest days of European settlement. Although prejudice against Roman Catholics, Quakers, and Jews persisted, adherents to minority religions still found relative freedom in the American colonies. One of the first acts of the revolutionary government in Virginia was to disestablish the Anglican church, so that the public would no longer be taxed to support it. The 1776 Virginia Declaration of Rights espoused the principle of religious liberty, as did other governing documents throughout the rebellious colonies. Jefferson intended the Statute of Religious Freedom to uphold the principle stated in the declaration; however, the proposed statute did not receive enough legislative support to become law while Jefferson was governor. Only when James Madison took up the cause years later as part of another political battle did the proposed bill become law, on January 16, 1786.

Primary Source

I. Whereas Almighty God hath created the mind free; that all attempts to influence it by temporal punishments or burthens, or by civil incapacitations, tend only to beget habits of hypocrisy and meanness, and are a departure from the plan of the Holy author of our religion, who being Lord both of body and mind, yet chose not to propagate it by coercions on either, as it was in his Almighty power to do; that the impious presumption of legislators and rulers, civil as well as ecclesiastical, who being themselves but fallible and uninspired men, have assumed dominion over the faith of others, setting up their own opinions and modes of thinking as the only true and infallible, and as such endeavouring to impose them on others, hath established and maintained false religions over the greatest part of the world, and through all time; that to compel a man to furnish contributions of money for the propagation of opinions which he disbelieves, is sinful and tyrannical; that even the forcing him to support this or that teacher of his own religious persuasion, is depriving him of the comfortable liberty of giving his contributions to the particular pastor, whose morals he would make his pattern, and whose powers he feels most persuasive to righteousness, and is withdrawing from the ministry those temporary rewards, which proceeding from an approbation of their personal conduct, are an additional incitement to earnest and unremitting labours for the instruction of mankind; that our civil rights have no dependence on our religious opinions, any more than our opinions in physics or geometry; that therefore the proscribing any citizen as unworthy the public confidence by laying upon him an incapacity of being called to offices of trust and emolument, unless he profess or renounce this or that religious opinion, is depriving him injuriously of those privileges and advantages to which in common with his fellow-citizens he has a natural right; that it tends only to corrupt the principles of that religion it is meant to encourage, by bribing with a monopoly of worldly honours and emoluments, those who will externally profess and conform to it; that though indeed these are criminal who do not withstand such temptation, yet neither are those innocent who lay the bait in their way; that to suffer the civil magistrate to intrude his powers into the field of opinion, and to restrain the profession or propagation of principles on supposition of their ill tendency, is a dangerous fallacy, which at once destroys all religious liberty, because he being of course judge of that tendency will make his opinions the rule of judgment, and approve or condemn the sentiments of others only as they shall square with or differ from his own; that it is time enough for the rightful purposes of civil government, for its officers to interfere when principles break out into overt acts against peace and good order; and finally, that truth is great and will prevail if left to herself, that she is the proper and sufficient antagonist to error, and has nothing to fear from the conflict, unless by human interposition disarmed of her natural weapons, free argument and debate, errors ceasing to be dangerous when it is permitted freely to contradict them.

II. Be it enacted by the General Assembly, That no man shall be compelled to frequent or support any religious worship, place, or ministry whatsoever, nor shall be enforced, restrained, molested, or burthened in his body or goods, nor shall otherwise suffer on account of his religious opinions or belief; but that all men shall be free to profess, and by argument to maintain, their opinion in matters of religion, and that the same shall in no wise diminish enlarge, or affect their civil capacities.

III. And though we well know that this assembly elected by the people for the ordinary purposes of legislation only, have no power to restrain the acts of succeeding assemblies, constituted with powers equal to our own, and that therefore to declare this act to be irrevocable would be of no effect in law; yet we are free to declare, and do declare, that the rights hereby asserted are of the natural rights of mankind, and that if any act shall be hereafter passed to repeal the present, or to narrow its operation, such act shall be an infringement of natural right.

> *Source:* Hening, William Waller, ed., *The Statutes at Large; Being a Collection of all the Laws of Virginia* (Richmond: Printed for The Editor By George Cochran, 1823)

6. Article III of the Constitution of the United States of America, 1787

In addition to Article III, this excerpt includes

Introduction

Article III of the U.S. Constitution establishes the judicial branch of the federal government. Courts that have been established under Article III of the Constitution, including the Supreme Court of the United States, U.S. Courts of Appeals, and U.S. District Courts, are called constitutional, or Article III, courts. Article III of the U.S. Constitution establishes the judicial power of the federal government. The Supreme Court of the United States was created by Article III, Section 1, of the Constitution. The judicial branch comprises the Supreme Court of the United States and lower courts as created by Congress. A federal court may be an Article III, Article I, or Article IV tribunal. These courts are described in reference to the article of the Constitution from which their authority stems. The constitutional provisions for the judiciary reflected the conventions' debate on the appointment of judges, the institutional independence of the third branch, and the value of lower federal courts.

Primary Source

ARTICLE III

Section 1.
The judicial Power of the United States shall be vested in one Supreme Court, and in such inferior Courts as the Congress may from time to time ordain and establish. The Judges, both of the supreme and inferior Courts, shall hold their Offices during good Behaviour, and shall, at stated Times, receive for their Services, a Compensation, which shall not be diminished during their Continuance in Office.

Section 2.
The judicial Power shall extend to all Cases, in Law and Equity, arising under this Constitution, the Laws of the United States, and Treaties made, or which shall be made, under their Authority;—to all Cases affecting Ambassadors, other public Ministers and Consuls;—to all Cases of admiralty and maritime Jurisdiction;—to Controversies to which the United States shall be a Party;—to Controversies

between two or more States;—between a State and Citizens of another State;—between Citizens of different States;—between Citizens of the same State claiming Lands under Grants of different States, and between a State, or the Citizens thereof, and foreign States, Citizens or Subjects.

In all Cases affecting Ambassadors, other public Ministers and Consuls, and those in which a State shall be Party, the Supreme Court shall have original Jurisdiction. In all the other Cases before mentioned, the Supreme Court shall have appellate Jurisdiction, both as to Law and Fact, with such Exceptions, and under such Regulations as the Congress shall make.

The Trial of all Crimes, except in cases of Impeachment, shall be by Jury; and such Trial shall be held in the State where the said Crimes shall have been committed; but when not committed within any State, the Trial shall be at such Place or Places as the Congress may by Law have directed.

Section 3.
Treason against the United States shall consist only in levying War against them, or in adhering to their Enemies, giving them Aid and Comfort. No Person shall be convicted of Treason unless on the Testimony of two Witnesses to the same overt Act, or on Confession in open Court.

The Congress shall have Power to declare the Punishment of Treason, but no Attainder of Treason shall work Corruption of Blood, or Forfeiture except during the Life of the Person attainted.

ARTICLE IV

Section 1.
Full Faith and Credit shall be given in each State to the public Acts, Records, and judicial Proceedings of all other States. And the Congress may by general Laws prescribe the Manner in which such Acts, Records and Proceedings shall be proved, and the Effect thereof.

Section 2.
The Citizens of each State shall be entitled to all Privileges and Immunities of Citizens in the several States.

A Person charged in any State with Treason, Felony, or other Crime, who shall flee from Justice, and be found in another State, shall on Demand of the executive Authority of the State from which he fled, be delivered up, to be removed to the State having Jurisdiction of the Crime.

No Person held to Service or Labour in one State, under the Laws thereof, escaping into another, shall, in Consequence of any Law or Regulation therein, be discharged from such Service or Labour, but shall be delivered up on Claim of the Party to whom such Service or Labour may be due.

Section 3.
New States may be admitted by the Congress into this Union; but no new State shall be formed or erected within the Jurisdiction of any other State; nor any State be formed by the Junction of two or more States, or Parts of States, without the Consent of the Legislatures of the States concerned as well as of the Congress.

The Congress shall have Power to dispose of and make all needful Rules and Regulations respecting the Territory or other Property belonging to the United States; and nothing in this Constitution shall be so construed as to Prejudice any Claims of the United States, or of any particular State.

Section 4.
The United States shall guarantee to every State in this Union a Republican Form of Government, and shall protect each of them against Invasion; and on Application of the Legislature, or of the Executive (when the Legislature cannot be convened) against domestic Violence.

ARTICLE V

The Congress, whenever two thirds of both Houses shall deem it necessary, shall propose Amendments to this Constitution, or, on the Application of the Legislatures of two thirds of the several States, shall call a Convention for proposing Amendments, which, in either Case, shall be valid to all Intents and Purposes, as Part of this Constitution, when ratified by the Legislatures of three fourths of the several States, or by Conventions in three fourths thereof, as the one or the other Mode of Ratification may be proposed by the Congress; Provided that no Amendment which may be made prior to the Year One thousand eight hundred and eight shall in any Manner affect the first and fourth Clauses in the Ninth Section of the first Article; and that no State, without its Consent, shall be deprived of its equal Suffrage in the Senate.

ARTICLE VI

All Debts contracted and Engagements entered into, before the Adoption of this Constitution, shall be as valid against the United States under this Constitution, as under the Confederation.

This Constitution, and the Laws of the United States which shall be made in Pursuance thereof; and all Treaties made, or which shall be made, under the Authority of the United States, shall be the supreme Law of the Land; and the Judges in every State shall be the supreme Law of the Land; and the Judges in every State shall be bound thereby, any Thing in the Constitution or Laws or any State to the Contrary notwithstanding.

The Senators and Representatives before mentioned, and the Members of the several State Legislatures, and all executive and judicial Officers, both of the United States and of the several States, shall be bound by Oath or Affirmation, to support this Constitution; but no religious Test shall ever be required as a Qualification to any Office or public Trust under the United States.

ARTICLE VII

The Ratification of the Conventions of nine States, shall be sufficient for the Establishment of this Constitution between the States so ratifying the Same.

AMENDMENTS
[First 10 amendments ratified on December 15, 1791]

Amendment I
Congress shall make no law respecting an establishment of religion, or prohibiting the free exercise thereof; or abridging the freedom of speech, or of the press; or the right of the people peaceably to assemble, and to petition the Government for a redress of grievances.

Amendment II
A well regulated Militia, being necessary to the security of a free State, the right of the people to keep and bear Arms, shall not be infringed.

Amendment III
No Soldier shall, in time of peace be quartered in any house, without the consent of the Owner, nor in time of war, but in a manner to be prescribed by law.

Amendment IV
The right of the people to be secure in their persons, houses, papers, and effects, against unreasonable searches and seizures, shall not be violated, and no Warrants shall issue, but upon probable cause, supported by Oath or affirmation, and particularly describing the place to be searched, and the persons or things to be seized.

Amendment V

No person shall be held to answer for a capital, or otherwise infamous crime, unless on a presentment or indictment of a Grand Jury, except in cases arising in the land or naval forces, or in the Militia, when in actual service in time of War or public danger; nor shall any person be subject for the same offence to be twice put in jeopardy of life or limb; nor shall be compelled in any criminal case to be a witness against himself, nor be deprived of life, liberty, or property, without due process of law; nor shall private property be taken for public use, without just compensation.

Amendment VI

In all criminal prosecutions, the accused shall enjoy the right to a speedy and public trial, by an impartial jury of the State and district wherein the crime shall have been committed, which district shall have been previously ascertained by law, and to be informed of the nature and cause of the accusation; to be confronted with the witnesses against him; to have compulsory process for obtaining witnesses in his favor, and to have the Assistance of Counsel for his defence.

Amendment VII

In Suits at common law, where the value in controversy shall exceed twenty dollars, the right of trial by jury shall be preserved, and no fact tried by a jury, shall be otherwise re-examined in any Court of the United States, than according to the rules of the common law.

Amendment VIII

Excessive bail shall not be required, nor excessive fines imposed, nor cruel and unusual punishments inflicted.

Amendment IX

The enumeration in the Constitution, of certain rights, shall not be construed to deny or disparage others retained by the people.

Amendment X

The powers not delegated to the United States by the Constitution, nor prohibited by it to the States, are reserved to the States respectively, or to the people.

Amendment XI
[Ratified February 7, 1795]
The Judicial power of the United States shall not be construed to extend to any suit in law or equity, commenced or prosecuted against one of the United States by Citizens of another State, or by Citizens or Subjects of any Foreign State.

Amendment XII
[Ratified June 15, 1804]
The Electors shall meet in their respective states and vote by ballot for President and Vice-President, one of whom, at least, shall not be an inhabitant of the same state with themselves; they shall name in their ballots the person voted for as President, and in distinct ballots the person voted for as Vice-President, and they shall make distinct lists of all persons voted for as President, and of all persons voted for as Vice-President, and of the number of votes for each, which lists they shall sign and certify, and transmit sealed to the seat of the government of the United States, directed to the President of the Senate;—The President of the Senate shall, in the presence of the Senate and House of Representatives, open all the certificates and the votes shall then be counted;—The person having the greatest number of votes for President, shall be the President, if such number be a majority of the whole number of Electors appointed; and if no person have such majority, then from the persons having the highest numbers not exceeding three on the list of those voted for as President, the House of Representatives shall choose immediately, by ballot, the President. But in choosing the President, the votes shall be taken by states, the representation from each state having one vote; a quorum for this purpose shall consist of a member or members from two-thirds of the states, and a majority of all the states shall be necessary to a choice. And if the House of Representatives shall not choose a President whenever the right of choice shall devolve upon them, before the fourth day of March next following, then the Vice-President shall act as President, as in the case of the death or other constitutional disability of the President—The person having the greatest number of votes as Vice-President, shall be the Vice-President, if such number be a majority of the whole number of Electors appointed, and if no person have a majority, then from the two highest numbers on the list, the Senate shall choose the Vice-President; a quorum for the purpose shall consist of two-thirds of the whole number of Senators, and a majority of the whole number shall be necessary to a choice. But no person constitutionally ineligible to the office of President shall be eligible to that of Vice-President of the United States.

Amendment XIII
[Ratified December 6, 1865]
Section 1.
Neither slavery nor involuntary servitude, except as a punishment for crime whereof the party shall have been duly convicted, shall exist within the United States, or any place subject to their jurisdiction.

Section 2.
Congress shall have power to enforce this article by appropriate legislation.

Amendment XIV
[Ratified July 9, 1868]
Section 1.
All persons born or naturalized in the United States and subject to the jurisdiction thereof, are citizens of the United States and of the State wherein they reside. No State shall make or enforce any law which shall abridge the privileges or immunities of citizens of the United States; nor shall any State deprive any person of life, liberty, or property, without due process of law; nor deny to any person within its jurisdiction the equal protection of the laws.

Section 2.
Representatives shall be apportioned among the several States according to their respective numbers, counting the whole number of persons in each State, excluding Indians not taxed. But when the right to vote at any election for the choice of electors for President and Vice President of the United States, Representatives in Congress, the Executive and Judicial officers of a State, or the members of the Legislature thereof, is denied to any of the male inhabitants of such State, being twenty-one years of age, and citizens of the United States, or in any way abridged, except for participation in rebellion, or other crime, the basis of representation therein shall be reduced in the proportion which the number of such male citizens shall bear to the whole number of male citizens twenty-one years of age in such State.

Section 3.
No person shall be a Senator or Representative in Congress, or elector of President and Vice President, or hold any office, civil or military, under the United States, or under any State, who, having previously taken an oath, as a member of Congress, or as an officer of the United States, or as a member of any State legislature, or as an executive or judicial officer of any State, to support the Constitution of the United States, shall have engaged in insurrection or rebellion against the same, or given aid or comfort to the enemies thereof. But Congress may by a vote of two-thirds of each House, remove such disability.

Section 4.
The validity of the public debt of the United States, authorized by law, including debts incurred for payment of pensions and bounties for services in suppressing insurrection or rebellion, shall not be questioned. But neither the United States nor any State shall assume or pay any debt or obligation incurred in aid of insurrection or rebellion against the United States, or any claim for the loss or emancipation of any slave; but all such debts, obligations and claims shall be held illegal and void.

Section 5.
The Congress shall have power to enforce, by appropriate legislation, the provisions of this article.

Amendment XV
[Ratified February 3, 1870]
Section 1.
The right of citizens of the United States to vote shall not be denied or abridged by the United States or by any State on account of race, color, or previous condition of servitude.

Section 2.
The Congress shall have power to enforce this article by appropriate legislation.

Amendment XVI
[Ratified February 3, 1913]
The Congress shall have power to lay and collect taxes on incomes, from whatever source derived, without apportionment among the several States, and without regard to any census or enumeration.

Amendment XVII
[Ratified April 8, 1913]
The Senate of the United States shall be composed of two Senators from each State, elected by the people thereof, for six years; and each Senator shall have one vote. The electors in each State shall have the qualifications requisite for electors of the most numerous branch of the State legislatures.

When vacancies happen in the representation of any State in the Senate, the executive authority of such State shall issue writs of election to fill such vacancies: Provided, That the legislature of any State may empower the executive thereof to make temporary appointments until the people fill the vacancies by election as the legislature may direct.

This amendment shall not be so construed as to affect the election or term of any Senator chosen before it becomes valid as part of the Constitution.

Amendment XVIII
[Ratified January 16, 1919]
Section 1.
After one year from the ratification of this article the manufacture, sale, or transportation of intoxicating liquors within, the importation thereof into, or the expor-

tation thereof from the United States and all territory subject to the jurisdiction thereof for beverage purposes is hereby prohibited.

Section 2.
The Congress and the several States shall have concurrent power to enforce this article by appropriate legislation.

Section 3.
This article shall be inoperative unless it shall have been ratified as an amendment to the Constitution by the legislatures of the several States, as provided in the Constitution, within seven years from the date of the submission hereof to the States by the Congress.

Amendment XIX
[Ratified August 18, 1920]
The right of citizens of the United States to vote shall not be denied or abridged by the United States or by any State on account of sex.

Congress shall have power to enforce this article by appropriate legislation.

Amendment XX
[Ratified January 23, 1933]
Section 1.
The terms of the President and Vice President shall end at noon on the 20th day of January, and the terms of Senators and Representatives at noon on the 3rd day of January, of the years in which such terms would have ended if this article had not been ratified; and the terms of their successors shall then begin.

Section 2.
The Congress shall assemble at least once in every year, and such meeting shall begin at noon on the 3d day of January, unless they shall by law appoint a different day.

Section 3.
If, at the time fixed for the beginning of the term of the President, the President elect shall have died, the Vice President elect shall become President. If a President shall not have been chosen before the time fixed for the beginning of his term, or if the President elect shall have failed to qualify, then the Vice President elect shall act as President until a President shall have qualified; and the Congress may by law provide for the case wherein neither a President elect nor a Vice President elect shall have qualified, declaring who shall then act as President, or the manner in which

one who is to act shall be selected, and such person shall act accordingly until a President or Vice President shall have qualified.

Section 4.
The Congress may by law provide for the case of the death of any of the persons from whom the House of Representatives may choose a President whenever the right of choice shall have devolved upon them, and for the case of the death of any of the persons from whom the Senate may choose a Vice President whenever the right of choice shall have devolved upon them.

Section 5.
Sections 1 and 2 shall take effect on the 15th day of October following the ratification of this article.

Section 6.
This article shall be inoperative unless it shall have been ratified as an amendment to the Constitution by the legislatures of three-fourths of the several States within seven years from the date of its submission.

Amendment XXI
[Ratified December 5, 1933]
Section 1.
The eighteenth article of amendment to the Constitution of the United States is hereby repealed.

Section 2.
The transportation or importation into any State, Territory or possession of the United States for delivery or use therein of intoxicating liquors, in violation of the laws thereof, is hereby prohibited.

Section 3.
This article shall be inoperative unless it shall have been ratified as an amendment to the Constitution by conventions in the several States, as provided in the Constitution, within seven years from the date of the submission hereof to the States by the Congress.

Amendment XXII
[Ratified February 27, 1951]
Section 1.
No person shall be elected to the office of the President more than twice, and no person who has held the office of President, or acted as President, for more than two years of a term to which some other person was elected President shall be elected

to the office of the President more than once. But this Article shall not apply to any person holding the office of President when this Article was proposed by the Congress, and shall not prevent any person who may be holding the office of President, or acting as President, during the term within which this Article becomes operative from holding the office of President or acting as President during the remainder of such term.

Section 2.
This Article shall be inoperative unless it shall have been ratified as an amendment to the Constitution by the legislatures of three-fourths of the several States within seven years from the date of its submission to the States by the Congress.

Amendment XXIII
[Ratified March 29, 1961]
Section 1.
The District constituting the seat of Government of the United States shall appoint in such manner as the Congress may direct:

A number of electors of President and Vice President equal to the whole number of Senators and Representatives in Congress to which the District would be entitled if it were a State, but in no event more than the least populous State; they shall be in addition to those appointed by the States, but they shall be considered, for the purposes of the election of President and Vice President, to be electors appointed by a State; and they shall meet in the District and perform such duties as provided by the twelfth article of amendment.

Section 2.
The Congress shall have power to enforce this article by appropriate legislation.

Amendment XXIV
[Ratified January 23, 1964]
Section 1.
The right of citizens of the United States to vote in any primary or other election for President or Vice President, for electors for President or Vice President, or for Senator or Representative in Congress, shall not be denied or abridged by the United States or any State by reason of failure to pay any poll tax or other tax.

Section 2.
The Congress shall have power to enforce this article by appropriate legislation.

Amendment XXV
[Ratified February 10, 1967]

Section 1.

In case of the removal of the President from office or of his death or resignation, the Vice President shall become President.

Section 2.

Whenever there is a vacancy in the office of the Vice President, the President shall nominate a Vice President who shall take office upon confirmation by a majority vote of both Houses of Congress.

Section 3.

Whenever the President transmits to the President pro tempore of the Senate and the Speaker of the House of Representatives his written declaration that he is unable to discharge the powers and duties of his office, and until he transmits to them a written declaration to the contrary, such powers and duties shall be discharged by the Vice President as Acting President.

Section 4.

Whenever the Vice President and a majority of either the principal officers of the executive departments or of such other body as Congress may by law provide, transmit to the President pro tempore of the Senate and the Speaker of the House of Representatives their written declaration that the President is unable to discharge the powers and duties of his office, the Vice President shall immediately assume the powers and duties of the office as Acting President.

Thereafter, when the President transmits to the President pro tempore of the Senate and the Speaker of the House of Representatives his written declaration that no inability exists, he shall resume the powers and duties of his office unless the Vice President and a majority of either the principal officers of the executive department or of such other body as Congress may by law provide, transmit within four days to the President pro tempore of the Senate and the Speaker of the House of Representatives their written declaration that the President is unable to discharge the powers and duties of his office. Thereupon Congress shall decide the issue, assembling within forty-eight hours for that purpose if not in session. If the Congress, within twenty-one days after receipt of the latter written declaration, or, if Congress is not in session, within twenty-one days after Congress is required to assemble, determines by two-thirds vote of both houses that the President is unable to discharge the powers and duties of his office, the Vice President shall continue to discharge the same as Acting President; otherwise, the President shall resume the powers and duties of his office.

Amendment XXVI
[Ratified July 1, 1971]

Section 1.
The right of citizens of the United States, who are eighteen years of age or older, to vote shall not be denied or abridged by the United States or by any State on account of age.

Section 2.
The Congress shall have power to enforce this article by appropriate legislation.

Amendment XXVII
[Ratified May 7, 1992]
No law, varying the compensation for the services of the senators and representatives shall take effect, until an election of representatives shall have intervened.

Source: National Archives

7. Judiciary Act, 1789

Introduction

The Judiciary Act of 1789 was largely drafted by Oliver Ellsworth of Connecticut, who would later serve as the nation's second chief justice. The law has been credited with upholding the principle of federal supremacy while at the same time serving as a compromise between states' rights and centralization. Enacted on September 24, 1789, the Judiciary Act created a three-tiered system of national courts that, with some modifications, remains in effect today.

<u>Primary Source</u>

An Act to establish the Judicial Courts of the United States.

Section 1. Be it enacted by the Senate and House of Representatives of the United States of America in Congress assembled, That the supreme court of the United States shall consist of a chief justice and five associate justices, any four of whom shall be a quorum, and shall hold annually at the seat of government two sessions, the one commencing the first Monday of February, and the other the first Monday of August. That the associate justices shall have precedence according to the date of their commissions, or when the commissions of two or more of them bear date on the same day, according to their respective ages.

Section 2. And be it further enacted, That the United States shall be and they hereby are divided into thirteen districts. . . .

Section 3. And be it further enacted, That there be a court called a District Court, in each of the aforementioned districts, to consist of one judge, who shall reside in the district for which he is appointed, and shall be called a District Judge, and shall hold annually four sessions. . . .

Section 4. And be it further enacted, That the before mentioned districts, except those of Maine and Kentucky, shall be divided into three circuits, and be called the eastern, the middle, and the southern circuit . . . and that there shall be held annually in each district of said circuits, two courts, which shall be called Circuit Courts, and shall consist of any two justices of the Supreme Court, and the district judge of such districts, any two of whom shall constitute a quorum: Provided, that no district judge shall give a vote in any case of appeal or error from his own decision; but may assign the reasons of such his decision. . . .

Section 8. And be it further enacted, That the justices of the Supreme Court, and the district judges, before they proceed to execute the duties of their respective offices, shall take the following oath or affirmation, to wit: "I, A. B., do solemnly swear or affirm, that I will administer justice without respect to persons, and do equal right to the poor and to the rich, and that I will faithfully and impartially discharge, and perform all the duties incumbent on me as _____, according to the best of my abilities and understanding, agreeably to the constitution and laws of the United States. So help me God."

Section 9. And be it further enacted, That the district courts . . . shall have, exclusively of the courts of the several States, cognizance of all crimes and offences that shall be cognizable under the authority of the United States, committed within their respective districts, or upon the high seas; where no other punishment than whipping, not exceeding thirty stripes, a fine not exceeding one hundred dollars, or a term of imprisonment, not exceeding six months, is to be inflicted; and shall also have exclusive original cognizance of all civil causes of admiralty and maritime jurisdiction, including all seizures under laws of impose, navigation or trade of the United States, where the seizures are made, on waters which are navigable from the sea by vessels of ten or more tons burthen, within their respective districts as well as upon the high seas; saving to suitors, in all cases, the right of a common law remedy, where the common law is competent to give it; and shall also have exclusive original cognizance of all seizures on land, or other waters than as aforesaid, made, and of all suits for penalties and forfeitures incurred, under the laws of the United States. And shall also have cognizance, concurrent with the courts of the several States, or the circuit courts, as the case may be, of all causes where an alien sues for a tort only in violation of the law of nations or a treaty of the United States. And shall also have cognizance, concurrent as last mentioned, of all suits at common law where the United States sue, and the matter in dispute amounts, exclusive of costs, to the sum or value of one hundred dollars. And shall exclusive of costs, to the sum or value of one hundred dollars. And shall also have jurisdiction exclusively of the courts of the several States, of all suits against consuls or vice-consuls, except for offences above the description aforesaid. And the trial of issues in fact, in the district courts, in all causes except civil causes of admiralty and maritime jurisdiction, shall be by jury. . . .

Section 11. And be it further enacted, That the circuit courts shall have original cognizance, concurrent with the courts of the several States, of all suits of a civil nature at common law or in equity, where the matter in dispute exceeds, exclusive of costs, the sum or value of five hundred dollars, and the United States are plaintiffs, or petitioners; or an alien is a party, or the suit is between a citizen of the State where the suit is brought, and a citizen of another State. And shall have exclusive cognizance of all crimes and offences cognizable under the authority of the United States, except where this act otherwise provides, or the laws of the United States shall otherwise direct, and concurrent jurisdiction with the district courts of the crimes and offences cognizable therein. But no person shall be arrested in one district for trial in another, in any civil action before a circuit or district court. And no civil suit shall be brought before either of said courts against an inhabitant of the United States, by any original process in any other district than that whereof he is an inhabitant, or in which he shall be found at the time of serving the writ, nor shall any district or circuit court have cognizance of any suit to recover the contents of any promissory note or other chose in action in favour of an assignee, unless a suit might have been prosecuted in such court to recover the said contents if no assignment had been made, except in cases of foreign bills of exchange. And the circuit courts shall also have appellate jurisdiction from the district courts under the regulations and restrictions herein after provided. . . .

Section 12. And be it further enacted, That if a suit be commenced in any state court against an alien, or by a citizen of another state, and the matter in dispute exceeds the aforesaid sum or value of five hundred dollars, exclusive of costs, to be made to appear to the satisfaction of the court; and the defendant shall, at the time of entering his appearance in such state court, file a petition for the removal of the cause of trail into the next circuit court, to be held in the district where the suit is pending, . . . and offer good and sufficient surety, and proceed no further in the cause, and any bail that may have been originally taken shall be discharged, and the said copies being entered as aforesaid, in such court of the United States, the cause shall there proceed in the same manner as if it had been brought there by original process. And any attachment of the goods or estate of the defendant by the original process, shall hold the goods or estate so attached, to answer the final judgment in the same manner as by the laws of such state they would have been holden to answer final judgment, had it been rendered by the court in which the suit commenced. And if in any action commenced in a state court, the title of land be concerned, and the parties are citizens of the same state, and the matter in dispute exceeds the sum or value of five hundred dollars, exclusive of costs, the sum or value being made to appear to the satisfaction of the court, either party, before the trial, shall state to the court and make affidavit if they require it, that he claims and shall rely upon a right or title to the land, under a grant from a state other than that in which the suit is pending, and produce the original grant or an exemplification of it, except where the loss of public records shall put it out of his power, and shall move that the adverse party inform the court, whether he claims a right or title to the land under a grant from the state in which the suit is pending; the said land under a grant from the state in which the suit is pending; the said adverse [party] shall give such information, or otherwise not be allowed to plead such grant, or give it in evidence upon the trial, and if he informs that he does claim under such grant, the party claiming under the grant first mentioned may then, on motion, remove the cause of trial to the next circuit court to be holden in such district . . . but if he is the defendant, shall do it under the same regulations as in the before-mentioned case of the removal of a cause into such court by an alien; and neither party removing the cause, shall be allowed to plead or give evidence of any other title than that by him stated as aforesaid, as the ground of his claim; and the trial of issues in fact in the circuit courts shall, in all suits, except those of equity, and of admiralty, and maritime jurisdiction, be by jury. . . .

Section 13. And be it further enacted, That the Supreme Court shall have exclusive jurisdiction of all controversies of a civil nature, where a state is a party, except between a state and its citizens; and except also between a state and citizens of other states, or aliens, in which latter case it shall have original but not exclusive jurisdiction. And shall have exclusively all such jurisdiction of suits or proceedings against ambassadors, or other public ministers, or their domestics, or domestic servants, as a court of law can have or exercise consistently with the law of nations; and original, but not exclusive jurisdiction of all suits brought by ambassadors, or other public ministers, or in which a consul, or vice consul, shall be a party. And the trial of issues in fact in the Supreme Court, in all actions at law against citizens of the United States, shall be by jury. The Supreme Court shall also have appellate jurisdiction from the circuit courts and courts of the several states, in the cases herein after specially provided for; and shall have power to issue writs of prohibition to the district courts, when proceeding as courts of admiralty and maritime jurisdiction, and writs of mandamus, in cases warranted by the principles and usages of law, to any courts appointed, or persons holding office, under the authority of the United States.

Section 14. And be it further enacted, That all the before-mentioned courts of the United States, shall have power to issue writs of scire facias, habeas corpus, and all other writs not specially provided for by statute, which may be necessary for the exercise of their respective jurisdictions, and agreeable to the principles and usages of law. And that either of the justices of the supreme court, as well as judges of the district courts, shall have power to grant writs of habeas corpus for the purpose of an inquiry into the cause of commitment.—Provided, That writs of habeas corpus shall in no case extend to prisoners in gaol [jail], unless where they are in custody, under or by colour of the authority of the United States, or are committed for trial before some court of the same, or are necessary to be brought into court to testify.

Section 15. And be it further enacted, That all the said courts of the United States, shall have power in the trial of actions at law, on motion and due notice thereof being given, to require the parties to produce books or writings in their possession or power, which contain evidence pertinent to the issue, in cases and under circumstances where they might be compelled to produce the same by the ordinary rules of proceeding in chancery; and if a plaintiff shall fail to comply with such order, to produce books or writings, it shall be lawful for the courts respectively, on motion, to give the like judgment for the defendant as in cases of nonsuit; and if a defendant shall fail to comply with such order, to produce books or writings, it shall be lawful for the courts respectively on motion as aforesaid, to give judgment against him or her by default. . . .

Section 16. And be it further enacted, That suits in equity shall not be sustained in either of the courts of the United States, in any case where plain, adequate and complete remedy may be had at law. . . .

Section 17. And be it further enacted, That all the said courts of the United States shall have power to grant new trials, in cases where there has been a trial by jury for reasons for which new trials have usually been granted in the courts of law; and shall have power to impose and administer all necessary oaths or affirmations, and to punish by fine or imprisonment, at the discretion of said courts, all contempts of authority in any cause or hearing before the same; and to make and establish all necessary rules for the orderly conducting business in the said courts, provided such rules are not repugnant to the laws of the United States. . . .

Section 20. And be it further enacted, That where in a circuit court, a plaintiff in an action, originally brought there, or a petitioner in equity, other than the United States, recovers less than the sum or value of five hundred dollars, or a libellant, upon his own appeal, less than the sum or value of three hundred dollars, he shall not be allowed, but at the discretion of the court, may be adjudged to pay costs. . . .

Section 27. And be it further enacted, That a marshal shall be appointed in and for each district for the term of four years, but shall be removable from office at pleasure, whose duty it shall be to attend the district and circuit courts when sitting therein, and also the Supreme Court in the district in which that court shall sit. And to execute throughout the district, all lawful precepts directed to him, and issued under the authority of the United States, and he shall have power to command all necessary assistance in the execution of his duty, and to appoint as there shall be occasion, one or more deputies, who shall be removable from office by the judge of the district court, or the circuit court sitting within the district, at the pleasure of either; and before he enters on the duties of his office, he shall become bound for the faithful performance of the same, by himself and by his deputies before the judge of the district court to the United States, jointly and severally, with two good and sufficient sureties, inhabitants and freeholders of such district, to be approved by the district judge, in the sum of twenty thousand dollars, and shall take before said judge, as shall also his deputies, before they enter on the duties of their appointment, the following oath of office: "I, A. B., do solemnly swear or affirm, that I will faithfully execute all lawful precepts directed to the marshal of the district of _____ under the authority of the United States, and true returns make, and in all things well and truly, and without malice or partiality, perform the duties of the office of marshal (or marshal's deputy, as the case may be) and take only my lawful fees. So help me God." . . .

Section 29. And be it further enacted, That in cases punishable with death, the trial shall be had in the county where the offence was committed, or where that cannot be done without great inconvenience, twelve petit jurors at least shall be summoned thence. And jurors in all cases to serve in the courts of the United States shall be designated by lot or otherwise in each State respectively according to the mode of forming juries therein now practised, so far as the laws of the same shall render such designation practicable by the courts or marshals of the United States; and the jurors shall have the same qualifications as are requisite for jurors by the laws of the State of which they are citizens, to serve in the highest courts of law of such State, and shall be returned as there shall be occasion for them, from such parts of the district from time to time as the court shall direct, so as shall be most favourable to an impartial trial, and so as not to incur an unnecessary expense, or unduly to burthen the citizens of any part of the district with such services. And writs of venire facias when directed by the court shall issue from the clerk's office, and shall be served and returned by the marshal in his proper person, or by his deputy, or in case the marshal or his deputy is not an indifferent person, or is interested in the event of the cause, by such fit person as the court shall specially appoint for that purpose, to whom they shall administer an oath or affirmation that he will truly and impartially serve and return such writ. And when from challenges or otherwise there shall not be a jury to determine any civil or criminal cause, the marshal or his deputy shall, by order of the court where such defect of jurors shall happen, return jurymen de talibus circustantibus sufficient to complete the pannel; and when the marshal or his deputy are disqualified as aforesaid, jurors may be returned by such disinterested person as the court shall appoint.

Section 30. And be it further enacted, That the mode of proof by oral testimony and examination of witnesses in open court shall be the same in all the courts of the United States, as well in the trial of causes in equity and of admiralty and maritime jurisdiction, as of actions at common law. And when the testimony of any person shall be necessary in any civil cause depending in any district in any court of the United States, who shall live at a greater distance from the place of trial than one hundred miles, or is bound on a voyage to sea, or is about to go out of the United States, or out of such district, and to a greater distance from the place of trial than as aforesaid, before the time of trial, or is ancient or very infirm, the deposition of such person may be taken de bene esse before any justice or judge of any of the courts of the United States, or before any chancellor, justice or judge of a supreme or superior court, mayor or chief magistrate of a city, or judge of a county court or court of common please of any of the United States, not being of counsel or attorney to either of the parties, or interested in the event of the cause, provided that a notification from the magistrate before whom the deposition is to be taken to the adverse party, to be present at the taking of the same, and to put interrogatories, if he think fit, be first made out and served on the adverse party or his attorney as either may be nearest, if either is within one hundred miles of the place of such caption. . . . And any person may be compelled to appear and depose as aforesaid in the same manner as to appear and testify in court. And in the trail of any cause of admiralty or maritime jurisdiction in a district court, the decree in which may be appealed from, if either party shall suggest to and satisfy the court that probably it will not be in his power to produce the witnesses there testifying before the circuit court should an appeal be had, and shall move that their testimony be taken down in writing, it shall be so done by the clerk of the court. And, if an appeal be had, such testimony may be used on the trial of the same, if it shall appear to the satisfaction of the court which shall try the appeal, that the witnesses are then dead or gone out of the United States, or to a greater distance than as aforesaid from the place where the court is sitting, or that by reason of age, sickness, bodily infirmity or imprisonment, they are unable to travel and appear at court, but not otherwise. And unless the same shall be made to appear on the trial of any cause, with respect to witnesses whose depositions may have been taken therein, such depositions shall not be admitted or used in the cause. Provided, That nothing herein shall be construed to prevent any court of the United States from granting a dedimus potestatem to take depositions according to common usage, when it may be necessary to prevent a failure or delay of justice. . . .

Section 31. And be it [further] enacted, That where any suit shall be depending in any court of the United States, and either of the parties shall die before final judgment, the executor or administrator of such deceased party who was plaintiff, petitioner, or defendant, in case the cause of action doth by law survive, shall have full power to prosecute or defend any such suit or action until final judgment; and the defendant or defendants are hereby obliged to answer thereto accordingly; and the court before whom such cause may be depending, is hereby empowered and directed to hear and determine the same, and to render judgment for or against the executor or administrator, as the case may require. . . .

Section 33. And be it further enacted, That for any crime or offence against the United States, the offender may, by any justice or judge of the United States, or by any justice of the peace, or other magistrate of any of the United States where he may be found agreeably to the usual mode of process against offenders in such state, and at the expense of the United States, be arrested, and imprisoned or bailed, as the case may be, for trial before such court of the United States as by this act has cognizance of the offence. . . .

Section 34. And be it further enacted, that the laws of the several states, except where the constitution, treaties or statutes of the United States shall otherwise require or provide, shall be regarded as rules of decision in trials at common law in the courts of the United States in cases where they apply. . . .

Section 35. And be it further enacted, That in all the courts of the United States, the parties may plead and manage their own causes personally or by the assistance of such counsel or attorneys at law as by the rules of the said courts respectively shall be permitted to manage and conduct causes therein. And there shall be appointed in each district a meet person learned in the law to act as attorney for the United States in such district, who shall be sworn or affirmed to the faithful execution of his office, whose duty it shall be to prosecute in such district all delinquents for crimes and offences, cognizable under the authority of the United States, and all civil actions in which the United States shall be concerned, except before the supreme court in the district in which that court shall be holden. And he shall receive as compensation for his services such fees as shall be taxed therefor in the respective courts before which the suits or prosecutions shall be. And there shall also be appointed a meet person, learned in the law, to act as attorney-general of the United States, who shall be sworn or affirmed to a faithful execution of his office; whose duty it shall be to prosecute and conduct all suits in the Supreme Court in which the United States shall be concerned, and to give his advice and opinion upon questions of law when required by the President of the United States, or when requested by the heads of any of the departments, touching any matters that may concern their departments, and shall receive such compensation for his services as shall by law be provided. . . .

Source: Statutes at Large, 1st Congress, 1st Session, Vol. 1, Ch. 20, Pg. 73

8. Alien and Sedition Acts, 1798

Introduction

A series of four laws championed by the Federalists in the U.S. Congress and President John Adams, the Alien and Sedition Acts made it more difficult for immigrants to obtain U.S. citizenship, enacted stricter laws against immigrants that increased the risk of deportation, and limited the rights of freedom of assembly and freedom of the press for U.S. citizens under the guise of preparing the United States for its entry into the Napoleonic Wars against France. Democratic-Republicans maintained that the acts were a weapon to suppress political dissent, and the acts themselves proved wildly unpopular. The laws included here are the Alien Enemies Act (passed July 6) and the Sedition Act (passed July 14). The other two laws were the Naturalization Act (passed June 18) and the Alien Act (passed June 25).

Primary Source

ALIEN ENEMIES ACT

Section 1. Be it enacted by the Senate and House of Representatives of the United States of America in Congress assembled, That whenever there shall be a declared war between the United States and any foreign nation or government, or any invasion or predatory incursion shall be perpetrated, attempted, or threatened against the territory of the United States, by any foreign nation or government, and the President of the United States shall make public proclamation of the event, all natives, citizens, denizens, or subjects of the hostile nation or government, being males of the age of fourteen years and upwards, who shall be within the United States, and not actually naturalized, shall be liable to be apprehended, restrained, secured and removed, as alien enemies. And the President of the United States shall be, and he is hereby authorized, in any event, as aforesaid, by his proclamation thereof, or other public act, to direct the conduct to be observed, on the part of the United States, towards the aliens who shall become liable, as aforesaid; the manner and degree of the restraint to which they shall be subject, and in what cases, and upon what security their residence shall be permitted, and to provide for the removal of those, who, not being permitted to reside within the United States, shall refuse or neglect to depart therefrom; and to establish any other regulations which shall be found necessary in the premises and for the public safety: Provided, that aliens resident within the United States, who shall become liable as enemies, in the manner aforesaid, and who shall not be chargeable with actual hostility, or other crime against the public safety, shall be allowed, for the recovery, disposal, and removal of their goods and effects, and for their departure, the full time which is, or shall be stipulated by any treaty, where any shall have been between the United States, and the hostile nation or government, of which they shall be natives, citizens, denizens or subjects: and where no such treaty shall have existed, the President of the United States may ascertain and declare such reasonable time as may be consistent with the public safety, and according to the dictates of humanity and national hospitality.

Section 2. And be it further enacted, That after any proclamation shall be made as aforesaid, it shall be the duty of the several courts of the United States, and of each state, having criminal jurisdiction, and of the several judges and justices of the courts of the United States, and they shall be, and are hereby respectively, authorized upon complaint, against any alien or alien enemies, as aforesaid, who shall be resident and at large within such jurisdiction or district, to the danger of the public peace or safety, and contrary to the tenor or intent of such proclamation, or other regulations which the President of the United States shall and may establish in the premises, to cause such alien or aliens to be duly apprehended and convened before such court, judge or justice; and after a full examination and hearing on such complaint. and sufficient cause therefor appearing, shall and may order such alien or aliens to be removed out of the territory of the United States, or to give sureties of their good behaviour, or to be otherwise restrained, conformably to the proclamation or regulations which shall and may be established as aforesaid, and may imprison, or otherwise secure such alien or aliens, until the order which shall and may be made, as aforesaid, shall be performed.

Section 3. And be it further enacted, That it shall be the duty of the marshal of the district in which any alien enemy shall be apprehended, who by the President of the United States, or by order of any court, judge or justice, as aforesaid, shall be required to depart, and to be removed, as aforesaid, to provide therefor, and to execute such order, by himself or his deputy, or other discreet person or persons to be employed by him, by causing a removal of such alien out of the territory of the United States; and for such removal the marshal shall have the warrant of the President of the United States, or of the court, judge or justice ordering the same, as the case may be.

SEDITION ACT

Section 1. Be it enacted That if any persons shall unlawfully combine or conspire together, with intent to oppose any measure or measures of the government of the United States, which are or shall be directed by proper authority, or to impede the operation of any law of the United States, or to intimidate or prevent any person holding a place or office in or under the government of the United States, from undertaking, performing or executing his trust or duty; and if any person or persons, with intent as aforesaid, shall counsel, advise or attempt to procure any insurrection, riot. unlawful assembly, or combination, whether such conspiracy, threatening, counsel, advice, or attempt shall have the proposed effect or not, he or they shall be deemed guilty of a high misdemeanor, and on conviction, before any court of the United States having jurisdiction thereof, shall be punished by a fine not exceeding five thousand dollars, and by imprisonment during a term not less than six months nor exceeding five years; and further, at the discretion of the court may be holden to find sureties for his good behaviour in such sum, and for such time, as the said court may direct.

Section 2. That if any person shall write, print, utter, or publish, or shall cause or procure to be written, printed, uttered or published, or shall knowingly and willingly assist or aid in writing, printing, uttering or publishing any false, scandalous and malicious writing or writings against the government of the United States, or either house of the Congress of the United States, or the President of the United States, with intent to defame the said government, or either house of the said Congress, or the said President, or to bring them. or either of them, into contempt or disrepute; or to excite against them, or either or any of them, the hatred of the good people of the United States, or to excite any unlawful combinations therein, for opposing or resisting any law of the United States, or any act of the President of the United States, done in pursuance of any such law, or of the powers in him vested by the constitution of the United States, or to resist, oppose, or defeat any such law or act, or to aid, encourage or abet any hostile designs of any foreign nation against the United States, their people or government, then such person, being thereof convicted before any court of the United States having jurisdiction thereof, shall be punished by a fine not exceeding two thousand dollars, and by imprisonment not exceeding two years.

Section 3. That if any person shall be prosecuted under this act, for the writing or publishing any libel aforesaid, it shall be lawful for the defendant, upon the trial of the cause, to give in evidence in his defence, the truth of the matter contained in the publication charged as a libel. And the jury who shall try the cause, shall have a right to determine the law and the fact, under the direction of the court, as in other cases.

Section 4. That this act shall continue to be in force until March 3, 1801, and no longer.

Source: National Archives

9. Judiciary Act, 1801

Introduction

Passed by the lame-duck Federalists in Congress on February 13, 1801, after the election of Democratic-Republican president Thomas Jefferson, the Judiciary Act of 1801 was a blend of needed judicial reform and partisan politics. The law reduced membership on the U.S. Supreme Court from six to five, added six new circuit courts to replace the original three created by the Judiciary Act of 1789, and relieved Supreme Court justices from their responsibility of circuit-riding. In the process, the act also created 16 new judgeships, along with their support staffs, for outgoing Federalist president John Adams to fill. These judgeships later became the source of controversy leading to the U.S. Supreme Court case *Marbury v. Madison* (1803). Most of the Judiciary Act of 1801 was replaced by the Democratic-Republican-backed Judiciary Act of 1802.

Primary Source

An Act to provide for the more convenient organization of the Courts of the United States.

Section 1. Be it enacted by the Senate and House of Representatives of the United States of America in Congress assembled, That from and after the next session of the Supreme Court of the United States, the said court shall be holden by the justices thereof, or any four of them, at the city of Washington, and shall have two sessions in each and every year thereafter, to commence on the first Monday of June and December respectively; and that if four of the said justices shall not attend within ten days after the times hereby appointed for the commencement of the said sessions respectively, the said court shall be continued over till the next stated session thereof: Provided always, that any one or more of the said justices, attending as aforesaid, shall have power to make all necessary orders touching any suit, action, appeal, writ of error, process, pleadings, or proceeding, returned to the said court or depending therein, preparatory to the hearing, trial or decision of such action, suit, appeal, writ of error, process, pleadings or proceedings.

Section 2. And be it further enacted, That the said court shall have power, and is hereby authorized, to issue writs of prohibition, mandamus, scire facias, habeas corpus, certiorari, procedendo, and all other writs not specially provided for by statute, which may be necessary for the exercise of its jurisdiction, and agreeable to the principles and usages of law.

Section 3. And be it further enacted, That from and after the next vacancy that shall happen in the said court, it shall consist of five justices only; that is to say, of one chief justice, and four associate justices.

Section 4. And be it further enacted, That for the better establishment of the circuit courts of the United States, the said states shall be, and hereby are divided into districts, in manner following; that is to say, one to consist of that part of the state of Massachusetts, which is called the district of Maine, and to be called the district of Maine; one to consist of the state of New Hampshire, and to be called the district of New Hampshire; one to consist of the remaining part of the state of Massachusetts, and to be called the district of Massachusetts; one to consist of the state of Rhode Island and Providence Plantations, and to be called the district of Rhode Island; one to consist of the state of Connecticut, and to be called the district of Connecticut; one to consist of the state of Vermont, and to be called the district of Vermont; one to consist of that part of the state of New York which lies north of the counties of Dutchess and Ulster, and to be called the district of Albany; one to consist of the remaining part of the state of New York, and to be called the district of New York; one to consist of the state of New Jersey, and to be called the district of Jersey; one to consist of that part of the state of Pennsylvania which lies east of the river Susquehanna, and the northeast branch thereof, to the line betwixt Northumberland and Luzerne counties; thence westwardly along said line, betwixt Northumberland and Luzerne, and betwixt Luzerne and Lycoming counties, until the same strikes the line of the state of New York, and to be called the Eastern district of Pennsylvania; one to consist of the remaining part of the state of Pennsylvania, and to be called the Western district of Pennsylvania; one to consist of the state of Delaware, and to be called the district of Delaware; one to consist of the state of Maryland, and to be called the district of Maryland; one to consist of that part of the state of Virginia, which lies to the eastward of a line to be drawn from the river Potomac at Harper's ferry, along the Blue Ridge, with the line which divides the counties on the east side thereof from those on the west side thereof, to the North Carolina line, to be called the Eastern district of Virginia; one to consist of the remaining part of the said state of Virginia, to be called the Western district of Virginia; one to consist of the state of North Carolina, and to be called the district of North Carolina; one to consist of the state of South Carolina, and to be called the district of South Carolina; one to consist of the state of Georgia, and to be called the district of Georgia; one to consist of that part of the state of Tennessee which lies on the east side of Cumberland mountain, and to be called the district of East Tennessee; one to consist of the remaining part of said state, and to be called the district of West Tennessee; one to consist of the state of Kentucky, and to be called the district of Kentucky; and one to consist of the territory of the United States northwest of the Ohio, and the Indiana territory, and to be called the district of Ohio.

Section 5. And be it further enacted, That where any two adjoining districts of the United States shall be divided from each other, in whole or in part, by any river, bay, water, water-course or mountain, the whole width of such river, bay, water, water-course or mountain, as the case may be, shall be taken and deemed, to all intents and purposes, to be within both of the districts so to be divided thereby.

Section 6. And be it further enacted, That the said districts shall be classed into six circuits in manner following; that is to say: The first circuit shall consist of the districts of Maine, New Hampshire, Massachusetts, and Rhode Island; the second, of the districts of Connecticut, Vermont, Albany and New York; the third, of the districts of Jersey, the Eastern and Western districts of Pennsylvania, and Delaware; the fourth, of the districts of Maryland, and the Eastern and Western districts of Virginia; the fifth, of the districts of North Carolina, South Carolina, and Georgia; and the sixth, of the districts of East Tennessee, West Tennessee, Kentucky, and Ohio.

Section 7. And be it further enacted, That there shall be in each of the aforesaid circuits, except the sixth circuit, three judges of the United States, to be called circuit judges, one of whom shall be commissioned as chief judge; and that there shall be a circuit court of the United States, in and for each of the aforesaid circuits, to be composed of the circuit judges within the five first circuits respectively, and in the sixth circuit, by a circuit judge, and the judges of the district courts of Kentucky and Tennessee; the duty of all of whom it shall be to attend, but any two of whom shall form a quorum; and that each and every of the said circuit courts shall hold two sessions annually, at the times and places following, in and for each district contained within their several circuits respectively; that is to say, the circuit court of the first circuit, at Providence on the eighth day of May, and at Newport on the first day of November, in and for the district of Rhode Island; at Boston, in and for the district of Massachusetts, on the twenty-second day of May and fifteenth day of October; at Portsmouth on the eighth day of June, and at Exeter on the twenty-ninth day of September, in and for the district of New Hampshire; in and for the district of Maine, at Portland on the fifteenth day of June, and at Wiscasset on the twenty-second day of September. The circuit court of the second circuit, at New Haven on the fifteenth day of April, and at Hartford, on the twenty-fifth day of September, in and for the district of Connecticut; at Windsor on the fifth day of May, and at Rutland on the fifteenth day of October, in and for the district of Vermont; at the city of Albany, in and for the district of Albany, on the twentieth day of May and twenty-fifth day of October; at the city of New York, in and for the district of New York, on the fifth day of June and the tenth day of November. The circuit court of the third circuit, at Trenton, in and for the district of Jersey, on the second days of May and October; at the city of Philadelphia, in and for the Eastern district of Pennsylvania, on the eleventh day of May and eleventh day of October; at Bedford, in and for the Western district of Pennsylvania, on the twenty-fifth day of June and twenty-fifth day of November; and at Dover, in and for the district of Delaware, on the third day of June and twenty-seventh day of October. The circuit court of the fourth circuit, at Baltimore, in and for the district of Maryland, on the twentieth day of March and fifth day of November; at Lexington in Rockbridge county, in and for the Western district of Virginia, on the fifth day of April and twentieth day of November; and at the city of Richmond, in and for the Eastern district of Virginia, on the twenty-fifth day of April, and fifth day of December. The circuit court of the fifth circuit, at Raleigh, in and for the district of North Carolina, on the first day of June and the first day of November; at Charleston on the sixth day of May, and at Columbia on the thirtieth day of November, in and for the district of South Carolina; at Savannah on the tenth day of April, and at Augusta on the fifteenth day of December, in and for the district of Georgia; and the circuit court of the sixth circuit, at Knoxville, in and for the district of East Tennessee, on the twenty-fifth day of March and twenty-fifth day of September; at Nashville, in and for the district of West Tennessee, on the twentieth day of April and twentieth day of October; and at Bairdstown, in and for the district of Kentucky, on the fifteenth day of May and fifteenth day of November; and at Cincinnati in and for the district of Ohio, on the tenth day of June and on the tenth day of December; and so on the several days and at the several places aforesaid, in each and every year afterwards: Provided always, that when any of the said days shall happen on Sunday, then the said court hereby directed to be holden on such day, shall be holden on the next day thereafter; and provided also, that there shall be appointed, in the sixth circuit, a judge of the United States, to be called a circuit judge, who together with the district judges of Tennessee and Kentucky, shall hold the circuit courts, hereby directed to be holden, within the said circuit; and that whenever the office of district judge, in the districts of Kentucky and Tennessee respectively, shall become vacant, such vacancies shall respectively be supplied by the appointment of two additional circuit judges, in the said circuit, who, together with the circuit judge first aforesaid, shall compose the circuit court of the said circuit.

Section 8. Provided always, and be it further enacted, That the said circuit courts hereby established shall have power, and hereby are authorized, to hold special sessions, for the trial of criminal causes, at any other time or times than is hereby directed, at their discretion.

Section 9. And provided also, and be it further enacted, That if in the opinion of any judge of any of the said circuit courts, it shall be dangerous to hold the next stated session of such court, for any district within the circuit to which such judge shall belong, at the place by law appointed for holding the same; it shall be lawful for such judge to issue his order, under his hand and seal, to the marshal of such court, directing him to adjourn the said session, to such other place within the same district as the said judge shall deem convenient; which said marshal shall, thereupon, adjourn the said court pursuant to such order, by making, in one or more public papers, printed within the said district, publication of such order and adjournment, from the time when he shall receive such order to the time appointed by law for commencing such stated session: and that the court so to be held, according to, and by virtue of such adjournment, shall have the same powers and authorities, and shall proceed in the same manner, as if the same had been held at the place appointed by law for that purpose.

Section 10. And be it further enacted, That the circuit courts shall have, and hereby are invested with, all the powers heretofore granted by law to the circuit courts of the United States, unless where otherwise provided by this act.

Section 11. And be it further enacted, That the said circuit courts respectively shall have cognizance of all crimes and offences cognizable under the authority of the United States, and committed within their respective districts, or upon the high seas; and also of all cases in law or equity, arising under the constitution and laws of the United States, and treaties made, or which shall be made, under their authority; and also of all actions, or suits of a civil nature, at common law, or in equity, where the United States shall be plaintiffs or complainants; and also of all seizures on land or water, and all penalties and forfeitures, made, arising or accruing under the laws of the United States; which cognizance of all penalties and forfeitures, shall be exclusively of the state courts, in the said circuit courts, where the offence, by which the penalty or forfeiture is incurred, shall have been committed within fifty miles of the place of holding the said courts; and also of all actions, or suits, matters or things cognizable by the judicial authority of the United States, under and by virtue of the constitution thereof, where the matter in dispute shall amount to four hundred dollars, and where original jurisdiction is not given by the constitution of the United States to the supreme court thereof, or exclusive jurisdiction by law to the district courts of the United States: Provided always, that in all cases where the title, or bounds of land shall come into question, the jurisdiction of the said circuit courts shall not be restrained, by reason of the value of the land in dispute.

Section 12. And be it further enacted, That the said circuit courts respectively shall have cognizance concurrently with the district courts, of all cases which shall arise, within their respective circuits, under the act to establish an uniform system of bankruptcy throughout the United States; and that each circuit judge, within his respective circuit, shall and may perform all and singular the duties enjoined by the said act, upon a judge of a district court: and that the proceedings under a commission of bankruptcy, which shall issue from a circuit judge, shall in all respects be conformable to the proceedings under a commission of bankruptcy, which shall issue from a district judge, mutatis mutandis.

Section 13. And be it further enacted, That where any action or suit shall be, or shall have been commenced, in any state court within the United States, against an alien, or by a citizen or citizens of the state in which such suit or action shall be, or shall have been commenced against a citizen or citizens of another state, and the matter in dispute, except in cases where the title or bounds of land shall be in question, shall exceed the sum or value of four hundred dollars, exclusive of costs, and the defendant or defendants in such suit or action shall be personally served with the original process therein, or shall appear thereto; or where, in any suit or action, so commenced or to be commenced, final judgment, for a sum exceeding four hundred dollars, exclusive of costs, shall have been rendered in such state court, against such defendant or defendants, without return of personal service on him, her, or them, of the original process in such suit or action, and without an appearance thereto, by him, her, or them, and a writ of error, or writ of review, shall be brought by such defendant or defendants, in such state court, to reverse the said judgment; or where any suit or action shall have been, or shall be commenced in any such court, against any person or persons, in any case arising under the constitution or laws of the United States, or treaties made or to be made under their authority; then, and in any of the said cases, it shall be lawful for the defendant or defendants, in such suit or action, at the time of entering his, her, or their appearance thereto, and for the plaintiff, or plaintiffs in such writ of error, or writ of review, at the time when such writ shall be returnable, to file in such court a petition for the removal of such suit, action, writ of error, or writ of review, to the next circuit court of the United States, hereby directed to be holden in and for the district within which such state court shall be holden, and to offer to such state court good and sufficient surety for entering, in such circuit court, on the first day of its next ensuing session, true copies of the process and proceedings, in such action, suit, writ of error, or writ of review, and also for his, her, or their appearance in the said circuit court, at the period aforesaid, and then and there entering special bail, in the said suit, or action, if special bail was originally demandable, and demanded therein; whereupon it shall be the duty of the said state court to accept the said security, and to stay all further proceedings in such suit, action, writ of error, or writ of review, and to discharge any bail that may have been given therein; and that the said copies being filed as aforesaid in such circuit court, and special bail, in manner aforesaid, being given therein, such suit, action, writ of error, or writ of review, shall be therein proceeded on, tried, heard and determined, in the same manner as if there originally commenced or brought: Provided always, that any attachment of the goods or estate of the defendant, by the original process in such suit or action, shall hold the goods or estate so attached, to answer the final judgment in the said circuit court, in the same manner as by the laws of the state they would have been holden, to answer the final judgment, had it been rendered by the court in which the suit or action was commenced.

Section 14. And be it further enacted, That when any suit or action, commenced, or to be commenced, in any state court within the United States, between citizens of the same state, the title or bounds of land shall come into question, it shall be lawful for either party, before trial, to state to the said court, and make affidavit if thereby required, that he, she, or they, doth or do claim under, and at the hearing or trial shall rely upon a right or title to the lands in dispute, under a grant, or grants, from a state other than that wherein such suit or action is, or shall be pending; and to produce to the said court the original grant, or grants, so claimed under, or exemplifications thereof, except in cases where the loss of public records shall put it out of his, her or their power so to do; and to move that the adverse party do inform the said court, forthwith, whether he, she, or they, doth or do claim the land in dispute, under a grant or grants from the state wherein such suit or action is, or shall be pending; whereupon the said adverse party shall give such information, or otherwise not be allowed to plead, or give in evidence, in the cause any such grant; and that if it shall appear from such information, that the said adverse party doth claim the said lands, under any such grant, or grants, then it shall be lawful for the party moving for such information, if plaintiff or complainant in the said suit or action, to remove the same, by motion, to the next circuit court of the United States, hereby directed to be holden in and for the district within which such state court shall be holden; and if defendant in the said suit or action, then to remove the same, as aforesaid, in the same manner, and under the like regulations, terms, and conditions, as are provided in and by the preceding section of this act, in the cases of actions thereby directed to be removed; and that the said circuit courts respectively, into which such suit or action shall be removed, pursuant to the provisions in this section contained, shall proceed in, try, hear and determine the same, in like manner as if therein brought by original process: Provided always, that neither party, so removing any suit or action, shall be allowed, on the trial or hearing thereof, to plead, give evidence of, or rely on, any other title than that by him, her, or them, so stated as aforesaid, as the ground of his, her, or their claim.

Section 15. And be it further enacted, That any one judge of any of the said circuit courts shall be, and hereby is, authorized and empowered, to hold the same from day to day, not exceeding five days, to impannel and charge the grand jury, to order process on any indictment or presentment found in the said court; to direct subpoenas for witnesses to attend the same, and the requisite process on the non-attendance of witnesses or jurors; to receive any presentment or indictment from the grand jury; to take recognizance for the attendance of any witness, or for the appearance of any person, presented or indicted; to award and issue process, and order commitment for contempts; to commit any person presented or indicted, for want of security or otherwise; to order publication of testimony; to issue commissions for the examination of witnesses, where allowable by law; to grant rules and orders of survey; to take order, where necessary, relative to jurors, to serve at the next stated session of the said court; to direct the examination of witnesses de bene esse, where allowed by law; to make rules of reference by consent of parties; and to grant continuances on the motion of either party, upon such terms and conditions, as shall be agreeable to practice and the usages of law; and that if some other judge of the said court shall not attend the same within five days after the commencement thereof, inclusive, then the said court shall, by virtue of this act, be continued over to the next stated session thereof; in which case, all writs, process, and recognizances, returned and returnable to the said court, and all actions, suits, process, pleadings, and other proceedings of what nature or kind soever, depending before the said court, shall, by virtue of this act, be continued to the next stated session of the same.

Section 16. And be it further enacted, That no person shall be arrested in one of the said districts, for trial in another, before any of the said circuit courts in any civil action; and that no civil action or suit shall be brought before any of the said courts, by any original process, against an inhabitant of the United States, in any other district than that whereof he is an inhabitant, or in which he shall be found at the time of serving the writ; nor shall any district or circuit court have cognizance of any suit to recover the contents of any promissory note, or other chose in action, in favour of an assignee, unless a suit might have been prosecuted in such court to recover the said contents, if no assignment had been made, except in cases of foreign bills of exchange.

Section 17. And be it further enacted, That the trials of all issues of fact, before any of the circuit courts hereby established, except in cases of equity, and admiralty and maritime jurisdiction, shall be by jury.

Section 18. And be it further enacted, That any judge of any of the said circuit courts shall be, and hereby is authorized and empowered, in all cases cognizable by the circuit court, whereof he shall be a judge, to grant writs of ne-exeat, and writs of injunction to stay waste, or to stay proceedings at law, on any judgment rendered by such circuit court, upon the like terms and conditions as such writs may be now granted, by the justices of the Supreme Court of the United States.

Section 19. And be it further enacted, That if in the opinion of any circuit judge, of the circuit within which such district may be situated, the life or lives of any person or persons, confined in the prison of such district, under or by virtue of any law of the United States, shall be in imminent danger, arising from the place of such confinement, it shall, in such case, be lawful for such judge, and he is hereby authorized and empowered, to direct the marshal of such district to remove, or cause to be removed, the person or persons so confined, to the next adjacent prison, there to be confined, until he, she, or they, may safely be removed back, to the place of his, her, or their first confinement; and that the said removals shall be at the expense of the United States.

Section 20. And be it further enacted, That all actions, suits, process, pleadings, and other proceedings of what nature or kind soever, depending or existing in any of the present circuit courts of the United States, or in any of the present district courts of the United States, acting as circuit courts, shall be, and hereby are, continued over to the circuit courts established by this act, in manner following, that is to say: all such as shall, on the fifteenth day of June next, be depending and un-determined, or shall then have been commenced and made returnable before the district court of Maine, acting as a circuit court, to the next circuit court hereby directed to be holden within and for the district of Maine; all such as shall be de-pending and undetermined before the circuit court for the district of New Hamp-shire, to the next circuit court hereby directed to be holden, within and for the district of New Hampshire; all such as shall be depending and undetermined before the circuit court for the district of Massachusetts, to the next circuit court hereby directed to be holden, within and for the district of Massachusetts; all such as shall be depending and undetermined before the circuit court of the district of Rhode Island, to the next circuit court hereby directed to be holden, within and for the district of Rhode Island; all such as shall be depending or undetermined before the circuit court for the district of Connecticut, to the next circuit court hereby directed to be holden, within and for the district of Connecticut; all such as shall be depend-ing and undetermined before the circuit court for the district of Vermont, to the next circuit court hereby directed to be holden, within and for the district of Vermont; all such as shall be depending and undetermined before the circuit court for the district of New York, to the next circuit court hereby directed to be holden, within and for the district of New York; all such as shall be depending and undetermined before the circuit court for the district of New Jersey, to the next circuit court hereby directed to be holden, within and for the district of Jersey; all such as shall be depending and undetermined before the circuit court for the district of Pennsyl-vania, to the next circuit court hereby directed to be holden, within and for the eastern district of Pennsylvania; all such as shall be depending and undetermined before the circuit court for the district of Delaware, to the next circuit court hereby directed to be holden, within and for the district of Delaware; all such as shall be depending and undetermined before the circuit court for the district of Maryland, to the next circuit court hereby directed to be holden, within and for the district of Maryland; all such as shall be depending and undetermined before the circuit court for the district of Virginia, to the next circuit court hereby directed to be holden, within and for the eastern district of Virginia; all such as shall be depending and undetermined before the circuit court for the district of North Carolinia, to the next circuit court hereby directed to be holden, within and for the district of North Caro-lina; all such as shall be depending and undetermined before the circuit court for the district of South Carolina, to the next circuit court hereby directed to be holden, within and for the district of South Carolina; all such as shall be depending and undetermined before the circuit court for the district of Georgia, to the next circuit court hereby directed to be holden, within and for the district of Georgia; all such as shall be depending and undetermined before the district court of Tennessee, act-ing as a circuit court, to the next circuit court hereby directed to be holden, within and for the district of East Tennessee; all such as shall be depending and undeter-mined before the district court of Kentucky, acting as a circuit court, to the next circuit court hereby directed to be holden, within and for the district of Kentucky; and shall there be equally regular and effectual, and shall be proceeded in, in the same manner as they could have been, if this act had not been made.

Section 21. And be it further enacted, That for the better dispatch of the business of district courts of the United States, in the districts of Jersey, Maryland, Virginia, and North Carolina, additional district courts shall be established therein, in manner following, that is to say: The said district of Jersey shall be divided into two districts; one to consist of that part thereof, which is called East New Jersey, and to be called the district of East Jersey; a district court, in and for which, shall be holden at New Brunswick, by the district judge of the district of Jersey, on the fourth Tuesday in May, and on the fourth Tuesday in November, in each and every year; and one other, to consist of the remaining part of the said district of Jersey, and to be called the district of West Jersey, a district court, in and for which, shall be holden at Burlington, by the district judge last aforesaid, on the fourth Tuesday in February, and on the fourth Tuesday in August, in each and every year. And a new district shall be established, in the districts of Maryland and Virginia, to consist of the territory of Columbia, of all that part of the district of Maryland, which lies west and southwest of the river Patuxent, and of the western branch thereof, and south of the line which divides the county of Montgomery in the last mentioned district, from the county of Frederick, and of a line to be drawn from the termination of the last mentioned line, a northeast course to the western branch of the Patuxent; and of all that part of the district of Virginia, which lies north of the river Rappahannock, and east of the line which divides the counties of Fauquier and Loudon, in the last mentioned district from the counties of Fairfax, Prince William, and Stafford; which new district shall be called the district of Potomac, and a district court in and for the same, shall be holden at Alexandria, by the district judge of the district of Maryland, on the first Tuesday in April, and the first Tuesday in October, in each and every year. And there shall be a new district established in the district of Virginia, to be called the district of Norfolk, and to consist of all that part of the said district of Virginia, which is contained within the counties of Isle of Wight, Nansemond, Norfolk, Princess Anne, James City, New Kent, Warwick, York, Elizabeth City, Gloucester, Matthews, Middlesex, Accomac, and Northampton; a district court, in and for which district of Norfolk, shall be holden at Norfolk, by the district judge of the district of Virginia, on the first Tuesday in February, on the first Tuesday in May, on the first Tuesday in August, and on the first Tuesday in November, in each and every year. And the district of North Carolina shall be divided into three districts; one to consist of all that part thereof, which by the laws of the state of North Carolina, now forms the districts of Edenton and Halifax; which district shall be called the district of Albemarle, and a district court, in and for the same, shall be holden at Edenton, by the district judge of the district of North Carolina, on the third Tuesday in April, on the third Tuesday in August, and on the third Tuesday in December, in each and every year; one other to be called the district of Pamptico, and to consist of all that part of the district of North Carolina aforesaid, which by the laws of the said state now forms the district of Newbern and Hillsborough, together with all that part of the district of Wilmington, which lies to the northward and eastward of the river called New River, and for which district of Pamptico, a district court shall be holden at Newbern, by the district judge last aforesaid, on the first Tuesday in April, on the first Tuesday in August, and on the first Tuesday in December, in each and every year. And one other to consist of the remaining part of the said district of North Carolina, and to be called the district of Cape Fear, in and for which a district court shall be holden at Wilmington, by the district judge last aforesaid, on the last Tuesday in March, on the last Tuesday in July, and on the last Tuesday in November, in each and every year; which said courts, hereby directed to be holden, shall severally and respectively have and exercise, within their several and respective districts, the same powers, authority, and jurisdiction, in all cases and respects whatsoever, which are vested by law in the district courts of the United States.

Section 22. And be it further enacted, That there shall be clerks for each of the said courts to be appointed by the judge thereof, which clerks shall reside and keep the records of the said courts, at the places of holding the courts, whereto they respectively shall belong, and shall perform the same duties, and be entitled to and receive the same emoluments and fees, which are established by law, for the clerks of the district courts of the United States respectively; and that the marshals and attornies of the United States, for the districts, which are hereby divided, or within the limits of which new districts are hereby erected, shall continue to be marshals and attornies for the courts hereby appointed to be holden within the limits of their present districts respectively, and shall have, exercise, and perform, within the jurisdictions of those courts respectively, all the powers and duties, and receive all the fees and emoluments, appointed and established by law, for the marshals and attornies of the United States.

Section 23. And be it further enacted, That the stated sessions of the district court of the district of Maryland shall hereafter be holden at Baltimore only.

Section 24. And be it further enacted, That the district courts of the United States, in and for the districts of Tennessee and Kentucky, shall be, and hereby are, abolished; and that all and singular the powers, authority and jurisdiction of the said courts respectively shall be and hereby are vested in, and shall be exercised by the circuit courts, by this act directed to be holden in and for the districts of East Tennessee, West Tennessee and Kentucky, respectively, within the limits of their respective jurisdictions; and that the circuit judges to be appointed for the sixth circuit aforesaid, severally, shall be invested with, possess and exercise, all and singular the powers, now vested by law in the district judges of the United States.

Section 25. And be it further enacted, That in case of the inability of the district judge of either of the districts of the United States, to perform the duties of his office, and satisfactory evidence thereof being shown to the circuit court, in and for such district, it shall be the duty of such circuit court, from time to time, as occasion may require, to direct one of the judges of said circuit court, to perform the duties of such district judge, within and for said district, for and during the period the inability of the district judge shall continue. And it shall be the duty of the circuit judge, to whom the duties of the district judge shall be assigned in manner aforesaid, and he is hereby authorized to perform the duties of said district judge, during the continuance of his disability.

Section 26. And be it further enacted, That the several circuit courts hereby established shall have power to appoint clerks for their respective courts; that is to say, one for each district within which such court is or shall be directed by law to be holden; which clerks respectively shall take the same oath or affirmation, and give the like bonds, as are by law required to be taken and given by the clerk of the supreme court of the United States; and shall be entitled to demand and receive, for their services respectively, the same fees, to be recovered in the same manner, as have heretofore been allowed by law, for the like services, to the clerks of the circuit and district courts of the United States.

Section 27. And be it further enacted, That the circuit courts of the United States, heretofore established, shall cease and be abolished; and that the records and office papers of every kind, belonging to those courts respectively, shall be safely kept by the clerks thereof, who shall continue in all respects to act as heretofore in the business of the said courts, until it shall otherwise be ordered by the courts hereby established.

Section 28. And be it further enacted, That the supreme, circuit and district courts of the United States, shall be, and hereby are, constituted courts of record.

Section 29. And be it further enacted, That all writs and processes whatsoever, issuing from any of the circuit courts, hereby established, shall, after the first day of April next, bear test of the presiding judge of such court; before which time they shall bear test of the chief justice of the United States; all which said writs and processes shall be signed by the clerks of the courts respectively, from which the same shall issue, and shall be made returnable to the next stated or special session of such court, and all writs and processes which have issued, or which may issue before the first day of April next, returnable to the circuit courts heretofore estab-lished, or to any district court acting as a circuit court, shall be returned to the circuit courts hereby established, and shall be there proceeded in, in the same man-ner as they could, had they been originally returnable to the circuit courts hereby established.

Section 30. And be it further enacted, That every justice of the supreme court of the United States, and every judge of any circuit or district court shall be, and hereby is authorized and empowered, to grant writs of habeas corpus, for the purpose of inquiring into the cause of commitment, and thereupon to discharge from confine-ment, on bail or otherwise: Provided always, that no writ of habeas corpus, to be granted under this act, shall extend to any prisoner or prisoners in gaol [jail], unless such prisoner or prisoners be in custody, under or by colour of the authority of the United States, or be committed for trial before some court of the same; or be neces-sary to be brought into court to give testimony.

Section 31. And be it further enacted, That the several courts of the United States shall be, and hereby are authorized and empowered to grant new trials and rehear-ings, on motion and cause shown, and to make and establish all necessary rules and regulations, for returning writs, filing pleas, and other proceedings; and for regulat-ing the practice and enforcing the orderly conduct of business, in the said courts respectively: Provided always, that the said rules and regulations be not repugnant to the laws of the United States; and that all the courts of the United States, and each of the justices and judges thereof, shall be, and hereby are, authorized and em-powered to administer all necessary oaths and affirmations, and to bind to the peace or good behaviour, with surety where necessary, in all cases, arising under the au-thority of the United States.

Section 32. And be it further enacted, That every person who shall be appointed a judge of any circuit court, hereby established, shall, before he shall begin to exer-cise the duties of his said office, take the following oath or affirmation; that is to say: "I, A. B. do solemnly swear" (or affirm) "that I will administer justice without respect to persons; and will do equal right to all persons; and will, in all things, faithfully and impartially discharge and perform, all the duties incumbent on me as a judge of according to the best of my abilities and understanding, and to the con-stitution and laws of the United States."

Section 33. And be it further enacted, That from all final judgments or decrees, in any of the district courts of the United States, an appeal, where the matter in dis-pute, exclusive of costs, shall exceed the sum or value of fifty dollars, shall be al-lowed to the circuit court next to be holden, in the district where such final judgment or judgments, decree or decrees, may be rendered; and the circuit court or courts are hereby authorized and required to receive, hear and determine such appeal; and that from all final judgments or decrees in any circuit court, in any cases of equity, of admiralty and maritime jurisdiction, and of prize or no prize, an appeal, where the matter in dispute, exclusive of costs, shall exceed the sum or value of two thousand dollars, shall be allowed to the supreme court of the United States; and that upon such appeal, a transcript of the libel, bill, answer, depositions, and all other proceedings of what kind soever in the cause, shall be transmitted to the said supreme court; and that no new evidence shall be received in the said court, on the hearing of such appeal; and that such appeals shall be subject to the same rules, regulations and restrictions, as are prescribed by law in case of writs of error; and that the said supreme court shall be, and hereby is authorized and required, to receive, hear and determine such appeals.

Section 34. And be it further enacted, That all final judgments in civil actions at common law, in any of the circuit courts hereby established, whether brought by original process in such court, or removed thereto from any state court, and all final judgments in any of the district courts of the United States may, where the matter in dispute, exclusive of costs, shall exceed the sum or value of two thousand dollars, be reexamined and reversed or affirmed, in the supreme court of the United States, by writ of error: whereto shall be annexed, and returned therewith at the day and place therein mentioned, an authenticated transcript of the record and assignment of errors, and prayer for reversal, and also a citation to the adverse party, signed by a judge of such circuit court, or by the district judge as the case may be; which citation shall be served on the adverse party personally, or by leaving a true copy thereof at his or their usual place or places of residence, at least thirty days before the time mentioned in such writ of error, for the return thereof.

Section 35. And be it further enacted, That the stipulation, bond or security, taken upon any writ of error or appeal to be brought or allowed as aforesaid, shall be returned by the judge taking the same, to the clerk or register of the court where the judgment or decree complained of was rendered, to be by him annexed to the transcript of the record, hereby directed to be sent up to the supreme court of the United States.

Section 36. And be it further enacted, That there shall be appointed, in and for each of the districts established by this act, a marshal, whose duty it shall be to attend the circuit courts of the United States hereby established, when sitting within such district, and who shall have and exercise, within such district, the same powers, perform the same duties, be subject to the same penalties, give the same bond with sureties, take the same oath, be entitled to and receive the same compensation and emoluments, and in all respects be subject to the same regulations, as are now prescribed by law, in respect to the marshals of the United States heretofore appointed:

Provided always, that the several marshals of the United States, now in office, shall, during the periods for which they were respectively appointed, unless sooner removed by the President of the United States, be and continue marshals for the several districts hereby established, within which they respectively reside; and shall perform the duties, exercise the powers, and receive the emoluments, hereby directed to be performed, exercised and received, by marshals therein.

Section 37. And be it further enacted, That there shall be appointed for each of the districts hereby established, a person learned in the law, to act as attorney for the United States within such district, and in the circuit and district courts which may be holden therein; which attorney shall take an oath or affirmation for the faithful performance of the duties of his office, and shall prosecute, in such district, all delinquents for crimes and offences cognizable under the authority of the United States, and all civil actions or suits in which the United States shall be concerned, except actions or suits in the supreme court of the United States; and shall be entitled to, and receive, for their services respectively, such compensations, emoluments and fees, as by law are or shall be allowed, to the district attornies of the United States: Provided always, that the district attornies of the United States now in office shall, severally and respectively, be attornies for those districts hereby established, within which they reside, until removed by the President of the United States; and shall perform the duties, exercise the powers, and receive the emoluments, hereby directed to be performed, exercised and received, by the attorney of the United States therein.

Section 38. And be it further enacted, That jurors and witnesses attending any of the courts, hereby established, shall be entitled to and receive the same compensations respectively, as heretofore have been allowed by law to jurors and witnesses, attending the circuit and district courts of the United States.

Section 39. And be it further enacted, That the records of the several circuit courts, hereby established, shall hereafter be kept at the respective places at which the said courts are hereby directed to be holden: Provided always, that in the district wherein there are more than one place directed by this act for holding said circuit courts, the records of the circuit court in such district shall hereafter be kept in either of such places, as the said court in such district shall direct.

Section 40. And be it further enacted, That the privilege from arrest of every person going to, attending at, or returning from, any court of the United States, shall be computed and continue, from the time of his or her departure from his or her habitation, until his or her return thereto: Provided, that such time shall not exceed one day, Sundays excluded, for every twenty miles of the distance, which such person must necessarily travel in so going and returning, over and above the time of attendance.

Section 41. And be it further enacted, That each of the circuit judges of the United States, to be appointed by virtue of this act, shall be allowed as a compensation for his services, an annual salary of two thousand dollars, to be paid quarter-yearly at the treasury of the United States; except the judges of the sixth circuit, who shall be allowed the sum of fifteen hundred dollars each, to be paid in like manner; and that the salaries of the district judges of Kentucky and Tennessee shall be, and hereby are, severally augmented to the like sum of fifteen hundred dollars, annually, to be paid in like manner.

Source: Statutes at Large, 6th Congress, 2nd Session, Vol. 2, Ch. 4, Pg. 89

10. Judiciary Act, 1802

Introduction

Having repealed the Judiciary Act of 1801 in 1802, Democratic-Republicans adopted an amendatory Judiciary Act in the same year, on April 29. This law increased the number of circuit courts from three to six, and it also reduced the circuit-riding duties of Supreme Court justices to one circuit rather than two. Whereas the Supreme Court had previously met for two two-week terms a year, the new law consolidated those into a single four-week term, reducing the number of times the justices had to assemble in Washington. The law had the effect of postponing the Supreme Court's session from June 1802 to February 1803. It was in that session that Chief Justice John Marshall issued the Court's historic decision in *Marbury v. Madison*, which established judicial review of federal laws.

Primary Source

An Act to amend the Judicial System of the United States.

Section 1. Be it enacted by the Senate and House of Representatives of the United States of America in Congress assembled, That from and after the passing of this act, the Supreme Court of the United States shall be holden by the justices thereof, or any four of them, at the city of Washington, and shall have one session in each and every year, to commence on the first Monday of February annually, and that if four of the said justices shall not attend within ten days after the time hereby appointed for the commencement of the said session, the business of the said court shall be continued over till the next stated session thereof. Provided always, that any one or more of the said justices attending as aforesaid shall have power to make all necessary orders touching any suit, action, writ of error, process, pleadings or proceedings returned to the said court or depending therein, preparatory to the hearing, trial or decision of such action, suit, appeal, writ of error, process, pleadings or proceedings. And so much of the act, intituled "An act to establish the judicial courts of the United States," passed the twenty-fourth day of September, seventeen hundred and eighty-nine, as provides for the holding a session of the supreme court of the United States on the first Monday of August, annually, is hereby repealed.

Section 2. And be it further enacted, That it shall be the duty of the associate justice resident in the fourth circuit formed by this act, to attend at the city of Washington on the first Monday of August next, and on the first Monday of August each and every year thereafter, who shall have power to make all necessary orders touching any suit, action, appeal, writ of error, process, pleadings or proceedings, returned to the said court or depending therein, preparatory to the hearing, trial or decision of such action, suit, appeal, writ of error, process, pleadings or proceedings: and that all writs and process may be returnable to the said court on the said first Monday in August, in the same manner as to the session of the said court, herein before directed to be holden on the first Monday in February, and may also bear teste on the said first Monday in August, as though a session of the said court was holden on that day, and it shall be the duty of the clerk of the supreme court to attend the said justice on the said first Monday of August, in each and every year, who shall make due entry of all such matters and things as shall or may be ordered as aforesaid by the said justice, and at each and every such August session, all actions, pleas, and other proceedings relative to any cause, civil or criminal, shall be continued over to the ensuing February session.

Section 3. And be it further enacted, That all actions, suits, process, pleadings and other proceedings, of what nature or kind soever, civil or criminal, which were continued from the supreme court of the United States, which was begun and holden on the first Monday of December last, to the next court to have been holden on the first Monday of June, under the act which passed on the thirteenth day of February, one thousand eight hundred and one, intituled, "An act to provide for the more convenient organization of the courts of the United States," and all writs, process and proceedings, as aforesaid, which are or may be made returnable to the same June session, shall be continued, returned to, and have day, in the session to be holden by this act, on the first Monday of August next; and such proceedings shall be had thereon, as is herein before provided.

Section 4. And be it further enacted, That the districts of the United States (excepting the districts of Maine, Kentucky, and Tennessee) shall be formed into six circuits, in manner following:

The districts of New Hampshire, Massachusetts and Rhode Island, shall constitute the first circuit;

The districts of Connecticut, New York and Vermont, shall constitute the second circuit;

The districts of New Jersey and Pennsylvania shall constitute the third circuit;

The districts of Maryland and Delaware shall constitute the fourth circuit;

The districts of Virginia and North Carolina shall constitute the fifth circuit; and

The districts of South Carolina and Georgia shall constitute the sixth circuit.

And there shall be holden annually in each district of the said circuits, two courts, which shall be called circuit courts. In the first circuit, the said circuit court shall consist of the justice of the supreme court residing within the said circuit, and the district judge of the district where such court shall be holden: and the sessions of the said court, in the district of New Hampshire, shall commence on the nineteenth day of May, and the second day of November, annually; in the district of Massachusetts, on the first day of June, and the twentieth day of October, annually; in the district of Rhode Island, on the fifteenth day of June, and the fifteenth day of November, annually.

In the second circuit, the said circuit court shall consist of the senior associate justice of the supreme court residing within the fifth circuit, and the district judge of the district, where such court shall be holden: and the sessions of the said court in the district of Connecticut, shall commence on the thirteenth day of April, and the seventeenth day of September, annually; in the district of New York, on the first day of April, and the first day of September, annually; in the district of Vermont, on the first day of May, and the third day of October, annually.

In the third circuit, the said circuit court shall consist of the justice of the supreme court residing within the said circuit; and the district judge of the district where such court shall be holden: and the sessions of the said court, in the district of New Jersey, shall commence on the first day of April, and the first day of October, annually; in the district of Pennsylvania, on the eleventh day of April, and the eleventh day of October, annually.

In the fourth circuit, the said circuit court shall consist of the justice of the supreme court residing within the said circuit, and the district judge of the district where such court shall be holden: and the sessions of the said court, in the district of Delaware, shall commence on the third day of June, and the twenty-seventh day of October, annually; in the district of Maryland, on the first day of May, and the seventh day of November, annually; to be holden hereafter at the city of Baltimore only.

In the fifth circuit, the circuit court shall consist of the present chief justice of the supreme court, and the district judge of the district where such court shall be holden: and the sessions of the said court, in the district of Virginia, shall commence on the twenty-second day of May, and the twenty-second day of November, annually; in the district of North Carolina, on the fifteenth day of June, and the twenty-ninth day of December, annually.

In the sixth circuit, the said circuit court shall consist of the junior associate justice of the supreme court, in the fifth circuit, and the district judge of the district where such court shall be holden: and the sessions of the said court, in the district of South Carolina, shall commence at Charleston on the twentieth day of May, and at Columbia on the thirtieth day of November, annually; in the district of Georgia, on the sixth day of May at Savannah, and on the fourteenth day of December hereafter at Louisville, annually: Provided, that when only one of the judges hereby directed to hold the circuit courts, shall attend, such circuit court may be held by the judge so attending; and that when any of the said days shall happen on a Sunday, then the said court hereby directed to be holden on such day, shall be holden on the next day thereafter; and the circuit courts constituted by this act, shall be held at the same place or places in each district of every circuit, as by law they were respectively required to be held previous to the thirteenth day of February, one thousand eight hundred and one, excepting as is herein before directed. And none of the said courts shall be holden until after the first day of July next, and the clerk of each district court shall be also clerk of the circuit court in such district, except as is herein after excepted.

Section 5. And be it further enacted, That on every appointment which shall be hereafter made of a chief justice or associate justice, the said chief justice and associate justices shall allot themselves among the aforesaid circuits as they shall think fit, and shall enter such allotment on record. And in case no such allotment shall be made by them at their session next succeeding such appointment, and also, after the appointment of any judge, as aforesaid, and before any allotment shall have been made, it shall and may be lawful for the President of the United States to make such allotment as he shall deem proper, which allotment made in either case, shall be binding until another allotment shall be made; and the circuit courts constituted by this act, shall have all the power, authority and jurisdiction within the several districts of their respective circuits that before the thirteenth day of February, one thousand eight hundred and one, belonged to the circuit courts of the United States, and in all cases which, by appeal or writ of error, are or shall be removed from a district to a circuit court, judgment shall be rendered in conformity to the opinion of the judge of the supreme court presiding in such circuit court.

Section 6. And be it further enacted, That whenever any question shall occur before a circuit court, upon which the opinions of the judges shall be opposed, the point upon which the disagreement shall happen, shall, during the same term, upon the request of either party, or their counsel, be stated under the direction of the judges, and certified under the seal of the court, to the supreme court, at their next session to be held thereafter; and shall, by the said court, be finally decided. And the decision of the supreme court, and their order in the premises, shall be remitted to the circuit court, and be there entered of record, and shall have effect according to the nature of the said judgment and order: Provided, that nothing herein contained shall prevent the cause from proceeding, if, in the opinion of the court, farther proceedings can be had without prejudice to the merits: and provided also, that imprisonment shall not be allowed, nor punishment in any case be inflicted, where the judges of the said court are divided in opinion upon the question touching the said imprisonment or punishment.

Section 7. And be it further enacted, That the district of North Carolina shall be divided into three districts, one to consist of all that part thereof which, by the laws of the state of North Carolina, now forms the districts of Edenton and Halifax, which district shall be called the district of Albemarle, and a district court in and for the same shall be holden at Edenton by the district judge of North Carolina, on the third Tuesday in April, on the third Tuesday in August, and on the third Tuesday in December, in each and every year; one other to be called the district of Pamptico, and to consist of all that part of North Carolina which by the laws of the said state now forms the districts of Newbern and Hillsborough, together with all that part of the district of Wilmington which lies to the northward and eastward of New river; for which district of Pamptico, a district court shall be holden at Newbern by the district judge last aforesaid on the second Tuesday in April, on the second Tuesday in August, and on the second Tuesday in December in each and every year; and one other to consist of the remaining part of the said district of North Carolina, and to be called the district of Cape Fear, in and for which a district court shall be holden at Wilmington by the district judge last aforesaid, on the first Tuesday in April, on the first Tuesday in August, and on the first Tuesday in December, in each and every year; which said district courts hereby directed to be holden shall respectively have and exercise within their several districts, the same powers, authority and jurisdiction, which are vested by law in the district courts of the United States.

Section 8. And be it further enacted, That the circuit court and district courts for the district of North Carolina shall appoint clerks for the said courts respectively, which clerks shall reside and keep the records of the said courts at the places of holding the courts whereto they shall respectively belong, and shall perform the same duties and be entitled to and receive the same emoluments and fees, respectively, which are by law established for the clerks of the circuit and district courts of the United States respectively.

Section 9. And be it further enacted, That all actions, causes, pleas, process and other proceedings relative to any cause, civil or criminal, which shall be returnable to, or depending in the several circuit or district courts of the United States on the first day of July next, shall be and are hereby declared to be respectively transferred, returned and continued to the several circuit and district courts constituted by this act, at the times herein before and herein after appointed for the holding of each of the said courts, and shall be heard, tried and determined therein in the same manner and with the same effect, as if no change had been made in the said courts. And it shall be the duty of the clerk of each and every court hereby constituted, to receive and to take into his safe keeping the writs, process, pleas, proceedings and papers of all those causes and actions which by this act shall be transferred, returned or continued to such court, and also all the records and office papers of every kind respectively belonging to the courts abolished by the repeal of the act, intituled "An act to provide for the more convenient organization of the courts of the United States," and from which the said causes shall have been transferred as aforesaid.

Section 10. And be it further enacted, That all suits, process, pleadings and other proceedings, of what nature or kind soever, depending in the circuit court in the district of Ohio, and which shall have been, or may hereafter be commenced within the territory of the United States northwest of the river Ohio, in the said court, shall, from and after the first day of July next, be continued over, returned, and made cognizable, in the superior court of the said territory next thereafter to be holden, and all actions, suits, process, pleadings, and other proceedings as aforesaid depending in the circuit court of the said district, and which shall have been or may hereafter be commenced within the Indiana territory in said court, shall, from and after the first day of July next, be continued over, returned and made cognizable in the superior court of the said Indiana territory, next thereafter to be holden.

Section 11. And be it further enacted, That in all cases in which proceedings shall, on the said first day of July next, be pending under a commission of bankruptcy issued in pursuance of the aforesaid act, intituled "An act to provide for the more convenient organization of the courts of the United States," the cognizance of the same shall be, and hereby is transferred to, and vested in, the district judge of the district within which such commission shall have issued, who is hereby empowered to proceed therein in the same manner and to the same effect, as if such commission of bankruptcy had been issued by his order.

Section 12. And be it further enacted, That from and after the first day of July next, the district judges of Kentucky and Tennessee shall be and hereby are severally entitled to a salary of fifteen hundred dollars, annually, to be paid quarter-yearly at the treasury of the United States.

Section 13. And be it further enacted, That the marshals and attornies of the United States, for the districts which were not divided, or within the limits of which, new districts were not erected, by the act intituled "An act to provide for the more con-venient organization of the courts of the United States," passed the thirteenth day of February, one thousand eight hundred and one, shall continue to be marshals and attornies for such districts respectively, unless removed by the President of the United States, and in all other districts which were divided or within the limits of which new districts were erected by the last recited act, the President of the United States be and hereby is empowered from and after the first day of July next to dis-continue all such supernumerary marshals and district attornies of the United States in such districts respectively as he shall deem expedient, so that there shall be but one marshal and district attorney to each district; and every marshal and district attorney who shall be continued in office, or appointed by the President of the United States in such districts, shall have and exercise the same powers, perform the same duties, give the same bond with sureties, take the same oath, be subject to the same penalties and regulations as are, or may be prescribed by law, in respect to the marshals and district attornies of the United States. And every marshal and district attorney who shall be so discontinued as aforesaid shall be holden to de-liver over all papers, matters and things in relation to their respective offices, to such marshals and district attornies respectively who shall be so continued or ap-pointed as aforesaid in such district, in the same manner as is required by law in cases of resignation or removal from office.

Section 14. And be it further enacted, That there shall be appointed by the Presi-dent of the United States, from time to time, as many general commissioners of bankruptcy, in each district of the United States, as he may deem necessary: and upon petition to the judge of a district court for a commission of bankruptcy he shall proceed as is provided in and by an act, intituled "An act to establish an uni-form system of bankruptcy throughout the United States," and appoint, not exceed-ing three of the said general commissioners as commissioners of the particular bankrupt petitioned against; and the said commissioners, together with the clerk, shall each be allowed as a full compensation for their services, when sitting and act-ing under their commissions, at the rate of six dollars per day for every day which they may be employed in the same business, to be apportioned among the several causes on which they may act on the same day, and to be paid out of the respective bankrupt's estates: Provided, that the commissioners, who may have been, or may be appointed in any district before notice shall be given of the appointment of com-missioners for such district by the President in pursuance of this act, and who shall not then have completed their business, shall be authorized to proceed and finish the same, upon the terms of their original appointment.

Section 15. And be it further enacted, That the stated session of the district court, for the district of Virginia, heretofore directed to be holden in the city of Williams-burg shall be holden in the town of Norfolk from and after the first day of July next,

822 | 10. Judiciary Act, 1802

and the stated sessions of the district court for the district of Maryland, shall hereafter be holden in the city of Baltimore only, and in the district of Georgia, the stated sessions of the district court shall be held in the city of Savannah only.

Section 16. And be it further enacted, That for the better establishment of the courts of the United States within the state of Tennessee, the said state shall be divided in two districts, one to consist of that part of said state, which lies on the east side of Cumberland mountain, and to be called the district of East Tennessee, the other to consist of the remaining part of said state, and to be called the district of West Tennessee.

Section 17. And be it further enacted, That the district judge of the United States, who shall hereafter perform the duties of district judge, within the state of Tennessee, shall annually hold four sessions, two at Knoxville, on the fourth Monday of April, and the fourth Monday of October, in and for the district of East Tennessee, and two at Nashville, on the fourth Monday of May, and the fourth Monday of November, in and for the district of West Tennessee.

Section 18. And be it further enacted, That there shall be a clerk for each of the said districts of East and West Tennessee, to be appointed by the judge thereof, who shall reside and keep the records of the said courts, at the places of holding the courts, whereto they respectively shall belong, and shall perform the same duties, and be entitled to, and receive the same emoluments and fees, which are established by law for the clerks of the district courts of the United States, respectively.

Section 19. And be it further enacted, That there shall be appointed, in and for each of the districts of East and West Tennessee, a marshal, whose duty it shall be to attend the district courts hereby established, and who shall have and exercise within such district, the same powers, perform the same duties, be subject to the same penalties, give the same bond with sureties, take the same oath, be entitled to the same allowance, as a full compensation for all extra services, as hath heretofore been allowed to the marshal of the district of Tennessee, by a law, passed the twenty-eighth day of February, one thousand seven hundred and ninety-nine, and shall receive the same compensation and emoluments, and in all respects be subject to the same regulations as are now prescribed by law, in respect to the marshals of the United States, heretofore appointed: Provided, that the marshals of the districts of East and West Tennessee, now in office, shall, during the periods for which they have been appointed, unless sooner removed by the President of the United States, be and continue marshals for the several districts hereby established, within which they respectively reside.

Section 20. And be it further enacted, That there shall be appointed for each of the districts of East and West Tennessee, a person learned in the law, to act as attorney for the United States within such district; which attorney shall take an oath or affirmation for the faithful performance of the duties of his office, and shall prosecute in such district, all delinquencies, for crimes and offences, cognizable under the authority of the United States, and all civil actions or suits, in which the United States shall be concerned; and shall be entitled to the same allowance, as a full compensation for all extra services, as hath heretofore been allowed to attornies of the district of Tennessee, by a law passed the twenty-eighth day of February, one thousand seven hundred and ninety-nine, and shall receive such compensation, emoluments and fees, as by law are or shall be allowed to the district attornies of the United States, respectively: Provided, that the district attornies of East and West Tennessee, now in office, shall severally and respectively be attornies for those districts within which they reside, until removed by the President of the United States.

Section 21. And be it further enacted, That all actions, suits, process, pleadings and proceedings, of what nature or kind soever, which shall be depending or existing in the sixth circuit of the United States within the circuit courts of the districts of East and West Tennessee, shall be and hereby are continued over to the district courts established by this act in manner following, that is to say: All such as shall on the first day of July next, be depending and undetermined, or shall then have been commenced, and made returnable before the circuit court of East Tennessee, to the next district court hereby directed to be holden, within and for the district of East Tennessee; all such as shall be depending and undetermined, or shall have been commenced and made returnable before the circuit court of West Tennessee, to the next district court, hereby directed to be holden, within and for the district of West Tennessee, and all the said suits shall then be equally regular and effectual, and shall be proceeded in, in the same manner as they could have been if the law, authorizing the establishment of the sixth circuit of the United States, had not been repealed.

Section 22. And be it further enacted, That the next session of the district court for the district of Maine, shall be holden on the last Tuesday in May next; and that the session of the said court heretofore holden on the third Tuesday of June annually, shall thereafter be holden, annually, on the last Tuesday in May.

Section 23. And be it further enacted, That all writs and process which shall have been issued, and all recognizances returnable, and all suits and other proceedings which have been continued to the said district court on the third Tuesday in June next, shall be returned and held continued to the said last Tuesday of May next.

Section 24. And be it further enacted, That the chief judge of the district of Columbia shall hold a district court of the United States, in and for the said district, on the first Tuesday of April, and on the first Tuesday of October in every year; which court shall have and exercise, within the said district, the same powers and jurisdiction which are by law vested in the district courts of the United States.

Section 25. And be it further enacted, That in all suits in equity, it shall be in the discretion of the court, upon the request of either party, to order the testimony of the witnesses therein to be taken by depositions; which depositions shall be taken in conformity to the regulations prescribed by law for the courts of the highest original jurisdiction in equity, in cases of a similar nature, in that state in which the court of the United States may be holden: Provided however, that nothing herein contained shall extend to the circuit courts which may be holden in those states, in which testimony in chancery is not taken by deposition.

Section 26. And be it further enacted, That there shall be a clerk for the district court of Norfolk, to be appointed by the judge thereof, which clerk shall reside and keep the records of the said court at Norfolk aforesaid, and shall perform the same duties, and be entitled to, and receive the same fees and emoluments which are established by law for the clerks of the district courts of the United States.

Section 27. And be it further enacted, That from and after the first day of July next, there shall be holden, annually, in the district of Vermont, two stated sessions of the district court, which shall commence on the tenth day of October, at Rutland, and on the seventh day of May, at Windsor, in each year; and when either of the said days shall happen on a Sunday, the said court, hereby directed to be holden on such day, shall be holden on the day next thereafter.

Section 28. And be it further enacted, That the act, intituled "An act altering the time of holding the district court in Vermont," and so much of the second section of the act, intituled "An act giving effect to the laws of the United States within the state of Vermont," as provides for the holding four sessions, annually, of the said district court, in said district, from and after the first day of July next, be and hereby are repealed.

Section 29. And be it further enacted, That the clerk of the said district court shall not issue a process to summon, or cause to be returned, to any session of the said district court, a grand jury, unless by special order of the district judge, and at the request of the district attorney; nor shall he cause to be summoned or returned, a petit jury to such sessions of the said district court, in which there shall appear to be no issue proper for the trial by jury, unless by special order of the judge as aforesaid. And it shall be the duty of the circuit court in the district of Vermont, at their stated sessions, to give in charge to the grand juries, all crimes, offences and misdemeanors, as are cognizable, as well in the said district court, as the said circuit court, and such bills of indictment as shall be found in the circuit court, and cognizable in the said district court, shall, at the discretion of the said circuit court, be transmitted by the clerk of the said court, pursuant to the order of the said circuit court, with all matters and things relating thereto, to the district court next thereafter to be holden, in said district, and the same proceedings shall be had thereon in said district court, as though said bill of indictment had originated and been found in the said district court. And all recognizances of witnesses, taken by any magistrate in said district, for their appearance to testify in any case cognizable in either of the said courts, shall be to the circuit court next thereafter to be holden in said district.

Section 30. And be it further enacted, That from and after the passing of this act, no special juries shall be returned by the clerks of any of the said circuit courts; but that in all cases in which it was the duty of the said clerks to return special juries before the passing of this act, it shall be the duty of the marshal for the district where such circuit court may be held, to return special juries, in the same manner and form, as, by the laws of the respective states, the said clerks were required to return the same.

Source: Statutes at Large, 7th Congress, 1st Session, Vol. 2, Ch. 31, Pg. 156

11. *Marbury v. Madison,* 1803

Introduction

Marbury v. Madison was pivotal in establishing the doctrine of judicial review of laws made in Congress and thus helped to shape the government of the United States. In England, Parliament is considered to be supreme. Because it exercises such legislative sovereignty and because Great Britain has no single written constitution, a formal amendment process is not necessary. By contrast, in the United States, the Constitution is supreme over ordinary acts of legislation. If Congress wishes to alter the Constitution, it must proceed via the Article V amending processes. In large part, this system emerged because of the extraordinarily important decision that Chief Justice John Marshall authored in *Marbury v. Madison.*

Primary Source

MR. JUSTICE MARSHALL delivered the opinion of the Court.

In the order in which the court has viewed this subject, the following questions have been considered and decided.

1. Has the applicant a right to the commission he demands?

2. If he has a right, and that right has been violated, do the laws of his country afford him a remedy?

3. If they do afford him a remedy, is it a mandamus issuing from this court?
. . . It is . . . the opinion of the court,

1. That, by signing the commission of Mr. Marbury, the President of the United States appointed him a justice of peace, for the county of Washington in the District of Columbia; and that the seal of the United States, affixed thereto by the Secretary of State, is conclusive testimony of the verity of the signature, and of the completion of the appointment; and that the appointment conferred on him a legal right to the office for the space of five years.

2. That, having this legal title to the office, he has a consequent right to the commission; a refusal to deliver which, is a plain violation of that right, for which the laws of this country afford him a remedy.
It remains to be enquired whether,

3. He is entitled to the remedy for which applies. This depends on,

1. The nature of the writ applied for and

2. The power of this court.

. . . This, then, is a plain case for mandamus, either to deliver the commission, or a copy of it from the record; and it only remains to be enquired, whether it can issue from this court.

The act to establish the judicial courts of the United States authorizes the Supreme Court "to issue writs of mandamus in cases warranted by the principles and usages of law, to any courts appointed, or persons holding office, under the authority of the United States."

The Secretary of State, being a person holding an office under the authority of the United States, is precisely within the letter of the description and if this court is not authorized to issue a writ of mandamus to such an officer, it must be because the law is unconstitutional, and therefore absolutely incapable of conferring the authority, and assigning the duties which its words purport to confer and assign.

The Constitution vests the whole judicial power of the United States in one supreme court, and such inferior courts as Congress shall, from time to time, ordain and establish. This power is expressly extended to all cases arising under the laws of the United States; and, consequently, in some form, may be exercised over the present case; because the right claimed is given by a law of the United States.

In the distribution of this power it is declared that "the Supreme Court shall have original jurisdiction in all cases affecting ambassadors, other public ministers and consuls, and those in which a state shall be a party. In all other cases, the Supreme Court shall have appellate jurisdiction."

It has been insisted at the bar, that, as the original grant of jurisdiction to the Supreme and inferior courts, is general, and the clause assigning original jurisdiction to the Supreme Court contains no negative or restrictive words, the power remains to the legislature to assign original jurisdiction to that court in other cases than those specified in the article which has been recited; provided those cases belong to the judicial power of the United States.

If it had been intended to leave it in the discretion of the legislature to apportion the judicial power between the Supreme and inferior courts according to the will of that body, it would certainly have been useless to have proceeded further than to have defined the judicial power, and the tribunals in which it should be vested. The subsequent part of the section is mere surplusage, is entirely without meaning. If Congress remains at liberty to give this court appellate jurisdiction, where the Constitution has declared their jurisdiction shall be original; and original jurisdiction where the Constitution has declared it shall be appellate, the distribution of jurisdiction made in the Constitution is form without substance.

Affirmative words are often, in their operation, negative of other objects than those affirmed; and in this case, a negative or exclusive sense must be given to them, or they have no operation at all.

It cannot he presumed that any clause in the Constitution is intended to be without effect; and, therefore, such a construction is inadmissible unless the words require it.

. . . To enable this court, then to issue a mandamus, it must be shown to be an exercise of appellate jurisdiction, or to be necessary to enable them to exercise appellate jurisdiction.

It has been stated at the bar that the appellate jurisdiction may be exercised in a variety of forms, and that, if it be the will of the legislature that a mandamus should be used for that purpose, that will must be obeyed. This is true, yet the jurisdiction must be appellate, not original.

It is the essential criterion of appellate jurisdiction that it revises and corrects the proceedings in a cause already instituted, and does not create that cause. Although, therefore, a mandamus may be directed to courts, yet to issue such a writ to an officer for the delivery of a paper is in effect the same as to sustain an original action for that paper, and, therefore, seems not to belong to appellate, but to original jurisdiction. Neither is it necessary, in such a case as this, to enable the court to exercise its appellate jurisdiction.

The authority, therefore, given to the Supreme Court by the act establishing the judicial courts of the United States, to issue writs of mandamus to public officers, appears not to be warranted by the Constitution; and it becomes necessary to inquire whether a jurisdiction so conferred can be exercised.

The question, whether an act repugnant to the Constitution can become the law of the land, is a question deeply interesting to the United States; but, happily, not of an intricacy proportioned to its interest. It seems only necessary to recognize certain principles, supposed to have been long and well established, to decide it.

That the people have an original right to establish, for their future government, such principles as, in their opinion, shall most conduce to their own happiness is the basis on which the whole American fabric had been erected. The exercise of this original right is a very great exertion; nor can it, nor ought it, to be frequently repeated. The principles, therefore, so established, are deemed fundamental. And as the authority from which they proceed is supreme, and can seldom act, they are designed to be permanent.

This original and supreme will organizes the government, and assigns to different departments their respective powers. It may either stop here, or establish certain limits not to be transcended by those departments.

The government of the United States is of the latter description. The powers of the legislature are defined and limited; and that those limits may not be mistaken, or forgotten, the Constitution is written. To what purpose are powers limited, and to what purpose is that limitation committed to writing, if these limits may, at any time, be passed by those intended to be restrained? The distinction between a government with limited and unlimited powers is abolished if those limits do not confine the persons on whom they are imposed, and if acts prohibited and acts allowed are of equal obligation. It is a proposition too plain to be contested, that the Constitution controls any legislative act repugnant to it; or, that the legislature may alter the Constitution by an ordinary act.

Between these alternatives there is no middle ground. The Constitution is either a superior paramount law, unchangeable by ordinary means, or it is on a level with ordinary legislative acts, and, like other acts, is alterable when the legislature shall please to alter it.

If the former part of the alternative be true, then a legislative act contrary to the Constitution is not law: if the latter part be true, then written constitutions are absurd attempts on the part of the people to limit a power in its own nature illimitable.

Certainly all those who have framed written constitutions contemplate them as forming the fundamental and paramount law of the nation, and consequently, the theory of every such government must be, that an act of the legislature, repugnant to the constitution, is void.

This theory is essentially attached to a written constitution, and is, consequently, to be considered by this court as one of the fundamental principles of our society. It is not therefore to be lost sight of in the further consideration of this subject.

If an act of the legislature, repugnant to the Constitution, is void, does it, notwithstanding its invalidity, bind the courts, and oblige them to give it effect? Or, in other words, though it be not law, does it constitute a rule as operative as if it was a law? This would be to overthrow in fact what was established in theory; and would seem at first view, an absurdity too gross to be insisted on. It shall, however, receive a more attentive consideration.

It is emphatically the province and duty of the judicial department to say what the law is. Those who apply the rule to particular cases must, of necessity, expound and interpret that rule. If two laws conflict with each other, the courts must decide on the operation of each.

So if a law be in opposition to the Constitution; if both the law and the constitution apply to a particular case, so that the court must either decide that case conformably to the law, disregarding the Constitution; or conformably to the Constitution, disregarding the law; the court must determine which of these conflicting rules governs the case. This is of the very essence of judicial duty.

If, then, the courts are to regard the Constitution, and the Constitution is superior to any ordinary act of the legislature, the Constitution, and not such ordinary act, must govern the case to which they both apply.

Those, then, who controvert the principle that the Constitution is to be considered, in court, as a paramount law, are reduced to the necessity of maintaining that courts must close their eyes on the Constitution, and see only the law.

This doctrine would subvert the very foundation of all written constitutions. It would declare that an act which, according to the principles and theory of our government, is entirely void, is yet, in practice, completely obligatory. It would declare that if the legislature shall do what is expressly forbidden, such act, not-withstanding the express prohibition, is in reality effectual. It would be giving to the legislature a practical and real omnipotence, with the same breath which pro-fesses to restrict their powers within narrow limits. It is prescribing limits and de-claring that those limits may be passed at pleasure.

That it thus reduces to nothing what we have deemed the greatest improvement on political institutions—a written constitution—would of itself be sufficient, in America, where written constitutions have been viewed with so much reverence, for rejecting the construction. But the peculiar expressions of the Constitution of the United States furnish additional arguments in favor of its rejection.

The judicial power of the United States is extended to all cases arising under the Constitution.

Could it be the intention of those who gave this power to say that, in using it, the Constitution should not be looked into? That a case arising under the Constitution should be decided without examining the instrument under which it rises?

This is too extravagant to be maintained.

In some cases then, the Constitution must be looked into by the judges. And if they can open it at all, what part of it are they forbidden to read or to obey?

There are many other parts of the Constitution which serve to illustrate this subject.

It is declared that "no tax or duty shall be laid on articles exported from any state." Suppose a duty on the export of cotton, of tobacco, or of flour; and a suit instituted to recover it. Ought judgment to be rendered in such a case? Ought the judges to close their eyes on the Constitution, and see only the law?

The Constitution declares that "no bill of attainder or ex post facto law shall be passed."

If, however, such a bill should be passed and a person should be prosecuted under it; must the court condemn to death those victims who the Constitution endeavours to preserve?

"No person," says the Constitution, "shall be convicted of treason unless on the testimony of two witnesses to the same overt act, or on confession in open court."

Here the language of the Constitution is addressed especially to the courts. It prescribes, directly for them, a rule of evidence not to be departed from. If the legislature should change that rule, and declare one witness, or a confession out of court, sufficient for conviction, must the constitutional principle yield to the legislative act?

From these, and many other selections which might be made, it is apparent that the framers of the Constitution contemplated that instrument as a rule for the government of courts, as well as of the legislature.

Why otherwise does it direct the judges to take an oath to support it? This oath certainly applies in an especial manner to their conduct in their official character. How immoral to impose it on them, if they were to be used as the instruments, and the knowing instruments, for violating what they swear to support?

The oath of office, too, imposed by the legislature, is completely demonstrative of the legislative opinion on this subject. It is in these words: "I do solemnly swear that I will administer justice without respect to persons, and do equal right to the poor and to the rich; and that I will faithfully and impartially discharge all the duties incumbent on me as—, according to the best of my abilities and understanding agreeably to the Constitution and laws of the United States."

Why does a judge swear to discharge his duties agreeably to the Constitution of the United States, if that Constitution forms no rule for his government? If it is closed upon him, and cannot be inspected by him?

If such be the real state of things, this is worse than solemn mockery. To prescribe, or take this oath, becomes equally a crime.

It is also not entirely unworthy of observation that, in declaring what shall be the supreme law of the land, the Constitution itself is first mentioned; and not the laws of the United States generally, but those only which shall be made in pursuance of the Constitution, have that rank.

Thus, the particular phraseology of the Constitution of the United States confirms and strengthens the principle, supposed to be essential to all written constitutions, that a law repugnant to the Constitution is void; and that courts, as well as other departments, are bound by that instrument.

The rule must be
Discharged.

Source: McCulloch v. Maryland, 17 U.S. 316 (1819)

12. Establishment of the Seventh Circuit, 1807

Introduction

For the first time since the establishment of the federal judiciary in 1789, the Congress in 1807 increased the number of justices on the Supreme Court. The act authorizing the appointment of a seventh justice came in response to the geographic expansion of the nation and the increased caseload of the district courts in the west. The act established a Seventh Circuit, consisting of Ohio, Kentucky, and Tennessee, and specified that the new justice be assigned to preside over the U.S. circuit courts within that circuit. In an effort to ensure attendance at the circuit courts, which met twice a year in each district, Congress required that the new justice reside within the circuit as well. The act was the first in a series increasing the size of the Supreme Court to accommodate new circuits formed from recently admitted states, although no such residency requirement was ever applied to another Supreme Court seat.

Primary Source

February 24, 1807.
2 Stat. 420.

CHAP. XVI.—An Act establishing Circuit Courts, and abridging the jurisdiction of the district courts of Kentucky, Tennessee and Ohio.

Be it enacted by the Senate and House of Representatives of the United States of America in Congress assembled, That so much of any act or acts of Congress, as vests in the district courts of the United States, in the districts of Kentucky, East and West Tennessee and Ohio, the powers, authority and jurisdiction of the circuit courts of the United States, shall be, and the same is hereby repealed.

SEC. 2. Be it further enacted, That for the purpose of holding therein the circuit courts, to be established by this act; the state of Kentucky shall constitute one district, the state of Tennessee one district, and the state of Ohio one district, and the said districts of Kentucky, Tennessee, and Ohio, shall constitute and be denominated the seventh circuit. And there shall be holden annually in each district of the said circuit, two courts, to be called circuit courts, and to consist of one justice of the supreme court of the United States, and the judge of the district where such court shall be holden. And the sessions of the said courts, in the district of Kentucky, shall be held at Frankfort, and commence on the first Monday in May and November, annually; in the district of Tennessee, at Knoxville and Nashville, alternately, to commence on the first Monday in June and third Monday in October, annually, beginning at Nashville; and in the district of Ohio, at Chilicothe, to commence on the first Monday in January and September, annually. And the circuit court of Tennessee, shall designate at which of the two places where the said court is hereby directed to be holden, the office of clerk thereof shall be kept.

SEC. 3. Be it further enacted, That all the authority, powers and jurisdiction, vested in the several circuit courts of the United States, or the judges thereof, or either of them, shall be, and hereby are vested in, and may be exercised by the several circuit courts of the seventh circuit, and the judges thereof: and that all actions, causes, pleas, process, and other proceedings, relative to any cause, civil or criminal, which shall be returnable to, or depending in the several district courts of Kentucky, Tennessee and Ohio, acting as circuit courts, on the first day of May next, shall be, and hereby are declared to be respectively transferred, returnable, and continued, to the several circuit courts constituted by this act, at the times herein appointed for the session of each of the said courts, and shall be heard, tried, and determined therein, in the same manner, and with the same effect, as if no change, had been made hereby in the courts of the said district. And, the said circuit courts of the seventh circuit, shall be governed by the same laws and regulations as apply to the other circuit courts of the United States, and shall appoint clerks for the said courts respectively, who shall reside, and keep the records of the said courts, at the places of holding the courts, whereto they shall respectively belong, except as herein before provided, and shall perform the same duties, and be entitled to, and receive the same emoluments and fees, respectively, which are by law established for the clerks of the other circuit courts of the United States.

SEC. 4. Be it further enacted, That the state of Tennessee shall be divided into two districts, for the purpose of holding district courts in the same, one to consist of that part thereof, which by the laws of the said state, now forms the districts of Washington and Hamilton, which shall be called the district of East Tennessee; and one other to consist of all that part of the state of Tennessee, which by the laws of the said state now forms the districts of Winchester, Mero and Robertson, which shall be called the district of West Tennessee; and all the authority, powers and jurisdiction, vested in the several district courts of the United States, and the judges thereof, in those districts in which circuit courts are now held, shall be retained, and may be exercised by the several district courts of Kentucky, East and West Tennessee, and Ohio, and the several judges thereof. And the sessions of the said district courts shall, after the first day of May next, be as follows: in Kentucky, at Frankfort, two sessions, to commence on the first Mondays in June and December, annually; in East Tennessee, at Knoxville, two sessions, to commence on the third Monday in April and second Monday in October, annually; and at Nashville, two sessions, to commence on the fourth Mondays in May and November, annually; and in Ohio, at Chilicothe, three sessions, to commence on the first Mondays in February, June and October, annually; and all actions, causes, pleas, process, and other proceedings, relative to any cause, civil or criminal, which shall have been issued, and shall be returnable to, or depending in the said several district courts of the United States, acting as district courts, on the said first day of May next, shall be returned and held continued to the said several district courts, respectively, at the times herein before appointed for holding the same.

SEC. 5. Be it further enacted, That the supreme court of the United States shall hereafter consist of a chief justice, and six associate justices, any law to (the) contrary notwithstanding. And for this purpose there shall be appointed a sixth associate justice, to reside in the seventh circuit, whose duty it shall be, until he is otherwise allotted, to attend the circuit courts of the said seventh circuit, and the supreme court of the United States, and who shall take the same oath, and be entitled to the same salary as are required of, and provided for the other associate justices of the United States.

APPROVED, February 24, 1807.

Source: Statutes at Large, 9th Congress, 1st Session, Vol. 2, Ch. 16, Pg. 420

13. Establishment of the Eighth and Ninth Circuits, 1837

Introduction

In each of the eight western states admitted between 1812 and 1837, Congress established a district court with the authority to exercise the trial jurisdiction of circuit courts. By the 1820s, Congress faced growing demands that these states receive the same access to the courts of the federal judiciary as states that were within a circuit. In 1836 and 1837 two more states entered the Union without being included within a circuit. In 1837 Congress approved the establishment of two additional circuits and two new seats on the Supreme Court. Once again, Congress increased the size of the Supreme Court to support the circuit court system rather than in response to the caseload of the high Court itself. In the following years, Congress allowed further exceptions as some justices found it difficult to travel twice a year to all of the districts within their assigned circuits.

Primary Source

March 3, 1837.
5 Stat. 176.

CHAP. XXXIV.—.An Act supplementary to the act entitled An act to amend the judicial system of the United States.(a)

Be it enacted, by the Senate and House of Representatives of the United States of America in Congress assembled, That the Supreme Court of the United States shall hereafter consist of a chief justice, and eight associate judges, any five of whom shall constitute a quorum; and for this purpose there shall be appointed two additional justices of said court, with the like powers, and to take the same oaths, perform the same duties, and be entitled to the same salary, as the other associate judges.

Hereafter, the districts of Vermont, Connecticut, and New York, shall constitute the second circuit; the district of New Jersey, the eastern and western districts of Pennsylvania, shall constitute the third circuit; the district of Maryland and the district of Delaware shall constitute the fourth circuit; the districts of Virginia and the district of North Carolina shall constitute the fifth circuit; the districts of South Carolina and Georgia shall constitute the sixth circuit; the districts of Ohio, Indiana, Illinois and Michigan, shall constitute the seventh circuit; and the circuit courts shall be held at Columbus, in the

Ohio district, on the third Mondays in May, and December; at Detroit, in the Michigan district, on the fourth Monday in June; at Indianapolis, in the Indiana district, on the first Monday in December; at Vandalia, in the Illinois district, on the last Monday in November, in each year; the districts of Kentucky, east and west Tennessee, and Missouri, shall form and be called the eighth circuit; and the districts of Alabama, the eastern district of Louisiana, the district of Mississippi, and the district of Arkansas, shall form and be called the ninth circuit.

SEC. 2. And be it further enacted, That the sessions of said circuit courts shall be held twice in each year in the following districts, to wit: commencing in the eastern district of Louisiana, at New Orleans, on the third Monday of May and on the third Monday of November, annually; in the district of Mississippi, at Jackson, on the first Monday of May and on the first Monday of November, annually; in the southern district of Alabama, at Mobile, on the second Monday of April and the second Monday of October, annually; in the western district of

Pennsylvania, at Pittsburg, on the third Mondays of May and November, annually; in the district of Delaware, at Newcastle on the Tuesday next following the fourth Monday of May, and at Dover on the Tuesday next following the third Monday of October, annually; and in the district of Maryland, at Baltimore, on the first Monday of April and the first Monday of October, annually; in the northern district of New York, at Albany, on the second Tuesday of June and the third Tuesday of October, annually; and there shall be holden a term of said circuit courts, annually, at Lewisburg, in the western district of Virginia, commencing on the first Monday of August; at Huntsville, in the northern district of Alabama, commencing on the first Monday of June; at St. Louis, in the district of

Missouri, commencing on the first Monday of April; and at Little Rock, in the district of Arkansas, on the fourth Monday of March; and that no process, recognizance, or bail bond, returnable to the next term of either of said courts, shall be avoided or impaired, or affected by this change, as to the commencement of said term; but that all process, bail bonds, and recognizances returnable to the next term of either of said courts, shall be returnable and returned to the court next held, according to this act, in the same manner as if so made returnable on the face thereof, and shall have full effect accordingly; and that all continuances in either of said courts shall be from the last term to the court appointed by this act, and the day herein appointed for the commencement of the next session thereof:

Provided, That nothing herein contained shall prevent the judge of the northern district of New York from holding the courts at Utica, nor the judge of the western district of Pennsylvania from holding the courts at Williamsport, at the same time and with the same power and jurisdiction as heretofore.

SEC. 3. And be it further enacted, That so much of any act or acts of Congress as vests in the district courts of the United States for the districts of Indiana, Illinois, Missouri, Arkansas, the eastern district of Louisiana, the district of Mississippi, the northern district of New York, the western district of Virginia, and the western district of Pennsylvania, and the districts of Alabama, or either of them, the power and jurisdiction of circuit courts, be, and the same is hereby, repealed; and there shall hereafter be circuit courts held for said districts by the chief or associate justices of the

Supreme Court, assigned or allotted to the circuit to which such districts may respectively belong, and the district judges of such districts severally and respectively; either of whom shall constitute a quorum; which circuit courts, and the judges thereof, shall have like powers and exercise like jurisdiction as other circuit courts and the judges thereof; and the said district courts, and the judges thereof, shall have like powers and exercise like jurisdiction as the district courts, and the judges thereof, in the other circuits.

From all judgments and decrees, rendered in the district courts of the United States for the western district of Louisiana, writs of error and appeals shall lie to the circuit court in the other district in said State, in the same manner as from decrees and judgments rendered in the districts within which a circuit court is provided by this act.

SEC. 4. And be it further enacted, That all actions, suits, prosecutions, causes, pleas, process, and other proceedings, relative to any cause, civil or criminal, (which might have been brought, and could have been, originally, cognizable in a circuit court,) now pending in, or returnable to, the several district courts of Indiana, Illinois,

Missouri, Mississippi, Arkansas, Michigan, the eastern district of Louisiana, the districts of Alabama, the northern district of New York, the western district of

Pennsylvania, and western district of Virginia, acting as circuit courts on the first day of April next, shall be, and are hereby declared to be, respectively transferred, returnable, and continued to, the several circuit courts constituted by this act, to be holden within the said districts respectively; and shall be heard, tried and determined therein, in the same manner as if originally brought, entered, prosecuted, or had, in such circuit courts.

And the said circuit courts shall be governed by the same laws and regulations as apply to the other circuit courts of the United States; and the clerks of the said courts, respectively, shall perform the same duties, and shall be entitled to receive the same fees and emoluments, which are by law established for the clerks of the other circuit courts of the United States. The allotment of their chief justice and the associate justices of the said Supreme Court to the several circuits shall be made as heretofore.

SEC. 5. And be it further enacted, That all acts and provisions inconsistent with this act be, and the same are hereby, repealed.

APPROVED, March 3, 1837.

Source: Statutes at Large, 24th Congress, Session 2, Vol. 5, Ch. 34, Pg. 176

14. Declaration of Sentiments, 1848

Introduction

The birth of the woman's suffrage movement is generally traced to the Seneca Falls Convention, held in Seneca Falls, New York, on July 19–20, 1848. Called by Lucretia Mott, Elizabeth Cady Stanton, and other prominent women, the delegates to the convention cleverly decided to model their declaration after the Declaration of Independence of 1776. The actual address was read to the convention's 240 delegates by Stanton. In addition to the Declaration of Sentiments, the Seneca Falls Convention adopted a number of resolutions proclaiming women's equality and demanding equal treatment. A number of these resolutions were premised on the idea that women were morally superior to men and that their participation in the public sphere would accordingly have an uplifting and refining influence on politics. The only resolution that was not adopted unanimously was the one advocating equal woman's suffrage.

Primary Source

Whereas, the great precept of nature is conceded to be that "man shall pursue his own true and substantial happiness," Blackstone in his Commentaries remarks that this law of nature being coeval with mankind, and dictated by God himself, is of course superior in obligation to any other. It is binding over all the globe, in all countries and at all times; no human laws are of any validity if contrary to this, and such of them as are valid, derive all their force, and all their validity, and all their authority, immediately from this original; therefore:

Resolved, that all laws which prevent woman from occupying such a station in society as her conscience shall dictate, or which place her in a position inferior to that of man, are contrary to the great precept of nature, and therefore of no force or authority.

Resolved, that woman is man's equal—was intended to be so by the Creator, and the highest good of the race demands that she should be recognized as such.

Resolved, that the women of this country ought to be enlightened in regard to the laws under which they live, that they may no longer publish their degradation by declaring themselves satisfied with their present position, nor their ignorance by asserting that they have all the rights they want.

Resolved, that inasmuch as man, while claiming for himself intellectual superiority, does accord to woman moral superiority, it is preeminently his duty to encourage her to speak and teach, as she has an opportunity, in all religious assemblies.

Resolved, that the same amount of virtue, delicacy, and refinement of behavior that is required of woman in the social state, should also be required of man, and the same transgressions should be visited with equal severity on both man and woman.

Resolved, that the objection of indelicacy and impropriety, which is so often brought against woman when she addresses a public audience, comes with a very ill grace from those who encourage, by their attendance, her appearance on the stage, in the concert, or in feats of the circus.

Resolved, that woman has too long rested satisfied in the circumscribed limits which corrupt customs and a perverted application of the Scriptures have marked out for her, and that it is time she should move in the enlarged sphere which her great Creator has assigned her.

Resolved, that it is the duty of the women of this country to secure to themselves their sacred right to the elective franchise.

Resolved, that the equality of human rights results necessarily from the fact of the identity of the race in capabilities and responsibilities.

Resolved, that the speedy success of our cause depends upon the zealous and untiring efforts of both men and women, for the overthrow of the monopoly of the pulpit, and for the securing to women an equal participation with men in the various trades, professions, and commerce.

Resolved, therefore, that, being invested by the Creator with the same capabilities, and the same consciousness of responsibility for their exercise, it is demonstrably the right and duty of woman, equally with man, to promote every righteous cause by every righteous means; and especially in regard to the great subjects of morals and religion, it is self-evidently her right to participate with her brother in teaching them, both in private and in public, by writing and by speaking, by any instrumentalities proper to be used, and in any assemblies proper to be held; and this being a self-evident truth growing out of the divinely implanted principles of human nature, any custom or authority adverse to it, whether modern or wearing the hoary sanction of antiquity, is to be regarded as a self-evident falsehood, and at war with mankind.

Source: Library of Congress

15. New York Married Woman's Property Act, 1848

Introduction

The New York Married Woman's Property Act of 1848, passed three months before the Seneca Falls, New York, gathering, gave women control over the property they owned at the time of their marriage. The Seneca Falls Convention resulted in a Declaration of Sentiments and is considered the first convention in the United States called to discuss women's rights and issues.

Primary Source

AN ACT for the effectual protection of the property of married women.

The People of the State of New York, represented in Senate and Assembly do enact as follows:

Sec. 1. The real and personal property of any female who may hereafter marry, and which she shall own at the time of marriage, and the rents issues and profits thereof shall not be subject to the disposal of her husband, nor be liable for his debts, and shall continue her sole and separate property, as if she were a single female.

Sec. 2. The real and personal property, and the rents issues and profits thereof of any female now married shall not be subject to the disposal of her husband; but shall be her sole and separate property as if she were a single female except so far as the same may be liable for the debts of her husband heretofore contracted.

Sec. 3. It shall be lawful for any married female to receive, by gift, grant devise or bequest, from any person other than her husband and hold to her sole and separate use, as if she were a single female, real and personal property, and the rents, issues and profits thereof, and the same shall not be subject to the disposal of her husband, nor be liable for his debts.

Sec. 4. All contracts made between persons in contemplation of marriage shall remain in full force after such marriage takes place.

Passed April 7, 1848.

Source: New York Laws 307 (1848)

16. Compromise of 1850

Introduction

Like the Missouri Compromise of 1820, the Compromise of 1850 was an attempt to reconcile Northern and Southern interests in the years before the Civil War. Concern over slavery had been heightened by quarrels over the status of slavery in territories recently won during the Mexican-American War and by applications for statehood from California. Although many other men played important roles in hammering out the compromise, this controversy is remembered as the last crisis in which the three congressional titans of the day—Henry Clay, Daniel Webster, and John C. Calhoun—all played a part.

Primary Source

It being desirable, for the peace, concord, and harmony of the Union of these States, to settle and adjust amicably all existing questions of controversy between them arising out of the institution of slavery upon a fair, equitable and just basis: therefore,

1. Resolved, That California, with suitable boundaries, ought, upon her application to be admitted as one of the States of this Union, without the imposition by Congress of any restriction in respect to the exclusion or introduction of slavery within those boundaries.

2. Resolved, That as slavery does not exist by law, and is not likely to be introduced into any of the territory acquired by the United States from the republic of Mexico, it is inexpedient for Congress to provide by law either for its introduction into, or

exclusion from, any part of the said territory; and that appropriate territorial governments ought to be established by Congress in all of the said territory, not assigned as the boundaries of the proposed State of California, without the adoption of any restriction or condition on the subject of slavery.

3. Resolved, That the western boundary of the State of Texas ought to be fixed on the Rio del Norte, commencing one marine league from its mouth, and running up that river to the southern line of New Mexico; thence with that line eastwardly, and so continuing in the same direction to the line as established between the United States and Spain, excluding any portion of New Mexico, whether lying on the east or west of that river.

4. Resolved, That it be proposed to the State of Texas, that the United States will provide for the payment of all that portion of the legitimate and bona fide public debt of that State contracted prior to its annexation to the United States, and for which the duties on foreign imports were pledged by the said State to its creditors, not exceeding the sum of —— dollars, in consideration of the said duties so pledged having been no longer applicable to that object after the said annexation, but having thenceforward become payable to the United States; and upon the condition, also, that the said State of Texas shall, by some solemn and authentic act of her legislature or of a convention, relinquish to the United States any claim which it has to any part of New Mexico.

5. Resolved, That it is inexpedient to abolish slavery in the District of Columbia whilst that institution continues to exist in the State of Maryland, without the consent of that State, without the consent of the people of the District, and without just compensation to the owners of slaves within the District.

6. But, resolved, That it is expedient to prohibit, within the District, the slave trade in slaves brought into it from States or places beyond the limits of the District, either to be sold therein as merchandise, or to be transported to other markets without the District of Columbia.

7. Resolved, That more effectual provision ought to be made by law, according to the requirement of the constitution, for the restitution and delivery of persons bound to service or labor in any State, who may escape into any other State or Territory in the Union. And,

8. Resolved, That Congress has no power to promote or obstruct the trade in slaves between the slaveholding States; but that the admission or exclusion of slaves brought from one into another of them, depends exclusively upon their own particular laws.

Source: Motions, and Orders of the 31st Congress, ca. 03/1849–ca. 03/1851; Record Group 46; Records of the United States Senate, 1789–1990; National Archives

17. Fugitive Slave Act, 1850

Introduction

Passed on February 12, 1793, and signed into law by President George Washington, the Fugitive Slave Act implemented Article IV, Section 2 of the Constitution, which prohibited states from freeing persons "held to Service or Labour" and required states to return fugitive slaves to the state from which they had fled. The Fugitive Slave Act made it a federal offense to assist escapees and permitted the seizure of escaped slaves—as well as any children subsequently born to them—in any state of the union for as long as they lived. The act also specifically recognized the role of agents—known as slave-catchers—in securing escaped slaves, and it authorized judges and magistrates to approve the transfer of slaves. However, Northern states passed laws that made the Fugitive Slave Act more difficult to enforce. As part of the Compromise of 1850, Congress strengthened the Fugitive Slave Act. The new act imposed harsh penalties for assisting or failing to return runaway slaves, at the same time stripping free blacks of any legal right to challenge the claims of slave owners. Under the Fugitive Slave Acts, free blacks were frequently forced into slavery. Abolitionists, now legally required to assist slave owners, defiantly supported the Underground Railroad, organized to help slaves escape to Canada, where they were safe from American laws.

Primary Source

Section 1

Be it enacted by the Senate and House of Representatives of the United States of America in Congress assembled, That the persons who have been, or may hereafter be, appointed commissioners, in virtue of any act of Congress, by the Circuit Courts of the United States, and Who, in consequence of such appointment, are authorized to exercise the powers that any justice of the peace, or other magistrate of any of the United States, may exercise in respect to offenders for any crime or offense against the United States, by arresting, imprisoning, or bailing the same under and by the virtue of the thirty-third section of the act of the twenty-fourth of September seventeen hundred and eighty-nine, entitled "An Act to establish the judicial courts of the United States" shall be, and are hereby, authorized and required to exercise and discharge all the powers and duties conferred by this act.

Section 2

And be it further enacted, That the Superior Court of each organized Territory of the United States shall have the same power to appoint commissioners to take acknowledgments of bail and affidavits, and to take depositions of witnesses in civil causes, which is now possessed by the Circuit Court of the United States; and all commissioners who shall hereafter be appointed for such purposes by the Superior Court of any organized Territory of the United States, shall possess all the powers, and exercise all the duties, conferred by law upon the commissioners appointed by the Circuit Courts of the United States for similar purposes, and shall moreover exercise and discharge all the powers and duties conferred by this act.

Section 3
And be it further enacted, That the Circuit Courts of the United States shall from time to time enlarge the number of the commissioners, with a view to afford reasonable facilities to reclaim fugitives from labor, and to the prompt discharge of the duties imposed by this act.

Section 4
And be it further enacted, That the commissioners above named shall have concurrent jurisdiction with the judges of the Circuit and District Courts of the United States, in their respective circuits and districts within the several States, and the judges of the Superior Courts of the Territories, severally and collectively, in term-time and vacation; shall grant certificates to such claimants, upon satisfactory proof being made, with authority to take and remove such fugitives from service or labor, under the restrictions herein contained, to the State or Territory from which such persons may have escaped or fled.

Section 5
And be it further enacted, That it shall be the duty of all marshals and deputy marshals to obey and execute all warrants and precepts issued under the provisions of this act, when to them directed; and should any marshal or deputy marshal refuse to receive such warrant, or other process, when tendered, or to use all proper means diligently to execute the same, he shall, on conviction thereof, be fined in the sum of one thousand dollars, to the use of such claimant, on the motion of such claimant, by the Circuit or District Court for the district of such marshal; and after arrest of such fugitive, by such marshal or his deputy, or whilst at any time in his custody under the provisions of this act, should such fugitive escape, whether with or without the assent of such marshal or his deputy, such marshal shall be liable, on his official bond, to be prosecuted for the benefit of such claimant, for the full value of the service or labor of said fugitive in the State, Territory, or District whence he escaped: and the better to enable the said commissioners, when thus appointed, to execute their duties faithfully and efficiently, in conformity with the requirements of the Constitution of the United States and of this act, they are hereby authorized and empowered, within their counties respectively, to appoint, in writing under their hands, any one or more suitable persons, from time to time, to execute all such

warrants and other process as may be issued by them in the lawful performance of their respective duties; with authority to such commissioners, or the persons to be appointed by them, to execute process as aforesaid, to summon and call to their aid the bystanders, or posse comitatus of the proper county, when necessary to ensure a faithful observance of the clause of the Constitution referred to, in conformity with the provisions of this act; and all good citizens are hereby commanded to aid and assist in the prompt and efficient execution of this law, whenever their services may be required, as aforesaid, for that purpose; and said warrants shall run, and be executed by said officers, any where in the State within which they are issued.

Section 6
And be it further enacted, That when a person held to service or labor in any State or Territory of the United States, has heretofore or shall hereafter escape into another State or Territory of the United States, the person or persons to whom such service or labor may be due, or his, her, or their agent or attorney, duly authorized, by power of attorney, in writing, acknowledged and certified under the seal of some legal officer or court of the State or Territory in which the same may be executed, may pursue and reclaim such fugitive person, either by procuring a warrant from some one of the courts, judges, or commissioners aforesaid, of the proper circuit, district, or county, for the apprehension of such fugitive from service or labor, or by seizing and arresting such fugitive, where the same can be done without process, and by taking, or causing such person to be taken, forthwith before such court, judge, or commissioner, whose duty it shall be to hear and determine the case of such claimant in a summary manner; and upon satisfactory proof being made, by deposition or affidavit, in writing, to be taken and certified by such court, judge, or commissioner, or by other satisfactory testimony, duly taken and certified by some court, magistrate, justice of the peace, or other legal officer authorized to administer an oath and take depositions under the laws of the State or Territory from which such person owing service or labor may have escaped, with a certificate of such magistracy or other authority, as aforesaid, with the seal of the proper court or officer thereto attached, which seal shall be sufficient to establish the competency of the proof, and with proof, also by affidavit, of the identity of the person whose service or labor is claimed to be due as aforesaid, that the person so arrested does in fact owe service or labor to the person or persons claiming him or her, in the State or Territory from which such fugitive may have escaped as aforesaid, and that said person escaped, to make out and deliver to such claimant, his or her agent or attorney, a certificate setting forth the substantial facts as to the service or labor due from such fugitive to the claimant, and of his or her escape from the State or Territory in which he or she was arrested, with authority to such claimant, or his or her agent or attorney, to use such reasonable force and restraint as may be necessary, under the circumstances of the case, to take and remove such fugitive person back to the State or Territory whence he or she may have escaped as aforesaid. In no trial

or hearing under this act shall the testimony of such alleged fugitive be admitted in evidence; and the certificates in this and the first [fourth] section mentioned, shall be conclusive of the right of the person or persons in whose favor granted, to remove such fugitive to the State or Territory from which he escaped, and shall prevent all molestation of such person or persons by any process issued by any court, judge, magistrate, or other person whomsoever.

Section 7

And be it further enacted, That any person who shall knowingly and willingly obstruct, hinder, or prevent such claimant, his agent or attorney, or any person or persons lawfully assisting him, her, or them, from arresting such a fugitive from service or labor, either with or without process as aforesaid, or shall rescue, or attempt to rescue, such fugitive from service or labor, from the custody of such claimant, his or her agent or attorney, or other person or persons lawfully assisting as aforesaid, when so arrested, pursuant to the authority herein given and declared; or shall aid, abet, or assist such person so owing service or labor as aforesaid, directly or indirectly, to escape from such claimant, his agent or attorney, or other person or persons legally authorized as aforesaid; or shall harbor or conceal such fugitive, so as to prevent the discovery and arrest of such person, after notice or knowledge of the fact that such person was a fugitive from service or labor as aforesaid, shall, for either of said offences, be subject to a fine not exceeding one thousand dollars, and imprisonment not exceeding six months, by indictment and conviction before the District Court of the United States for the district in which such offence may have been committed, or before the proper court of criminal jurisdiction, if committed within any one of the organized Territories of the United States; and shall moreover forfeit and pay, by way of civil damages to the party injured by such illegal conduct, the sum of one thousand dollars for each fugitive so lost as aforesaid, to be recovered by action of debt, in any of the District or Territorial Courts aforesaid, within whose jurisdiction the said offence may have been committed.

Section 8

And be it further enacted, That the marshals, their deputies, and the clerks of the said District and Territorial Courts, shall be paid, for their services, the like fees as may be allowed for similar services in other cases; and where such services are rendered exclusively in the arrest, custody, and delivery of the fugitive to the claimant, his or her agent or attorney, or where such supposed fugitive may be discharged out of custody for the want of sufficient proof as aforesaid, then such fees are to be paid in whole by such claimant, his or her agent or attorney; and in all cases where the proceedings are before a commissioner, he shall be entitled to a fee of ten dollars in full for his services in each case, upon the delivery of the said certificate to the claimant, his agent or attorney; or a fee of five dollars in cases where the proof shall not, in the opinion of such commissioner, warrant such certificate and delivery, inclusive of all services incident to such arrest and examination, to be paid, in either case, by the claimant, his or her agent or attorney. The person or persons authorized to execute the process to be issued by such commissioner for the arrest and detention of fugitives from service or labor as aforesaid, shall also be entitled to a fee of five dollars each for each person he or they may arrest, and take before any commissioner as aforesaid, at the instance and request of such claimant, with such other fees as may be deemed reasonable by such commissioner for such other additional services as may be necessarily performed by him or them; such as attending at the examination, keeping the fugitive in custody, and providing him with food and lodging during his detention, and until the final determination of such commissioners; and, in general, for performing such other duties as may be required by such claimant, his or her attorney or agent, or commissioner in the premises, such fees to be made up in conformity with the fees usually charged by the officers of the courts of justice within the proper district or county, as near as may be practicable, and paid by such claimants, their agents or attorneys, whether such supposed fugitives from service or labor be ordered to be delivered to such claimant by the final determination of such commissioner or not.

Section 9

And be it further enacted, That, upon affidavit made by the claimant of such fugitive, his agent or attorney, after such certificate has been issued, that he has reason to apprehend that such fugitive will he rescued by force from his or their possession before he can be taken beyond the limits of the State in which the arrest is made, it shall be the duty of the officer making the arrest to retain such fugitive in his custody, and to remove him to the State whence he fled, and there to deliver him to said claimant, his agent, or attorney. And to this end, the officer aforesaid is hereby authorized and required to employ so many persons as he may deem necessary to overcome such force, and to retain them in his service so long as circumstances may require. The said officer and his assistants, while so employed, to receive the same compensation, and to be allowed the same expenses, as are now allowed by law for transportation of criminals, to be certified by the judge of the district within which the arrest is made, and paid out of the treasury of the United States.

Section 10

And be it further enacted, That when any person held to service or labor in any State or Territory, or in the District of Columbia, shall escape therefrom, the party to whom such service or labor shall be due, his, her, or their agent or attorney, may apply to any court of record therein, or judge thereof in vacation, and make satisfactory proof to such court, or judge in vacation, of the escape aforesaid, and that the person escaping owed service or labor to such party. Whereupon the court shall cause a record to be made of the matters so proved, and also a general description of the person so escaping, with such convenient certainty as may be; and a transcript of such record, authenticated by the attestation of the clerk and of the seal of the said court, being produced in any other State, Territory, or district in which the person so escaping may be found, and being exhibited to any judge, commissioner, or other office, authorized by the law of the United States to cause persons escaping from service or labor to be delivered up, shall be held and taken to be full and conclusive evidence of the fact of escape, and that the service or labor of the person escaping is due to the party in such record mentioned. And upon the production by the said party of other and further evidence if necessary, either oral or by affidavit, in addition to what is contained in the said record of the identity of the person escaping, he or she shall be delivered up to the claimant, And the said court, commissioner, judge, or other person authorized by this act to grant certificates to claimants or fugitives, shall, upon the production of the record and other evidences aforesaid, grant to such claimant a certificate of his right to take any such person identified and proved to be owing service or labor as aforesaid, which certificate shall authorize such claimant to seize or arrest and transport such person to the State or Territory from which he escaped: Provided, That nothing herein contained shall be construed as requiring the production of a transcript of such record as evidence as aforesaid. But in its absence the claim shall be heard and determined upon other satisfactory proofs, competent in law.

Source: U.S. Statutes at Large, 9 (1850): 462

18. Establishment of the Circuit Court for California, 1855

Introduction

When California was admitted as a state in 1850, the distance from Washington, D.C. to the Pacific coast, compounded by the lack of any connecting rail lines, made it impractical to assign a Supreme Court justice to any circuit court in the new state. Like the courts in most new states that had not been incorporated in a circuit, California's district courts exercised the jurisdiction of district and circuit courts. Congress granted the U.S. Circuit Court for the districts of California the same original and appellate jurisdiction exercised by other circuit courts within the federal judiciary. The organizing statute repealed the circuit court jurisdiction of the California district courts, although those two courts continued to hear appeals from the board of commissioners established to confirm private land claims. Only one judge, Matthew McAllister, ever served on the California circuit court, and soon after he resigned in 1863 Congress abolished the court and established the Tenth Circuit.

Primary Source

March 2, 1855.
10 Stat. 631.

CHAP. CXLII. — An Act to establish a Circuit Court of the United States in and for the State of California.

Be it enacted by the Senate and House of Representatives of the United States of America in Congress assembled, That a judicial circuit shall be, and the same is hereby, constituted, in and for the State of California, to be known as the circuit court of the United States for the districts of California, a term of which court shall be held annually, in the city of San Francisco, on the first Monday of July in each and every year; and for this purpose a judge shall be appointed, and a court hereby organized shall, in all things, have and exercise the same original jurisdiction as is vested in the several circuit courts of the United States, as organized under existing laws, and shall also have and exercise the same appellate jurisdiction over the district courts of the United States for the northern and southern districts of California as by existing laws is vested in the several circuit courts of the United States over the district courts of the United States in their respective circuits; and the said judge shall appoint a clerk, who shall have the power to appoint a deputy, which clerk shall reside, and keep the records of the court, in the said city of San Francisco, and shall receive for the services he may perform double the fees allowed to the clerk of the southern district of New York.

SEC. 2. And be it further enacted, That said judge shall have power to order and hold such special or extra terms of said court as he may deem expedient, and at such time or times as he shall, by his order, under his hand and seal, direct, addressed to the marshal and clerk of said court, at least thirty days previous to the commencement of such special or extra term or terms, which order shall be published intermediately in two or more of the gazettes of the State of California; and at any or all of such special terms the business of said court shall have reference, to the immediately preceding regular or special term, and be proceeded with in the same manner; and such proceedings shall be, to all intents and purposes, as valid as if the same had taken place at a regular term of said court; all which terms shall be held at such place, in the said city of San Francisco, as the marshal of the United States for the northern district of California, whose duty it shall be to act as the marshal of said court, shall procure for the purpose, under the directions of said judge; and appeals from the proceedings of the court organized under this act shall be taken to the Supreme Court of the United States, in the same manner, and on the same conditions, as appeals are taken under existing laws from the other circuit courts of the United States.

SEC. 3. And be it further enacted, That the judge of said court shall have the same power to issue writs of habeas corpus and other writs as is vested by law in the other judges of the United States.

SEC. 4. And be it further enacted, That in case the judge of said court shall fail to attend at the time and place of holding any regular or special term of said court, before the close of the fourth day after the commencement of such term, the business pending, before said court shall stand adjourned until the next regular term of said court, or until the next special term of the court, should one be ordered under the authority of this act previous to such regular term.

SEC. 5. And be it further enacted, That the district courts of the United States for the northern and southern districts of California, shall hereafter exercise only the ordinary duties and powers of the district courts of the United States, except the special jurisdiction vested in the said district courts of California over the decisions of the board of commissioners for the settlement of private land claims in California under existing laws; and that appeals from the judgments, orders, and decrees of either of said district courts of California, in the exercise of its ordinary jurisdiction, shall be taken to the circuit court organized by this act, in the same manner and upon the same conditions as appeals may be taken from the judgments, orders, or decrees of the district courts to the circuit courts of the United States.

SEC. 6. And be it further enacted, That the judge appointed under this act shall, from time to time, or at any time when in his opinion the business of his own court will permit, and that of the courts of the northern and southern districts of California shall require, form part of, and preside over, the said district courts when either of them is engaged in the discharge of the appellate jurisdiction vested in it over the decisions of the board of commissioners for the settlement of private land claims in the State of California, under the act of Congress entitled "An act to ascertain and settle the private land claims in the State of California," passed March third, eighteen hundred and fifty-one, and by another act entitled "An act making appropriations for the civil and diplomatic expenses of the government for the year ending thirtieth of June, eighteen hundred and fifty-three, and for other purposes," passed thirty-first of August, eighteen hundred and fifty-two; and it shall be the duty of the clerks of the respective district courts of California to give thirty days' written notice to the judge of the court organized under this act, of the time and place of the sitting of such district court for the discharge of such appellate jurisdiction; and in case the judge of such district court shall fail, from sickness or other casualty, to attend at such time and place, the judge of the court organized under this act, is hereby authorized to hold said court, and proceed with the business of the court, in accordance with the provisions prescribed for the regulation of said district court in the act of Congress hereinbefore referred to; and all appeals to the Supreme Court of the United States from the decisions of said district court, whether held by the last-mentioned judge, or by him in conjunction with the district judge, or by the district judge alone, shall be taken in the manner prescribed by the act of Congress passed on the third day of March, eighteen hundred and fifty-one, entitled "An act to ascertain and settle the private land claims in the State of California."

SEC. 7. And be it further enacted, That the salary of the judge appointed under this act shall be four thousand five hundred dollars per annum, commence from the date of his appointment.

SEC. 8. And be it further enacted, That all laws and parts of laws militating against this act be, and the same are hereby, repealed.

APPROVED, March 2, 1855.

Source: Statutes at Large, 34th Congress, 2nd Session, Vol. 10, Ch. 142, Pg. 631

19. Homestead Act, 1862

Introduction

The Homestead Act granted 160 acres of land, at no cost, to anyone who lived on and worked the land for at least five years. Any person over the age of twenty-one who was the head of a family, and was a born or soon to be naturalized American citizen, could avail themselves of a grant by essentially becoming a squatter on the unclaimed public lands in the west. The decades-long drive for free distribution of public land had been stoutly resisted. Easterners did not want to lose laborers and feared that the value of their own property would fall. People in the slaveholding states saw homesteading as a threat to the spread of slavery. The outbreak of the Civil War removed the major political obstacle to passage of the act posed by the slaveholding states. The 1862 act specifically denied homesteading privileges to people who had borne arms against the United States or aided the nation's enemies, effectively excluding Confederates. However, the act was amended after the war to include former Confederates. The Homestead Act was subject to abuse, with speculators erecting mere shacks and fraudulently claiming ownership only to sell the free land for a profit. The act was the greatest single factor in the rapid settlement of the Great Plains after the Civil War, with more than a million people claiming over eighty million acres from 1863 to 1900. This in turn resulted in decades of warfare with the Plains Indians.

Primary Source

Be it enacted, That any person who is the head of a family, or who has arrived at the age of twenty-one years, and is a citizen of the United States, or who shall have filed his declaration of intention to become such, as required by the naturalization laws of the United States, and who has never borne arms against the United States Government or given aid and comfort to its enemies, shall, from and after the first of January, eighteen hundred and sixty-three, be entitled to enter one quarter-section or a less quantity of unappropriated public lands, upon which said person may have filed a pre-emption claim, or which may, at the time the application is made, be subject to pre-emption at one dollar and twenty-five cents, or less, per acre; or eighty acres or less of such unappropriated lands, at two dollars and fifty cents per acre, to be located in a body, in conformity to the legal subdivisions of the public lands, and after the same shall have been surveyed: *Provided,* That any person owning or residing on land may, under the provisions of this act, enter other land lying contiguous to his or her said land, which shall not, with the land so already owned and occupied, exceed in the aggregate one hundred and sixty acres.

Sec. 2. That the person applying for the benefit of this act shall, upon application to the register of the land office in which he or she is about to make such entry, make affidavit before the said register or receiver that he or she is the head of a family, or is twenty-one or more years of age, or shall have performed service in the Army or Navy of the United States, and that he has never borne arms against the Government of the United States or given aid and comfort to its enemies, and that such application is made for his or her exclusive use and benefit, and that said entry is made for the purpose of actual settlement and cultivation, and not, either directly or indirectly, for the use or benefit of any other person or persons whomsoever, and upon filing the said affidavit with the register or receiver, and on payment of ten dollars, he or she shall thereupon be permitted to enter the quantity of land specified: *Provided, however,* That no certificate shall be given or patent issued therefor until the expiration of five years from the date of such entry; and if, at the expiration of such time, or at any time within two years thereafter, the person making such entry—or if he be dead, his widow; or in case of her death, his heirs or devisee; or in case of a widow making such entry, her heirs or devisee, in case of her death—shall prove by two credible witnesses that he, she or they have resided upon or cultivated the same for the term of five years immediately succeeding the time of filing the affidavit aforesaid, and shall make affidavit that no part of said land has been alienated, and that he has borne true allegiance to the Government of the United States; then, in such case, he, she, or they, if at that time a citizen of the United States, shall be entitled to a patent, as in other cases provided for by law: *And provided, further,* That in case of the death of both father and mother, leaving an infant child or children under twenty-one years of age, the right and fee shall inure to the benefit of said infant child or children; and the executor, administrator, or guardian may, at any time within two years after the death of the surviving parent, and in accordance with the laws of the States in which such children for the time being have their domicile, sell said land for the benefit of said infants, but for no other purpose; and the purchaser shall acquire the absolute title by the purchase, and be entitled to a patent from the United States, on payment of the office fees and sum of money herein specified. . . .

Source: Public Law 37-64 (1862)

20. Abraham Lincoln's Emancipation Proclamation, 1863

Introduction

A war measure signed by President Abraham Lincoln on September 22, 1862, to take effect on January 1, 1863, the Emancipation Proclamation freed the slaves in all areas rebelling against the Union at that point. Technically, therefore, the proclamation did not free any slaves, as slaves from conquered Confederate territory had already been freed under a series of Confiscation Acts regarding captured contraband. Slaves in areas still within the control of the Confederacy were obviously not affected by the proclamation, nor were slaves residing in the border states that had remained loyal to the Union. Despite the limited practical impact of the proclamation, however, it had an enormous psychological impact, elevating the abolition of slavery to one of the North's stated war aims and leading the way for the adoption of the Thirteenth Amendment after the war ended in Union victory in 1865.

Primary Source

Whereas, on the 22nd day of September, in the year of our Lord 1862, a proclamation was issued by the President of the United States, containing, among other things, the following, to wit:

"That on the 1st day of January, in the year of our Lord 1863, all persons held as slaves within any state or designated part of a state, the people whereof shall then be in rebellion against the United States, shall be then, thenceforward, and forever free; and the executive government of the United States, including the military and naval authority thereof, will recognize and maintain the freedom of such persons and will do no act or acts to repress such persons, or any of them, in any efforts they may make for their actual freedom.

That the executive will, on the 1st day of January aforesaid, by proclamation, designate the states and parts of states, if any, in which the people thereof, respectively, shall then be in rebellion against the United States; and the fact that any state or the people thereof shall on that day be in good faith represented in the Congress of the United States by members chosen thereto at elections wherein a majority of the qualified voters of such states shall have participated shall, in the absence of strong countervailing testimony, be deemed conclusive evidence that such state and the people thereof are not then in rebellion against the United States."

Now, therefore, I, Abraham Lincoln, President of the United States, by virtue of the power in me vested as a commander in chief of the Army and Navy of the United States, in time of actual armed rebellion against the authority and government of the United States, and as a fit and necessary war measure for suppressing said rebellion, do, on this 1st day of January, in the year of our Lord 1863, and in accordance with my purpose so to do, publicly proclaimed for the full period of 100 days from the day first above mentioned, order and designate as the states and parts of states wherein the people thereof, respectively, are this day in rebellion against the United States the following, to wit:

Arkansas, Texas, Louisiana (except the parishes of St. Bernard, Plaquemines, Jefferson, St. John, St. Charles, St. James, Ascension, Assumption, Terrebonne, Lafourche, St. Mary, St. Martin, and Orleans, including the city of New Orleans), Mississippi, Alabama, Florida, Georgia, South Carolina, North Carolina, and Virginia (except the forty-eight counties designated as West Virginia, and also the counties of Berkeley, Accomac, Northampton, Elizabeth City, York, Princess Anne, and Norfolk, including the cities of Norfolk and Portsmouth), and which excepted parts are for the present left precisely as if this proclamation were not issued.

And, by virtue of the power and for the purpose aforesaid, I do order and declare that all persons held as slaves within said designated states and parts of states are, and henceforward shall be, free; and that the executive government of the United States, including the military and naval authorities thereof, will recognize and maintain the freedom of said persons.

And I hereby enjoin upon the people so declared to be free to abstain from all violence, unless in necessary self-defense; and I recommend to them that, in all cases when allowed, they labor faithfully for reasonable wages.

And I further declare and make known that such persons of suitable condition will be received into the armed service of the United States to garrison forts, positions, stations, and other places, and to man vessels of all sorts in said service.

And upon this act, sincerely believed to be an act of justice, warranted by the Constitution upon military necessity, I invoke the considerate judgment of mankind and the gracious favor of Almighty God.

Source: National Archives

21. Establishment of the Tenth Circuit, 1863

Introduction

Congress in 1929 created a new judicial circuit to accommodate the increased number of states and the expansion of caseloads in the federal courts. This was the first such expansion in more than 65 years. The 12 states that entered the Union between 1866 and 1912 had been incorporated into the Eighth and Ninth Circuits. The Eighth Circuit, encompassing 13 states stretching from Canada to Mexico and from the Mississippi to beyond the Rocky Mountains, became the largest in the nation. By the 1920s, the Eighth Circuit Court of Appeals was meeting in three divisions, and district court judges were recruited regularly to assist the six circuit judges. Various groups representing the bar and the judiciary feared that such a large circuit threatened the efficient administration of justice in regionally-defined courts. The 1929 statute grouped Minnesota, Iowa, North Dakota, South Dakota, Nebraska, Missouri, and Arkansas as the Eighth Circuit and established a Tenth Circuit consisting of Wyoming, Colorado, Utah, New Mexico, Kansas, and Oklahoma. Sitting circuit judges were reassigned according to residence, and three new judgeships were authorized. Five judges would serve the Eighth Circuit, and four would sit in the Tenth.

Primary Source

March 3, 1863.
12 Stat. 794.

CHAP. C. — An Act to provide Circuit Courts for the Districts of

California and Oregon, and for other Purposes.

Be it enacted by the Senate and House of Representatives of the United States of America in Congress assembled, That the supreme court of the United States shall hereafter consist of a chief justice and nine associate justices, any six of whom shall constitute a quorum; and for this purpose there shall be appointed one additional associate justice of said court, with the like powers, and to take the same oaths, perform the same duties, and be entitled to the same salary, as the other associate justices. The districts of California and Oregon shall constitute the tenth circuit, and the other circuits shall remain as now constituted by law.

SEC. 2. And be it further enacted, That so much of any act or acts of Congress as vests in the district courts in and for the said States of California and Oregon, or either of them, the power and jurisdiction of circuit courts, and the act entitled "An act to establish a circuit court of the United States in and for the State of California," approved March second, eighteen hundred and fifth-five [sic], be, and the same are hereby, repealed, and the said circuit court is hereby abolished; and there shall hereafter be circuit courts held for the districts of the States of California and Oregon by the chief justice, or one of the associate justices of the supreme court of the United States assigned or allotted to the circuit to which such districts may respectively belong, and the district judges of such districts, severally and respectively, either of whom shall constitute a quorum, which circuit courts and the judges thereof shall have like powers and exercise like jurisdiction as other circuit courts and the judges thereof; and the district courts in and for the several districts in and for said States of California and Oregon, and the judges thereof, shall have like powers and exercise like jurisdiction as the district courts and the judges thereof in the other circuit courts

SEC. 3. And be it further enacted, That all actions, suits, prosecutions, causes, pleas, process, and other proceedings, relative to any cause, civil or criminal, (which might have been brought and could have been originally cognizable in a circuit court as established by this act,) now pending in or returnable to the several district courts of the United States in the said States of California and Oregon, or now pending in or returnable to the circuit court of California, by this act abolished, acting as circuit courts (or so empowered to act) shall be, and are hereby declared to be, respectively, transferred, returnable, and continued to the several circuit courts constituted by this act, to be holden within said districts respectively, and shall be heard, tried, and determined therein, in the same manner as if originally brought, entered, prosecuted, or had in such circuit courts; and no bail-bond or recognizance taken in any of said actions, suits, prosecutions, or causes transferred to said circuit courts by this act shall thereby be avoided, impaired, or invalidated; and the said circuit courts shall be governed by the same laws and regulations as apply to the other circuit courts of the United States, and the clerks of said courts, respectively, shall perform the same duties, and shall be entitled to receive the same fees and emoluments which are by law established for the clerks of the other circuit courts of the United States.

SEC. 4. And be it further enacted, That the circuit court for the districts in California shall be held at the city of San Francisco, and the city of Los Angeles, in said State, at the same times now prescribed by law for holding terms of the district courts of the northern and southern districts of said State at said places; and the circuit court for the State of Oregon shall be held at Portland, in said State, at the same times now fixed by law for holding terms of the district court for the district of Oregon at that place.

SEC. 5. And be it further enacted, That the judge assigned to the tenth circuit, as constituted by this act, shall receive, in addition to his salary hereinbefore provided, the sum of one thousand dollars for his travelling expenses for each year in which he may actually attend a session of the supreme court of the United States.

APPROVED, March 3, 1863.

Source: Statutes at Large, 70th Congress, 2nd Session, Vol. 45, Ch. 363, Pg. 1346

22. Black Codes of Mississippi, 1865

Introduction

A series of laws passed by state legislatures throughout the South in the early days of Reconstruction, black codes were intended to impose limits on the newly freed African Americans by enacting strict regulations regarding everything in black life from jobs to marriage. Mississippi was among the first to enact such codes and imposed the most stringent limits of all the Southern states. The codes were a direct attempt by the former Confederate states to subvert federal Reconstruction policies, and they were surprisingly successful in establishing a form of second-class citizenship for African Americans that would later develop into the system of Jim Crow laws and segregation that the U.S. Supreme Court recognized in *Plessy v. Ferguson* (1896).

Primary Source

An Act to Confer Civil Rights on Freedmen, and for other Purposes

Section 1. All freedmen, free negroes and mulattoes may sue and be sued, implead and be impleaded, in all the courts of law and equity of this State, and may acquire personal property, and chooses in action, by descent or purchase, and may dispose of the same in the same manner and to the same extent that white persons may: Provided, That the provisions of this section shall not be so construed as to allow any freedman, free negro or mulatto to rent or lease any lands or tenements except in incorporated cities or towns, in which places the corporate authorities shall control the same.

Section 2. All freedmen, free negroes and mulattoes may intermarry with each other, in the same manner and under the same regulations that are provided by law for white persons: Provided, that the clerk of probate shall keep separate records of the same.

Section 3. All freedmen, free negroes or mullatoes who do now and have herebefore lived and cohabited together as husband and wife shall be taken and held in law as legally married, and the issue shall be taken and held as legitimate for all purposes; and it shall not be lawful for any freedman, free negro or mulatto to intermarry with any white person; nor for any person to intermarry with any freedman, free negro or mulatto; and any person who shall so intermarry shall be deemed guilty of felony, and on conviction thereof shall be confined in the State penitentiary for life; and those shall be deemed freedmen, free negroes and mulattoes who are of pure negro blood, and those descended from a negro to the third generation, inclusive, though one ancestor in each generation may have been a white person.

Section 4. In addition to cases in which freedmen, free negroes and mulattoes are now by law competent witnesses, freedmen, free negroes or mulattoes shall be competent in civil cases, when a party or parties to the suit, either plaintiff or plaintiffs, defendant or defendants; also in cases where freedmen, free negroes and mulattoes is or are either plaintiff or plaintiffs, defendant or defendants. They shall also be competent witnesses in all criminal prosecutions where the crime charged is alleged to have been committed by a white person upon or against the person or property of a freedman, free negro or mulatto: Provided, that in all cases said witnesses shall be examined in open court, on the stand; except, however, they may be examined before the grand jury, and shall in all cases be subject to the rules and tests of the common law as to competency and credibility.

Section 5. Every freedman, free negro and mulatto shall, on the second Monday of January, one thousand eight hundred and sixty-six, and annually thereafter, have a lawful home or employment, and shall have written evidence thereof as follows, to wit: if living in any incorporated city, town, or village, a license from that mayor thereof; and if living outside of an incorporated city, town, or village, from the member of the board of police of his beat, authorizing him or her to do irregular and job work; or a written contract, as provided in Section 6 in this act; which license may be revoked for cause at any time by the authority granting the same.

Section 6. All contracts for labor made with freedmen, free negroes and mulattoes for a longer period than one month shall be in writing, and a duplicate, attested and read to said freedman, free negro or mulatto by a beat, city or county officer, or two disinterested white persons of the county in which the labor is to performed, of which each party shall have one: and said contracts shall be taken and held as entire contracts, and if the laborer shall quit the service of the employer before the expiration of his term of service, without good cause, he shall forfeit his wages for that year up to the time of quitting.

Section 7. Every civil officer shall, and every person may, arrest and carry back to his or her legal employer any freedman, free negro, or mulatto who shall have quit the service of his or her employer before the expiration of his or her term of service without good cause; and said officer and person shall be entitled to receive for arresting and carrying back every deserting employee aforesaid the sum of five dollars, and ten cents per mile from the place of arrest to the place of delivery; and the same shall be paid by the employer, and held as a set off for so much against the wages of said deserting employee: Provided, that said arrested party, after being so returned, may appeal to the justice of the peace or member of the board of police of the county, who, on notice to the alleged employer, shall try summarily whether said appellant is legally employed by the alleged employer, and has good cause to quit said employer. Either party shall have the right of appeal to the county court, pending which the alleged deserter shall be remanded to the alleged employer or otherwise disposed of, as shall be right and just; and the decision of the county court shall be final.

Section 8. Upon affidavit made by the employer of any freedman, free negro or mulatto, or other credible person, before any justice of the peace or member of the board of police, that any freedman, free negro or mulatto legally employed by said employer has illegally deserted said employment, such justice of the peace or member of the board of police issue his warrant or warrants, returnable before himself or other such officer, to any sheriff, constable or special deputy, commanding him to arrest said deserter, and return him or her to said employer, and the like proceedings shall be had as provided in the preceding section; and it shall be lawful for any officer to whom such warrant shall be directed to execute said warrant in any county in this State; and that said warrant may be transmitted without endorsement to any like officer of another county, to be executed and returned as aforesaid; and the said employer shall pay the costs of said warrants and arrest and return, which shall be set off for so much against the wages of said deserter.

Section 9. If any person shall persuade or attempt to persuade, entice, or cause any freedman, free negro or mulatto to desert from the legal employment of any person before the expiration of his or her term of service, or shall knowingly employ any such deserting freedman, free negro or mullato, or shall knowingly give or sell to any such deserting freedman, free negro or mulatto, any food, raiment, or other thing, he or she shall be guilty of a misdemeanor, and, upon conviction, shall be fined not less than twenty-five dollars and not more than two hundred dollars and costs; and if the said fine and costs shall not be immediately paid, the court shall sentence said convict to not exceeding two months imprisonment in the county jail, and he or she shall moreover be liable to the party injured in damages: Provided, if any person shall, or shall attempt to, persuade, entice, or cause any freedman, free negro or mullatto to desert from any legal employment of any person, with the view to employ said freedman, free negro or mullato without the limits of this State, such costs; and if said fine and costs shall not be immediately paid, the court shall sentence said convict to not exceeding six months imprisonment in the county jail.

Section 10. It shall be lawful for any freedman, free negro, or mulatto, to charge any white person, freedman, free negro or mulatto by affidavit, with any criminal offense against his or her person or property, and upon such affidavit the proper process shall be issued and executed as if said affidavit was made by a white person, and it shall be lawful for any freedman, free negro, or mulatto, in any action, suit or controversy pending, or about to be instituted in any court of law equity in this State, to make all needful and lawful affidavits as shall be necessary for the institution, prosecution or defense of such suit or controversy.

Section 11. The penal laws of this state, in all cases not otherwise specially provided for, shall apply and extend to all freedman, free negroes and mulattoes.

> *Source: An Act to Confer Civil Rights on Freedmen, and for other purposes. Laws of Mississippi, 1865*

23. Civil Rights Act, 1866

Introduction

The Civil Rights Act of 1866 was passed by Congress to enforce the end of slavery and protect the rights of the newly freed African Americans before the passage of the Fourteenth Amendment in 1868. The act was originally vetoed by President Andrew Johnson, but the Radical Republican Congress overrode Johnson's veto. After this episode, however, some of the act's congressional supporters feared the law might be found unconstitutional by a U.S. Supreme Court packed with justices opposed to civil rights. Therefore, they began drafting the legislation that eventually became the Fourteenth Amendment so that it could withstand any judicial challenges.

Primary Source

An Act to Protect All Persons in the United States in Their Civil Rights, and Furnish the Means of their Vindication.

Be it enacted, That all persons born in the United States and not subject to any foreign power, excluding Indians not taxed, are hereby declared to be citizens of the United States; and such citizens, of every race and color, without regard to any previous condition of slavery or involuntary servitude, except as a punishment for crime whereof the party shall have been duly convicted, shall have the same right, in every State and Territory in the United States, to make and enforce contracts, to sue, be parties, and give evidence, to inherit, purchase, lease, sell, hold, and convey real and personal property and to full and equal benefit of all laws and proceedings for the security of person and property, as is enjoyed by white citizens, and shall be subject to like punishment, pains, and penalties, and to none other, any law, statute, ordinance, regulation, or custom, to the contrary notwithstanding.

Section 2. And be it further enacted, That any person who, under color of any law, statute, ordinance, regulation, or custom, shall subject, or cause to be subjected, any inhabitant of any State or Territory to the deprivation of any right secured or protected by this act, or to different punishment, pains, or penalties on account of such person having at any time been held in a condition of slavery or involuntary servitude, except as a punishment for crime whereof the party shall have been duly convicted or by reason of his color, or race, than is prescribed for the punishment of white persons, shall be deemed guilty of a misdemeanor, and, on conviction, shall be punished by fine not exceeding one thousand dollars, or imprisonment not exceeding one year, or both, in the discretion of the court.

Section 3. And be it further enacted, That the district courts of the United States . . . shall have, exclusively of the courts of the several States, cognizance of all crimes and offences committed against the provisions of this act, and also, concurrently with the circuit court of the United States, of all causes, civil and criminal, affecting persons who are denied or cannot enforce in the courts or judicial tribunals of the State or locality where they may be any of the rights secured to them by the first section of this act. . . .

Section 4. And be it further enacted, That the district attorneys, marshals, and deputy marshals of the United States, the commissioners appointed by the Circuit and territorial courts of the United States, with powers of arresting, imprisoning, or bailing offenders against the laws of the United States, the officers and agents of the Freedmen's Bureau, and every other officer who may be specially empowered by the President of the United States, shall be, and they are hereby, specially authorized and required, at the expense of the United States, to institute proceedings against all and every person who shall violate the provisions of this act, and cause him or them to be arrested and imprisoned, or bailed, as the case may be, for trial before such court of the United States or territorial court as by this act has cognizance of the offence. . . .

Section 8. And be it further enacted, That whenever the President of the United States shall have reason to believe that offences have been or are likely to be committed against the provisions of this act within any judicial district, it shall be lawful for him, in his discretion, to direct the judge, marshal, and district attorney of such district to attend at such place within the district, and for such time as he may designate, for the purpose of the more speedy arrest and trial of persons charged with a violation of this act; and it shall be the duty of every judge or other officer, when any such requisition shall be received by him, to attend at the place and for the time therein designated.

Section 9. And be it further enacted, That it shall be lawful for the President of the United States, or such person as he may empower for that purpose, to employ such part of the land or naval forces of the United States, or of the militia, as shall be necessary to prevent the violation and enforce the due execution of this act.

Section 10. And be it further enacted, That upon all questions of law arising in any cause under the provisions of this act a final appeal may be taken to the Supreme Court of the United States.

Source: Civil Rights Act of 1866. U.S. Statutes at Large 14 (1866): 27

24. Reorganization of the Judicial Circuits, 1866

Introduction

After the Civil War, Congress redrew the boundaries of the judicial circuits and reduced the number of circuits from ten to nine. It also provided for the gradual elimination of seats on the Supreme Court until there would be seven justices rather than the ten authorized in 1863. Although Congress would increase the size of the Supreme Court within three years, the geographical outline of the circuits has since remained largely the same except for the addition of new states to existing circuits and the division of two large circuits in the twentieth century.

Primary Source

July 23, 1866.
14 Stat. 209.

CHAP. CCX. — An Act to fix the Number of the Judges of the Supreme Court of the United States, and to change certain Judicial Circuits.

Be it enacted by the Senate and House of Representatives of the United States of America in Congress assembled, That no vacancy in the office of associate justice of the supreme court shall be filled by appointment until the number of associate justices shall be reduced to six; and thereafter the said supreme court shall consist of a chief justice of the United States and six associate justices, any four of whom shall be a quorum; and the said court shall hold one term annually at the seat of government, and such adjourned or special terms as it may find necessary for the despatch of business.

SEC. 2. And be it further enacted, That the first and second circuits shall remain as now constituted; that the districts of Pennsylvania, New Jersey, and Delaware shall constitute the third circuit; that the districts Maryland, West Virginia, Virginia, North Carolina, and South Carolina shall constitute the fourth circuit; that the districts of Georgia, Florida, Alabama, Mississippi, Louisiana, and Texas shall constitute the fifth circuit; that the districts of Ohio, Michigan, Kentucky, and Tennessee shall constitute the sixth circuit; that the districts of Indiana, Illinois, and Wisconsin, shall constitute the seventh circuit; that the districts of Minnesota, Iowa, Missouri, Kansas, and Arkansas shall constitute the eighth circuit; and the districts of California, Oregon, and Nevada shall constitute the ninth circuit.

APPROVED, July 23, 1866.

Source: Statutes at Large, 39th Congress, 1st Session, Vol. 14, Ch. 210, Pg. 209

25. The Judiciary Act of 1869 (Circuit Judges Act)

Introduction

In the midst of Reconstruction, the Act of 1869 increased the size of the Supreme Court, established separate judgeships for the U.S. circuit courts, and included the first provision allowing judges to retire without losing their salary. After a period of six years in which the number of authorized seats on the Supreme Court shifted from nine to ten to seven, the act of 1869 restored the number of justices to nine, the number of circuits established in 1866. Justices were required to attend each circuit court within their assigned circuit only once every two years. Congress approved the appointment of circuit judges, who in all matters related to the circuit courts exercised the same authority as the justices. A circuit court could be held by the circuit judge, the justice appointed to the circuit, the district judge, or by any combination of two of them, thus making possible the simultaneous meeting of circuit courts within a given circuit. The more efficient distribution of judicial responsibilities and the retirement clause offered promise of a more active federal judiciary, but by adhering to the system of dual trial courts and maintaining the circuit duty of Supreme Court justices, the act fell short of proposals for the elimination of the circuit courts and the creation of a middle tier of appellate courts.

Primary Source

April 10, 1869.
16 Stat. 44.

CHAP. XXII.— An Act to amend the Judicial System of the United States.

Be it enacted by the Senate and House of Representatives of the United States of America in Congress assembled, That the Supreme Court of the United States shall hereafter consist of the Chief Justice of the United States and eight associate justices, any six of whom shall constitute a quorum; and for the purposes of this act there shall be appointed an additional associate justice of said court.

SEC. 2. And be it further enacted, That for each of the nine existing judicial circuits there shall be appointed a circuit judge, who shall reside in his circuit, and shall possess the same power and jurisdiction therein as the justice of the Supreme Court allotted to the circuit. The circuit courts in each circuit shall be held by the justice of the Supreme Court allotted to the circuit, or by the circuit judge of the circuit, or by the district judge of the district sitting alone, or by the justice of the Supreme Court and circuit judge sitting together, in which case the justice of the Supreme Court shall preside, or in the absence of either of them by the other, (who shall preside,) and the district judge. And such courts may be held at the same time in the different districts of the same circuits, and cases may be heard and tried by each of the judges holding any such court sitting apart by direction of the presiding justice or judge, who shall designate the business to be done by each. The circuit judges shall each receive an annual salary of five thousand dollars.

SEC. 3. And be it further enacted, That nothing in this act shall affect the powers of the justices of the Supreme Court as judges of the circuit court, except in the appointment of clerks of the circuit courts, who in each circuit shall be appointed by the circuit judge of that circuit, and the clerks of the district courts shall be appointed by the judges thereof respectively: Provided, That the present clerks of said courts shall continue in office till other appointments be made in their place, or they be otherwise removed.

SEC. 4. And be it further enacted, That it shall be the duty of the Chief Justice and of each justice of the Supreme Court to attend at least one term of the circuit court in each district of his circuit during every period of two years.

SEC. 5. And be it further enacted, That any judge of any court of the United States, who, having held his commission as such at least ten years, shall, after having attained to the age of seventy years, resign his office, shall thereafter, during the residue of his natural life, receive the same salary which was by law payable to him at the time of his resignation.

SEC. 6. And be it further enacted, That this act shall take effect on the first Monday of December, eighteen hundred and sixty-nine.

APPROVED, April 10, 1869.

Source: Public Law No. 18. *Acts and Resolutions of the United States of America Passed at the Third Session of the Fortieth Congress and the First Session of the Forty-First Congress*, Washington, D.C.: Government Printing Office, 1869, Pg. 196

26. *Minor v. Happersett,* 1872

Introduction

Despite the expanded recognition of rights in the Thirteenth through Fifteenth Amendments and extensions of suffrage to women in the Wyoming and Utah territories, the 19th century did not prove to be a good time for advocates of women's rights at the national level. Declaring in *Bradwell v. Illinois* (1873) that "the law of the Creator" mandated that "the paramount destiny and mission of woman are to fulfill the noble and benign offices of wife and mother," the Supreme Court refused to overturn the decision of the Illinois bar to exclude Myra Bradwell from the practice of law simply because she was a woman. In *Minor v. Happersett,* Chief Justice Morrison Waite wrote the Court's unanimous decision to uphold a registrar's refusal to allow Virginia Minor to vote in the presidential election of 1872. Susan B. Anthony had asserted a similar privilege, but her case had not made it to the Supreme Court.

Primary Source

JUSTICE C.J. WAITE delivered the opinion of the Court

The plaintiff, Virginia L. Minor (with whom is joined her husband, Francis Minor, as required by the law of Missouri), states, that under the Constitution and law of Missouri, all persons wishing to vote at any election, must previously have been registered in the manner pointed out by law, this being a condition precedent to the exercise of the elective franchise.

That on the fifteenth day of October, 1872 (one of the days fixed by law for the registration of voters), and long prior thereto, she was a native-born, free white citizen of the United States, and of the State of Missouri, and on the day last mentioned she was over the age of twenty-one years.

That on said day, the plaintiff was a resident of the thirteenth election district of the city and county of St. Louis, in the State of Missouri, and had been residing in said county and election district, for the entire period of twelve months and more, immediately preceding said fifteenth day of October, 1872, and for more than twenty years had been and is a tax-paying, law-abiding citizen of the county and State aforesaid.

That on said last mentioned day, the defendant, having been duly and legally appointed Registrar and entered upon the discharge of the duties thereof at the office of registration, to wit: No. 2004 Market Street, in said city and county of St. Louis, it became and was then and there his duty to register all citizens, resident in said district as aforesaid, entitled to the elective franchise, who might apply to him for that purpose.

The plaintiff further states, that wishing to exercise her privilege as a citizen of the United States, and vote for Electors for President and Vice-President of the United States, and for a Representative in Congress, and for other officers, at the General Election held in November, 1872: While said defendant was so acting as Registrar, on said 15th day of October, 1872, she appeared before him, at his office aforesaid, and then and there offered to take and subscribe the oath to support the Constitution of the United States and of the State of Missouri, as required by the registration law of said State, approved March 10, 1871, and respectfully applied to him to be registered as a lawful voter, which said defendant then and there refused to do.

The plaintiff further states, that the defendant, well knowing that she, as a citizen of the United States and of the State of Missouri, resident as aforesaid, was then and there entitled to all the privileges and immunities of citizenship, chief among which is the elective franchise, and as such, was entitled to be registered, in order to exercise said privilege: yet, unlawfully intending, contriving, and designing to deprive the plaintiff of said franchise or privilege, then and there knowingly, willfully, maliciously, and corruptly refused to place her name upon the list of registered voters, whereby she was deprived of her right to vote.

Defendant stated to plaintiff, that she was not entitled to be registered, or to vote, because she was not a "male" citizen, but a woman! that by the Constitution of Missouri, Art. II., Sec. 18, and by the aforesaid registration law of said State, approved March 10, 1871, it is provided and declared, that only "male citizens" of the United States, etc., are entitled or permitted to vote.

But the plaintiff protests against such decision, and she declares and maintains that said provisions of the Constitution and registration law of Missouri aforesaid, are in conflict with, and repugnant to the Constitution of the United States, which is paramount to State authority; and that they are especially in conflict with the following articles and clauses of said Constitution of the United States, to wit:

Art. I. Sec. 9. Which declares that no Bill of Attainder shall be passed.

Art. I. Sec. 10. No State shall pass any Bill of Attainder, or grant any title of nobility.

Art. IV. Sec. 2. The citizens of each State shall be entitled to all privileges and immunities of citizens in the several States.

Art. IV. Sec. 4. The United States shall guarantee to every State a republican form of government.

Art. VI. This Constitution and the laws of the United States which shall be made in pursuance thereof, shall be the supreme law of the land, anything in the Constitutions or laws of any State to the contrary notwithstanding.
Amendments

Art. V. No person shall be . . . deprived of life, liberty, or property without due process of law.

Art. IX. The enumeration in the Constitution of certain rights, shall not be construed to deny or disparage others retained by the people.

Art. XIV. Sec. 1. All persons born or naturalized in the United States, and subject to the jurisdiction thereof, are citizens of the United States and of the State wherein they reside. No State shall make or enforce any law which shall abridge the privileges or immunities of citizens of the United States. Nor shall any State deprive any person of life, liberty, or property, without due process of law; nor deny to any person within its jurisdiction, the equal protection of the laws.

The plaintiff states, that by reason of the wrongful act of the defendant as aforesaid, she has been damaged in the sum of ten thousand dollars, for which she prays judgment. . . .

Source: Minor v. Happersett, 88 U.S. 162 (1875)

27. Civil Rights Act [Excerpt], 1875

Introduction

Sponsored by Senator Charles Sumner of Massachusetts, the 1875 Civil Rights Act was passed by Congress to secure for African Americans the rights and privileges of social contact that whites already enjoyed. Basically, the act covered discrimination in public transportation, public accommodations, restaurants and other places of dining, and on grand and petit juries. In 1880, the act was challenged when the Civil Rights Cases came before the U.S. Supreme Court, which ruled the law unconstitutional.

Primary Source

An Act to Protect All Citizens in Their Civil and Legal Rights.

Whereas it is essential to just government we recognize the equality of all men before the law, and hold that it is the duty of government in its dealings with the people to mete out equal and exact justice to all, of whatever nativity, race, color, or persuasion, religious or political; and it being the appropriate object of legislation to enact great fundamental principles into law: Therefore,

Be it enacted, That all persons within the jurisdiction of the United States shall be entitled to the full and equal enjoyment of the accommodations, advantages, facilities, and privileges of inns, public conveyances on land or water, theaters, and other places of public amusement; subject only to the conditions and limitations established by law, and applicable alike to citizens of every race and color, regardless of any previous condition of servitude.

Sec. 2. That any persons who shall violate the foregoing section by denying to any citizen, except for reasons by law applicable to citizens of every race and color, and regardless of any previous condition of servitude, the full enjoyment of any of the accommodations, advantages, facilities, or privileges in said section enumerated, or by aiding or inciting such denial, shall, for every such offense, forfeit and pay the sum of five hundred dollars to the person aggrieved thereby . . . and shall also, for every such offense, be deemed guilty of a misdemeanor, and upon conviction thereof, shall be fined not less than five hundred nor more than one thousand dollars, or shall be imprisoned not less than thirty days nor more than one year. . . .

Sec. 3. That the district and circuit courts of the United States shall have, exclusively of the courts of the several States, cognizance of all crimes and offenses against, and violations of, the provisions of this act. . . .

Sec. 4. That no citizen possessing all other qualifications which are or may be prescribed by law shall be disqualified for service as grand or petit juror in any court of the United States, or of any State, on account of race, color, or previous condition of servitude; and any officer or other person charged with any duty in the selection or summoning of jurors who shall exclude or fail to summon any citizen for the cause aforesaid shall, on conviction thereof, be deemed guilty of a misdemeanor, and be fined not more than five thousand dollars.

Sec. 5. That all cases arising under the provisions of this act . . . shall be renewable by the Supreme Court of the United States, without regard to the sum in controversy. . . .

Source: Civil Rights Act of 1875. U.S. Statutes at Large 18 (1875): 335

28. The Jurisdiction and Removal Act of 1875

Introduction

Since 1789, federal jurisdiction had been divided between the federal courts and state courts, with the latter hearing most cases involving federal law if both parties were residents of the state. In the first half of the nineteenth century, Congress occasionally expanded the right of removal to federal courts in order to protect specific areas of federal authority. A series of acts expanded the authority of the federal judiciary after the Civil War. In 1875, Congress granted the U.S. circuit courts the jurisdiction to hear all cases arising under the Constitution and the laws of the United States, as long as the dispute concerned more than $500. The statute also made it possible for plaintiffs and defendants in cases before state courts to remove a case to a U.S. circuit court whenever the matter involved a question of federal law or if any members of the parties were from different states. By establishing the full federal jurisdiction permitted by the Constitution, the act of 1875 fundamentally changed the role of the federal courts.

Primary Source

March 3, 1875.
18 Stat. 470.

CHAP. 137. – An act to determine the jurisdiction of circuit courts of the United States, and to regulate the removal of causes from State courts, and for other purposes.

Be it enacted by the Senate and House of Representatives of the United States of America in Congress assembled, That the circuit courts of the United States shall have original cognizance, concurrent with the courts of the several States, of all suits of a civil nature at common law or in equity, where the matter in dispute exceeds, exclusive of costs, the sum or value of five hundred dollars, and arising under the Constitution or laws of the United States, or treaties made, or which shall be made, under their authority, or in which the United States are plaintiffs or petitioners, or in which there shall be a controversy between citizens of different States or a controversy between citizens of the same State claiming lands under grants of different States, or a controversy between citizens of a State and foreign states, citizens, or subjects; and shall have exclusive cognizance of all crimes and offenses cognizable under the authority of the United States, except as otherwise provided by law, and concurrent jurisdiction with the district courts of the crimes and offenses cognizable therein. But no person shall be arrested in one district for trial in another in any civil action before a circuit or district court. And no civil suit shall be brought before either of said courts against any person by any original process or proceeding in any other district than that whereof he is an inhabitant, or in which he shall be found at the time of serving such process or commencing such proceeding, except as hereinafter provided; nor shall any circuit or district court have cognizance of any suit founded on contract in favor of an assignee, unless a suit might have been prosecuted in such court to recover thereon if no assignment had been made, except in cases of promissory notes negotiable by the law merchant and bills of exchange. And the circuit courts shall also have appellate jurisdiction from the district courts under the regulations and restrictions prescribed by law.

SEC. 2. That any suit of a civil nature, at law or in equity, now pending or hereafter brought in any State court where the matter in dispute exceeds, exclusive of costs, the sum or value of five hundred dollars, and arising under the Constitution or laws of the United States, or treaties made, or which shall be made, under their authority, or in which the United States shall be plaintiff or petitioner, or in which there shall be a controversy between citizens of different States, or a controversy between citizens of the same State claiming lands under grants of different States, or a controversy between citizens of a State and foreign States, citizens, or subjects, either party may remove said suit into the circuit court of the United States for the proper district. And when in any suit mentioned in this section there shall be a controversy which is wholly between citizens of different States, and which be fully determined as between them, then either one or more of the plaintiffs or defendants actually interested in such controversy may remove said suit to the circuit court of the United States for the proper district.

SEC. 3. That whenever either party, or any one or more of the plaintiffs or defendants entitled to remove any suit mentioned in the next preceding section shall desire to remove such suit from a State court to the circuit court of the United States, he or they may make and file a petition in such suit in such State court before or at the term at which said cause could be first tried and before the trial thereof for the removal of such suit into the circuit court to be held in the district where such suit is pending, and shall make and file therewith a bond, with good and sufficient surety, for his or their entering in such circuit court, on the first day of its then next session, a copy of the record in such suit, and for paying of all costs that may be awarded by the said circuit court, if said court shall hold that such suit was wrongfully or improperly removed thereto, and also for there appearing and entering special bail in such suit, if special bail was originally requisite therein, it shall then be the duty of the State court to accept said petition and bond, and proceed no further in such suit, and any bail that may have been originally taken shall be discharged; and the said copy being entered as aforesaid in the said circuit court of the United States, the cause shall then proceed in the same manner as if it had been originally commenced in the said circuit court; and if in any action commenced in a State court the title of land be concerned, and the parties are citizens of the same State, and the matter in dispute exceed the sum or value of five hundred dollars, exclusive of costs, the sum or value being made to appear, one or more of the plaintiffs or defendants, before the trial, may state to the court, and make affidavit, if the court require it, that he or they claim and shall rely upon a right or title to the land under a grant from a State, and produce the original grant, or an exemplification of it, except where the loss of public records shall put it out of his or their power, and shall move that any one or more of the adverse party inform the court whether he or they claim a right or title to the land under a grant from some other State, the party or parties so required shall give such information, or otherwise not be allowed to plead such grant, or give it in evidence upon the trial; and if he or they inform that he or they do claim under such grant, any one or more of the party moving for such information may then, on petition and bond as hereinbefore mentioned in this act, remove the cause for trial to the circuit court of the United States next to be holden in such district; and any one of either party removing the cause shall not be allowed to plead or give evidence of any other title than that by him or them stated as aforesaid as the ground of his or their claim, and the trial of issues of fact in the circuit courts shall, in all suits except those of equity and of admiralty and maritime jurisdiction, be by jury.

SEC. 4. That when any suit shall be removed from a State court to a circuit court of the United States, any attachment or sequestration of the goods or estate of the defendant had in such suit in the State court shall hold the goods or estate so attached or sequestered to answer the final judgment or decree in the same manner as by law they would have been held to answer final judgment or decree had it been rendered by the court in which such suit was commenced; and all bonds, undertakings, or security given by either party in suit prior to its removal shall remain valid and effectual, nothwithstanding said removal; and all injunctions, orders, and other proceedings had in such suit prior to its removal shall remain in full force and effect until dissolved or modified by the court to which such suit shall be removed.

SEC. 5. That if, in any suit commenced in a circuit court or removed from a State court to a circuit court of the United States, it shall appear to the satisfaction of said circuit court, at any time after such suit has been brought or removed thereto, that suit does not really and substantially involve a dispute or controversy properly within the jurisdiction of said circuit court, or that the parties to said suit have been improperly or collusively made or joined, either as plaintiffs or defendants, for the purpose of creating a case cognizable or removable under this act, the said circuit court shall proceed no further therein, but shall dismiss the suit or remand it to the court from which it was removed as justice may require, and shall make such order as to costs as shall be just; but the order of said circuit court dismissing or remanding said cause to the State court shall be reviewable by the Supreme Court on writ of error or appeal, as the case may be.

SEC. 6. That the circuit court of the United States shall, in all suits removed under the provisions of this act, proceed therein as if the suit had been originally commenced in said circuit court, and the same proceedings had been taken in such suit in said circuit court as shall have been had therein in said State court prior to its removal.

SEC. 7. That in all causes removable under this act, if the term of the circuit court to which the same is removable, then next to be holden, shall commence within twenty days after filing the petition and bond in the State court for its removal, then he or they who apply to remove the same shall have twenty days from such application to file said copy of record in said circuit court, and enter appearance therein; and if done within said twenty days, such filing and appearance shall be taken to satisfy the said bond in that behalf; that if the clerk of the State court in which any such cause shall be pending, shall refuse to any one or more of the parties or persons applying to remove the same, a copy of the record therein, after tender of legal fees for such copy, said clerk so offending shall be deemed guilty of a misdemeanor, and, on conviction thereof in the circuit court of the United States to which said action, or proceeding was removed, shall be punished by imprisonment not more than one year, or by fine not exceeding one thousand dollars, or both in the discretion of the court.

And the circuit court to which any cause, shall be removable under this act shall have power to issue a writ of certiorari to said State court commanding such State court to make return of the record in any such cause removed as aforesaid, or in which any one or more of the plaintiffs or defendants have complied with the provisions of this act for the removal of the same, and enforce said writ according to law; and if it shall be impossible for the parties or persons removing any cause under this act, or complying with the provision for the removal thereof, to obtain such copy, for the reason that the clerk of said State court refuses to furnish a copy, on payment of legal fees, or for any other reason, the circuit court shall make an order requiring the prosecutor in any such action or proceeding to enforce forfeiture or recover penalty as aforesaid, to file a copy of the paper or proceeding by which the same was commenced, within such time as the court may determine; and in default thereof the court shall dismiss the said action or proceeding; but if said order shall be complied with, then said circuit-court shall require the other party to plead, and said action, or proceeding shall proceed to final judgment; and the said circuit court may make an order requiring the parties thereto to plead de novo; and the bond given, conditioned as aforesaid, shall be discharged so far as it requires copy of the record to be filed as aforesaid.

SEC. 8. That when in any suit, commenced in any circuit court of the United States, to enforce any legal or equitable lien upon, or claim to, or to remove any incumbrance or lien or cloud upon the title to real or personal property within the district where such suit is brought, one or more of the defendants therein shall not be an inhabitant of, or found within, the said district, or shall not voluntarily appear thereto, it shall be lawful for the court to make an order directing such absent defendant or defendants to appear, plead, answer, or demur, by a day certain to be designated, which order shall be served on such absent defendant or defendants, if practicable, wherever found, and also upon the person or persons in possession or charge of said property, if any there be; or where such personal service upon such absent defendant or defendants is not practicable, such order shall be published in such manner as the court may direct, not less than once a week for six consecutive weeks; and in case such absent defendant shall not appear, plead, answer, or demur within the time so limited, or within some further time, to be allowed by the court, in its discretion, and upon proof of the service or publication of said order, and of the performance of the directions contained in the same, it shall be lawful for the court to entertain jurisdiction, and proceed to the hearing and adjudication of such suit in the same manner as if such absent defendant had been served with process within the said district; but said adjudication shall, as regards said absent defendant or defendants without appearance, affect only the property which shall have been the subject of the suit and under the jurisdiction of the court therein, within such district. And when a part of the said real or personal property against which such proceeding shall be taken shall be within another district, but within the same State, said suit may be brought in either district in said State; Provided, however, That any defendant or defendants not actually personally notified as above provided may, at any time within one year after final judgment in any suit mentioned in this section, enter his appearance in said suit in said circuit court, and thereupon the said court shall make an order setting aside the judgment therein, and permitting said defendant or defendants to plead therein on payment by him or them of such costs as the court shall deem just; and thereupon said suit shall be proceeded with to final judgment according to law.

SEC. 9. That whenever either party to a final judgment or decree which has been or shall be rendered in any circuit court has died or shall die before the time allowed for taking an appeal or bringing a writ of error has expired, it shall not be necessary to revive the suit by any formal proceedings aforesaid. The representative of such deceased party may file in the office of the clerk of such circuit court a duly certified copy of his appointment and thereupon may enter an appeal or bring writ of error as the party he represents might have done. If the party in whose favor such judgment or decree is rendered has died before appeal taken or writ of error brought, notice to his representatives shall be given from the Supreme court, as provided in case of the death of a party after appeal taken or writ of error brought.

SEC. 10. That all acts and parts of acts in conflict with the provisions of this act hereby repealed.

Approved, March 3. 1875.

> *Source:* Statutes at Large, 43rd Congress, 2nd Session, Vol. 18, Ch. 137, Pg. 470

29. Chinese Exclusion Act, 1882

Introduction

Enacted on May 6, 1882, the Chinese Exclusion Act placed a ban on Chinese immigrants entering the United States or being naturalized as U.S. citizens for ten years. Originally vetoed by President Chester A. Arthur, the president eventually signed the law after some minor alterations. The Chinese had been entering the country in record numbers for several years previously, particularly in California, and were typically forced to work for extremely low wages and live in conditions of poverty. Many of them lived as near slaves while employed building railroad lines across the West. They were also frequently victims of attacks by workingmen and other immigrant groups, who believed the Chinese were taking jobs away from them.

Primary Source

An act to execute certain treaty stipulations relating to Chinese.

WHEREAS, in the opinion of the Government of the United States the coming of Chinese laborers to this country endangers the good order of certain localities within the territory thereof: Therefore,

Be it enacted by the Senate and House of Representatives of the United States of America in Congress assembled, That from and after the expiration of ninety days next after the passage of this act, and until the expiration of ten years next after the passage of this act, the coming of Chinese laborers to the United States be, and the same is hereby, suspended; and during such suspension it shall not be lawful for any Chinese laborer to come, or, having so come after the expiration of said ninety days, to remain within the United States.

Section 2. That the master of any vessel who shall knowingly bring within the United States on such vessel, and land or permit to be landed, any Chinese laborer, from any foreign port or place, shall be deemed guilty of a misdemeanor, and on conviction thereof shall be punished by a fine of not more than five hundred dollars for each and every such Chinese laborer so brought, and may be also imprisoned for a term not exceeding one year.

Section 3. That the two foregoing sections shall not apply to Chinese laborers who were in the United States on the seventeenth day of November, eighteen hundred and eighty, or who shall have come into the same before the expiration of ninety days next after the passage of this act, and who shall produce to such master before going on board such vessel, and shall produce to the collector of the port in the United States at which such vessel shall arrive, the evidence hereinafter in this act required of his being one of the laborers in this section mentioned; nor shall the two foregoing sections apply to the case of any master whose vessel, being bound to a port not within the United States, shall come within the jurisdiction of the United States by reason of being in distress or in stress of weather, or touching at any port of the United States on its voyage to any foreign port or place: Provided, That all Chinese laborers brought on such vessel shall depart with the vessel on leaving port.

Section 4. That for the purpose of properly identifying Chinese laborers who were in the United States on the seventeenth day of November, eighteen hundred and eighty, or who shall have come into the same before the expiration of ninety days next after the passage of this act, and in order to furnish them with the proper evidence of their right to go from and come to the United States of their free will and accord, as provided by the treaty between the United States and China dated November seventeenth, eighteen hundred and eighty, the collector of customs of the district from which any such Chinese laborer shall depart from the United States shall, in person or by deputy, go on board each vessel having on board any such Chinese laborer and cleared or about to sail from his district for a foreign port, and on such vessel make a list of all such Chinese laborers, which shall be entered in registry-books to be kept for that purpose, in which shall be stated the name, age, occupation, last place of residence, physical marks or peculiarities, and all facts necessary for the identification of each of such Chinese laborers, which books shall be safely kept in the custom-house; and every such Chinese laborer so departing from the United States shall be entitled to, and shall receive, free of any charge or cost upon application therefor, from the collector or his deputy, at the time such list is taken, a certificate, signed by the collector or his deputy and attested by his seal of office, in such form as the Secretary of the Treasury shall prescribe, which certificate shall contain a statement of the name, age, occupation, last place of residence, personal description, and facts of identification of the Chinese laborer to whom the certificate is issued, corresponding with the said list and registry in all particulars. In case any Chinese laborer after having received such certificate shall leave such vessel before her departure he shall deliver his certificate to the master of the vessel, and if such Chinese laborer shall fail to return to such vessel before her departure from port the certificate shall be delivered by the master to the collector of customs for cancellation. The certificate herein provided for shall entitle the Chinese laborer to whom the same is issued to return to and reenter the United States upon producing and delivering the same to the collector of customs of the district at which such Chinese laborer shall seek to reenter; and upon delivery of such certificate by such Chinese laborer to the collector of customs at the time of reentry in the United States, said collector shall cause the same to be filed in the custom-house and duly canceled.

Section 5. That any Chinese laborer mentioned in section four of this act being in the United States, and desiring to depart from the United States by land, shall have the right to demand and receive, free of charge or cost, a certificate of identification similar to that provided for in section four of this act to be issued to such Chinese laborers as may desire to leave the United States by water; and it is hereby made the duty of the collector of customs of the district next adjoining the foreign country to which said Chinese laborer desires to go to issue such certificate, free of charge or cost, upon application by such Chinese laborer, and to enter the same upon registry-books to be kept by him for the purpose, as provided for in section four of this act.

Section 6. That in order to the faithful execution of articles one and two of the treaty in this act before mentioned, every Chinese person other than a laborer who may be entitled by said treaty and this act to come within the United States, and who shall be about to come to the United States, shall be identified as so entitled by the Chinese Government in each case, such identity to be evidenced by a certificate issued under the authority of said government, which certificate shall be in the English language or (if not in the English language) accompanied by a translation into English, stating such right to come, and which certificate shall state the name, title, or official rank, if any, the age, height, and all physical peculiarities, former and present occupation or profession, and place of residence in China of the person to whom the certificate is issued and that such person is entitled conformably to the treaty in this act mentioned to come within the United States. Such certificate shall be prima-facie evidence of the fact set forth therein, and shall be produced to the collector of customs, or his deputy, of the port in the district in the United States at which the person named therein shall arrive.

Section 7. That any person who shall knowingly and falsely alter or substitute any name for the name written in such certificate or forge any such certificate, or knowingly utter any forged or fraudulent certificate, or falsely personate any person named in any such certificate, shall be deemed guilty of a misdemeanor; and upon conviction thereof shall be fined in a sum not exceeding one thousand dollars, and imprisoned in a penitentiary for a term of not more than five years.

Section 8. That the master of any vessel arriving in the United States from any foreign port or place shall, at the same time he delivers a manifest of the cargo, and if there be no cargo, then at the time of making a report of the entry of the vessel pursuant to law, in addition to the other matter required to be reported, and before landing, or permitting to land, any Chinese passengers, deliver and report to the collector of customs of the district in which such vessels shall have arrived a separate list of all Chinese passengers taken on board his vessel at any foreign port or place, and all such passengers on board the vessel at that time. Such list shall show the names of such passengers (and if accredited officers of the Chinese Government traveling on the business of that government, or their servants, with a note of such facts), and the names and other particulars, as shown by their respective certificates; and such list shall be sworn to by the master in the manner required by law in relation to the manifest of the cargo. Any willful refusal or neglect of any such master to comply with the provisions of this section shall incur the same penalties and forfeiture as are provided for a refusal or neglect to report and deliver a manifest of the cargo.

Section 9. That before any Chinese passengers are landed from any such vessel, the collector, or his deputy, shall proceed to examine such passengers, comparing the certificates with the list and with the passengers; and no passenger shall be allowed to land in the United States from such vessel in violation of law.

Section 10. That every vessel whose master shall knowingly violate any of the provisions of this act shall be deemed forfeited to the United States, and shall be liable to seizure and condemnation in any district of the United States into which such vessel may enter or in which she may be found.

Section 11. That any person who shall knowingly bring into or cause to be brought into the United States by land, or who shall knowingly aid or abet the same, or aid or abet the landing in the United States from any vessel of any Chinese person not lawfully entitled to enter the United States, shall be deemed guilty of a misdemeanor, and shall, on conviction thereof, be fined in a sum not exceeding one thousand dollars, and imprisoned for a term not exceeding one year.

Section 12. That no Chinese person shall be permitted to enter the United States by land without producing to the proper office of customs the certificate in this act required of Chinese persons seeking to land from a vessel. And any Chinese person found unlawfully within the United States shall be caused to be removed therefrom to the country from whence he came, by direction of the President of the United States, and at the cost of the United States, after being brought before some justice, judge, or commissioner of a court of the United States and found to be one not lawfully entitled to be or remain in the United States.

Section 13. That this act shall not apply to diplomatic and other officers of the Chinese Government traveling upon the business of that government, whose credentials shall be taken as equivalent to the certificate in this act mentioned, and shall exempt them and their body and household servants from the provisions of this act as to other Chinese persons.

Section 14. That hereafter no State court or court of the United States shall admit Chinese to citizenship; and all laws in conflict with this act are hereby repealed.

Section 15. That the words "Chinese laborers," whenever used in this act, shall be construed to mean both skilled and unskilled laborers and Chinese employed in mining.

Source: Chinese Exclusion Act. U.S. Statutes at Large 22 (1882): 58

30. Dawes Act, 1887

Introduction

Considered the most important piece of U.S. federal legislation dealing with Native American land rights, this act became law on February 8, 1887. Also known as the General Allotment Act, it was named after its principal congressional sponsor, Senator Henry Dawes of Massachusetts. It provided for the subdivision and allocation of Indian reservation land into individual holdings. In addition, Indians not residing on reservations could apply to local land offices for title to non-reservation land. In passing the act, Congress was responding in part to public demands for reform by conferring on Indians the right to secure individual land ownership. However, the Dawes Act also extended the jurisdiction of U.S. laws over reservations. This provision undermined tribal authority in the attempt to make Indian reservations more similar to white society. Another underlying purpose was to encourage Indians to settle in one place and take up agriculture. The law gave rise to widespread abuses that resulted in the Indians losing some ninety million acres— two-thirds of their total land—by selling it to white speculators. Not until 1934, however, did the federal government pass legislation to supersede the Dawes Act and reestablish the authority of traditional tribal structures.

Primary Source

An act to provide for the allotment of lands in severalty to Indians on the various reservations, and to extend the protection of the laws of the United States and the Territories over the Indians, and for other purposes.

Be it enacted by the Senate and House of Representatives of the United States of America in Congress assembled, That in all cases where any tribe or band of Indians has been, or shall hereafter be, located upon any reservation created for their use, either by treaty stipulation or by virtue of an act of Congress or executive order setting apart the same for their use, the President of the United States be, and he hereby is, authorized, whenever in his opinion any reservation or any part thereof of such Indians is advantageous for agricultural and grazing purposes, to cause said reservation, or any part thereof, to be surveyed, or resurveyed if necessary, and to allot the lands in said reservation in severalty to any Indian located thereon in quantities as follows:

To each head of a family, one-quarter of a section;

To each single person over eighteen years of age, one-eighth of a section;

To each orphan child under eighteen years of age, one-eighth of a section; and

To each other single person under eighteen years now living, or who may be born prior to the date of the order of the President directing an allotment of the lands embraced in any reservation, one-sixteenth of a section: *Provided*, That in case there is not sufficient land in any of said reservations to allot lands to each individual of the classes above named in quantities as above provided, the lands embraced in such reservation or reservations shall be allotted to each individual of each of said classes pro rata in accordance with the provisions of this act: *And provided further*, That where the treaty or act of Congress setting apart such reservation provides the allotment of lands in severalty in quantities in excess of those herein provided, the President, in making allotments upon such reservation, shall allot the lands to each individual Indian belonging thereon in quantity as specified in such treaty or act: *And provided further*, That when the lands allotted are only valuable for grazing purposes, an additional allotment of such grazing lands, in quantities as above provided, shall be made to each individual.

SEC. 2. That all allotments set apart under the provisions of this act shall be selected by the Indians, heads of families selecting for their minor children, and the agents shall select for each orphan child, and in such manner as to embrace the improvements of the Indians making the selection. where the improvements of two or more Indians have been made on the same legal subdivision of land, unless they shall otherwise agree, a provisional line may be run dividing said lands between them, and the amount to which each is entitled shall be equalized in the assignment of the remainder of the land to which they are entitled under his act: *Provided*, That if any one entitled to an allotment shall fail to make a selection within four years after the President shall direct that allotments may be made on a particular reservation, the Secretary of the Interior may direct the agent of such tribe or band, if such there be, and if there be no agent, then a special agent appointed for that purpose, to make a selection for such Indian, which selection shall be allotted as in cases where selections are made by the Indians, and patents shall issue in like manner.

SEC. 3. That the allotments provided for in this act shall be made by special agents appointed by the President for such purpose, and the agents in charge of the respective reservations on which the allotments are directed to be made, under such rules and regulations as the Secretary of the Interior may from time to time prescribe, and shall be certified by such agents to the Commissioner of Indian Affairs, in duplicate, one copy to be retained in the Indian Office and the other to be transmitted to the Secretary of the Interior for his action, and to be deposited in the General Land Office.

SEC. 4. That where any Indian not residing upon a reservation, or for whose tribe no reservation has been provided by treaty, act of Congress, or executive order, shall make settlement upon any surveyed or unsurveyed lands of the United States not otherwise appropriated, he or she shall be entitled, upon application to the local land-office for the district in which the lands arc located, to have the same allotted to him or her, and to his or her children, in quantities and manner as provided in this act for Indians residing upon reservations; and when such settlement is made upon unsurveyed lands, the grant to such Indians shall be adjusted upon the survey of the lands so as to conform thereto; and patents shall be issued to them for such lands in the manner and with the restrictions as herein provided. And the fees to which the officers of such local land-office would have been entitled had such lands been entered under the general laws for the disposition of the public lands shall be paid to them, from any moneys in the Treasury of the United States not otherwise appropriated, upon a statement of an account in their behalf for such fees by the Commissioner of the General Land Office, and a certification of such account to the Secretary of the Treasury by the Secretary of the Interior.

SEC. 5. That upon the approval of the allotments provided for in this act by the Secretary of the Interior, he shall cause patents to issue therefor in the name of the allottees, which patents shall be of the legal effect, and declare that the United States does and will hold the land thus allotted, for the period of twenty-five years, in trust for the sole use and benefit of the Indian to whom such allotment shall have been made, or, in case of his decease, of his heirs according to the laws of the State or Territory where such land is located, and that at the expiration of said period the United States will convey the same by patent to said Indian, or his heirs as aforesaid, in fee, discharged of said trust and free of all charge or incumbrance whatsoever: *Provided*, That the President of the United States may in any case in his discretion extend the period. And if any conveyance shall be made of the lands set apart and allotted as herein provided, or any contract made touching the same, before the expiration of the time above mentioned, such conveyance or contract shall be absolutely null and void: *Provided*, That the law of descent and partition in force in the State or Territory where such lands are situate shall apply thereto after patents therefor have been executed and delivered, except as herein otherwise provided; and the laws of the State of Kansas regulating the descent and partition of real estate shall, so far as practicable, apply to all lands in the Indian Territory which may be allotted in severalty under the provisions of this act: And provided further, That at any time after lands have been allotted to all the Indians of any tribe as herein provided, or sooner if in the opinion of the President it shall be for the best interests of said tribe, it shall be lawful for the Secretary of the Interior to negotiate with such Indian tribe for the purchase and release by said tribe, in conformity with the treaty or statute under which such reservation is held, of such portions of its reservation not allotted as such tribe shall, from time to time, consent to sell, on such terms and conditions as shall be considered just and equitable between the United States and said tribe of Indians, which purchase shall not be complete until ratified by Congress, and the form and manner of executing such release prescribed by Congress: *Provided however*, That all lands adapted to agriculture, with or without irrigation so sold or released to the United States by any Indian tribe shall be held by the United States for the sole purpose of securing homes to actual settlers and shall be disposed of by the United States to actual and bona fide settlers only tracts not exceeding one hundred and sixty acres to any one person, on such terms as Congress shall prescribe, subject to grants which Congress may make in aid of education: *And provided further*, That no patents shall issue therefor except to the person so taking the same as and homestead, or his heirs, and after the expiration of five years occupancy thereof as such homestead; and any conveyance of said lands taken as a homestead, or any contract touching the same, or lieu thereon, created prior to the date of such patent, shall be null and void. And the sums agreed to be paid by the United States as purchase money for any portion of any such reservation shall be held in the Treasury of the United States for the sole use of the tribe or tribes Indians; to whom such reservations belonged; and the same, with interest thereon at three per cent per annum, shall be at all times subject to appropriation by Congress for the education and civilization of such tribe or tribes of Indians or the members thereof. The patents aforesaid shall be recorded in the General Land Office, and afterward delivered, free of charge, to the allottee entitled thereto. And if any religious society or other organization is now occupying any of the public lands to which this act is applicable, for religious or educational work among the Indians, the Secretary of the Interior is hereby authorized to confirm such occupation to such society or organization, in quantity not exceeding one hundred and sixty acres in any one tract, so long as the same shall be so occupied, on such terms as he shall deem just; but nothing herein contained shall change or alter any claim of such society for religious or educational purposes heretofore granted by law. And hereafter in the employment of Indian police, or any other employees in the public service among any of the Indian tribes or bands affected by this act, and where Indians can perform the duties required, those Indians who have availed themselves of the provisions of this act and become citizens of the United States shall be preferred.

SEC. 6. That upon the completion of said allotments and the patenting of the lands to said allottees, each and every number of the respective bands or tribes of Indians to whom allotments have been made shall have the benefit of and be subject to the laws, both civil and criminal, of the State or Territory in which they may reside; and no Territory shall pass or enforce any law denying any such Indian within its jurisdiction the equal protection of the law. And every Indian born within the territorial limits of the United States to whom allotments shall have been made under the provisions of this act, or under any law or treaty, and every Indian born within the territorial limits of the United States who has voluntarily taken up, within said limits, his residence separate and apart from any tribe of Indians therein, and has adopted the habits of civilized life, is hereby declared to be a citizen of the United States, and is entitled to all the rights, privileges, and immunities of such citizens, whether said Indian has been or not, by birth or otherwise, a member of any tribe of Indians within the territorial limits of the United States without in any manner affecting the right of any such Indian to tribal or other property.

SEC. 7. That in cases where the use of water for irrigation is necessary to render the lands within any Indian reservation available for agricultural purposes, the Secretary of the Interior be, and he is hereby, authorized to prescribe such rules and regulations as he may deem necessary to secure a just and equal distribution thereof among the Indians residing upon any such reservation; and no other appropriation or grant of water by any riparian proprietor shall permitted to the damage of any other riparian proprietor.

SEC. 8. That the provisions of this act shall not extend to the territory occupied by the Cherokees, Creeks, Choctaws, Chickasaws, Seminoles, and Osage, Miamies and Peorias, and Sacs and Foxes, in the Indian Territory, nor to any of the reservations of the Seneca Nation of New York Indians in the State of New York, nor to that strip of territory in the State of Nebraska adjoining the Sioux Nation on the south added by executive order.

SEC. 9. That for the purpose of making the surveys and resurveys mentioned in section two of this act, there be, and hereby is, appropriated, out of any moneys in the Treasury not otherwise appropriated, the sum of one hundred thousand dollars, to be repaid proportionately out of the proceeds of the sales of such land as may be acquired from the Indians under the provisions of this act.

SEC. 10. That nothing in this act contained shall be so construed to affect the right and power of Congress to grant the right of way through any lands granted to an Indian, or a tribe of Indians, for railroads or other highways, or telegraph lines, for the public use, or condemn such lands to public uses, upon making just compensation.

SEC. 11. That nothing in this act shall be so construed as to prevent the removal of the Southern Ute Indians from their present reservation in Southwestern Colorado to a new reservation by and with consent of a majority of the adult male members of said tribe.

Source: Dawes Severalty Act of 1887. U.S. Statutes at Large, 24 (1887): 388–91

31. Interstate Commerce Act, 1887

Introduction

The Interstate Commerce Act attempted to regulate the growing railway industry in the United States and established the Interstate Commerce Commission (ICC), the first federal regulatory commission. The second half of the nineteenth century witnessed an explosion in the growth of railroads in the United States. Concern about unfair and discriminatory railroad pricing policies helped stir the Granger Movement in the American Midwest and resulted in increased calls for governmental regulation of the railroad industry. The Interstate Commerce Act of 1887 is important not only because it represented a congressional response to the calls for railroad regulations but also because it established the first of many federal regulatory commissions, the ICC. The ICC was abolished in 1996, and the Transportation Department assumed some of its earlier functions.

Primary Source

Be it enacted . . . , That the provisions of this act shall apply to any common carrier or carriers engaged in the transportation of passengers or property wholly by railroad, or partly by railroad and partly by water when both are used, under a common control, management, or arrangement, for a continuous carriage or shipment, from one State or Territory of the United States, or the District of Columbia, or from any place in the United States through a foreign country to any other place in the United States, and also to the transportation in like manner of property shipped from any place in the United States to a foreign country and carried from such place to a port of transshipment, or shipped from a foreign country to any other place in the United States, and also to the transportation in like manner of property shipped from any place in the United States to a foreign country and carried from such place to a port of entry either in the United States or an adjacent foreign country: Provided, however, That the provisions of this act shall not apply to the transportation of passengers or property, or to the receiving, delivering, storage, or handling of property, wholly within one State, and not shipped to or from a foreign country from or to any State or Territory as aforesaid.

The term "railroad" as used in this act shall include all bridges and ferries used or operated in connection with any railroad, and also all the road in use by any corporation operating a railroad, whether owned or operated under a contract, agreement, or lease; and the term "transportation" shall include all instrumentalities of shipment or carriage.

All charges made for any service rendered or to be rendered in the transportation of passengers or property as aforesaid, or in connection therewith, or for the receiving, delivering, storage, or handling of such property, shall be reasonable and just; and every unjust and unreasonable charge for such service is prohibited and declared to be unlawful.

Section 2. That if any common carrier subject to the provisions of this act shall, directly or indirectly, by any special rate, rebate, drawback, or other device, charge, demand, collect, or receive from any person or persons a greater or less compensation for any service rendered, or to be rendered, in the transportation of passengers or property, subject to the provisions of this act, than it charges, demands, collects, or receives from any other person or persons for doing for him or them a like and contemporaneous service in the transportation of a like kind of traffic under substantially similar circumstances and conditions, such common carrier shall be deemed guilty of unjust discrimination, which is hereby prohibited and declared to be unlawful.

Section 3. That it shall be unlawful for any common carrier subject to the provisions of this act to make or give any undue or unreasonable preference or advantage to any particular person, company, firm, corporation, or locality, or any particular description of traffic, in any respect whatsoever, or to subject any particular person, company, firm, corporation, or locality, or any particular description of traffic, to any undue or unreasonable prejudice or disadvantage in any respect whatsoever.

Every common carrier subject to the provisions of this act shall, according to their respective powers, afford all reasonable, proper, and equal facilities for the interchange of traffic between their respective lines, and for the receiving, forwarding, and delivering of passengers and property to and from their several lines and those connecting therewith, and shall not discriminate in their rates and charges between such connecting lines; but this shall not be construed as requiring any such common carrier to give the use of its tracks or terminal facilities to another carrier engaged in like business.

Section 4. That it shall be unlawful for any common carrier subject to the provisions of this act to charge or receive any greater compensation in the aggregate for the transportation of passengers or of like kind of property, under substantially similar circumstances and conditions, for a shorter than for a longer distance over the same line, in the same direction, the shorter being included within the longer distance; but this shall not be construed as authorizing any common carrier within the terms of this act to charge and receive as great compensation for a shorter as for a longer distance: Provided, however, That upon application to the Commission appointed under the provisions of this act, such common carrier may, in special cases, after investigation by the Commission, be authorized to charge less for longer than for shorter distances for the transportation of passengers or property; and the Commission may from time to time prescribe the extent to which such designated common carrier may be relieved from the operation of this section of this act.

Section 5. That it shall be unlawful for any common carrier subject to the provisions of this act to enter into any contract, agreement, or combination with any other common carrier or carriers for the pooling of freights of different and competing railroads, or to divide between them the aggregate or net proceeds of the earnings of such railroads, or any portion thereof; and in any case of an agreement for the pooling of freights as aforesaid, each day of its continuation shall be deemed a separate offense.

Section 6. That every common carrier subject to the provisions of this act shall print and keep for public inspection schedules showing the rates and fares and charges for the transportation of passengers and property which any such common carrier has established and which are in force at the time upon its railroad, as defined by the first section of this act. . . .

No advance shall be made in the rates, fares, and charges which have been established and published as aforesaid by any common carrier in compliance with the requirements of this section, except after ten days' public notice, which shall plainly state the changes proposed to be made in the schedule then in force, and the time when the increased rates, fares, or charges will go into effect. . . .

And when any such common carrier shall have established and published its rates, fares, and charges in compliance with the provisions of this section, it shall be unlawful for such common carrier to charge, demand, collect, or receive from any person or persons a greater or less compensation for the transportation of passengers or property, or for any services in connection therewith, than is specified in such published schedule of rates, fares, and charges as may at the time be in force.

Every common carrier subject to the provisions of this act shall file with the Commission hereinafter provided for copies of its schedules of rates, fares, and charges which have been established and published in compliance with the requirements of this section, and shall promptly notify said Commission of all changes made in the same. Every such common carrier shall also file with said Commission copies of all contracts, agreements, or arrangements with other common carriers in relation to any traffic affected by the provisions of this act to which it may be a party. . . .

Section 9. That any person or persons claiming to be damaged by any common carrier subject to the provisions of this act may either make complaint to the Commission as hereinafter provided for, or may bring suit in his or their own behalf for the recovery of the damages for which such common carrier may be liable under the provisions of this act, in any district or circuit court of the United States of competent jurisdiction. . . .

Section 10. That any common carrier subject to the provisions of this act, or, wherever such common carrier is a corporation, any director or officer thereof, or any receiver, trustee, lessee, agent, or person acting for or employed by such corporation, who, alone or with any other corporation, company, person, or party, . . . shall be guilty of any infraction of this act, or shall aid or abet therein, shall be deemed guilty of a misdemeanor, and shall, upon conviction thereof in any district court of the United States within the jurisdiction of which such offense was committed, be subject to a fine of not to exceed five thousand dollars for each offense.

Section 11. That a Commission is hereby created and established to be known as the Inter-State Commerce Commission, which shall be composed of five Commissioners, who shall be appointed by the President, by and with the advice and consent of the Senate. The Commissioners first appointed under this act shall continue in office for the term of two, three, four, five, and six years, respectively, from January 1, 1887, the term of each to be designated by the President; but their successors shall be appointed for terms of six years. . . . Any Commissioner may be removed by the President for inefficiency, neglect of duty, or malfeasance in office. Not more than three of the Commissioners shall be appointed from the same political party. No person in the employ of or holding any official relation to any common carrier subject to the provisions of this act, or owning stock or bonds thereof, or who is in any manner pecuniarily interested therein, shall enter upon the duties of or hold such office. Said Commissioners shall not engage in any other business, vocation, or employment. No vacancy in the Commission shall impair the right of the remaining Commissioners to exercise all the powers of the Commission.

Section 12. That the Commission hereby created shall have authority to inquire into the management of the business of all common carriers subject to the provisions of this act, and shall keep itself informed as to the manner and method in which the same is conducted, and shall have the right to obtain from such common carriers full and complete information necessary to enable the Commission to perform the duties and carry out the objects for which it was created; and for the purposes of this act the Commission shall have power to require the attendance and testimony of witnesses and the production of all books, papers, tariffs, contracts, agreements, and documents relating to any matter under investigation, and to that end may invoke the aid of any court of the United States in requiring the attendance and testimony of witnesses and the production of books, papers, and documents under the provisions of this section. . . .

Section 13. That any person, firm, corporation, or association, or any mercantile, agricultural, or manufacturing society, or any body politic or municipal organization complaining of anything done or omitted to be done by any common carrier subject to the provisions of this act, in contravention of the provisions thereof, may apply to said Commission by petition, which shall briefly state the facts; whereupon a statement of the charges thus made shall be forwarded by the Commission to such common carrier, who shall be called upon to satisfy the complaint or to answer the same in writing within a reasonable time, to be specified by the Commission. . . . If there shall appear to be any reasonable ground for investigating said complaint, it shall be the duty of the Commission to investigate the matters complained of in such manner and by such means as it shall deem proper.

Said Commission shall in like manner investigate any complaint forwarded by the railroad commissioner or railroad commission of any State or Territory, at the request of such commissioner or commission, and may institute any inquiry on its own motion in the same manner and to the same effect as though complaint had been made. . . .

Section 16. That whenever any common carrier, . . . shall violate or refuse to neglect to obey any lawful order or requirement of the Commission on this act named, it shall be the duty of the Commission, and lawful for any company or person interested in such order or requirement, to apply, in a summary way, by petition, to the circuit court of the United States sitting in equity in the judicial district in which the common carrier complained of has its principal office, or in which the violation or disobedience of such order or requirements shall happen, alleging such violation or disobedience, as the case may be; and the said court shall have power to hear and determine the matter, on such short notice to the common carrier complained of as the court shall deem reasonable. . . .

Section 20. That the Commission is hereby authorized to require annual reports from all common carriers subject to the provisions of this act, fix the time and prescribe the manner in which such reports shall be made, and to require from such carriers specific answers to all questions upon which the Commission may need information. Such reports shall also contain such information in relation to rates or regulations concerning fares or freights, or agreements, arrangements, or contracts with other common carriers, as the Commission may require; and the said Commission may, within its discretion, for the purpose of enabling it the better to carry out the purposes of this act, prescribe (if in the opinion of the Commission it is practicable to prescribe such uniformity and methods of keeping accounts) a period of time within which all common carriers subject to the provisions of this act shall have, as near as may be, a uniform system of accounts, and the manner in which such accounts shall be kept. . . .

Source: Interstate Commerce Act. U.S. Statutes at Large, 24 (1887): 379

32. Sherman Antitrust Act, 1890

Introduction

In 1890, after months of heated debate, Congress passed the Sherman Antitrust Act, the first federal law to regulate large corporations and trusts and eliminate monopolies. It was the first of a series of antitrust laws based on the constitutional power of Congress to oversee interstate commerce. Promoted by Senator John Sherman of Ohio, the act outlawed any contract, combination, or conspiracy that restrained trade or monopolized any market. The Sherman Antitrust Act established a precedent for subsequent antitrust legislation and laid the groundwork for the trust-busting campaigns of President Theodore Roosevelt in the early twentieth century.

Primary Source

Sec. 1. Every contract, combination in the form of trust or otherwise; or conspiracy, in restraint of trade or commerce among the several States, or with foreign nations, is hereby declared to be illegal. Every person who shall make any such contract or engage in any such combination or conspiracy, shall be deemed guilty of a misdemeanor, and, on conviction thereof, shall be punished by fine not exceeding five thousand dollars, or by imprisonment not exceeding one year, or by both said punishments, in the discretion of the court.

Sec. 2. Every person who shall monopolize, or attempt to monopolize, or combine or conspire with any other person or persons, to monopolize any part of the trade or commerce among the several States, or with foreign nations, shall be deemed guilty of a misdemeanor, and, on conviction thereof, shall be punished by fine not exceeding five thousand dollars, or by imprisonment not exceeding one year, or by both said punishments, in the discretion of the court.

Sec. 3. Every contract, combination in form of trust or otherwise, or conspiracy, in restraint of trade or commerce in any Territory of the United States or of the District of Columbia, or in restraint of trade or commerce between any such Territory and another, or between any such Territory or Territories and any State or States or the District of Columbia, or with foreign nations, or between the District of Columbia and any States or States or foreign nations, is hereby declared illegal. Every person who shall make any such contract or engage in any such combination or conspiracy, shall be deemed guilty of a misdemeanor, and, on conviction thereof, shall be punished by fine not exceeding five thousand dollars, or by imprisonment not exceeding one year, or by both said punishments, in the discretion of the court.

Sec. 4. The several circuit courts of the United States are hereby invested with jurisdiction to prevent and restrain violations of this act; and it shall be the duty of the several district attorneys of the United States, in their institute proceedings in equity to prevent and restrain such violations. Such proceedings may be by way of petition setting forth the case and praying that such violation shall be enjoined or otherwise prohibited. When the parties complained of shall have been duly notified of such petition the courts shall proceed, as soon as may be, to the hearing and determination of the case; and pending such petition and before final decrees, the court many at any time make such temporary restraining order or prohibition as shall be deemed just in the premises.

Sec. 5. Whenever it shall appear to the court before which any proceeding under Section four of this act may be pending, that the ends of justice require that other parties should be brought before the court, the court may cause them to be summoned, whether they reside in the district in which the court is held or not; and subpoenas to that end may be served in any district by the marshal thereof.

Sec. 6. Any property owned under any contract or by any combination, or pursuant to any conspiracy (and being the subject thereof) mentioned in section one of this act, and being in the course of transportation from one State to another, or to a foreign country, shall be forfeited to the United States, and may be seized and condemned by like proceedings as those provided by law for the forfeiture, seizure, and condemnation of property imported into the United States contrary to law.

Sec. 7. Any person who shall be injured in his business or property by any other person or corporation by reason of anything forbidden or declared to be unlawful by this act, may sue therefor in any circuit court of the United States in the district in which the defendant resides or is found, without respect to the amount in controversy, and shall recover threefold the damages by him sustained, and the costs of suit, including a reasonable attorney's fee.

Sec. 8. That the word "person," or "persons," wherever used in this act shall be deemed to include corporations and associations existing under or authorized by the laws of either the United States, the laws of any of the Territories, and the laws of any State, or the laws of any foreign country.

Source: U.S. Statutes at Large, 26 (1890): 209

33. Establishment of the U.S. Circuit Courts of Appeals (Evarts Act, 1891)

Introduction

In 1891 Congress established a separate tier of appeals courts and granted the Supreme Court limited authority to determine the cases it heard. The 1891 Evarts Act established a court of appeals in each of the nine circuits but maintained the circuit courts to operate as trial courts alongside the district courts. It also established an additional judgeship for each circuit and authorized the circuit justice, the circuit judges, or district judges to preside over each three-person court of appeals. The impact of the act was quickly apparent as the number of new cases before the Supreme Court fell from 623 in 1890 to 379 in 1891 and 275 in 1892.

Primary Source

March 3, 1891.
26 Stat. 826.

CHAP. 517. — An Act to establish circuits courts of appeals and to define and regulate in certain cases the jurisdiction of the courts of the United States, and for other purposes.

Be it enacted by the Senate and House of Representatives of the United States of America in Congress assembled, That there shall be appointed by the President of the United States, by and with the advice and consent of the Senate, in each circuit an additional circuit judge, who shall have the same qualifications, and shall have the same power and jurisdiction therein that the circuit judges of the United States, within their respective circuits, now have under existing laws, and who shall be entitled to the same compensation as the circuit judges of the United States in their respective circuits now have.

SEC. 2. That there is hereby created in each circuit a circuit court of appeals, which shall consist of three judges, of whom two shall constitute a quorum, and which shall be a court of record with appellate jurisdiction, as is hereafter limited and established. Such court shall prescribe the form and style of its seal and the form of writs and other process and procedure as may be conformable to the exercise of its jurisdiction as shall be conferred by law. It shall have the appointment of the marshal of the court with the same duties and powers under the regulations of the court as are now provided for the marshal of the Supreme Court of the United States, so far as the same may be applicable. The court shall also appoint a clerk, who shall perform and exercise the same duties and powers in regard to all matters within its jurisdiction as are now exercised and performed by the clerk of the Supreme Court of the United States, so far as the same may be applicable. The salary of the marshal of the court shall be twenty-five hundred dollars a year, and the salary of the clerk of the court shall be three thousand dollars a year, to be paid in equal proportions quarterly. The costs and fees in the Supreme Court now provided for by law shall be costs and fees in the circuit courts of appeals; and the same shall be expended, accounted for, and paid for, and paid over to the Treasury Department of the United States in the same manner as is provided in respect of the costs and fees in the Supreme Court.

The court shall have power to establish all rules and regulations for the conduct of the business of the court within its jurisdiction as conferred by law.

SEC. 3. That the Chief-Justice and the associate justices of the Supreme Court assigned to each circuit, and the circuit judges within each circuit, and the several district judges within each circuit, shall be competent to sit as judges of the circuit court of appeals within their respective circuits in the manner hereinafter provided. In case the Chief-Justice or an associate justice of the Supreme Court should attend at any session of the circuit court of appeals he shall preside, and the circuit judges in attendance upon the court in the absence of the Chief-Justice or associate justice of the Supreme Court shall preside in the order of the seniority of their respective commissions.

In case the full court at any time shall not be made up by the attendance of the Chief-Justice or an associate justice of the Supreme Court and circuit judges, one or more district judges within the circuit shall be competent to sit in the court according to such order or provision among the district judges as either by general or particular assignment shall be designated by the court: Provided, That no justice or judge before whom a cause or question may have been tried or heard in a district court, or existing circuits court, shall sit on the trial or hearing of such cause or question in the circuit court of appeals. A term shall be held annually by the circuit court of appeals in the several judicial circuits at the following places: In first the circuit, in the city of Boston; in the second circuit, in the city of New York; in the third circuit, in the city of Philadelphia; in the fourth circuit, in the city of Richmond; in the fifth circuit, in the city of New Orleans; in the sixth circuit, in the city of Cincinnati; in the seventh circuit, in the city of Chicago; in the eighth circuit, in the city of St. Louis; in the ninth circuit, in the city of San Francisco; and in such other places in each of the above circuits as said court may from time to time designate. The first terms of said courts shall be held on the second Monday in January, eighteen hundred and ninety-one, and thereafter at such times as may be fixed by said courts

SEC. 4. That no appeal, whether by writ of error or otherwise, shall hereafter be taken or allowed from any district court to the existing circuit courts, and no appellate jurisdiction shall hereafter be exercised or allowed by said existing circuit courts, but all appeals by writ of error otherwise, from said district courts shall only be subject to review in the Supreme Court of the United States or in the circuit court of appeals hereby established, as is hereinafter provided, and the review, by appeal, by writ of error, or otherwise, from the existing circuit courts shall be had only in the Supreme Court of the United States or in the circuit courts of appeals hereby established according to the provisions of this act regulating the same.

SEC. 5. That appeals or writs of error may be taken from the district courts or from the existing circuit courts direct to the Supreme Court in the following cases:

In any case in which the jurisdiction of the court is in issue; in such cases the question of jurisdiction alone shall be certified to the Supreme Court from the court below for decision.

From the final sentences and decrees in prize causes.

In cases of conviction of a capital or otherwise infamous crime.

In any case that involves the construction or application of the Constitution of the United States.

In any case in which the constitutionality of any law of the United States, or the validity or construction of any treaty made under its authority is drawn in question.

In any case in which the constitution or law of a State is claimed to be in contravention of the Constitution of the United States.

Nothing in this act shall affect the jurisdiction of the Supreme Court in cases appealed from the highest court of a State, nor the construction of the statute providing for review of such cases.

SEC. 6. That the circuit courts of appeals established by this act shall exercise appellate jurisdiction to review by appeal or by writ of error final decision in the district court and the existing circuit courts in all cases other than those provided for in the preceding section of this act, unless otherwise provided by law, and the judgments or decrees of the circuit courts of appeals shall be final in all cases in which the jurisdiction is dependent entirely upon the opposite parties to the suit or controversy, being aliens and citizens of the United States citizens or citizens of different States; also in all cases arising under the patent laws, under the revenue laws, and under criminal laws as in admiralty cases, excepting that in every such subject within its appellate jurisdiction the circuit court of appeals at any time may certify to the Supreme Court of the United States any questions or propositions of law concerning which it desires the instruction of that court for its proper decision. And thereupon the Supreme Court may either give its instruction on the questions and propositions certified to it, which shall be binding upon the circuit courts of appeals in such case, or it may require that the whole record and cause may be sent up to it for its consideration, and thereupon shall decide the whole matter in controversy in the same manner as if it had been brought there for review by writ of error or appeal.

And excepting also that in any such case as is hereinbefore made final in the circuit court of appeals it shall be competent for the Supreme Court to require, by certiorari or otherwise, any such case to be certified to the Supreme Court for its review and determination with the same power and authority in the case as if it had been carried by appeal or writ of error to the Supreme Court.

In all cases not hereinbefore, in this section, made final there shall be of right an appeal or writ of error or review of the case by the Supreme Court of the United States where the matter in controversy shall exceed one thousand dollars besides costs. But no such appeal shall be taken or writ of error sued out unless within one year after the entry of the order, judgment, or decree sought to be reviewed.

SEC. 7. That where, upon a hearing in equity in a district court, or in an existing circuit court, an injunction shall be granted or continued by an interlocutory order or decree, in a cause in which an appeal from a final decree may be taken under the provisions of this act to the circuit court of appeals, an appeal may be taken from such interlocutory order or decree granting or continuing such injunction to the circuit court of appeals: Provided, That the appeal must be taken within thirty days from the entry of such order or decree, and it shall take precedence in the appellate court; and the proceedings in other respects in the court below shall not be stayed unless otherwise ordered by that court during the pendency of such appeal.

SEC. 8. That any justice or judge, who, in pursuance of the provisions of this act, shall attend the circuit court of appeals held at any place other than where he resides shall, upon his written certificate, be paid by the marshal of the district in which the court shall be held his reasonable expenses for travel and attendance, not to exceed ten dollars per day, and such payments shall be allowed the marshal in the settlement of his accounts with the United States.

SEC. 9. That the marshals of the several districts in which said circuit court of appeals may be held shall, under the direction of the Attorney-General of the United States, and with his approval, provide such rooms in the public buildings of the United States as may be necessary, and pay all incidental expenses of said court, including criers, bailiffs, and messengers: Provided, however, That in case proper rooms can not be provided in such buildings, then the said marshals, with the approval of the Attorney-General of the United States, may, from time to time, lease such rooms as may be necessary for such courts. That the marshals, criers, clerks, bailiffs, and messengers shall be allowed the same compensation for their respective services as are allowed for similar services in the existing circuit courts.

SEC. 10. That whenever on appeal or writ of error or otherwise a case coming directly from the district court or existing circuit court shall be reviewed and determined in the Supreme Court the cause shall be remanded to the proper district or circuit court for further proceedings to be taken in pursuance of such determination. And whenever on appeal or writ of error or otherwise a case coming from a circuit court of appeals shall be reviewed and determined in the Supreme Court the cause shall be remanded by the Supreme Court to the proper district or circuit court for further proceedings in pursuance of such determination. Whenever on appeal or writ or error or otherwise a case coming from a district or circuit court shall be reviewed and determined in the circuit court of appeals in a case in which the decision in the circuit court of appeals is final such cause shall be remanded to the said district or circuit court for further proceedings to be there taken in pursuance of such determination.

SEC. 11. That no appeal or writ of error by which any order, judgment, or decree may be reviewed in the circuit courts of appeals under the provisions of this act shall be taken or sued out except within six months after the entry of the order, judgment, or decree sought to be reviewed: Provided however, That in all cases in which a lesser time is now by law limited for appeals or writs of error such limits of time shall apply to appeals or writs of error in such cases taken to or sued out from the circuit courts of appeals. And all provisions of law now in force regulating the methods and system of review, through appeals or writs of error, shall regulate the methods and system of appeals and writs of error provided for in this act in respect of the circuit courts of appeals, including all provisions for bonds or other securities to be required and taken on such appeals and writs of error, and any judge of the circuit courts of appeals, in respect of cases to be brought to that court, shall have the same powers and duties as to the allowance of appeals or writs of error, and the conditions of such allowance, as now by law belong to the justices or judges in respect of the existing courts of the United States respectively.

SEC. 12. That the circuit court of appeals shall have the powers specified in section seven hundred and sixteen of the Revised Statutes of the United States.

SEC. 13. Appeals and writs of error may be taken and prosecuted from the decisions of the United States court in the Indian Territory to the Supreme Court of the

United States, or to the circuit court of appeals in the eighth circuit, in the same manner and under the same regulations as from the circuit or district courts of the United States, under this act.

SEC. 14. That section six hundred and ninety-one of the Revised Statutes of the United States and section three of an act entitled "An act to facilitate the disposition of cases in the Supreme Court, and for other purposes," approved February sixteenth, eighteen hundred and seventy-five, be, and the same are hereby repealed. And all acts and parts of acts relating to appeals or writs of error inconsistent with the provisions for review by appeals or writs of error in the preceding sections five and six of this act are hereby repealed.

SEC. 15. That the circuit court of appeal in cases in which the judgments of the circuit courts of appeal are made final by this act shall have the same appellate jurisdiction, by writ of error or appeal, to review the judgments, orders, and decrees of the supreme courts of the several Territories as by this act they may have to review judgments, orders, and decrees of the district court and circuit courts; and for that purpose the several Territories shall, by orders of the Supreme court, to be made from time to time, be assigned to particular circuits.

APPROVED, March 3, 1891.

Source: Statutes at Large, 55th Congress, 2nd Session, Vol. 26, Ch. 517, Pg. 826

34. *Plessy v. Ferguson*, 1896

Introduction

Plessy v. Ferguson was one of the most important decisions about the meaning of the Thirteenth and Fourteenth Amendments to be handed down during the nineteenth century. In the Civil Rights Cases (1883), the Supreme Court ruled that Congress did not have the power to remedy individual acts of racial discrimination that were not the result of state action. By contrast, in *Plessy v. Ferguson*, the Court upheld one of Louisiana's Jim Crow laws requiring that white and black passengers be seated in separate train cars. This law was challenged by Homer Plessy, who was seven-eighths white and one-eighth black, after he was denied seating on a car reserved for whites.

Primary Source

MR. JUSTICE BROWN, after stating the facts in the foregoing language, delivered the opinion of the Court.

This case turns upon the constitutionality of an act of the general assembly of the state of Louisiana, passed in 1890, providing for separate railway carriages for the white and colored races.

The first section of the statute enacts "that all railway companies carrying passengers in their coaches in this state, shall provide equal but separate accommodations for the white, and colored races, by providing two or more passenger coaches for each passenger train, or by dividing the passenger coaches by a partition so as to secure separate accommodations: provided, that this section shall not be construed to apply to street railroads. No person or persons shall be permitted to occupy seats in coaches, other than the ones assigned to them, on account of the race they belong to."

By the second section it was enacted "that the officers of such passenger trains shall have power and are hereby required to assign each passenger to the coach or compartment used for the race to which such passenger belongs; any passenger insisting on going into a coach or compartment to which by race he does not belong, shall be liable to a fine of twenty-five dollars, or in lieu thereof to imprisonment for a period of not more than twenty days in the parish prison, and any officer of any railroad insisting on assigning a passenger to a coach or compartment other than the one set aside for the race to which said passenger belongs, shall be liable to a fine of twenty-five dollars, or in lieu thereof to imprisonment for a period of not more than twenty days in the parish prison; and should any passenger refuse to occupy the coach or compartment to which he or she is assigned by the officer of such railway, said officer shall have power to refuse to carry such passenger on his train, and for such refusal neither he nor the railway company which he represents shall be liable for damages in any of the courts of this state."

The third section provides penalties for the refusal or neglect of the officers, directors, conductors, and employees of railway companies to comply with the act, with a proviso that "nothing in this act shall be construed as applying to nurses attending children of the other race." The fourth section is immaterial.

The information filed in the criminal district court charged, in substance, that Plessy, being a passenger between two stations within the state of Louisiana, was assigned by officers of the company to the coach used for the race to which he belonged, but he insisted upon going into a coach used by the race to which he did not belong. Neither in the information nor plea was his particular race or color averred.

The petition for the writ of prohibition averred that petitioner was seven-eighths Caucasian and one-eighth African blood; that the mixture of colored blood was not discernible in him; and that he was entitled to every right, privilege, and immunity secured to citizens of the United States of the white race; and that, upon such theory, he took possession of a vacant seat in a coach where passengers of the white race were accommodated, and was ordered by the conductor to vacate said coach, and take a seat in another, assigned to persons of the colored race, and, having refused to comply with such demand, he was forcibly ejected, with the aid of a police officer, and imprisoned in the parish jail to answer a charge of having violated the above act.

The constitutionality of this act is attacked upon the ground that it conflicts both with the thirteenth amendment of the constitution, abolishing slavery, and the fourteenth amendment, which prohibits certain restrictive legislation on the part of the states.

1. That it does not conflict with the thirteenth amendment, which abolished slavery and involuntary servitude, except a punishment for crime, is too clear for argument. Slavery implies involuntary servitude,-a state of bondage; the ownership of mankind as a chattel, or, at least, the control of the labor and services of one man for the benefit of another, and the absence of a legal right to the disposal of his own person, property, and services. This amendment was said in the *Slaughter-House Cases*, to have been intended primarily to abolish slavery, as it had been previously known in this country, and that it equally forbade Mexican peonage or the Chinese coolie trade, when they amounted to slavery or involuntary servitude, and that the use of the word "servitude" was intended to prohibit the use of all forms of involuntary slavery, of whatever class or name. It was intimated, however, in that case, that this amendment was regarded by the statesmen of that day as insufficient to protect the colored race from certain laws which had been enacted in the Southern states, imposing upon the colored race onerous disabilities and burdens, and curtailing their rights in the pursuit of life, liberty, and property to such an extent that their freedom was of little value; and that the fourteenth amendment was devised to meet this exigency.

So, too, in the *Civil Rights Cases*, it was said that the act of a mere individual, the owner of an inn, a public conveyance or place of amusement, refusing accommodations to colored people, cannot be justly regarded as imposing any badge of slavery or servitude upon the applicant, but only as involving an ordinary civil injury, properly cognizable by the laws of the state, and presumably subject to redress by those laws until the contrary appears. "It would be running the slavery question into the ground," said Mr. Justice Bradley, "to make it apply to every act of discrimination which a person may see fit to make as to the guests he will entertain, or as to the people he will take into his coach or cab or car, or admit to his concert or theater, or deal with in other matters of intercourse or business."

A statute which implies merely a legal distinction between the white and colored races—a distinction which is founded in the color of the two races, and which must always exist so long as white men are distinguished from the other race by color—has no tendency to destroy the legal equality of the two races, or re-establish a state of involuntary servitude. Indeed, we do not understand that the thirteenth amendment is strenuously relied upon by the plaintiff in error in this connection.

2. By the fourteenth amendment, all persons born or naturalized in the United States, and subject to the jurisdiction thereof, are made citizens of the United States and of the state wherein they reside; and the states are forbidden from making or enforcing any law which shall abridge the privileges or immunities of citizens of the United States, or shall deprive any person of life, liberty, or property without due process of law, or deny to any person within their jurisdiction the equal protection of the laws.

The proper construction of this amendment was first called to the attention of this court in the *Slaughter-House Cases*, which involved, however, not a question of race, but one of exclusive privileges. The case did not call for any expression of opinion as to the exact rights it was intended to secure to the colored race, but it was said generally that its main purpose was to establish the citizenship of the negro, to give definitions of citizenship of the United States and of the states, and to protect from the hostile legislation of the states the privileges and immunities of citizens of the United States, as distinguished from those of citizens of the states. The object of the amendment was undoubtedly to enforce the absolute equality of the two races before the law, but, in the nature of things, it could not have been intended to abolish distinctions based upon color, or to enforce social, as distinguished from political, equality, or a commingling of the two races upon terms unsatisfactory to either. Laws permitting, and even requiring, their separation, in places where they are liable to be brought into contact, do not necessarily imply the inferiority of either race to the other, and have been generally, if not universally, recognized as within the competency of the state legislatures in the exercise of their police power. The most common instance of this is connected with the establishment of separate schools for white and colored children, which have been held to be a valid exercise of the legislative power even by courts of states where the political rights of the colored race have been longest and most earnestly enforced.

One of the earliest of these cases is that of *Roberts v. City of Boston*, in which the supreme judicial court of Massachusetts held that the general school committee of Boston had power to make provision for the instruction of colored children in separate schools established exclusively for them, and to prohibit their attendance upon the other schools. "The great principle," said Chief Justice Shaw, "advanced by the learned and eloquent advocate for the plaintiff [Mr. Charles Sumner], is that, by the constitution and laws of Massachusetts, all persons, without distinction of age or sex, birth or color, origin or condition, are equal before the law. . . . But, when this great principle comes to be applied to the actual and various conditions of persons in society, it will not warrant the assertion that men and women are legally clothed with the same civil and political powers, and that children and adults are legally to have the same functions and be subject to the same treatment; but only that the rights of all, as they are settled and regulated by law, are equally entitled to the paternal consideration and protection of the law for their maintenance and security." It was held that the powers of the committee extended to the establishment of separate schools for children of different ages, sexes and colors, and that they might also establish special schools for poor and neglected children, who have become too old to attend the primary school, and yet have not acquired the rudiments of learning, to enable them to enter the ordinary schools. Similar laws have been enacted by congress under its general power of legislation over the District of Columbia, as well as by the legislatures of many of the states, and have been generally, if not uniformly, sustained by the courts. . . .

Laws forbidding the intermarriage of the two races may be said in a technical sense to interfere with the freedom of contract, and yet have been universally recognized as within the police power of the state.

The distinction between laws interfering with the political equality of the negro and those requiring the separation of the two races in schools, theaters, and railway carriages has been frequently drawn by this court. Thus, in *Strauder v. West Virginia*, it was held that a law of West Virginia limiting to white male persons 21 years of age, and citizens of the state, the right to sit upon juries, was a discrimination which implied a legal inferiority in civil society, which lessened the security of the right of the colored race, and was a step towards reducing them to a condition of servility. Indeed, the right of a colored man that, in the selection of jurors to pass upon his life, liberty, and property, there shall be no exclusion of his race, and no discrimination against them because of color, has been asserted in a number of cases. . . . So, where the laws of a particular locality or the charter of a particular railway corporation has provided that no person shall be excluded from the cars on account of color, we have held that this meant that persons of color should travel in the same car as white ones, and that the enactment was not satisfied by the company providing cars assigned exclusively to people of color, though they were as good as those which they assigned exclusively to white persons.

Upon the other hand, where a statute of Louisiana required those engaged in the transportation of passengers among the states to give to all persons traveling within that state, upon vessels employed in that business, equal rights and privileges in all parts of the vessel, without distinction on account of race or color, and subjected to an action for damages the owner of such a vessel who excluded colored passengers on account of their color from the cabin set aside by him for the use of whites, it was held to be, so far as it applied to interstate commerce, unconstitutional and void. The court in this case, however, expressly disclaimed that it had anything whatever to do with the statute as a regulation of internal commerce, or affecting anything else than commerce among the states.

In the *Civil Rights Cases*, it was held that an act of congress entitling all persons within the jurisdiction of the United States to the full and equal enjoyment of the accommodations, advantages, facilities, and privileges of inns, public conveyances, on land or water, theaters, and other places of public amusement, and made applicable to citizens of every race and color, regardless of any previous condition of servitude, was unconstitutional and void, upon the ground that the fourteenth amendment was prohibitory upon the states only, and the legislation authorized to be adopted by congress for enforcing it was not direct legislation on matters respecting which the states were prohibited from making or enforcing certain laws, or doing certain acts, but was corrective legislation, such as might be necessary or proper for counter-acting and redressing the effect of such laws or acts. In delivering the opinion of the court, Mr. Justice Bradley observed that the fourteenth amendment "does not invest congress with power to legislate upon subjects that are within the domain of state legislation, but to provide modes of relief against state legislation or state action of the kind referred to. It does not authorize congress to create a code of municipal law for the regulation of private rights, but to provide modes of redress against the operation of state laws, and the action of state officers, executive or judicial, when these are subversive of the fundamental rights specified in the amendment. Positive rights and privileges are undoubtedly secured by the fourteenth amendment; but they are secured by way of prohibition against state laws and state proceedings affecting those rights and privileges, and by power given to congress to legislate for the purpose of carrying such prohibition into effect; and such legislation must necessarily be predicated upon such supposed state laws or state proceedings, and be directed to the correction of their operation and effect."

Much nearer, and, indeed, almost directly in point, is the case of the *Louisville, N. O. & T. Ry. Co. v. State*, wherein the railway company was indicted for a violation of a statute of Mississippi, enacting that all railroads carrying passengers should provide equal, but separate, accommodations for the white and colored races, by providing two or more passenger cars for each passenger train, or by dividing the passenger cars by a partition, so as to secure separate accommodations. The case was presented in a different aspect from the one under consideration, inasmuch as it was an indictment against the railway company for failing to provide the separate accommodations, but the question considered was the constitutionality of the law. In that case, the supreme court of Mississippi had held that the statute applied solely to commerce within the state, and, that being the construction of the state statute by its highest court, was accepted as conclusive. "If it be a matter," said the court, "respecting commerce wholly within a state, and not interfering with commerce between the states, then, obviously, there is no violation of the commerce clause of the federal constitution. . . . No question arises under this section as to the power of the state to separate in different compartments interstate passengers, or affect, in any manner, the privileges and rights of such passengers. All that we can consider is whether the state has the power to require that railroad trains within her limits shall have separate accommodations for the two races. That affecting only commerce within the state is no invasion of the power given to congress by the commerce clause."

A like course of reasoning applies to the case under consideration, since the supreme court of Louisiana, in the case of *State v. Judge*, held that the statute in question did not apply to interstate passengers, but was confined in its application to passengers traveling exclusively within the borders of the state. The case was decided largely upon the authority of *Louisville, N. O. & T. Ry. Co. v. State*, and affirmed by this court. . . . In the present case no question of interference with interstate commerce can possibly arise, since the East Louisiana Railway appears to have been purely a local line, with both its termini within the state of Louisiana. Similar statutes for the separation of the two races upon public conveyances were held to be constitutional in *Railroad v. Miles, Day v. Owen, Railway Co. v. Williams, Railroad Co. v. Wells, Railroad Co. v. Benson, Logwood v. Railroad Co., McGuinn v. Forbes, People v. King* . . . , *Houck v. Railway Co., Heard v. Railroad Co.*

While we think the enforced separation of the races, as applied to the internal commerce of the state, neither abridges the privileges or immunities of the colored man, deprives him of his property without due process of law, nor denies him the equal protection of the laws, within the meaning of the fourteenth amendment, we are not prepared to say that the conductor, in assigning passengers to the coaches according to their race, does not act at his peril, or that the provision of the second section of the act that denies to the passenger compensation in damages for a refusal to receive him into the coach in which he properly belongs is a valid exercise of the legislative power. Indeed, we understand it to be conceded by the state's attorney that such part of the act as exempts from liability the railway company and its officers is unconstitutional. The power to assign to a particular coach obviously implies the power to determine to which race the passenger belongs, as well as the power to determine who, under the laws of the particular state, is to be deemed a white, and who a colored, person. This question, though indicated in the brief of the plaintiff in error, does not properly arise upon the record in this case, since the only issue made is as to the unconstitutionality of the act, so far as it requires the railway to provide separate accommodations, and the conductor to assign passengers according to their race.

It is claimed by the plaintiff in error that, in an mixed community, the reputation of belonging to the dominant race, in this instance the white race, is "property," in the same sense that a right of action or of inheritance is property. Conceding this to be so, for the purposes of this case, we are unable to see how this statute deprives him of, or in any way affects his right to, such property. If he be a white man, and assigned to a colored coach, he may have his action for damages against the company for being deprived of his so-called "property." Upon the other hand, if he be a colored man, and be so assigned, he has been deprived of no property, since he is not lawfully entitled to the reputation of being a white man.

In this connection, it is also suggested by the learned counsel for the plaintiff in error that the same argument that will justify the state legislature in requiring railways to provide separate accommodations for the two races will also authorize them to require separate cars to be provided for people whose hair is of a certain color, or who are aliens, or who belong to certain nationalities, or to enact laws requiring colored people to walk upon one side of the street, and white people upon the other, or requiring white men's houses to be painted white, and colored men's black, or their vehicles or business signs to be of different colors, upon the theory that one side of the street is as good as the other, or that a house or vehicle of one color is as good as one of another color. The reply to all this is that every exercise of the police power must be reasonable, and extend only to such laws as are enacted in good faith for the promotion of the public good, and not for the annoyance or oppression of a particular class. Thus, in *Yick Wo v. Hopkins*, it was held by this court that a municipal ordinance of the city of San Francisco, to regulate the carrying on of public laundries within the limits of the municipality, violated the provisions of the constitution of the United States, if it conferred upon the municipal authorities arbitrary power, at their own will, and without regard to discretion, in the legal sense of the term, to give or withhold consent as to persons or places, without regard to the competency of the persons applying or the propriety of the places selected for the carrying on of the business. It was held to be a covert attempt on the part of the municipality to make an arbitrary and unjust discrimination against the Chinese race. While this was the case of a municipal ordinance, a like principle has been held to apply to acts of a state legislature passed in the exercise of the police power. . . .

So far, then, as a conflict with the fourteenth amendment is concerned, the case reduces itself to the question whether the statute of Louisiana is a reasonable regulation, and with respect to this there must necessarily be a large discretion on the part of the legislature. In determining the question of reasonableness, it is at liberty to act with reference to the established usages, customs, and traditions of the people, and with a view to the promotion of their comfort, and the preservation of the public peace and good order. Gauged by this standard, we cannot say that a law which authorizes or even requires the separation of the two races in public conveyances is unreasonable, or more obnoxious to the fourteenth amendment than the acts of congress requiring separate schools for colored children in the District of Columbia, the constitutionality of which does not seem to have been questioned, or the corresponding acts of state legislatures.

We consider the underlying fallacy of the plaintiff's argument to consist in the assumption that the enforced separation of the two races stamps the colored race with a badge of inferiority. If this be so, it is not by reason of anything found in the act, but solely because the colored race chooses to put that construction upon it. The argument necessarily assumes that if, as has been more than once the case, and is not unlikely to be so again, the colored race should become the dominant power in the state legislature, and should enact a law in precisely similar terms, it would thereby relegate the white race to an inferior position. We imagine that the white race, at least, would not acquiesce in this assumption. The argument also assumes that social prejudices may be overcome by legislation, and that equal rights cannot be secured to the negro except by an enforced commingling of the two races. We cannot accept this proposition. If the two races are to meet upon terms of social equality, it must be the result of natural affinities, a mutual appreciation of each other's merits, and a voluntary consent of individuals. As was said by the court of appeals of New York in *People v. Gallagher*: "This end can neither be accomplished nor promoted by laws which conflict with the general sentiment of the community upon whom they are designed to operate. When the government, therefore, has secured to each of its citizens equal rights before the law, and equal opportunities for improvement and progress, it has accomplished the end for which it was organized, and performed all of the functions respecting social advantages with which it is endowed." Legislation is powerless to eradicate racial instincts, or to abolish distinctions based upon physical differences, and the attempt to do so can only result in accentuating the difficulties of the present situation. If the civil and political rights of both races be equal, one cannot be inferior to the other civilly or politically. If one race be inferior to the other socially, the constitution of the United States cannot put them upon the same plane.

It is true that the question of the proportion of colored blood necessary to constitute a colored person, as distinguished from a white person, is one upon which there is a difference of opinion in the different states; some holding that any visible admixture of black blood stamps the person as belonging to the colored race; others, that it depends upon the preponderance of blood; and still others, that the predominance of white blood must only be in the proportion of three-fourths. But these are questions to be determined under the laws of each state, and are not properly put in issue in this case. Under the allegations of his petition, it may undoubtedly become a question of importance whether, under the laws of Louisiana, the petitioner belongs to the white or colored race.

The judgment of the court below is therefore affirmed.

Source: Plessy v. Ferguson, 163 U.S. 537 (1896)

35. *Lone Wolf v. Hitchcock,* 1903

Introduction

The case of Kiowa Chief Lone Wolf and his failed battle against the U.S. government to stop the allotment of the Kiowa reservation was a watershed event in the jurisprudential history of federal government policy toward American Indians. In a unanimous ruling, the Supreme Court granted Congress almost limitless powers in dealing with American Indians.

Primary Source

MR. JUSTICE WHITE delivered the opinion of the Court:

By the sixth article of the first of the two treaties referred to in the preceding statement, proclaimed on August 25, 1868 . . . , it was provided that heads of families of the tribes affected by the treaty might select, within the reservation, a tract of land of not exceeding 320 acres in extent, which should thereafter cease to be held in common, and should be for the exclusive possession of the Indian making the selection so long as he or his family might continue to cultivate the land. The twelfth article reads as follows:

Article 12. No treaty for the cession of any portion or part of the reservation herein in described, which may be held in common, shall be of any validity or force, as against the said Indians, unless executed and signed by at least three fourths of all the adult male Indians occupying the same, and no cession by the tribe shall be understood or construed in such manner as to deprive, without his consent, any individual member of the tribe of his rights to any tract of land selected by him as provided in article 3 of this treaty.

The appellants base their right to relief on the proposition that by the effect of the article just quoted the confederated tribes of Kiowas, Comanches, and Apaches were vested with an interest in the lands held in common within the reservation, which interest could not be devested by Congress in any other mode than that specified in the said twelfth article, and that as a result of the said stipulation the interest of the Indians in the common lands fell within the protection of the 5th Amendment to the Constitution of the United States, and such interest—indirectly at least—came under the control of the judicial branch of the government. We are unable to yield our assent to this view.

The contention in effect ignores the status of the contracting Indians and the relation of dependency they bore and continue to bear towards the government of the United States. To uphold the claim would be to adjudge that the indirect operation of the treaty was to materially limit and qualify the controlling authority of Congress in respect to the care and protection of the Indians, and to deprive Congress, in a possible emergency, when the necessity might be urgent for a partition and disposal of the tribal lands, of all power to act, if the assent of the Indians could not be obtained.

Now, it is true that in decisions of this court, the Indian right of occupancy of tribal lands, whether declared in a treaty or otherwise created, has been stated to be sacred, or, as sometimes expressed, as sacred as the fee of the United States in the same lands. *Johnson v. M'Intosh* (1823) . . . ; *Cherokee Nation v. Georgia* (1831) . . . ; *Worcester v. Georgia* (1832) . . . ; *United States v. Cook* (1873) . . . ; *Leavenworth, L. & G. R. Co. v. United States* (1875) . . . ; *Beecher v. Wetherby* (1877). . . . But in none of these cases was there involved a controversy between Indians and the government respecting the power of Congress to administer the property of the Indians. The questions considered in the cases referred to, which either directly or indirectly had relation to the nature of the property rights of the Indians, concerned the character and extent of such rights as respected states or individuals. In one of the cited cases it was clearly pointed out that Congress possessed a paramount power over the property of the Indians, by reason of its exercise of guardianship over their interests, and that such authority might be implied, even though opposed to the strict letter of a treaty with the Indians. Thus, in *Beecher v. Weherby* . . . , discussing the claim that there had been a prior reservation of land by treaty to the use of a certain tribe of Indians, the court said . . . :

But the right which the Indians held was only that of occupancy. The fee was in the United States, subject to that right, and could be transferred by them whenever they chose. The grantee, it is true, would take only the naked fee, and could not disturb the occupancy of the Indians; that occupancy could only be interfered with or determined by the United States. It is to be presumed that in this matter the United States would be governed by such considerations of justice as would control a Christian people in their treatment of an ignorant and dependent race. Be that is it may, the propriety or justice of their action towards the Indians with respect to their lands is a question of governmental policy, and is not a matter open to discussion in a controversy between third parties, neither of whom derives title from the Indians.

Plenary authority over the tribal relations of the Indians has been exercised by Congress from the beginning, and the power has always been deemed a political one, not subject to be controlled by the judicial department of the government. Until the year 1871 the policy was pursued of dealing with the Indian tribes by means of treaties, and, of course, a moral obligation rested upon Congress to act in good faith in performing the stipulations entered into on its behalf. But, as with treaties made with foreign nations (*Chinese Exclusion Case* . . .), the legislative power might pass laws in conflict with treaties made with the Indians. *Thomas v. Gay* . . . ; *Ward v. Race Horse* . . . ; *Spalding v. Chandler* . . . ; *Missouri, K. & T. R. Co. v. Roberts* . . . ; *Cherokee Tobacco* . . . *Half Pound Papers of Smoking Tobacco v. United States.* . . .

The power exists to abrogate the provisions of an Indian treaty, though presumably such power will be exercised only when circumstances arise which will not only justify the government in disregarding the stipulations of the treaty, but may demand, in the interest of the country and the Indians themselves, that it should do so. When, therefore, treaties were entered into between the United States and a tribe of Indians it was never doubted that the power to abrogate existed in Congress, and that in a contingency such power might be availed of from considerations of governmental policy, particularly if consistent with perfect good faith towards the Indians. In *United States v. Kagama* (1885) . . . , speaking of the Indians, the court said . . . :

After an experience of a hundred years of the treaty-making system of government Congress has determined upon a new departure,—to govern them by acts of Congress. This is seen in the act of March 3, 1871, embodied in 2079 of the Revised Statutes: "No Indian nation or tribe, within the territory of the United States, shall be acknowledged or recognized as an independent nation, tribe, or power with whom the United States may contract by treaty; but no obligation of any treaty lawfully made and ratified with any such Indian nation or tribe prior to March 3d, 1871, shall be hereby invalidated or impaired."

In upholding the validity of an act of Congress which conferred jurisdiction upon the courts of the United States for certain crimes committed on an Indian reservation within a state, the court said . . . : "It seems to us that this is within the competency of Congress. These Indian tribes are the wards of the nation. They are communities dependent on the United States. Dependent largely for their daily food. Dependent for their political rights. They own no allegiance to the states, and receive from them no protection. Because of the local ill feeling, the people of the states where they are found are often their deadliest enemies. From their very weakness and helplessness, so largely due to the course of dealing of the Federal government with them and the treaties in which it has been promised, there arises the duty of protection, and with it the power. This has always been recognized by the executive and by Congress, and by this court, whenever the question has arisen. . . . The power of the general government over these remnants of a race once powerful, now weak and diminished in numbers, is necessary to their protection, as well as to the safety of those among whom they dwell. It must exist in that government, because it never has existed anywhere else, because the theater of its exercise is within the geographical limits of the United States, because it has never been denied, and because it alone can enforce its laws on all the tribes."

That Indians who had not been fully emancipated from the control and protection of the United States are subject, at least so far as the tribal lands were concerned, to be controlled by direct legislation of Congress, is also declared in *Choctaw Nation v. United States* . . . and *Stephens v. Choctaw Nation.* . . .

In view of the legislative power possessed by Congress over treaties with the Indians and Indian tribal property, we may not specially consider the contentions pressed upon our notice that the signing by the Indians of the agreement of October 6, 1892, was obtained by fraudulent misrepresentations, and concealment, that the requisite three fourths of adult male Indians had not signed, as required by the twelfth article of the treaty of 1867, and that the treaty as signed had been amended by Congress without submitting such amendments to the action of the Indians since all these matters, in any event, were solely within the domain of the legislative authority, and its action is conclusive upon the courts.

The act of June 6, 1900, which is complained of in the bill, was enacted at a time when the tribal relations between the confederated tribes of Kiowas, Comanches, and Apaches still existed, and that statute and the statutes supplementary thereto dealt with the disposition of tribal property, and purported to give an adequate consideration for the surplus lands not allotted among the Indians or reserved for their benefit. Indeed, the controversy which this case presents is concluded by the decision in *Cherokee Nation v. Hitchcock* . . . , decided at this term, where it was held that full administrative power was possessed by Congress over Indian tribal property. In effect, the action of Congress now complained of was but an exercise of such power, a mere change in the form of investment of Indian tribal property, the property of those who, as we have held, were in substantial effect the wards of the government. We must presume that Congress acted in perfect good faith in the dealings with the Indians of which complaint is made, and that the legislative branch of the government exercised its best judgment in the premises. In any event, as Congress possessed full power in the matter, the judiciary cannot question or inquire into the motives which prompted the enactment of this legislation. If injury was occasioned, which we do not wish to be understood as implying, by the use made by Congress of its power, relief must be sought by an appeal to that body for redress, and not to the courts. The legislation in question was constitutional, and the demurrer to the bill was therefore rightly sustained.

The motion to dismiss does not challenge jurisdiction over the subject-matter. Without expressly referring to the propositions of fact upon which it proceeds, suffice it to say that we think it need not be further adverted to, since, for the reasons previously given and the nature of the controversy, we think the decree below should be affirmed.

And it is so ordered.

> *Source: Lone Wolf, Principal Chief of the Kiowas, et al., Appts., v. Ethan A. Hitchcock, Secretary of the Interior, et al.,* 187 U.S. 553 (1903)

36. *Lochner v. New York,* 1905

Introduction

When a New York state law limited to ten the number of hours that a baker could work each day, and limited the number of hours per week to 60, bakery owners sued. By a 5–4 vote, the Supreme Court rejected the state's argument that the law was necessary to protect the health of bakers. Lochner was one of the most controversial decisions in the Supreme Court's history. During the so-called Lochner era, roughly spanning from the Progressive Era at the turn of the twentieth century through the height of the Great Depression of the 1930s, the Court upheld some economic regulations, such as antitrust laws, but also issued decisions invalidating federal and state statutes that sought to improve working conditions. This pattern is seen as a measure of the Justice's struggle over balancing personal and property rights (especially the "liberty of contract") against the "police" powers of government to regulate for the common good. The Lochner era is often considered to have ended with *West Coast Hotel Co. v. Parrish* (1937), in which the Supreme Court questioned the wisdom of a laissez faire philosophy and took a much broader view of the government's power to regulate economic activities.

Primary Source

Justice Peckham delivered the opinion of the Court.

The statute necessarily interferes with the right of contract between the employer and employees, concerning the numbers of hours in which the latter may labor in the bakery of the employer. The general right to make a contract in relation to his business is part of the liberty of the individual protected by the Fourteenth Amendment of the Federal Constitution. . . .

. . . There are, however, certain powers, existing in the sovereignty of each State in the Union, somewhat vaguely termed police powers, the exact description and limitation of which have not been attempted by the courts. These powers, broadly stated and without, at present, any attempt at a more specific definition, relate to the safety, health, morals and general welfare of the public. . . .

The State, therefore, has power to prevent the individual from making certain kinds of contracts, and in regard to them the Federal Constitution offers no protection. If the contract be one which the State, in the legitimate exercise of its police power, has the right to prohibit, it is not prevented from prohibiting it by the Fourteenth Amendment. . . .

This court has recognized the existence and upheld the exercise of the police powers of the States in many cases which might fairly be considered as border ones, and it has, in the course of its determination of questions regarding the asserted invalidity of such statutes, on the ground of their violation of the rights secured by the federal Constitution, been guided by rules of a very liberal nature, the application of which has resulted, in numerous instances, in upholding the validity of state statutes thus assailed. Among the later cases where the state law has been upheld by this court is that of *Holden* v. *Hardy.* . . .

It must, of course, be conceded that there is a limit to the valid exercise of the police power by the State. There is no dispute concerning this general proposition. Otherwise the Fourteenth Amendment would have no efficacy and the legislatures of the States would have unbounded power, and it would be enough to say that any piece of legislation was enacted to conserve the morals, the health, or the safety of the people; such legislation would be valid, no matter how absolutely without foundation the claim might be. The claim of the police power would be a mere pretext—because another and delusive name for the supreme sovereignty of the State to be exercised free from constitutional restraint. This is not contended for. In every case that comes before this court, therefore, where legislation of this character is concerned, and where the protection of the federal Constitution is sought, the question necessarily arises: Is this a fair, reasonable, and appropriate exercise of the police power of the State, or is it an unreasonable, unnecessary, and arbitrary interference with the right to the individual to his personal liberty or to enter into those contracts in relation to labor which may seem to him appropriate or necessary for the support of himself and his family? Of course the liberty of contract relating to labor includes both parties to it. The one has as much right to purchase as the other to sell labor.

This is not a question of substituting the judgment of the court for that of the legislature. If the act be within the power of the State it is valid, although the judgment of the court might be totally opposed to the enactment of such a law. But the question would still remain: Is it within the police power of the State? and the question must be answered by the court.

The question whether this act is valid as a labor law, pure and simple, may be dismissed in a few words. There is no reasonable ground for interfering with the liberty of person or the right of free contract, by determining the hours of labor, in the occupation of a baker. There is no contention that bakers as a class are not equal in intelligence and capacity to men in other trades or manual occupations, or that they are not able to assert their rights and care for themselves without the protecting arm of the State, interfering with their independence of judgment and of action. They are in no sense wards of the State. Viewed in the light of a purely labor law, with no reference whatever to the question of health, we think that the law like the one before us involves neither the safety, the morals, nor the welfare, of the public, and that the interest of the public is not in the slightest degree affected by such an act. The law must be upheld, if at all, as a law pertaining to the health of the individual engaged in the occupation of a baker. It does not affect any other portion of the public than those who are engaged in that occupation. Clean and wholesome bread does not depend upon whether the baker works but ten hours per day or only sixty hours a week. The limitation of the hours of labor does not come within the police power on that ground.

It is a question of which of two powers or rights shall prevail—the power of the State to legislate or the right of the individual to liberty of person and freedom of contract. The mere assertion that the subject relates, though but in a remote degree, to the public health, does not necessarily render the enactment valid. The act must have a more direct relation, as a means to an end, and the end itself must be appropriate and legitimate, before an act can be held to be valid which interferes with the general right of an individual to be free in his person and in his power to contract in relation to his own labor. . . .

We think the limit of the police power has been reached and passed in this case. There is, in our judgment, no reasonable foundation for holding this to be necessary or appropriate as a health law to safeguard the public health, or the health of the individuals who are following the trade of a baker. If this statute be valid, and if, therefore, a proper case is made out in which to deny the right of an individual, *sui juris,* as employer or employee, to make contracts for the labor of the latter under the protection of the provisions of the federal Constitution, there would seem to be no length to which legislation of this nature might not go. . . .

It is impossible for us to shut our eyes to the fact that many of the laws of this character, while passed under what is claimed to be the police power for the purposes of protecting the public health or welfare, are, in reality, passed from other motives. We are justified in saying so when, from the character of the law and the subject upon which it legislates, it is apparent that the public health or welfare bears but the most remote relation to the law. The purpose of a statute must be determined from the natural and legal effect of the language employed; and whether it is or is not repugnant to the Constitution of the United States must be determined from the natural effect of such statutes when put into operation, and not from their proclaimed purpose. . . . The court looks beyond the mere letter of the law in such cases.

. . . The act is not, within any fair meaning of the term, a health law, but is an illegal interference with the rights of individuals, both employers and employees, to make contracts regarding labor upon such terms as they may think best, or which they may agree upon with the other parties to such contracts. Statutes of the nature of that under review, limiting the hours in which grown and intelligent men may labor to earn their living, are mere meddlesome interferences with the rights of the individual, and they are not saved from condemnation by the claim that they are passed in the exercise of the police power and upon the subject of the health of the individual whose rights are interfered with, unless there be some fair ground, reasonable in and of itself, to say that there is material danger to the public health, or to the health of the employees, if the hours of labor are not curtailed. . . .

It is manifest to us that the limitation of the hours of labor as provided for in this section of the statute . . . has no such direct relation to and no such substantial effect upon the health of the employee, as to justify us in regarding the section as really a health law. It seems to us that the real object and purpose were simply to regulate the hours of labor between the master and his employees . . . in a private business, not dangerous in any degree to morals or in any real and substantial degree, to the health of the employees. Under such circumstances the freedom of master and employee to contract with each other in relation to their employment, and in defining the same, cannot be prohibited or interfered with, without violating the Federal Constitution.

Judgment reversed.

Justice Holmes, dissenting.

The case is decided upon an economic theory which a large part of the country does not entertain. If it were a question whether I agreed with that theory, I should desire to study it further and long before making up my mind. But I do not conceive that to be my duty, because I strongly believe that my agreement or disagreement has nothing to do with the right of a majority to embody their opinions in law. It is settled by various decisions of this court that state constitutions and state laws may regulate life in many ways which we as legislators might think as injudicious, or if you like as tyrannical, as this, and which, equally with this, interfere with the liberty to contract. Sunday laws and usury laws are ancient examples. A more modern one is the prohibition of lotteries. The liberty of the citizen to do as he likes so long as he does not interfere with the liberty of others to do the same, which has been a shibboleth for some well-known writers, is interfered with by school laws, by the post-office, by every state or municipal institution which takes his money for purposes though desirable, whether he likes it or not. The Fourteenth Amendment does not enact Mr. Herbert Spencer's Social Statics. . . . United States and state statutes and decisions cutting down the liberty to contract by way of combination are familiar to this court. . . . Some of these laws embody convictions or prejudices which judges are likely to share. Some may not. But a constitution is not intended to embody a particular economic theory, whether of paternalism and the organic relation of the citizen to the state or of *laissez faire*. It is made for people of fundamentally differing views, and the accident of our finding certain opinions natural and familiar, or novel, and even shocking, ought not to conclude our judgments upon the question whether statutes embodying them conflict with the Constitution of the United States.

General propositions do not decide concrete cases. The decision will depend on a judgment or intuition more subtle than any articulate major premise. But I think that the proposition just stated, if it is accepted, will carry us far toward the end. Every opinion tends to become a law. I think that the word "liberty," in the Fourteenth Amendment, is perverted when it is held to prevent the natural outcome of a dominant opinion, unless it can be said that a rational and fair man necessarily would admit that the statute proposed would infringe fundamental principles as they have been understood by the traditions of our people and our law. It does not need research to show that no such sweeping condemnation can be passed upon the statute before us. A reasonable man might think it a proper measure on the score of health. Men whom I certainly could not pronounce unreasonable would uphold it as a first installment of a general regulation of the hours of work. Whether in the latter aspect is would be open to the charge of inequality I think it unnecessary to discuss.

Source: Lochner v. New York, 198 U.S. 45 (1905)

37. *Muller v. Oregon,* 1908

Introduction

The unanimous opinion by the Supreme Court in *Muller v. Oregon* accepted a limit on the working hours of women in the state of Oregon. The decision came at a time when the Court was invalidating many attempts to protect laborers (as in *Lochner v. New York* of 1905) on the basis that they interfered with the liberty of contract thought to be inherent in the due process clause of the Fourteenth Amendment. *Muller v. Oregon* is therefore considered a victory not only for progressive efforts to protect women workers but also for the Brandeis brief that attorney Louis Brandeis (later a Supreme Court justice) filed on behalf of the state.

Primary Source

MR. JUSTICE BREWER delivered the opinion of the Court:

On February 19, 1903, the legislature of the state of Oregon passed an act the first section of which is in these words:

Sec. 1. That no female (shall) be employed in any mechanical establishment, or factory, or laundry in this state more than ten hours during any one day. The hours of work may be so arranged as to permit the employment of females at any time so that they shall not work more than ten hours during the twenty-four hours of any one day.

Sec. 3 made a violation of the provisions of the prior sections a misdemeanor subject to a fine of not less than $10 nor more than $25. On September 18, 1905, an information was filed in the circuit court of the state for the county of Multnomah, charging that the defendant "on the 4th day of September, A. D. 1905, in the county of Multnomah and state of Oregon, then and there being the owner of a laundry, known as the Grand Laundry, in the city of Portland, and the employer of females therein, did then and there unlawfully permit and suffer one Joe Haselbock, he, the said Joe Haselbock, then and there being an overseer, superintendent, and agent of said Curt Muller, in the said Grand Laundry, to require a female, to wit, one Mrs. E. Gotcher, to work more than ten hours in said laundry on said 4th day of September, A. D. 1905, contrary to the statutes in such cases made and provided, and against the peace and dignity of the state of Oregon."

A trial resulted in a verdict against the defendant, who was sentenced to pay a fine of $10. The supreme court of the state affirmed the conviction, whereupon the case was brought here on writ of error.

The single question is the constitutionality of the statute under which the defendant was convicted, so far as it affects the work of a female in a laundry. That it does not conflict with any provisions of the state Constitution is settled by the decision of the supreme court of the state. The contentions of the defendant, now plaintiff in error, are thus stated in his brief:

(1) Because the statute attempts to prevent persons sui juris from making their own contracts, and thus violates the provisions of the 14th Amendment, as follows: "No state shall make or enforce any law which shall abridge the privileges or immunities of citizens of the United States; nor shall any state deprive any person of life, liberty, or property, without due process of law; nor deny to any person within its jurisdiction the equal protection of the laws."

(2) Because the statute does not apply equally to all persons similarly situated, and is class legislation.

(3) The statute is not a valid exercise of the police power. The kinds of work prescribed are not unlawful, nor are they declared to be immoral or dangerous to the public health; nor can such a law be sustained on the ground that it is designed to protect women on account of their sex. There is no necessary or reasonable connection between the limitation prescribed by the act and the public health, safety, or welfare.

It is the law of Oregon that women, whether married or single, have equal contractual and personal rights with men. As said by Chief Justice Wolverton, in *First Nat. Bank v. Leonard*, after a review of the various statutes of the state upon the subject:

We may therefore say with perfect confidence that, with these three sections upon the statute book, the wife can deal, not only with her separate property, acquired from whatever source, in the same manner as her husband can with property belonging to him, but that she may make contracts and incur liabilities, and the same may be enforced against her, the same as if she were a feme sole. There is now no residuum of civil disability resting upon her which is not recognized as existing against the husband. The current runs steadily and strongly in the direction of the emancipation of the wife, and the policy, as disclosed by all recent legislation upon the subject in this state, is to place her upon the same footing as if she were a feme sole, not only with respect to her separate property, but as it affects her right to make binding contracts; and the most natural corollary to the situation is that the remedies for the enforcement of liabilities incurred are made coextensive and coequal with such enlarged conditions.

It thus appears that, putting to one side the elective franchise, in the matter of personal and contractual rights they stand on the same plane as the other sex. Their rights in these respects can no more be infringed than the equal rights of their brothers. We held in *Lochner v. New York* a law providing that no laborer shall be required or permitted to work in bakeries more than sixty hours in a week or ten hours in a day was not as to men a legitimate exercise of the police power of the state, but an unreasonable, unnecessary, and arbitrary interference with the right and liberty of the individual to contract in relation to his labor, and as such was in conflict with, and void under, the Federal Constitution. That decision is invoked by plaintiff in error as decisive of the question before us. But this assumes that the difference between the sexes does not justify a different rule respecting a restriction of the hours of labor.

In patent cases counsel are apt to open the argument with a discussion of the state of the art. It may not be amiss, in the present case, before examining the constitutional question, to notice the course of legislation, as well as expressions of opinion from other than judicial sources. In the brief filed by Mr. Louis D. Brandeis for the defendant in error is a very copious collection of all these matters, an epitome of which is found in the margin. While there have been but few decisions bearing directly upon the question, the following sustain the constitutionality of such legislation: *Com. v. Hamilton Mfg. Co., Wenham v. State, State v. Buchanan, Com. v. Beatty*; against them is the case of *Ritchie v. People*.

The legislation and opinions referred to in the margin may not be, technically speaking, authorities, and in them is little or no discussion of the constitutional question presented to us for determination, yet they are significant of a widespread belief that woman's physical structure, and the functions she performs in consequence thereof, justify special legislation restricting or qualifying the conditions under which she should be permitted to toil. Constitutional questions, it is true, are not settled by even a consensus of present public opinion, for it is the peculiar value of a written constitution that it places in unchanging form limitations upon legislative action, and thus gives a permanence and stability to popular government which otherwise would be lacking. At the same time, when a question of fact is debated and debatable, and the extent to which a special constitutional limitation goes is affected by the truth in respect to that fact, a widespread and long continued belief concerning it is worthy of consideration. We take judicial cognizance of all matters of general knowledge.

It is undoubtedly true, as more than once declared by this court, that the general right to contract in relation to one's business is part of the liberty of the individual, protected by the 14th Amendment to the Federal Constitution; yet it is equally well settled that this liberty is not absolute and extending to all contracts, and that a state may, without conflicting with the provisions of the 14th Amendment, restrict in many respects the individual's power of contract. Without stopping to discuss at length the extent to which a state may act in this respect, we refer to the following cases in which the question has been considered: *Allgeyer v. Louisiana, Holden v. Hardy, Lochner v. New York.*

That woman's physical structure and the performance of maternal functions place her at a disadvantage in the struggle for subsistence is obvious. This is especially true when the burdens of motherhood are upon her. Even when they are not, by abundant testimony of the medical fraternity continuance for a long time on her feet at work, repeating this from day to day, tends to injurious effects upon the body, and, as healthy mothers are essential to vigorous offspring, the physical well-being of woman becomes an object of public interest and care in order to preserve the strength and vigor of the race.

Still again, history discloses the fact that woman has always been dependent upon man. He established his control at the outset by superior physical strength, may, without conflicting with the provisions and this control in various forms, with diminishing intensity, has continued to the present. As minors, thought not to the same extent, she has been looked upon in the courts as needing especial care that her rights may be preserved. Education was long denied her, and while now the doors of the schoolroom are opened and her opportunities for acquiring knowledge are great, yet even with that and the consequent increase of capacity for business affairs it is still true that in the struggle for subsistence she is not an equal competitor with her brother. Though limitations upon personal and contractual rights may be removed by legislation, there is that in her disposition and habits of life which will operate against a full assertion of those rights. She will still be where some legislation to protect her seems necessary to secure a real equality of right. Doubtless there are individual exceptions, and there are many respects in which she has an advantage over him; but looking at it from the viewpoint of the effort to maintain an independent position in life, she is not upon an equality. Differentiated by these matters from the other sex, she is properly placed in a class by herself, and legislation designed for her protection may be sustained, even when like legislation is not necessary for men, and could not be sustained. It is impossible to close one's eyes to the fact that she still looks to her brother and depends upon him. Even though all restrictions on political, personal, and contractual rights were taken away, and she stood, so far as statutes are concerned, upon an absolutely equal plane with him, it would still be true that she is so constituted that she will rest upon and look to him for protection; that her physical structure and a proper discharge of her maternal functions—having in view not merely her own health, but the well-being of the race—justify legislation to protect her from the greed as well as the passion of man. The limitations which this statute places upon her contractual powers, upon her right to agree with her employer as to the time she shall labor, are not imposed solely for her benefit, but also largely for the benefit of all. Many words cannot make this plainer. The two sexes differ in structure of body, in the functions to be performed by each, in the amount of physical strength, in the capacity for long continued labor, particularly when done standing, the influence of vigorous health upon the future well-being of the race, the self-reliance which enables one to assert full rights, and in the capacity to maintain the struggle for subsistence. This difference justifies a difference in legislation, and upholds that which is designed to compensate for some of the burdens which rest upon her.

We have not referred in this discussion to the denial of the elective franchise in the state of Oregon, for while that may disclose a lack of political equality in all things with her brother, that is not of itself decisive. The reason runs deeper, and rests in the inherent difference between the two sexes, and in the different functions in life which they perform.

For these reasons, and without questioning in any respect the decision in *Lochner v. New York*, we are of the opinion that it cannot be adjudged that the act in question is in conflict with the Federal Constitution, so far as it respects the work of a female in a laundry, and the judgment of the Supreme Court of Oregon is affirmed.

Source: Muller v. Oregon, 208 U.S. 412 (1908).

38. The Judicial Code of 1911 [Excerpt]

Introduction

Established by the Judiciary Act of 1789, the circuit courts served as the most important trial courts of the federal judiciary for over a century. The circuit courts lost their limited appellate jurisdiction in the 1891 act creating the U.S. courts of appeals, but as part of the political compromise behind the act of 1891, the circuit courts continued to serve as trial courts alongside the district courts for the next 20 years. In 1911, Congress created a single code encompassing all statutes related to the judiciary and took the opportunity to revise and unify existing laws. At the same time, Congress abolished the U.S. circuit courts as of the effective date of the statute, January 1, 1912. By abolishing the circuit courts and transferring their jurisdiction and pending business to the district courts, Congress instituted a judicial system with a single type of trial court and eliminated the inefficiencies associated with administering two types of court that were often presided over by the same judge.

Primary Source

March 3, 1911.
36 Stat. 1087, 1167.

CHAPTER THIRTEEN.

GENERAL PROVISIONS.

SEC. 289. The circuit courts of the United States, upon the taking effect of this Act, shall be, and hereby are, abolished; and thereupon, on said date, the clerks of said courts shall deliver to the clerks of the district courts of the United States for their respective districts all the journals, dockets, books, files, records, and other books and papers of or belonging to or in any manner connected with said circuit courts; and shall also on said date deliver to the clerks of said district courts all moneys, from whatever source received, then remaining in their hands or under their control as clerks of said circuit courts, or received by them by virtue of their said offices. The journals, dockets, books, files, records, and other books and papers so delivered to the clerks of the several district courts shall be and remain a part of the official records of said district courts, and copies thereof, when certified under the hand and seal of the clerk of the district court, shall be received as evidence equally with the originals thereof; and the clerks of the several district courts shall have the same authority to exercise all the powers and to perform all the duties with respect thereto as the clerks of the several circuit courts had prior to the taking effect of this Act.

SEC. 290. All suits and proceedings pending in said circuit courts on the date of the taking effect of this Act, whether originally brought therein or certified thereto from the district courts, shall thereupon and thereafter be proceeded with and disposed of in the district courts in the same manner and with the same effect as if originally begun therein, the record thereof being entered in the records of the circuit courts so transferred as above provided.

SEC. 291. Wherever, in any law not embraced within this Act, any reference is made to, or any power or duty is conferred or imposed upon, the circuit courts, such reference shall, upon the taking effect of this Act, be deemed and held to refer to, and to confer such power and impose such duty upon, the district courts.

SEC. 292. Wherever, in any law not contained within this Act, a reference is made to any law revised or embraced herein, such reference, upon the taking effect hereof, shall be construed to refer to the section of this Act into which has been carried or revised the provision of law to which reference is so made.

SEC. 293. The provisions of sections one to five, both inclusive, of the Revised Statutes, shall apply to and govern the construction of the provisions of this Act. The words "this title," wherever they occur herein, shall be construed to mean this Act.

SEC. 294. The provisions of this Act, so far as they are substantially the same as existing statutes, shall be construed as continuations thereof, and not as new enactments, and there shall be no implication of a change of intent by reason of a change of words in such statute, unless such change of intent shall be clearly manifest.

SEC. 295. The arrangement and classification of the several sections of this Act have been made for the purpose of a more convenient and orderly arrangement of the same, and therefore no inference or presumption of a legislative construction is to be drawn by reason of the chapter under which any particular section is placed.

SEC. 296. This Act may be designated and cited as "The Judicial Code."

> *Source:* Hopkins, James Love. *The Judicial Code: Being the Judiciary Act of the Congress of the United States, Approved March 3, A.D. 1911*, Callaghan & Co., 1911

39. Establishment of the Conference of Senior Circuit Judges, 1922

Introduction

The establishment of an annual Conference of Senior Circuit Judges, later to be known as the Judicial Conference of the United States, provided the first formal mechanism by which members of the federal judiciary might develop national administrative policies, reassign judges temporarily, and recommend legislation. Chief Justice William Howard Taft (a former U.S. president appointed to the Supreme Court in 1921) had led a public campaign for federal judicial reform since leaving the White House in 1913. Congress in 1922 enacted a new form of court administration that advanced the institutionalization of an independent judiciary by establishing an annual conference of the chief justice and the senior circuit judge (now called the chief judge) from each judicial circuit and charged the conference with a general mandate to offer advice on the administrative needs of the federal courts. The act required the senior judge in each district to prepare an annual report of the business of the district's court. The conference would use these reports to prepare suggestions for the temporary transfer of judges, pending the approval of all courts involved.

Primary Source

September 14, 1922.
42 Stat. 837.

CHAP. 306. — An Act For the appointment of an additional circuit judge for the Fourth Judicial Circuit, for the appointment of additional district judges for certain districts, providing for an annual conference of certain judges, and for other purposes.

Be it further enacted by the Senate and House of Representative of the United States of America in Congress assembled, That the President be, and he is hereby, authorized to appoint, by and with the advice and consent of the Senate, the following number of district judges for the United States district courts in the district specified in addition to those now authorized by law:

For the district of Massachusetts, two; for the eastern district of New York, one; for the southern district of New York, two; for the district of New Jersey, one; for the eastern district of Pennsylvania, one; for the western district of Pennsylvania, one; for the northern district of Texas, one; for the southern district of Florida, one; for the eastern district of Michigan, one; for the northern district of Ohio, one; for the middle district of Tennessee, one; for the northern district of Illinois, one; for the eastern district of Illinois, one; for the district of Minnesota, one; for the eastern district of Missouri, one; for the western district of Missouri, one; for the eastern district of Oklahoma, one; for the district of Montana, one; for the northern district of California, one; for the southern district of California, one; for the district of New Mexico, one; and for the district of Arizona, one.

A vacancy occurring, more than two years after the passage of this Act, in the office of any district judge appointed pursuant to this Act, except for the middle district of Tennessee, shall not be filled unless Congress shall so provide, and if an appointment is made to fill such a vacancy occurring within two years a vacancy thereafter occurring in said office shall not be filled unless Congress shall so provide; Provided, however, That in case a vacancy occurs in the district of New Mexico at any time after the passage of this Act, there shall thereafter be but one judge for said district until otherwise provided by law.

Every judge shall reside in the district or circuit or one of the districts or circuits for which he is appointed.

SEC. 2. It shall be the duty of the Chief Justice of the United States, or in case of his disability, of one of the other justices of the Supreme Court, in order of their seniority, as soon as may be after the passage of this Act, and annually thereafter, to summon to a conference on the last Monday in September, at Washington, District of Columbia, or at such other time and place in the United States as the Chief Justice, or, in case of his disability, any of said justices in order of their seniority, may designate, the senior circuit judge of each judicial circuit. If any senior circuit judge is unable to attend, the Chief Justice, or in case of his disability, the justice of the Supreme Court calling said conference, may summon any other circuit or district judge in the judicial circuit whose senior circuit judge is unable to attend, that each circuit may be adequately represented at said conference. It shall be the duty of every judge thus summoned to attend said conference, and to remain throughout its proceedings, unless excused by the Chief Justice, and to advise as to the needs of his circuit and as to any matters in respect of which the administration of justice in the courts of the United States may be improved.

The senior district judge of each United States district court, on or before the first day of August in each year, shall prepare and submit to the senior circuit judge of the judicial district in which said district is situated, a report setting forth the condition of business in said district court, including the number and character of cases on the docket, the business in arrears, and cases disposed of, and such other facts pertinent to the business dispatched and pending as said district judge may deem proper, together with recommendations as to the need of additional judicial assistance for the disposal of business for the year ensuing. Said reports shall be laid before the conference herein provided, by said senior circuit judge, or, in his absence, by the judge representing the circuit at the conference, together with such recommendations as he may deem proper.

The Chief Justice, or, in his absence, the senior associate justice, shall be the presiding officer of the conference. Said conference shall make a comprehensive survey of the condition of business in the courts of the United States and prepare plans for assignment and transfer of judges to or from circuits or districts where the state of the docket or condition of business indicates the need therefor, and shall submit such suggestions to the various courts as may seem in the interest of uniformity and expedition of business.

The Attorney General shall, upon request of the Chief Justice, report to said conference on matters relating to the business of the several courts of the United States, with particular reference to causes or proceedings in which the United States may be a party.

The Chief Justice and each justice or judge summoned and attending said conference shall be allowed his actual expenses of travel and his necessary expenses for subsistence, not to exceed $10 per day, which payments shall be made by the marshal of the Supreme Court of the United States upon the written certificate of the judge incurring such expenses, approved by the Chief Justice.

SEC. 3. Section 13 of the Judicial Code is hereby amended to read as follows:

"SEC. 13. Whenever any district judge by reason of any disability or necessary absence from his district or the accumulation or urgency of business is unable to perform speedily the work of his district, the senior circuit judge of that circuit, or, in his absence, the circuit justice thereof, may, if in his judgment the public interest requires, designate and assign any district judge of any district court within the same judicial circuit to act as district judge in such district and to discharge all the judicial duties of a judge thereof for such time as the business of the said district court may require. Whenever it is found impracticable to designate and assign another district judge within the same judicial circuit as above provided and a certificate of the needs of any such district is presented by said senior circuit judge or said circuit justice to the Chief Justice the United States, he, or in his absence the senior associate justice, may, if in his judgment the public interest so requires, designate and assign a district judge of an adjoining judicial circuit if practicable, or if not practicable, then of any judicial circuit, to perform the duties of district judge and hold a district court in any such district as above provided: Provided, however, That before any such designation or assignment is made the senior circuit judge of the circuit from which the designated or assigned judge is to be taken shall consent thereto. All designations and assignments made hereunder shall be filed in the office of the clerk and entered on the minutes of both the court from and to which a judge is designated and assigned."

SEC. 4. Section 15 of the Judicial Code is hereby amended to read as follows:

"SEC. 15. Each district judge designated and assigned under the provision 5 of Section 13 may hold separately and at the same time a district court in the district or territory to which such judge is designated and assigned and discharge all the judicial duties of the district or territorial judge therein."

SEC. 5. Section 18 of the Judicial Code is hereby amended to read as follows:

"SEC. 18. The Chief Justice of the United States, or the circuit justice of any judicial circuit, or the senior circuit judge thereof, may, if the public interest requires, designate and assign any circuit judge of a judicial circuit to hold a district court within such circuit. The judges of the United States Court of Customs Appeals, or any of them, whenever the business of that court will permit, may, if in the judgment of the Chief Justice of the United States the public interest requires, be designated and assigned by him for service from time to time, and until he shall otherwise direct, in the Supreme Court of the District of Columbia or the Court of Appeals of the District of Columbia, when requested by the Chief Justice or either of said courts.

"During the period of service of any judge designated and assigned under this Act he shall have all the powers, and rights, and perform all the duties, of the district, or a justice of the court, to which he has been assigned (excepting the power of appointment to a statutory position or of permanent designation of newspaper or depository of funds): Provided, however, That in case a trial has been has entered upon before such period of service has expired and has not been concluded, the period of service shall be deemed to be extended until the trial has been concluded.

"Any designated and assigned judge who has held court in another district than his own shall answer, notwithstanding his absence from such district and the expiration of the time limit in his designation, to decide all matters, which have been submitted to him within such district, to decide motions for new trials, settle bills of exceptions, certify or authenticate narratives of testimony, or perform any other act required by law or the rules to be performed in order to prepare any case so tried by him for review in an appellate court; and his action thereon in writing filed with the clerk of the court where the trial or hearing was had shall be as valid as if such action had been taken by him within that district and within the period of his designation."

SEC. 6. Section 118 of the Judicial Code, as amended, is hereby further amended to read as follows:

"SEC. 118. There shall be in the second, seventh, and eighth circuits, respectively, four circuit judges; and in each of the other circuits, three circuit judges, to be appointed by the President, by and with the advice and consent of the Senate. All circuit judges shall receive a salary of $8,500.00 a year each, payable monthly. Each circuit judge shall reside within his circuit, and when appointed shall be a resident of the circuit for which he is appointed. The circuit judges in each circuit shall be judges of the circuit court of appeals in that circuit, and it shall be the duty of each circuit judge in each circuit to sit as one of the judges of the circuit court of appeals in that circuit from time to time according to the law: Provided, That nothing in this section shall be construed to prevent any circuit judge holding district court or otherwise, as provided by other sections of the Judicial Code."

SEC. 7. All laws or parts thereof inconsistent or in conflict with the provisions of this Act are hereby repealed.

Approved, September 14, 1922.

Source: Statutes at Large, 67th Congress, 2nd Session, Vol. 42, Ch. 306, Pg. 837

40. The Judges' Bill, 1925

Introduction

The Judges' Bill of 1925 redefined the Supreme Court's role within the federal judiciary by repealing much of the mandatory jurisdiction of the Court. The act preserved an automatic right of appeal to the Court in a few types of cases, but in other areas, cases would come to the High Court only when the justices granted a writ of certiorari in response to a petition from a party in a case before a lower court. While the circuit courts of appeals issued the final decisions in the great majority of appeals cases, the Supreme Court has since exercised its power to choose cases to become the nation's main forum for deciding questions of constitutional principle.

Primary Source

February 13, 1925.
43 Stat. 936.

CHAP. 229.—An Act To amend the Judicial Code, and to further define the jurisdiction of the circuit courts of appeals and of the Supreme Court, and for other purposes.

Be it enacted by the Senate and House of Representatives of the United States of America in Congress assembled, That sections 128, 129, 237, 238, 239, and 240 of the Judicial Code as now existing be, and they are severally, amended and re-enacted to read as follows:

SEC. 128. (a) The circuit courts of appeal shall have appellate jurisdiction to review by appeal or writ of error final decisions—

"First. In the district courts, in all cases save where a direct review of the decision may be had in the Supreme Court under section 238.

"Second. In the United States district courts for Hawaii and for Porto Rico in all cases.

"Third. In the district courts for Alaska or any division thereof, and for the Virgin Islands, in all cases, civil and criminal, wherein the Constitution or a statute or treaty of the United States or any authority exercised thereunder is involved; in all other civil cases wherein the value in controversy, exclusive of interest and costs, exceeds $1,000; in all other criminal cases where the offense charged is punishable by imprisonment for a term exceeding one year or by death, and in all habeas corpus proceedings; and in the district court for the Canal Zone in the cases and mode prescribed in the Act approved September 21, 1922, amending prior laws relating to the Canal Zone.

"Fourth. In the Supreme Courts of the Territory of Hawaii and of Porto Rico, in all civil cases, civil or criminal, wherein the Constitution or a statute or treaty of the United States or any authority exercised thereunder is involved; in all other civil cases wherein the value in controversy, exclusive of interest and costs, exceeds $5,000, and in all habeas corpus proceedings.

"Fifth. In the United States Court for China, in all cases.

"(b) The circuit court of appeals shall also have appellate jurisdiction—

"First. To review the interlocutory orders or decrees of the district courts which are specified in section 129.

"Second. To review decisions of the district courts sustaining or overruling exceptions to awards in arbitrations, as provided in section 8 of an Act entitled 'An Act providing for mediation, conciliation, and arbitration in controversies between certain employers and their employees,' approved July 15, 1913.

"(c) The circuit courts of appeal shall also have an appellate and supervisory jurisdiction under sections 24 and 25 of the Bankruptcy Act of July 1, 1898, over all proceedings, controversies, and cases had or brought in the district courts under that Act or any of its amendments, and shall exercise the same in the manner prescribed in those sections; and the jurisdiction of the Circuit Court of Appeals for the Ninth Circuit in this regard shall cover the courts of bankruptcy in Alaska and Hawaii, and that of the Circuit Court of Appeals for the First Circuit shall cover the court of bankruptcy in Porto Rico.

"(d) The review under this section shall be in the following circuit courts of appeal: The decisions of a district court of the United States within a State in the circuit court of appeals for the circuit embracing such State; those of the District Court of Alaska or any division thereof, the United States district court, and the Supreme Court of Hawaii, and the United States Court for China, in the Circuit Court of Appeals for the Ninth Circuit; those of the United States district court and the Supreme Court of Porto Rico in the Circuit Court of Appeals for the First Circuit; those of the District Court of the Virgin Islands in the Circuit Court of Appeals for the Third Circuit; and those of the District Court of the Canal Zone in the Circuit Court of Appeals for the Fifth Circuit.

"(e) The circuit courts of appeal are further empowered to enforce, set aside, or modify orders of the Federal Trade Commission, as provided in section 5 of 'An

Act to create a Federal Trade Commission, to define its powers and duties, and for other purposes,' approved September 26, 1914; and orders of the Interstate Commerce Commission, the Federal Reserve Board, and the Federal Trade Commission, as provided in section 11 of 'An Act to supplement existing laws against unlawful restraints and monopolies, and for other purposes,' approved October 15, 1914.

"SEC. 129. Where, upon a hearing in a district court, or by a judge thereof in vacation, an injunction is granted, continued, modified, refused, or dissolved by an interlocutory order or decree, or an application to dissolve or modify an injunction is refused, or an interlocutory order or decree is made appointing a receiver, or refusing an order to wind up a pending receivership or to take the appropriate steps to accomplish the purposes thereof, such as directing a sale or other disposal of property held thereunder, an appeal may be taken from such interlocutory order or decree to the circuit court of appeals; and sections 239 and 240 shall apply to such cases in the circuit courts of appeals as to other cases therein: Provided, That the appeal to the circuit courts of appeals must be applied for within thirty days from the entry of such order or decree, and shall take precedence in the appellate court; and the proceedings in other respects in the district court shall not be stayed during the pendency of such appeal unless otherwise ordered by the court, or the appellate court, or a judge thereof: Provided, however, That the district court may, in its discretion, require an additional bond as a condition of the appeal."

SEC. 237. (a) A final judgment or decree in any suit in the highest court of a State in which a decision in the suit could be had, where is drawn in question the validity of a treaty or statute of the United States, and the decision is against its validity; or where is drawn, in question the validity of a statute of any State, on the ground of its being repugnant to Constitution, treaties, or laws of the United States, and the decision is in favor of its validity, may be reviewed by the Supreme Court upon a writ of error. The writ shall have the same effect as if the judgment or decree had been rendered or passed in a court of the United States. The Supreme Court may reverse, modify, or affirm the judgment of such State court, and may, in its discretion, award execution or remand the cause to the court from which it was removed by the writ.

"(b) It shall be competent for the Supreme Court, by certiorari, to require that there be certified to it for review and determination, with the same power and authority and with like effect as if brought up by writ of error, any cause wherein a final judgment or decree has been rendered or passed by the highest court of a State in which a decision could be had where is drawn in question the validity of a treaty or statute of the United States; or where is drawn in question the validity of a statute of any State on the ground of its being repugnant to the Constitution, treaties, or laws of the United States; or where any title, right, privilege, or immunity is specially set up or claimed by either party under the Constitution, or any treaty or statute of, or commission held or authority exercised under, the United States; and the power to review under this paragraph may be exercised as well where the Federal claim in sustained as where it is denied. Nothing in this paragraph shall be construed to limit or detract from the right to a review on a writ of error in a case where such a right is conferred by the preceding paragraph; nor shall the fact that a review on a writ of error might be obtained under the preceding paragraph be an obstacle to granting a review on certiorari under this paragraph.

"(c) If a writ of error be improvidently sought and allowed under this section in a case where the proper mode of invoking a review is by a petition for certiorari, this alone shall not be a ground for dismissal; but the papers whereon the writ of error was allowed shall be regarded and acted on as a petition for certiorari and as if duly presented to the Supreme Court at the time they were presented to the court or judge by whom the writ of error was allowed: Provided, That where in such a case there appears to be no reasonable ground for granting a petition for certiorari it shall be competent for the Supreme Court to adjudge to the respondent reasonable damages for his delay, and single or double costs, as provided in section 1010 of the Revised Statutes."

"SEC. 238. A direct review by the Supreme Court of an interlocutory or final judgment or decree of a district court may be had where it is so provided in the following Acts or parts of Acts, and not otherwise:

"(1) Section 2 of the Act of February 11, 1903, 'to expedite the hearing and determination' of certain suits brought by the United States under the antitrust or interstate commerce laws, and so forth.

"(2) The Act of March 2, 1907, 'providing for writs of error in certain instances in criminal cases' where the decision of the district court is adverse to the United States.

"(3) An Act restricting the issuance of interlocutory injunctions to suspend the enforcement of the statute of a State or of an order made by an administrative board or commission created by and acting under the statute of a State, approved March 4, 1913, which Act is hereby amended by adding at the end thereof, 'The requirement respecting the presence of three judges shall also apply to the final hearing in such suit in the district court; and a direct appeal to the Supreme Court may be taken from a final decree granting or denying a permanent injunction in such suit.'

"(4) So much of 'An Act making appropriations to supply urgent deficiencies in appropriations for the fiscal year 1913, and for other purposes,' approved October 22, 1913, as relates to the review of interlocutory and final judgments and decrees in suits to enforce, suspend, or set aside orders of the Interstate Commerce Commission other than for the payment of money.

"(5) Section 316 of 'An Act to regulate interstate and foreign commerce in livestock, livestock products, dairy products, poultry, poultry products, and eggs, and for other purposes' approved August 15, 1921."

"SEC. 239. In any case, civil or criminal, in a circuit court of appeals, or in the Court of Appeals of the District of Columbia, the court at any time may certify to the Supreme Court of the United States any questions or propositions of law concerning which instructions are desired for the proper decision of the cause; and thereupon the Supreme Court may either give binding instructions on the questions and propositions certified or may require that the entire record in the cause be sent up for its consideration; and thereupon shall decide the whole matter in controversy in the same manner as if it had been brought there by writ of error or appeal."

SEC. 240. (a) In any case, civil or criminal, in a circuit court of appeals, or in the Court of Appeals of the District of Columbia, it shall be competent for the Supreme Court of the United States, upon the petition of any party thereto, whether Government or other litigant, to require by certiorari, either before or after a judgment or decree by such lower court, that the cause be certified to the Supreme Court for determination by it with the same power and authority, and with like effect, as if the cause had been brought there by unrestricted writ of error or appeal.

"(b) Any case in a circuit court of appeals where is drawn in question the validity of a statute of any State, on the ground of its being repugnant to the Constitution, treaties, or laws of the United States, and the decision is against its validity, may, at the election of the party relying on such State statute, be taken to the Supreme Court for review on writ of error or appeal; but in that event a review on certiorari shall not be allowed at the instance of such party, and the review on such writ of error or appeal shall be restricted to an examination and decision of the Federal questions presented in the case.

"(c) No judgment or decree of a circuit court of appeals or of the Court of Appeals of the District of Columbia shall be subject to review by the Supreme Court otherwise than as provided in this section."

SEC. 2. That cases in a circuit court of appeals under section 8 of "An Act providing for mediation, conciliation, and arbitration in controversies between certain employers and their employees," approved July 15, 1913; under section 5 of "An Act to create a Federal Trade Commission, to define its powers and duties, and for other purposes," approved September 26, 1914; and under section 11 of "An Act to supplement existing laws against unlawful restraints and monopolies, and for other purposes," approved October 15, 1914, are included among the cases to which sections 239 and 240 of the Judicial Code shall apply.

SEC. 3 (a) That in any case in the Court of Claims, including those begun under section 180 of the Judicial Code, that court at any time may certify to the Supreme Court any definite and distinct questions of law concerning which instructions are desired for the proper disposition of the cause; and thereupon the Supreme Court may give appropriate instructions on the questions certified and transmit the same to the Court of Claims for its guidance in the further progress of the cause.

(b) In any case in the Court of Claims, including those begun under section 180 of the Judicial Code, it shall be competent for the Supreme Court, upon the petition of either party, whether Government or claimant, to require, by certiorari, that the cause, including the findings of fact and the judgment or decree, but omitting the evidence, be certified to it for review and determination with the same power and authority, and with like effect, as if the cause had been brought there by appeal.

(c) All judgments and decrees of the Court of Claims shall be subject to review by the Supreme Court as provided in this section, and not otherwise.

SEC. 4. That in cases in the district courts wherein they exercise concurrent jurisdiction with the Court of Claims or adjudicate claims against the United States the judgments shall be subject to review in the circuit courts of appeals like other judgments of the district courts; and sections 239 and 240 of the Judicial Code shall apply to such cases in the circuit courts of appeals as to other cases therein.

SEC. 5. That the Court of Appeals of the District of Columbia shall have the same appellate and supervisory jurisdiction over proceedings, controversies, and cases in bankruptcy in the District of Columbia that a circuit court of appeals has over such proceedings, controversies, and cases within its circuit, and shall exercise that jurisdiction in the same manner as a circuit court of appeals is required to exercise it.

SEC. 6. (a) In a proceeding in habeas corpus in a district court, or before a district judge or a circuit judge, the final order shall be subject to review, on appeal, by the circuit court of appeals of the circuit wherein the proceeding is had. A circuit judge shall have the same power to grant writs of habeas corpus within his circuit that a district judge has within his district; and the order of the circuit judge shall be entered in the records of the district court of the district wherein the restraint complained of is had.

(b) In such a proceeding in the Supreme Court of the District of Columbia, or before a justice thereof, the final order shall be subject to review, on appeal, by the Court of Appeals of that District.

(c) Sections 239 and 240 of the Judicial Code shall apply to habeas corpus cases in the circuit courts of appeals and in the Court of Appeals of the District of Columbia as to other cases therein.

(d) The provisions of sections 765 and 766 of the Revised Statutes, and the provisions of an Act entitled "An Act restricting in certain cases the right of appeal to the Supreme Court in habeas corpus proceedings," approved March 10, 1908, shall apply to appellate proceedings under this section as they heretofore have applied to direct appeals to the Supreme Court.

SEC. 7. That in any case in the Supreme Court of the Philippine Islands wherein the Constitution, or any statute or treaty of the United States is involved, or wherein the value in controversy exceeds $25,000, or wherein the title or possession of real estate exceeding in value the sum of $25,000 is involved or brought in question, it shall be competent for the Supreme Court of the United States, upon the petition of a party aggrieved by the final judgment or decree to require, by certiorari, that the cause be certified to it for review and determination with the same power and authority, and with like effect, as if the cause had been brought before it on writ of error or appeal; and, except as provided in this section, the judgments and decrees of the Supreme Court of the Philippine Islands shall not be subject to appellate review.

SEC. 8. (a) That no writ of error, appeal, or writ of certiorari, intended to bring any judgment or decree before the Supreme Court for review shall be allowed or entertained unless application therefor be duly made within three months after the entry of such judgment or decree, excepting that writs of certiorari to the Supreme Court of the Philippine Islands may be granted where application therefor is made within six months: Provided, That for good cause shown either of such periods for applying for a writ of certiorari may be extended not exceeding sixty days by a justice of the Supreme Court.

(b) Where an application for a writ of certiorari is made with the purpose of securing a removal of the case to the Supreme Court from a circuit court of appeals or the Court of Appeals of the District of Columbia before the court wherein the same is pending has given a judgment or decree the application may be made at any and time prior to the hearing and submission in that court.

(c) No writ of error or appeal intended to bring any judgment or decree before a circuit court of appeals for review shall be allowed unless application therefor be duly made within three months after the entry of such judgment or decree.

(d) In any case in which the final judgment or decree of any court is subject to review by the Supreme Court on writ of certiorari, the execution and enforcement of such judgment or decree, may be stayed for a reasonable time to enable the party aggrieved to apply for and to obtain a writ of certiorari from the Supreme Court. The stay may be granted by a judge of the court rendering the judgment or decree or by a justice of the Supreme Court, and may be conditioned on the giving of good and sufficient security, to be approved by such judge or justice, that if the aggrieved party fails to make application for such writ within the period allotted therefor, or fails to obtain an order granting his application, or fails to make his plea good in the Supreme Court, he shall answer for all damages and costs which the other party may sustain by reason of the stay.

SEC. 9. That in any case where the power to review, whether in the circuit courts of appeals or in the Supreme Court, depends upon the amount or value in controversy, such amount or value, if not otherwise satisfactorily disclosed upon the record, may be shown and ascertained by the oath of a party to the cause or by other competent evidence.

SEC. 10. That no court having power to review a judgment or decree of another shall dismiss a writ of error solely because an appeal should have been taken, or dismiss an appeal solely because a writ of error should have been sued out; but where such error occurs the same shall be disregarded and the court shall proceed as if in that regard its power to review were properly invoked.

SEC. 11. (a) That where, during the pendency of an action, suit, or other proceeding brought by or against an officer of the United States, or of the District of Columbia, or the Canal Zone, or of a Territory or an insular possession of the United States, or of a county, city, or other governmental agency of such Territory or insular possession, and relating to the present or future discharge of his official duties, such officer dies, resigns, or otherwise ceases to hold such office, it shall be competent for the court wherein the action, suit, or proceeding is pending, whether the court be one of first instance or an appellate tribunal, to permit the cause to be continued and maintained by or against the successor in office of such officer, if within six months after his death or separation from the office it be satisfactorily shown to the court that there is a substantial need for so continuing and maintaining the cause and obtaining an adjudication of the questions involved.

(b) Similar proceedings may had and taken where an action, suit, or proceeding brought by or against an officer of a State, or of a county, city, or other governmental agency of a State, is pending in a court of the United States at the time of the officer's death or separation from the office.

(c) Before a substitution under this section is made, the party or officer to be affected, unless expressly consenting thereto, must be given reasonable notice of the application therefor and accorded an opportunity to present any objection which he may have.

SEC. 12. That no district court shall have jurisdiction of any action or suit by or against any corporation upon the ground that it was incorporated by or under an Act of Congress: Provided, That this section shall not apply to any suit, action, or proceeding brought by or against a corporation incorporated by or under an Act of Congress wherein the Government of the United States is the owner of more than one-half of its capital stock.

SEC. 13. That the following statutes and parts of statutes be, and they are, repealed:

Sections 130, 131, 133, 134, 181, 182, 236, 241, 242, 243, 244, 245, 246, 247, 248, 249, 250, 251, and 252 of the Judicial Code.

Sections 2, 4, and 5 of "An Act to amend an Act entitled 'An Act to codify, revise, and amend the laws relating to the judiciary,' approved March 3, 1911," approved January 28, 1915.

Sections 2, 3, 4, 5, and 6 of "An Act to amend the Judicial Code, to fix the time when the annual term of the Supreme Court shall commence, and further to define the jurisdiction of that court," approved September 6, 1916.

Section 27 of "An Act to declare the purpose of the people of the United States as to the future political status of the people of the Philippine Islands, and to provide a more autonomous government for those islands," approved

August 29, 1916.

So much of sections 4, 9, and 10 of "An Act to provide for the bringing of suits against the Government of the United States," approved March 3, 1887, as provides for a review by the Supreme Court on writ of error or appeal in the cases therein named.

So much of "An Act restricting in certain cases the right of appeal to the Supreme Court in habeas corpus proceedings," approved March 10, 1908, as permits a direct appeal to the Supreme Court.

So much of sections 24 and 25 of the Bankruptcy Act of July 1, 1898, as regulates the mode of review by the Supreme Court in the proceedings, controversies, and cases therein named.

So much of "An Act to provide a civil government for Porto Rico, and for other purposes," approved March 2, 1917, as permits a direct review by the Supreme Court of cases in the courts in Porto Rico.

So much of the Hawaiian Organic Act, as amended by the Act of July 9, 1921, as permits a direct review by the Supreme Court of cases in the courts in Hawaii.

So much of section 9 of the Act of August 24, 1912, relating to the government of the Canal Zone as designates the cases in which, and the courts by which, the judgments and decrees of the district court of the Canal Zone may be reviewed.

Sections 763 and 764 of the Revised Statutes.

An Act entitled "An Act amending section 764 of the Revised Statutes," approved March 3, 1885.

An Act entitled "An Act to prevent the abatement of certain actions," approved February 8, 1899.

An Act entitled "An Act to amend section 237 of the Judicial Code," approved February 17, 1922.

An Act entitled "An Act to amend the Judicial Code in reference to appeals and writs of error," approved September 14, 1922.

All other Acts and parts of Acts in so far as they are embraced within and superseded by this Act or are inconsistent therewith.

SEC. 14. That this Act shall take effect three months after its approval; but it shall not affect cases then pending in the Supreme Court, nor shall it affect the right to a review, or the mode or time for exercising the same, as respects any judgment or decree entered prior to the date when it takes effect.

Approved, February 13, 1925.

Source: Statutes at Large, 68th Congress, 2nd Session, Vol. 43, Pg. 936

41. Establishment of the Tenth Judicial Circuit, 1929

Introduction

Congress in 1929 created a new judicial circuit to accommodate the increased number of states and the expansion of the caseload in the federal courts. This was the first such expansion in more than 65 years. The 12 states that entered the Union between 1866 and 1912 had been incorporated into the Eighth and Ninth Circuits. The Eighth Circuit, encompassing 13 states stretching from Canada to Mexico and from the Mississippi to beyond the Rocky Mountains, became the largest in the nation. By the 1920s, the Eighth Circuit Court of Appeals was meeting in three divisions, and district court judges were recruited regularly to assist the six circuit judges. Various groups representing the bar and the judiciary feared that such a large circuit threatened the efficient administration of justice in regionally defined courts. The 1929 statute grouped Minnesota, Iowa, North Dakota, South Dakota, Nebraska, Missouri, and Arkansas as the Eighth Circuit and established a Tenth Circuit consisting of Wyoming, Colorado, Utah, New Mexico, Kansas, and Oklahoma. Sitting circuit judges were reassigned according to residence, and three new judgeships were authorized. Five judges would serve the Eighth Circuit, and four would sit in the Tenth.

Primary Source

February 29, 1929.
45 Stat. 1346.

CHAP. 363.–An Act To amend sections 116, 118, and 126 of the Judicial Code, as amended, to divide the eighth judicial circuit of the United States, and to create a tenth judicial circuit.

Be it enacted by the Senate and House of Representatives of the United States of America in Congress assembled, That section 116 of the Judicial Code, as amended [U. S. C., title 28, §211], is amended to read as follows:

"SEC. 116. There shall be ten judicial circuits of the United States, constituted as follows:

"First. The first circuit shall include the districts of Rhode Island, Massachusetts, New Hampshire, Maine, and Porto Rico.

"Second. The second circuit shall include the districts of Vermont, Connecticut, and New York.

"Third. The third circuit shall include the districts of Pennsylvania, New Jersey, and Delaware.

"Fourth. The fourth circuit shall include the districts of Maryland, Virginia, West Virginia, North Carolina and South Carolina.

"Fifth. The fifth circuit shall include the district of Georgia, Florida, Alabama, Mississippi, Louisiana, and Texas.

"Sixth. The sixth circuit shall include the districts Ohio, Michigan, Kentucky, and Tennessee.

"Seventh. The seventh circuits shall include the districts of Indiana, Illinois, and Wisconsin.

"Eighth. The eighth circuit shall include the districts of Minnesota, North Dakota, South Dakota, Iowa, Nebraska, Missouri, and Arkansas.

"Ninth. The ninth circuit shall include the districts of California, Oregon, Nevada, Washington, Idaho, Montana, Hawaii, and Arizona.

"Tenth. The tenth circuit shall include the districts of Colorado, Wyoming, Utah, Kansas, Oklahoma, and New Mexico."

SEC. 2. Section 118 of the Judicial Code, as amended [U. S. C., title 28, § 213; 45 Stat. at Large 492; Public No. 664, 70th Congress], is amended to read as follows:

"SEC. 118. There shall be in the sixth, seventh, and tenth circuits, respectively, four circuit judges; and in the second and eighth circuits, respectively, five circuit judges; and in each of the other circuits three circuit judges, to be appointed by the President, by and with the advice and consent of the Senate. Each circuit judge shall receive a salary of $12,500 a year, payable monthly. Each circuit judge shall reside within his circuit, and when appointed shall be a resident of the circuit for which he is appointed. The circuit judges in each circuit shall be judges of the circuit court of appeals in that circuit, and it shall be the duty of each circuit judge in each circuit to sit as one of the judges of the circuit court of appeals in that circuit from time to time according to law. Nothing in this section shall be construed to prevent any circuit judge holding district court or otherwise, as provided by other sections of the Judicial Code."

SEC. 3. Section 126 of the Judicial Code, as amended [U. S. C., title 28, § 223; U. S. C., Sup. I, title 28, § 223], is amended to read as follows:

"SEC. 126. A term shall be held annually by the circuit courts of appeals in the several judicial circuits at the following places, and at such times as may be fixed by said courts, respectively: In the first circuit, in Boston, and when in its judgment the public interests require in San Juan, Porto Rico; in the second circuit, in New York; in the third circuit, in Philadelphia; in the fourth circuit, in Richmond and in Asheville, North Carolina; in the fifth circuit, in New Orleans, Atlanta, Fort Worth, and Montgomery; in the sixth circuit, in Cincinnati; in the seventh circuit, in Chicago; in the eighth circuit, in Saint Louis, Kansas City, Omaha, and Saint Paul; in the ninth circuit, in San Francisco, and each year in two other places in said circuit to be designated by the judges of said court; in the tenth circuit, in Denver, Wichita, and Oklahoma City, provided that suitable rooms and accommodations for holding court at Oklahoma City are furnished free of expense to the United States; and in each of the above circuits terms may be held at such other times and in such other places as said courts, respectively, may from time to time designate, except that terms shall be held in Atlanta on the first Monday in October, in Fort Worth on the first Monday in November, and in Montgomery on the third Monday in October. All appeals and other appellate proceedings which may be taken or prosecuted from the district courts of the United States in the State of Georgia, in the State of Texas, and in the State of Alabama, to the circuit court of appeals for the fifth judicial circuit shall be heard and disposed of, respectively, by said court at the terms held in Atlanta, in Fort Worth, and in Montgomery, except that appeals in cases of injunctions and in all other cases which, under the statutes and rules, or in the opinion of the court, are entitled to be brought to a speedy hearing, may be heard and disposed of wherever said court may be sitting. All appeals and other appellate proceedings which may be taken or prosecuted from the district court of the United States at Beaumont, Texas, to the circuit court of appeals for the fifth circuit, shall be heard and disposed of by the said circuit court of appeals at the terms of court held at New Orleans, except that appeals in cases of injunctions and in all other cases which, under the statutes and rules, or in the opinion of the court, are entitled to be brought to a speedy hearing, may be heard and disposed of wherever said court may be sitting."

SEC. 4. Any circuit judge of the eighth circuit as constituted before the effective date of this Act, who resides within the eighth circuit as constituted by this Act, is assigned as a circuit judge to such part of the former eighth circuit as is constituted by this Act the eighth circuit, and shall be a circuit judge thereof; and any circuit judge of the eighth circuit as constituted before the effective date of this Act, who resides within the tenth circuit as constituted by this Act, is assigned as a circuit judge of such part of the former eighth circuit as is constituted by this Act the tenth circuit, and shall be a circuit judge thereof.

SEC. 5. Where before the effective date of this Act any appeal or other proceeding has been filed with the circuit court of appeals for the eighth circuit as constituted before the effective date of this Act—

(1) If any hearing before said court has been held in the case, or if the case has been submitted for decision, then further proceedings in respect of the case shall be had in the same manner and with the same effect as if this Act had not been enacted.

(2) If no hearing before said court has been held in the case, and the case has not been submitted for decision, then the appeal, or other proceeding, together with the original papers, printed records, and record entries duly certified, shall, by appropriate orders duly entered of record, be transferred to the circuit court of appeals to which it would have gone had this Act been in full force and effect at the time such appeal was taken or other proceeding commenced, and further proceedings in respect of the case shall be had in the same manner and with the same effect as if the appeal or other proceeding had been filed in said court.

SEC. 6. This Act shall take effect thirty days after its enactment.

Approved, February 28, 1929.

Source: Statutes at Large, 70th Congress, 2nd Session, Vol. 45, Ch. 363, Pg. 1346

42. Fireside Chat on Reorganization of the Judiciary, 1937

Introduction

President Franklin D. Roosevelt addressed the nation on his plan to reorganize the Supreme Court, March 9, 1937.

Primary Source

March 9, 1937

Last Thursday I described in detail certain economic problems which everyone admits now face the Nation. For the many messages which have come to me after that speech, and which it is physically impossible to answer individually, I take this means of saying "thank you."

Tonight, sitting at my desk in the White House, I make my first radio report to the people in my second term of office.

I am reminded of that evening in March, four years ago, when I made my first radio report to you. We were then in the midst of the great banking crisis.

Soon after, with the authority of the Congress, we asked the Nation to turn over all of its privately held gold, dollar for dollar, to the Government of the United States.

Today's recovery proves how right that policy was.

But when, almost two years later, it came before the Supreme Court its constitutionality was upheld only by a five-to-four vote. The change of one vote would have thrown all the affairs of this great Nation back into hopeless chaos. In effect, four Justices ruled that the right under a private contract to exact a pound of flesh was more sacred than the main objectives of the Constitution to establish an enduring Nation.

In 1933 you and I knew that we must never let our economic system get completely out of joint again—that we could not afford to take the risk of another great depression.

We also became convinced that the only way to avoid a repetition of those dark days was to have a government with power to prevent and to cure the abuses and the inequalities which had thrown that system out of joint.

We then began a program of remedying those abuses and inequalities—to give balance and stability to our economic system—to make it bomb-proof against the causes of 1929.

Today we are only part-way through that program—and recovery is speeding up to a point where the dangers of 1929 are again becoming possible, not this week or month perhaps, but within a year or two.

National laws are needed to complete that program. Individual or local or state effort alone cannot protect us in 1937 any better than ten years ago.

It will take time—and plenty of time—to work out our remedies administratively even after legislation is passed. To complete our program of protection in time, therefore, we cannot delay one moment in making certain that our National Government has power to carry through.

Four years ago action did not come until the eleventh hour. It was almost too late.

If we learned anything from the depression we will not allow ourselves to run around in new circles of futile discussion and debate, always postponing the day of decision.

The American people have learned from the depression. For in the last three national elections an overwhelming majority of them voted a mandate that the Congress and the President begin the task of providing that protection—not after long years of debate, but now.

The Courts, however, have cast doubts on the ability of the elected Congress to protect us against catastrophe by meeting squarely our modern social and economic conditions.

We are at a crisis in our ability to proceed with that protection. It is a quiet crisis. There are no lines of depositors outside closed banks. But to the far-sighted it is far-reaching in its possibilities of injury to America.

I want to talk with you very simply about the need for present action in this crisis— the need to meet the unanswered challenge of one-third of a Nation ill-nourished, ill-clad, ill-housed.

Last Thursday I described the American form of Government as a three horse team provided by the Constitution to the American people so that their field might be plowed. The three horses are, of course, the three branches of government—the Congress, the Executive and the Courts. Two of the horses are pulling in unison today; the third is not. Those who have intimated that the President of the United States is trying to drive that team, overlook the simple fact that the President, as Chief Executive, is himself one of the three horses.

It is the American people themselves who are in the driver's seat.

It is the American people themselves who want the furrow plowed.

It is the American people themselves who expect the third horse to pull in unison with the other two.

I hope that you have re-read the Constitution of the United States in these past few weeks. Like the Bible, it ought to be read again and again.

It is an easy document to understand when you remember that it was called into being because the Articles of Confederation under which the original thirteen States tried to operate after the Revolution showed the need of a National Government with power enough to handle national problems. In its Preamble, the Constitution states that it was intended to form a more perfect Union and promote the general welfare; and the powers given to the Congress to carry out those purposes can be best described by saying that they were all the powers needed to meet each and every problem which then had a national character and which could not be met by merely local action.

But the framers went further. Having in mind that in succeeding generations many other problems then undreamed of would become national problems, they gave to the Congress the ample broad powers "to levy taxes . . . and provide for the common defense and general welfare of the United States."

That, my friends, is what I honestly believe to have been the clear and underlying purpose of the patriots who wrote a Federal Constitution to create a National Government with national power, intended as they said, "to form a more perfect union . . . for ourselves and our posterity."

For nearly twenty years there was no conflict between the Congress and the Court. Then Congress passed a statute which, in 1803, the Court said violated an express provision of the Constitution. The Court claimed the power to declare it unconstitutional and did so declare it. But a little later the Court itself admitted that it was an extraordinary power to exercise and through Mr. Justice Washington laid down this limitation upon it: "It is but a decent respect due to the wisdom, the integrity and the patriotism of the legislative body, by which any law is passed, to presume in favor of its validity until its violation of the Constitution is proved beyond all reasonable doubt."

But since the rise of the modern movement for social and economic progress through legislation, the Court has more and more often and more and more boldly asserted a power to veto laws passed by the Congress and State Legislatures in complete disregard of this original limitation.

In the last four years the sound rule of giving statutes the benefit of all reasonable doubt has been cast aside. The Court has been acting not as a judicial body, but as a policy-making body.

When the Congress has sought to stabilize national agriculture, to improve the conditions of labor, to safeguard business against unfair competition, to protect our national resources, and in many other ways, to serve our clearly national needs, the majority of the Court has been assuming the power to pass on the wisdom of these acts of the Congress—and to approve or disapprove the public policy written into these laws.

That is not only my accusation. It is the accusation of most distinguished justices of the present Supreme Court. I have not the time to quote to you all the language used by dissenting justices in many of these cases. But in the case holding the Railroad Retirement Act unconstitutional, for instance, Chief Justice Hughes said in a dissenting opinion that the majority opinion was "a departure from sound principles," and placed "an unwarranted limitation upon the commerce clause." And three other justices agreed with him.

In the case of holding the AAA unconstitutional, Justice Stone said of the majority opinion that it was a "tortured construction of the Constitution." And two other justices agreed with him.

In the case holding the New York minimum wage law unconstitutional, Justice Stone said that the majority were actually reading into the Constitution their own "personal economic predilections," and that if the legislative power is not left free to choose the methods of solving the problems of poverty, subsistence, and health of large numbers in the community, then "government is to be rendered impotent." And two other justices agreed with him.

In the face of these dissenting opinions, there is no basis for the claim made by some members of the Court that something in the Constitution has compelled them regretfully to thwart the will of the people.

In the face of such dissenting opinions, it is perfectly clear that, as Chief Justice Hughes has said, "We are under a Constitution, but the Constitution is what the judges say it is."

The Court in addition to the proper use of its judicial functions has improperly set itself up as a third house of the Congress—a super-legislature, as one of the justices has called it—reading into the Constitution words and implications which are not there, and which were never intended to be there.

We have, therefore, reached the point as a nation where we must take action to save the Constitution from the Court and the Court from itself. We must find a way to take an appeal from the Supreme Court to the Constitution itself. We want a Supreme Court which will do justice under the Constitution and not over it. In our courts we want a government of laws and not of men.

I want—as all Americans want—an independent judiciary as proposed by the framers of the Constitution. That means a Supreme Court that will enforce the Constitution as written, that will refuse to amend the Constitution by the arbitrary exercise of judicial power—in other words by judicial say-so. It does not mean a judiciary so independent that it can deny the existence of facts which are universally recognized.

How then could we proceed to perform the mandate given us? It was said in last year's Democratic platform, "If these problems cannot be effectively solved within the Constitution, we shall seek such clarifying amendment as will assure the power to enact those laws, adequately to regulate commerce, protect public health and safety, and safeguard economic security." In other words, we said we would seek an amendment only if every other possible means by legislation were to fail.

When I commenced to review the situation with the problem squarely before me, I came by a process of elimination to the conclusion that, short of amendments, the only method which was clearly constitutional, and would at the same time carry out other much needed reforms, was to infuse new blood into all our Courts. We must have men worthy and equipped to carry out impartial justice. But, at the same time, we must have Judges who will bring to the Courts a present-day sense of the Constitution—Judges who will retain in the Courts the judicial functions of a court, and reject the legislative powers which the courts have today assumed.

In forty-five out of the forty-eight States of the Union, Judges are chosen not for life but for a period of years. In many States Judges must retire at the age of seventy. Congress has provided financial security by offering life pensions at full pay for Federal Judges on all Courts who are willing to retire at seventy. In the case of Supreme Court Justices, that pension is $20,000 a year. But all Federal Judges, once appointed, can, if they choose, hold office for life, no matter how old they may get to be.

What is my proposal? It is simply this: whenever a Judge or Justice of any Federal Court has reached the age of seventy and does not avail himself of the opportunity to retire on a pension, a new member shall be appointed by the President then in office, with the approval, as required by the Constitution, of the Senate of the United States.

That plan has two chief purposes. By bringing into the judicial system a steady and continuing stream of new and younger blood, I hope, first, to make the administration of all Federal justice speedier and, therefore, less costly; secondly, to bring to the decision of social and economic problems younger men who have had personal experience and contact with modern facts and circumstances under which average men have to live and work. This plan will save our national Constitution from hardening of the judicial arteries.

The number of Judges to be appointed would depend wholly on the decision of present Judges now over seventy, or those who would subsequently reach the age of seventy.

If, for instance, any one of the six Justices of the Supreme Court now over the age of seventy should retire as provided under the plan, no additional place would be created. Consequently, although there never can be more than fifteen, there may be only fourteen, or thirteen, or twelve. And there may be only nine.

There is nothing novel or radical about this idea. It seeks to maintain the Federal bench in full vigor. It has been discussed and approved by many persons of high authority ever since a similar proposal passed the House of Representatives in 1869.

Why was the age fixed at seventy? Because the laws of many States, the practice of the Civil Service, the regulations of the Army and Navy, and the rules of many of our Universities and of almost every great private business enterprise, commonly fix the retirement age at seventy years or less.

The statute would apply to all the courts in the Federal system. There is general approval so far as the lower Federal courts are concerned. The plan has met opposition only so far as the Supreme Court of the United States itself is concerned. If such a plan is good for the lower courts it certainly ought to be equally good for the highest Court from which there is no appeal.

Those opposing this plan have sought to arouse prejudice and fear by crying that I am seeking to "pack" the Supreme Court and that a baneful precedent will be established.

What do they mean by the words "packing the Court"?

Let me answer this question with a bluntness that will end all honest misunderstanding of my purposes.

If by that phrase "packing the Court" it is charged that I wish to place on the bench spineless puppets who would disregard the law and would decide specific cases as I wished them to be decided, I make this answer: that no President fit for his office would appoint, and no Senate of honorable men fit for their office would confirm, that kind of appointees to the Supreme Court.

But if by that phrase the charge is made that I would appoint and the Senate would confirm Justices worthy to sit beside present members of the Court who understand those modern conditions, that I will appoint Justices who will not undertake to override the judgment of the Congress on legislative policy, that I will appoint Justices who will act as Justices and not as legislators—if the appointment of such Justices can be called "packing the Courts," then I say that I and with me the vast majority of the American people favor doing just that thing—now.

Is it a dangerous precedent for the Congress to change the number of the Justices? The Congress has always had, and will have, that power. The number of justices has been changed several times before, in the Administration of John Adams and Thomas Jefferson—both signers of the Declaration of Independence—Andrew Jackson, Abraham Lincoln and Ulysses S. Grant.

I suggest only the addition of Justices to the bench in accordance with a clearly defined principle relating to a clearly defined age limit. Fundamentally, if in the future, America cannot trust the Congress it elects to refrain from abuse of our Constitutional usages, democracy will have failed far beyond the importance to it of any king of precedent concerning the Judiciary.

We think it so much in the public interest to maintain a vigorous judiciary that we encourage the retirement of elderly Judges by offering them a life pension at full salary. Why then should we leave the fulfillment of this public policy to chance or make independent on upon the desire or prejudice of any individual Justice?

It is the clear intention of our public policy to provide for a constant flow of new and younger blood into the Judiciary. Normally every President appoints a large number of District and Circuit Court Judges and a few members of the Supreme Court. Until my first term practically every President of the United States has appointed at least one member of the Supreme Court. President Taft appointed five members and named a Chief Justice; President Wilson, three; President Harding, four, including a Chief Justice; President Coolidge, one; President Hoover, three, including a Chief Justice.

Such a succession of appointments should have provided a Court well-balanced as to age. But chance and the disinclination of individuals to leave the Supreme bench have now given us a Court in which five Justices will be over seventy-five years of age before next June and one over seventy. Thus a sound public policy has been defeated.

I now propose that we establish by law an assurance against any such ill-balanced Court in the future. I propose that hereafter, when a Judge reaches the age of seventy, a new and younger Judge shall be added to the Court automatically. In this way I propose to enforce a sound public policy by law instead of leaving the composition of our Federal Courts, including the highest, to be determined by chance or the personal indecision of individuals.

If such a law as I propose is regarded as establishing a new precedent, is it not a most desirable precedent?

Like all lawyers, like all Americans, I regret the necessity of this controversy. But the welfare of the United States, and indeed of the Constitution itself, is what we all must think about first. Our difficulty with the Court today rises not from the Court as an institution but from human beings within it. But we cannot yield our constitutional destiny to the personal judgment of a few men who, being fearful of the future, would deny us the necessary means of dealing with the present.

This plan of mine is no attack on the Court; it seeks to restore the Court to its rightful and historic place in our Constitutional Government and to have it resume its high task of building anew on the Constitution "a system of living law." The Court itself can best undo what the Court has done.

I have thus explained to you the reasons that lie behind our efforts to secure results by legislation within the Constitution. I hope that thereby the difficult process of constitutional amendment may be rendered unnecessary. But let us examine the process.

There are many types of amendment proposed. Each one is radically different from the other. There is no substantial groups within the Congress or outside it who are agreed on any single amendment.

It would take months or years to get substantial agreement upon the type and language of the amendment. It would take months and years thereafter to get a two-thirds majority in favor of that amendment in both Houses of the Congress.

Then would come the long course of ratification by three-fourths of all the States. No amendment which any powerful economic interests or the leaders of any powerful political party have had reason to oppose has ever been ratified within anything like a reasonable time. And thirteen states which contain only five percent of the voting population can block ratification even though the thirty-five States with ninety-five percent of the population are in favor of it.

A very large percentage of newspaper publishers, Chambers of Commerce, Bar Association, Manufacturers' Associations, who are trying to give the impression that they really do want a constitutional amendment would be the first to exclaim as soon as an amendment was proposed, "Oh! I was for an amendment all right, but this amendment you proposed is not the kind of amendment that I was thinking about. I am therefore, going to spend my time, my efforts and my money to block the amendment, although I would be awfully glad to help get some other kind of amendment ratified."

Two groups oppose my plan on the ground that they favor a constitutional amendment. The first includes those who fundamentally object to social and economic legislation along modern lines. This is the same group who during the campaign last Fall tried to block the mandate of the people.

Now they are making a last stand. And the strategy of that last stand is to suggest the time-consuming process of amendment in order to kill off by delay the legislation demanded by the mandate.

To them I say: I do not think you will be able long to fool the American people as to your purposes.

The other groups is composed of those who honestly believe the amendment process is the best and who would be willing to support a reasonable amendment if they could agree on one.

To them I say: we cannot rely on an amendment as the immediate or only answer to our present difficulties. When the time comes for action, you will find that many of those who pretend to support you will sabotage any constructive amendment which is proposed. Look at these strange bed-fellows of yours. When before have you found them really at your side in your fights for progress?

And remember one thing more. Even if an amendment were passed, and even if in the years to come it were to be ratified, its meaning would depend upon the kind of Justices who would be sitting on the Supreme Court Bench. An amendment, like the rest of the Constitution, is what the Justices say it is rather than what its framers or you might hope it is.

This proposal of mine will not infringe in the slightest upon the civil or religious liberties so dear to every American.

My record as Governor and President proves my devotion to those liberties. You who know me can have no fear that I would tolerate the destruction by any branch of government of any part of our heritage of freedom.

The present attempt by those opposed to progress to play upon the fears of danger to personal liberty brings again to mind that crude and cruel strategy tried by the same opposition to frighten the workers of America in a pay-envelope propaganda against the Social Security Law. The workers were not fooled by that propaganda then. The people of America will not be fooled by such propaganda now.

I am in favor of action through legislation:

First, because I believe that it can be passed at this session of the Congress.

Second, because it will provide a reinvigorated, liberal-minded Judiciary necessary to furnish quicker and cheaper justice from bottom to top.

Third, because it will provide a series of Federal Courts willing to enforce the Constitution as written, and unwilling to assert legislative powers by writing into it their own political and economic policies.

During the past half century the balance of power between the three great branches of the Federal Government has been tipped out of balance by the Courts in direct contradiction of the high purposes of the framers of the Constitution. It is my purpose to restore that balance. You who know me will accept my solemn assurance that in a world in which democracy is under attack, I seek to make American democracy succeed. You and I will do our part.

Source: Franklin D. Roosevelt Library

43. Senate Judiciary Committee, Adverse Report on Roosevelt's Proposed Reorganization of the Federal Judiciary, 1937

Introduction

The Judicial Procedures Reform Bill of 1937, frequently called the court-packing plan, was a legislative initiative proposed by President Franklin Roosevelt to add more justices to the Supreme Court. The most controversial provision would have granted the president the power to appoint an additional justice, up to a maximum of six, for every sitting member over the age of 70 years, 6 months. Roosevelt's purpose was to increase the possibility of obtaining favorable rulings on New Deal legislation that had been previously ruled unconstitutional by the dominant conservative justices. The president's initiative ultimately failed due to adverse public opinion, the retirement of one justice, and unexpected resistance in the Senate. Although changing circumstances ultimately allowed the New Deal to continue, the court-packing episode is seen as a mistake on Roosevelt's part.

Primary Source

It is essential to the continuance of our constitutional democracy that the judiciary be completely independent of both the executive and legislative branches of the Government, and we assert that independent courts are the last safeguard of the citizen, where his rights, reserved to him by the express and implied provisions of the Constitution, come in conflict with the power of governmental agencies. . . .

The condition of the world abroad must of necessity cause us to hesitate at this time and to refuse to enact any law that would impair the independence of or destroy the people's confidence in an independent judicial branch of our Government. We unhesitatingly assert that any effort looking to the impairment of an independent judiciary of necessity operates toward centralization of power in the other branches of a tripartite form of government. We declare for the continuance and perpetuation of government and rule by law, as distinguished from government and rule by men, and in this we are but reasserting the principles basic to the Constitution of the United States. . . .

The whole bill prophesies and permits executive and legislative interferences with the independence of the Court, a prophecy and a permission which constitute an affront to the spirit of the Constitution. . . .

If interference with the judgment of an independent judiciary is to be countenanced in any degree, then it is permitted and sanctioned in all degrees. There is no constituted power to say where the degree ends or begins, and the political administration of the hour may apply the essential "concepts of justice" by equipping the courts with one strain of "new blood," while the political administration of another day may use a different light and a different blood test. Thus would influence run riot. Thus perpetuity, independence, and stability belonging to the judicial arm of the Government and relied on by lawyers and laity, are lost. Thus is confidence extinguished.

> *Source:* Senate Committee on the Judiciary, *Reorganization of the Federal Judiciary*, 75th Cong., 1st sess., 1937, S. Rep. 711

44. Establishment of the Administrative Office of the U.S. Courts, 1939

Introduction

By the late 1930s, a coalition of judges, lawyers, academics, and Justice Department officials agreed that the efficient administration of justice, as well as the principle of judicial independence, required a separate agency with officers appointed by and responsible to a body of judges. In 1939, with the establishment of the Administrative Office of the U.S. Courts and the circuit judicial councils, Congress provided the judiciary with budgetary and personnel management agencies that were independent of the executive branch. The 1939 act established circuit judicial councils through which the court of appeals judges would review the caseload reports of the Administrative Office and instruct district judges on what was necessary to expedite the courts' business. It also mandated annual circuit conferences at which circuit and district judges would meet with members of the bar to discuss judicial administration.

Primary Source

August 7, 1939.
53 Stat. 1223.

AN ACT

To provide for the administration of the United States courts, and for other purposes.

Be it enacted by the Senate and House of Representatives of United States of America in Congress assembled, That the Judicial Code is hereby amended by adding at the end thereof a new chapter to be numbered XV and entitled "The Administration of the United States Courts", as follows:

"CHAPTER XV—THE ADMINISTRATION OF THE UNITED STATES COURTS

"SEC. 302. There shall be at the seat of government an establishment to be known as the Administrative Office of the United States Courts, with a Director at the head thereof who shall be appointed by the Supreme Court of the United States and hold office at the pleasure of and be subject to removal by the aforesaid Court. There shall be in said establishment an Assistant Director, to be appointed and hold office in like manner, who shall perform such duties as may be assigned to him by the Director and, during the absence or incapacity of the Director or during a vacancy in that office, shall act as Director. The Director and Assistant Director shall receive annual salaries of $10,000 and $7,500, respectively. The Director shall cause a seal of office to be made for the said establishment of such design as the Supreme Court of the United States shall approve, and judicial notice shall be taken of the said seal.

"SEC. 303. The Director, with the approval of the Supreme Court, shall have authority, subject to the civil-service laws, to appoint such employees as are deemed necessary to perform the functions and duties vested in said establishment by this chapter, and the Director shall fix their compensation according to the Classification Act of 1923, as amended. During his term of office or employment, no officer or employee of said establishment shall engage directly or indirectly in the practice of law in any of the courts of the United States.

"SEC. 304. The Director shall be the administrative officer of the United States courts and shall have charge, under the supervision and direction of the conference of senior circuit judges, of—

"(1) All administrative matters related to the offices of the clerks and other clerical and administrative personnel of the courts, but nothing contained in this chapter shall be construed as affecting the authority of the courts to appoint their administrative or clerical personnel, or the authority of the Attorney General respecting United States marshals and their deputies, United States attorneys and their assistants;

"(2) Examining the state of the dockets of the various courts and securing information as to their needs for assistance, if any, and the preparation of statistical data and reports of the business transacted by the courts, and promptly transmitting the information so obtained quarterly to the senior circuit judges of the respective circuits, to the end that proper action may be taken action taken with respect thereto, but inspections of the dockets of the courts outside of the continental United States shall be made through officials of the United States Government residing within the jurisdiction, respectively, of the said courts;

"(3) The disbursement, directly and through the several United States marshals as now provided by law, of moneys appropriated for the maintenance, support, and operation of the courts;

"(4) The purchase, exchange, transfer, and distribution of equipment and supplies;

"(5) The examination and audit of vouchers and accounts of the officials and employees covered by this chapter;

"(6) The providing of accommodations for the use of the courts and the various officials and employees covered by this chapter; and

"(7) Such other matters as may be assigned to him by the Supreme Court and the conference of the senior circuit judges. The clerks of the district courts, their deputies and assistants, and all other employees of said courts shall comply with any and all requests made by the Director or one of his assistants for information and statistical data bearing on the state of the dockets of such courts.

"SEC. 305. The Director, under the supervision of the conference of senior circuit judges, shall prepare and submit annually to the Bureau of the Budget estimates of the expenditures and appropriations necessary for the maintenance and operation of the United States courts and the administrative office of the United States courts, and such supplemental and deficiency estimates as may be required time to time for the same purposes, in accordance with the provisions of the Budget and Accounting Act. Such estimates in respect of the circuit courts of appeals, the district courts of the United States, and courts hereinafter referred to in the Territories and possessions, and of the administrative office shall be approved by the conference of senior circuit judges before their presentation to the Bureau of the Budget. Such estimates in respect to the United States Court of Customs and Patent Appeals, the Court of Claims, and the United States Customs Court shall be approved by the judges of such courts, respectively, before submission to the Bureau of the Budget. All estimates so submitted shall be included in the Budget without revision (but subject to the recommendations of the Bureau of the Budget thereon), in the same manner as is provided for the estimates of the Supreme Court by section 201 of said Act. The Director shall submit annually to the conference of senior circuit judges a report of the activities of the administrative office and of the state of business of the courts, together with the statistical data compiled and submitted by him to the senior circuit judges as provided by clause 2 of section 304, with his recommendations. Such report shall be filed at least two weeks prior to the annual meeting of the conference, and a copy thereof shall also be filed with the Congress and with the Attorney General. Such report shall be a public document.

"SEC. 306. To the end that the work of the district courts shall be effectively and expeditiously transacted, it shall be the duty of the senior circuit judge of each circuit to call at such time and place as he shall designate, but at least twice in each year, a council composed of the circuit judges for such circuit, who are hereby designated a council for that purpose, at which council the senior circuit judge shall preside. The senior judge shall submit to the council the quarterly reports of the Director required to be filed by the provisions of section 304, clause (2), and such action shall be taken thereon by the council as may be necessary. It shall be the duty of the district judges promptly to carry out the directions of the council as to the administration of the business of their respective courts. Nothing contained in this section shall affect the provisions of existing law relating to the assignment of district judges to serve outside of the districts for which they, respectively, were appointed.

"SEC. 307. A conference shall be held annually in each judicial circuit, at such time and place, as shall be designated by the senior circuit judge thereof, which conference shall be composed of circuit and district judges in such circuit who reside within the continental United States, with participation in such conference on the part of members of the bar under rules to be prescribed by the circuit courts of appeals, for the purpose of considering the state of the business of the courts and advising ways and means of improving the administration of justice within the circuit. The senior circuit judge and each judge summoned and attending such conferences shall be allowed his actual expenses of travel and his necessary expenses for subsistence, not to exceed $10 per day, which payments shall be made by the United States marshal for the district in which the conference is held, upon the written certificate of the judge incurring such expenses.

"SEC. 308. The provisions of this chapter shall apply to the several United States circuit courts of appeals, the United States Court Appeals for the District of Columbia, the several district courts of the United States in the continental United States, the Court of Claims, the United States Court of Customs and Patent Appeals, the United States Customs Court, the District Court for the District of Alaska, the District Court for the District of Hawaii, the District Court of the

United States for Puerto Rico, the United States District Court for the District of the Canal Zone, the District Court of the Virgin Islands, and the United States Court for China. The term 'courts' as used in this chapter means the courts specified in this section. The term 'continental United States' as used in this chapter means the States of the Union and the District of Columbia. For the purposes of this chapter, the District of Columbia shall be deemed to be a judicial circuit. The chief justice of the United States Court of Appeals for the District of Columbia shall have the duties, powers, and authority of the senior circuit judge for such circuit, and the associate justices of the United States Court of Appeals for the District of Columbia shall have the duties, powers, and authority of circuit judges for such circuit."

SEC. 2. The following quoted provision of the Act making appropriations for the Departments of State and Justice, and for the Department of Commerce (H. R. 6392) for the fiscal year ending June 30, 1940, approved June 29, 1939, Public Act Numbered 156, Seventy-sixth Congress, first session, to wit: "That no part of this appropriation shall be used to defray the salary or expenses of any probation officer whose work fails to comply with the official orders, regulations, and probation standards promulgated by the Attorney General: Provided further, That no funds herein appropriated shall be used to defray the salary or expenses of any probation officer unless the district judge shall have so far as possible required the appointee to conform with the qualifications prescribed by the Attorney General: Provided further, That nothing herein contained shall be construed to abridge the right of the district judges to appoint probation officers, or to make such orders as may be necessary to govern probation officers in their own courts:" is hereby repealed.

SEC. 3. Those employees of the Department of Justice engaged in the audit of accounts and vouchers referred to in section 304 of the Judicial Code shall, as far as practicable, be transferred to the Administrative Office of the United States Courts. In such event, the appropriations available for the current fiscal year, from which such employees are paid, shall be apportioned between the Department of Justice and the Administrative Office of the United States Courts, on the basis of duties transferred to the latter office. All records, documents, and papers relating to the audit of accounts referred to in section 304 of the Judicial Code shall be transferred from the Department of Justice to the Administrative Office of the United States Courts.

SEC. 4. All unexpended appropriations for the support, maintenance, and operation of the courts specified in section 306 of the Judicial Code for the current fiscal year, and all unexpended appropriations covering judicial personnel as specified in section 304 (1) of the Judicial Code, including appropriations for the salaries of justices and judges who have retired or who have resigned under the provisions of section 260 of the Judicial Code (U. S. C., title 28, sec. 375), are hereby transferred to the control of the Administrative Office of the United States Courts.

SEC. 5. All powers and duties now conferred or imposed by law upon the Department of Justice or the Attorney General, relating to the administrative audit of the accounts and vouchers referred to in section 304 of the Judicial Code, are hereby transferred to and vested in the Administrative Office of the United States Courts.

SEC. 6. All administrative powers and duties now conferred or imposed by law upon the Department of Justice or the Attorney General, respecting clerks of courts, deputy clerks of courts and clerical assistants, law clerks, secretaries, and stenographers to the judges, and librarians in charge of libraries of the courts, and such other employees of the courts not excluded by section 304 of chapter XV as hereinbefore set forth, are hereby vested in the Administrative Office of the United States Courts.

SEC. 7. This Act shall take effect ninety days after its approval.

Approved, August 7, 1939.

Source: Statutes at Large, 70th Congress, 2nd Session, Vol. 53, Ch. 15, Pg. 1223

45. Franklin D. Roosevelt: Executive Order 8802, 1941

Introduction

On June 25, 1941, President Franklin D. Roosevelt signed Executive Order 8802, "Reaffirming Policy of Full Participation in the Defense Program by All Persons, Regardless of Race, Creed, Color, or National Origin, and Directing Certain Action in Furtherance of Said Policy." It ended discriminatory practices in the defense industry as the United States prepared for its possible entry into World War II.

Primary Source

WHEREAS it is the policy of the United States to encourage full participation in the national defense program by all citizens of the United States, regardless of race, creed, color, or national origin, in the firm belief that the democratic way of life within the Nation can be defended successfully only with the help and support of all groups within its borders; and

WHEREAS there is evidence that available and needed workers have been barred from employment in industries engaged in defense production solely because of considerations of race, creed, color, or national origin, to the detriment of workers' morale and national unity:

NOW, THEREFORE, by virtue of the authority vested in me by the Constitution and the statutes, and as a prerequisite to the successful conduct of our national defense production effort, I do hereby reaffirm the policy of the United States that there shall be no discrimination in the employment of workers in defense industries or government because of race, creed, color, or national origin, and I do hereby declare that it is the duty of employers and of labor organizations, in furtherance of said policy and of this order, to provide for the full and equitable participation of all workers in defense industries, without discrimination because of race, creed, color, or national origin:

And it is hereby ordered as follows:

1. All departments and agencies of the Government of the United States concerned with vocational and training programs for defense production shall take special measures appropriate to assure that such programs are administered without discrimination because of race, creed, color, or national origin;

2. All contracting agencies of the Government of the United States shall include in all defense contracts hereafter negotiated by them a provision obligating the contractor not to discriminate against any worker because of race, creed, color, or national origin;

3. There is established in the Office of Production Management a Committee on Fair Employment Practice, which shall consist of a chairman and four other members to be appointed by the President. The chairman and members of the Committee shall serve as such without compensation but shall be entitled to actual and necessary transportation, subsistence and other expenses incidental to performance of their duties. The Committee shall receive and investigate complaints of discrimination in violation of the provisions of this order and shall take appropriate steps to redress grievances which it finds to be valid. The Committee shall also recommend to the several departments and agencies of the Government of the United States and to the President all measures which may be deemed by it necessary or proper to effectuate the provisions of this order.

Franklin D. Roosevelt
The White House,
June 25, 1941.

Source: Roosevelt, Franklin D. Executive Order no. 8802. *Federal Register*, 6 FR3109, June 27, 1941

46. Executive Order 9066, 1942

Introduction

Signed by President Franklin D. Roosevelt on February 19, 1942, Executive Order 9066, or the Japanese Internment Order, authorized the secretary of war to prescribe military areas and was presented to the public as a necessary wartime measure to aid the United States in fighting World War II. The order was used to authorize the internment of over one hundred thousand Japanese Americans during the war. Both the U.S. government and much of the public feared that Japanese Americans would commit acts of sabotage in the United States to undermine the U.S. war effort and assist the Japanese. The government forced Japanese Americans into camps throughout the West, where they suffered from deprivation, despair, and disease for much of the war, even as Japanese-American units distinguished themselves in the U.S. military.

Primary Source

WHEREAS the successful prosecution of the war requires every possible protection against espionage and against sabotage to national-defense material, national-defense premises, and national-defense utilities as defined in Section 4, Act of April 20, 1918, 40 Stat. 533, as amended by the Act of November 30, 1940, 54 Stat. 1220, and the Act of August 21, 1941, 55 Stat. 655 (U.S.C. Title 50, Sec. 104):

NOW, THEREFORE, by virtue of the authority vested in me as President of the United States, and Commander in Chief of the Army and Navy, I hereby authorize and direct the Secretary of War, and the Military Commanders whom he may from time to time designate, whenever he or any designated Commander deems such action necessary or desirable, to prescribe military areas in such places and of such extent as he or the appropriate Military Commander may determine, from which any or all persons may be excluded, and with respect to which, the right of any person to enter, remain in, or leave shall be subject to whatever restrictions the Secretary of War or the appropriate Military Commander may impose in his discretion. The Secretary of War is hereby authorized to provide for residents of any such area who are excluded therefrom, such transportation, food, shelter, and other accommodations as may be necessary in the judgment of the Secretary of War or the said Military Commander, and until other arrangements are made, to accomplish the purpose of this order. The designation of military areas in any region or locality shall supersede designations or prohibited and restricted areas by the Attorney General under the Proclamations of December 7 and 8, 1941, and shall supersede the responsibility and authority of the Attorney General under the said Proclamations in respect of such prohibited and restricted areas.

I hereby further authorize and direct the Secretary of War and the said Military Commanders to take such other steps as he or the appropriate Military Commander may deem advisable to enforce compliance with the restrictions applicable to each Military area hereinabove authorized to be designated, including the use of Federal troops and other Federal Agencies, with authority to accept assistance of state and local agencies.

I hereby further authorize and direct all Executive Departments, independent establishments and other Federal Agencies, to assist the Secretary of War or the said Military Commanders in carrying out this Executive Order, including the furnishing of medical aid, hospitalization, food, clothing, transportation, use of land, shelter, and other supplies, equipment, utilities, facilities, and services.

This order shall not be construed as modifying or limiting in any way the authority heretofore granted under Executive Order No. 8972, dated December 12, 1941, nor shall it be construed as limiting or modifying the duty and responsibility of the Federal Bureau of Investigation, with respect to the investigation of alleged acts of sabotage or the duty and responsibility of the Attorney General and the Department of Justice under the Proclamations of December 7, and 8, 1941, prescribing regulations for the conduct and control of alien enemies, except as such duty and responsibility is superseded by the designation of military areas hereunder.

Franklin D. Roosevelt
The White House,
February 19, 1942.

> *Source:* General Records of the United States Government; Record Group 11; National Archives

47. *Hirabayashi v. United States,* 1943

Introduction

In this controversial opinion, the Supreme Court decided that a law establishing a curfew during wartime for those of Japanese ancestry was constitutional because of military necessity. The case arose during World War II when military necessity was used as an excuse to limit the freedom of movement of Japanese Americans. It was one of several challenges to those laws.

Primary Source

MR. CHIEF JUSTICE STONE delivered the opinion of the Court.

Appellant, an American citizen of Japanese ancestry, was convicted in the district court of violating the Act of Congress of March 21, 1942, which makes it a misdemeanor knowingly to disregard restrictions made applicable by a military commander to persons in a military area prescribed by him as such, all as authorized by an Executive Order of the President.

The questions for our decision are whether the particular restriction violated, namely that all persons of Japanese ancestry residing in such an area be within their place of residence daily between the hours of 8:00 p.m. and 6:00 a.m., was adopted by the military commander in the exercise of an unconstitutional delegation by Congress of its legislative power, and whether the restriction unconstitutionally discriminated between citizens of Japanese ancestry and those of other ancestries in violation of the Fifth Amendment.

The indictment is in two counts. The second charges that appellant, being a person of Japanese ancestry, had on a specified date, contrary to a restriction promulgated by the military commander of the Western Defense Command, Fourth Army, failed to remain in his place of residence in the designated military area between the hours of 8:00 o'clock p.m. and 6:00 a.m. The first count charges that appellant, on May 11 and 12, 1942, had, contrary to a Civilian Exclusion Order issued by the military commander, failed to report to the Civil Control Station within the designated area, it appearing that appellant's required presence there was a preliminary step to the exclusion from that area of persons of Japanese ancestry.

By demurrer and plea in abatement, which the court overruled, appellant asserted that the indictment should be dismissed because he was an American citizen who had never been a subject of and had never borne allegiance to the Empire of Japan, and also because the Act of March 21, 1942, was an unconstitutional delegation of Congressional power. On the trial to a jury it appeared that appellant was born in Seattle in 1918, of Japanese parents who had come from Japan to the United States, and who had never afterward returned to Japan; that he was educated in the Washington public schools and at the time of his arrest was a senior in the University of Washington; that he had never been in Japan or had any association with Japanese residing there.

The evidence showed that appellant had failed to report to the Civil Control Station on May 11 or May 12, 1942, as directed, to register for evacuation from the military area. He admitted failure to do so, and stated it had at all times been his belief that he would be waiving his rights as an American citizen by so doing. The evidence also showed that for like reason he was away from his place of residence after 8:00 p.m. on May 9, 1942. The jury returned a verdict of guilty on both counts and appellant was sentenced to imprisonment for a term of three months on each, the sentences to run concurrently.

On appeal the Court of Appeals for the Ninth Circuit certified to us questions of law upon which it desired instructions for the decision of the case. Acting under the authority conferred upon us by that section we ordered that the entire record be certified to this Court so that we might proceed to a decision of the matter in controversy in the same manner as if it had been brought here by appeal. Since the sentences of three months each imposed by the district court on the two counts were ordered to run concurrently, it will be unnecessary to consider questions raised with respect to the first count if we find that the conviction on the second count, for violation of the curfew order, must be sustained.

The curfew order which appellant violated, and to which the sanction prescribed by the Act of Congress has been deemed to attach, purported to be issued pursuant to an Executive Order of the President. In passing upon the authority of the military commander to make and execute the order, it becomes necessary to consider in some detail the official action which preceded or accompanied the order and from which it derives its purported authority.

On December 8, 1941, one day after the bombing of Pearl Harbor by a Japanese air force, Congress declared war against Japan. On February 19, 1942, the President promulgated Executive Order No. 9066. 7 Federal Register 1407. The Order recited that "the successful prosecution of the war requires every possible protection against espionage and against sabotage to national-defense material, national-defense premises, and national-defense utilities as defined in Section 4, Act of April 20, 1918, as amended by the Act of November 30, 1940, and the Act of August 21, 1941." By virtue of the authority vested in him as President and as Commander in Chief of the Army and Navy, the President purported to "authorize and direct the Secretary of War, and the Military Commanders whom he may from time to time designate, whenever he or any designated Commander deems such action necessary or desirable, to prescribe military areas in such places and of such extent as he or the appropriate Military Commander may determine, from which any or all persons may be excluded, and with respect to which, the right of any person to enter, remain in, or leave shall be subject to whatever restrictions the Secretary of War or the appropriate Military Commander may impose in his discretion."

On February 20, 1942, the Secretary of War designated Lt. General J. L. DeWitt as Military Commander of the Western Defense Command, comprising the Pacific Coast states and some others, to carry out there the duties prescribed by Executive Order No. 9066. On March 2, 1942, General DeWitt promulgated Public Proclamation No. 1. 7 Federal Register 2320. The proclamation recited that the entire Pacific Coast "by its geographical location is particularly subject to attack, to attempted invasion by the armed forces of nations with which the United States is now at war, and, in connection therewith, is subject to espionage and acts of sabotage, thereby requiring the adoption of military measures necessary to establish safeguards against such enemy operations." It stated that "the present situation requires as matter of military necessity the establishment in the territory embraced by the Western Defense Command of Military Areas and Zones thereof"; it specified and designated as military areas certain areas within the Western Defense Command; and it declared that "such persons or classes of persons as the situation may require" would, by subsequent proclamation, be excluded from certain of these areas, but might be permitted to enter or remain in certain others, under regulations and restrictions to be later prescribed. Among the military areas so designated by Public Proclamation No. 1 was Military Area No. 1, which embraced, besides the southern part of Arizona, all the coastal region of the three Pacific Coast states, including the City of Seattle, Washington, where appellant resided. Military Area No. 2. designated by the same proclamation, included those parts of the coastal states and of Arizona not placed within Military Area No. 1.

Public Proclamation No. 2 of March 16, 1942, issued by General DeWitt, made like recitals and designated further military areas and zones. It contained like provisions concerning the exclusion, by subsequent proclamation, of certain persons or classes of persons from these areas, and the future promulgation of regulations and restrictions applicable to persons remaining within them.

An Executive Order of the President, No. 9102, of March 18, 1942, established the War Relocation Authority, in the Office for Emergency Management of the Executive Office of the President; it authorized the Director of War Relocation Authority to formulate and effectuate a program for the removal, relocation, maintenance and supervision of persons designated under Executive Order No. 9066, already referred to; and it conferred on the Director authority to prescribe regulations necessary or desirable to promote the effective execution of the program.

Congress, by the Act of March 21, 1942, 18 U.S.C.A. 97a, provided: "That whoever shall enter, remain in, leave, or commit any act in any military area or military zone prescribed, under the authority of an Executive order of the President, by the Secretary of War, or by any military commander designated by the Secretary of War, contrary to the restrictions applicable to any such area or zone or contrary to the order of the Secretary of War or any such military commander, shall, if it appears that he knew or should have known of the existence and extent of the restrictions or order and that his act was in violation thereof, be guilty of a misdemeanor and upon conviction shall be liable" to fine or imprisonment, or both.

Three days later, on March 24, 1942, General DeWitt issued Public Proclamation No. 3. After referring to the previous designation of military areas by Public Proclamations No. 1 and 2, it recited that ". . . the present situation within these Military Areas and Zones requires as a matter or military necessity the establishment of certain regulations pertaining to all enemy aliens and all persons of Japanese ancestry within said Military Areas and Zones. . . ." It accordingly declared and established that from and after March 27, 1942, "all alien Japanese, all alien Germans, all alien Italians, and all persons of Japanese ancestry residing or being within the geographical limits of Military Area No. 1 . . . shall be within their place of residence between the hours of 8:00 P.M. and 6:00 A.M., which period is hereinafter referred to as the hours of curfew." It also imposed certain other restrictions on persons of Japanese ancestry, and provided that any person violating the regulations would be subject to the criminal penalties provided by the Act of Congress of March 21, 1942.

Beginning on March 24, 1942, the military commander issued a series of Civilian Exclusion Orders pursuant to the provisions of Public Proclamation No. 1. Each such order related to a specified area within the territory of his command. The order applicable to appellant was Civilian Exclusion Order No. 57 of May 10, 1942. It directed that from and after 12:00 noon, May 16, 1942, all persons of Japanese ancestry, both alien and non-alien, be excluded from a specified portion of Military Area No. 1 in Seattle, including appellant's place of residence, and it required a member of each family, and each individual living alone, affected by the order to report on May 11 or May 12 to a designated Civil Control Station in Seattle. Meanwhile the military commander had issued Public Proclamation No. 4 of March 27, 1942, which recited the necessity of providing for the orderly evacuation and resettlement of Japanese within the area, and prohibited all alien Japanese and all persons of Japanese ancestry from leaving the military area until future orders should permit.

Appellant does not deny that he knowingly failed to obey the curfew order as charged in the second count of the indictment, or that the order was authorized by the terms of Executive Order No. 9066, or that the challenged Act of Congress purports to punish with criminal penalties disobedience of such an order. His contentions are only that Congress unconstitutionally delegated its legislative power to the military commander by authorizing him to impose the challenged regulation, and that, even if the regulation were in other respects lawfully authorized, the Fifth Amendment prohibits the discrimination made between citizens of Japanese descent and those of other ancestry.

It will be evident from the legislative history that the Act of March 21, 1942, contemplated and authorized the curfew order which we have before us. The bill which became the Act of March 21, 1942, was introduced in the Senate on March 9th and in the House on March 10th at the request of the Secretary of War who, in letters to the Chairman of the Senate Committee on Military Affairs and to the Speaker of the House, stated explicitly that its purpose was to provide means for the enforcement of orders issued under Executive Order No. 9066. This appears in the committee reports on the bill, which set out in full the Executive Order and the Secretary's letter. And each of the committee reports expressly mentions curfew orders as one of the types of restrictions which it was deemed desirable to enforce by criminal sanctions.

When the bill was under consideration, General DeWitt had published his Proclamation No. 1 of March 2, 1942, establishing Military Areas Nos. 1 and 2, and that Proclamation was before Congress. A letter of the Secretary to the Chairman of the House Military Affairs Committee, of March 14, 1942, informed Congress that "General DeWitt is strongly of the opinion that the bill, when enacted, should be broad enough to enable the Secretary of War or the appropriate military commander to enforce curfews and other restrictions within military areas and zones"; and that General DeWitt had "indicated that he was prepared to enforce certain restrictions at once for the purpose of protecting certain vital national defense interests but did not desire to proceed until enforcement machinery had been set up."

The Chairman of the Senate Military Affairs Committee explained on the floor of the Senate that the purpose of the proposed legislation was to provide means of enforcement of curfew orders and other military orders made pursuant to Executive Order No. 9066. He read General DeWitt's Public Proclamation No. 1, and statements from newspaper reports that "evacuation of the first Japanese aliens and American-born Japanese" was about to begin. He also stated to the Senate that "reasons for suspected widespread fifth-column activity among Japanese" were to be found in the system of dual citizenship which Japan deemed applicable to American-born Japanese, and in the propaganda disseminated by Japanese consuls, Buddhist priests and other leaders, among American-born children of Japanese. Such was stated to be the explanation of the contemplated evacuation from the Pacific Coast area of persons of Japanese ancestry, citizens as well as aliens. Congress also had before it the Preliminary Report of a House Committee investigating national defense migration, of March 19, 1942, which approved the provisions of Executive Order No. 9066, and which recommended the evacuation, from military areas established under the Order, of all persons of Japanese ancestry, including citizens. The proposed legislation provided criminal sanctions for violation of orders, in terms broad enough to include the curfew order now before us, and the legislative history demonstrates that Congress was advised that curfew orders were among those intended, and was advised also that regulation of citizen and alien Japanese alike was contemplated.

The conclusion is inescapable that Congress, by the Act of March 21, 1942, ratified and confirmed Executive Order No. 9066. *Prize Cases (The Amy Warwick)*; *Hamilton v. Dillin*; *United States v. Heinszen & Co.*; *Tiaco v. Forbes*; *Isbrandtsen-Moller Co. v. United States*; *Swayne & Hoyt, Ltd. v. United States*; *Mason Co. v.*

Tax Comm'n. And so far as it lawfully could, Congress authorized and implemented such curfew orders as the commanding officer should promulgate pursuant to the Executive Order of the President. The question then is not one of Congressional power to delegate to the President the promulgation of the Executive Order, but whether, acting in cooperation, Congress and the Executive have constitutional authority to impose the curfew restriction here complained of. We must consider also whether, acting together, Congress and the Executive could leave it to the designated military commander to appraise the relevant conditions and on the basis of that appraisal to say whether, under the circumstances, the time and place were appropriate for the promulgation of the curfew order and whether the order itself was an appropriate means of carrying out the Executive Order for the "protection against espionage and against sabotage" to national defense materials, premises and utilities. For reasons presently to be stated, we conclude that it was within the constitutional power of Congress and the executive arm of the Government to prescribe this curfew order for the period under consideration and that its promulgation by the military commander involved no unlawful delegation of legislative power.

Executive Order No. 9066, promulgated in time of war for the declared purpose of prosecuting the war by protecting national defense resources from sabotage and espionage, and the Act of March 21, 1942, ratifying and confirming the Executive Order, were each an exercise of the power to wage war conferred on the Congress and on the President, as Commander in Chief of the armed forces, by Articles I and II of the Constitution. See *Ex parte Quirin.* We have no occasion to consider whether the President, acting alone, could lawfully have made the curfew order in question, or have authorized others to make it. For the President's action has the support of the Act of Congress, and we are immediately concerned with the question whether it is within the constitutional power of the national government, through the joint action of Congress and the Executive, to impose this restriction as an emergency war measure. The exercise of that power here involves no question of martial law or trial by military tribunal. Cf. *Ex parte Milligan*; *Ex parte Quirin*, supra. Appellant has been tried and convicted in the civil courts and has been subjected to penalties prescribed by Congress for the acts committed.

The war power of the national government is "the power to wage war successfully." See Charles Evans Hughes, *War Powers Under the Constitution.* It extends to every matter and activity so related to war as substantially to affect its conduct and progress. The power is not restricted to the winning of victories in the field and the repulse of enemy forces. It embraces every phase of the national defense, including the protection of war materials and the members of the armed forces from injury and from the dangers which attend the rise, prosecution and progress of war. *Prize Cases*, supra; *Miller v. United States*; *Stewart v. Kahn*; *Selective Draft Law Cases (Arver v. United States)*; *McKinley v. United States*; *United States v.*

Macintosh. Since the Constitution commits to the Executive and to Congress the exercise of the war power in all the vicissitudes and conditions of warfare, it has necessarily given them wide scope for the exercise of judgment and discretion in determining the nature and extent of the threatened injury or danger and in the selection of the means for resisting it. *Ex parte Quirin,* supra; cf. *Prize Cases,* supra; *Martin v. Mott.* Where, as they did here, the conditions call for the exercise of judgment and discretion and for the choice of means by those branches of the Government on which the Constitution has placed the responsibility of warmaking, it is not for any court to sit in review of the wisdom of their action or substitute it judgment for theirs.

The actions taken must be appraised in the light of the conditions with which the President and Congress were confronted in the early months of 1942, many of which since disclosed, were then peculiarly within the knowledge of the military authorities. On December 7, 1941, the Japanese air forces had attacked the United States Naval Base at Pearl Harbor without warning, at the very hour when Japanese diplomatic representatives were conducting negotiations with our State Department ostensibly for the peaceful settlement of differences between the two countries. Simultaneously or nearly so, the Japanese attacked Malaysia, Hong Kong, the Philippines, and Wake and Midway Islands. On the following day their army invaded Thailand. Shortly afterwards they sank two British battleships. On December 13th, Guam was taken. On December 24th and 25th they captured Wake Island and occupied Hong Kong. On January 2, 1942, Manila fell, and on February 10th Singapore, Britain's great naval base in the East, was taken. On February 27th the battle for the Java Sea resulted in a disastrous naval defeat to the United Nations. By the 9th of March Japanese forces had established control over the Netherlands East Indies; Rangoon and Burma were occupied; Bataan and Corregidor were under attack.

Although the results of the attack on Pearl Harbor were not fully disclosed until much later, it was known that the damage was extensive, and that the Japanese by their successes had gained a naval superiority over our forces in the Pacific which might enable them to seize Pearl Harbor, our largest naval base and the last stronghold of defense lying between Japan and the west coast. That reasonably prudent men charged with the responsibility of our national defense had ample ground for concluding that they must face the danger of invasion, take measures against it, and in making the choice of measures consider our internal situation, cannot be doubted.

The challenged orders were defense measures for the avowed purpose of safeguarding the military area in question, at a time of threatened air raids and invasion by the Japanese forces, from the danger of sabotage and espionage. As the curfew was made applicable to citizens residing in the area only if they were of Japanese ancestry, our inquiry must be whether in the light of all the facts and circumstances there was any substantial basis for the conclusion, in which Congress and the military commander united, that the curfew as applied was a protective measure necessary to meet the threat of sabotage and espionage which would substantially affect the war effort and which might reasonably be expected to aid a threatened enemy invasion. The alternative which appellant insists must be accepted is for the military authorities to impose the curfew on all citizens within the military area, or on none. In a case of threatened danger requiring prompt action, it is a choice between inflicting obviously needless hardship on the many, or sitting passive and unresisting in the presence of the threat. We think that constitutional government, in time of war, is not so powerless and does not compel so hard a choice if those charged with the responsibility of our national defense have reasonable ground for believing that the threat is real.

When the orders were promulgated there was a vast concentration, within Military Areas No. 1 and 2, of installations and facilities for the production of military equipment, especially ships and airplanes. Important Army and Navy bases were located in California and Washington. Approximately one-fourth of the total value of the major aircraft contracts then let by Government procurement officers were to be performed in the State of California. California ranked second, and Washington fifth, of all the states of the Union with respect to the value of shipbuilding contracts to be performed. In the critical days of March, 1942, the danger to our war production by sabotage and espionage in this area seems obvious. The German invasion of the Western European countries had given ample warning to the world of the menace of the "fifth column." Espionage by persons in sympathy with the Japanese Government had been found to have been particularly effective in the surprise attack on Pearl Harbor. At a time of threatened Japanese attack upon this country, the nature of our inhabitants' attachments to the Japanese enemy was consequently a matter of grave concern. Of the 126,000 persons of Japanese descent in the United States, citizens and non-citizens, approximately 112,000 resided in California, Oregon and Washington at the time of the adoption of the military regulations. Of these approximately two-thirds are citizens because born in the United States. Not only did the great majority of such persons reside within the Pacific Coast states but they were concentrated in or near three of the large cities, Seattle, Portland and Los Angeles, all in Military Area No. 1.

There is support for the view that social, economic and political conditions which have prevailed since the close of the last century, when the Japanese began to come to this country in substantial numbers, have intensified their solidarity and have in large measure prevented their assimilation as an integral part of the white population. In addition, large numbers of children of Japanese parentage are sent to Japanese language schools outside the regular hours of public schools in the locality.

Some of these schools are generally believed to be sources of Japanese nationalistic propaganda, cultivating allegiance to Japan. Considerable numbers, estimated to be approximately 10,000, of American-born children of Japanese parentage have been sent to Japan for all or a part of their education.

Congress and the Executive, including the military commander, could have attributed special significance, in its bearing on the loyalties of persons of Japanese descent, to the maintenance by Japan of its system of dual citizenship. Children born in the United States of Japanese alien parents, and especially those children born before December 1, 1924, are under many circumstances deemed, by Japanese law, to be citizens of Japan. No official census of those whom Japan regards as having thus retained Japanese citizenship is available, but there is ground for the belief that the number is large.

The large number of resident alien Japanese, approximately one-third of all Japanese inhabitants of the country, are of mature years and occupy positions of influence in Japanese communities. The association of influential Japanese residents with Japanese Consulates has been deemed a ready means for the dissemination of propaganda and for the maintenance of the influence of the Japanese Government with the Japanese population in this country.

As a result of all these conditions affecting the life of the Japanese, both aliens and citizens, in the Pacific Coast area, there has been relatively little social intercourse between them and the white population. The restrictions, both practical and legal, affecting the privileges and opportunities afforded to persons of Japanese extraction residing in the United States, have been sources of irritation and may well have tended to increase their isolation, and in many instances their attachments to Japan and its institutions.

Viewing these data in all their aspects, Congress and the Executive could reasonably have concluded that these conditions have encouraged the continued attachment of members of this group to Japan and Japanese institutions. These are only some of the many considerations which those charged with the responsibility for the national defense could take into account in determining the nature and extent of the danger of espionage and sabotage, in the event of invasion or air raid attack. The extent of that danger could be definitely known only after the event and after it was too late to meet it. Whatever views we may entertain regarding the loyalty to this country of the citizens of Japanese ancestry, we cannot reject as unfounded the judgment of the military authorities and of Congress that there were disloyal members of that population, whose number and strength could not be precisely and quickly ascertained. We cannot say that the war-making branches of the Government did not have ground for believing that in a critical hour such persons could not readily be isolated and separately dealt with, and constituted a menace to the national defense and safety, which demanded that prompt and adequate measures be taken to guard against it.

Appellant does not deny that, given the danger, a curfew was an appropriate measure against sabotage. It is an obvious protection against the perpetration of sabotage most readily committed during the hours of darkness. If it was an appropriate exercise of the war power its validity is not impaired because it has restricted the citizen's liberty. Like every military control of the population of a dangerous zone in war time, it necessarily involves some infringement of individual liberty, just as does the police establishment of fire lines during a fire, or the confinement of people to their houses during an air raid alarm—neither of which could be thought to be an infringement of constitutional right. Like them, the validity of the restraints of the curfew order depends on all the conditions which obtain at the time the curfew is imposed and which support the order imposing it. But appellant insists that the exercise of the power is inappropriate and unconstitutional because it discriminates against citizens of Japanese ancestry, in violation of the Fifth Amendment. The Fifth Amendment contains no equal protection clause and it restrains only such discriminatory legislation by Congress as amounts to a denial of due process. *Detroit Bank v. United States*, and cases cited. Congress may hit at a particular danger where it is seen, without providing for others which are not so evident or so urgent. *Keokee Consol. Coke Co. v. Taylor.*

Distinctions between citizens solely because of their ancestry are by their very nature odious to a free people whose institutions are founded upon the doctrine of equality. For that reason, legislative classification or discrimination based on race alone has often been held to be a denial of equal protection. *Yick Wo v. Hopkins*; *Yu Cong Eng v. Trinidad*; *Hill v. Texas*. We may assume that these considerations would be controlling here were it not for the fact that the danger of espionage and sabotage, in time of war and of threatened invasion, calls upon the military authorities to scrutinize every relevant fact bearing on the loyalty of populations in the danger areas. Because racial discriminations are in most circumstances irrelevant and therefore prohibited, it by no means follows that, in dealing with the perils of war, Congress and the Executive are wholly precluded from taking into account those facts and circumstances which are relevant to measures for our national defense and for the successful prosecution of the war, and which may in fact place citizens of one ancestry in a different category from others. "We must never forget, that it is a constitution we are expounding," "a constitution intended to endure for ages to come, and, consequently, to be adapted to the various crises of human affairs." *McCulloch v. Maryland.* The adoption by Government, in the crisis of war and of threatened invasion, of measures for the public safety, based upon the recognition of facts and circumstances which indicate that a group of one national extraction may menace that safety more than others, is not wholly beyond the limits of the Constitution and is not to be condemned merely because in other and in most circumstances racial distinctions are irrelevant. Cf. *State of Ohio ex rel. Clarke v. Deckebach*, and cases cited.

Here the aim of Congress and the Executive was the protection against sabotage of war materials and utilities in areas thought to be in danger of Japanese invasion and air attack. We have stated in detail facts and circumstances with respect to the American citizens of Japanese ancestry residing on the Pacific Coast which support the judgment of the warwaging branches of the Government that some restrictive measure was urgent. We cannot say that these facts and circumstances, considered in the particular war setting, could afford no ground for differentiating citizens of Japanese ancestry from other groups in the United States. The fact alone that attack on our shores was threatened by Japan rather than another enemy power set these citizens apart from others who have no particular associations with Japan.

Our investigation here does not go beyond the inquiry whether, in the light of all the relevant circumstances preceding and attending their promulgation, the challenged orders and statute afforded a reasonable basis for the action taken in imposing the curfew. We cannot close our eyes to the fact, demonstrated by experience, that in time of war residents having ethnic affiliations with an invading enemy may be a greater source of danger than those of a different ancestry. Nor can we deny that Congress, and the military authorities acting with its authorization, have constitutional power to appraise the danger in the light of facts of public notoriety. We need not now attempt to define the ultimate boundaries of the war power. We decide only the issue as we have defined it—we decide only that the curfew order as applied, and at the time it was applied, was within the boundaries of the war power. In this case it is enough that circumstances within the knowledge of those charged with the responsibility for maintaining the national defense afforded a rational basis for the decision which they made. Whether we would have made it is irrelevant.

What we have said also disposes of the contention that the curfew order involved an unlawful delegation by Congress of its legislative power. The mandate of the Constitution, that all legislative power granted "shall be vested in a Congress" has never been thought, even in the administration of civil affairs, to preclude Congress from resorting to the aid of executive or administrative officers in determining by findings whether the facts are such as to call for the application of previously adopted legislative standards or definitions of Congressional policy.

The purpose of Executive Order No. 9066, and the standard which the President approved for the orders authorized to be promulgated by the military commander—as disclosed by the preamble of the Executive Order—was the protection of our war resources against espionage and sabotage. Public Proclamations No. 1 and 2, by General DeWitt, contain findings that the military areas created and the measures to be prescribed for them were required to establish safeguards against espionage and sabotage. Both the Executive Order and the Proclamations were before Congress when the Act of March 21, 1942, was under consideration. To the extent that the Executive Order authorized orders to be promulgated by the military commander to accomplish the declared purpose of the Order, and to the extent that the findings in the Proclamations establish that such was their purpose, both have been approved by Congress.

It is true that the Act does not in terms establish a particular standard to which orders of the military commander are to conform, or require findings to be made as a prerequisite to any order. But the Executive Order, the Proclamations and the statute are not to be read in isolation from each other. They were parts of a single program and must be judged as such. The Act of March 21, 1942, was an adoption by Congress of the Executive Order and of the Proclamations. The Proclamations themselves followed a standard authorized by the Executive Order—the necessity of protecting military resources in the designated areas against espionage and sabotage. And by the Act, Congress gave its approval to that standard. We have no need to consider now the validity of action if taken by the military commander without conforming to this standard approved by Congress, or the validity of orders made without the support of findings showing that they do so conform. Here the findings of danger from espionage and sabotage, and of the necessity of the curfew order to protect against them, have been duly made. General DeWitt's Public Proclamation No. 3, which established the curfew, merely prescribed regulations of the type and in the manner which Public Proclamations No. 1 and 2 had announced would be prescribed at a future date, and was thus founded on the findings of Proclamations No. 1 and 2.

The military commander's appraisal of facts in the light of the authorized standard, and the inferences which he drew from those facts, involved the exercise of his informed judgment. But as we have seen, those facts, and the inferences which could be rationally drawn from them, support the judgment of the military commander, that the danger of espionage and sabotage to our military resources was imminent, and that the curfew order was an appropriate measure to meet it.

Where, as in the present case, the standard set up for the guidance of the military commander, and the action taken and the reasons for it, are in fact recorded in the military orders, so that Congress, the courts and the public are assured that the orders, in the judgment of the commander, conform to the standards approved by the President and Congress, there is no failure in the performance of the legislative function. *Opp Cotton Mills v. Administrator*, and cases cited. The essentials of that function are the determination by Congress of the legislative policy and its approval of a rule of conduct to carry that policy into execution. The very necessities which attend the conduct of military operations in time of war in this instance as in many others preclude Congress from holding committee meetings to determine whether there is danger, before it enacts legislation to combat the danger.

The Constitution as a continuously operating charter of government does not demand the impossible or the impractical. The essentials of the legislative function are preserved when Congress authorizes a statutory command to become operative, upon ascertainment of a basic conclusion of fact by a designated representative of the Government.... The present statute, which authorized curfew orders to be made pursuant to Executive Order No. 9066 for the protection of war resources from espionage and sabotage, satisfies those requirements. Under the Executive Order the basic facts, determined by the military commander in the light of knowledge then available, were whether that danger existed and whether a curfew order was an appropriate means of minimizing the danger. Since his findings to that effect were, as we have said, not without adequate support, the legislative function was performed and the sanction of the statute attached to violations of the curfew order. It is unnecessary to consider whether or to what extent such findings would support orders differing from the curfew order.

The conviction under the second count is without constitutional infirmity. Hence we have no occasion to review the conviction on the first count since, as already stated, the sentences on the two counts are to run concurrently and conviction on the second is sufficient to sustain the sentence. For this reason also it is unnecessary to consider the Government's argument that compliance with the order to report at the Civilian Control Station did not necessarily entail confinement in a relocation center.

AFFIRMED.

Source: Hirabayashi v. United States, 320 U.S. 81 (1943)

48. *Korematsu v. United States,* 1944

Introduction

Korematsu v. United States was a landmark U.S. Supreme Court case concerning the constitutionality of the internment of Japanese Americans in camps during World War II. In 1942, President Franklin Roosevelt signed Executive Order 9066, allowing the federal government to declare portions of the United States to be military areas, from which specific groups of people could be excluded for security purposes. Many Japanese Americans, including whole families, were forced from their homes, transported long distances, and placed in internment camps. Frank Korematsu, a U.S.-born citizen of Japanese descent, defied the order to be relocated. He was arrested and convicted of violating the law. On appeal, the Supreme Court considered whether relocation and related processes based on Executive Order 9066 were constitutional. In a 6–3 decision the Court upheld Korematsu's conviction on the grounds that national security concerns during wartime trumped his individual rights. Korematsu's conviction was eventually overturned in 1983, although the ruling concerning the creation of exclusion orders has never been overturned.

Primary Source

Mr. Justice Black delivered the opinion of the Court.

The petitioner, an American citizen of Japanese descent, was convicted in a federal district court for remaining in San Leandro, California, a "Military Area," contrary to Civilian Exclusion Order No. 34 of the Commanding General of the Western Command, U.S. Army, which directed that, after May 9, 1942, all persons of Japanese ancestry should be excluded from that area. No question was raised as to petitioner's loyalty to the United States. The Circuit Court of Appeals affirmed, and the importance of the constitutional question involved caused us to grant certiorari.

It should be noted, to begin with, that all legal restrictions which curtail the civil rights of a single racial group are immediately suspect. That is not to say that all such restrictions are unconstitutional. It is to say that courts must subject them to the most rigid scrutiny. Pressing public necessity may sometimes justify the existence of such restrictions; racial antagonism never can.

In the instant case, prosecution of the petitioner was begun by information charging violation of an Act of Congress, of March 21, 1942, 56 Stat. 173, which provides that

> . . . whoever shall enter, remain in, leave, or commit any act in any military area or military zone prescribed, under the authority of an Executive order of the President, by the Secretary of War, or by any military commander designated by the Secretary of War, contrary to the restrictions applicable to any such area or zone or contrary to the order of the Secretary of War or any such military commander, shall, if it appears that he knew or should have known of the existence and extent of the restrictions or order and that his act was in violation thereof, be guilty of a misdemeanor and upon conviction shall be liable to a fine of not to exceed $5,000 or to imprisonment for not more than one year, or both, for each offense.

Exclusion Order No. 34, which the petitioner knowingly and admittedly violated, was one of a number of military orders and proclamations, all of which were substantially based upon Executive Order No. 9066, 7 Fed. Reg. 1407. That order, issued after we were at war with Japan, declared that

> the successful prosecution of the war requires every possible protection against espionage and against sabotage to national defense material, national defense premises, and national defense utilities. . . .

One of the series of orders and proclamations, a curfew order, which, like the exclusion order here, was promulgated pursuant to Executive Order 9066, subjected all persons of Japanese ancestry in prescribed West Coast military areas to remain in their residences from 8 p.m. to 6 a.m. As is the case with the exclusion order here, that prior curfew order was designed as a "protection against espionage and against sabotage." In *Hirabayashi v. United States,* . . . we sustained a conviction obtained for violation of the curfew order. The Hirabayashi conviction and this one thus rest on the same 1942 Congressional Act and the same basic executive and military orders, all of which orders were aimed at the twin dangers of espionage and sabotage.

The 1942 Act was attacked in the *Hirabayashi* case as an unconstitutional delegation of power; it was contended that the curfew order and other orders on which it rested were beyond the war powers of the Congress, the military authorities, and of the President, as Commander in Chief of the Army, and, finally, that to apply the curfew order against none but citizens of Japanese ancestry amounted to a constitutionally prohibited discrimination solely on account of race. To these questions, we gave the serious consideration which their importance justified. We upheld the curfew order as an exercise of the power of the government to take steps necessary to prevent espionage and sabotage in an area threatened by Japanese attack.

In the light of the principles we announced in the *Hirabayashi* case, we are unable to conclude that it was beyond the war power of Congress and the Executive to exclude those of Japanese ancestry from the West Coast war area at the time they did. True, exclusion from the area in which one's home is located is a far greater deprivation than constant confinement to the home from 8 p.m. to 6 a.m. Nothing short of apprehension by the proper military authorities of the gravest imminent danger to the public safety can constitutionally justify either. But exclusion from a threatened area, no less than curfew, has a definite and close relationship to the prevention of espionage and sabotage. The military authorities, charged with the primary responsibility of defending our shores, concluded that curfew provided inadequate protection and ordered exclusion. They did so, as pointed out in our *Hirabayashi* opinion, in accordance with Congressional authority to the military to say who should, and who should not, remain in the threatened areas.

In this case, the petitioner challenges the assumptions upon which we rested our conclusions in the *Hirabayashi* case. He also urges that, by May, 1942, when Order No. 34 was promulgated, all danger of Japanese invasion of the West Coast had disappeared. After careful consideration of these contentions, we are compelled to reject them. . . .

It is said that we are dealing here with the case of imprisonment of a citizen in a concentration camp solely because of his ancestry, without evidence or inquiry concerning his loyalty and good disposition towards the United States. Our task would be simple, our duty clear, were this a case involving the imprisonment of a loyal citizen in a concentration camp because of racial prejudice. Regardless of the true nature of the assembly and relocation centers—and we deem it unjustifiable to call them concentration camps, with all the ugly connotations that term implies—we are dealing specifically with nothing but an exclusion order. To cast this case into outlines of racial prejudice, without reference to the real military dangers which were presented, merely confuses the issue. Korematsu was not excluded from the Military Area because of hostility to him or his race. He was excluded because we are at war with the Japanese Empire, because the properly constituted military authorities feared an invasion of our West Coast and felt constrained to take proper security measures, because they decided that the military urgency of the situation demanded that all citizens of Japanese ancestry be segregated from the West Coast temporarily, and, finally, because Congress, reposing its confidence in this time of war in our military leaders—as inevitably it must—determined that they should have the power to do just this. There was evidence of disloyalty on the part of some, the military authorities considered that the need for action was great, and time was short. We cannot—by availing ourselves of the calm perspective of hindsight—now say that, at that time, these actions were unjustified. . . .

Mr. Justice Murphy, dissenting.

The judicial test of whether the Government, on a plea of military necessity, can validly deprive an individual of any of his constitutional rights is whether the deprivation is reasonably related to a public danger that is so "immediate, imminent, and impending" as not to admit of delay and not to permit the intervention of ordinary constitutional processes to alleviate the danger. . . . Civilian Exclusion Order No. 34, banishing from a prescribed area of the Pacific Coast "all persons of Japanese ancestry, both alien and non-alien," clearly does not meet that test. Being an obvious racial discrimination, the order deprives all those within its scope of the equal protection of the laws as guaranteed by the Fifth Amendment. It further deprives these individuals of their constitutional rights to live and work where they will, to establish a home where they choose and to move about freely. In excommunicating them without benefit of hearings, this order also deprives them of all their constitutional rights to procedural due process. Yet no reasonable relations to an "immediate, imminent, and impending" public danger is evident to support this racial restriction, which is one of the most sweeping and complete deprivations of constitutional rights in the history of this nation in the absence of martial law. . . .

Racial discrimination in any form and in any degree has no justifiable part whatever in our democratic way of life. It is unattractive in any setting, but it is utterly revolting among a free people who have embraced the principles set forth in the Constitution of the United States. All residents of this nation are kin in some way by blood or culture to a foreign land. Yet they are primarily and necessarily a part of the new and distinct civilization of the United States. They must, accordingly, be treated at all times as the heirs of the American experiment, and as entitled to all the rights and freedoms guaranteed by the Constitution.

Source: Korematsu v. United States, 323 U.S. 214 (1944)

49. Harry Truman: Executive Order 9981, 1948

Introduction

Signed by President Harry Truman on July 26, 1948, Executive Order 9981 created the President's Committee on Equality of Treatment and Opportunity in the Armed Forces. It quickly led to the desegregation of the U.S. military. Truman had promised presidential action on the issue of civil rights in a speech before Congress on February 2, 1948. This executive order, in conjunction with Executive Order 9980 (which established the Fair Employment Board in the Civil Service Commission), fulfilled that promise.

Primary Source

WHEREAS it is essential that there be maintained in the armed services of the United States the highest standards of democracy, with equality of treatment and opportunity for all those who serve in our country's defense:

NOW, THEREFORE, by virtue of the authority vested in me as President of the United States, by the Constitution and the statutes of the United States, and as Commander in Chief of the armed services, it is hereby ordered as follows:

1. It is hereby declared to be the policy of the President that there shall be equality of treatment and opportunity for all persons in the armed services without regard to race, color, religion or national origin. This policy shall be put into effect as rapidly as possible, having due regard to the time required to effectuate any necessary changes without impairing efficiency or morale.

2. There shall be created in the National Military Establishment an advisory committee to be known as the President's Committee on Equality of Treatment and Opportunity in the Armed Services, which shall be composed of seven members to be designated by the President.

3. The Committee is authorized on behalf of the President to examine into the rules, procures and practices of the armed services in order to determine in what respect such rules, procedures and practices may be altered or improved with a view to carrying out the policy of this order. The Committee shall confer and advise with the Secretary of Defense, the Secretary of the Army, the Secretary of the Navy, and the Secretary of the Air Force, and shall make such recommendations to the President and to said Secretaries as in the judgment of the Committee will effectuate the policy hereof.

4. All executive departments and agencies of the Federal Government are authorized and directed to cooperate with the Committee in its work, and to furnish the Committee such information or the services of such persons as the Committee may require in the performance of its duties.

5. When requested by the Committee to do so, persons in the armed services or in any of the executive departments and agencies of the Federal Government shall testify before the Committee and shall make available for the use of the Committee such documents and other information as the Committee may require.

6. The Committee shall continue to exist until such time as the President shall terminate its existence by Executive order.

HARRY S. TRUMAN
THE WHITE HOUSE,
July 26, 1948.

   Source: Federal Register, 13 FR4313 (July 28, 1948)

50. *Brown v. Board of Education,* 1954

Introduction

Few, if any, twentieth-century cases better demonstrate the ability of the Supreme Court to alter understandings of the Constitution—and thus provide a substitute for constitutional amendment—than *Brown v. Board of Education*. Here, the Court overturned the doctrine of separate but equal that had been sanctioned in *Plessy v. Ferguson* (1896) and declared that segregation would have no place in U.S. public education. This opinion, in turn, sparked both support and opposition, including numerous attempts to trim the power of the Court in succeeding decades.

Primary Source

MR. CHIEF JUSTICE WARREN delivered the opinion of the Court.

These cases come to us from the States of Kansas, South Carolina, Virginia, and Delaware. They are premised on different facts and different local conditions, but a common legal question justifies their consideration together in this consolidated opinion.

In each of the cases, minors of the Negro race, through their legal representatives, seek the aid of the courts in obtaining admission to the public schools of their community on a nonsegregated basis. In each instance, they had been denied admission to schools attended by white children under laws requiring or permitting segregation according to race. This segregation was alleged to deprive the plaintiffs of the equal protection of the laws under the Fourteenth Amendment. In each of the cases other than the Delaware case, a three-judge federal district court denied relief to the plaintiffs on the so-called "separate but equal" doctrine announced by this Court in *Plessy v. Ferguson.* Under that doctrine, equality of treatment is accorded when the races are provided substantially equal facilities, even though these facilities be separate. In the Delaware case, the Supreme Court of Delaware adhered to that doctrine, but ordered that the plaintiffs be admitted to the white schools because of their superiority to the Negro schools.

The plaintiffs contend that segregated public schools are not "equal" and cannot be made "equal," and that hence they are deprived of the equal protection of the laws. Because of the obvious importance of the question presented, the Court took jurisdiction. Argument was heard in the 1952 Term, and reargument was heard this Term on certain questions propounded by the Court.

Reargument was largely devoted to the circumstances surrounding the adoption of the Fourteenth Amendment in 1868. It covered exhaustively consideration of the Amendment in Congress, ratification by the states, then existing practices in racial segregation, and the views of proponents and opponents of the Amendment. This discussion and our own investigation convince us that, although these sources cast some light, it is not enough to resolve the problem with which we are faced. At best, they are inconclusive. The most avid proponents of the post-War Amendments undoubtedly intended them to remove all legal distinctions among "all persons born or naturalized in the United States." Their opponents, just as certainly, were antagonistic to both the letter and the spirit of the Amendments and wished them to have the most limited effect. What others in Congress and the state legislatures had in mind cannot be determined with any degree of certainty.

An additional reason for the inconclusive nature of the Amendment's history, with respect to segregated schools, is the status of public education at that time. In the South, the movement toward free common schools, supported by general taxation, had not yet taken hold. Education of white children was largely in the hands of private groups. Education of Negroes was almost nonexistent, and practically all of the race were illiterate. In fact, any education of Negroes was forbidden by law in some states. Today, in contrast, many Negroes have achieved outstanding success in the arts and sciences as well as in the business and professional world. It is true that public school education at the time of the Amendment had advanced further in the North, but the effect of the Amendment on Northern States was generally ignored in the congressional debates. Even in the North, the conditions of public education did not approximate those existing today. The curriculum was usually rudimentary; ungraded schools were common in rural areas; the school term was but three months a year in many states; and compulsory school attendance was virtually unknown. As a consequence, it is not surprising that there should be so little in the history of the Fourteenth Amendment relating to its intended effect on public education.

In the first cases in this Court construing the Fourteenth Amendment, decided shortly after its adoption, the Court interpreted it as proscribing all state-imposed discriminations against the Negro race. The doctrine of "separate but equal" did not make its appearance in this Court until 1896 in the case of *Plessy v. Ferguson*, involving not education but transportation. American courts have since labored with the doctrine for over half a century. In this Court, there have been six cases involving the "separate but equal" doctrine in the field of public education. In *Cumming v. County Board of Education*, and *Gong Lum v. Rice*, the validity of the doctrine itself was not challenged. In more recent cases, all on the graduate school level, inequality was found in that specific benefits enjoyed by white students were denied to Negro students of the same educational qualifications. . . . In none of these cases was it necessary to re-examine the doctrine to grant relief to the Negro plaintiff. And in *Sweatt v. Painter*, the Court expressly reserved decision on the question whether *Plessy v. Ferguson* should be held inapplicable to public education.

In the instant cases, that question is directly presented. Here, unlike *Sweatt v. Painter*, there are findings below that the Negro and white schools involved have been equalized, or are being equalized, with respect to buildings, curricula, qualifications and salaries of teachers, and other "tangible" factors. Our decision, therefore, cannot turn on merely a comparison of these tangible factors in the Negro and white schools involved in each of the cases. We must look instead to the effect of segregation itself on public education.

In approaching this problem, we cannot turn the clock back to 1868 when the Amendment was adopted, or even to 1896 when *Plessy v. Ferguson* was written. We must consider public education in the light of its full development and its present place in American life throughout the Nation. Only in this way can it be determined if segregation in public schools deprives these plaintiffs of the equal protection of the laws.

Today, education is perhaps the most important function of state and local governments. Compulsory school attendance laws and the great expenditures for education both demonstrate our recognition of the importance of education to our democratic society. It is required in the performance of our most basic public responsibilities, even service in the armed forces. It is the very foundation of good citizenship. Today it is a principal instrument in awakening the child to cultural values, in preparing him for later professional training, and in helping him to adjust normally to his environment. In these days, it is doubtful that any child may reasonably be expected to succeed in life if he is denied the opportunity of an education. Such an opportunity, where the state has undertaken to provide it, is a right which must be made available to all on equal terms.

We come then to the question presented: Does segregation of children in public schools solely on the basis of race, even though the physical facilities and other "tangible" factors may be equal, deprive the children of the minority group of equal educational opportunities? We believe that it does.

In *Sweatt v. Painter*, in finding that a segregated law school for Negroes could not provide them equal educational opportunities, this Court relied in large part on "those qualities which are incapable of objective measurement but which make for greatness in a law school." In *McLaurin v. Oklahoma State Regents*, the Court, in requiring that a Negro admitted to a white graduate school be treated like all other students, again resorted to intangible considerations: ". . . his ability to study, to engage in discussions and exchange views with other students, and, in general, to learn his profession." Such considerations apply with added force to children in grade and high schools. To separate them from others of similar age and qualifications solely because of their race generates a feeling of inferiority as to their status in the community that may affect their hearts and minds in a way unlikely ever to be undone. The effect of this separation on their educational opportunities was well stated by a finding in the Kansas case by a court which nevertheless felt compelled to rule against the Negro plaintiffs:

Segregation of white and colored children in public schools has a detrimental effect upon the colored children. The impact is greater when it has the sanction of the law; for the policy of separating the races is usually interpreted as denoting the inferiority of the negro group. A sense of inferiority affects the motivation of a child to learn. Segregation with the sanction of law, therefore, has a tendency to [retard] the educational and mental development of negro children and to deprive them of some of the benefits they would receive in a racial[ly] integrated school system.

Whatever may have been the extent of psychological knowledge at the time of *Plessy v. Ferguson*, this finding is amply supported by modern authority. Any language in *Plessy v. Ferguson* contrary to this finding is rejected.

We conclude that in the field of public education the doctrine of "separate but equal" has no place. Separate educational facilities are inherently unequal. Therefore, we hold that the plaintiffs and others similarly situated for whom the actions have been brought are, by reason of the segregation complained of, deprived of the equal protection of the laws guaranteed by the Fourteenth Amendment. This disposition makes unnecessary any discussion whether such segregation also violates the Due Process Clause of the Fourteenth Amendment.

Because these are class actions, because of the wide applicability of this decision, and because of the great variety of local conditions, the formulation of decrees in these cases presents problems of considerable complexity. On reargument, the consideration of appropriate relief was necessarily subordinated to the primary question—the constitutionality of segregation in public education. We have now announced that such segregation is a denial of the equal protection of the laws. In order that we may have the full assistance of the parties in formulating decrees, the cases will be restored to the docket, and the parties are requested to present further argument on Questions 4 and 5 previously propounded by the Court for the reargument this Term. The Attorney General of the United States is again invited to participate. The Attorneys General of the states requiring or permitting segregation in public education will also be permitted to appear as amici curiae upon request to do so by September 15, 1954, and submission of briefs by October 1, 1954.

It is so ordered.

> *Source: Oliver Brown et al. v. Board of Education of Topeka, Kansas,* 347 U.S. 483 (1954)

51. *Brown v. Board of Education,* 1955

Introduction

In *Brown v. Board of Education* (1954), the U.S. Supreme Court ruled that the system of separate but equal in education and other fields would have to end. Because that system of racial segregation had been in place for so long, the Court recognized that immediate implementation of the decision might be impossible. It accordingly asked the parties to reargue the implementation issue. The following year *Brown v. Board of Education* (1955) was the result.

Primary Source

MR. CHIEF JUSTICE WARREN delivered the opinion of the Court.

These cases were decided on May 17, 1954. The opinions of that date, declaring the fundamental principle that racial discrimination in public education is unconstitutional, are incorporated herein by reference. All provisions of federal, state, or local law requiring or permitting such discrimination must yield to this principle. There remains for consideration the manner in which relief is to be accorded.

Because these cases arose under different local conditions and their disposition will involve a variety of local problems, we requested further argument on the question of relief. In view of the nationwide importance of the decision, we invited the Attorney General of the United States and the Attorneys General of all states requiring or permitting racial discrimination in public education to present their views on that question. The parties, the United States, and the States of Florida, North Carolina, Arkansas, Oklahoma, Maryland, and Texas filed briefs and participated in the oral argument.

These presentations were informative and helpful to the Court in its consideration of the complexities arising from the transition to a system of public education freed of racial discrimination. The presentations also demonstrated that substantial steps to eliminate racial discrimination in public schools have already been taken, not only in some of the communities in which these cases arose, but in some of the states appearing as amici curiae, and in other states as well. Substantial progress has been made in the District of Columbia and in the communities in Kansas and Delaware involved in this litigation. The defendants in the cases coming to us from South Carolina and Virginia are awaiting the decision of this Court concerning relief.

Full implementation of these constitutional principles may require solution of varied local school problems. School authorities have the primary responsibility for elucidating, assessing, and solving these problems; courts will have to consider whether the action of school authorities constitutes good faith implementation of the governing constitutional principles. Because of their proximity to local conditions and the possible need for further hearings, the courts which originally heard these cases can best perform this judicial appraisal. Accordingly, we believe it appropriate to remand the cases to those courts.

In fashioning and effectuating the decrees, the courts will be guided by equitable principles. Traditionally, equity has been characterized by a practical flexibility in shaping its remedies and by a facility for adjusting and reconciling public and private needs. These cases call for the exercise of these traditional attributes of equity power. At stake is the personal interest of the plaintiffs in admission to public schools as soon as practicable on a nondiscriminatory basis. To effectuate this interest may call for elimination of a variety of obstacles in making the transition to school systems operated in accordance with the constitutional principles set forth in our May 17, 1954, decision. Courts of equity may properly take into account the public interest in the elimination of such obstacles in a systematic and effective manner. But it should go without saying that the vitality of these constitutional principles cannot be allowed to yield simply because of disagreement with them.

While giving weight to these public and private considerations, the courts will require that the defendants make a prompt and reasonable start toward full compliance with our May 17, 1954, ruling. Once such a start has been made, the courts may find that additional time is necessary to carry out the ruling in an effective manner. The burden rests upon the defendants to establish that such time is necessary in the public interest and is consistent with good faith compliance at the earliest practicable date. To that end, the courts may consider problems related to administration, arising from the physical condition of the school plant, the school transportation system, personnel, revision of school districts and attendance areas into compact units to achieve a system of determining admission to the public schools on a nonracial basis, and revision of local laws and regulations which may be necessary in solving the foregoing problems. They will also consider the adequacy of any plans the defendants may propose to meet these problems and to effectuate a transition to a racially nondiscriminatory school system. During this period of transition, the courts will retain jurisdiction of these cases.

The judgments below, except that in the Delaware case, are accordingly reversed and the cases are remanded to the District Courts to take such proceedings and enter such orders and decrees consistent with this opinion as are necessary and proper to admit to public schools on a racially nondiscriminatory basis with all deliberate speed the parties to these cases. The judgment in the Delaware case—ordering the immediate admission of the plaintiffs to schools previously attended only by white children—is affirmed on the basis of the principles stated in our May 17, 1954, opinion, but the case is remanded to the Supreme Court of Delaware for such further proceedings as that Court may deem necessary in light of this opinion.

It is so ordered.

Source: Brown v. Board of Education, 349 U.S. 294 (1955)

52. Executive Order 10730, 1957

Introduction

In 1954, the U.S. Supreme Court handed down its decision in *Brown v. Board of Education*, which declared segregated ("separate but equal") public schools unconstitutional. Many white Americans, citing states' rights, responded with promises to organize acts of "massive resistance" against the ensuing federal court orders to desegregate schools. One dramatic confrontation began with the refusal by Arkansas state governor Orval Faubus to honor a federal judge's order to integrate the schools. Under Executive Order 10730, President Dwight Eisenhower placed the Arkansas National Guard under federal control and sent Army troops to escort nine black students (the "Little Rock Nine") into Little Rock Central High School, an all-white public school.

Primary Source

PROVIDING ASSISTANCE FOR THE REMOVAL OF AN OBSTRUCTION OF JUSTICE WITHIN THE STATE OF ARKANSAS

WHEREAS on September 23, 1957, I issued Proclamation No. 3204 reading in part as follows:

WHEREAS certain persons in the state of Arkansas, individually and in unlawful assemblages, combinations, and conspiracies, have wilfully obstructed the enforcement of orders of the United States Court for the Eastern District of Arkansas with respect to matters relating to enrollment and attendance at public schools, particularly at Central High School, located in Little Rock school district, Little Rock, Arkansas: and

WHEREAS such wilful obstruction of justice hinders the execution of the laws of the state and of the United States, and makes it impracticable to enforce such laws by the ordinary course of judicial proceeding; and

WHEREAS such obstruction of justice constitutes a denial of the equal protection of the laws secured by the Constitution of the United States and impedes the course of justice under those laws;

NOW THEREFORE, I, Dwight D. Eisenhower, President of the United States, under and by virtue of the authority vested in me by the Constitution and the statutes of the United States, including Chapter 15 of Title 10 of the United States Code, particularly Sections 332, 333, and 334 thereof, do command all persons engaged in such obstruction of justice to cease and desist therefrom, and to disperse forthwith; and

WHEREAS the command contained in that proclamation has not been obeyed and wilful obstruction of enforcement of said court orders still exists and threatens to continue:

Now, therefore, by virtue of the authority vested in me by the Constitution and statutes of the United States, including Chapter 15 of Title 10, particularly Sections 332, 333, and 334 thereof, and Section 301 of Title 3 of the United States Code, it is hereby ordered as follows:

Section 1. I hereby authorize and direct the Secretary of Defense to order into the active military service of the United States as he may deem appropriate to carry out the purposes of this order, any or all of the units of the National Guard of the United States and of the Air National Guard of the United States within the state of Arkansas to serve in the active military service of the United States for an indefinite period and until relieved by appropriate orders.

Section 2. The Secretary of Defense is authorized and directed to take all appropriate steps to enforce any orders of the United States District Court for the Eastern District of Arkansas for the removal of obstruction of justice in the state of Arkansas with respect to matters relating to enrollment and attendance at public schools in the Little Rock School District, Little Rock, Arkansas. To carry out the provisions of this section, the Secretary of Defense is authorized to use the units, and members thereof, ordered into the active military service of the United States pursuant to Section 1 of this order.

Section 3. In furtherance of the enforcement of the aforementioned orders of the United States District Court for the Eastern District of Arkansas, the Secretary of Defense is authorized to use such of the armed forces of the United States as he may deem necessary.

Section 4. The Secretary of Defense is authorized to delegate to the Secretary of the Army or the Secretary of the Air Force, or both, any of the authority conferred upon him by this order.

DWIGHT D. EISENHOWER
THE WHITE HOUSE,
September 24, 1957

Source: Executive Order 10730, 3 CFR 89 (Supp. 1957)

53. Equal Pay Act, 1963

Introduction

Enacted on June 10, 1963, the Equal Pay Act required equal pay for both genders for jobs requiring substantially equal skill, effort, and responsibility and for jobs that have similar working conditions. One of several federal efforts to eradicate sex discrimination, the Equal Pay Act remains in effect today, although the inequality between women's and men's pay continues to exist. Many women's rights activists have criticized the law's narrow focus.

Primary Source

An Act to prohibit discrimination on account of sex in the payment of wages by employers engaged in commerce or in the production of goods for commerce. Be it enacted by the Senate and House of Representatives of the United States of America in Congress assembled. That this Act may be cited as the "Equal Pay Act of 1963."

Declaration of Purpose

Section 2.

(a) The Congress hereby finds that the existence in industries engaged in commerce or in the production of goods for commerce of wage differentials based on sex—

(1) depressed wages and living standards for employees necessary for their health and efficiency:

(2) prevents the maximum utilization of the available labor resources;

(3) tends to cause labor disputes, thereby burdening, affecting, and obstructing commerce;

(4) burdens commerce and the free flow of goods in commerce; and

(5) constitutes an unfair method of competition.

(b) It is hereby declared to be the policy of this Act, through exercise by Congress of its power to regulate commerce among the several States and with foreign nations, to correct the conditions above referred to in such industries.

Section 3. Section 6 of the Fair Labor Standards Act of 1938, as amended (29 U.S.C. et seq.), is amended by adding thereto a new subsection (d) as follows:

"(d)(1) No employer having employees subject to any provisions of this section shall discriminate, within any establishment in which such employees are employed, between employees on the basis of sex by paying wages to employees in such establishment at a rate less than the rate at which he pays wages to employees of the opposite sex in such establishment for equal work on jobs the performance of which requires equal skill, effort, and responsibility, and which are performed under similar working conditions, except where such payment is made pursuant to (i) a seniority system; (ii) a merit system; (iii) a system which measures earnings by quantity or quality of production; or (iv) a differential based on any other factor other than sex: Provided, That an employer who is paying a wage rate differential in violation of this subsection shall not, in order to comply with the provisions of this subsection, reduce the wage rate of any employee.

"(2) No labor organization, or its agents, representing employees of an employer having employees subject to any provisions of this section shall cause or attempt to cause such an employer to discriminate against an employee in violation of paragraph (1) of this subsection.

"(3) For purpose of administration and enforcement, any amounts owing to any employee which have been withheld in violation of this subsection shall be deemed to be unpaid minimum wages or unpaid overtime compensation under this Act.

"(4) As used in this subsection, the term 'labor organization' means any organization of any kind, or any agency or employee representation committee or plan, in which employees participate and which exists for the purpose, in whole or in part, of dealing with employers concerning grievances, labor disputes, wages, rates of pay, hours of employment or conditions of work."

Section 4. The amendments made by this Act shall take effect upon the expiration of one year from the date of its enactment: Provided, That in the case of employees covered by a bona fide collective bargaining agreement in effect at least thirty days prior to the date of enactment of this Act, entered into by a labor organization (as defined in section 6(d) (4) of the Fair Labor Standards Act of 1938, as amended), the amendments made by this Act shall take effect upon the termination of such collective bargaining agreement or upon the expiration of two years from the date of enactment of this Act, whichever shall first occur.

Source: Public Law 88-38, *U.S. Statutes at Large* 77 (1963): 56

54. Civil Rights Act, 1964

Introduction

The Civil Rights Act of 1964, a landmark in American legal history, provided much of the legal basis for the modern civil rights movement. Enacted on July 2, 1964, the law is lengthy and covers many areas of discrimination, most notably voting rights and segregation. Although it was originally passed to protect the rights of African Americans, sections of the law have since been used by a variety of groups in their fight against discrimination.

Primary Source

AN ACT to enforce the constitutional right to vote, to confer jurisdiction upon the district courts of the United States to provide injunctive relief against discrimination in public accommodations, to authorize the Attorney General to institute suits to protect constitutional rights in public facilities and public education, to extend the Commission on Civil Rights, to prevent discrimination in federally assisted programs, to establish a Commission on Equal Employment Opportunity, and for other purposes.

Be it enacted by the Senate and House of Representatives of the United States of America in Congress assembled. That this Act may be cited as the "Civil Rights Act of 1964."

TITLE I—VOTING RIGHTS

Section 101.
Section 2004 of the Revised Statutes (42 U.S.C. 1971), as amended by section 131 of the Civil Rights Act of 1957 (71 Stat. 637), and as further amended by section 601 of the Civil Rights Act of 1960 (74 Stat. 90), is further amended as follows:

(a) Insert "1" after "(a)" in subsection (a) and add at the end of subsection (a) the following new paragraphs:

"(2) No person acting under color of law shall—

"(A) in determining whether any individual is qualified under State law or laws to vote in any Federal election, apply any standard, practice, or procedure different from the standards, practices, or procedures applied under such law or laws to other individuals within the same county, parish, or similar political subdivision who have been found by State officials to be qualified to vote;

"(B) deny the right of any individual to vote in any Federal election because of an error or omission on any record or paper relating to any application, registration, or other act requisite to voting, if such error or omission is not material in determining whether such individual is qualified under State law to vote in such election; or

"(C) employ any literacy test as a qualification for voting in any Federal election unless (i) such test is administered to each individual and is conducted wholly in writing, and (ii) a certified copy of the test and of the answers given by the individual is furnished to him within twenty-five days of the submission of his request made within the period of time during which records and papers are required to be retained and preserved pursuant to Title III of the Civil Rights Act of 1960 (42 U.S.C. 1974-74e; 74 Stat. 88): Provided, however, That the Attorney General may enter into agreements with appropriate State or local authorities that preparation, conduct, and maintenance of such tests in accordance with the provisions of applicable State or local law, including such special provisions as are necessary in the preparation, conduct, and maintenance of such tests for persons who are blind or otherwise physically handicapped, meet the purposes of this subparagraph and constitute compliance therewith.

"(3) For purposes of this subsection—

"(A) the term 'vote' shall have the same meaning as in subsection (e) of this section;

"(B) the phrase 'literacy test' includes any test of the ability to read, write, understand, or interpret any matter."

(b) Insert immediately following the period at the end of the first sentence of subsection (c) the following new sentence: "If in any such proceeding literacy is a relevant fact there shall be a rebuttable presumption that any person who has not been adjudged an incompetent and who has completed the sixth grade in a public school in, or a private school accredited by, any State or territory, the District of Columbia, or the Commonwealth of Puerto Rico where instruction is carried on predominantly in the English language, possesses sufficient literacy, comprehension, and intelligence to vote in any Federal election."

(c) Add the following subsection "(f)" and designate the present subsection "(f)" as subsection "(g)": "(f) When used in subsection (a) or (c) of this section, the words 'Federal election' shall mean any general, special, or primary election held solely or in part for the purpose of electing or selecting any candidate for the office of President, Vice President, presidential elector, Member of the Senate, or Member of the House of Representatives."

(d) Add the following subsection "(h)":

"(h) In any proceeding instituted by the United States in any district court of the United States under this section in which the Attorney General requests a finding of a pattern or practice of discrimination pursuant to subsection (e) of this section the Attorney General, at the time he files the complaint, or any defendant in the proceeding, within twenty days after service upon him of the complaint, may file with the clerk of such court a request that a court of three judges be convened to hear and determine the entire case. A copy of the request for a three-judge court shall be immediately furnished by such clerk to the chief judge of the circuit (or in his absence, the presiding circuit judge of the circuit) in which the case is pending. Upon receipt of the copy of such request it shall be the duty of the chief judge of the circuit or the presiding circuit judge, as the case may be, to designate immediately three judges in such circuit, of whom at least one shall be a circuit judge and another of whom shall be a district judge of the court in which the proceeding who instituted, to hear and determine such case, and it shall be the duty of the judges so designated to assign the case for hearing at the earliest practicable date, to participate in the hearing and determination thereof, and to cause the case to be in every way expedited.

An appeal from the final judgment of such court will lie to the Supreme Court.

"In any proceeding brought under subsection (c) of this section to enforce subsection (b) of this section, or in the event neither the Attorney General nor any defendant files a request for a three-judge court in any proceeding authorized by this subsection, it shall be the duty of the chief judge of the district (or in his absence, the acting chief judge) in which the case is pending immediately to designate a judge in such district to hear and determine the case. In the event that no judge in the district, or the acting chief judge, as the case may be, shall certify this fact to the chief judge of the circuit (or, in his absence, the acting chief judge) who shall then designate a district or circuit judge of the circuit to hear and determine the case.

"It shall be the duty of the judge designated pursuant to this section to assign the case for hearing at the earliest practicable date and to cause the case to be in every way expedited."

TITLE II—INJUNCTIVE RELIEF AGAINST DISCRIMINATION IN PLACES OF PUBLIC ACCOMMODATION

Section 201.
(a) All persons shall be entitled to the full and equal enjoyment of the goods, services, facilities, privileges, advantages, and accommodations of any place of public accommodation, as defined in this section, without discrimination or segregation on the ground of race, color, religion, or national origin.

(b) Each of the following establishments which serves the public is a place of public accommodation within the meaning of this title if its operations affect commerce, if discrimination or segregation by it is supported by State action:

(1) any inn, hotel, motel, or other establishment which provides lodging to transient guests, other than an establishment located within a building which contains not more than five rooms for rent or hire and which is actually occupied by the proprietor of such establishment as his residence;

(2) any restaurant, cafeteria, lunchroom, lunch counter, soda fountain, or other facility principally engaged in selling food for consumption on the premises, including, but not limited to, any such facility located on the premises of any retail establishment; or any gasoline station;

(3) any motion picture house, theater, concert hall, sports arena, stadium or other place of exhibition or entertainment; and

(4) any establishment (A) (i) which is physically located within the premises of any establishment otherwise covered by this subsection, or (ii) within the premises of which is physically located any such covered establishment, and (B) which holds itself out as serving patrons of such covered establishment.

(c) The operations of an establishment affect commerce within the meaning of this title if (1) it is one of the establishments described in paragraph (1) of subsection (b); (2) in the case of an establishment described in paragraph (2) of subsection (b), it serves or offers to serve interstate travelers or a substantial portion of the food which it serves, or gasoline or other products which it sells, has moved in commerce; (3) in the case of an establishment described in paragraph (3) of subsection (b), it customarily present films, performances, athletic teams, exhibitions, or other sources of entertainment which move in commerce; and (4) in the case of an establishment which move in commerce; and (4) in the case of an establishment described in paragraph (4) of subsection (b), it is physically located within the premises of, or there is physically located within its premises, an establishment the operations of which affect commerce within the meaning of this subsection. For purposes of this section, "commerce" means travel, trade, traffic, commerce, transportation, or communication among the several States, or between the District of Columbia and any State, or between any foreign country or any territory or possession and any State or the District of Columbia, or between points in the same State but through any other State or the District of Columbia or a foreign country.

(d) Discrimination or segregation by an establishment is supported by State action within the meaning of this title if such discrimination or segregation (1) is carried on under color of any law, statute, ordinance, or regulation; or (2) is carried on under color of any custom or usage required or enforced by officials of the State or political subdivision thereof; or (3) is required by action of the State or political subdivision thereof.

(e) The provisions of this title shall not apply to a private club or other establishment not in fact open to the public, except to the extent that the facilities of such establishment are made available to the customers or patrons of an establishment within the scope of subsection (b).

Section 202.
All persons shall be entitled to be free, at any establishment or place, from discrimination or segregation of any kind on the ground of race, color, religion, or national origin, if such discrimination or segregation is or purports to be required by any law, statute, ordinance, regulation, rule, or order of a State or any agency or political subdivision thereof.

Section 203.
No person shall (a) withhold, deny, or attempt to withhold or deny, or deprive or attempt to deprive, any person of any right or privilege secured by section 201 or 202, or (b) intimidate, threaten, or coerce, or attempt to intimidate, threaten, or coerce any person with the purpose of interfering with any right or privilege secured by section 201 or 202, or (c) punish or attempt to punish any person for exercising or attempting to exercise any right or privilege secured by section 201 or 202., or (b) intimidate, threaten, or coerce, or attempt to intimidate, threaten, or coerce any person with the purpose of interfering with any right or privilege secured by section 201 or 202, or (c) punish or attempt to punish any person for exercising or attempting to exercise any right or privilege secured by section 201 or 202.

Section 204.
(a) Whenever any person has engaged or there are reasonable grounds to believe that any person is about to engage in any act or practice prohibited by section 203, a civil action for preventive relief, including an application for a permanent or temporary injunction, restraining order, or other order, may be instituted by the person aggrieved and, upon timely application, the court may, in its discretion, permit the Attorney General to intervene in such civil action if he certifies that the case is of general public importance. Upon application by the complainant and in such circumstances as the court may deem just, the court may appoint an attorney for such complainant and may authorize the commencement of the civil action without the payment of fees, costs, or security.

(b) In any action commenced pursuant to this title, the court, in its discretion, may allow the prevailing party, other than the United States, a reasonable attorney's fee as part of the costs, and the United States shall be liable for costs the same as a private person.

(c) In the case of an alleged act or practice prohibited by this title which occurs in a State, or political subdivision of a State, which has a State or local law prohibiting such act or practice and establishing or authorizing a State or local authority to grant or seek relief from such practice or to institute criminal proceedings with respect thereto upon receiving notice thereof, no civil action may be brought under subsection (a) before the expiration of thirty days after written notice of such alleged act or practice has been given to the appropriate State or local authority by registered mail or in person, provided that the court may stay proceedings in such civil action pending the termination of State or local enforcement proceedings.

(d) In the case of an alleged act or practice prohibited by this title which occurs in a State, or political subdivision of a State, which has no State or local law prohibiting such act or practice, a civil action may be brought under subsection (a): Provided, That the court may refer the matter to the Community Relations Service established by title X of this Act for as long as the court believes there is a reasonable possibility of obtaining voluntary compliance, but for not more than sixty days: Provided further, That upon expiration of such sixty-day period, the court may extend such period for an additional period, not to exceed a cumulative total of one hundred and twenty days, if it believes there then exists a reasonable possibility of securing voluntary compliance.

Section 205.
The Service is authorized to make a full investigation of any complaint referred to it by the court under section 204(d) and may hold such hearing with respect thereto as may be necessary. The Service shall conduct any hearings with respect to any such complaint in executive session, and shall not release any testimony given therein except by agreement of all parties involved in the complaint with the permission of the court, and the Service shall endeavor to bring about a voluntary settlement between the parties.

Section 206.
(a) Whenever the Attorney General has reasonable cause to believe that any person or group of persons is engaged in a pattern or practice of resistance to the full enjoyment of any of the rights secured by this title, and that the pattern or practice is of such a nature and is intended to deny the full exercise of the rights herein described,

the Attorney General may bring a civil action in the appropriate district court of the United States by filing with it a complaint

(1) signed by him (or in his absence the Acting Attorney General),

(2) setting forth facts pertaining to such pattern or practice, and

(3) requesting such preventive relief, including an application for a permanent or temporary injunction, restraining order or other order against the person or persons responsible for such pattern or practice, as he deems necessary to insure the full enjoyment of the rights herein described.

(b) In any such proceeding the Attorney General may file with the clerk of such court a request that a court of three judges to be convened to hear and determine the case. Such request by the Attorney General shall be accompanied by a certificate that, in his opinion, the case is of general public importance. A copy of the certificate and request for a three-judge court shall be immediately furnished by such clerk to the chief judge of the circuit (or in his absence, the presiding circuit judge of the circuit) in which the case is pending. Upon receipt of the copy of such request it shall be the duty of the chief judge of the circuit or the presiding circuit judge, as the case may be, to designate immediately three judges in such circuit, of whom at least one shall be a circuit judge and another of whom shall be a district judge of the court in which the proceeding was instituted, to hear and determine such case, and it shall be the duty of the judges so designated to assign the case for hearing at the earliest practicable date, to participate in the hearing and determination thereof, and to cause the case to be in every way expedited. An appeal from the final judgment of such court will lie to the Supreme Court.

In the event the Attorney General fails to file such a request in any such proceeding, it shall be the duty of the chief judge of the district (or in his absence, the acting chief judge) in which the case is pending immediately to designate a judge in such district to hear and determine the case. In the event that no judge in the district is available to hear and determine the case, the chief judge of the district, or the acting chief judge, as the case may be, shall certify this fact to the chief judge of the circuit (or in his absence, the acting chief judge) who shall then designate a district or circuit judge of the circuit to hear and determine the case.

It shall be the duty of the judge designated pursuant to this section to assign the case for hearing at the earliest practicable date and to cause the case to be in every way expedited.

Section 207.

(a) The district courts of the United States shall have jurisdiction of proceedings instituted pursuant to this title and shall exercise the same without regard to whether the aggrieved party shall have exhausted any administrative or other remedies that may be provided by law.

(b) The remedies provided in this title shall be the exclusive means of enforcing the rights based on this title, but nothing in this title shall preclude any individual or any State or local agency from asserting any right based on any other Federal or State law not inconsistent with this title, including any statute or ordinance requiring nondiscrimination in public establishments or accommodations, or from pursuing any remedy, civil or criminal, which may be available for the vindication or enforcement of such right.

TITLE III—DESEGREGATION OF PUBLIC FACILITIES

Section 301.

(a) Whenever the Attorney General receives a complaint in writing signed by an individual to the effect that he is being deprived of or threatened with the loss of his right to the equal protection of the laws, on account of his race, color, religion, or national origin, by being denied equal utilization of any public facility which is owned, operated, or managed by or on behalf of any State or subdivision thereof, other than a public school or public college as defined in section 401 of title IV hereof, and the Attorney General believes the complaint is meritorious and certifies that the signer or signers of such complaint are unable, in his judgment, to initiate and maintain appropriate legal proceedings for relief and that the institution of an action will materially further the orderly progress of desegregation in public facilities, the Attorney General is authorized to institute for or in the name of the United States a civil action in any appropriate district court of the United States against such parties and for such relief as may be appropriate, and such court shall have and shall exercise jurisdiction of proceedings instituted pursuant to this section. The Attorney General may implead as defendants such additional parties as are or become necessary to the grant of effective relief hereunder.

(b) The Attorney General may deem a person or persons unable to initiate and maintain appropriate legal proceedings within the meaning of subsection (a) of this section when such person or persons are unable, either directly or through other interested persons or organizations, to bear the expense of the litigation or to obtain effective legal representation: or whenever he is satisfied that the institution of such litigation would jeopardize the personal safety, employment, or economic standing of such person or persons, their families, or their property.

Section 302.
In any action or proceeding under this title the United States shall be liable for costs, including a reasonable attorney's fee, the same as a private person.

Section 303.
Nothing in this title shall affect adversely the right of any person to sue for or obtain relief in any court against discrimination in any facility covered by this title.

Section 304.
A complaint as used in this title is a writing or document within the meaning of section 1001, title 18, United States Code.

TITLE IV—DESEGREGATION OF PUBLIC EDUCATION

Section 401. Definitions
As used in this title—

(a) "Commissioner" means the Commissioner of Education.

(b) "Desegregation" means the assignment of students to public schools and within such schools without regard to their race, color, religion, or national origin, but "desegregation" shall not mean the assignment of students to public schools in order to overcome racial imbalance.

(c) "Public school" means any elementary or secondary educational institution, and "public college" means any institution of higher education or any technical or vocational school above the secondary school level, provided that such public school or public college is operated by a State, subdivision of a State, or governmental agency within a State, or operated wholly or predominantly from or through the use of governmental funds or property, or funds or property derived from a governmental source.

(d) "School board" means any agency or agencies which administer a system of one or more public schools and any other agency which is responsible for the assignment of students to or within such system.

Section 402. Survey and Report of Educational Opportunities
The Commissioner shall conduct a survey and make a report to the President and the Congress, within two years of the enactment of this title, concerning the lack of availability of equal educational opportunities for individuals by reason of race, color, religion, or national origin in public educational institutions at all levels in the United States, its territories and possessions, and the District of Columbia.

Section 403. Technical Assistance

The Commissioner is authorized, upon the application of any school board, State, municipality, school district, or other governmental unit legally responsible for operating a public school or schools, to render technical assistance to such applicant in the preparation, adoption, and implementation of plans for the desegregation of public schools. Such technical assistance may, among other activities, include making available to such agencies information regarding effective methods of coping with special educational problems occasioned by desegregation, and making available to such agencies personnel of the Office of Education or other persons specially equipped to advise and assist them in coping with such problems.

Section 404. Training Institutes

The Commissioner is authorized to arrange, through grants or contracts, with institutions of higher education for the operation of short-term or regular session institutes for special training designed to improve the ability of teachers, supervisors, counselors, and other elementary or secondary school personnel to deal effectively with special education problems occasioned by desegregation. Individuals who attend such an institute on a full-time basis may be paid stipends for the period of their attendance at such institute in amounts specified by the Commissioner in regulations, including allowances for travel to attend such institute.

Section 405. Grants

(a) The Commissioner is authorized, upon the application of a school board, to make grants to such board to pay, in whole or in part, the cost of—

(1) giving to teachers and other school personnel inservice training in dealing with problems incident to desegregation, and

(2) employing specialists to advise in problems incident to desegregation.

(b) In determining whether to make a grant, and in fixing the amount thereof and the terms and conditions on which it will be made, the Commissioner shall take into consideration the amount available for grants under this section and the other applications which are pending before him; the financial condition of the applicant and the other resources available to it; the nature, extent, and gravity of its problems incident to desegregation; and such other factors as he finds relevant.

Section 406. Payments

Payments pursuant to a grant or contract under this title may be made (after necessary adjustments on account of previously made overpayments or underpayments) in advance or by way of reimbursement, and in such installments, as the Commissioner may determine.

Section 407. Suits By the Attorney General
(a) Whenever the Attorney General receives a complaint in writing—

(1) signed by a parent or group of parents to the effect that his or their minor children, as members of a class of persons similarly situated, are being deprived by a school board of the equal protection of the laws, or

(2) signed by an individual, or his parent, to the effect that he has been denied admission to or not permitted to continue in attendance at a public college by reason of race, color, religion, or national origin, and the Attorney General believes the complaint is meritorious and certifies that the signer or signers of such complaint are unable, in his judgment, to initiate and maintain appropriate legal proceedings for relief and that the institution of an action will materially further the orderly achievement of desegregation in public education, the Attorney General is authorized, after giving notice of such complaint to the appropriate school board or college authority and after certifying that he is satisfied that such board or authority has had a reasonable time to adjust the conditions alleged in such complaint, to institute for or in the name of the United States a civil action in any appropriate district court of the United States against such parties and for such relief as may be appropriate, and such court shall have and shall exercise jurisdiction of proceedings instituted pursuant to this section, provided that nothing herein shall empower any official or court of the United States to issue any order seeking to achieve a racial balance in any school by requiring the transportation of pupils or students from one school to another or one school district to another in order to achieve such racial balance, or otherwise enlarge the existing power of the court to insure compliance with constitutional standards. The Attorney General may implead as defendants such additional parties as are or become necessary to the grant of effective relief hereunder.

(b) The Attorney General may deem a person or persons unable to initiate and maintain appropriate legal proceedings within the meaning of subsection (a) of this section when such person or persons are unable, either directly or through other interested persons or organizations, to bear the expense of the litigation or to obtain effective legal representation: or whenever he is satisfied that the institution of such litigation would jeopardize the personal safety, employment, or economic standing of such person or persons, their families, or their property.

(c) The term "parent" as used in this section includes any person standing in loco parentis. A "complaint" as used in this section is a writing or document within the meaning of section 1001, title 18, United States Code.

Section 408.
In any action or proceeding under this title the United States shall be liable for costs the same as a private person.

Section 409.
Nothing in this title shall prohibit classification ad assignment for reasons other than race, color, religion, or national origin.

TITLE V—COMMISSION ON CIVIL RIGHTS

Section 501.
Section 102 of the Civil Rights Act of 1957 (42 U.S.C. 1975a; 71 Stat. 634) is amended to read as follows:

"rules of procedure of the Commission hearings

"Sec. 102.
(a) At least thirty days prior to the commencement of any hearing, the Commission shall cause to be published in the Federal Register notice of the date on which such hearing is to commence, the place at which it is to be held and the subject of the hearing. The Chairman, or one designated by him to act as Chairman at a hearing of the Commission, shall announce in an opening statement the subject of the hearing.

"(b) A copy of the Commission's rules shall be made available to any witness before the Commission, and a witness compelled to appear before the Commission or required to produce written or other matter shall be served with a copy of the Commission's rules at the time of service of the subpena.

"(c) Any person compelled to appear in person before the Commission shall be accorded the right to be accompanied and advised by counsel, who shall have the right to subject his client to reasonable examination, and to make objections on the record and to argue briefly the basis for such objections. The Commission shall proceed with reasonable dispatch to conclude any hearing in which it is engaged. Due regard shall be had for the convenience and necessity of witnesses.

"(d) The Chairman or Acting Chairman may punish breaches of order and decorum by censure and exclusion from the hearings.

"(e) If the Commission determines that evidence or testimony at any hearing may tend to defame, degrade, or incriminate any person, it shall receive such evidence or testimony or summary of such evidence or testimony in executive session. The Commission shall afford any person defamed, degraded, or incriminated by such evidence or testimony an opportunity to appear and be heard in executive session, with a reasonable number of additional witnesses requested by him, before deciding to use such evidence or testimony. In the event the Commission determines to release or use such evidence or testimony in such manner as to reveal publicly the identity of the person defamed, degraded, or incriminated, such evidence or testimony. In the event the Commission determines to release or use such evidence or testimony in such manner as to reveal publicly the identity of the person defamed, degraded, or incriminated, such evidence or testimony, prior to such public release or use, shall be given at a public session, and the Commission shall afford such person an opportunity to appear as a voluntary witness or to file a sworn statement in his behalf and to submit brief and pertinent sworn statements of others. The Commission shall receive and dispose of requests from such person to subpena additional witnesses.

"(f) Except as provided in sections 102 and 105(f) of this Act the Chairman shall receive and the Commission shall dispose of requests to subpena additional witnesses.

"(g) No evidence or testimony or summary of evidence or testimony taken in executive session may be released or used in public sessions without the consent of the Commission. Whoever releases or uses in public without the consent of the Commission such evidence or testimony taken in executive session shall be fined not more than $1,000, or imprisoned for not more than one year.

"(h) In the discretion of the Commission, witnesses may submit brief and pertinent sworn statements in writing for inclusion in the record. The Commission shall determine the pertinency of testimony and evidence adduced at its hearings.

"(i) Every person who submits data or evidence shall be entitled to retain or, on payment of lawfully prescribed costs, procure a copy or transcript thereof, except that a witness in a hearing held in executive session may for good cause be limited to inspection of the official transcript of his testimony. Transcript copies of public sessions may be obtained by the public upon the payment of the cost thereof. An accurate transcript shall be made of the testimony of all witnesses at all hearings, either public or executive sessions, of the Commission or of any subcommittee thereof.

"(j) A witness attending any session of the Commission shall receive $6 for each day's attendance and for the time necessarily occupied in going to and returning from the same, and 10 cents per mile for going from and returning to his place of residence. Witnesses who attend at points so far removed from their respective residences as to prohibit return thereto from day to day shall be entitled to an additional allowance of $10 per day for expenses of subsistence, including the time necessarily occupied in going to and returning from the place of attendance. Mileage payments shall be tendered to the witness upon service of a subpena issued on behalf of the Commission or any subcommittee thereof.

"(k) The Commission shall not issue any subpena for the attendance and testimony of witnesses or for the production of written or other matter which would require the presence of the party subpenaed at a hearing to be held outside of the State wherein the witness is found or resides or is domiciled or transacts business, or has appointed an agent for receipt of service of process except that, in any event, the Commission may issue subpenas for the attendance and testimony of witnesses and the production of written or other matter at a hearing held within fifty miles of the place where the witness is found or resides or is domiciled or transacts business or has appointed an agent for receipt of service of process.

"(l) The Commission shall separately state and currently publish in the Federal Register (1) descriptions of its central and field organization including the established places at which, and methods whereby, the public may secure information or makes requests; (2) statements of the general course and method by which its functions are channeled and determined, and (3) rules adopted as authorized by law. No person shall in any manner be subject to or required to resort to rules, organization, or procedure not so published.

Section 502.
Section 103(a) of the Civil Rights of Act of 1957 (42 U.S.C. 1975b(a); 71 Stat. 634) is amended to read as follows:

"Sec. 103.
(a) Each member of the Commission who is not otherwise in the service of the Government of the United States shall receive the sum of $75 per day for each day spent in the work of the Commission, shall be paid actual travel expenses, and per diem in lieu of subsistence expenses when away from his usual place of residence, in accordance with section 5 of the Administrative Expenses Act of 1946, as amended (5 U.S.C. 73b-2; 60 Stat. 808)."

Section 503.
Section 103(b) of the Civil Rights of Act of 1957 (42 U.S.C. 1975b(b); 71 Stat. 635) is amended to read as follows:

"(b) Each member of the Commission who is not otherwise in the service of the Government of the United States shall serve without compensation in addition to that received for such other service, but while engaged in the work of the Commission, shall be paid actual travel expenses, and per diem in lieu of subsistence expenses when away from his usual place of residence, in accordance with the provisions of the Travel Expenses Act of 1949, as amended (5 U.S.C. 835—42; 63 Stat. 166)."

Section 504.
Section 104(a) of the Civil Rights of Act of 1957 (42 U.S.C. 1975c(a); 71 Stat. 635) as amended, is further amended to read as follows:

"Duties of the Commission

"Sec. 104. (a) The Commission shall—

"(1) investigate allegations in writing under oath or affirmation that certain citizens of the United States are being deprived of their right to vote and have that vote counted by reason of their color, race, religion, or national origin; when writing, under oath or affirmation, shall set forth the facts upon which such belief or beliefs are based;

"(2) study and collect information concerning legal developments constituting a denial of equal protection of the laws under the Constitution because of race, color, religion or national origin or in the administration of justice;

"(3) appraise the laws and policies of the Federal Government with respect to denials of equal protection of the laws under the Constitution because of race, color, religion or national origin or in the administration of justice;

"(4) serve as a national clearinghouse for information in respect to denials of equal protection of the laws because of race, color, religion or national origin or including but not limited to the fields of voting, education, housing, employment, the use of public facilities, and transportation, or in the administration of justice;

"(5) investigate allegations in writing under oath or affirmation, that citizens of the United States are unlawfully being accorded or denied the right to vote, or to have their votes properly counted, in any election of presidential electors. Members of the United States Senate, or of the House of Representatives, as a result of any patterns or practice of fraud or discrimination in the conduct of such election; and

"(6) Nothing in this or any other Act shall be construed as authorizing the Commission, its Advisory Committees, or any person under its supervision or control to inquire into or investigate any membership practices or internal operations of any fraternal organization, any college or university fraternity or sorority, any private club or any religious organization."

(b) Section 104(b) of the Civil Rights Act of 1957 (42 U.S.C. 1975c(b); 71 Stat. 635), as amended, is further amended by striking out the present subsection "(b)" and by substituting therefor:

"(b) The Commission shall submit interim reports to the President and to the Congress at such times as the Commission, the Congress or the President shall deem desirable, and shall submit to the President and to the Congress a final report of its activities, findings, and recommendations not later than January 31, 1968."

Section 505.
Section 105(a) of the Civil Rights Act of 1957 (42 U.S.C. 1975d(a);71 Stat. 636) is amended by striking out in the first sentence thereof "$50 per diem" and inserting in lieu thereof "$75 per diem."

Section 506.
Section 105(f) and section 105(g) of the Civil Rights Act of 1957 (42 U.S.C. 1975d (f) and (g); (71 Stat. 637), are amended to read as follows:

"(f) The Commission, or on the authorization of the Commission any subcommittee of two or more members, at least one of whom shall be of each major political party, may, for the purpose of carrying out the provisions of this Act, hold such hearings and act at such times and places as the Commission or such authorized subcommittee may deem advisable. Subpenas for the attendance and testimony of witnesses or the production of written or other matter may be issued in accordance with the rules of the Commission as contained in section 102 (j) and (k) of this Act, over the signature of the Chairman of the Commission or of such subcommittee, and may be served by any person designated by such Chairman. The holding of hearings by the Commission, or the appointment of a subcommittee to hold hearings pursuant to this subparagraph, must be approved by a majority of the Commission, or by a majority of the members present at a meeting at which at least a quorum of four members is present.

"(g) In case of contumacy or refusal to obey a subpena, any district court of the United States or the United States court of any territory or possession, or the District Court of the United States for the District of Columbia, within the jurisdiction of which the inquiry is carried on or within the jurisdiction of which said person guilty of contumacy or refusal to obey is found or resides or is domiciled or transacts business, or has appointed an agent for receipt of service of process, upon application by the Attorney General of the United States shall have jurisdiction to issue to such person an order requiring such person to appear before the Commission or a subcommittee thereof, there to produce pertinent, relevant and nonprivileged evidence if so ordered, or there to give testimony touching the matter under investigation; and any failure to obey such order of the court may be punished by said court as a contempt thereof."

Section 507.
Section 105 of the Civil Rights Act of 1957 (42 U.S.C. 1975d; 71 Stat. 636), as amended by section 401 of the Civil Rights Act of 1960 (42 U.S.C. 1975d(h): 74

Stat. 89), is further amended by adding a new subsection at the end to read as follows:

"(i) The Commission shall have the power to make such rules and regulations as are necessary to carry out the purposes of this Act."

TITLE VI—NONDISCRIMINATON IN FEDERALLY ASSISTED PROGRAMS

Section 601.

No person in the United States shall, on the ground of race, color, or national origin, be excluded from participation in, be denied the benefits of, or be subjected to discrimination under any program or activity receiving Federal financial assistance.

Section 602.

Each Federal department and agency which is empowered to extend Federal financial assistance to any program or activity, by way of grant, loan, or contract other than a contract of insurance or guaranty, is authorized and directed to effectuate the provisions of section 601 with respect to such program or activity by issuing rules, regulations, or orders of general applicability which shall be consistent with achievement of the connection with which the action is taken. No such rule, regulation, or order shall become effective unless and until approved by the President. Compliance with any requirement adopted pursuant to this section may be effected (1) by the termination of or refusal to grant or to continue assistance under such program or activity to any recipient as to whom there has been an express finding on the record, after opportunity for hearing, of a failure to comply with such requirement, but such termination or refusal shall be limited to the particular political entity, or part thereof, or other recipient as to whom such a finding has been made and, shall be limited in its effect to the particular program, or part thereof, in which such noncompliance has been so found, or (2) by any other means authorized by law: Provided, however, That no such action shall be taken until the department or agency concerned has advised the appropriate person or persons of the failure to comply with the requirement and has determined that compliance cannot be secured by voluntary means. In the case of any action terminating, or refusing to grant or continue, assistance because of failure to comply with a requirement imposed pursuant to this section, the head of the Federal department or agency shall file with the committees of the House and Senate having legislative jurisdiction over the program or activity involved a full written report of the circumstances and the grounds for such action. No such action shall become effective until thirty days have elapsed after the filing of such report.

Section 603.

Any department or agency action taken pursuant to section 602 shall be subject to such judicial review as may otherwise be provided by law for similar action taken by such department or agency on other grounds. In the case of action, not otherwise subject to judicial review, terminating or refusing to grant or to continue financial assistance upon a finding of failure to comply with any requirement imposed pursuant to section 602, any person aggrieved (including any State or political subdivision thereof and any agency of either) may obtain judicial review of such action in accordance with section 10 of the Administrative Procedure Act, and such action shall not be deemed committed to unreviewable agency discretion within the meaning of that section.

Section 604.

Nothing contained in this title shall be construed to authorize action under this title by any department or agency with respect to any employment practice of any employer, employment agency, or labor organization except where a primary objective of the Federal financial assistance is to provide employment.

Section 605.

Nothing in this title shall add to or detract from any existing authority with respect to any program or activity under which Federal financial assistance is extended by way of a contract of insurance or guaranty.

TITLE VII—EQUAL EMPLOYMENT OPPORTUNITY

Section 701.

For the purposes of this title—

(a) The term "person" includes one or more individuals, labor unions, partnerships, associations, corporations, legal representatives, mutual companies, joint-stock companies, trusts, unincorporated organizations, trustees, trustees in bankruptcy, or receivers.

(b) The term "employer" means a person engaged in an industry affecting commerce who has twenty-five or more employees for each working day in each of twenty or more calendar weeks in the current or preceding calendar year, and any agent of such a person, but such term does not include (1) the United States, a corporation wholly owned by the Government of the United States, an Indian tribe, or a State or political subdivision thereof, (2) a bona fide private membership club (other than a labor organization) which is exempt from taxation under section 501(c) of the Internal Revenue Code of 1954: Provided, That during the first year after the effective date prescribed in subsection (a) of section 716, persons having fewer than one hundred employees (and their agents) shall not be considered employers, and, during the second year after such date, persons having fewer than seventy-five employees (and their agents) shall not be considered employers, and, during the third year after such date, persons having fewer than fifty employees (and their agents) shall not be considered employers: Provided further, That it shall be the policy of United States to insure equal employment opportunities for Federal employees without discrimination because of race, color, religion, sex or national origin and the President shall utilize his existing authority to effectuate this policy.

(c) The term "employment agency" means any person regularly undertaking with or without compensation to procure employees for an employer or to procure for employees opportunities to work for an employer and includes an agent of such a person; but shall not include an agency of the United States, or an agency of a State or political subdivision of a State, except that such term shall include the United States Employment Service and the system of State and local employment services receiving Federal assistance.

(d) The term "labor organization" means a labor organization engaged in an industry affecting commerce, and any agent of such an organization, and includes any organization of any kind, any agency, or employee representation committee, group, association, or plan so engaged in which employees participate and which exists for the purpose, in whole or in part, of dealing with employers concerning grievances, labor disputes, wages, rates of pay, hours, or other terms or conditions of employment, and any conference, general committee, joint or system board, or joint council so engaged which is subordinate to a national or international labor organization.

(e) A labor organization shall be deemed to be engaged in an industry affecting commerce if (1) it maintains or operates a hiring hall or hiring office which procures employees for an employer or procures for employees opportunities to work for an employer, or (2) the number of its members (or, where it is a labor organization composed of other labor organizations or their representatives, if the aggregate number of the members of such other labor organization) is (A) one hundred or more during the year after the effective date prescribed in subsection (a) of section 716, (B) seventy-five or more during the second year after such date or fifty or more during the third year, or (C) twenty-five or more thereafter, and such labor organization—

(1) is the certified representative of employees under the provisions of the National Labor Relations Act, as amended, or the Railway Labor Act, as amended;

(2) although not certified, is a national or international labor organization or a local labor organization recognized or acting as the representative of employees of an employer or employers engaged in an industry affecting commerce; or

(3) has chartered a local labor organization or subsidiary body which is representing or actively seeking to represent employees of employers within the meaning of paragraph (1) or (2); or

(4) has been chartered by a labor organization representing or actively seeking to represent employees within the meaning of paragraph (1) or (2) as the local or subordinate body through which such employees may enjoy membership or become affiliated with such labor organization; or

(5) is a conference, general committee, joint or system board, or joint council subordinate to a national or international labor organization, which includes a labor organization engaged in an industry affecting commerce within the meaning of any of the preceding paragraphs of this subsection.

(f) The term "employee" means an individual employed by an employer.

(g) The term "commerce" means trade, traffic, commerce, transportation, transmission, or communication among the several States; or between a State and any place outside thereof; or within the District of Columbia, or a possession of the United States; or between points in the same State but through a point outside thereof.

(h) The term "industry affecting commerce" means any activity, business, or industry in commerce or in which a labor dispute would hinder or obstruct commerce or the free flow of commerce and includes any activity or industry "affecting commerce" within the meaning of the Labor-Management Reporting and Disclosure Act of 1959.

(i) The term "State" includes a State of the United States, the District of Columbia, Puerto Rico, the Virgin Islands, American Samoa, Guam, Wake Island, the Canal Zone, and Outer Continental Shelf lands defined in the Outer Continental Shelf Lands Act.

Section 702. Exemption
This title shall not apply to an employer with respect to the employment of aliens outside any State, or to a religious corporation association, or society with respect to the employment of individuals of a particular religion to perform work connected with the carrying on by such corporation, association, or society of its religious activities or to an educational institution with respect to the employment of individuals to perform work connected with the educational activities of such institution.

Section 703. Discrimination Because of Race, Color, Religion, Sex, or National Origin

(a) It shall be an unlawful employment practice for an employer—

(1) to fail or refuse to hire or to discharge any individual, or otherwise to discriminate against any individual with respect to his compensation, terms, conditions, or privileges of employment, because of such individual's race, color, religion, sex, or national origin; or

(2) to limit, segregate, or classify his employees in any way which would deprive or tend to deprive any individual of employment opportunities or otherwise adversely affect his status as an employee, because of such individual's race, color, religion, sex, or national origin.

(b) It shall be an unlawful employment practice for an employment agency to fail or refuse to refer for employment, or otherwise to discriminate against, any individual because of his race, color, religion, sex, or national origin, or to classify or refer for employment any individual on the basis of his race, color, religion, sex, or national origin.

(c) It shall be an unlawful employment practice for a labor organization—

(1) to exclude or to expel from its membership, or otherwise to discriminate against, any individual because of his race, color, religion, sex, or national origin;

(2) to limit, segregate, or classify its membership, or to classify or fail or refuse to refer for employment any individual, in anyway which would deprive or tend to deprive any individual of employment opportunities, or would limit such employment opportunities or otherwise adversely affect his status as an employee or as an applicant for employment, because of such individual's race, color, religion, sex, or national origin; or

(3) to cause or attempt to cause an employer to discriminate against an individual in violation of this section.

(d) It shall be an unlawful employment practice for any employer, labor organization, or joint labor-management committee controlling apprenticeship or other training or retraining, including on-the-job training programs to discriminate against any individual because of his race, color, religion, sex, or national origin in admission to, or employment in, any program established to provide apprenticeship or other training.

(e) Notwithstanding any other provision of this title, (1) it shall not be an unlawful employment practice for an employer to hire and employ employees, for an employment agency to classify, or refer for employment any individual, for a labor organization to classify its membership or to classify or refer for employment any individual, or for an employer, labor organization, or joint labor-management committee controlling apprenticeship or other training or retraining programs to admit or employ any individual in any such program, on the basis of his religion, sex, or national origin in those certain instances where religion, sex, or national origin is a bona fide occupational qualification reasonably necessary to the normal operation of that particular business or enterprise, and

(2) it shall not be an unlawful employment practice for a school, college, university, or other educational institution or institution of learning to hire and employ employees of particular religion if such school, college, university, or other educational institution or institution of learning is, in whole or in substantial part, owned, supported, controlled, or managed by a particular religion or by a particular religious corporation, association, or society, or if the curriculum of such school, college, university, or other educational institution or institution of learning is directed toward the propagation of particular religion.

(f) As used in this title, the phrase "unlawful employment practice" shall not be deemed to include any action or measure taken by an employer, labor organization, joint labor-management committee, or employment agency with respect to an individual who is a member of the Communist Party of the United States or of any other organization required to register as a Commission-action or Commission-front organization by final order of the Subversive Activities Control Board pursuant to the Subversive Activities Control Act of 1950.

(g) Notwithstanding any other provision of this title, it shall not be an unlawful employment practice for an employer to fail or refuse to hire and employ any individual for any position, for an employer to discharge any individual from any position, or for an employment agency to fail or refuse to refer any individual for employment in any position, if—

(1) the occupancy of such position, or access to the premises in or upon which any part of the duties of such position is performed or is to be performed, is subject to any requirement imposed in the interest of the national security of the United States under any security program in effect pursuant to or administered under any statute of the United States or any Executive order of the President; and

(2) such individual has not fulfilled or has ceased to fulfill that requirement.

(h) Notwithstanding any other provision of this title, it shall not be an unlawful employment practice for an employer to apply different standards of compensation, or different terms, conditions, or privileges of employment pursuant to a bona fide seniority or merit system, or a system which measures earnings by quantity or quality of production or to employees who work in different locations, provided that such differences are not the result of an intention to discriminate because of race, color, religion, sex, or national origin, nor shall it be an unlawful employment practice for an employer to give and to act upon the results of any professionally developed ability test provided that such test, its administration or action upon the results is not designed, intended or used to discriminate because of race, color, religion, sex or national origin. It shall not be an unlawful employment practice under this title for any employer to differentiate upon the basis of sex in determining the amount of the wages of compensation paid or to be paid to employees of such employer if such differentiation is authorized by the provisions of section 6(d) of the Fair Labor Standards Act of 1938, as amended (29 U.S.C. 206 (d)).

(i) Nothing contained in this title shall apply to any business or enterprise on or near an Indian reservation with respect to any publicly announced employment practice of such business or enterprise under which a preferential treatment is given to any individual because he is an Indian living on or near a reservation.

(j) Nothing contained in this title shall be interpreted to require any employer, employment agency, labor organization, or joint labor-management committee subject to this title to grant preferential treatment to any individual or to any group because of the race, color, religion, sex, or national origin of such individual or group on account of an imbalance which may exist with respect to the total number or percentage of persons of any race, color, religion, sex, or national origin employed by an employer, referred or classified for employment by any employment agency or labor organization, admitted to membership or classified by any labor organization, or admitted to, or employed in, any apprenticeship or other training program, in comparison with the total number or percentage of persons of such race, color, religion, sex, or national origin in any community, State, section, or other area, or in the available work force in any community, State, section, or other area.

Section 704. Other Unlawful Employment Practices

(a) It shall be an unlawful employment practice for an employer to discriminate against any of his employees or applicants for employment, for an employment agency to discriminate against any individual, or for a labor organization to discriminate against any member thereof or applicant for membership, because he has opposed any practice made an unlawful employment practice by this title, or because he has made a charge, testified, assisted, or participated in any manner in an investigation, proceeding, or hearing under this title.

(b) It shall be an unlawful employment practice for an employer, labor organization, or employment agency to print or publish or cause to be printed or published any notice or advertisement relating to employment by such an employer or membership in or any classification or referral for employment by such a labor organization, or relating to any classification or referral for employment by such an employment agency, indicating any preference, limitation, specification, or discrimination, based on race, color, religion, sex, or national origin, except that such a notice or advertisement may indicate a preference, limitation, specification, or discrimination based on religion, sex, or national origin when religion, sex, or national origin is a bona fide occupational qualification for employment.

Section 705. Equal Employment Opportunity Commission

(a) There is hereby created a Commission to be known as the Equal Employment Opportunity Commission, which shall be composed of five members, not more than three of whom shall be members of the same political party, who shall be appointed by the President by and with the advice and consent of the Senate. One of the original members shall be appointed for a term of one year, one for a term of two years, one for a term of three years, one for a term of four years, and one for a term of five years, beginning from the date of enactment of this title, but their successors shall be appointed for terms of five years each, except that any individual chosen to fill a vacancy shall be appointed only for the unexpired term of the member whom he shall succeed. The President shall designate one member to serve as Chairman of the Commission, and one member to serve as Vice Chairman. The Chairman shall be responsible on behalf of the Commission for the administrative operations of the Commission, and shall appoint, in accordance with the civil service laws, such officers, agents, attorneys, and employees as it deems necessary to assist it in the performance of its functions and to fix their compensation in accordance with the Classification Act of 1949, as amended. The Vice Chairman shall act as Chairman in the absence or disability of the Chairman or in the event of a vacancy in that office.

(b) A vacancy in the Commission shall not impair the right of the remaining members to exercise all the powers of the Commission and three members thereof shall constitute a quorum.

(c) The Commission shall have an official seal which shall be judicially noticed.

(d) The Commission shall at the close of each fiscal year report to the Congress and to the President concerning the action it has taken; the names, salaries, and duties of all individuals in its employ and the moneys it has disbursed; and shall make such further reports on the cause of and means of eliminating discrimination and such recommendations for further reports on the cause of and means of eliminating discrimination and such recommendations for further legislation as may appear desirable.

(e) The Federal Executive Pay Act of 1956, as amended (5 U.S.C. 2201-2209), is further amended—

(1) by adding to section 105 thereof (5 U.S.C. 2204) the following clause:

"(32) Chairman, Equal Employment Opportunity Commission"; and

(2) by adding to clause (45) of section 1069(a) thereof (5 U.S.C. 2205 9(a)) the following: "Equal Employment Opportunity Commission (4)."

(f) The principal office of the Commission shall be in or near the District of Columbia, but it may meet or exercise any or all its powers at any other place. The Commission may establish such regional or State offices as it deems necessary to accomplish the purpose of this title.

(g) The Commission shall have power—

(1) to cooperate with and, with their consent, utilize regional, State, local, and other agencies, both public and private, and individuals;

(2) to pay to witnesses whose depositions are taken or who are summoned before the Commission or any of its agents the same witness and mileage fees as are paid to witnesses in the courts of the United States;

(3) to furnish to persons subject to this title such technical assistance as they may request to further their compliance with this title or an order issued thereunder;

(4) upon the request of (i) any employer, whose employees or some of them, or (ii) any labor organization, whose members or some of them, refuse or threaten to refuse to cooperate in effectuating the provisions of this title, to assist in such effectuation by conciliation or such other remedial action as is provided by this title;

(5) to make such technical studies as are appropriate to effectuate the purposes and policies of this title and to make the results of such studies available to the public;

(6) to refer matters to the Attorney General with recommendations for intervention in a civil action brought by an aggrieved party under section 706, or for the institution of a civil action by the Attorney General under section 707, and to advise, consult, and assist the Attorney General on such matters.

(h) Attorneys appointed under this section may, at the direction of the Commission, appear for and represent the Commission in any case in court.

(i) The Commission shall, in any of its educational or promotional activities, cooperate with other departments and agencies in the performance of such educational and promotional activities.

(j) All officers, agents, attorneys, and employees of the Commission shall be subject to the provisions of section 9 of the Act of August 2, 1939, as amended (the Hatch Act), notwithstanding any exemption contained in such section.

Section 706. Prevention of Unlawful Employment Practices
(a) Whenever it is charged in writing under oath by a person claiming to be aggrieved, or a written charge has been filed by a member of the Commission where he has reasonable cause to believe a violation of this title has occurred (and such charge sets forth the facts upon which it is based) that an employer, employment agency, or labor organization has engaged in an unlawful employment practice, the Commission shall furnish such employer, employment agency, or labor organization (hereinafter referred to as the "respondent") with a copy of such charge and shall make an investigation of such charge, provided that such charge shall not be made public by the Commission. If the Commission shall determine, after such investigation, that there is reasonable cause to believe that the charge is true, the Commission shall endeavor to eliminate any such alleged unlawful employment practice by informal methods of conference, conciliation, and persuasion. Nothing said or done during and as apart of such endeavors may be made public by the Commission without the written consent of the parties, or used as evidence in a subsequent proceeding. Any officer or employee of the Commission, who shall make public in any manner whatever any information in violation of this subsection shall be deemed guilty of a misdemeanor and upon conviction thereof shall be fined not more than $1,000 or imprisoned not more than one year.

(b) In the case of alleged unlawful employment practice occurring in a State, or political subdivision of a State, which has a State or local law prohibiting the unlawful employment practice alleged and establishing or authorizing a State or local authority to grant or seek relief from such practice or to institute criminal proceedings with respect thereto upon receiving notice thereof, no charge may be filed under subsection (a) by the person aggrieved before the expiration of sixty days after proceedings have been commenced under the State or local law, unless such proceedings have been earlier terminated, provided that such sixty-day period shall be extended to one hundred and twenty days during the first year after the effective date of such State or local law. If any requirement for the commencement of such proceedings is imposed by a State or local authority other than a requirement of the filing of a written and signed statement of the facts upon which the proceeding is based, the proceeding shall be deemed to have been commenced for the purposes of this subsection at the time such statement is sent by registered mail to the appropriate State or local authority.

(c) In the case of any charge filed by a member of the Commission alleging an unlawful employment practice occurring in a State or political subdivision of a State, which has a State or local law prohibiting the practice alleged and establishing or authorizing a State or local authority to grant or seek relief from such practice or to institute criminal proceedings with respect thereto upon receiving notice thereof, the Commission shall, before taking any action with respect to such charge, notify the appropriate State or local officials and upon request, afford them a reasonable time, but not less than sixty days (provided that such sixty-day period shall be extended to one hundred and twenty days during the first year after the effective day of such State or local law), unless a shorter period is requested, to act under such State or local law to remedy the practice alleged.

(d) A charge under subsection (a) shall be filed within ninety days after the alleged unlawful employment practice occurred, except that in the case of an unlawful employment practice with respect to which the person aggrieved has followed the procedure set out in subsection (b), such charge shall be filed by the person aggrieved within two hundred and ten days after the alleged unlawful employment practice occurred, or within thirty days after receiving notice that the State or local agency has terminated the proceedings under the State or local law, whichever is earlier, and a copy of such charge shall be filed by the Commission with the State or local agency.

(e) If within thirty days after a charge is filed with the Commission or within thirty days after expiration of any period of reference under subsection (c) (except that in either case such period may be extended to not more than sixty days upon a determination by the Commission that further efforts to secure voluntary compliance are warranted), the Commission has been unable to obtain voluntary compliance with this title, the Commission shall so notify the person aggrieved and a civil action may, within thirty days thereafter, be brought against the respondent named in the charge (1) by the person claiming to be aggrieved, or (2) if such charge was filed by a member of the Commission, by any person whom the charge alleges was aggrieved by the alleged unlawful employment practice. Upon application by the complainant and in such circumstances as the court may deem just, the court may appoint an attorney for such complainant and may authorize the commencement of the action without the payment of fees, costs, or security. Upon timely application, the court may, in its discretion, permit the Attorney General to intervene in such civil action if he certifies that the case is of general public importance. Upon request, the court may, in its discretion, stay further proceedings for not more than sixty days pending the termination of State or local proceedings described in subsection (b) or the efforts of the Commission to obtain voluntary compliance.

(f) Each United States district court and each United States court of a place subject to the jurisdiction of the United States shall have jurisdiction of actions brought under this title. Such an action may be brought in any judicial district in the State in which the unlawful employment practice is alleged to have been committed, in the judicial district in which the employment records relevant to such practice are maintained and administered, or in the judicial district in which the plaintiff would have worked but for the alleged unlawful employment practice, but if the respondent is not found within any such district, such an action may be brought with the judicial district in which the respondent has his principal office. For purposes of sections 1404 and 1406 of title 28 of the United States Code, the judicial district in which the respondent has his principal office shall in all cases be considered a district in which the action might have been brought.

(g) If the court finds that the respondent has intentionally engaged in or is intentionally engaging in an unlawful employment practice charged in the complaint, the court may enjoin the respondent from engaging in such unlawful employment practice, and order such affirmative action as may be appropriate, which may include reinstatement or hiring of employees, with or without back pay (payable by the employer, employment agency, or labor organization, as the case may be, responsible for the unlawful employment practice). Interim earnings or amounts earnable with reasonable diligence by the person or persons discriminated against shall operate to reduce the back pay otherwise allowable. No order of the court shall require the admission or reinstatement of an individual as a member of a union or the hiring, reinstatement, or promotion of an individual as an employee, or the payment to him of any back pay, if such individual was refused admission, suspended, or expelled or was refused employment or advancement or was suspended or discharged for any reason other than discrimination on account of race, color, religion, sex or national origin or in violation of section 704 (a).

(h) The provisions of the Act entitled "An Act to amend the Judicial Code and to define and limit the jurisdiction of courts sitting in equity, and for other purposes," approved March 23, 1932 (29 U.S.C. 101-115), shall not apply with respect to civil actions brought under this section.

(i) In any case in which an employer, employment agency, or labor organization fails to comply with an order of a court issued in a civil action brought under subsection (e), the Commission may commence proceedings to compel compliance with such order.

(j) Any civil action brought under subsection (e) and any proceedings brought under subsection (i) shall be subject to appeal as provided in sections 1291 and 1292, title 28. United States Code.

(k) In any action or proceeding under this title the court, in its discretion, may allow the prevailing party, other than the Commission or the United States a reasonable attorney's fee as part of the costs, and the Commission and the United States shall be liable for costs the same as a private person.

Section 707.
(a) Whenever the Attorney General has reasonable cause to believe that any person or group of persons is engaged in a pattern or practice of resistance to the full enjoyment of any of the rights secured by this title, and that the pattern or practice is of such a nature and is intended to deny the full exercise of the rights herein described, the Attorney General may bring a civil action in the appropriate district court of the United States by filing with it a complaint

(1) signed by him (or in his absence the Acting Attorney General);

(2) setting forth facts pertaining to such pattern or practice, and

(3) requesting such relief, including an application for a permanent or temporary injunction, restraining order or other order against the person or persons responsible for such pattern or practice, as he deems necessary to insure the full enjoyment of the rights herein described.

(b) The district courts of the United States shall have and shall exercise jurisdiction of proceedings instituted pursuant to this section, and in any such proceeding the Attorney General may file with the clerk of such court a request that a court of three judges be convened to hear and determine the case. Such request by the Attorney General shall be accompanied by a certificate that, in his opinion, the case is of general public importance. A copy of the certificate and request for a three-judge court shall be immediately furnished by such clerk to the chief judge of the circuit (or in his absence, the presiding circuit judge of the circuit) in which the case is pending. Upon receipt of such request it shall be the duty of the chief judge of the circuit or the presiding circuit judge, as the case may be, to designate immediately three judges in such circuit, of whom at least one shall be a circuit judge and another of whom shall be a district judge of the court in which the proceeding was instituted, to hear and determine such case for hearing at the earliest practicable date, to participate in the hearing and determination thereof, and to cause the case to be in every way expedited. An appeal from the final judgment of such court will lie to the Supreme Court.

In the event the Attorney General fails to file such a request in any such proceeding, it shall be the duty of the chief judge of the district (or in his absence, the acting chief judge) in which the case is pending immediately to designate a judge in such district to hear and determine the case. In the event that no judge in the district is available to hear and determine the case, the chief judge of the district, or the acting chief judge, as the case may be, shall certify this fact to the chief judge of the circuit (or in his absence, the acting chief judge) who shall then designate a district or circuit judge of the circuit to hear and determine the case.

It shall be the duty of the judge designated pursuant to this section to assign the case for hearing at the earliest practicable date and to cause the case to be in every way expedited.

Section 708. Effect On State Laws
Nothing in this title shall be deemed to exempt or relieve any person from any liability, duty, penalty, or punishment provided by any present or future law of any State or political subdivision of a State, other than any such law which purports to require or permit the doing of any act which would be an unlawful employment practice under this title.

Section 709. Investigations, Inspections, Records, State Agencies
(a) In connection with any investigation of a charge filed under section 706, the Commission or its designated representative shall at all reasonable times have access to, for the purposes of examination, and the right to copy any evidence of any person being investigated or proceeded against that relates to unlawful employment practices covered by this title and is relevant to the charge under investigation.

(b) The Commission may cooperate with State and local agencies charged with the administration of State fair employment practices laws and, with the consent of such agencies, may for the purpose of carrying out its functions and duties under this title and within the limitation of funds appropriated specifically for such purpose, utilize the services of such agencies and their employees and, notwithstanding any other provision of law, may reimburse such agencies and their employees for services rendered to assist the Commission in carrying out this title. In furtherance of such cooperative efforts, the Commission may enter into written agreements with such State or local agencies and such agreements may include provisions under which the Commission shall refrain from processing a charge in any cases or class of cases specified in such agreements and under which no person may bring a civil action under section 706 in any cases or class of cases so specified, or under which the Commission shall relieve any person or class of persons in such State or locality from requirements imposed under this section. The Commission shall rescind any such agreement whenever it determines that the agreement no longer serves the interest of effective enforcement of this title.

(c) Except as provided in subsection (d), every employer, employment agency, and labor organization subject to this title shall (1) make and keep such records relevant to the determinations of whether unlawful employment practices have been or are being committed, (2) preserve such records for such periods, and (3) make such reports therefrom, as the Commission shall prescribe by regulation or order, after public hearing, as reasonable, necessary, or appropriate for the enforcement of this title or the regulations or orders thereunder. The Commission shall, by regulation, require each employer, labor organization, and joint labor-management committee subject to this title which controls an apprenticeship or other training program to maintain such records as are reasonably necessary to carry out the purpose of this title, including, but not limited to, a list of applicants who wish to participate in such program, including the chronological order in which such applications were received, and shall furnish to the Commission, upon request, a detailed description of the manner in which persons are selected to participate in the apprenticeship or other training program. Any employer, employment agency, labor organization, or joint labor-management committee which believes that the application to it of any regulation or order issued under this section would result in undue hardship may (1) apply to the Commission for an exemption from the application of such regulation or order or (2) bring a civil action in the United States district court for the district where such records are kept. If the Commission or the court, as the case may be, finds that the application of the regulation or order to the employer, employment agency, or labor organization in question would impose an undue hardship, the Commission or the court, as the case may be, may grant appropriate relief.

(d) The provisions of subsection (c) shall not apply to any employer, employment agency, labor organization, or joint labor-management committee with respect to matters occurring in any State or political subdivision thereof which has a fair employment practice law during any period in which such employer, employment agency, labor organization, or joint labor-management committee is subject to such law, except that the Commission may require such notations on records which such employer, employment agency, labor organization, or joint labor-management committee keeps or is required to keep as are necessary because of differences in coverage or methods of enforcement between the State or local law and the provisions of this title. Where an employer is required by Executive Order 10925, issued March 6, 1961, or by any other Executive order prescribing fair employment practices for Government contractors and subcontractors, or by rules or regulations issued thereunder, to file reports relating to his employment practices with any Federal agency or committee, and he substantially in compliance with such requirements, the Commission shall not require him to file additional reports pursuant to subsection (c) of this section.

(e) It shall be unlawful for any officer or employee of the Commission to make public in any manner whatever any information obtained by the Commission pursuant to its authority under this section prior to the institution of any proceeding under this title involving such information. Any officer or employee of the Commission who shall make public in any manner whatever any information in violation of this subsection shall be guilty of a misdemeanor and upon conviction thereof, shall be fined not more than $1,000, or imprisoned not more than one year.

Section 710. Investigatory Powers
(a) For the purposes of any investigation of a charge filed under the authority contained in section 706, the Commission shall have authority to examine witnesses under oath and to require the production of documentary evidence relevant or material to the charge under investigation.

(b) If the respondent named in a charge filed under section 706 fails or refuses to comply with a demand of the Commission for permission to examine or to copy evidence in conformity with the provisions of section 709(a), or if any person required to comply with the provisions of section 709 (c) or (d) fails or refuses to do so, or if any person fails or refuses to comply with a demand by the Commission to give testimony under oath, the United States district court for the district in which such person is found, resides, or transacts business, shall, upon application of the Commission, have jurisdiction to issue to such person an order requiring him to comply with the provisions of section 709 (c) or (d) or to comply with the demand of the Commission, but the attendance of a witness may not be required outside the State where he is found, resides, or transacts business and the production of evidence may not be required outside the State where such evidence is kept.

(c) Within twenty days after the service upon any person charged under section 706 of a demand by the Commission for the production of documentary evidence or for permission to examine or to copy evidence in conformity with the provisions of section 709(a), such person may file in the district court of the United States for the judicial district in which he resides, is found, or transacts business, and serve upon the Commission a petition for an order of such court modifying or setting aside such demand. The time allowed for compliance with the demand in whole or in part as deemed proper and ordered by the court shall not run during the pendency of such petition in the court. Such petition shall specify each ground upon which the petitioner relies in seeking such relief, and may be based upon any failure of such demand to comply with the provisions of this title or with the limitations generally applicable to compulsory process or upon any constitutional or other legal right or privilege of such person. No objection which is not raised by such a petition may be urged in the defense to a proceeding initiated by the Commission under subsection (b) for enforcement of such a demand unless such proceeding is commenced by the Commission prior to the expiration of the twenty-day period, or unless the court determines that the defendant could not reasonably have been aware of the availability of such ground of objection.

(d) In any proceeding brought by the Commission under subsection (b), except as provided in subsection (c) of this section, the defendant may petition the court for an order modifying or setting aside the demand of the Commission.

Section 711. Notices To Be Posted
(a) Every employer, employment agency, and labor organization, as the case may be, shall post and keep posted in conspicuous places upon its premises where notices to employees, applicants for employment, and members are customarily posted a notice to be prepared or approved by the Commission setting forth excerpts from or, summaries of, the pertinent provisions of this title and information pertinent to the filing of a complaint.

(b) A willful violation of this section shall be punishable by a fine of not more than $100 for each separate offense.

Section 712. Veterans' Preference
Nothing contained in this title shall be construed to repeal or modify any Federal, State, territorial, or local law creating special rights or preference for veterans.

Section 713. Rules and Regulations
(a) The Commission shall have authority from time to time to issue, amend, or rescind suitable procedural regulations to carry out the provisions of this title. Regulations issued under this section shall be in conformity with the standards and limitations of the Administrative Procedure Act.

(b) In any action or proceeding based on any alleged unlawful employment practice, no person shall be subject to any liability or punishment for or on account of (1) the commission by such person of an unlawful employment practice if he pleads and proves that the act or omission complained of was in good faith, in conformity with, and in reliance on any written interpretation or opinion of the Commission, or (2) the failure of such person to publish and file any information required by any provision of this title if he pleads and proves that he failed to publish and file such information in good faith, in conformity with the instructions of the Commission issued under this title regarding the filing of such information. Such a defense, if established, shall be a bar to the action or proceeding, notwithstanding that (A) after such act or omission, such interpretation or opinion is modified or rescinded or is determined by judicial authority to be invalid or no legal effect, or (B) after publishing or filing the description and annual reports, such publication or filing is determined by judicial authority not to be in conformity with the requirements of this title.

Section 714. Forcibly Resisting the Commission or Its Representatives
The provisions of section 111, title 18, United States Code, shall apply to officers, agents, and employees of the Commission in the performance of their official duties.

Section 715. Special Study by Secretary of Labor
The Secretary of Labor shall make a full and complete study of the factors which might tend to result in discrimination in employment because of age and of the consequences of such discrimination on the economy and individuals affected. The Secretary of Labor shall make a report to the Congress not later than June 30, 1965, containing the results of such study and shall include in such report such recommendations for legislation to prevent arbitrary discrimination in employment because of age as he determines advisable.

Section 716. Effective Date
(a) This title shall become effective one year after the date of its enactment.

(b) Notwithstanding subsection (a), sections of this title other than sections 703, 704, 706, and 707 shall become effective immediately.

(c) The President shall, as soon as feasible after the enactment of this title, convene one or more conferences for the purpose of enabling the leaders of groups whose members will be affected by this title to become familiar with the rights afforded and obligations imposed by its provisions, and for the purpose of making plans which will result in the fair and effective administration of this title when all of its provisions become effective. The President shall invite the participation in such conference or conferences of (1) the members of the President's Committee on Equal Employment Opportunity, (2) the members of the Commission on Civil Rights, (3) representatives of State and local agencies engaged in furthering equal employment opportunity, (4) representatives of private agencies engaged in furthering equal employment opportunity, and (5) representatives of employers, labor organizations, and employment agencies who will be subject to this title.

TITLE VIII—REGISTRATION AND VOTING STATISTICS

Section 801.

The Secretary of Commerce shall promptly conduct a survey to compile registration and voting statistics in such geographic areas as may be recommended by the Commission on Civil Rights. Such a survey and compilation shall, to the extent recommended by the Commission on Civil Rights, only include a count of persons of voting age by race, color, and national origin, and determination of the extent to which such persons are registered to vote, and have voted in any statewide primary or general election in which the Members of the United States House of Representatives are nominated or elected, since January 1, 1960. Such information shall also be collected and compiled in connection with the Nineteenth Decennial Census, and at such other times as the Congress may prescribe. The provisions of section 9 and chapter 7 of title 13, United States Code, shall apply to any survey, collection, or compilation of registration and voting statistics carried out under this title: Provided, however, that no person shall be compelled to disclose his race, color, national origin, or questioned about his political party affiliation, how he voted, or the reasons therefore, nor shall any penalty be imposed for his failure or refusal to make such disclosure. Every person interrogated orally, by written survey or questionnaire or by any other means with respect to such information shall be fully advised with respect to his right to fail or refuse to furnish such information.

TITLE IX—INTERVENTION AND PROCEDURE AFTER REMOVAL IN CIVIL RIGHTS CASES

Section 901.

Title 28 of the United States Code, section 1447 (d), is amended to read as follows:

"An order remanding a case to the State court from which it was removed is not reviewable on appeal or otherwise, except that an order remanding a case to the State court from which it was removed pursuant to section 1443 of this title shall be reviewable by appeal or otherwise."

Section 902.

Whenever an action has been commenced in any court of the United States seeking relief from the denial of equal protection of the laws under the fourteenth amendment to the Constitution on account of race, color, religion, or national origin, the Attorney General for or in the name of the United States may intervene in such action upon timely application if the Attorney General certifies that the case is of general public importance. In such action the United States shall be entitled to the same relief as if it has instituted the action.

TITLE X—ESTABLISHMENT OF COMMUNITY RELATIONS SERVICE

Section 1001.

(a) There is hereby established in and as a part of the Department of Commerce a Community Relations Service (hereinafter referred to as the "Service"), which shall be headed by a Director who shall be appointed by the President with the advise and consent of the Senate for a term of four years. The Director is authorized to appoint, subject to the civil service laws and regulations, such other personnel as may be necessary to enable the Service to carry out its functions and duties, and to fix their compensation in accordance with the Classification Act of 1949, as amended. The Director is further authorized to procure services as authorized by section 15 of the Act of August 2, 1946 (60 Stat. 810; 5 U.S.C. 55(a)), but at rates for individuals not in excess of $75 per diem.

(b) Section 106(a) of the Federal Executive Pay Act of 1956, as amended (5 U.S.C. 2205(a)), is further amended by adding the following clause thereto:

"(52) Director, Community Relations Service."

Section 1002.

It shall be the function of the Service to provide assistance to communities and persons therein in resolving disputes, disagreements, or difficulties relating to discriminatory practices based on race, color, or national origin which impair the rights of persons in such communities under the Constitution or laws of the Unites States or which affect or may affect interstate commerce. The Service may offer its services in cases of such disputes, disagreements, or difficulties whenever, in its judgment, peaceful relations among the citizens of the community involved are threatened thereby, and it may offer its services either upon its own motion or upon the request of an appropriate State or local official or other interested person.

Section 1003.

(a) The Service shall, whenever possible, in performing its functions, seek and utilize the cooperation of appropriate State or local, public, or private agencies.

(b) The activities of all officers and employees of the Service in providing conciliation assistance shall be conducted in confidence and without publicity, and the Service shall hold confidential any information acquired in the regular performance of its duties upon the understanding that it would be so held. No officer or employee of the Service shall engage in the performance of investigative or prosecuting functions of any department or agency in any litigation arising out of a dispute in which he acted on behalf of the Service. Any officer or other employee of the Service, who shall make public in any manner whatever any information in violation of this subsection, shall be deemed guilty of a misdemeanor and, upon conviction thereof, shall be fined not more than $1,000 or imprisoned not more than one year.

Section 1004.

Subject to the provisions of sections 205 and 1003(b), the Director shall, on or before January 31 of each year, submit to the Congress a report of the activities of the Service during the preceding fiscal year.

TITLE XI—MISCELLANEOUS

Section 1101.

In any proceeding for criminal contempt arising under title II, III, IV, V, VI, or VII of this Act, the accused, upon demand therefor, shall be entitled to a trial by jury, which shall conform as near as may be to the practice in criminal cases. Upon conviction, the accused shall not be fined more than $1,000 or imprisoned for more than six months.

This section shall not apply to contempts committed in the presence of the court, or so near thereto as to obstruct the administration of justice, nor to the misbehavior, misconduct, or disobedience of any officer of the court in respect to writs, orders, or process of the court. No person shall be convicted of criminal contempt hereunder unless the act or omission constituting such contempt shall have been intentional, as required in other cases of criminal contempt.

Nor shall anything herein be construed to deprive courts of their power, by civil contempt proceedings, without a jury, to secure compliance with or to prevent obstruction of, as distinguished from punishment for violations of, any lawful writ, process, order, rule, decree, or command of the court in accordance with the prevailing usages of law and equity, including the power of detention.

Section 1102.

No person should be put twice in jeopardy under the laws of the United States for the same act or omission. For this reason, an acquittal or conviction in a prosecution for a specific crime under the laws of the United States shall bar a proceeding for criminal contempt, which is based upon the same act or omission and which arises under the provisions of this Act; and an acquittal or conviction in a proceeding for criminal contempt, which arises under the provisions of this Act, shall bar a prosecution for a specific crime under the laws of the United States based upon the same act or omission.

Section 1103.

Nothing in this Act shall be construed to deny, impair, or otherwise affect any right or authority of the Attorney General or of the United States or any agency or officer thereof under existing law to institute or intervene in any action or proceeding.

Section 1104.

Nothing contained in any title of this Act shall be construed as indicating an intent on the part of Congress to occupy the field in which any such title operates to the exclusion of State laws on the same subject matter, nor shall any provision of this Act be construed as invalidating any provision of State law unless such provision is inconsistent with any of the purposes of this Act, or any provision thereof.

Section 1105.

There are hereby authorized to be appropriated such sums as are necessary to carry out the provisions of this Act.

Section 1106.

If any provision of this Act or the application thereof to any person or circumstances is held invalid, the remainder of the Act and the application of the provision to other persons not similarly situated or to other circumstances shall not be affected thereby.

> *Source: Civil Rights Act of 1964.* Public Law 88-352. *U.S. Statutes at Large* 78 (1964): 241

55. *Griswold v. Connecticut,* 1965

Introduction

In *Griswold v. Connecticut*, the Supreme Court overturned a Connecticut statute of 1879 that made the use of any birth control device illegal. The case sparked intense debate not only on the issue of birth control but on the scope of judicial interpretation and the degree to which legislative action or constitutional amendment is necessary to strike down unwise laws. The executive director and medical director of the Planned Parenthood League of Connecticut had been convicted of giving instruction and medical advice to married people about ways to prevent conception. The conviction was upheld by Connecticut courts but reversed with a 7–2 majority by the U.S. Supreme Court.

Primary Source

MR. JUSTICE DOUGLAS delivered the opinion of the Court.

Appellant Griswold is Executive Director of the Planned Parenthood League of Connecticut. Appellant Buxton is a licensed physician and a professor at the Yale Medical School who served as Medical Director for the League at its Center in New Haven—a center open and operating from November 1 to November 10, 1961, when appellants were arrested.

They gave information, instruction, and medical advice to married persons as to the means of preventing conception. They examined the wife and prescribed the best contraceptive device or material for her use. Fees were usually charged, although some couples were serviced free.

The statutes whose constitutionality is involved in this appeal are 53-32 and 54-196 of the General Statutes of Connecticut (1958 rev.). The former provides:

Any person who uses any drug, medicinal article or instrument for the purpose of preventing conception shall be fined not less than fifty dollars or imprisoned not less than sixty days nor more than one year or be both fined and imprisoned.

Section 54-196 provides:

Any person who assists, abets, counsels, causes, hires or commands another to commit any offense may be prosecuted and punished as if he were the principal offender.

The appellants were found guilty as accessories and fined $100 each, against the claim that the accessory statute as so applied violated the Fourteenth Amendment. The Appellate Division of the Circuit Court affirmed. The Supreme Court of Errors affirmed that judgment. We noted probable jurisdiction.

We think that appellants have standing to raise the constitutional rights of the married people with whom they had a professional relationship. *Tileston v. Ullman* is different, for there the plaintiff seeking to represent others asked for a declaratory judgment. In that situation we thought that the requirements of standing should be strict, lest the standards of "case or controversy" in Article III of the Constitution become blurred. Here those doubts are removed by reason of a criminal conviction for serving married couples in violation of an aiding-and-abetting statute. Certainly the accessory should have standing to assert that the offense which he is charged with assisting is not, or cannot constitutionally be, a crime.

This case is more akin to *Truax v. Raich*, where an employee was permitted to assert the rights of his employer; to *Pierce v. Society of Sisters*, where the owners of private schools were entitled to assert the rights of potential pupils and their parents; and to *Barrows v. Jackson,* where a white defendant, party to a racially restrictive covenant, who was being sued for damages by the covenantors because she had conveyed her property to Negroes, was allowed to raise the issue that enforcement of the covenant violated the rights of prospective Negro purchasers to equal protection, although no Negro was a party to the suit. And see *Meyer v. Nebraska*; *Adler v. Board of Education*; *NAACP v. Alabama*; *NAACP v. Button.* The rights of husband and wife, pressed here, are likely to be diluted or adversely affected unless those rights are considered in a suit involving those who have this kind of confidential relation to them.

Coming to the merits, we are met with a wide range of questions that implicate the Due Process Clause of the Fourteenth Amendment. Overtones of some arguments suggest that *Lochner v. New York* should be our guide. But we decline that invitation as we did in *West Coast Hotel Co. v. Parrish, Olsen v. Nebraska, Lincoln Union v. Northwestern Co., Williamson v. Lee Optical Co., Giboney v. Empire Storage Co.* We do not sit as a super-legislature to determine the wisdom, need, and propriety of laws that touch economic problems, business affairs, or social conditions. This law, however, operates directly on an intimate relation of husband and wife and their physician's role in one aspect of that relation.

The association of people is not mentioned in the Constitution nor in the Bill of Rights. The right to educate a child in a school of the parents' choice—whether public or private or parochial—is also not mentioned. Nor is the right to study any particular subject or any foreign language. Yet the First Amendment has been construed to include certain of those rights.

By *Pierce v. Society of Sisters*, the right to educate one's children as one chooses is made applicable to the States by the force of the First and Fourteenth Amendments. By *Meyer v. Nebraska*, the same dignity is given the right to study the German language in a private school. In other words, the State may not, consistently with the spirit of the First Amendment, contract the spectrum of available knowledge. The right of freedom of speech and press includes not only the right to utter or to print, but the right to distribute, the right to receive, the right to read and freedom of inquiry, freedom of thought, and freedom to teach (see *Wieman v. Updegraff*)—indeed the freedom of the entire university community. . . . Without those peripheral rights the specific rights would be less secure. And so we reaffirm the principle of the *Pierce* and the *Meyer* cases.

In *NAACP v. Alabama*, we protected the "freedom to associate and privacy in one's associations," noting that freedom of association was a peripheral First Amendment right. Disclosure of membership lists of a constitutionally valid association, we held, was invalid "as entailing the likelihood of a substantial restraint upon the exercise by petitioner's members of their right to freedom of association." In other words, the First Amendment has a penumbra where privacy is protected from governmental intrusion. In like context, we have protected forms of "association" that are not political in the customary sense but pertain to the social, legal, and economic benefit of the members. In *Schware v. Board of Bar Examiners*, we held it not permissible to bar a lawyer from practice, because he had once been a member of the Communist Party. The man's "association with that Party" was not shown to be "anything more than a political faith in a political party" and was not action of a kind proving bad moral character.

Those cases involved more than the "right of assembly"—a right that extends to all irrespective of their race or ideology. The right of "association," like the right of belief (*Board of Education v. Barnette*), is more than the right to attend a meeting; it includes the right to express one's attitudes or philosophies by membership in a group or by affiliation with it or by other lawful means. Association in that context is a form of expression of opinion; and while it is not expressly included in the First Amendment its existence is necessary in making the express guarantees fully meaningful.

The foregoing cases suggest that specific guarantees in the Bill of Rights have penumbras, formed by emanations from those guarantees that help give them life and substance. See *Poe v. Ullman* (dissenting opinion). Various guarantees create zones of privacy. The right of association contained in the penumbra of the First Amendment is one, as we have seen. The Third Amendment in its prohibition against the quartering of soldiers "in any house" in time of peace without the consent of the owner is another facet of that privacy. The Fourth Amendment explicitly affirms the "right of the people to be secure in their persons, houses, papers, and effects, against unreasonable searches and seizures." The Fifth Amendment in its Self-Incrimination Clause enables the citizen to create a zone of privacy which government may not force him to surrender to his detriment. The Ninth Amendment provides: "The enumeration in the Constitution, of certain rights, shall not be construed to deny or disparage others retained by the people."

The Fourth and Fifth Amendments were described in *Boyd v. United States*, as protection against all governmental invasions "of the sanctity of a man's home and the privacies of life." We recently referred in *Mapp v. Ohio*, to the Fourth Amendment as creating a "right to privacy, no less important than any other right carefully and particularly reserved to the people." . . .

We have had many controversies over these penumbral rights of "privacy and repose." See, e.g., *Breard v. Alexandria, Public Utilities Comm'n v. Pollak, Monroe v. Pape, Lanza v. New York, Frank v. Maryland, Skinner v. Oklahoma.* These cases bear witness that the right of privacy which presses for recognition here is a legitimate one.

The present case, then, concerns a relationship lying within the zone of privacy created by several fundamental constitutional guarantees. And it concerns a law which, in forbidding the use of contraceptives rather than regulating their manufacture or sale, seeks to achieve its goals by means having a maximum destructive impact upon that relationship. Such a law cannot stand in light of the familiar principle, so often applied by this Court, that a "governmental purpose to control or prevent activities constitutionally subject to state regulation may not be achieved by means which sweep unnecessarily broadly and thereby invade the area of protected freedoms." Would we allow the police to search the sacred precincts of marital bedrooms for telltale signs of the use of contraceptives? The very idea is repulsive to the notions of privacy surrounding the marriage relationship.

We deal with a right of privacy older than the Bill of Rights—older than our political parties, older than our school system. Marriage is a coming together for better or for worse, hopefully enduring, and intimate to the degree of being sacred. It is an association that promotes a way of life, not causes; a harmony in living, not political faiths; a bilateral loyalty, not commercial or social projects. Yet it is an association for as noble a purpose as any involved in our prior decisions.

Reversed.

> *Source: Griswold et al. v. Connecticut*, 381 U.S. 479; 85 S. Ct. 1678; 14 L. Ed. 2d 510; 1965

56. Voting Rights Act, 1965

Introduction

The Voting Rights Act of 1965 is possibly the most successful civil rights act ever passed by Congress. The law was enacted on August 9, 1965, with the support of President Lyndon B. Johnson. It was the first national law to guarantee fully the voting rights of all Americans. Despite the adoption of the Fifteenth Amendment in 1870, Southern states had used a variety of means to deny African Americans the right to vote. The Voting Rights Act authorized the use of federal voting registrars and prevented states from changing their election laws without clearance from the national government. Furthermore, the act suspended the use of literacy tests in portions of eight states. Within two years, the act helped to raise African-American voter registration rates from 52 percent to 62 percent. The Supreme Court upheld the act as appropriate congressional enforcement under Section 2 of the Fifteenth

Amendment in *South Carolina v. Katzenbach* (1966). In *Katzenbach v. Morgan* (1966), the Court also upheld a provision of the law (applying chiefly to New York City) that eliminated English literacy tests for individuals who had six years or more of education in another language. The Voting Rights Act was extended in 1970, in 1975, and in 1992.

Primary Source

Section 1971. Voting rights

(a) Race, color, or previous condition not to affect right to vote; uniform standards for voting qualifications; errors or omissions from papers; literacy tests; agreements between Attorney General and State or local authorities; definitions

(1) All citizens of the United States who are otherwise qualified by law to vote at any election by the people in any State, Territory, district, county, city, parish, township, school district, municipality, or other territorial subdivision, shall be entitled and allowed to vote at all such elections, without distinction of race, color, or previous condition of servitude; any constitution, law, custom, usage, or regulation of any State or Territory, or by or under its authority, to the contrary notwithstanding.

(2) No person acting under color of law shall—

(A) in determining whether any individual is qualified under State law or laws to vote in any election, apply any standard, practice, or procedure different from the standards, practices, or procedures applied under such law or laws to other individuals within the same county, parish, or similar political subdivision who have been found by State officials to be qualified to vote;

(B) deny the right of any individual to vote in any election because of an error or omission on any record or paper relating to any application, registration, or other act requisite to voting, if such error or omission is not material in determining whether such individual is qualified under State law to vote in such election; or

(C) employ any literacy test as a qualification for voting in any election unless (i) such test is administered to each individual and is conducted wholly in writing, and (ii) a certified copy of the test and of the answers given by the individual is furnished to him within twenty-five days of the submission of his request made within the period of time during which records and papers are required to be retained and preserved pursuant to title III of the Civil Rights Act of 1960 (42 U.S.C. 1974 et seq.): Provided, however, That the Attorney General may enter into agreements with appropriate State or local authorities that preparation, conduct, and maintenance of such tests in accordance with the provisions of applicable State or local law, including such special provisions as are necessary in the preparation, conduct, and maintenance of such tests for persons who are blind or otherwise physically handicapped, meet the purposes of this subparagraph and constitute compliance therewith.

(3) For purposes of this subsection—

(A) the term "vote" shall have the same meaning as in subsection (e) of this section;

(B) the phrase "literacy test" includes any test of the ability to read, write, understand, or interpret any matter.

(b) **Intimidation, threats, or coercion.** No person, whether acting under color of law or otherwise, shall intimidate, threaten, coerce, or attempt to intimidate, threaten, or coerce any other person for the purpose of interfering with the right of such other person to vote or to vote as he may choose, or of causing such other person to vote for, or not to vote for, any candidate for the office of President, Vice President, presidential elector, Member of the Senate, or Member of the House of Representatives, Delegates or Commissioners from the Territories or possessions, at any general, special, or primary election held solely or in part for the purpose of selecting or electing any such candidate.

(c) **Preventive relief; injunction; rebuttable literacy presumption; liability of United States for costs; State as party defendant.** Whenever any person has engaged or there are reasonable grounds to believe that any person is about to engage in any act or practice which would deprive any other person of any right or privilege secured by subsection (a) or (b) of this section, the Attorney General may institute for the United States, or in the name of the United States, a civil action or other proper proceeding for preventive relief, including an application for a permanent or temporary injunction, restraining order, or other order. If in any such proceeding literacy is a relevant fact there shall be a rebuttable presumption that any person who has not been adjudged an incompetent and who has completed the sixth grade in a public school in, or a private school accredited by, any State or territory, the District of Columbia, or the Commonwealth of Puerto Rico where instruction is carried on predominantly in the English language, possesses sufficient literacy, comprehension, and intelligence to vote in any election. In any proceeding hereunder the United States shall be liable for costs the same as a private person. Whenever, in a proceeding instituted under this subsection any official of a State or subdivision thereof is alleged to have committed any act or practice constituting a deprivation of any right or privilege secured by subsection (a) of this section, the act or practice shall also be deemed that of the State and the State may be joined as a party defendant and, if, prior to the institution of such proceeding, such official has resigned or has been relieved of his office and no successor has assumed such office, the proceeding may be instituted against the State.

(d) **Jurisdiction; exhaustion of other remedies.** The district courts of the United States shall have jurisdiction of proceedings instituted pursuant to this section and shall exercise the same without regard to whether the party aggrieved shall have exhausted any administrative or other remedies that may be provided by law.

(e) **Order qualifying person to vote; application; hearing; voting referees; transmittal of report and order; certificate of qualification; definitions.** In any proceeding instituted pursuant to subsection (c) of this section in the event the court finds that any person has been deprived on account of race or color of any right or privilege secured by subsection (a) of this section, the court shall upon request of the Attorney General and after each party has been given notice and the opportunity to be heard make a finding whether such deprivation was or is pursuant to a pattern or practice. If the court finds such pattern or practice, any person of such race or color resident within the affected area shall, for one year and there-after until the court subsequently finds that such pattern or practice has ceased, be entitled, upon his application therefor, to an order declaring him qualified to vote, upon proof that at any election or elections (1) he is qualified under State law to vote, and (2) he has since such finding by the court been (a) deprived of or denied under color of law the opportunity to register to vote or otherwise to qualify to vote, or (b) found not qualified to vote by any person acting under color of law. Such order shall be effective as to any election held within the longest period for which such applicant could have been registered or otherwise qualified under State law at which the applicant's qualifications would under State law entitle him to vote.

Notwithstanding any inconsistent provision of State law or the action of any State officer or court, an applicant so declared qualified to vote shall be permitted to vote in any such election. The Attorney General shall cause to be transmitted certified copies of such order to the appropriate election officers. The refusal by any such officer with notice of such order to permit any person so declared qualified to vote to vote at an appropriate election shall constitute contempt of court.

An application for an order pursuant to this subsection shall be heard within ten days, and the execution of any order disposing of such application shall not be stayed if the effect of such stay would be to delay the effectiveness of the order beyond the date of any election at which the applicant would otherwise be enabled to vote.

The court may appoint one or more persons who are qualified voters in the judicial district, to be known as voting referees, who shall subscribe to the oath of office required by section 3331 of title 5, to serve for such period as the court shall determine, to receive such applications and to take evidence and report to the court findings as to whether or not at any election or elections

(1) any such applicant is qualified under State law to vote, and

(2) he has since the finding by the court heretofore specified been (a) deprived of or denied under color of law the opportunity to register to vote or otherwise to qualify to vote, or (b) found not qualified to vote by any person acting under color of law. In a proceeding before a voting referee, the applicant shall be heard ex parte at such times and places as the court shall direct. His statement under oath shall be prima facie evidence as to his age, residence, and his prior efforts to register or otherwise qualify to vote. Where proof of literacy or an understanding of other subjects is required by valid provisions of State law, the answer of the applicant, if written, shall be included in such report to the court; if oral, it shall be taken down stenographically and a transcription included in such report to the court.

Upon receipt of such report, the court shall cause the Attorney General to transmit a copy thereof to the State attorney general and to each party to such proceeding together with an order to show cause within ten days, or such shorter time as the court may fix, why an order of the court should not be entered in accordance with such report. Upon the expiration of such period, such order shall be entered unless prior to that time there has been filed with the court and served upon all parties a statement of exceptions to such report. Exceptions as to matters of fact shall be considered only if supported by a duly verified copy of a public record or by affidavit of persons having personal knowledge of such facts or by statements or matters contained in such report; those relating to matters of law shall be supported by an appropriate memorandum of law. The issues of fact and law raised by such exceptions shall be determined by the court or, if the due and speedy administration of justice requires, they may be referred to the voting referee to determine in accordance with procedures prescribed by the court. A hearing as to an issue of fact shall be held only in the event that the proof in support of the exception disclose the existence of a genuine issue of material fact. The applicant's literacy and understanding of other subjects shall be determined solely on the basis of answers included in the report of the voting referee.

The court, or at its direction the voting referee, shall issue to each applicant so declared qualified a certificate identifying the holder thereof as a person so qualified.

Any voting referee appointed by the court pursuant to this subsection shall to the extent not inconsistent herewith have all the powers conferred upon a master by rule 53(c) of the Federal Rules of Civil Procedure. The compensation to be allowed to any persons appointed by the court pursuant to this subsection shall be fixed by the court and shall be payable by the United States.

Applications pursuant to this subsection shall be determined expeditiously. In the case of any application filed twenty or more days prior to an election which is undetermined by the time of such election, the court shall issue an order authorizing the applicant to vote provisionally: Provided, however, That such applicant shall be qualified to vote under State law. In the case of an application filed within twenty days prior to an election, the court, in its discretion, may make such an order. In either case the order shall make appropriate provision for the impounding of the applicant's ballot pending determination of the application. The court may take any other action, and may authorize such referee or such other person as it may designate to take any other action, appropriate or necessary to carry out the provisions of this subsection and to enforce its decrees.

This subsection shall in no way be construed as a limitation upon the existing powers of the court.

When used in the subsection, the word "vote" includes all action necessary to make a vote effective including, but not limited to, registration or other action required by State law prerequisite to voting, casting a ballot, and having such ballot counted and included in the appropriate totals of votes cast with respect to candidates for public office and propositions for which votes are received in an election; the words "affected area" shall mean any subdivision of the State in which the laws of the State relating to voting are or have been to any extent administered by a person found in the proceeding to have violated subsection (a) of this section; and the words "qualified under State law" shall mean qualified according to the laws, customs, or usages of the State, and shall not, in any event, imply qualifications more stringent than those used by the persons found in the proceeding to have violated subsection (a) in qualifying persons other than those of the race or color against which the pattern or practice of discrimination was found to exist.

(f) **Contempt; assignment of counsel; witnesses.** Any person cited for an alleged contempt under this Act shall be allowed to make his full defense by counsel learned in the law; and the court before which he is cited or tried, or some judge thereof, shall immediately, upon his request, assign to him such counsel, not exceeding two, as he may desire, who shall have free access to him at all reasonable hours. He shall be allowed, in his defense to make any proof that he can produce by lawful witnesses, and shall have the like process of the court to compel his witnesses to appear at his trial or hearing, as is usually granted to compel witnesses to appear on behalf of the prosecution. If such person shall be found by the court to be financially unable to provide for such counsel, it shall be the duty of the court to provide such counsel.

(g) **Three-judge district court: hearing, determination, expedition of action, review by Supreme Court; single-judge district court: hearing, determination, expedition of action.** In any proceeding instituted by the United States in any district court of the United States under this section in which the Attorney General requests a finding of a pattern or practice of discrimination pursuant to subsection (e) of this section the Attorney General, at the time he files the complaint, or any defendant in the proceeding, within twenty days after service upon him of the complaint, may file with the clerk of such court a request that a court of three judges be convened to hear and determine the entire case. A copy of the request for a three-judge court shall be immediately furnished by such clerk to the chief judge of the circuit (or in his absence, the presiding circuit judge of the circuit) in which the case is pending. Upon receipt of the copy of such request it shall be the duty of the chief judge of the circuit or the presiding circuit judge, as the case may be, to designate immediately three judges in such circuit, of whom at least one shall be a circuit judge and another of whom shall be a district judge of the court in which the proceeding was instituted, to hear and determine such case, and it shall be the duty of the judges so designated to assign the case for hearing at the earliest practicable date, to participate in the hearing and determination thereof, and to cause the case to be in every way expedited. An appeal from the final judgment of such court will lie to the Supreme Court.

In any proceeding brought under subsection (c) of this section to enforce subsection (b) of this section, or in the event neither the Attorney General nor any defendant files a request for a three-judge court in any proceeding authorized by this subsection, it shall be the duty of the chief judge of the district (or in his absence, the acting chief judge) in which the case is pending immediately to designate a judge in such district to hear and determine the case. In the event that no judge in the district is available to hear and determine the case, the chief judge of the district, or the acting chief judge, as the case may be, shall certify this fact to the chief judge of the circuit (or, in his absence, the acting chief judge) who shall then designate a district or circuit judge of the circuit to hear and determine the case.

It shall be the duty of the judge designated pursuant to this section to assign the case for hearing at the earliest practicable date and to cause the case to be in every way expedited.

Source: Public Law 89-110, *U.S. Statutes at Large* 79 (1965): 437, codified at *U.S. Code* 42, § 1973

57. Establishment of the Federal Judicial Center, 1967

Introduction

The Federal Judicial Center conducts research and educational programs designed to improve judicial administration of the federal courts. It was established by Congress in 1967 on the recommendation of Chief Justice Earl Warren and other members of the judiciary, who hoped that regular programs of research and education would improve the efficiency of the federal courts and also relieve the backlog of cases in the lower courts. The Federal Judicial Center's board consists of the chief justice, a rotating group of judges selected by the Judicial Conference, and the director of the Administrative Office. The Center conducts and supports research on the operation of the courts, offers education and training for judges and court personnel, and assists and advises the Judicial Conference on matters related to the administration and management of the courts. Subsequent legislation has expanded the Center's mandate to include, among other things, programs related to the history of the federal judiciary.

Primary Source

December 20, 1967.
81 Stat. 664.

AN ACT

To provide for the establishment of a Federal Judicial Center, and for other purposes.

Be it enacted by the Senate and House of Representatives of the United States of America in Congress assembled,

TITLE I—FEDERAL JUDICIAL CENTER

SEC. 101. Title 28, United States Code, is amended by inserting, immediately following chapter 41, a new chapter as follows:

"Chapter 42.—FEDERAL JUDICIAL CENTER

"Sec.

"620. Federal Judicial Center.

"621. Board; composition, tenure of members, compensation.

"622. Meetings; conduct of business.

"623. Duties of the Board.

"624. Powers of the Board.

"625. Director and staff.

"626. Compensation of the Director.

"627. Retirement; employee benefits.

"628. Appropriations and accounting.

"629. Organizational provisions.

"§ 620. Federal Judicial Center

"(a) There is established within the judicial branch of the Government a Federal Judicial Center, whose purpose it shall be to further the development and adoption of improved judicial administration in the courts of the United States.

"(b) The Center shall have the following functions:

"(1) to conduct research and study of the operation of the courts of the United States, and to stimulate and coordinate such research and study on the part of other public and private persons and agencies;

"(2) to develop and present for consideration by the Judicial Conference of the United States recommendations for improvement of the administration and management of the courts of the United States;

"(3) to stimulate, create, develop, and conduct programs of continuing education and training for personnel of the judicial branch of the Government including, but not limited to, judges, referees, clerks of court, probation officers, and United States commissioners; and

"(4) insofar as it may be consistent with the performance of the other functions set forth in this section, to provide staff, research, and planning assistance to the Judicial Conference of the United States and its committees.

"§ 621. Board; composition, tenure of members, compensation

"(a) The activities of the Center shall be supervised by a Board to be composed of—

"(1) the Chief Justice of the United States, who shall be the permanent Chairman of the Board;

"(2) two active judges of the courts of appeals of the United States and three active judges of the district courts of the United States elected by vote of the members of the Judicial Conference of the United States: Provided, however, That the judges so elected shall not be members of the Judicial Conference of the United States; and

"(3) the Director of the Administrative Office of the United States Courts, who shall be a permanent member of the Board.

"(b) The term of office of each elected member of the Board shall be four years: Provided, however, That section 629 of this chapter shall govern the terms of office of the first members elected to the Board: And provided however, That a member elected to serve for an unexpired term arising by virtue of the death, disability, retirement, or resignation of a member shall be elected only for such unexpired term.

"(c) No member elected for a four-year term shall be eligible for reelection to the Board.

"(d) Members of the Board shall serve without additional compensation, but shall be reimbursed for actual and necessary expenses incurred in the performance of their official duties.

"§ 622. Meetings; conduct of business

"(a) Regular meetings of the Board shall be held quarterly. Special meetings shall be held from time to time upon the call of the Chairman, acting at his own discretion or pursuant to the petition of any four members.

"(b) Each member of the Board shall be entitled to one vote. A simple majority of the membership shall constitute a quorum for the conduct of business. The Board shall act upon the concurrence of a simple majority of the members present and voting.

"§ 623. Duties of the Board

"(a) In its direction and supervision of the activities of the Federal Judicial Center, the Board shall—

"(1) establish such policies and develop such programs for the Federal Judicial Center as will further achievement of its purpose and performance of its functions;

"(2) formulate recommendations for improvements in the administration of the courts of the United States, in the training of the personnel of those courts, and in the management of their resources;

"(3) submit to the Judicial Conference of the United States, at least one month in advance of its annual meeting, a report of the activities of the Center and such recommendations as the Board may propose for the consideration of the Conference;

"(4) present to other government departments, agencies and instrumentalities whose programs or activities relate to the administration of justice in the courts of the United States the recommendations of the Center for the improvement of such programs or activities;

"(5) study and determine ways in which automatic data processing and systems procedures may be applied to the administration of the courts of the United States, and include in the annual report required by paragraph (3) of this subsection details of the results of the studies and determinations made pursuant to this paragraph; and

"(6) consider and recommend to both public and private agencies aspects of the operation of the courts of the United States deemed worthy of special study.

"(b) The Board shall transmit to Congress and to the Attorney General of the United States copies of all reports and recommendations submitted to the Judicial Conference of the United States. The Board shall also keep the Committees on the Judiciary of the United States Senate and House of Representatives fully and currently informed with respect to the activities of the Center.

"**§ 624. Powers of the Board**

"The Board is authorized—

"(1) to appoint and fix the duties of the Director of the Federal Judicial Center, who shall serve at the pleasure of the Board;

"(2) to request from any department, agency, or independent instrumentality of the Government any information it deems necessary to the performance of the functions of the Federal Judicial Center set forth in this chapter, and each such department, agency, or instrumentality is directed to cooperate with the Board and, to the extent permitted by law, to furnish such information to the Center upon request of the Chairman or upon request of the Director when the Board has delegated this authority to him;

"(3) to contract with and compensate government and private agencies or persons for research projects and other services, without regard to section 3709 of the Revised Statutes, as amended (41 U.S.C. 5), and to delegate such contract authority to the Director of the Federal Judicial Center, who is hereby empowered to exercise such delegated authority.

"§ 625. Director and staff

"(a) The Director shall supervise the activities of persons employed by the Center and perform other duties assigned to him by the Board.

"(b) The Director shall appoint and fix the compensation of such additional professional personnel as the Board may deem necessary, without regard to the provisions of title 5, United States Code, governing appointments in competitive service, or the provisions of chapter 51 and subchapter III of chapter 53 of such title, relating to classification and General Schedule pay rates: Provided, however, That the compensation of any person appointed under this subsection shall not exceed the annual rate of basic pay of level V of the Executive Schedule pay rates, section 5316, title 5, United States Code: And provided further, That the salary of a reemployed annuitant under the Civil Service Retirement Act shall be adjusted pursuant to the provisions of section 8344, title 5, United States Code.

"(c) The Director shall appoint and fix the compensation of such secretarial and clerical personnel as he may deem necessary, subject to the provisions of title 5, United States Code, governing appointments in competitive service and the provisions of chapter 5 and subchapter III of chapter 53 of such title, relating to classification and General Schedule pay rates.

"(d) The Director may procure personal services as authorized by section 3109 of title 5, United States Code, at rates not to exceed the daily equivalent of the highest rate payable under General Schedule pay rates, section 5332, title 5, United States Code.

"(e) The Director is authorized to incur necessary travel and other miscellaneous expenses incident to the operation of the Center.

"§ 626. Compensation of the Director

"The compensation of the Director of the Federal Judicial Center shall be the same as that of the Director of the Administrative Office of the United States Courts, and his appointment and salary shall not be subject to the provisions of title 5, United States Code, governing appointments in competitive service, or the provisions of chapter 51 and subchapter III of chapter 53 of such title, relating to classification and General Schedule pay rates: Provided, however, That any Director who is a justice or judge of the United States in active or retired status shall serve without additional compensation.

"§ 627. Retirement; employee benefits

"(a) A Director of the Federal Judicial Center who attains the age of seventy years shall be retired from that office.

"(b) The Director, the professional staff, and the clerical and secretarial employees of the Federal Judicial Center shall be deemed to be officers and employees of the judicial branch of the United States Government within the meaning of subchapter III of chapter 83 (relating to civil service retirement), chapter 87 (relating to Federal employees' life insurance program), and chapter 89 (relating to Federal employees' health benefits program) of title 5, United States Code: Provided, however, That the Director, upon written notice filed with the Director of the Administrative Office of the United States Courts within six months after the date on which he takes office, may waive coverage under subchapter III of chapter 83 of title 5, United States Code (relating to civil service retirement), and elect coverage under the retirement and disability provisions of this section: And provided further, That upon his non-retirement separation from the Federal Judicial Center, such waiver and election shall not operate to foreclose to the Director such opportunity as the law may provide to secure civil service retirement credit for service as Director by depositing with interest the amount required by section 8334 of title 5, United States Code.

"(c) Upon the retirement of a Director who has elected coverage under this section and who has served at least fifteen years and attained the age of sixty-five years the Director of the Administrative Office of the United States Courts shall pay him an annuity for life equal to 80 per centum of the salary of the office at the time of his retirement.

"Upon the retirement of a Director who has elected coverage under this section and who has served at least ten years, but who is not eligible to receive an annuity under the first paragraph of this subsection, the Administrative Office of the United States Courts shall pay him an annuity for life equal to that proportion of 80 per centum of the salary of the office at the time of his retirement that the number of years of his service bears to fifteen, reduced by one-quarter of 1 per centum for each full month, if any, he is under the age of sixty-five at the time of separation from service.

"(d) A Director who has elected coverage under this section and who becomes permanently disabled to perform the duties of his office shall be retired and shall receive an annuity for life equal to 80 per centum of the salary of the office at the time of his retirement if he has served at least fifteen years, or equal to that proportion of 80 per centum of such salary that the aggregate number of years of his service bears to fifteen if he has served less than fifteen years, but in no event less than 50 per centum of such salary.

"(e) For the purpose of this section, 'service' means service, whether or not continuous, as Director of the Federal Judicial Center, and any service, not to exceed five years, as a judge of the United States, a Senator or Representative in Congress, or a civilian official appointed by the President, by and with the advice and consent of the Senate.

"§ 628. Appropriations and accounting

"There are hereby authorized to be appropriate such sums as may be necessary to carry out the provisions of this chapter. The Administrative Office of the United States Courts shall provide accounting, disbursing, auditing, and other fiscal services for the Federal Judicial Center.

"§ 629. Organizational provisions

"(a) The terms of office of the members first elected to the Board shall commence on the thirtieth day after the first meeting of the Judicial Conference after the date on which this chapter shall take effect.

"(b) The members first elected to the Board shall continue in office for terms of one, two, three, three, and four years, respectively, the term of each to be designated by the Judicial Conference of the United States at the time of his election.

"(c) Members first elected to the Board who are designated by the Judicial Conference of the United States to serve terms of office of less than four years shall be eligible for reelection to one full term of office."

TITLE II—ADDITIONAL AMENDMENTS TO TITLE 28, UNITED STATES CODE

SEC. 201. (a) Chapter 41 of title 28, United States Code, is amended by adding at the end thereof a new section as follows:

"§ 611. Retirement of Director

"(a) The Director may, by written election filed with the Chief Justice of the United States within six months after the date on which he takes office, waive coverage under subchapter III (relating to civil service retirement) of chapter 83, title 5, United States Code, and bring himself within the purview of this section. Such waiver and election shall not operate to foreclose to the Director, upon separation from service other than by retirement, such opportunity as the law may provide to secure civil service retirement credit for service as Director by depositing with interest the amount required by section 8334 of title 5, United States Code.

"(b) Upon the retirement of a Director who has elected coverage under this section and who has served at least fifteen years and attained the age of sixty-five years the Administrative Office of the United States Courts shall pay him an annuity for life equal to 80 per centum of the salary of the office at the time of his retirement.

"Upon the retirement of a Director who has elected coverage under this section and who has served at least ten years, but who is not eligible to receive an annuity under the first paragraph of this subsection, the Administrative Office of the United States Courts shall pay him an annuity for life equal to that proportion of 80 per centum of the salary of the office at the time of his retirement that the number of years of his service bears to fifteen, reduced by one-quarter of 1 per centum for each full month, if any, he is under the age of sixty-five at the time of separation from service.

"(c) A Director who has elected coverage under this section and who becomes permanently disabled to perform the duties of his office shall be retired and shall receive an annuity for life equal to 80 per centum of the salary of the office at the time of his retirement if he has served at least fifteen years, or equal to that proportion of 80 per centum of such salary that the aggregate number of years of his service bears to fifteen if he has served less than fifteen years, but in no event less than 50 per centum of such salary.

"(d) For the purpose of this section, 'service' means service, whether or not continuous, as Director of the Administrative Office of the United States Courts, and any service, not to exceed five years, as a judge of the United States, a Senator or Representative in Congress, or a civilian official appointed by the President, by and with the advice and consent of the Senate."

(b) The table of contents preceding such chapter is amended by inserting at the end thereof the following new item:

"611. Retirement of Director."

SEC. 202. Section 376, title 28, United States Code, is amended by adding the following new subsections:

"(r) The Director of the Federal Judicial Center shall be deemed a judge of the United States for the purposes of this section and shall be entitled to bring himself within the purview of this section by filing an election as provided in subsection (a) of this section within the time therein specified. As applied to a Director of the Federal Judicial Center, the phrase 'retirement from office by resignation on salary under section 371(a) of this title' as used in subsections (b), (c), (g), (i), and (n) of this section shall mean 'retirement from office under subsection (c) or (d) of section 627 of this title or by removal after not less than ten years service', the phrase 'salary paid after retirement' as used in subsection (b) of this section shall mean 'annuity paid after retirement under subsection (c) or (d) of section 627 of this title', and the phrase 'resigns from office other than on salary under section 371(a) of this title' as used in subsection (f) of this section shall mean 'resigns from office otherwise than on retirement under subsection (c) or (d) of section 627 of this title or is removed after less than ten years service'.

"(s) The Director of the Administrative Office of the United States Courts shall be deemed a judge of the United States for the purposes of this section and shall be entitled to bring himself within the purview of this section by filing an election as provided in subsection (a) of this section within the time therein specified. As applied to a Director of the Administrative Office of the United States Courts, the phrase 'retirement from office by resignation on salary under section 371 (a) of this title' as used in subsections (b), (c), (g), (i), and (n) of this section shall mean 'retirement from office under section 611 of this title or by removal after not less than ten years service', the phrase 'salary paid after retirement' as used in subsection (b) of this section shall mean 'annuity paid after retirement under section 611 of this title', and the phrase 'resigns from office other than on salary under section 371(a) of this title' as used in subsection (f) of this section shall mean 'resigns from office otherwise than on retirement under section 611 of this title or is removed after less than ten years service'."

SEC. 203. Subsection (a) of section 604, title 28, United States Code, is amended by amending:

(a) Paragraph (7) to read as follows:

"(7) Regulate and pay annuities to widows and surviving dependent children of judges, Directors of the Federal Judicial Center, and Directors of the Administrative Office, and necessary travel and subsistence expenses incurred by judges, court officers and employees, and officers and employees of the Administrative Office, and the Federal Judicial Center, while absent from their official stations on official business,";

(b) Paragraph (9), to insert between the word "courts" and the word "and" a comma and the words "the Federal Judicial Center,";

(c) Paragraphs (10) and (11), to insert between the word "courts" and the word "and" a comma and the words "the Federal Judicial Center,".

SEC. 204. The table of contents to "Part III.—COURT OFFICERS AND EM-PLOYEES" of title 28, United States Code, is amended by inserting after

"41. Administrative Office of the United States Courts_ _ _ _ _ _ _ _ _ _ _ 601" a new chapter reference as follows:

"42. Federal Judicial Center _ 620".

SEC. 205. (a) Except as provided in subsection (b), the amendments made by this title, insofar as they relate to retirement and survivorship benefits of the Director of the Administrative Office of the United States Courts, shall be applicable only with respect to persons first appointed to such office after the date of enactment of this Act.

(b) The provisions of section 611(a), first paragraph of section 611(b), and section 376(s), of title 28, United States Code, as added by such amendments, shall be applicable to a Director or former Director of the Administrative Office of the United States Courts who was first appointed prior to the date of enactment of this Act if at the time such Director or former Director left or leaves such office he had, or shall have, attained the age of sixty-five years and completed fifteen years of service as Director of the Administrative Office of the United States Courts and if, on or before the expiration of six months following the date of enactment of this Act, he makes the election referred to in section 611(a) or section 376(s), or both, as the case may be.

Approved December 20, 1967.

Source: 28 U.S.C. §§ 620–629

58. Federal Magistrates Act, 1968

Introduction

In 1968 Congress abolished the position and title of United States Commisioners and created the position and titles of federal magistrates who continued to perform the same duties. The Federal Magistrates Act of 1968 instructed the Judicial Conference to determine the number of magistrates necessary in each judicial district and authorized the district judges to appoint the approved number. Magistrates continued to carry out the commissioners' duties, such as issuing warrants, conducting hearings, and establishing bail. District judges could assign other duties related to service as special masters, pretrial and discovery proceedings, and applications for post-trial relief. Magistrates also were granted the authority to conduct trials of persons accused of minor offenses and to sentence those convicted, although defendants were granted the right to choose a trial with a district judge or to appeal the magistrate's ruling to the district court. Subsequent legislation expanded the magistrates' trial authority, especially in civil cases. The Judicial Improvements Act of 1990 (104 Stat. 5089) changed the title of the office to Magistrate Judge.

Primary Source

October 17, 1968.
82 Stat. 1668.

AN ACT

To abolish the office of United States commissioner, to establish in place thereof within the judicial branch of the Government the office of United States magistrate, and for other purposes.

Be it enacted by the Senate and House of Representatives of the United States of America in Congress assembled, That this Act may be cited as the "Federal Magistrates Act".

TITLE I—UNITED STATES MAGISTRATES

SEC. 101. Chapter 43, title 28, United States Code, relating to United States commissioners, is amended to read as follows:

"Chapter 43.—UNITED STATES MAGISTRATES

"Sec.

"631. Appointment and tenure.

"632. Character of service.

"633. Determination of number, locations, and salaries of magistrates.

"634. Compensation.

"635. Expenses.

"636. Jurisdiction and powers.

"637. Training.

"638. Dockets and forms; United States Code; seals.

"639. Definitions.

"§ 631. Appointment and tenure

"(a) The judges of each United States district court shall appoint United States magistrates in such numbers and to serve at such locations within the judicial district as the conference may determine under this chapter. Where there is more than one judge of a district, court, the appointment, whether an original appointment or a reappointment, shall be by the concurrence of a majority of all the judges of such district court, and when there is no such concurrence, then by the chief judge. Where an area under the administration of the National Park Service, or the United States Fish and Wildlife Service, or any other Federal agency, extends into two or more judicial districts and it is deemed desirable by the conference that the territorial jurisdiction of a magistrate's appointment include the entirety of such area, the appointment or reappointment shall he made by the concurrence of a majority of all judges of the district courts of the judicial districts involved, and where there is no such concurrence by the concurrence of the chief judges of such district courts.

"(b) No individual may be appointed or serve as a magistrate under this chapter unless:

"(1) He is a member in good standing of the bar of the highest court of the State in which he is to serve, or, in the case of an individual appointed to serve—

"(A) in the District of Columbia, a member in good standing of the bar of the United States district court for the District of Columbia;

"(B) in the Commonwealth of Puerto Rico, a member in good standing of the bar of the Supreme Court of Puerto Rico; or

"(C) in an area under the administration of the National Park Service, the United States Fish and Wildlife Service, or any other Federal agency that extends into two or more States, a member in good standing of the bar of the highest court of one of those States;

except that an individual who does not meet the bar membership requirements of the first sentence of this paragraph may be appointed and serve as a part-time magistrate if the appointing court or courts and the conference find that no qualified individual who is a member of the bar is available to serve at a specific location;

"(2) He is determined by the appointing district court or courts to be competent to perform the duties of the office;

"(3) In the case of an individual appointed to serve in a national park, he resides within the exterior boundaries of that park, or at someplace reasonably adjacent thereto;

"(4) He is not related by blood or marriage to a judge of the appointing court or courts at the time of his initial appointment.

"(c) A magistrate may hold no other civil or military office or employment under the United States: Provided, however, That, with the approval of the conference, a part-time referee in bankruptcy or a clerk or deputy clerk of a court of the United States may be appointed and serve as a part-time United States magistrate, but the conference shall fix the aggregate amount of compensation to be received for performing the duties of part-time magistrate and part-time referee bankruptcy, clerk or deputy clerk: And provided further, That retired officers and retired enlisted personnel of the Regular and Reserve components of the Army, Navy, Air Force, Marine Corps, and Coast Guard, members of the Reserve components of the Army, Navy, Air Force, Marine Corps, and Coast Guard, and members of the Army National Guard of the United States, the Air National Guard of the United States, and the Naval Militia and of the National Guard of a State or territory, or the District of Columbia, except the National Guard disbursing officers who are on a full-time salary basis, may be appointed and serve as United States magistrates.

"(d) No individual may serve under this chapter after having attained the age of seventy years: Provided, however, That upon the unanimous vote of all the judges of the appointing court or courts, a magistrate who has attained the age of seventy years may continue to serve and may be reappointed under this chapter.

"(e) The appointment of any individual as a full-time magistrate shall be for a term of eight years, and the appointment of any individuals as a part-time magistrate shall be for a term of four years, except that the term of a full-time or part-time magistrate appointed under subsection (j) shall expire upon—

"(1) the expiration of the absent magistrate's term,

"(2) the reinstatement of the absent magistrate in regular service in office as a magistrate,

"(3) the failure of the absent magistrate to make timely application under subsection (i) of this section for reinstatement in regular military service in office as a magistrate after discharge or release from military service,

"(4) the death or resignation of the absent magistrate, or

"(5) the removal from office of the absent magistrate pursuant to subsection (h) of this section, whichever may first occur.

"(f) Each individual appointed as a magistrate under this section shall take the oath or affirmation prescribed by section 453 of this title before performing the duties of his office.

"(g) Each appointment made by a judge or judges of a district court shall be entered of record in such court, and notice of such appointment shall be given at once by the clerk of that court to the Director.

"(h) Removal of a magistrate during the term for which he is appointed shall be only for incompetency, misconduct, neglect of duty, or physical or mental disability, but a magistrate's office shall be terminated if the conference determines that the services performed by his office are no longer needed. Removal shall be by the judges of the district court for the judicial district in which the magistrate serves; where there is more than one judge of a district court, removal shall not occur unless a majority of all the judges of such court concur in the order of removal; and when there is a tie vote of the judges of the district court on the question of the removal or retention in office of a magistrate, then removal shall be only by a concurrence of a majority of all the judges of the council. In the case of a magistrate appointed under the third sentence of subsection (a) of this section, removal shall not occur unless a majority of all the judges of the appointing district courts concur in the order of removal; and where there is a tie vote on the question of the removal or retention in office of a magistrate, then removal shall be only by a concurrence of a majority of all the judges of the council or councils. Before any order or removal shall be entered, a full specification of the charges shall be furnished to the magistrate, and he shall be accorded by the judge or judges of the removing court, courts, council, or councils an opportunity to be heard on the charges.

"(i) (1) A magistrate who is inducted into the Armed Forces of the United States pursuant to the Military Selective Service Act of 1967 (50 U.S.C. App. 451 et seq.), or is otherwise ordered to active duty with such forces for a period of more than thirty days, and who makes application for a leave of absence to the district court or courts which appointed him, shall be granted a leave of absence without compensation for such period as he is required to serve in such forces. Every application for a leave of absence under this subsection shall include a copy of the official orders requiring the magistrate's military service. The granting of a leave of absence under this subsection shall not operate to extend the term of office of any magistrate.

"(2) A magistrate granted a leave of absence under this subsection who—

"(A) receives a certificate of service under section 9(a) of the Military Selective Service Act of 1967 (50 U.S.C. App. 459(a)), or is released under honorable conditions from the military service,

"(B) makes application for reinstatement to regular service in office as a magistrate within ninety days after he is released from such service or training or from hospitalization continuing after discharge for a period of not more than one year, and

"(C) is determined by the appointing court or courts in the manner specified in subsection (a) of this section to be still qualified to perform the duties of such position,

shall be reinstated in regular service in such office.

"(j) Upon the grant by the appropriate district, court or courts of a leave of absence to a magistrate entitled to such relief under the terms of subsection (i) of this section, such court or courts may proceed to appoint, in the manner specified in subsection (a) of this section, another magistrate, qualified for appointment and service under subsections (b), (c), and (d) of this section, who shall serve for the period specified in subsection (e) of this section.

"§ 632. Character of service

"(a) Full-time United States magistrates may not engage in the practice of law, and may not engage in any other business, occupation, or employment inconsistent with the expeditious, proper, and impartial performance of their duties as judicial officers.

"(b) Part-time United States magistrates shall render such service as judicial officers as is required by law. While so serving they may engage in the practice of law, but may not serve as counsel in any criminal action in any court of the United States, nor act in any capacity that is, under such regulations as the conference may establish, inconsistent with the proper discharge of their office. Within such restrictions, they may engage in any other business, occupation, or employment which is not inconsistent with the expeditious, proper, and impartial performance of their duties as judicial officers.

"§ 633. Determination of number, locations, and salaries of magistrates

"(a) SURVEYS BY THE DIRECTOR.—

"(1) The Director shall, within one year immediately following the date of the enactment of the Federal Magistrates Act, make a careful survey of conditions in judicial districts to determine (A) the number of appointments of full-time magistrates and part-time magistrates required to be made under this chapter to provide for the expeditious and effective administration of justice, (B) the locations at which such officers shall serve, and (C) their respective salaries under section 634 of this title. Thereafter, the Director shall, from time to time, make such surveys, general or local, as the conference shall deem expedient.

"(2) In the course of any survey, the Director shall take into account local conditions in each judicial district, including the areas and the populations to be served, the transportation and communications facilities available, the amount and distribution of business of the type expected to arise before officers appointed under this chapter (including such matters as may be assigned under section 636(b) of this chapter), and any other material factors. The Director shall give consideration to suggestions from any interested parties, including district judges, United States commissioners or officers appointed under this chapter, United States attorneys, bar associations, and other parties having relevant experience or information.

"(3) The surveys shall be made with a view toward creating and maintaining a system of full-time United States magistrates. However, should the Director find, as a result of any such surveys, areas in which the employment of a full-time magistrate would not be feasible or desirable, he shall recommend the appointment of part-time United States magistrates in such numbers and at such locations as may be required to permit prompt and efficient issuance of process and to permit individuals charged with criminal offenses against the United States to be brought before a judicial officer of the United States promptly after arrest.

"(b) DETERMINATION BY THE CONFERENCE.—Upon the completion of the initial surveys required by subsection (a) of this section, the Director shall report to the district courts, the councils, and the conference his recommendations concerning the number of full-time magistrates and part-time magistrates, their respective locations, and the amount of their respective salaries under section 643 of this title. The district courts shall advise their respective councils, stating their recommendations and the reasons therefor; the councils shall advise the conference, stating their recommendations and the reasons therefor, and shall also report to the conference the recommendations of the district courts. The conference shall determine, in the light of the recommendations of the Director the district courts, and the councils, the number of full-time United States magistrates and part-time United States magistrates, the locations at which they shall serve, and their respective salaries. Such determinations shall take effect in each judicial district at such time as the district court for such judicial district shall determine, but in no event later than one year after they are promulgated.

"(c) CHANGES IN NUMBER, LOCATIONS, AND SALARIES.—Except as otherwise provided in this chapter, the conference may, from time to time, in the light of the recommendations of the Director, the district courts, and the councils, change the number, locations, and salaries of full-time and part-time magistrates as the expeditious administration of justice may require. Such determinations shall take effect sixty days after they are promulgated.

"§ 634. Compensation

"(a) Officers appointed under this chapter shall receive as full compensation for their services salaries to be fixed by the conference pursuant to section 633 of this title, at rates not more than $22,500 per annum for full-time United States magistrates, and not more than $11,000 per annum nor less than $100 per annum for part-time United States magistrates. In fixing the amount of salary to be paid to any officer appointed under this chapter, consideration shall be given to the average number and the nature of matters that have arisen during the immediately preceding period of five years, and that may be expected thereafter to arise, over which such officer would have jurisdiction and to such other factors as may be material. Disbursement of salaries shall be made by or pursuant to the order of the Director.

"(b) Except as provided by section 8344, title 5, relating to reductions of the salaries of reemployed annuitants under subchapter III of chapter 83 of such title and unless the office has been terminated as provided in this chapter, the salary of a full-time United States magistrate shall not be reduced, during the term in which he is serving, below the salary fixed for him at the beginning of that term.

"(c) All United States magistrates effective upon their taking die oath or affirmation of office, and all necessary clerical and secretarial assistants employed in the offices of full-time United States magistrates shall be deemed to be officers and employees in the judicial branch of the United States Government within the meaning of subsection III (relating to civil service retirement) of chapter 83, chapter 87 (relating to Federal employees' group life insurance), and chapter 89 (relating to Federal employees' health benefits program) of title.

5. Part-time magistrates shall not be excluded from coverage under these chapters solely for lack of a prearranged regular tour of duty.

"§ 635. Expenses

"(a) Full-time United States magistrates serving under this chapter shall be allowed their actual and necessary expenses incurred in the performance of their duties, including the compensation of necessary clerical and secretarial assistance. Such expenses and compensation shall be determined and paid by the Director under such regulations as the Director shall prescribe with the approval of the conference. The Administrator of General Services shall provide such magistrates with necessary courtrooms, office space, furniture and facilities within United States courthouses or office buildings owned or occupied by departments or agencies of the United States, or should suitable courtroom and office space not be available within any such courthouse or office building, the Administrator of General Services, at the request of the Director, shall procure and pay for suitable courtroom and office space, furniture and facilities for such magistrate in another building, but only if such request hat has been approved as necessary by the judicial council of the appropriate circuit.

"(b) Under such regulations as the Director shall prescribe with the approval of the conference, the Director shall reimburse part-time magistrates for actual expenses necessarily incurred by them in the performance of their duties under this chapter. Such reimbursement may be made, at rates not exceeding those prescribed by such regulations, for expenses incurred by such part-time magistrates for clerical and secretarial assistance, stationery, telephone and other communications services, travel, and such other expenses as may be determined to be necessary for the proper performance of the duties of such officers: Provided, however, That no reimbursement shall be made for all or any portion of the expense incurred by such part-time magistrates for the procurement of office space.

"§ 636. Jurisdiction and powers

"(a) Each United States magistrate serving under this chapter shall have within the territorial jurisdiction prescribed by his appointment—

"(1) all powers and duties conferred or imposed upon United States commissioners by law or by the Rules of Criminal Procedure for the United States District Courts

"(2) the power to administer oaths and affirmations, impose conditions of release under section 3146 of title 18, and take acknowledgements, affidavits, and depositions; and

"(3) the power to conduct trials under section 3401, title 18, United States Code, in conformity with and subject to the limitations of that section.

"(b) Any district court of the United States, by the concurrence of a majority of all the judges of such district court, may establish rules pursuant to which any full-time United States magistrate, or, where there is no full-time magistrate reasonably available, any part-time magistrate specially designated by the court, may be assigned within the territorial jurisdiction of such court such additional duties as are not inconsistent with the Constitution and laws of the United States. The additional duties authorized by rule may include, but are not restricted to—

"(1) service as a special master in an appropriate civil action, pursuant to the applicable provisions of this title and the Federal Rules of Civil Procedure for the United States district courts;

"(2) assistance to a district judge in the conduct of pretrial or discovery proceedings in civil or criminal actions; and

"(3) preliminary review of applications for posttrial relief made by individuals convicted of criminal offenses, and submission of a report and recommendations to facilitate the decision of the district judge having jurisdiction over the case as to whether there should be a hearing.

"(c) The practice and procedure for the trial of cases before officers serving under this chapter, and for the taking and hearing of appeals to the district courts, shall conform to rules promulgated by the Supreme Court pursuant to section 3402 of title 18, United States Code.

"(d) In a proceeding before a magistrate, any of the following acts or conduct shall constitute a contempt of the district court for the district wherein the magistrate is sitting: (1) disobedience or resistance to any lawful order, process or writ; (2) misbehavior at a hearing or other proceeding, or so near the place thereof as to obstruct the same; (3) failure to produce, after having been ordered to do so, any pertinent document; (4) refusing to appear after having been subpenaed or, upon appearing, refusal to take the oath or affirmation as a witness, or, having taken the oath or affirmation, refusal to be examined according to law; or (5) any other act or conduct which if committed before a judge of the district court would constitute contempt of such court. Upon the commission of any such act or conduct, the magistrate shall forthwith certify the facts to a judge of the district court and may serve or cause to be served upon any person whose behavior is brought into question under this section an order requiring such person to appear before a judge of that court upon a day certain to show cause why he should not be adjudged in contempt by reason of the facts so certified. A judge of the district court shall thereupon, in a summary manner, hear the evidence as to the act or conduct complained of and, if it is such as to warrant punishment, punish such person in the same manner and to the same extent as for a contempt committed before a judge of the court, or commit such person upon the conditions applicable in the case of defiance of the process of the district court or misconduct in the presence of a judge of that court.

"§ 637. Training

"The Federal Judicial Center shall conduct periodic training programs and seminars for both full-time and part-time United States magistrates, including an introductory training program for new magistrates, to be held within one year after initial appointment.

"§ 638. Dockets and forms; United States Code; seals

"(a) The Director shall furnish to United States magistrates adequate docket books and forms prescribed by the Director. The Director shall also furnish to each such officer a copy of the current edition of the United States Code.

"(b) All property furnished to any such officer shall remain the property of the United States and, upon the termination of his term of office, shall be transmitted to his successor in office or otherwise disposed of as the Director orders.

"(c) The Director shall furnish to each United States magistrate appointed under this chapter an official impression seal in a form prescribed by the conference. Each such officer shall affix his seal to every jurat or certificate of his official acts without fee.

"§ 639. Definitions

"As used in this chapter—

"(1) 'Conference' shall mean the Judicial Conference of the United States;

"(2) 'Council' shall mean the Judicial Council of the Circuit;

"(3) 'Director' shall mean the Director of the Administrative Office of the United States Courts;

"(4) 'Full-time magistrate' shall mean a full-time United States magistrate; and

"(5) 'Part-time magistrate' shall mean a part-time United States magistrate; and

"(6) 'United States magistrate' and 'magistrate' shall mean both full-time and part-time United States magistrates."

SEC. 102. (a) The item relating to United States commissioners contained in the chapter analysis of part III, title 28, United States Code, is amended to read as follows:

"43. United States magistrates_ _631."

(b) The item relating to United States commissioners contained in the part and chapter analysis immediately following the title caption of title 28, United States Code, is amended to read as follows:

"43. United States magistrates_ _631."

TITLE II—ADMINISTRATIVE OFFICE OF THE UNITED STATES COURTS

SEC. 201. (a) Paragraph (9) of subsection (a) of section 604, title 28, United States Code, is amended by striking out the words "United States Commissioners", and inserting in lieu thereof the words "United States magistrates".

(b) Section 604, title 28, United States Code, is amended by adding at the end thereof the following new subsections:

"(d) The Director, under the supervision and direction of the conference, shall:

"(1) supervise all administrative matters relating to the offices of the United States magistrates;

"(2) gather, compile, and evaluate all statistical and other information required for the performance of his duties and the duties of the conference with respect to such officers;

"(3) lay before Congress annually statistical tables and other information which will accurately reflect the business which has come before the various United States magistrates;

"(4) prepare and distribute a manual, with annual supplements and periodic revisions, for the use of such officers, which shall set forth their powers and duties, describe all categories of proceedings that may arise before them, and contain such other information as may be required to enable them to discharge their powers and duties promptly, effectively, and impartially.

"(e) The Director may promulgate appropriate rules and regulations approved by the conference and not inconsistent with any provision of law, to assist him in the performance of the duties conferred upon him by subsection (d) of this section. Magistrates shall keep such records and make such reports as are specified in such rules and regulations."

TITLE III—AMENDMENTS TO TITLE 18, UNITED STATES CODE

TECHNICAL AMENDMENTS

SEC. 301. (a) Except as otherwise specifically provided by this title, part II, title 18, United States Code (relating to criminal procedure) is amended by:

(1) striking out the words "United States commissioner" wherever they appear therein, and inserting in lieu thereof the words "United States magistrate";

(2) striking out the words "United States commissioners" wherever they appear therein, and inserting in lieu thereof the words "United States magistrates";

(3) striking out the word "commissioner" wherever it appears in relation to a United States Commissioner, and inserting in lieu thereof the word "magistrate";

(4) striking out the word "Commissioners" wherever it appears relation to United States commissioners, and inserting in lieu thereof the word "magistrates".

(b) Section 202(a) of title 18, United States Code, is amended by striking out words "or a part-time United States Commissioner", and inserting in lieu thereof the words "a part-time United States commissioner, or a part-time United States magistrate".

(c) The chapter caption of chapter 219, part II, title 18, United States Code, is amended to read as follows:

"Chapter 219.—TRIAL BY UNITED STATES MAGISTRATES"

TRIAL BY MAGISTRATES

SEC. 302. (a) Section 3401, title 18, United States Code, is amended to read as follows:

"§ 3401. Minor offenses; application of probation laws

"(a) When specially designated to exercise such jurisdiction by the district court or courts he serves, and under such conditions as may be imposed by the terms of the special designation, any United States magistrate shall have jurisdiction to try persons accused of, and sentence persons convicted of, minor offenses committed within that judicial district.

"(b) Any person charged with a minor offense may elect, however, to be tried before a judge of the district court of the district in which the offense was committed. The magistrate shall carefully explain to the defendant that he has a right to trial before a judge of the district court and that he may have a right to trial by jury before such judge and shall not proceed to try the case unless the defendant, after such explanation, signs a written consent to be tried before the magistrate that specifically waives both a trial before a judge of the district court and any right to trial by jury that he may have.

"(c) A magistrate who exercises trial jurisdiction under this section, and before whom a person is convicted or pleads either guilty or nolo contendere, may, with the approval of a judge of the district court, direct the probation service of the court to conduct a presentence investigation on that person and render a report to the magistrate prior to the imposition of sentence.

"(d) The probation laws shall be applicable to persons tried by a magistrate under this section, and such officer shall have power to grant probation and to revoke or reinstate the probation of any person granted probation by him.

"(e) Proceedings before United States magistrates under this section shall be taken down by a court reporter or recorded by suitable sound recording equipment. For purposes of appeal a copy of the record of such proceedings shall be made available at the expense of the United States to a person who makes affidavit that he is unable to pay or give security therefor, and the expense of such copy shall be paid by the Director of the Administrative Office of the United States Courts.

"(f) As used in this section, the term 'minor offenses' means misdemeanors punishable under the laws of the United States, the penalty for which does not exceed imprisonment for a period of one year, or a fine of not more than $1,000, or both, except that such term does not include any offense punishable under any of the following provisions of law: Section 102 of the Revised Statutes, as amended (2 U.S.C. 192); section 314(a) of the Federal Corrupt Practices Act, 1925 (2 U.S.C. 252(a)); and sections 210, 211, 242, 594, 597, 599, 600, 601, 1304, 1504, 1508, 1509, 2234, 2235, and 2236 of title 18, United States Code."

(b) Section 3402, title 18, United States Code, is amended to read as follows:

"§ 3402. Rules of procedure; practice and appeal

"In all cases of conviction by a United States magistrate an appeal of right shall lie from the judgment of the magistrate to a judge of the district court of the district in which the offense was committed.

"The Supreme Court shall prescribe rules of procedure and practice for the trial of cases before magistrates and for taking and hearing of appeals to the judges of the district courts of the United States."

(c) The item related to section 3401, title 18, United States Code, contained in the chapter analysis of chapter 219, title 18, United States Code, is amended to read as follows:

"3401. Minor offenses; application of probation laws."

SEC. 303. (a) Section 3060, title 18, United States Code, is amended to read as follows:

"§ 3060. Preliminary examination

"(a) Except as otherwise provided by this section, a preliminary examination shall be held within the time set by the judge or magistrate pursuant to subsection (b) of this section, to determine whether there is probable cause to believe that an offense has been committed and that the arrested person has committed it.

"(b) The date for the preliminary examination shall be fixed by the judge or magistrate at the initial appearance of the arrested person. Except as provided by subsection (c) of this section, or unless the arrested person waives the preliminary examination, such examination shall be held within a reasonable time following initial appearance, but in any event not later than—

"(1) the tenth day following the date of the initial appearance of the arrested person before such officer if the arrested person is held in custody without any provision for release, or is held in custody for failure to meet the conditions of release imposed, or is released from custody only during specified hours of the day; or

"(2) the twentieth day following the date of the initial appearance if the arrested person is released from custody under any condition other than a condition described in paragraph (1) of this subsection.

"(c) With the consent of the arrested person, the date fixed by the judge or magistrate for the preliminary examination may be a date later than that prescribed by subsection (b), or may be continued one or more times to a date subsequent to the date initially fixed therefor. In the absence of such consent of the accused, the date fixed for the preliminary hearing may be a date later than that prescribed by subsection (b), or may be continued to a date subsequent to the date initially fixed therefor, only upon the order of a judge of the appropriate United States district court after a finding that extraordinary circumstances exist, and that the delay of the preliminary hearing is indispensable to the interests of justice.

"(d) Except as provided by subsection (e) of this section, an arrested person who has not been accorded the preliminary examination required by subsection (a) within the period of time fixed by the judge or magistrate in compliance with subsections (b) and (c), shall be discharged from custody or from the requirement of bail or any other condition of release, without prejudice, however, to the institution of further criminal proceedings against him upon the charge upon which he was arrested.

"(e) No preliminary examination in compliance with subsection (a) of this section shall be required to be accorded an arrested person, nor shall such arrested person be discharged from custody or from the requirement of bail or any other condition of release pursuant to subsection (d), if at any time subsequent to the initial appearance of such person before a judge or magistrate and prior to the date fixed for the preliminary examination pursuant to subsections (b) and (c) an indictment is returned or, in appropriate cases, an information is filed against such person in a court of the United States.

"(f) Proceedings before United States magistrates under this section shall be taken down by a court reporter or recorded by suitable sound recording equipment. A copy of the record of such proceeding shall be made available at the expense of the United States to a person who makes affidavit that he is unable to pay or give security therefor, and the expense of such copy shall be paid by the Director of the Administrative Office of the United States Courts."

(b) The item relating to section 3060 contained in the section analysis of chapter 203, title 18, United States Code, is amended to read as follows:

"3060. Preliminary examination."

TITLE IV—TRANSITIONAL PROVISIONS

APPOINTMENT OF MAGISTRATES

SEC. 401. (a) No individual may serve as a United States commissioner within any judicial district after the date on which a United States magistrate assumes office in such judicial district.

(b) An individual serving as a United States commissioner within any judicial district on the date of enactment of this Act who is a member in good standing of the bar of the highest court of any State may be appointed to the office of United States magistrate for an initial term, and may be reappointed to such office for successive terms, notwithstanding his failure to meet the bar membership qualification imposed by section 631(b) (1) of chapter 43, title 28, United States Code: Provided, however, That any appointment or reappointment of such an individual must be by unanimous vote of all the judges of the appointing district court or courts.

APPLICABLE LAW

SEC. 402. (a) All provisions of law relating to the powers, duties, jurisdiction, functions, service, compensation, and facilities of United States commissioners, as such provisions existed on the day preceding the date of enactment of this Act, shall continue in effect in each judicial district until but not on or after (1) the date on which the first United States magistrate assumes office within such judicial district pursuant to section 631 of chapter 43, title 28, United States Code, as amended by this Act, or (2) the third anniversary of the date of enactment of this Act, whichever date is earlier.

(b) On and after the date on which the first United States magistrate assumes office within any judicial district pursuant to section 631 of chapter 43, title 28, United States Code, as amended by this Act or the third anniversary of the date of enactment of this Act, whichever date is earlier—

(1) the provisions of chapter 43, title 28, United States Code as amended by this Act, shall be effective within such judicial district except as otherwise specifically provided by section 401 (b) of this title; and

(2) within such judicial district every reference to a United States commissioner contained in any previously enacted statute of the United States (other than sections 8331(1) (E), 8332(i), 8701(a) (7), and 8901(1) (G) of title 5), any previously promulgated rule of any court of the United States, or any previously promulgated regulation of any executive department or agency of the United States, shall be deemed to be a reference to a United States magistrate duly appointed under section 631 of chapter 43, title 28, United States Code, as amended by this Act.

(c) The administrative powers and duties of the Director of the Administrative Office of the United States Courts with respect to United States commissioners under the provisions of chapter 41, title 28, United States Code, as such provisions existed on the day preceding the date of enactment of this Act, shall continue in effect until no United States commissioner remains in service.

EFFECTIVE DATE

SEC. 403. Except as otherwise provided by sections 401 and 402 of this title, this Act shall take effect on the date of its enactment.

TITLE V—SEVERABILITY

SEC. 501. If any provision of this Act or the application thereof to any person or circumstances is held invalid, the validity of the remainder of the Act and of its application to other persons and circumstances shall not be affected.

Approved October 17, 1968.

Source: 28 U.S.C. § 631 et seq.

59. *Roe v. Wade,* 1973

Introduction

Roe v. Wade is one of the most controversial and far-reaching decisions of the twentieth century, striking down state laws that restricted abortion with a 72 majority. Led by Justice Harry Blackmun, the Supreme Court based its decision on the constitutional right of privacy, which it had recognized in *Griswold v. Connecticut* (1965) and other cases. The case spawned a great deal of opposition and many calls for amendments that would eliminate legal abortions.

Primary Source

Mr. Justice Blackmun delivered the opinion of the Court.

This Texas federal appeal and its Georgia companion, *Doe v. Bolton, post*, . . . present constitutional challenges to state criminal abortion legislation. The Texas statutes under attack here are typical of those that have been in effect in many States for approximately a century. The Georgia statutes, in contrast, have a modern cast, and are a legislative product that, to an extent at least, obviously reflects the influences of recent attitudinal change, of advancing medical knowledge and techniques, and of new thinking about an old issue. . . .

Jane Roe, a single woman who was residing in Dallas County, Texas, instituted this federal action in March 1970 against the District Attorney of the county. She sought a declaratory judgment that the Texas criminal abortion statutes were unconstitutional on their face, and an injunction restraining the defendant from enforcing the statutes.

Roe alleged that she was unmarried and pregnant; that she wished to terminate her pregnancy by an abortion "performed by a competent, licensed physician, under safe, clinical conditions"; that she was unable to get a "legal" abortion in Texas because her life did not appear to be threatened by the continuation of her pregnancy; and that she could not afford to travel to another jurisdiction in order to secure a legal abortion under safe conditions. She claimed that the Texas statutes were unconstitutionally vague and that they abridged her right of personal privacy, protected by the First, Fourth, Fifth, Ninth, and Fourteenth Amendments. By an amendment to her complaint, Roe purported to sue "on behalf of herself and all other women" similarly situated.

James Hubert Hallford, a licensed physician, sought and was granted leave to intervene in Roe's action. In his complaint, he alleged that he had been arrested previously for violations of the Texas abortion statutes, and that two such prosecutions were pending against him. He described conditions of patients who came to him seeking abortions, and he claimed that for many cases he, as a physician, was unable to determine whether they fell within or outside the exception recognized by Article 1196. He alleged that, as a consequence, the statutes were vague and uncertain, in violation of the Fourteenth Amendment, and that they violated his own and his patients' rights to privacy in the doctor-patient relationship and his own right to practice medicine, rights he claimed were guaranteed by the First, Fourth, Fifth, Ninth, and Fourteenth Amendments.

John and Mary Doe, a married couple, filed a companion complaint to that of Roe. They also name the District Attorney as defendant, claimed like constitutional deprivations, and sought declaratory and injunctive relief. The Does alleged that they were a childless couple; that Mrs. Doe was suffering from a "neural-chemical" disorder; that her physician had "advised her to avoid pregnancy until such time as her condition has materially improved" (although a pregnancy at the present time would not present "a serious risk" to her life); that, pursuant to medical advice, she had discontinued use of birth control pills; and that, if she should become pregnant, she would want to terminate the pregnancy by an abortion performed by a competent, licensed physician under safe, clinical conditions. By an amendment to their complaint, the Does purported to sue "on behalf of themselves and all couples similarly situated."

The two actions were consolidated and heard together by a duly convened three-judge district court. The suits thus presented the situations of the pregnant single woman, the childless couple, with the wife not pregnant, and the licensed practicing physician, all joining in the attack on the Texas criminal abortion statutes. Upon the filing of affidavits, motions were made for dismissal and for summary judgment. The court held that Roe and members of her class, and Dr. Hallford, had standing to sue and presented justiciable controversies, but that the Does had failed to allege facts sufficient to state a present controversy, and did not have standing. It concluded that, with respect to the requests for a declaratory judgment, abstention was not warranted. On the merits, the District Court held that the

> fundamental right of single women and married persons to choose whether to have children is protected by the Ninth Amendment, through the Fourteenth Amendment,

and that the Texas criminal abortion statutes were void on their face because they were both unconstitutionally vague and constituted an overbroad infringement of the plaintiffs' Ninth Amendment rights. The court then held that abstention was warranted with respect to the requests for an injunction. It therefore dismissed the Does' complaint, declared the abortion statutes void, and dismissed the application for injunctive relief. . . .

The plaintiffs Roe and Doe and the intervenor Hallford, . . . have appealed to this Court from that part of the District Court's judgment denying the injunction. The defendant District Attorney has purported to cross-appeal, pursuant to the same statute, from the court's grant of declaratory relief to Roe and Hallford. Both sides also have taken protective appeals to the United States Court of Appeals for the Fifth Circuit. That court ordered the appeals held in abeyance pending decision here. We postponed decision on jurisdiction to the hearing on the merits. . . .

The Constitution does not explicitly mention any right of privacy. In a line of decisions, however, going back perhaps as far as *Union Pacific R. Co. v. Botsford* [1891], . . . the Court has recognized that a right of personal privacy, or a guarantee of certain areas or zones of privacy, does exist under the Constitution. In varying contexts, the Court or individual Justices have, indeed, found at least the roots of that right in the First Amendment, *Stanley v. Georgia* [1969], . . . in the Fourth and Fifth Amendments, *Terry v. Ohio* [1968], . . . *Katz v. United States* [1967], . . . *Boyd v. United States* [1886], . . . *see Olmstead v. United States* [1928], . . . (Brandeis, J., dissenting); in the penumbras of the Bill of Rights, *Griswold v. Connecticut* [1965], . . . in the Ninth Amendment, . . . (Goldberg, J., concurring); or in the concept of liberty guaranteed by the first section of the Fourteenth Amendment, *see Meyer v. Nebraska* [1923] . . . . These decisions make it clear that only personal rights that can be deemed "fundamental" or "implicit in the concept of ordered liberty," *Palko v. Connecticut* [1937], . . . are included in this guarantee of personal privacy. They also make it clear that the right has some extension to activities relating to marriage, *Loving v. Virginia* [1967], . . . procreation, *Skinner v. Oklahoma* [1942], . . . contraception, *Eisenstadt v. Baird* [1972], . . . (White, J., concurring in result); family relationships, *Prince v. Massachusetts* [1944], . . . and childrearing and education, *Pierce v. Society of Sisters,* . . . *Meyer v. Nebraska.* . . .

The Court's decisions recognizing a right of privacy also acknowledge that some state regulation in areas protected by that right is appropriate. As noted above, a State may properly assert important interests in safeguarding health, in maintaining medical standards, and in protecting potential life. At some point in pregnancy, these respective interests become sufficiently compelling to sustain regulation of the factors that govern the abortion decision. The privacy right involved, therefore, cannot be said to be absolute. In fact, it is not clear to us that the claim asserted by some *amici* that one has an unlimited right to do with one's body as one pleases bears a close relationship to the right of privacy previously articulated in the Court's decisions. The Court has refused to recognize an unlimited right of this kind in the past. . . .

We, therefore, conclude that the right of personal privacy includes the abortion decision, but that this right is not unqualified, and must be considered against important state interests in regulation. . . .

Although the results are divided, most of these courts have agreed that the right of privacy, however based, is broad enough to cover the abortion decision; that the right, nonetheless, is not absolute, and is subject to some limitations; and that, at some point, the state interests as to protection of health, medical standards, and prenatal life, become dominant. We agree with this approach.

Where certain "fundamental rights" are involved, the Court has held that regulation limiting these rights may be justified only by a "compelling state interest," *Kramer v. Union Free School District* [1969]. . . .

With respect to the State's important and legitimate interest in the health of the mother, the "compelling" point, in the light of present medical knowledge, is at approximately the end of the first trimester. This is so because of the now-established medical fact, . . . that, until the end of the first trimester mortality in abortion may be less than mortality in normal childbirth. It follows that, from and after this point, a State may regulate the abortion procedure to the extent that the regulation reasonably relates to the preservation and protection of maternal health. Examples of permissible state regulation in this area are requirements as to the qualifications of the person who is to perform the abortion; as to the licensure of that person; as to the facility in which the procedure is to be performed, that is, whether it must be a hospital or may be a clinic or some other place of less-than-hospital status; as to the licensing of the facility; and the like.

This means, on the other hand, that, for the period of pregnancy prior to this "compelling" point, the attending physician, in consultation with his patient, is free to determine, without regulation by the State, that, in his medical judgment, the patient's pregnancy should be terminated. If that decision is reached, the judgment may be effectuated by an abortion free of interference by the State.

With respect to the State's important and legitimate interest in potential life, the "compelling" point is at viability. This is so because the fetus then presumably has the capability of meaningful life outside the mother's womb. State regulation protective of fetal life after viability thus has both logical and biological justifications. If the State is interested in protecting fetal life after viability, it may go so far as to proscribe abortion during that period, except when it is necessary to preserve the life or health of the mother. . . .

Mr. Justice Rehnquist, dissenting. . . .

To reach its result, the Court necessarily has had to find within the scope of the Fourteenth Amendment a right that was apparently completely unknown to the drafters of the Amendment. As early as 1821, the first state law dealing directly with abortion was enacted by the Connecticut Legislature. . . . By the time of the adoption of the Fourteenth Amendment in 1868, there were at least 36 laws enacted by state or territorial legislatures limiting abortion. While many States have amended or updated their laws, 21 of the laws on the books in 1868 remain in effect today. Indeed, the Texas statute struck down today was, as the majority notes, first enacted in 1857, and "has remained substantially unchanged to the present time." . . .

There apparently was no question concerning the validity of this provision or of any of the other state statutes when the Fourteenth Amendment was adopted. The only conclusion possible from this history is that the drafters did not intend to have the Fourteenth Amendment withdraw from the States the power to legislate with respect to this matter. . . .

Source: Roe et al. v. Wade, District Attorney of Dallas County, 410 U.S. 113 (1973)

60. "The Notion of a Living Constitution"* by William H. Rehnquist,** 1976

Introduction

William H. Rehnquist (1924–2005) was the sixteenth chief justice of the United States. He was appointed to the court in 1971, as an associate justice, and elevated to chief justice in 1986. Rehnquist was regarded as a conservative jurist, a proponent of judicial restraint and strict construction of the U.S. Constitution. In "The Notion of a Living Constitution," first published in the *Texas Law Review*, Rehnquist articulated the role of the court in a democratic society, concluding that judicial restraint and deference to legislative majorities are essential elements of a responsible judicial system. The contrary liberal concept of a living constitution, sometimes referred to as loose construction, is a mode of constitutional interpretation that claims that the conditions of contemporary society should be taken into account when interpreting the Constitution. Rehnquist decried this view, arguing that the appeal to a living document would allow judges to substitute their own political views for the views of the people and their representatives.

Primary Source

At least one of the more than half-dozen persons nominated during the past decade to be an Associate Justice of the Supreme Court of the United States has been asked by the Senate Judiciary Committee at his confirmation hearings whether he believed in a living Constitution.[1] It is not an easy question to answer; the phrase "living Constitution" has about it a teasing imprecision that makes it a coat of many colors.

One's first reaction tends to be along the lines of public relations or ideological sex appeal, I suppose. At first blush it seems certain that a *living* Constitution is better than what must be its counterpart, a *dead* Constitution. It would seem that only a necrophile could disagree. If we could get one of the major public opinion research firms in the country to sample public opinion concerning whether the United States Constitution should be *living* or *dead*, the overwhelming majority of the responses doubtless would favor a *living* Constitution.

If the question is worth asking a Supreme Court nominee during his confirmation hearings, however, it surely deserves to be analyzed in more than just the public relations context. While it is undoubtedly true, as Mr. Justice Holmes said, that "general propositions do not decide concrete cases,"[2] general phrases such as this have a way of subtly coloring the way we think about concrete cases.

Professor McBain of the Columbia University Law School published a book in 1927 entitled *The Living Constitution*.[3] Professor Reich of the Yale Law School entitled his contribution to a book-length symposium on Mr. Justice Black *The Living Constitution and the Court's Role*.[4] I think I do no injustice to either of these scholars when I say that neither of their works attempts any comprehensive definition of the phrase "living Constitution." The phrase is really a shorthand expression that is susceptible of at least two quite different meanings.

The first meaning was expressed over a half-century ago by Mr. Justice Holmes in *Missouri v. Holland*[5] with his customary felicity when he said:

> When we are dealing with words that also are a constituent act, like the Constitution of the United States, we must realize that they have called into life a being the development of which could not have been foreseen completely by the most gifted of its begetters. It was enough for them to realize or to hope that they had created an organism; it has taken a century and has cost their successors much sweat and blood to prove that they created a nation."[6]

I shall refer to this interpretation of the phrase "living Constitution," with which scarcely anyone would disagree, as the Holmes version.

The framers of the Constitution wisely spoke in general language and left to succeeding generations the task of applying that language to the unceasingly changing environment in which they would live. Those who framed, adopted, and ratified the Civil War amendments[7] to the Constitution likewise used what have been aptly described as "majestic generalities"[8] in composing the fourteenth amendment. Merely because a particular activity may not have existed when the Constitution was adopted, or because the framers could not have conceived of a particular method of transacting affairs, cannot mean that general language in the Constitution may not be applied to such a course of conduct. Where the framers of the Constitution have used general language, they have given latitude to those who would later interpret the instrument to make that language applicable to cases that the framers might not have foreseen.

In my reading and travels I have sensed a second connotation of the phrase "living Constitution," however, one quite different from what I have described as the Holmes version, but which certainly has gained acceptance among some parts of the legal profession. Embodied in its most naked form, it recently came to my attention in some language from a brief that had been filed in a United States District

Court on behalf of state prisoners asserting that the conditions of their confinement offended the United States Constitution. The brief urged:

> We are asking a great deal of the Court because other branches of government have abdicated their responsibility. . . . Prisoners are like other "discrete and insular' minorities for whom the Court must spread its protective umbrella because no other branch of government will do so. . . . This Court, as the voice and conscience of contemporary society, as the measure of the modem conception of human dignity, must declare that the [named prison] and all it represents offends the Constitution of the United States and will not be tolerated.

Here we have a living Constitution with a vengeance. Although the substitution of some other set of values for those which may be derived from the language and intent of the framers is not urged in so many words, that is surely the thrust of the message. Under this brief writer's version of the living Constitution, nonelected members of the federal judiciary may address themselves to a social problem simply because other branches of government have failed or refused to do so. These same judges, responsible to no constituency whatever, are nonetheless acclaimed as "the voice and conscience of contemporary society."

If we were merely talking about a slogan that was being used to elect some candidate to office or to persuade the voters to ratify a constitutional amendment, elaborate dissection of a phrase such as "living Constitution" would probably not be warranted. What we are talking about, however, is a suggested philosophical approach to be used by the federal judiciary, and perhaps state judiciaries, in exercising the very delicate responsibility of judicial review. Under the familiar principle of judicial review, the courts in construing the Constitution are, of course, authorized to invalidate laws that have been enacted by Congress or by a state legislature but that those courts find to violate some provision of the Constitution. Nevertheless, those who have pondered the matter have always recognized that the ideal of judicial review has basically antidemocratic and antimajoritarian facets that require some justification in this Nation, which prides itself on being a self-governing representative democracy.

All who have studied law, and many who have not, are familiar with John Marshall's classic defense of judicial review in his opinion for the Court in *Marbury v. Madison*.[9] I will summarize very briefly the thrust of that answer, with which I fully agree, because while it supports the Holmes version of the phrase "living Constitution," it also suggests some outer limits for the brief writer's version.

The ultimate source of authority in this Nation, Marshall said, is not Congress, not the states, not for that matter the Supreme Court of the United States. The people are the ultimate source of authority; they have parceled out the authority that originally resided entirely with them by adopting the original Constitution and by later amending it. They have granted some authority to the federal government and have reserved authority not granted it to the states or to the people individually. As between the branches of the federal government, the people have given certain authority to the President, certain authority to Congress, and certain authority to the federal judiciary. In the Bill of Rights they have erected protections for specified individual rights against the actions of the federal government. From today's perspective we might add that they have placed restrictions on the authority of the state governments in the thirteenth, fourteenth, and fifteenth amendments.

In addition, Marshall said that if the popular branches of government—state legislatures, the Congress, and the Presidency—are operating within the authority granted to them by the Constitution, their judgment and not that of the Court must obviously prevail. When these branches overstep the authority given them by the Constitution, in the case of the President and the Congress, or invade protected individual rights, and a constitutional challenge to their action is raised in a lawsuit brought in federal court, the Court must prefer the Constitution to the government acts.

John Marshall's justification for judicial review makes the provision for an independent federal judiciary not only understandable but also thoroughly desirable. Since the judges will be merely interpreting an instrument framed by the people, they should be detached and objective. A mere change in public opinion since the adoption of the Constitution, unaccompanied by a constitutional amendment, should not change the meaning of the Constitution. A merely temporary majoritarian groundswell should not abrogate some individual liberty truly protected by the Constitution.

Clearly Marshall's explanation contains certain elements of either ingenuousness or ingeniousness, which tend to grow larger as our constitutional history extends over a longer period of time. The Constitution is in many of its parts obviously not a specifically worded document but one couched in general phraseology. There is obviously wide room for honest difference of opinion over the meaning of general phrases in the Constitution; any particular Justice's decision when a question arises under one of these general phrases will depend to some extent on his own philosophy of constitutional law. One may nevertheless concede all of these problems that inhere in Marshall's justification of judicial review, yet feel that his justification for nonelected judges exercising the power of judicial review is the only one consistent with democratic philosophy of representative government.

Marshall was writing at a time when the governing generation remembered well not only the deliberations of the framers of the Constitution at Philadelphia in the summer of 1787 but also the debates over the ratification of the Constitution in the thirteen colonies. The often heated discussions that took place from 1787, when Delaware became the first state to ratify the Constitution,[10] until 1790, when recalcitrant Rhode Island finally joined the Union,[11] were themselves far more representative of the give-and-take of public decisionmaking by a constituent assembly than is the ordinary enactment of a law by Congress or by a state legislature. Patrick Henry had done all he could to block ratification in Virginia,[12] and the opposition of the Clinton faction in New York had provoked Jay, Hamilton, and Madison to their brilliant effort in defense of the Constitution, the *Federalist Papers*.[13] For Marshall, writing the *Marbury v. Madison* opinion in 1803, the memory of the debates in which the people of the thirteen colonies had participated only a few years before could well have fortified his conviction that the Constitution was, not merely in theory but in fact as well, a fundamental charter that had emanated from the people.

One senses no similar connection with a popularly adopted constituent act in what I have referred to as the brief writer's version of the living Constitution. The brief writer's version seems instead to be based upon the proposition that federal judges, perhaps judges as a whole, have a role of their own, quite independent of popular will, to play in solving society's problems. Once we have abandoned the idea that the authority of the courts to declare laws unconstitutional is somehow tied to the language of the Constitution that the people adopted, a judiciary exercising the power of judicial review appears in a quite different light. Judges then are no longer the keepers of the covenant; instead they are a small group of fortunately situated people with a roving commission to second-guess Congress, state legislatures, and state and federal administrative officers concerning what is best for the country. Surely there is no justification for a third legislative branch in the federal government, and there is even less justification for a federal legislative branch's reviewing on a policy basis the laws enacted by the legislatures of the fifty states. Even if one were to disagree with me on this point, the members of a third branch of the federal legislature at least ought to be elected by and responsible to constituencies, just as in the case of the other two branches of Congress. If there is going to be a council of revision, it ought to have at least some connection with popular feeling. Its members either ought to stand for reelection on occasion, or their terms should expire and they should be allowed to continue serving only if reappointed by a popularly elected Chief Executive and confirmed by a popularly elected Senate.

The brief writer's version of the living Constitution is seldom presented in its most naked form, but is instead usually dressed in more attractive garb. The argument in favor of this approach generally begins with a sophisticated wink—why pretend that there is any ascertainable content to the general phrases of the Constitution as they are written since, after all, judges constantly disagree about their meaning? We are all familiar with Chief Justice Hughes' famous aphorism that "We are under a Constitution, but the Constitution is what the judges say it is."[14] We all know the basis of Marshall's justification for judicial review, the argument runs, but it is necessary only to keep the window dressing in place. Any sophisticated student of the subject knows that judges need not limit themselves to the intent of the framers, which is very difficult to determine in any event. Because of the general language used in the Constitution, judges should not hesitate to use their authority to make the Constitution relevant and useful in solving the problems of modern society. The brief writer's version of the living Constitution envisions all of the above conclusions.

At least three serious difficulties flaw the brief writer's version of the living Constitution. First, it misconceives the nature of the Constitution, which was designed to enable the popularly elected branches of government, not the judicial branch, to keep the country abreast of the times. Second, the brief writer's version ignores the Supreme Court's disastrous experiences when in the past it embraced contemporary, fashionable notions of what a living Constitution should contain. Third, however socially desirable the goals sought to be advanced by the brief writer's version, advancing them through a freewheeling, non-elected judiciary is quite unacceptable in a democratic society.

It seems to me that it is almost impossible, after reading the record of the Founding Fathers' debates in Philadelphia, to conclude that they intended the Constitution itself to suggest answers to the manifold problems that they knew would confront succeeding generations. The Constitution that they drafted was indeed intended to endure indefinitely, but the reason for this very well-founded hope was the general language by which national authority was granted to Congress and the Presidency. These two branches were to furnish the motive power within the federal system, which was in turn to coexist with the state governments; the elements of government having a popular constituency were looked to for the solution of the numerous and varied problems that the future would bring. Limitations were indeed placed upon both federal and state governments in the form of both a division of powers and express protection for individual rights. These limitations, however, were not themselves designed to solve the problems of the future, but were instead designed to make certain that the constituent branches, when *they* attempted to solve those problems, should not transgress these fundamental limitations.

Although the Civil War Amendments[15] were designed more as broad limitations on the authority of state governments, they too were enacted in response to practices that the lately seceded states engaged in to discriminate against and mistreat the newly emancipated freed men. To the extent that the language of these amendments is general, the courts are of course warranted in giving them an application coextensive with their language. Nevertheless, I greatly doubt that even men like Thad Stevens and John Bingham, leaders of the radical Republicans in Congress, would have thought any portion of the Civil War Amendments, except section five of the fourteenth amendment,[16] was designed to solve problems that society might confront a century later. I think they would have said that those amendments were designed to prevent from ever recurring abuses in which the states had engaged prior to that time.

The brief writer's version of the living Constitution, however, suggests that if the states' legislatures and governors, or Congress and the President, have not solved a particular social problem, then the federal court may act. I do not believe that this argument will withstand rational analysis. Even in the face of a conceded social evil, a reasonably competent and reasonably representative legislature may decide to do nothing. It may decide that the evil is not of sufficient magnitude to warrant any governmental intervention. It may decide that the financial cost of eliminating the evil is not worth the benefit which would result from its elimination. It may decide that the evils which might ensue from the proposed solution are worse than the evils which the solution would eliminate.

Surely the Constitution does not put either the legislative branch or the executive branch in the position of a television quiz show contestant so that when a given period of time has elapsed and a problem remains unsolved by them, the federal judiciary may press a buzzer and take its turn at fashioning a solution.

The second difficulty with the brief writer's version of the living Constitution lies in its inattention to or rejection of the Supreme Court's historical experience gleaned from similar forays into problem solving.

Although the phrase "living Constitution" may not have been used during the nineteenth century and the first half of this century, the idea represented by the brief writer's version was very much in evidence during both periods. The apogee of the living Constitution doctrine during the nineteenth century was the Supreme Court's decision in *Dred Scott v. Sanford*.[17] In that case the question at issue was the status of a Negro who had been carried by his master from a slave state into a territory made free by the Missouri Compromise. Although thereafter taken back to a slave state, Dred Scott claimed that upon previously reaching free soil he had been forever emancipated. The Court, speaking through Chief Justice Taney, held that Congress was without power to legislate upon the issue of slavery even in a territory governed by it, and that therefore Dred Scott had never become free.[18] Congress, the Court held, was virtually powerless to check or limit the spread of the institution of slavery.

The history of this country for some thirty years before the *Dred Scott* decision demonstrates the bitter frustration which that decision brought to large elements of the population who opposed any expansion of slavery. In 1820 when Maine was seeking admission as a free state and Missouri as a slave state, a fight over the expansion of slavery engulfed the national legislative halls and resulted in the Missouri Compromise,[19] which forever banned slavery from those territories lying north of a line drawn through the southern boundary of Missouri.[20] This was a victory for the antislavery forces in the North, but the Southerners were prepared to live with it. At the time of the Mexican War in 1846, Representative David Wilmot of Pennsylvania introduced a bill, later known as the Wilmot Proviso,[21] that would have precluded the opening to slavery of any territory acquired as a result of the Mexican War.[22] This proposed amendment to the Missouri Compromise was hotly debated for years both in and out of Congress.[23] Finally in 1854 Senator Stephen A. Douglas shepherded through Congress the Kansas-Nebraska Act,[24] which in effect repealed the Missouri Compromise and enacted into law the principle of "squatter sovereignty": the people in each of the new territories would decide whether or not to permit slavery.[25] The enactment of this bill was, of course, a victory for the proslavery forces in Congress and a defeat for those opposed to the expansion of slavery. The great majority of the antislavery groups, as strongly as they felt about the matter, were still willing to live with the decision of Congress.[26] They were not willing, however, to live with the *Dred Scott* decision.

The Court in *Dred Scott* decided that all of the agitation and debate in Congress over the Missouri Compromise in 1820, over the Wilmot Proviso a generation later, and over the Kansas-Nebraska Act in 1854 had amounted to absolutely nothing. It was, in the words of Macbeth, "A tale told by an idiot, full of sound and fury, signifying nothing."[27] According to the Court, the decision had never been one that Congress was entitled to make; it was one that the Court alone, in construing the Constitution, was empowered to make.

The frustration of the citizenry, who had thought themselves charged with the responsibility for making such decisions, is well expressed in Abraham Lincoln's First Inaugural Address:

> [T]he candid citizen must confess that if the policy of the government, upon vital questions affecting the whole people, is to be irrevocably fixed by decisions of the Supreme Court, the instant they are made, in ordinary litigation between parties in personal actions, the people will have ceased to be their own rulers, having to that extent practically resigned their government into the hands of that eminent tribunal.[28]

The *Dred Scott* decision, of course, was repealed in fact as a result of the Civil War and in law by the Civil War amendments. The injury to the reputation of the Supreme Court that resulted from the *Dred Scott* decision, however, took more than a generation to heal. Indeed, newspaper accounts long after the *Dred Scott* decision bristled with attacks on the Court, and particularly on Chief Justice Taney, unequalled in their bitterness even to this day.

The brief writer's version of the living Constitution made its next appearance, almost as dramatically as its first, shortly after the turn of the century in *Lochner v. New York*.[29] The name of the case is a household word to those who have studied constitutional law, and it is one of the handful of cases in which a dissenting opinion has been overwhelmingly vindicated by the passage of time. In *Lochner* a New York law that limited to ten the maximum number of hours per day that could be worked by bakery employees was assailed on the ground that it deprived the bakery employer of liberty without due process of law. A majority of the Court held the New York maximum hour law unconstitutional, saying, "Statutes of the nature of that under review, limiting the hours in which grown and intelligent men may labor to earn their living, are mere meddlesome interferences with the rights of the individual. . . ."[30]

The fourteenth amendment, of course, said nothing about any freedom to make contracts upon terms that one thought best, but there was a very substantial body of opinion outside the Constitution at the time of *Lochner* that subscribed to the general philosophy of social Darwinism as embodied in the writing of Herbert Spencer in England and William Graham Sumner in this country. It may have occurred to some of the Justices who made up a majority in *Lochner*, hopefully subconsciously rather than consciously, that since this philosophy appeared eminently sound and since the language in the due process clause was sufficiently general not to rule out its inclusion, why not strike a blow for the cause? The answer, which has been vindicated by time, came in the dissent of Mr. Justice Holmes:

> [A] constitution is not intended to embody a particular economic theory, whether of paternalism and the organic relation of the citizen to the state or of *laissez faire*. It is made for people of fundamentally differing views, and the accident of our finding certain opinions natural and familiar or novel and even shocking ought not to conclude our judgment upon the question whether statutes embodying them conflict with the Constitution of the United States.[31]

One reads the history of these episodes in the Supreme Court to little purpose if he does not conclude that prior experimentation with the brief writer's expansive notion of a living Constitution has done the Court little credit. There remain today those, such as wrote the brief from which I quoted, who appear to cleave nevertheless to the view that the experiments of the Taney Court before the Civil War, and of the Fuller and Taft Courts in the first part of this century, ended in failure not because they sought to bring into the Constitution a principle that the great majority of objective scholars would have to conclude was not there but because they sought to bring into the Constitution the *wrong* extraconstitutional principle. This school of thought appears to feel that while added protection for slave owners was clearly unacceptable and safeguards for businessmen threatened with ever-expanding state regulation were not desirable, expansion of the protection accorded to individual liberties against the state or to the interest of "discrete and insular" minorities,[32] such as prisoners, must stand on a quite different, more favored footing. To the extent, of course, that such a distinction may legitimately be derived from the Constitution itself, these latter principles do indeed stand on an entirely different footing. To the extent that one must, however, go beyond even a generously fair reading of the language and intent of that document in order to subsume these principles, it seems to me that they are not really distinguishable from those espoused in *Dred Scott* and *Lochner*.

The third difficulty with the brief writer's notion of the living Constitution is that it seems to ignore totally the nature of political value judgments in a democratic society. If such a society adopts a constitution and incorporates in that constitution safeguards for individual liberty, these safeguards indeed do take on a generalized moral rightness or goodness. They assume a general social acceptance neither because of any intrinsic worth nor because of any unique origins in someone's idea of natural justice but instead simply because they have been incorporated in a constitution by the people. Within the limits of our Constitution, the representatives of the people in the executive branches of the state and national governments enact laws. The laws that emerge after a typical political struggle in which various individual value judgments are debated likewise take on a form of moral goodness because they have been enacted into positive law. It is the fact of their enactment that gives them whatever moral claim they have upon us as a society, however, and not any independent virtue they may have in any particular citizen's own scale of values.

Beyond the Constitution and the laws in our society, there simply is no basis other than the individual conscience of the citizen that may serve as a platform for the launching of moral judgments. There is no conceivable way in which I can logically demonstrate to you that the judgments of my conscience are superior to the judgments of your conscience, and vice versa. Many of us necessarily feel strongly and deeply about our own moral judgments, but they remain only personal moral judgments until in some way given the sanction of law.

As Mr. Justice Holmes said in his famous essay on natural law:

> Certitude is not the test of certainty. We have been cocksure of many things that were not so. . . . One cannot be wrenched from the rocky crevices into which one

is thrown for many years without feeling that one is attacked in one's life. What we most love and revere generally is determined by early associations. I love granite rocks and barberry bushes, no doubt because with them were my earliest joys that reach back through the past eternity of my life. But while one's experience thus makes certain preferences dogmatic for oneself, recognition of how they came to be so leaves one able to see that others, poor souls, may be equally dogmatic about something else. And this again means skepticism.[33]

This is not to say that individual moral judgments ought not to afford a springboard for action in society, for indeed they are without doubt the most common and most powerful wellsprings for action when one believes that questions of right and wrong are involved. Representative government is predicated upon the idea that one who feels deeply upon a question as a matter of conscience will seek out others of like view or will attempt to persuade others who do not initially share that view. When adherents to the belief become sufficiently numerous, he will have the necessary armaments required in a democratic society to press his views upon the elected representatives of the people, and to have them embodied into positive law.

Should a person fail to persuade the legislature, or should he feel that a legislative victory would be insufficient because of its potential for future reversal, he may seek to run the more difficult gauntlet of amending the Constitution to embody the view that he espouses. Success in amending the Constitution would, of course, preclude succeeding transient majorities in the legislature from tampering with the principle formerly added to the Constitution.

I know of no other method compatible with political theory basic to democratic society by which one's own conscientious belief may be translated into positive law and thereby obtain the only general moral imprimatur permissible in a pluralistic, democratic society. It is always time consuming, frequently difficult, and not infrequently impossible to run successfully the legislative gauntlet and have enacted some facet of one's own deeply felt value judgments. It is even more difficult for either a single individual or indeed for a large group of individuals to succeed in having such a value judgment embodied in the Constitution. All of these burdens and difficulties are entirely consistent with the notion of a democratic society. It should not be easy for any one individual or group of individuals to impose by law their value judgments upon fellow citizens who may disagree with those judgments. Indeed, it should not be easier just because the individual in question is a judge. We all have a propensity to want to do it, but there are very good reasons for making it difficult to do. The great English political philosopher John Stuart Mill observed:

> The disposition of mankind, whether as rulers or as fellow-citizens, to impose their own opinions and inclinations as a rule of conduct on others, is so energetically

supported by some of the best and by some of the worst feeling incident to human nature, that it is hardly ever kept under restraint by anything but want of power. . . .[34]

The brief writer's version of the living Constitution, in the last analysis, is a formula for an end run around popular government. To the extent that it makes possible an individual's persuading one or more appointed federal judges to impose on other individuals a rule of conduct that the popularly elected branches of government would not have enacted and the voters have not and would not have embodied in the Constitution, the brief writer's version of the living Constitution is genuinely corrosive of the fundamental values of our democratic society.

Source: Texas Law Review 54, no. 4 (1976): 693–706

Notes

*This observation is the revised text of the ninth annual Will E. Orgain Lecture, delivered at The University of Texas School of Law on March 12, 1976.

** Associate Justice, United States Supreme Court. B.A. 1948, LL.B. 1952, Stanford University; M.A. 1950, Harvard University.

1. See *Hearings on Nominations of William H. Rehnquist and Lewis F. Powell, Jr., Before the Senate Comm. on the Judiciary*, 92d Cong., 1st Sess. 87 (1971).

2. Lochner v. New York, 198 U.S. 45, 76 (1905) (Holmes, J., dissenting).

3. H. McBAIN, THE LIVING CONSTITUTION (1927).

4. Reich, *The Living Constitution and the Court's Role*, in HUGO BLACK AND THE SUPREME COURT 133 (S. Strickland ed. 1967).

5. 252 U.S. 416 (1920).

6. *Id*. at 433.

7. U.S. CONST. amends. XIII, XIV, XV.

8. Fay v. New York, 332 U.S. 261, 282 (1947) (Jackson, J.).

9. 5 U.S. (1 Cranch) 137 (1803).

10. 2 F. THORPE, THE CONSTITUTIONAL HISTORY OF THE UNITED STATES 18 (1901).

11. *Id*. at 191.

12. *Id*. at 81, 87, 91–95.

13. *Id*. at 134–39.

14. C. HUGHES, ADDRESSES 139 (1908).

15. U.S. CONST. amends. XIII, XIV, XV.

16. "The Congress shall have power to enforce, by appropriate legislation, the provisions of this article." U.S. CONST. amend. XIV, § 5.

17. 60 U.S. (19 How.) 393 (1857).

18. *Id*. at 452.

19. Act of March 6, 1820, ch. 22, 3 Stat. 545.

20. See 2 F. THORPE, supra note 10, at 366–71, 433.

21. Act of June 19, 1862, ch. 111, 12 Stat. 432.

22. 2 F. THORPE, supra note 10, at 430.

23. *Id*. at 430–32.

24. Act of May 30, 1854, ch. 59, 10 Stat. 277.

25. See 2 F. THORPE, supra note 10, at 518–21.

26. *See id.* at 524–36.

27. Shakespeare, *Macbeth*, V.v. 19.

28. First Inaugural Address by Abraham Lincoln, March 4, 1861, in A. LINCOLN, SPEECHES AND LETTERS 171–72 (M. Roe ed. 1894).

29. 198 U.S. 45 (1905).

30. *Id.* at 61.

31. *Id.* at 75–76 (Holmes, J., dissenting).

32. United States v. Carolene Prods. Co., 304 U.S. 144, 152 n.4 (1938).

33. O.W. HOLMES, *Natural Law*, in COLLECTED LEGAL PAPERS 310, 311 (1920).

34. J.S. MILL, ON LIBERTY, in 43 GREAT BOOKS OF THE WESTERN WORLD 273 (R. Hutchins ed. 1952).

61. Establishment of the U.S. Bankruptcy Courts [Excerpt], 1978

Introduction

The Bankruptcy Reform Act of 1978 established United States Bankruptcy Courts in each federal judicial district and made the new panels courts of record with their own clerks and other staff. The reform act also revised and codified Title 11 of the U.S. Code which contained the substantive and procedural laws of bankruptcy. The act authorized the president to nominate bankruptcy judges who would be confirmed by the U.S. Senate and serve a term of 14 years. The office of the trustees was placed under the direction of the Department of Justice. A Supreme Court ruling in 1982 questioned the constitutionality of the grant of bankruptcy jurisdiction to independent courts with judges who served limited terms. In 1984, Congress responded with an act (98 Stat. 333) that declared bankruptcy courts to be units of the U.S. district courts and provided for the appointment of bankruptcy judges by the U.S. courts of appeals.

Primary Source

November 6, 1978.

92 Stat. 2549, 2657.

TITLE II—AMENDMENTS TO TITLE 28 OF THE UNITED STATES CODE AND TO THE FEDERAL RULES OF EVIDENCE

SEC. 201. (a) Title 28 of the United States Code is amended by inserting immediately after chapter 5 the following:

"CHAPTER 6—BANKRUPTCY COURTS

"SEC.

"151. Creation and composition of bankruptcy courts.

"152. Appointment of bankruptcy judges.

"153. Tenure and residence of bankruptcy judges.

"154. Salaries of bankruptcy judges.

"155. Chief Judge; precedence of bankruptcy judges.

"156. Division of business among bankruptcy judges.

"157. Times of holding court.

"158. Accommodations at places for holding court.

"159. Vacant judgeship as affecting proceedings.

"160. Appellate panels.

"§ 151. Creation and composition of bankruptcy courts

"(a) There shall be in each judicial district, as an adjunct to the district court for such district, a bankruptcy court which shall be a court of record known as the United States Bankruptcy Court for the district.

"(b) Each bankruptcy court shall consist of the bankruptcy judge or judges for the district in regular active service. Justices or judges designated and assigned shall be competent to sit as judges of the bankruptcy court.

"(c) Except as otherwise provided by law, or rule or order of court, the judicial power of a bankruptcy court with respect to any action, suit or proceeding may be exercised by a single bankruptcy judge, who may preside alone and hold a regular or special session of court at the same time other sessions are held by other bankruptcy judges.

"§ 152. Appointment of bankruptcy judges

"The President shall appoint, by and with the advice and consent of the Senate, bankruptcy judges for the several judicial districts. In each instance, the President shall give due consideration to the recommended nominee or nominees of the Judicial Council of the Circuit within which an appointment is to be made.

"§ 153. Tenure and residence of bankruptcy judges

"(a) Each bankruptcy judge shall hold office for a term of 14 years, but may continue to perform the duties of his office until his successor takes office, unless such office has been eliminated.

"(b) Removal of a bankruptcy judge during the term for which he is appointed shall be only for incompetency, misconduct, neglect of duty, or physical or mental disability. Removal shall be by the judicial council of the circuit or circuits in which the bankruptcy judge serves, but removal may not occur unless a majority of all the judges of such circuit council or councils concur in the order of removal. Before any order of removal may be entered, a full specification of the charges shall be furnished to the bankruptcy judge, and he shall be accorded an opportunity to be heard on the charges. Any cause for removal of any bankruptcy judge coming to the knowledge of the Director of the Administrative Office of the United States Courts shall be reported by him to the chief judge of the circuit or circuits in which he serves, and a copy of the report shall at the same time be transmitted to the circuit council or councils and to the bankruptcy judge.

"(c) Each bankruptcy judge shall reside in the district or one of the districts for which he is appointed, or within 20 miles of his official station.

"(d) If the public interest and the nature of the business of a bankruptcy court require that a bankruptcy judge should maintain his abode at or near a particular part of the district the judicial council of the circuit may so declare and may make an appropriate order. If the bankruptcy judges of such a district are unable to agree as to which of them shall maintain his abode at or near the place or within the area specified in such an order the judicial council of the circuit may decide which of them shall do so.

"§ 154. Salaries of bankruptcy judges

"Each judge of a bankruptcy court shall receive a salary at an annual rate of $50,000, subject to adjustment under section 225 of the Federal Salary Act of 1967 (2 U.S.C. 351-361), and section 461 of this title.

"§ 155. Chief judge; precedence of bankruptcy judges

"(a) In each district having more than one judge the bankruptcy judge in regular active service who is senior in commission and under seventy years of age shall be the chief judge of the bankruptcy court. If all the bankruptcy judges in regular active service are 70 years of age or older the youngest shall act as chief judge until a judge has been appointed and qualified who is under 70 years of age, but a judge may not act as chief judge until he has served as a bankruptcy judge for one year.

"(b) The chief judge shall have precedence and preside at any session which he attends.

"Other bankruptcy judges shall have precedence and preside according to the seniority of their commissions. Judges whose commissions bear the same date shall have precedence according to seniority in age.

"(c) A judge whose commission extends over more than one district shall be junior to all bankruptcy judges except in the district in which he resided at the time he entered upon the duties of his office.

"(d) If the chief judge desires to be relieved of his duties as chief judge while retaining his active status as a bankruptcy judge, he may so certify to the chief judge of the court of appeals for the circuit in which the bankruptcy judge serves, and thereafter the bankruptcy judge in active service next in precedence and willing to serve shall be designated by the chief judge of the court of appeals as the chief judge of the bankruptcy court.

"(e) If a chief judge is temporarily unable to perform his duties as such, they shall be performed by the bankruptcy judge in active service, present in the district and able and qualified to act, who is next in precedence.

"(f) Service as a referee in bankruptcy or as a bankruptcy judge under the Bankruptcy Act shall be taken into account in the determination of seniority of commission under this section.

"§ 156. Division of business among bankruptcy judges

"The business of a bankruptcy court having more than one judge shall be divided among the judges as provided by the rules and orders of the court.

"The chief judge of the bankruptcy court shall be responsible for the observance of such rules and orders, and shall divide the business and assign the cases so far as such rules and orders do not otherwise prescribe.

"If the bankruptcy judges in any district are unable to agree upon the adoption of rules or orders for that purpose the judicial council of the circuit shall make the necessary orders.

"§ 157. Times of holding court

"(a) The bankruptcy court at each designated location shall be deemed to be in continuous session on all business days throughout the year.

"(b) Each bankruptcy court may establish by local rule or order schedules of court sessions at designated places of holding court other than the headquarters office of the court. Such schedules may be pretermitted by order of the court.

"(c) Bankruptcy court may be held at any place within the territory served, in any case, on order of the bankruptcy court, for the convenience of the parties, on such notice as the bankruptcy court orders.

"§ 158. Accommodations at places for holding court

"Court shall be held only at places where Federal quarters and accommodations are available, or suitable quarters and accommodations are furnished without cost to the United States. The foregoing restrictions shall not, however, preclude the Administrator of General Services, at the request of the Director of the Administrative Office of the United States Courts, from providing such court quarters and accommodations as the Administrator determines can appropriately be made available at places where court is authorized by law to be held, but only if such court quarters and accommodations have been approved as necessary by the judicial council of the appropriate circuit.

"§ 159. Vacant judgeship as affecting proceedings

"When the office of a bankruptcy judge becomes vacant, all pending process, pleadings and proceedings shall, when necessary, be continued by the clerk until a judge is appointed or designated to hold such court.

"§ 160. Appellate panels

"(a) If the circuit council of a circuit orders application of this section to a district within such circuit, the chief judge of each circuit shall designate panels of three bankruptcy judges to hear appeals from judgments, orders, and decrees of the bankruptcy court of the United States for such district. Except as provided in section 293(e) of this title, a panel shall be composed only of bankruptcy judges for districts located in the circuit in which the appeal arises. The chief judge shall designate a sufficient number of such panels so that appeals may be heard and disposed of expeditiously.

"(b) A panel designated under subsection (a) of this section may not hear an appeal from a judgment, order, or decree entered by a member of the panel.

"(c) When hearing an appeal, a panel designated under subsection (a) of this section shall sit at a place convenient to the parties to the appeal.".

"(b) The table of chapters of part I of title 28 of the United States Code is amended by inserting immediately after the item relating to chapter 5 of such title the following:

"6. Bankruptcy courts _151".

SEC. 202. Section 291(c) of title 28 of the United States Code is amended by inserting "or bankruptcy" immediately after "to hold a district".

SEC. 203. Section 292(b) of title 28 of the United States Code is amended by inserting "or a bankruptcy court" immediately after "to hold a district court".

SEC. 204. Section 292(d) of title 28 of the United States Code is amended—

(1) by striking out "either";

(2) by inserting "bankruptcy court," immediately after "in a"; and

(3) by inserting a comma immediately after "district court".

SEC. 205. Section 293 of title 28 of the United States Code is amended by adding at the end thereof the following:

"(e) (1) The Chief Justice of the United States may designate and assign temporarily a bankruptcy judge of one circuit for service in a bankruptcy court in another circuit upon presentation of a certificate of necessity by the chief judge or circuit justice of the circuit wherein the need arises.

"(2) The chief judge of a circuit may, in the public interest, designate and assign temporarily a bankruptcy judge of the circuit to hold a bankruptcy court in any district within the circuit.".

SEC. 206. Section 294 of title 28 of the United States Code is amended—

(1) in subsection (c), by deleting "or district" and inserting "district or bankruptcy judge"; and

(2) in subsection (d), by striking out "or district judge" and inserting in lieu thereof ", district judge or bankruptcy judge".

SEC. 207. Section 295 of title 28 of the United States Code is amended by striking out "or district" and inserting in lieu thereof "district, or bankruptcy".

SEC. 208. Section 331 of title 28 of the United States Code is amended—

(1) by striking out "and a district judge from each judicial circuit" in the first sentence of the first paragraph thereof and inserting "a district judge from each judicial circuit, and two bankruptcy judges" in lieu thereof;

(2) by inserting "circuit and district" in the second paragraph—

(A) immediately after "amended section the";

(B) immediately after "for one year, the"; and

(C) immediately after "two years and the";

(3) by inserting immediately after the second paragraph the following: "The bankruptcy judges to be summoned shall be chosen at large by all the bankruptcy judges. Each bankruptcy judge chosen shall serve as a member of the conference for three successive years, except that in the year following the effective date of this sentence the bankruptcy judges shall choose one bankruptcy judge to serve for two years."

(4) by inserting "or a bankruptcy judge chosen by the bankruptcy judges" immediately after "judges of the circuit" in the first sentence in the third paragraph; and

(5) by inserting "or any other bankruptcy judge" immediately before the period in the first sentence in the third paragraph.

SEC. 209. Section 332(d) of title 28 of the United States Code is amended by inserting "and bankruptcy judges" immediately after "The district judges".

SEC. 210. Section 333 of title 28 of the United States Code is amended by striking out "and district" and inserting in lieu thereof ", district, and bankruptcy".

SEC. 211. Section 376(a) (2) (A) of title 28 of the United States Code is amended by inserting ", or (iii) in the case of a bankruptcy judge, after retirement under section 337 of this title" immediately before the semicolon.

SEC. 213. Section 451 of title 28 of the United States Code is amended—

(1) by inserting a comma and "and bankruptcy courts, the judges of which are entitled to hold office for a term of 14 years" immediately before the period at the end of the paragraph beginning with "The term 'court of the United States'"; and

(2) by inserting a comma and "and judge of the bankruptcy courts, the judges of which are entitled to hold office for a term of 14 years" immediately before the period at the end of the paragraph beginning with "The term 'judge of the United States'".

SEC. 214. (a) Sections 455(a) and 455(e) of title 28 of the United States Code are each amended by striking out "magistrate, or referee in bankruptcy" each place it appears and inserting in lieu thereof "or magistrate".

(b) The heading for section 455 of title 28 of the United States Code is amended by striking out "magistrate, or referee in bankruptcy" and inserting in lieu thereof, "or magistrate".

(c) The item relating to section 455 in the table of sections of chapter 21 of title 28 of the United States Code is amended by striking out "magistrate, or referee in bankruptcy" and inserting in lieu thereof "or magistrate".

SEC. 215. Section 456 of title 28 of the United States Code is amended—

(1) by striking out "and the United States District Court for the District of Columbia," and inserting in lieu thereof "the United States District Court for the District of Columbia, and the United States Bankruptcy Court for the District of Columbia,";

(2) by striking out "and district" and inserting in lieu thereof "district and bankruptcy"; and

(3) by striking out "and each district judge" and inserting in lieu thereof ", each district judge; and each bankruptcy judge".

SEC. 216. Section 457 of title 28 of the United States Code is amended by inserting "of bankruptcy courts," immediately after "The record".

SEC. 217. (a) The heading for section 460 of title 28 of the United States Code is amended by striking out "Alaska,".

(b) The item relating to section 460 in the table of sections of chapter 21 of title 28 of the United States Code is amended by striking out "Alaska,".

SEC. 218. Section 506 of title 28 of the United States Code is amended by striking out "nine" and inserting in lieu thereof "ten".

SEC. 219. (a) Section 526 (a) (1) of title 28 of the United States Code is amended by striking out "and marshals" and inserting in lieu thereof ", marshals, and trustees".

(b) The heading for section 526 of title 28 of the United States Code is amended by striking out "and marshals" and inserting in lieu thereof ", marshals, and trustee".

(c) The item relating to section 526 in the table of sections of chapter 31 of title 28 of the United States Code is amended by striking out "and marshals" and inserting in lieu thereof ", marshals, and trustees".

SEC. 220. Section 526 (a) (2) of title 28 of the United States Code is amended—

(1) by striking out "referees,";

(2) by striking out "and receivers in bankruptcy" and inserting in lieu thereof "in cases under title 11"; and

(3) by striking out "commissioners" and inserting "magistrates" in lieu thereof.

SEC. 221. Section 569 (a) of title 28 of the United States Code is amended by striking out "of the district court" and inserting in lieu thereof "of the bankruptcy, of the district court,".

SEC. 222. Section 571 (a) of title 28 of the United States Code is amended—

(1) by striking out "and of the marshals" and inserting in lieu thereof "of the marshals"; and

(2) by inserting ", and of the United States trustees, their assistants, staff and other employees" immediately after "clerical assistance".

SEC. 223. Section 571(b) of title 28 of the United States Code is amended by striking out "and district" and inserting in lieu thereof "district, and bankruptcy".

SEC. 224. (a) Title 28 of the United States Code is amended by inserting immediately after chapter 37 the following:

"CHAPTER 39—UNITED STATES TRUSTEES

"SEC.

"581. United States trustees.

"582. Assistant United States trustees.

"583. Oath of office.

"584. Official stations.

"585. Vacancies.

"586. Duties; supervision by Attorney General

"587. Salaries.

"588. Expenses.

"589. Staff and other employees.

"§ 581. United States trustees

"(a) The Attorney General shall appoint one United States trustee for each of the following districts or groups of districts:

"(1) District of Maine, District of New Hampshire, District of Massachusetts, and District of Rhode Island.

"(2) Southern District of New York.

"(3) District of Delaware and District of New Jersey.

"(4) Eastern District of Virginia and District of District of Columbia.

"(5) Northern District of Alabama.

"(6) Northern District of Texas.

"(7) Northern District of Illinois.

"(8) District of Minnesota, District of North Dakota, District of South Dakota.

"(9) Central District of California.

"(10) District of Colorado and District of Kansas.

"(b) Each United States trustee shall be appointed for a term of seven years. On the expiration of his term, a United States trustee shall continue to perform the duties of his Office until his successor is appointed and qualifies.

"(c) Each United States trustee is subject to removal for cause by the Attorney General.

"§ 582. Assistant United States trustees

"(a) The Attorney General may appoint one or more assistant United States trustees in any district when the public interest so requires.

"(b) Each assistant United States trustee is subject to removal for cause by the Attorney General.

"§ 583. Oath of office

"Each United States trustee and assistant United States trustee, before taking office, shall take an oath to execute faithfully his duties.

"§ 584. Official stations

"The Attorney General may determine the official stations of the United States trustees and assistant United States trustees within the districts for which they were appointed.

"§ 585. Vacancies

"The Attorney General may appoint an acting United States trustee for a district in which the office of United States trustee is vacant, or may designate a United States trustee for another judicial district to serve as trustee for the district in which such vacancy exists. The individual so appointed or designated may serve until the earlier of 90 days after such appointment or designation, as the case may be, or the date on which the vacancy is filled by appointment under section 581 of this title.

"§ 586. Duties; supervision by Attorney General

"(a) Each United States trustee, within his district, shall—

"(1) establish, maintain, and supervise a panel of private trustees that are eligible and available to serve as trustees in cases under chapter 7 of title 11;

"(2) serve as and perform the duties of a trustee in a case under title 11 when required under title 11 to serve as trustee in such a case;

"(3) supervise the administration of cases and trustees in cases under chapter 7, 11, or 13 of title 11;

"(4) deposit or invest under section 345 of title 11 money received as trustee in cases under title 11;

"(5) perform the duties prescribed for the United States trustee under title 11; and

"(6) make such reports as the Attorney General directs.

"(b) If the number of cases under chapter 13 of title 11 commenced in a particular judicial district so warrant, the United States trustee for such district may, subject to the approval of the Attorney General, appoint one or more individuals to serve as standing trustee, or designate one or more assistant United States trustee, in cases under such chapter. The United States trustee for such district shall supervise any such individual appointed as standing trustee in the performance of the duties of standing trustee.

"(c) Each United States trustee shall be under the general supervision of the Attorney General, who shall provide general coordination and assistance to the United States trustees.

"(d) The Attorney General shall prescribe by rule qualifications for membership on the panels established by United States trustees under subsection (a) (1) of this section, and qualifications for appointment under subsection (b) of this section to serve as standing trustee in cases under chapter 13 of title 11. The Attorney General may not require that an individual be an attorney in order to qualify for appointment under subsection (b) of this section to serve as standing trustee in cases under chapter 13 of title 11.

"(e) (1) The Attorney General, after consultation with a United States trustee that has appointed an individual under subsection (b) of this section to serve as standing trustee in cases under chapter 13 of title 11, shall fix—

"(A) a maximum annual compensation for such individual, not to exceed the lowest annual rate of basic pay in effect for grade GS-16 of the General Schedule prescribed under section 5332 of title 5; and

"(B) a percentage fee, not to exceed ten percent, based on such maximum annual compensation and the actual, necessary expenses incurred by such individual as standing trustee.

"(2) Such individual shall collect such percentage fee from all payments under plans in the cases under chapter 13 of title 11 for which such individual serves as standing trustee. Such individual shall pay to the United States trustee, and the United States trustee shall pay to the Treasury—"(A) any amount by which the actual compensation of such individual exceeds five percent upon all payments under plans in cases under chapter 13 of title 11 for which such individual serves as standing trustee; and

"(B) any amount by which the percentage for all such cases exceeds—

"(i) such individual actual compensation for such cases, as adjusted under subparagraph (A) of this paragraph; plus

"(ii) the actual, necessary expenses incurred by such individual as standing trustee in such cases.

"§ 587. Salaries

"The Attorney General shall fix the annual salaries of United States trustees and assistant United States trustees at rates of compensation not to exceed the lowest annual rate of basic pay in effect for grade GS-16 of the General Schedule prescribed under section 5332 of title 5.

"§ 588. Expenses

"Necessary office expenses of the United States trustee shall be allowed when authorized by the Attorney General.

"§ 589. Staff and other employees

"The United States trustee may employ staff and other employees on approval of the Attorney General.".

(b) The table of chapters of part II of title 28 of the United States Code is amended by inserting at the end thereof the following:

"39. United States Trustees_ 581".

SEC. 225. (a) Section 604(a) of title 28 of the United States Code is amended—

(1) by redesignating paragraph (13) as paragraph (14); and

(2) by inserting immediately after paragraph (12) the following:

"(13) Lay before Congress, annually, statistical tables that will accurately reflect the business transacted by the several bankruptcy courts, and all other pertinent data relating to such courts;".

(b) Section 604 of title 28 of the United States Code, is amended by adding at the end thereof the following:

"(f) For each bankruptcy court, the Director shall name qualified persons to membership on the panel of trustees. The number and qualifications of persons named to membership on the panel of trustees shall be determined by rules and regulations to be adopted by the Director. An individual named to membership on the panel of trustees shall have a residency or office in the State served by the court or in any adjacent State. A corporation named to membership on the panel of trustees shall be authorized by its charter or by law to act as trustee and shall have an office in the State served by the court. The Director on his own initiative may at any time remove for cause a person named to a panel of trustees or remove a trustee appointed from the panel.".

SEC. 226. Section 610 of title 28 of the United States Code is amended by striking out "and district courts" and inserting in lieu thereof ", district courts, and bankruptcy courts".

SEC. 227. Section 620(b) (3) of title 28 of the United States Code is amended—

(1) by striking out "referees,"; and

(2) by striking out "commissioners" and inserting "magistrates" in lieu thereof.

SEC. 228. Section 621 (a) (2) of title 28 of the United States Code is amended by striking out "and three active judges of the district courts of the United States" and inserting in lieu thereof ", three active judges of the district courts of the United States, one active judge of the bankruptcy courts of the United States".

SEC. 229. Section 621(b) of title 28 of the United States Code is amended by striking out everything after "years" down through "That a" and inserting in lieu thereof ". A".

SEC. 230. Chapter 42 of title 28 of the United States Code is amended—

(1) by striking out section 629; and

(2) by striking out the item relating to section 629 in the table of sections.

SEC. 231. Section 631(c) of title 28 of the United States Code is amended—

(1) by striking out "of the conference, a part-time referee in bankruptcy or" and inserting in lieu thereof "of the conference,"; and

(2) by striking out "magistrate and part-time referee in bankruptcy," and inserting in lieu thereof "magistrate and".

SEC. 232. Section 634(a) of title 28 of the United States Code is amended by striking out "for full-time and part-time United States magistrates not to exceed the rates now or hereafter provided for full-time and part-time referees in bankruptcy, respectively, referred to in section 40a of the Bankruptcy Act (11 U.S.C. 68(a)), as amended,", and inserting in lieu thereof "not to exceed $48,500 per annum, subject to adjustment in accordance with section 225 of the Federal Salary Act of 1967 and section 461 of this title,".

SEC. 233. (a) Title 28 of the United States Code is amended by inserting immediately after chapter 49 the following:

"CHAPTER 50—BANKRUPTCY COURTS

"Sec.

"771. Clerks.

"772. Other employees.

"773. Records of proceedings; reporters.

"774. Power to appoint.

"775. Salaries of employees.

"§ 771. Clerks

"(a) Based on need each bankruptcy court may appoint a clerk who shall be subject to removal only by the court "(b) The clerk may appoint, with the approval of the court, necessary deputies, clerical assistants, and employees in such number as may be approved by the Director of the Administrative Office of the United States Courts. Such deputies, clerical assistants, and employees shall be subject to removal only by the clerk with the approval of the court. If there is no clerk, the Bankruptcy Judge shall perform the duties of this subsection.

"(c) The clerk of each bankruptcy court shall reside in the district for which he is appointed. The bankruptcy court may designate places within the district for the offices of the clerk and his deputies, and their official stations.

"(d) A clerk of a bankruptcy court or his deputy or assistant shall not receive any compensation or emoluments through any office or position to which he is appointed by the court, other than that received as such clerk, deputy or assistant, whether from the United States or from private litigants.

"(e) The clerk of each bankruptcy court shall pay into the Treasury all fees, costs and other moneys collected by him, except uncollected fees not required by Act of Congress to be prepaid.

"He shall make returns thereof to the Director of the Administrative Office of the United States Courts under regulations prescribed by him.

"§ 772. Other employees

"Bankruptcy judges may appoint necessary other employees, including law clerks and secretaries, subject to any limitation on the aggregate salaries of such employees which may be imposed by law.

"§ 773. Records of proceedings; reporters

"(a) The bankruptcy court shall require a record to be made, whenever practicable, of all proceedings in cases had in open court. The Judicial Conference shall prescribe that the record be taken by electronic sound recording means, by a court reporter appointed or employed by such bankruptcy court to take a verbatim record by shorthand or mechanical means, or by an employee of such court designated by such court to take such a verbatim record.

"(b) On the request of a party to a proceeding that has been recorded who has agreed to pay the fee for a transcript, or a judge of the bankruptcy court, a transcript of the original record of the requested parts of such proceeding shall be made and delivered promptly to such party or judge. Any such transcript that is certified shall be deemed prima facie a correct statement of the testimony taken and proceedings had. No transcript of the proceedings of the bankruptcy court shall be considered as official except those made from certified records.

"(c) Fees for transcripts furnished in proceedings to persons permitted to appeal in forma pauperis shall be paid by the United States out of money appropriated for that purpose if the trial judge or a circuit judge certifies that the appeal is not frivolous (but presents a substantial question).

"§ 774. Power to appoint

"Whenever a majority of the bankruptcy judges of any bankruptcy court cannot agree upon the appointment of any officer of such court, the chief judge shall make such appointment.

"§ 775. Salaries of employees

"The salary of an individual appointed or employed under section 771(a), 772, or 773(a) of this title shall be the same as the salary of an individual appointed or employed under section 751(a), 752, or 753(a) of this title, as the case may be. The salaries of individuals appointed under section 771(b) of this title shall be comparable to the salaries of individuals appointed under section 751(b) of this title.".

(b) The table of chapters of part III of title 28 of the United States Code is amended by inserting immediately after the item relating to chapter 49 the following:

"50. Bankruptcy Courts_ 771".

SEC. 234. Section 957(a) of title 28 of the United States Code is amended by inserting "or bankruptcy court" immediately after "district court".

SEC. 235. Section 959(b) of title 28 of the United States Code is amended by striking out "A" and inserting in lieu thereof "Except as provided in section 1166 of title 11, a

SEC. 236. (a) Chapter 83 of title 28 of the United States Code is amended by inserting immediately after section 1292 the following:

"§ 1293. Bankruptcy appeals

"(a) The courts of appeals shall have jurisdiction of appeals from all final decisions of panels designated under section 160(a) of this title.

"(b) Notwithstanding section 1482 of this title, a court of appeals shall have jurisdiction of an appeal from a final judgment, order, or decree of an appellate panel created under section 160 or a District court of the United States or from a final judgment, order, or decree of a bankruptcy court of the United States if the parties to such appeal agree to a direct appeal to the court of appeals.

(b) The table of sections of chapter 83 of title 28 of the United States Code is amended by inserting immediately after the item relating to section 1292 the following:

"1293. Bankruptcy appeals.".

SEC. 237. Section 1294 of title 28 of the United States Code is amended—

(1) by striking out "district and territorial" and inserting in lieu thereof "district, bankruptcy, and territorial";

(2) by striking out the period at the end thereof and inserting a semicolon; and

(3) by adding at the end thereof the following:

"(5) From a panel designated under section 160 (a) of this title to the court of appeals for the circuit in which the panel was so designated;

"(6) From a bankruptcy court of the United States to the court of appeals for the circuit embracing the district in which the bankruptcy court is located.".

SEC. 238. (a) Section 1334 of title 28 of the United States Code is amended to read as follows:

"§ 1334. Bankruptcy appeals

"(a) The district courts for districts for which panels have not been ordered appointed under section 160 of this title shall have jurisdiction of appeals from all final judgments, orders, and decrees of bankruptcy courts.

"(b) The district courts for such districts shall have jurisdiction of appeals from interlocutory orders and decrees of bankruptcy courts, but only by leave of the district court to which the appeal is taken.

"(c) A district court may not refer an appeal under that section to a magistrate or to a special master.".

(b) The table of sections of chapter 85 of title 28 of the United States Code is amended by striking out the item relating to section 1334 and inserting in lieu thereof the following:

"1334. Bankruptcy appeals.".

SEC. 239. Section 1360(a) of title 28 of the United States Code is amended by striking out "within the Territory" and inserting in lieu thereof "within the State".

SEC. 240. (a) Chapter 87 of title 28 of the United States Code is amended by adding at the end thereof the following:

"§ 1408. Bankruptcy appeals

"An appeal under section 1334 of this title from a judgment, order, or decree of a bankruptcy court may be brought only in the judicial district in which such bankruptcy court is located.".

(b) The table of sections of chapter 87 of title 28 of the United States Code is amended by adding at the end thereof the following:

"1408. Bankruptcy appeals.".

SEC. 241. (a) Title 28 of the United States Code is amended by inserting immediately after chapter 89 the following:

"CHAPTER 90—DISTRICT COURTS AND BANKRUPTCY COURTS

"SEC.

"1471. Jurisdiction.

"1472. Venue of cases under title II.

"1473. Venue of proceedings arising under or related to cases under title 11.

"1474. Venue of cases ancillary to foreign proceedings.

"1475. Change of venue.

"1476. Creation or alteration of district or division.

"1477. Cure or waiver of defects.

"1478. Removal to the bankruptcy courts.

"1479. Provisional remedies; security.

"1480. Jury trials.

"1481. Powers of bankruptcy court.

"1482. Appeals.

"§ 1471. Jurisdiction

"(a) Except as provided in subsection (b) of this section, the district courts shall have original and exclusive jurisdiction of all cases under title 11.

"(b) Notwithstanding any Act of Congress that confers exclusive jurisdiction on a court or courts other than the district courts, the district courts shall have original but not exclusive jurisdiction of all civil proceedings arising under title 11 or arising in or related to cases under title 11.

"(c) The bankruptcy court for the district in which a case under title 11 is commenced shall exercise all of the jurisdiction conferred by this section on the district courts.

"(d) Subsection (b) or (c) of this section does not prevent a district court or a bankruptcy court, in the interest of justice, from abstaining from hearing a particular proceeding arising under title 11 or arising in or related to a case under title 11. Such abstention, or a decision not to abstain, is not reviewable by appeal or otherwise.

"(e) The bankruptcy court in which a case under title 11 is commenced shall have exclusive jurisdiction of all of the property, wherever located, of the debtor, as of the commencement of such case.

§ 1472. Venue of cases under title 11

"Except as provided in section 1474 of this title, a case under title 11 may be commenced in the bankruptcy court for a district—

"(1) in which the domicile, residence, principal place of business, in the United States, or principal assets, in the United States, of the person or entity that is the subject of such case shall have been located for the 180 days immediately preceding such commencement, or for a longer portion of such 180-day period than the domicile, residence, principal place of business, in the United States, or principle assets, in the United States, of such person were located in any other district; or

"(2) in which there is pending a case under title 11 concerning such person's affiliate, general partner, or partnership.

"§ 1473. Venue of proceedings arising under or related to cases under title 11

"(a) Except as provided in subsections (b) and (d) of this section, a proceeding arising in or related to a case under title 11 may be commenced in the bankruptcy court in which such case is pending.

"(b) Except as provided in subsection (d) of this section, a trustee in a case under title 11 may commence a proceeding arising in or related to such case to recover a money judgment of or property worth less than $1,000 or a consumer debt of less than $5,000 only in the bankruptcy court for the district in which a defendant resides.

"(c) Except as provided in section (b) of this section, a trustee in a case under title 11 may commence a proceeding arising in or related to such case as statutory successor to the debtor or creditors under section 541 or 544(b) of title 11 in the bankruptcy court for the district where the State or Federal court sits in which, under applicable nonbankruptcy venue provisions, the debtor or creditors, as the case may be, may have commenced an action on which such proceeding is based if the case under title 11 had not been commenced.

"(d) A trustee may commence a proceeding arising under title 11 or arising in or related to a case under title 11 based on a claim arising after the commencement of such case from the operation of the business of the debtor only in the bankruptcy court for the district where a State or Federal court sits in which, under applicable nonbankruptcy venue provisions, an action on such claim may have been brought.

"(e) A proceeding arising in or related to a case under title 11, based on a claim arising after the commencement of such case from the operation of the business of the debtor, may be commenced against the representative of the estate in such case in the bankruptcy court for the district where the State or Federal court sits in which the party commencing such proceeding may, under applicable nonbankruptcy venue provisions, have brought an action on such claim, or in the bankruptcy court in which such case in pending.

"§ 1474. Venue of cases ancillary to foreign proceedings

"(a) A case under section 304 of title 11 to enjoin the commencement or continuation of an action or proceeding in a State or Federal court, or the enforcement of a judgment, may be commenced only in the bankruptcy court for the district where the State or Federal court sits in which is pending the action or proceeding against which the injunction is sought.

"(b) A case under section 304 of title 11 to enjoin the enforcement of a lien against property, or to require turnover of property of an estate, may be commenced only in the bankruptcy court for the district in which such property is found.

"(c) A case under section 304 of title 11, other than a case specified in subsection (a) or (b) of this section, may be commenced only in the bankruptcy court for the district in which is located the principal assets in the United States, of the estate that is the subject of such case.

"§ 1475. Change of venue

"A bankruptcy court may transfer a case under title 11 or a proceeding arising under or related to such a case to a bankruptcy court for another district, in the interest of justice and for the convenience of the parties.

"§ 1476. Creation or alteration of district or division

"Cases or proceedings pending at the time of the creation of a new district or division or transfer of a county or territory from one division or district to another may be tried in the district or division as it existed at the institution of the case or proceeding, or in the district or division so created or to which the county or territory is so transferred as the parties shall agree or the court direct.

"§ 1477. Cure or waiver of defects

"(a) The bankruptcy court of a district in which is filed a case or proceeding laying venue in the wrong division or district may, in the interest of justice and for the convenience of the parties, retain such case or proceeding, or may transfer, under section 1475 of this title, such case or proceeding to any other district or division.

"(b) Nothing in this chapter shall impair the jurisdiction of a bankruptcy court of any matter involving a party who does not interpose timely and sufficient objection to the venue.

"§ 1478. Removal to the bankruptcy courts

"(a) A party may remove any claim or cause of action in a civil action, other than a proceeding before the United States Tax Court or a civil action by a Government unit to enforce such governmental unit's police or regulatory power, to the bankruptcy court for the district where such civil action is pending, if the bankruptcy courts have jurisdiction over such claim or cause of action.

"(b) The court to which such claim or cause of action is removed may remand such claim or cause of action on any equitable ground. An order under this subsection remanding a claim or cause of action, or a decision not so remanding, is not reviewable by appeal or otherwise.

"§ 1479. Provisional remedies; security

"(a) Whenever any action is removed to a bankruptcy court under section 1478 of this title, any attachment or sequestration of the goods or estate of the defendant in such action shall hold the goods or estate to answer the final judgment or decree in the same manner as they would have been held to answer final judgment or decree had it been rendered by the court from which the action was removed, unless the attachment or sequestration is invalidated under applicable law.

"(b) Any bond, undertaking, or security given by either party in an action prior to removal under section 1478 of this title shall remain valid and effectual notwithstanding such removal, unless such bond, undertaking, or other security is invalidated under applicable law.

"(c) All injunctions, orders, or other proceedings in an action prior to removal of such action under section 1478 of this title shall remain in full force and effect until dissolved or modified by the bankruptcy court.

"§ 1480. Jury trials

"(a) Except as provided in subsection (b) of this section, this chapter and title 11 do not affect any right to trial by jury, in a case under title 11 or in a proceeding arising under title 11 or arising in or related to a case under title 11, that is provided by any statute in effect on September 30, 1979.

"(b) The bankruptcy court may order the issues arising under section 303 of title 11 to be tried without a jury.

"§ 1481. Powers of bankruptcy court

"A bankruptcy court shall have the powers of a court of equity, law, and admiralty, but may not enjoin another court or punish a criminal contempt not committed in the presence of the judge of the court or warranting a punishment of imprisonment.

"§ 1482. Appeals

"(a) Panels designated under section 160(a) of this title shall have jurisdiction of appeals from all final judgments, orders, and decrees of bankruptcy courts.

"(b) Panels designated under section 160(a) of this title shall have jurisdiction of appeals from interlocutory judgments, orders, and decrees of bankruptcy courts, but only by leave of the panel to which the appeal is taken.".

(b) The table of chapters of part IV of title 28 of the United States Code is amended by inserting immediately after the item relating to chapter 89 the following:

"90. District Courts and Bankruptcy Courts_ _ _ _ _ _ _ _ _ _ _ _ _ _ _ _ _ _1471".

SEC. 242. Section 1656 of title 28 of the United States Code is amended by inserting "or in a bankruptcy court" immediately after "a district court".

SEC. 243. Section 1869(f) of title 28 of the United States Code is amended by inserting "chapter 6 of title 28, United States Code," immediately after "chapter 5 of title 28, United States Code,".

SEC. 244. Section 1914(a) of title 28 of the United States Code is amended by striking out "$15" and inserting "$60" in lieu thereof.

SEC. 245. Section 1923(b) of title 28 of the United States Code is amended by inserting "and United States trustees" immediately after "United States attorneys".

SEC. 246. (a) Chapter 123 of title 28 of the United States Code is amended by inserting immediately after section 1929 the following:

"§ 1930. Bankruptcy courts

"(a) Notwithstanding section 1915 of this title, the parties commencing a case under title 11 shall pay to the clerk of the bankruptcy court the following filing fees:

"(1) For a case commenced under chapter 7 or 13 of title 11, $60.

"(2) For a case commenced under chapter 9 of title 11, $300.

"(3) For a case commenced under chapter 11 of title 11 that does not concern a railroad, as defined in section 101 of title 11, $200.

"(4) For a case commenced under chapter 11 of title 11 concerning a railroad, as so defined, $500.

An individual commencing a voluntary case or a joint case under title 11 may pay such fee in installments.

"(b) The Judicial Conference of the United States may prescribe additional fees in cases under title 11 of the same kind as the Judicial Conference prescribes under section 1914(b) of this title.

"(c) Upon the filing of any separate or joint notice of appeal or application for appeal or upon the receipt of any order allowing, or notice of the allowance of, an appeal or a writ of certiorari $5 shall be paid to the clerk of the bankruptcy court, by the appellant or petitioner.

"(d) Whenever any case or proceeding is dismissed in any bankruptcy court for want of jurisdiction, such court may order the payment of just costs.

"(e) The clerk of the bankruptcy court may collect only the fees prescribed under this section.".

(b) The table of sections of chapter 123 of title 28 of the United States Code is amended by adding at the end thereof the following:

"1930. Bankruptcy courts.".

SEC. 247. Section 2075 of title 28 of the United States Code is amended by—

(1) striking out "under the Bankruptcy Act" and inserting in lieu thereof "in cases under title 11"; and

(2) by striking out the last sentence thereof.

SEC. 248. Section 2107 of title 28 of the United States Code is amended—

(1) by inserting "or the bankruptcy court" immediately after "district court"; and

(2) by striking out the final paragraph.

SEC. 249. Section 2201 of title 28 of the United States Code is amended by inserting "or a proceeding under section 505 or 1146 of title 11" immediately after "the Internal Revenue Code of 1954".

SEC. 250. (a) Chapter 153 of title 28 of the United States Code is amended by adding at the end thereof the following:

"§ 2256. Habeas corpus from bankruptcy courts

"A bankruptcy court may issue a writ of habeas corpus—

"(1) when appropriate to bring a person before the court—

"(A) for examination;

"(B) to testify; or

"(C) to perform a duty imposed on such person under this title; or

"(2) ordering the release of a debtor in a case under title 11 in custody under the judgment of a Federal or State court if—

"(A) such debtor was arrested or imprisoned on process in any civil action;

"(B) such process was issued for the collection of a debt—

"(i) dischargeable under title 11; or

"(ii) that is or will be provided for in a plan under chapter 11 or 13 of title 11; and

"(C) before the issuance of such writ, notice and a hearing have been afforded the adverse party of such debtor in custody to contest the issuance of such writ.".

(b) The table of sections for chapter 153 of title 28 of the United States Code is amended by adding at the end thereof the following:

"2256. Habeas corpus from bankruptcy courts.".

SEC. 251. (a) Rule 1101(a) of the Federal Rules of Evidence is amended by striking out ", referees in bankruptcy,".

(b) Rule 1101(b) of the Federal Rules of Evidence is amended by striking out "the Bankruptcy Act" and inserting in lieu thereof "title 11, United States Code".

SEC. 252. Rule 1101(a) of the Federal Rules of Evidence is amended by inserting "the United States bankruptcy courts," immediately after "the United States district courts,".

Source: 11 U.S.C. § 101 et seq.

62. Establishment of the Eleventh Judicial Circuit, 1980

Introduction

By the early 1960s, the U.S. Court of Appeals for the Fifth Circuit had become the nation's busiest federal appeals court as well as the forum for dramatic civil rights cases. In 1980, in response to overcrowded dockets in the Fifth Circuit and elsewhere, Congress created an Eleventh Judicial Circuit, consisting of Florida, Georgia, and Alabama, three states that had been part of the Fifth Circuit since 1862. The act provided that Texas, Louisiana, and Mississippi would comprise a new Fifth Circuit.

Primary Source

October 14, 1980.
94. Stat. 1994.

An Act

To amend title 28, United States Code, to divide the fifth judicial circuit of the

United States into two circuits, and for other purposes.

Be it enacted by the Senate and House of Representatives of the United States of America in Congress assembled, That this Act may be cited as the "Fifth Circuit Court of Appeals Reorganization Act of 1980".

SEC. 2. Section 41 of title 28, United States Code, is amended—

(1) in the text before the table, by striking out "eleven" and inserting in lieu thereof "twelve";

(2) in the table, by striking out the item relating to the fifth circuit and inserting in lieu thereof the following new item:

"Fifth……………………………….……. District of the Canal Zone, Louisiana, Mississippi, Texas.";

and

(3) at the end of the table, by adding the following new item:

"Eleventh.................................. Alabama, Florida, Georgia.".

SEC. 3. The table in section 44(a) of title 28, United States Code, is amended—

(1) by striking out the item relating to the fifth circuit and inserting in lieu thereof the following new item:

"Fifth... 14";

and

(2) by adding at the end thereof the following new item:

"Eleventh.. 12".

SEC. 4. The table in section 48 of title 28, United States Code, is amended—

(1) by striking out the item relating to the fifth circuit and inserting in lieu thereof the following new item:

"Fifth............................... New Orleans, Fort Worth, Jackson.";

and

(2) by adding at the end thereof the following new item:

"Eleventh................................... Atlanta, Jacksonville, Montgomery.".

SEC. 5. Each circuit judge in regular active service of the former fifth circuit whose official station on the day before the effective date of this Act—

(1) is in Louisiana, Mississippi, or Texas is assigned as a circuit judge of the new fifth circuit; and

(2) is in Alabama, Florida, or Georgia is assigned as a circuit judge of the eleventh circuit.

SEC. 6. Each judge who is a senior judge of the former fifth circuit on the day before the effective date of this Act may elect to be assigned to the new fifth circuit or to the eleventh circuit and shall notify the Director of the Administrative Office of the United States Courts of such election.

SEC. 7. The seniority of each judge—

(1) who is assigned under section 5 of this Act; or

(2) who elects to be assigned under section 6 of this Act; shall run from the date of commission of such judge as a judge of the former fifth circuit.

SEC. 8. The eleventh circuit is authorized to hold terms or sessions of court at New Orleans, Louisiana, until such time as adequate facilities for such court are provided in Atlanta, Georgia.

SEC. 9. The provisions of the following paragraphs of this section apply to any case in which, on the date before the effective date of this Act, an appeal or other proceeding has been filed with the former fifth circuit:

(1) If the matter has been submitted for decision, further proceedings in respect of the matter shall be had in the same manner and with the same effect as if this Act had not been enacted.

(2) If the matter has not been submitted for decision, the appeal or proceeding, together with the original papers, printed records, and record entries duly certified, shall, by appropriate orders, be transferred to the court to which it would have gone had this Act been in full force and effect at the time such appeal was taken or other proceeding commenced, and further proceedings in respect of the case shall be had in the same manner and with the same effect as if the appeal or other proceeding had been filed in such court.

(3) A petition for rehearing or a petition for rehearing en banc in a matter decided before the effective date of this Act, or submitted before the effective date of this Act and decided on or after the effective date as provided in provided in paragraph (1) of this section, shall be treated in the same manner and with the same effect as though this Act had not been enacted. If a petition for rehearing en banc is granted, the matter shall be reheard by a court comprised as though this Act had not been enacted.

SEC. 10. As used in sections 5, 6, 7, 8, and 9 of this Act, the term—

(1) "former fifth circuit" means the fifth judicial circuit of the United States as in existence on the day before the effective date of this Act;

(2) the term "new fifth circuit" means the fifth judicial circuit of the United States established by the amendment made by section 2(2) of this Act; and

(3) the term "eleventh circuit" means the eleventh judicial circuit of the United States established by the amendment made by section 2(3) of this Act.

SEC. 11. The court of appeals for the fifth circuit as constituted on the day before the effective date of this Act may take such administrative action as may be required to carry out this Act. Such court shall cease to exist for administrative purposes on July 1, 1984.

SEC. 12. This Act and the amendments made by this Act shall take effect on October 1, 1981.

Approved October 14, 1980.

   Source: 11 U.S.C. § 101 et seq.

63. Establishment of the Federal Circuit, 1982

Introduction

In an effort to promote uniform federal jurisdiction and relieve the pressure on the dockets of the Supreme Court and the courts of appeals for the regional circuits, the Congress in 1982 established the Federal Circuit, the only U.S. court of appeals defined by its jurisdiction rather than geographical boundaries. The U.S. Court of Appeals for the Federal Circuit assumed the jurisdiction of the U.S. Court of Customs and Patent Appeals and the appellate jurisdiction of the U.S. Court of Claims. In addition, the new court was authorized to hear appeals from several federal administrative boards. Congress abolished the Court of Customs and Patent Appeals and the Court of Claims, reassigning judges to serve on the Federal Circuit. The act also established a U.S. Claims Court (now the U.S. Court of Federal Claims).

Primary Source

April 2, 1982.
96 Stat. 25.

An Act

To establish a United States Court of Appeals for the Federal Circuit, to establish a United States Claims Court, and for other purposes.

Be it enacted by the Senate and House of Representatives of the United States of America in Congress assembled, That this Act may be cited as the "Federal Courts Improvement Act of 1982".

TITLE I—UNITED STATES COURT OF APPEALS FOR THE FEDERAL CIRCUIT AND UNITED STATES CLAIMS COURT

Part A—Organization, Structure, and Jurisdiction

NUMBER AND COMPOSITION OF CIRCUITS

Sec. 101. Section 41 of title 28, United States Code, as amended by the Fifth Circuit Court of Appeals Reorganization Act of 1980 (Public Law 96-452; 94 Stat. 1994), is amended by striking out "twelve" and inserting in lieu thereof "thirteen" and by adding at the end thereof the following:

"Federal................................ All Federal judicial district.".

NUMBER OF CIRCUIT JUDGES

Sec. 102. (a) Section 44(a) of title 28, United States Code, as amended by the Fifth Circuit Court of Appeals Reorganization Act of 1980 (Public Law 96-452; 94 Stat. 1994), is amended by adding at the end thereof the following:

"Federal................................ 12".

(b) Section 44(c) of title 28, United States Code, is amended by adding the following sentence at the end thereof: "While in active service, each circuit judge of the Federal judicial circuit appointed after the effective date of this Act, and the chief judge of the Federal judicial circuit, whenever appointed, shall reside within fifty miles of the District of Columbia.".

PANELS OF JUDGES; NUMBER OF JUDGES FOR HEARINGS

Sec. 103. (a) Section 46(a) of title 28, United States Code, is amended by striking out "divisions" and inserting in lieu thereof "panels".

(b) Section 46(b) of title 28, United States Code, is amended—

(1) by striking out "divisions" each place it appears and inserting in lieu thereof "panels";

(2) by inserting immediately before the period at the end of the first sentence the following: ", at least a majority of whom shall be judges of that court, unless such judges cannot sit because recused or disqualified, or unless the chief judge of that court certifies that there is an emergency including, but not limited to, the unavailability of a judge of the court because of illness"; and

(3) by adding at the end thereof the following new sentence: "The United States Court of Appeals for the Federal Circuit shall determine by rule a procedure for the rotation of judges from panel to panel to ensure that all of the judges sit on a representative cross section of the cases heard and, notwithstanding the first sentence of this subsection, may determine by rule the number of judges, not less than three, who constitute a panel.".

(c) The first sentence of section 46(c) of title 28, United States Code, is amended by inserting immediately after "three judges" the following: "(except that the United States Court of Appeals for the Federal Circuit may sit in panels of more than three judges if its rules so provide)".

(d) Section 46(d) of title 28, United States Code, is amended by striking out "division" and inserting in lieu thereof "panel".

PLACES FOR HOLDING COURT

Sec. 104. (a) Section 48 of title 28, United States Code, is amended by striking out the first two sentences and inserting in lieu thereof the following:

"(a) The courts of appeals shall hold regular sessions at the places listed below, and at such other places within the respective circuit as each court may designate by rule.".

(b) Section 48 of title 28, United States Code, as amended by the Fifth Circuit Court of Appeals Reorganization Act of 1980 (Public Law 96-452; 94 Stat 1994), is amended further by inserting at the end of the table of circuits and places the following:

"Federal.............................. District of Columbia, and in any other place listed above as the court by rule directs.".

(c) Section 48 of title 28, United States Code, is amended further by striking out the final paragraph and inserting in lieu thereof the following:

"(b) Each court of appeals may hold special sessions at any place within its circuit as the nature of the business may require, and upon such notice as the court orders.

The court may transact any business at a special session which it might transact at a regular session.

"(c) Any court of appeals may pretermit, with the consent of the Judicial Conference of the United States, any regular session of court at any place for insufficient business or other good cause.

"(d) The times and places of the sessions of the Court of Appeals for the Federal Circuit shall be prescribed with a view to securing reasonable opportunity to citizens to appear before the court with as little inconvenience and expense to citizens as is practicable.".

JURISDICTION OF THE UNITED STATES COURT OF APPEALS FOR THE FEDERAL CIRCUIT

Sec. 127. (a) Chapter 83 of title 28, United States Code, is amended by adding at the end thereof the following new sections:

"§ 1295. Jurisdiction of the United States Court of Appeals for the Federal Circuit

"(a) The United States Court of Appeals for the Federal Circuit shall have exclusive jurisdiction—

"(1) of an appeal from a final decision of a district court of the United States, the United States District Court for the District of the Canal Zone, the District Court of Guam, the District Court of the Virgin Islands, or the District Court for the Northern Mariana Islands, if the jurisdiction of that court was based, in whole or in part, on section 1338 of this title, except that a case involving a claim arising under any Act of Congress relating to copyrights or trademarks and no other claims under section 1338(a) shall be governed by sections 1291, 1292, and 1294 of this title;

"(2) of an appeal from a final decision of a district court of the United States, the United States District Court for the District of the Canal Zone, the District Court of Guam, the District Court of the Virgin Islands, or the District Court for the Northern Mariana Islands, if the jurisdiction of that court was based, in whole or in part, on section 1346 of this title, except that jurisdiction of an appeal in a case brought in a district court under section 1346(a)(1), 1346(b), 1346(e), or 1346(f) of this title or under section 1346(a)(2) when the claim is founded upon an Act of Congress or a regulation of an executive department providing for internal revenue shall be governed by sections 1291, 1292, and 1294 of this title;

"(3) of an appeal from a final decision of the United States Claims Court;

"(4) of an appeal from a decision of—

"(A) the Board of Appeals or the Board of Patent Interferences of the Patent and Trademark Office with respect to patent applications and interferences, at the instance of an applicant for a patent or any party to a patent interference, and any such appeal shall waive the right of such applicant or party to proceed under section 145 or 146 of title 35;

"(B) the Commissioner of Patents and Trademarks or the Trademark Trial and Appeal Board with respect to applications for registration of marks and other proceedings as provided in section 21 of the Trademark Act of 1946 (15 U.S.C. 1071); or

"(C) a district court to which a case was directed pursuant to section 145 or 146 of title 35;

"(5) of an appeal from a final decision of the United States Court of International Trade;

"(6) to review the final determinations of the United States International Trade Commission relating to unfair practices in import trade, made under section 337 of the Tariff Act of 1930 (19 U.S.C. 1337);

"(7) to review, by appeal on questions of law only, findings of the Secretary of Commerce under headnote 6 to schedule 8, part 4, of the Tariff Schedules of the United States (relating to importation of instruments or apparatus);

"(8) of an appeal under section 71 of the Plant Variety Protection Act (7 U.S.C. 2461);

"(9) of an appeal from a final order or final decision of the Merit Systems Protection Board, pursuant to sections 7703(b)(1) and 7703(d) of title 5; and

"(10) of an appeal from a final decision of an agency board of contract appeals pursuant to section 8(g)(1) of the Contract Disputes Act of 1978 (41 U.S.C. 607(g)(1)).

"(b) The head of any executive department or agency may, with the approval of the Attorney General, refer to the Court of Appeals for the Federal Circuit for judicial review any final decision rendered by a board of contract appeals pursuant to the terms of any contract with the United States awarded by that department or agency which the head of such department or agency has concluded is not entitled to finality pursuant to the review standards specified in section 10(b) of the Contract Disputes Act of 1978 (41 U.S.C. 609(b)). The head of each executive department or agency shall make any referral under this section within one hundred and twenty days after the receipt of a copy of the final appeal decision.

"(c) The Court of Appeals for the Federal Circuit shall review the matter referred in accordance with the standards specified in section 10(b) of the Contract Disputes Act of 1978. The court shall proceed with judicial review on the administrative record made before the board of contract appeals on matters so referred as in other cases pending in such court, shall determine the issue of finality of the appeal decision, and shall, if appropriate, render judgment thereon, or remand the matter to any administrative or executive body or official with such direction as it may deem proper and just.

"§ 1296. Precedence of cases in the United States Court of Appeals for the Federal Circuit

"Civil actions in the United States Court of Appeals for the Federal Circuit shall be given precedence, in accordance with the law applicable to such actions, in such order as the court may by rule establish.".

(b) The section analysis of chapter 83 of title 28, United States Code, is amended by adding at the end thereof the following new items:

"1295. Jurisdiction of the United States Court of Appeals for the Federal Circuit.

"1296. Precedence of cases in the United States Court of Appeals for the Federal Circuit."

Source: Public Law 97-164, 96 Stat. (1982)

64. Defense of Marriage Act, 1996

Introduction

The Defense of Marriage Act of 1996 allows states to refuse to recognize gay marriages and prevents homosexuals from taking advantage of spousal benefits by defining marriage as "a legal union between one man and one woman as husband and wife."

Primary Source

An Act

To define and protect the institution of marriage.

Be it enacted by the Senate and House of Representatives of the United States of America in Congress assembled.

SECTION 1. SHORT TITLE.

This Act may be cited as the "Defense of Marriage Act".

SEC. 2. POWERS RESERVED TO THE STATES.

(a) In General.—Chapter 115 of title 28, United States Code, is amended by adding after section 1738B the following:

'Sec. 1738C. Certain acts, records, and proceedings and the effect thereof'

"No State, territory, or possession of the United States, or Indian tribe, shall be required to give effect to any public act, record, or judicial proceeding of any other State, territory, possession, or tribe respecting a relationship between persons of the same sex that is treated as a marriage under the laws of such other State, territory, possession, or tribe, or a right or claim arising from such Relationship.".

(b) Clerical Amendment.—The table of sections at the beginning of chapter 115 of title 28, United States Code, is amended by inserting after the item relating to section 1738B the following new item:

'1738C. Certain acts, records, and proceedings and the effect thereof.'.

SEC. 3. DEFINITION OF MARRIAGE.

(a) In General.—Chapter 1 of title 1, United States Code, is amended by adding at the end the following:

Sec. 7. Definition of "marriage" and "spouse"

"In determining the meaning of any Act of Congress, or of any ruling, regulation, or interpretation of the various administrative bureaus and agencies of the United States, the word 'marriage' means only a legal union between one man and one woman as husband and wife, and the word 'spouse' refers only to a person of the opposite sex who is a husband or a wife.".

(b) Clerical Amendment.—The table of sections at the beginning of chapter 1 of title 1, United States Code, is amended by inserting after the item relating to section 6 the following new item:

"7. Definition of 'marriage' and 'spouse'.".

Approved September 21, 1996.

Source: Public Law 104-199 (1996)

65. *Romer v. Evans,* 1996

Introduction

Romer v. Evans involved the constitutionality of an amendment to the Colorado state Constitution that had been adopted by referendum and prohibited and repealed all state and local statutes that extended special protection on the basis of sexual orientation.

Primary Source

JUSTICE KENNEDY delivered the opinion of the Court.

One century ago, the first Justice Harlan admonished this Court that the Constitution "neither knows nor tolerates classes among citizens." *Plessy v. Ferguson* . . . (1896) (dissenting opinion). Unheeded then, those words now are understood to state a commitment to the law's neutrality where the rights of persons are at stake. The Equal Protection Clause enforces this principle and today requires us to hold invalid a provision of Colorado's Constitution.

I.

The enactment challenged in this case is an amendment to the Constitution of the State of Colorado, adopted in a 1992 statewide referendum. The parties and the state courts refer to it as "Amendment 2," its designation when submitted to the voters. The impetus for the amendment and the contentious campaign that preceded its adoption came in large part from ordinances that had been passed in various Colorado municipalities. For example, the cities of Aspen and Boulder and the City and County of Denver each had enacted ordinances which banned discrimination in many transactions and activities, including housing, employment, education, public accommodations, and health and welfare services. . . . What gave rise to the statewide controversy was the protection the ordinances afforded to persons discriminated against by reason of their sexual orientation. See Boulder Rev. Code §12–1–1 (defining "sexual orientation" as "the choice of sexual partners, i.e., bisexual, homosexual or heterosexual"); Denver Rev. Municipal Code, Art. IV §28–92 (defining "sexual orientation" as "[t]he status of an individual as to his or her heterosexuality, homosexuality or bisexuality"). Amendment 2 repeals these ordinances to the extent they prohibit discrimination on the basis of "homosexual, lesbian or bisexual orientation, conduct, practices or relationships." . . .

Yet Amendment 2, in explicit terms, does more than repeal or rescind these provisions. It prohibits all legislative, executive or judicial action at any level of state or local government designed to protect the named class, a class we shall refer to as homosexual persons or gays and lesbians. The amendment reads: "No Protected Status Based on Homosexual, Lesbian, or Bisexual Orientation. Neither the State of Colorado, through any of its branches or departments, nor any of its agencies, political subdivisions, municipalities or school districts, shall enact, adopt or enforce any statute, regulation, ordinance or policy whereby homosexual, lesbian or bisexual orientation, conduct, practices or relationships shall constitute or otherwise be the basis of or entitle any person or class of persons to have or claim any minority status, quota preferences, protected status or claim of discrimination. This Section of the Constitution shall be in all respects self-executing." . . . Soon after Amendment 2 was adopted, this litigation to declare its invalidity and enjoin its enforcement was commenced in the District Court for the City and County of Denver. Among the plaintiffs (respondents here) were homosexual persons, some of them government employees. They alleged that enforcement of Amendment 2 would subject them to immediate and substantial risk of discrimination on the basis of their sexual orientation. Other plaintiffs (also respondents here) included the three municipalities whose ordinances we have cited and certain other governmental entities which had acted earlier to protect homosexuals from discrimination but would be prevented by Amendment 2 from continuing to do so. Although Governor Romer had been on record opposing the adoption of Amendment 2, he was named in his official capacity as a defendant, together with the Colorado Attorney General and the State of Colorado.

The trial court granted a preliminary injunction to stay enforcement of Amendment 2, and an appeal was taken to the Supreme Court of Colorado. Sustaining the interim injunction and remanding the case for further proceedings, the State Supreme Court held that Amendment 2 was subject to strict scrutiny under the Fourteenth Amendment because it infringed the fundamental right of gays and lesbians to participate in the political process. . . . To reach this conclusion, the state court relied on our voting rights cases, e.g., *Reynolds v. Sims* . . . (1964); *Carrington v. Rash* . . . (1965); *Harper v. Virginia Bd. of Elections* . . . (1966); *Williams v. Rhodes* . . . (1968), and on our precedents involving discriminatory restructuring of governmental decisionmaking, see, e.g., *Hunter v. Erickson* . . . (1969); *Reitman v. Mulkey* . . . (1967); *Washington v. Seattle School Dist. No. 1* . . . (1982); *Gordon v. Lance* . . . (1971). On remand, the State advanced various arguments in an effort to show that Amendment 2 was narrowly tailored to serve compelling interests, but the trial court found none sufficient. It enjoined enforcement of Amendment 2, and the Supreme Court of Colorado, in a second opinion, affirmed the ruling. . . . We granted certiorari and now affirm the judgment, but on a rationale different from that adopted by the State Supreme Court.

II.

The State's principal argument in defense of Amendment 2 is that it puts gays and lesbians in the same position as all other persons. So, the State says, the measure does no more than deny homosexuals special rights. This reading of the amendment's language is implausible. We rely not upon our own interpretation of the amendment but upon the authoritative construction of Colorado's Supreme Court. The state court, deeming it unnecessary to determine the full extent of the amendment's reach, found it invalid even on a modest reading of its implications. The critical discussion of the amendment, set out in *Evans I,* is as follows:

The immediate objective of Amendment 2 is, at a minimum, to repeal existing statutes, regulations, ordinances, and policies of state and local entities that barred discrimination based on sexual orientation. See Aspen, Colo., Mun. Code §13–98 (1977) (prohibiting discrimination in employment, housing and public accommodations on the basis of sexual orientation); Boulder, Colo., Rev. Code §§12–1–2 to –4 (1987) (same); Denver, Colo., Rev. Mun. Code art. IV, §§28–91 to –116 (1991) (same); Executive Order No. D0035 (December 10, 1990) (prohibiting employment discrimination for 'all state employees, classified and exempt' on the basis of sexual orientation); Colorado Insurance Code, §10–3–1104, 4A C. R. S. (1992 Supp.) (forbidding health insurance providers from determining insurability and premiums based on an applicant's, a beneficiary's, or an insured's sexual orientation); and various provisions prohibiting discrimination based on sexual orientation at state colleges. (Metropolitan State College of Denver prohibits college sponsored social clubs from discriminating in membership on the basis of sexual orientation and Colorado State University has an antidiscrimination policy which encompasses sexual orientation.)

The "ultimate effect" of Amendment 2 is to prohibit any governmental entity from adopting similar, or more protective statutes, regulations, ordinances, or policies in the future unless the state constitution is first amended to permit such measures. . . .

Sweeping and comprehensive is the change in legal status effected by this law. So much is evident from the ordinances that the Colorado Supreme Court declared would be void by operation of Amendment 2. Homosexuals, by state decree, are put in a solitary class with respect to transactions and relations in both the private and governmental spheres. The amendment withdraws from homosexuals, but no others, specific legal protection from the injuries caused by discrimination, and it forbids reinstatement of these laws and policies.

The change that Amendment 2 works in the legal status of gays and lesbians in the private sphere is far-reaching, both on its own terms and when considered in light of the structure and operation of modern anti-discrimination laws. That structure is well illustrated by contemporary statutes and ordinances prohibiting discrimination by providers of public accommodations. "At common law, innkeepers, smiths, and others who 'made profession of a public employment,' were prohibited from refusing, without good reason, to serve a customer." . . . The duty was a general one and did not specify protection for particular groups. The common law rules, however, proved insufficient in many instances, and it was settled early that the Fourteenth Amendment did not give Congress a general power to prohibit discrimination in public accommodations, *Civil Rights Cases* . . . (1883). In consequence, most States have chosen to counter discrimination by enacting detailed statutory schemes. . . .

Colorado's state and municipal laws typify this emerging tradition of statutory protection and follow a consistent pattern. The laws first enumerate the persons or entities subject to a duty not to discriminate. The list goes well beyond the entities covered by the common law. The Boulder ordinance, for example, has a comprehensive definition of entities deemed places of "public accommodation." They include "any place of business engaged in any sales to the general public and any place that offers services, facilities, privileges, or advantages to the general public or that receives financial support through solicitation of the general public or through governmental subsidy of any kind." Boulder Rev. Code §12–1–1(j) (1987). The Denver ordinance is of similar breadth, applying, for example, to hotels, restaurants, hospitals, dental clinics, theaters, banks, common carriers, travel and insurance agencies, and "shops and stores dealing with goods or services of any kind," Denver Rev. Municipal Code, Art. IV, §28–92.

These statutes and ordinances also depart from the common law by enumerating the groups or persons within their ambit of protection. Enumeration is the essential device used to make the duty not to discriminate concrete and to provide guidance for those who must comply. In following this approach, Colorado's state and local governments have not limited anti-discrimination laws to groups that have so far been given the protection of heightened equal protection scrutiny under our cases. . . . Rather, they set forth an extensive catalogue of traits which cannot be the basis for discrimination, including age, military status, marital status, pregnancy, parenthood, custody of a minor child, political affiliation, physical or mental disability of an individual or of his or her associates—and, in recent times, sexual orientation. . . .

Amendment 2 bars homosexuals from securing protection against the injuries that these public-accommodations laws address. That in itself is a severe consequence, but there is more. Amendment 2, in addition, nullifies specific legal protections for this targeted class in all transactions in housing, sale of real estate, insurance, health and welfare services, private education, and employment. . . .

Not confined to the private sphere, Amendment 2 also operates to repeal and forbid all laws or policies providing specific protection for gays or lesbians from discrimination by every level of Colorado government. The State Supreme Court cited two examples of protections in the governmental sphere that are now rescinded and may not be reintroduced. The first is Colorado Executive Order D0035 (1990), which forbids employment discrimination against "'all state employees, classified and exempt' on the basis of sexual orientation." . . . Also repealed, and now forbidden, are "various provisions prohibiting discrimination based on sexual orientation at state colleges." . . . The repeal of these measures and the prohibition against their future reenactment demonstrates that Amendment 2 has the same force and effect in Colorado's governmental sector as it does elsewhere and that it applies to policies as well as ordinary legislation.

Amendment 2's reach may not be limited to specific laws passed for the benefit of gays and lesbians. It is a fair, if not necessary, inference from the broad language of the amendment that it deprives gays and lesbians even of the protection of general laws and policies that prohibit arbitrary discrimination in governmental and private settings. See, e.g., Colo. Rev. Stat. §24–4–106(7) (1988) (agency action subject to judicial review under arbitrary and capricious standard); §18–8–405 (making it a criminal offense for a public servant knowingly, arbitrarily or capriciously to refrain from performing a duty imposed on him by law); §10–3–1104(1)(f) (prohibiting "unfair discrimination" in insurance); 4 Colo. Code of Regulations 801–1, Policy 11–1 (1983) (prohibiting discrimination in state employment on grounds of specified traits or "other non-merit factor"). At some point in the systematic administration of these laws, an official must determine whether homosexuality is an arbitrary and thus forbidden basis for decision. Yet a decision to that effect would itself amount to a policy prohibiting discrimination on the basis of homosexuality, and so would appear to be no more valid under Amendment 2 than the specific prohibitions against discrimination the state court held invalid.

If this consequence follows from Amendment 2, as its broad language suggests, it would compound the constitutional difficulties the law creates. The state court did not decide whether the amendment has this effect, however, and neither need we. In the course of rejecting the argument that Amendment 2 is intended to conserve resources to fight discrimination against suspect classes, the Colorado Supreme Court made the limited observation that the amendment is not intended to affect many anti-discrimination laws protecting non-suspect classes. . . . In our view that does not resolve the issue. In any event, even if, as we doubt, homosexuals could find some safe harbor in laws of general application, we cannot accept the view that Amendment 2's prohibition on specific legal protections does no more than deprive homosexuals of special rights. To the contrary, the amendment imposes a special disability upon those persons alone. Homosexuals are forbidden the safeguards that others enjoy or may seek without constraint. They can obtain specific protection against discrimination only by enlisting the citizenry of Colorado to amend the state constitution or perhaps, on the State's view, by trying to pass helpful laws of general applicability. This is so no matter how local or discrete the harm, no matter how public and widespread the injury. We find nothing special in the protections Amendment 2 withholds. These are protections taken for granted by most people either because they already have them or do not need them; these are protections against exclusion from an almost limitless number of transactions and endeavors that constitute ordinary civic life in a free society.

III.

The Fourteenth Amendment's promise that no person shall be denied the equal protection of the laws must co-exist with the practical necessity that most legislation classifies for one purpose or another, with resulting disadvantage to various groups or persons. . . . We have attempted to reconcile the principle with the reality by stating that, if a law neither burdens a fundamental right nor targets a suspect class, we will uphold the legislative classification so long as it bears a rational relation to some legitimate end. . . .

Amendment 2 fails, indeed defies, even this conventional inquiry. First, the amendment has the peculiar property of imposing a broad and undifferentiated disability on a single named group, an exceptional and, as we shall explain, invalid form of legislation. Second, its sheer breadth is so discontinuous with the reasons offered for it that the amendment seems inexplicable by anything but animus toward the class that it affects; it lacks a rational relationship to legitimate state interests.

Taking the first point, even in the ordinary equal protection case calling for the most deferential of standards, we insist on knowing the relation between the classification adopted and the object to be attained. The search for the link between classification and objective gives substance to the Equal Protection Clause; it provides guidance and discipline for the legislature, which is entitled to know what sorts of laws it can pass; and it marks the limits of our own authority. In the ordinary case, a law will be sustained if it can be said to advance a legitimate government interest, even if the law seems unwise or works to the disadvantage of a particular group, or if the rationale for it seems tenuous. See *New Orleans v. Dukes* . . . (1976) (tourism benefits justified classification favoring pushcart vendors of certain longevity); *Williamson v. Lee Optical of Okla., Inc.* . . . (1955) (assumed health concerns justified law favoring optometrists over opticians); *Railway Express Agency, Inc. v. New York* . . . (1949) (potential traffic hazards justified exemption of vehicles advertising the owner's products from general advertising ban);

Kotch v. Board of River Port Pilot Comm'rs for Port of New Orleans . . . (1947) (licensing scheme that disfavored persons unrelated to current river boat pilots justified by possible efficiency and safety benefits of a closely knit pilotage system). The laws challenged in the cases just cited were narrow enough in scope and grounded in a sufficient factual context for us to ascertain that there existed some relation between the classification and the purpose it served. By requiring that the classification bear a rational relationship to an independent and legitimate legislative end, we ensure that classifications are not drawn for the purpose of disadvantaging the group burdened by the law. See *United States Railroad Retirement Bd. v. Fritz* . . . (1980) (STEVENS, J., concurring) ("If the adverse impact on the disfavored class is an apparent aim of the legislature, its impartiality would be suspect.").

Amendment 2 confounds this normal process of judicial review. It is at once too narrow and too broad. It identifies persons by a single trait and then denies them protection across the board. The resulting disqualification of a class of persons from the right to seek specific protection from the law is unprecedented in our jurisprudence. The absence of precedent for Amendment 2 is itself instructive; "[d]iscriminations of an unusual character especially suggest careful consideration to determine whether they are obnoxious to the constitutional provision." . . .

It is not within our constitutional tradition to enact laws of this sort. Central both to the idea of the rule of law and to our own Constitution's guarantee of equal protection is the principle that government and each of its parts remain open on impartial terms to all who seek its assistance. "Equal protection of the laws is not achieved through indiscriminate imposition of inequalities." . . . Respect for this principle explains why laws singling out a certain class of citizens for disfavored legal status or general hardships are rare. A law declaring that in general it shall be more difficult for one group of citizens than for all others to seek aid from the government is itself a denial of equal protection of the laws in the most literal sense. "The guaranty of 'equal protection of the laws is a pledge of the protection of equal laws.'" . . . *Davis v. Beason* . . . (1890), not cited by the parties but relied upon by the dissent, is not evidence that Amendment 2 is within our constitutional tradition, and any reliance upon it as authority for sustaining the amendment is misplaced. In *Davis,* the Court approved an Idaho territorial statute denying Mormons, polygamists, and advocates of polygamy the right to vote and to hold office because, as the Court construed the statute, it "simply excludes from the privilege of voting, or of holding any office of honor, trust or profit, those who have been convicted of certain offences, and those who advocate a practical resistance to the laws of the Territory and justify and approve the commission of crimes forbidden by it." . . . To the extent *Davis* held that persons advocating a certain practice may be denied the right to vote, it is no longer good law. . . . To the extent it held that the groups designated in the statute may be deprived of the right to vote because of their status, its ruling could not stand without surviving strict scrutiny, a most doubtful outcome. . . . To the extent *Davis* held that a convicted felon may be denied the right to vote, its holding is not implicated by our decision and is unexceptionable. . . .

A second and related point is that laws of the kind now before us raise the inevitable inference that the disadvantage imposed is born of animosity toward the class of persons affected. "[I]f the constitutional conception of 'equal protection of the laws' means anything, it must at the very least mean that a bare . . . desire to harm a politically unpopular group cannot constitute a legitimate governmental interest." . . . Even laws enacted for broad and ambitious purposes often can be explained by reference to legitimate public policies which justify the incidental disadvantages they impose on certain persons. Amendment 2, however, in making a general announcement that gays and lesbians shall not have any particular protections from the law, inflicts on them immediate, continuing, and real injuries that outrun and belie any legitimate justifications that may be claimed for it. We conclude that, in addition to the far-reaching deficiencies of Amendment 2 that we have noted, the principles it offends, in another sense, are conventional and venerable; a law must bear a rational relationship to a legitimate governmental purpose, *Kadrmas v. Dickinson Public Schools* . . . (1988), and Amendment 2 does not.

The primary rationale the State offers for Amendment 2 is respect for other citizens' freedom of association, and in particular the liberties of landlords or employers who have personal or religious objections to homosexuality. Colorado also cites its interest in conserving resources to fight discrimination against other groups. The breadth of the Amendment is so far removed from these particular justifications that we find it impossible to credit them. We cannot say that Amendment 2 is directed to any identifiable legitimate purpose or discrete objective. It is a status-based enactment divorced from any factual context from which we could discern a relationship to legitimate state interests; it is a classification of persons undertaken for its own sake, something the Equal Protection Clause does not permit. "[C]lass legislation . . . [is] obnoxious to the prohibitions of the Fourteenth Amendment . . . ." Civil Rights Cases. . . .

We must conclude that Amendment 2 classifies homosexuals not to further a proper legislative end but to make them unequal to everyone else. This Colorado cannot do. A State cannot so deem a class of persons a stranger to its laws. Amendment 2 violates the Equal Protection Clause, and the judgment of the Supreme Court of Colorado is affirmed.

It is so ordered.

Source: Romer v. Evans, 517 U.S. 620 (1996)

66. *Bush v. Gore,* 2000

Introduction

Bush v. Gore is the U.S. Supreme Court decision that resolved the disputed 2000 presidential election in favor of George W. Bush, the Republican Party candidate. The Court majority ruled that the Florida Supreme Court's chosen method for recounting ballots would violate the Equal Protection Clause of the Fourteenth Amendment. The Court also ruled that no alternative method could be established within the time limits set by the State of Florida. Three concurring justices also asserted that the Florida Supreme Court had violated Article II, Section 1, clause 2 of the Constitution, by misinterpreting Florida election law that had been enacted by the Florida Legislature. The justices had taken on the politically charged case after previously attempting to resolve lesser technical disputes. Only eight days previous, the Court had unanimously decided the related case of *Bush v. Palm Beach County Canvassing Board*, and only three days earlier, it had preliminarily halted a recount of votes in Florida. The final decision effectively allowed to stand the Florida Secretary of State's previous certification of Bush as the winner of Florida's 25 electoral votes. This gave Bush 271 electoral votes in total, one more than the required 270 to win the Electoral College and defeat Democratic candidate Al Gore.

Primary Source

Per Curiam.

I

On December 8, 2000, the Supreme Court of Florida ordered that the Circuit Court of Leon County tabulate by hand 9,000 ballots in Miami-Dade County. It also ordered the inclusion in the certified vote totals of 215 votes identified in Palm Beach County and 168 votes identified in Miami-Dade County for Vice President Albert Gore, Jr., and Senator Joseph Lieberman, Democratic Candidates for President and Vice President. The Supreme Court noted that petitioner, Governor George W. Bush asserted that the net gain for Vice President Gore in Palm Beach County was 176 votes, and directed the Circuit Court to resolve that dispute on remand. ___ So. 2d, at ___ (slip op., at 4, n. 6). The court further held that relief would require manual recounts in all Florida counties where so-called "undervotes" had not been subject to manual tabulation. The court ordered all manual recounts to begin at once. Governor Bush and Richard Cheney, Republican Candidates for the Presidency and Vice Presidency, filed an emergency application for a stay of this mandate. On December 9, we granted the application, treated the application as a petition for a writ of certiorari, and granted certiorari. *Post,* p. ___.

The proceedings leading to the present controversy are discussed in some detail in our opinion in *Bush* v. *Palm Beach County Canvassing Bd., ante,* p. ____ *(per curiam) (Bush I).* On November 8, 2000, the day following the Presidential election, the Florida Division of Elections reported that petitioner, Governor Bush, had received 2,909,135 votes, and respondent, Vice President Gore, had received 2,907,351 votes, a margin of 1,784 for Governor Bush. Because Governor Bush's margin of victory was less than "one-half of a percent . . . of the votes cast," an automatic machine recount was conducted under §102.141(4) of the election code, the results of which showed Governor Bush still winning the race but by a diminished margin. Vice President Gore then sought manual recounts in Volusia, Palm Beach, Broward, and Miami-Dade Counties, pursuant to Florida's election protest provisions. Fla. Stat. §102.166 (2000). A dispute arose concerning the deadline for local county canvassing boards to submit their returns to the Secretary of State (Secretary). The Secretary declined to waive the November 14 deadline imposed by statute. §§102.111, 102.112. The Florida Supreme Court, however, set the deadline at November 26. We granted certiorari and vacated the Florida Supreme Court's decision, finding considerable uncertainty as to the grounds on which it was based. *Bush I, ante,* at ___—___ (slip. op., at 6—7). On December 11, the Florida Supreme Court issued a decision on remand reinstating that date. ___ So. 2d ___, ___ (slip op. at 30—31).

On November 26, the Florida Elections Canvassing Commission certified the results of the election and declared Governor Bush the winner of Florida's 25 electoral votes. On November 27, Vice President Gore, pursuant to Florida's contest provisions, filed a complaint in Leon County Circuit Court contesting the certification. Fla. Stat. §102.168 (2000). He sought relief pursuant to §102.168(3)(c), which provides that "[r]eceipt of a number of illegal votes or rejection of a number of legal votes sufficient to change or place in doubt the result of the election" shall be grounds for a contest. The Circuit Court denied relief, stating that Vice President Gore failed to meet his burden of proof. He appealed to the First District Court of Appeal, which certified the matter to the Florida Supreme Court.

Accepting jurisdiction, the Florida Supreme Court affirmed in part and reversed in part. *Gore* v. *Harris,* ___ So. 2d. ___ (2000). The court held that the Circuit Court had been correct to reject Vice President Gore's challenge to the results certified in Nassau County and his challenge to the Palm Beach County Canvassing Board's determination that 3,300 ballots cast in that county were not, in the statutory phrase, "legal votes."

The Supreme Court held that Vice President Gore had satisfied his burden of proof under §102.168(3)(c) with respect to his challenge to Miami-Dade County's failure to tabulate, by manual count, 9,000 ballots on which the machines had failed to detect a vote for President ("undervotes"). ___ So. 2d., at ___ (slip. op., at 22—23). Noting the closeness of the election, the Court explained that "[o]n this record, there can be no question that there are legal votes within the 9,000 uncounted votes sufficient to place the results of this election in doubt." *Id.*, at ___ (slip. op., at 35). A "legal vote," as determined by the Supreme Court, is "one in which there is a 'clear indication of the intent of the voter.' " *Id.*, at ___ (slip op., at 25). The court therefore ordered a hand recount of the 9,000 ballots in Miami-Dade County. Observing that the contest provisions vest broad discretion in the circuit judge to "provide any relief appropriate under such circumstances," Fla. Stat. §102.168(8) (2000), the Supreme Court further held that the Circuit Court could order "the Supervisor of Elections and the Canvassing Boards, as well as the necessary public officials, in all counties that have not conducted a manual recount or tabulation of the undervotes . . . to do so forthwith, said tabulation to take place in the individual counties where the ballots are located." ___ So. 2d, at ___ (slip. op., at 38).

The Supreme Court also determined that both Palm Beach County and Miami-Dade County, in their earlier manual recounts, had identified a net gain of 215 and 168 legal votes for Vice President Gore. *Id.*, at ___ (slip. op., at 3334). Rejecting the Circuit Court's conclusion that Palm Beach County lacked the authority to include the 215 net votes submitted past the November 26 deadline, the Supreme Court explained that the deadline was not intended to exclude votes identified after that date through ongoing manual recounts. As to Miami-Dade County, the Court concluded that although the 168 votes identified were the result of a partial recount, they were "legal votes [that] could change the outcome of the election." *Id.*, at (slip op., at 34). The Supreme Court therefore directed the Circuit Court to include those totals in the certified results, subject to resolution of the actual vote total from the Miami-Dade partial recount.

The petition presents the following questions: whether the Florida Supreme Court established new standards for resolving Presidential election contests, thereby violating Art. II, §1, cl. 2, of the United States Constitution and failing to comply with 3 U.S.C. § 5 and whether the use of standardless manual recounts violates the Equal Protection and Due Process Clauses. With respect to the equal protection question, we find a violation of the Equal Protection Clause.

II

A

The closeness of this election, and the multitude of legal challenges which have followed in its wake, have brought into sharp focus a common, if heretofore unnoticed, phenomenon. Nationwide statistics reveal that an estimated 2% of ballots cast do not register a vote for President for whatever reason, including deliberately choosing no candidate at all or some voter error, such as voting for two candidates or insufficiently marking a ballot. See Ho, More Than 2M Ballots Uncounted, AP Online (Nov. 28, 2000); Kelley, Balloting Problems Not Rare But Only In A Very Close Election Do Mistakes And Mismarking Make A Difference, Omaha

World-Herald (Nov. 15, 2000). In certifying election results, the votes eligible for inclusion in the certification are the votes meeting the properly established legal requirements.

This case has shown that punch card balloting machines can produce an unfortunate number of ballots which are not punched in a clean, complete way by the voter. After the current counting, it is likely legislative bodies nationwide will examine ways to improve the mechanisms and machinery for voting.

B

The individual citizen has no federal constitutional right to vote for electors for the President of the United States unless and until the state legislature chooses a statewide election as the means to implement its power to appoint members of the Electoral College. U.S. Const., Art. II, §1. This is the source for the statement in *McPherson* v. *Blacker*, 146 U.S. 1, 35 (1892), that the State legislature's power to select the manner for appointing electors is plenary; it may, if it so chooses, select the electors itself, which indeed was the manner used by State legislatures in several States for many years after the Framing of our Constitution. *Id.,* at 28–33. History has now favored the voter, and in each of the several States the citizens themselves vote for Presidential electors. When the state legislature vests the right to vote for President in its people, the right to vote as the legislature has prescribed is fundamental; and one source of its fundamental nature lies in the equal weight accorded to each vote and the equal dignity owed to each voter. The State, of course, after granting the franchise in the special context of Article II, can take back the power to appoint electors. See *id.,* at 35 ("[T]here is no doubt of the right of the legislature to resume the power at any time, for it can neither be taken away nor abdicated") (quoting S. Rep. No. 395, 43d Cong., 1st Sess.).

The right to vote is protected in more than the initial allocation of the franchise. Equal protection applies as well to the manner of its exercise. Having once granted the right to vote on equal terms, the State may not, by later arbitrary and disparate treatment, value one person's vote over that of another. See, *e.g., Harper* v. *Virginia Bd. of Elections,* 383 U.S. 663, 665 (1966) ("[O]nce the franchise is granted to the electorate, lines may not be drawn which are inconsistent with the Equal Protection Clause of the Fourteenth Amendment"). It must be remembered that "the right of suffrage can be denied by a debasement or dilution of the weight of a citizen's vote just as effectively as by wholly prohibiting the free exercise of the franchise." *Reynolds* v. *Sims,* 377 U.S. 533, 555 (1964).

There is no difference between the two sides of the present controversy on these basic propositions. Respondents say that the very purpose of vindicating the right to vote justifies the recount procedures now at issue. The question before us, however, is whether the recount procedures the Florida Supreme Court has adopted are consistent with its obligation to avoid arbitrary and disparate treatment of the members of its electorate.

Much of the controversy seems to revolve around ballot cards designed to be perforated by a stylus but which, either through error or deliberate omission, have not been perforated with sufficient precision for a machine to count them. In some cases a piece of the card—a chad—is hanging, say by two corners. In other cases there is no separation at all, just an indentation.

The Florida Supreme Court has ordered that the intent of the voter be discerned from such ballots. For purposes of resolving the equal protection challenge, it is not necessary to decide whether the Florida Supreme Court had the authority under the legislative scheme for resolving election disputes to define what a legal vote is and to mandate a manual recount implementing that definition. The recount mechanisms implemented in response to the decisions of the Florida Supreme Court do not satisfy the minimum requirement for non-arbitrary treatment of voters necessary to secure the fundamental right. Florida's basic command for the count of legally cast votes is to consider the "intent of the voter." *Gore* v. *Harris*, ___ So. 2d, at ___ (slip op., at 39). This is unobjectionable as an abstract proposition and a starting principle. The problem inheres in the absence of specific standards to ensure its equal application. The formulation of uniform rules to determine intent based on these recurring circumstances is practicable and, we conclude, necessary.

The law does not refrain from searching for the intent of the actor in a multitude of circumstances; and in some cases the general command to ascertain intent is not susceptible to much further refinement. In this instance, however, the question is not whether to believe a witness but how to interpret the marks or holes or scratches on an inanimate object, a piece of cardboard or paper which, it is said, might not have registered as a vote during the machine count. The factfinder confronts a thing, not a person. The search for intent can be confined by specific rules designed to ensure uniform treatment.

The want of those rules here has led to unequal evaluation of ballots in various respects. See *Gore* v. *Harris*, ___ So. 2d, at ___ (slip op., at 51) (Wells, J., dissenting) ("Should a county canvassing board count or not count a 'dimpled chad' where the voter is able to successfully dislodge the chad in every other contest on that ballot? Here, the county canvassing boards disagree"). As seems to have been acknowledged at oral argument, the standards for accepting or rejecting contested ballots might vary not only from county to county but indeed within a single county from one recount team to another.

The record provides some examples. A monitor in Miami-Dade County testified at trial that he observed that three members of the county canvassing board applied different standards in defining a legal vote. 3 Tr. 497, 499 (Dec. 3, 2000). And testimony at trial also revealed that at least one county changed its evaluative standards during the counting process. Palm Beach County, for example, began the process with a 1990 guideline which precluded counting completely attached chads, switched to a rule that considered a vote to be legal if any light could be seen through a chad, changed back to the 1990 rule, and then abandoned any pretense of a *per se* rule, only to have a court order that the county consider dimpled chads legal. This is not a process with sufficient guarantees of equal treatment.

An early case in our one person, one vote jurisprudence arose when a State accorded arbitrary and disparate treatment to voters in its different counties. *Gray* v. *Sanders*, 372 U.S. 368 (1963). The Court found a constitutional violation. We relied on these principles in the context of the Presidential selection process in *Moore* v. *Ogilvie,* 394 U.S. 814 (1969), where we invalidated a county-based procedure that diluted the influence of citizens in larger counties in the nominating process. There we observed that "[t]he idea that one group can be granted greater voting strength than another is hostile to the one man, one vote basis of our representative government." *Id.,* at 819.

The State Supreme Court ratified this uneven treatment. It mandated that the recount totals from two counties, Miami-Dade and Palm Beach, be included in the certified total. The court also appeared to hold *sub silentio* that the recount totals from Broward County, which were not completed until after the original November 14 certification by the Secretary of State, were to be considered part of the new certified vote totals even though the county certification was not contested by Vice President Gore. Yet each of the counties used varying standards to determine what was a legal vote. Broward County used a more forgiving standard than Palm Beach County, and uncovered almost three times as many new votes, a result markedly disproportionate to the difference in population between the counties.

In addition, the recounts in these three counties were not limited to so-called undervotes but extended to all of the ballots. The distinction has real consequences. A manual recount of all ballots identifies not only those ballots which show no vote but also those which contain more than one, the so-called overvotes. Neither category will be counted by the machine. This is not a trivial concern. At oral argument, respondents estimated there are as many as 110,000 overvotes statewide. As a result, the citizen whose ballot was not read by a machine because he failed to vote for a candidate in a way readable by a machine may still have his vote counted in a manual recount; on the other hand, the citizen who marks two candidates in a way discernable by the machine will not have the same opportunity to have his vote count, even if a manual examination of the ballot would reveal the requisite indicia of intent. Furthermore, the citizen who marks two candidates, only one of which is discernable by the machine, will have his vote counted even though it should have been read as an invalid ballot. The State Supreme Court's inclusion of vote counts based on these variant standards exemplifies concerns with the remedial processes that were under way.

That brings the analysis to yet a further equal protection problem. The votes certified by the court included a partial total from one county, Miami-Dade. The Florida Supreme Court's decision thus gives no assurance that the recounts included in a final certification must be complete. Indeed, it is respondent's submission that it would be consistent with the rules of the recount procedures to include whatever partial counts are done by the time of final certification, and we interpret the Florida Supreme Court's decision to permit this. See ____ So. 2d, at ____, n. 21 (slip op., at 37, n. 21) (noting "practical difficulties" may control outcome of election, but certifying partial Miami-Dade total nonetheless). This accommodation no doubt results from the truncated contest period established by the Florida Supreme Court in *Bush I*, at respondents' own urging. The press of time does not diminish the constitutional concern. A desire for speed is not a general excuse for ignoring equal protection guarantees.

In addition to these difficulties the actual process by which the votes were to be counted under the Florida Supreme Court's decision raises further concerns. That order did not specify who would recount the ballots. The county canvassing boards were forced to pull together ad hoc teams comprised of judges from various Circuits who had no previous training in handling and interpreting ballots. Furthermore, while others were permitted to observe, they were prohibited from objecting during the recount.

The recount process, in its features here described, is inconsistent with the minimum procedures necessary to protect the fundamental right of each voter in the special instance of a statewide recount under the authority of a single state judicial officer. Our consideration is limited to the present circumstances, for the problem of equal protection in election processes generally presents many complexities.

The question before the Court is not whether local entities, in the exercise of their expertise, may develop different systems for implementing elections. Instead, we are presented with a situation where a state court with the power to assure uniformity has ordered a statewide recount with minimal procedural safeguards. When a court orders a statewide remedy, there must be at least some assurance that the rudimentary requirements of equal treatment and fundamental fairness are satisfied.

Given the Court's assessment that the recount process underway was probably being conducted in an unconstitutional manner, the Court stayed the order directing the recount so it could hear this case and render an expedited decision. The contest provision, as it was mandated by the State Supreme Court, is not well calculated to sustain the confidence that all citizens must have in the outcome of elections. The State has not shown that its procedures include the necessary safeguards. The problem, for instance, of the estimated 110,000 overvotes has not been addressed, although Chief Justice Wells called attention to the concern in his dissenting opinion. See ____ So. 2d, at ____, n. 26 (slip op., at 45, n. 26).

Upon due consideration of the difficulties identified to this point, it is obvious that the recount cannot be conducted in compliance with the requirements of equal protection and due process without substantial additional work. It would require not only the adoption (after opportunity for argument) of adequate statewide standards for determining what is a legal vote, and practicable procedures to implement them, but also orderly judicial review of any disputed matters that might arise. In addition, the Secretary of State has advised that the recount of only a portion of the ballots requires that the vote tabulation equipment be used to screen out undervotes, a function for which the machines were not designed. If a recount of overvotes were also required, perhaps even a second screening would be necessary. Use of the equipment for this purpose, and any new software developed for it, would have to be evaluated for accuracy by the Secretary of State, as required by Fla. Stat. §101.015 (2000).

The Supreme Court of Florida has said that the legislature intended the State's electors to "participat[e] fully in the federal electoral process," as provided in 3 U.S.C. § 5. ___ So. 2d, at ___ (slip op. at 27); see also *Palm Beach Canvassing Bd. v. Harris,* 2000 WL 1725434, *13 (Fla. 2000). That statute, in turn, requires that any controversy or contest that is designed to lead to a conclusive selection of electors be completed by December 12. That date is upon us, and there is no recount procedure in place under the State Supreme Court's order that comports with minimal constitutional standards. Because it is evident that any recount seeking to meet the December 12 date will be unconstitutional for the reasons we have discussed, we reverse the judgment of the Supreme Court of Florida ordering a recount to proceed.

Seven Justices of the Court agree that there are constitutional problems with the recount ordered by the Florida Supreme Court that demand a remedy. See post, at 6 (Souter, J., dissenting); *post,* at 2, 15 (Breyer, J., dissenting). The only disagreement is as to the remedy. Because the Florida Supreme Court has said that the Florida Legislature intended to obtain the safe-harbor benefits of 3 U.S.C. § 5

Justice Breyer's proposed remedy–remanding to the Florida Supreme Court for its ordering of a constitutionally proper contest until December 18-contemplates action in violation of the Florida election code, and hence could not be part of an "appropriate" order authorized by Fla. Stat. §102.168(8) (2000).

* * *

None are more conscious of the vital limits on judicial authority than are the members of this Court, and none stand more in admiration of the Constitution's design to leave the selection of the President to the people, through their legislatures, and to the political sphere. When contending parties invoke the process of the courts, however, it becomes our unsought responsibility to resolve the federal and constitutional issues the judicial system has been forced to confront.

The judgment of the Supreme Court of Florida is reversed, and the case is remanded for further proceedings not inconsistent with this opinion.

Pursuant to this Court's Rule 45.2, the Clerk is directed to issue the mandate in this case forthwith.

It is so ordered.

Source: George W. Bush, et al. v. Albert Gore, Jr., et al., 531 U.S. 98, 121 S. Ct. 525 (2000)

67. Federal Courts Improvement Act, 2000

Introduction

The Federal Courts Improvement Act of 2000 (Public Law 106-518) was intended to enhance the Judiciary's effectiveness and efficiency. Among other provisions, the Act broadens the authority of magistrate judges by expanding their civil and criminal contempt authority. Magistrate judges now may punish by fine or imprisonment any misbehavior occurring in their presence, and they also have been given additional civil and criminal contempt authority in civil consent and misdemeanor cases. The act also increased certain fees for bankruptcy court proceedings.

Primary Source

An Act

To make improvements in the operation and administration of the Federal courts, and for other purposes.

Be it enacted by the Senate and House of Representatives of the United States of America in Congress assembled,

SECTION 1. SHORT TITLE AND TABLE OF CONTENTS.

(a) SHORT TITLE—This Act may be cited as the 'Federal Courts Improvement Act of 2000'.

(b) TABLE OF CONTENTS—The table of contents of this Act is as follows:

Sec. 1. Short title and table of contents.

TITLE I—JUDICIAL FINANCIAL ADMINISTRATION
Sec. 101. Extension of Judiciary Information Technology Fund.
Sec. 102. Disposition of miscellaneous fees.
Sec. 103. Increase in chapter 9 bankruptcy filing fee.
Sec. 104. Increase in fee for converting a chapter 7 or chapter 13 bankruptcy case to a chapter 11 bankruptcy case.
Sec. 105. Bankruptcy fees.

TITLE II—JUDICIAL PROCESS IMPROVEMENTS
Sec. 201. Extension of statutory authority for magistrate judge positions to be established in the district courts of Guam and the Northern Mariana Islands.
Sec. 202. Magistrate judge contempt authority.
Sec. 203. Consent to magistrate judge authority in petty offense cases and magistrate judge authority in misdemeanor cases involving juvenile defendants.
Sec. 204. Savings and loan data reporting requirements.
Sec. 205. Membership in circuit judicial councils.
Sec. 206. Sunset of civil justice expense and delay reduction plans.
Sec. 207. Repeal of Court of Federal Claims filing fee.
Sec. 208. Technical bankruptcy correction.
Sec. 209. Technical amendment relating to the treatment of certain bankruptcy fees collected.
Sec. 210. Maximum amounts of compensation for attorneys.
Sec. 211. Reimbursement of expenses in defense of certain malpractice actions.

TITLE III—JUDICIAL PERSONNEL ADMINISTRATION, BENEFITS, AND PROTECTIONS
Sec. 301. Judicial administrative officials retirement matters.
Sec. 302. Applicability of leave provisions to employees of the Sentencing Commission.

Sec. 303. Payments to military survivors benefits plan.
Sec. 304. Creation of certifying officers in the judicial branch.
Sec. 305. Amendment to the jury selection process.
Sec. 306. Authorization of a circuit executive for the Federal circuit.
Sec. 307. Residence of retired judges.
Sec. 308. Recall of judges on disability status.
Sec. 309. Personnel application and insurance programs relating to judges of the Court of Federal Claims.
Sec. 310. Lump-sum payment for accumulated and accrued leave on separation.
Sec. 311. Employment of personal assistants for handicapped employees.
Sec. 312. Mandatory retirement age for Director of the Federal Judicial Center.
Sec. 313. Reauthorization of certain Supreme Court Police authority.

TITLE IV—FEDERAL PUBLIC DEFENDERS
Sec. 401. Tort Claims Act amendment relating to liability of Federal public defenders.

TITLE V—MISCELLANEOUS PROVISIONS
Sec. 501. Extensions relating to bankruptcy administrator program.
Sec. 502. Additional place of holding court in the district of Oregon.

TITLE I—JUDICIAL FINANCIAL ADMINISTRATION

SEC. 101. EXTENSION OF JUDICIARY INFORMATION TECHNOLOGY FUND.

Section 612 of title 28, United States Code, is amended—

(1) by striking 'equipment' each place it appears and inserting 'resources';

(2) by striking subsection (f) and redesignating subsections (g) through (k) as subsections (f) through (j), respectively;

(3) in subsection (g), as so redesignated, by striking paragraph (3); and

(4) in subsection (i), as so redesignated—

(A) by striking 'Judiciary' each place it appears and inserting 'judiciary';

(B) by striking 'subparagraph (c)(1)(B)' and inserting 'subsection (c)(1)(B)'; and

(C) by striking 'under (c)(1)(B)' and inserting 'under subsection (c)(1)(B)'.

SEC. 102. DISPOSITION OF MISCELLANEOUS FEES.

For fiscal year 2001 and each fiscal year thereafter, any portion of miscellaneous fees collected as prescribed by the Judicial Conference of the United States under sections 1913, 1914(b), 1926(a), 1930(b), and 1932 of title 28, United States Code, exceeding the amount of such fees in effect on September 30, 2000, shall be deposited into the special fund of the Treasury established under section 1931 of title 28, United States Code.

SEC. 103. INCREASE IN CHAPTER 9 BANKRUPTCY FILING FEE.

Section 1930(a)(2) of title 28, United States Code, is amended by striking '$300' and inserting 'equal to the fee specified in paragraph (3) for filing a case under chapter 11 of title 11. The amount by which the fee payable under this paragraph exceeds $300 shall be deposited in the fund established under section 1931 of this title'.

SEC. 104. INCREASE IN FEE FOR CONVERTING A CHAPTER 7 OR CHAPTER 13 BANKRUPTCY CASE TO A CHAPTER 11 BANKRUPTCY CASE.

The flush paragraph at the end of section 1930(a) of title 28, United States Code, is amended by striking '$400' and inserting 'the amount equal to the difference between the fee specified in paragraph (3) and the fee specified in paragraph (1)'.

SEC. 105. BANKRUPTCY FEES.

Section 1930(a) of title 28, United States Code, is amended by adding at the end the following:

'(7) In districts that are not part of a United States trustee region as defined in section 581 of this title, the Judicial Conference of the United States may require the debtor in a case under chapter 11 of title 11 to pay fees equal to those imposed by paragraph (6) of this subsection. Such fees shall be deposited as offsetting receipts to the fund established under section 1931 of this title and shall remain available until expended.'.

TITLE II—JUDICIAL PROCESS IMPROVEMENTS

SEC. 201. EXTENSION OF STATUTORY AUTHORITY FOR MAGISTRATE JUDGE POSITIONS TO BE ESTABLISHED IN THE DISTRICT COURTS OF GUAM AND THE NORTHERN MARIANA ISLANDS.

Section 631 of title 28, United States Code, is amended—

(1) by striking the first two sentences of subsection (a) and inserting the following: 'The judges of each United States district court and the district courts of the Virgin Islands, Guam, and the Northern Mariana Islands shall appoint United States magistrate judges in such numbers and to serve at such locations within the judicial districts as the Judicial Conference may determine under this chapter. In the case of a magistrate judge appointed by the district court of the Virgin Islands, Guam, or the Northern Mariana Islands, this chapter shall apply as though the court appointing such a magistrate judge were a United States district court.'; and

(2) by inserting in the first sentence of paragraph (1) of subsection (b) after 'Commonwealth of Puerto Rico,' the following: 'the Territory of Guam, the Commonwealth of the Northern Mariana Islands,'.

SEC. 202. MAGISTRATE JUDGE CONTEMPT AUTHORITY.

Section 636(e) of title 28, United States Code, is amended to read as follows:

'(e) CONTEMPT AUTHORITY—

'(1) IN GENERAL—A United States magistrate judge serving under this chapter shall have within the territorial jurisdiction prescribed by the appointment of such magistrate judge the power to exercise contempt authority as set forth in this subsection.

'(2) SUMMARY CRIMINAL CONTEMPT AUTHORITY—A magistrate judge shall have the power to punish summarily by fine or imprisonment such contempt of the authority of such magistrate judge constituting misbehavior of any person in the magistrate judge's presence so as to obstruct the administration of justice. The order of contempt shall be issued under the Federal Rules of Criminal Procedure.

'(3) ADDITIONAL CRIMINAL CONTEMPT AUTHORITY IN CIVIL CONSENT AND MISDEMEANOR CASES—In any case in which a United States magistrate judge presides with the consent of the parties under subsection (c) of this section, and in any misdemeanor case proceeding before a magistrate judge under section 3401 of title 18, the magistrate judge shall have the power to punish, by fine or imprisonment, criminal contempt constituting disobedience or resistance to the magistrate judge's lawful writ, process, order, rule, decree, or command. Disposition of such contempt shall be conducted upon notice and hearing under the Federal Rules of Criminal Procedure.

'(4) CIVIL CONTEMPT AUTHORITY IN CIVIL CONSENT AND MISDE-MEANOR CASES—In any case in which a United States magistrate judge presides with the consent of the parties under subsection (c) of this section, and in any misdemeanor case proceeding before a magistrate judge under section 3401 of title 18, the magistrate judge may exercise the civil contempt authority of the district court. This paragraph shall not be construed to limit the authority of a magistrate judge to order sanctions under any other statute, the Federal Rules of Civil Procedure, or the Federal Rules of Criminal Procedure.

'(5) CRIMINAL CONTEMPT PENALTIES—The sentence imposed by a magistrate judge for any criminal contempt provided for in paragraphs (2) and (3) shall not exceed the penalties for a Class C misdemeanor as set forth in sections 3581(b)(8) and 3571(b)(6) of title 18.

'(6) CERTIFICATION OF OTHER CONTEMPTS TO THE DISTRICT COURT—Upon the commission of any such act—

'(A) in any case in which a United States magistrate judge presides with the consent of the parties under subsection (c) of this section, or in any misdemeanor case proceeding before a magistrate judge under section 3401 of title 18, that may, in the opinion of the magistrate judge, constitute a serious criminal contempt punishable by penalties exceeding those set forth in paragraph (5) of this subsection, or

'(B) in any other case or proceeding under subsection (a) or (b) of this section, or any other statute, where—

'(i) the act committed in the magistrate judge's presence may, in the opinion of the magistrate judge, constitute a serious criminal contempt punishable by penalties exceeding those set forth in paragraph (5) of this subsection,

'(ii) the act that constitutes a criminal contempt occurs outside the presence of the magistrate judge, or

'(iii) the act constitutes a civil contempt, the magistrate judge shall forthwith certify the facts to a district judge and may serve or cause to be served, upon any person whose behavior is brought into question under this paragraph, an order requiring such person to appear before a district judge upon a day certain to show cause why that person should not be adjudged in contempt by reason of the facts so certified. The district judge shall thereupon hear the evidence as to the act or conduct complained of and, if it is such as to warrant punishment, punish such person in the same manner and to the same extent as for a contempt committed before a district judge.

'(7) APPEALS OF MAGISTRATE JUDGE CONTEMPT ORDERS—The appeal of an order of contempt under this subsection shall be made to the court of appeals in cases proceeding under subsection (c) of this section. The appeal of any other order of contempt issued under this section shall be made to the district court.'.

SEC. 203. CONSENT TO MAGISTRATE JUDGE AUTHORITY IN PETTY OFFENSE CASES AND MAGISTRATE JUDGE AUTHORITY IN MISDEMEANOR CASES INVOLVING JUVENILE DEFENDANTS.

(a) AMENDMENTS TO TITLE 18—

(1) PETTY OFFENSE CASES—Section 3401(b) of title 18, United States Code, is amended by striking 'that is a class B misdemeanor charging a motor vehicle offense, a class C misdemeanor, or an infraction,' after 'petty offense'.

(2) CASES INVOLVING JUVENILES—Section 3401(g) of title 18, United States Code, is amended—

(A) by striking the first sentence and inserting the following: 'The magistrate judge may, in a petty offense case involving a juvenile, exercise all powers granted to the district court under chapter 403 of this title.';

(B) in the second sentence by striking 'any other class B or C misdemeanor case' and inserting 'the case of any misdemeanor, other than a petty offense,'; and

(C) by striking the last sentence.

(b) AMENDMENTS TO TITLE 28—Section 636(a) of title 28, United States Code, is amended by striking paragraphs (4) and (5) and inserting the following:

'(4) the power to enter a sentence for a petty offense; and

'(5) the power to enter a sentence for a class A misdemeanor in a case in which the parties have consented.'.

SEC. 204. SAVINGS AND LOAN DATA REPORTING REQUIREMENTS.

Section 604 of title 28, United States Code, is amended in subsection (a) by striking the second paragraph designated (24).

SEC. 205. MEMBERSHIP IN CIRCUIT JUDICIAL COUNCILS.

Section 332(a) of title 28, United States Code, is amended—

(1) by striking paragraph (3) and inserting the following:

'(3) Except for the chief judge of the circuit, either judges in regular active service or judges retired from regular active service under section 371(b) of this title may serve as members of the council. Service as a member of a judicial council by a judge retired from regular active service under section 371(b) may not be considered for meeting the requirements of section 371(f)(1) (A), (B), or (C).'; and

(2) in paragraph (5) by striking 'retirement,' and inserting 'retirement under section 371(a) or 372(a) of this title,'.

SEC. 206. SUNSET OF CIVIL JUSTICE EXPENSE AND DELAY REDUCTION PLANS.

Section 103(b)(2)(A) of the Civil Justice Reform Act of 1990 (Public Law 101-650; 104 Stat. 5096; 28 U.S.C. 471 note), as amended by Public Law 105-53 (111 Stat. 1173), is amended by inserting '471,' after 'sections'.

SEC. 207. REPEAL OF COURT OF FEDERAL CLAIMS FILING FEE.

Section 2520 of title 28, United States Code, and the item relating to such section in the table of contents for chapter 165 of such title, are repealed.

SEC. 208. TECHNICAL BANKRUPTCY CORRECTION.

Section 1228 of title 11, United States Code, is amended by striking '1222(b)(10)' each place it appears and inserting '1222(b)(9)'.

SEC. 209. TECHNICAL AMENDMENT RELATING TO THE TREATMENT OF CERTAIN BANKRUPTCY FEES COLLECTED.

(a) AMENDMENT—The first sentence of section 406(b) of the Departments of Commerce, Justice, and State, the Judiciary, and Related Agencies Appropriations Act, 1990 (Public Law 101-162; 103 Stat. 1016; 28 U.S.C. 1931 note) is amended by striking 'service enumerated after item 18' and inserting 'service not of a kind described in any of the items enumerated as items 1 through 7 and as items 9 through 18, as in effect on November 21, 1989,'.

(b) APPLICATION OF AMENDMENT—The amendment made by subsection (a) shall not apply with respect to fees collected before the date of enactment of this Act.

SEC. 210. MAXIMUM AMOUNTS OF COMPENSATION FOR ATTORNEYS.

Section 3006A(d)(2) of title 18, United States Code, is amended—

(1) in the first sentence—

(A) by striking '$3,500' and inserting '$5,200'; and

(B) by striking '$1,000' and inserting '$1,500';

(2) in the second sentence by striking '$2,500' and inserting '$3,700';

(3) in the third sentence—

(A) by striking '$750' and inserting '$1,200'; and

(B) by striking '$2,500' and inserting '$3,900';

(4) by inserting after the second sentence the following: 'For representation of a petitioner in a non-capital habeas corpus proceeding, the compensation for each attorney shall not exceed the amount applicable to a felony in this paragraph for representation of a defendant before a judicial officer of the district court. For representation of such petitioner in an appellate court, the compensation for each attorney shall not exceed the amount applicable for representation of a defendant in an appellate court.'; and

(5) in the last sentence by striking '$750' and inserting '$1,200'.

SEC. 211. REIMBURSEMENT OF EXPENSES IN DEFENSE OF CERTAIN MALPRACTICE ACTIONS.

Section 3006A(d)(1) of title 18, United States Code, is amended by striking the last sentence and inserting 'Attorneys may be reimbursed for expenses reasonably incurred, including the costs of transcripts authorized by the United States magistrate or the court, and the costs of defending actions alleging malpractice of counsel in furnishing representational services under this section. No reimbursement for expenses in defending against malpractice claims shall be made if a judgment of malpractice is rendered against the counsel furnishing representational services under this section. The United States magistrate or the court shall make determinations relating to reimbursement of expenses under this paragraph.'.

TITLE III—JUDICIAL PERSONNEL ADMINISTRATION, BENEFITS, AND PROTECTIONS

SEC. 301. JUDICIAL ADMINISTRATIVE OFFICIALS RETIREMENT MATTERS.

(a) DIRECTOR OF ADMINISTRATIVE OFFICE—Section 611 of title 28, United States Code, is amended—

(1) in subsection (d), by inserting 'a congressional employee in the capacity of primary administrative assistant to a Member of Congress or in the capacity of staff director or chief counsel for the majority or the minority of a committee or subcommittee of the Senate or House of Representatives,' after 'Congress,';

(2) in subsection (b)—

(A) by striking 'who has served at least fifteen years and' and inserting 'who has at least fifteen years of service and has'; and

(B) in the first undesignated paragraph, by striking 'who has served at least ten years,' and inserting 'who has at least ten years of service,'; and

(3) in subsection (c)—

(A) by striking 'served at least fifteen years,' and inserting 'at least fifteen years of service,'; and

(B) by striking 'served less than fifteen years,' and inserting 'less than fifteen years of service,'.

(b) DIRECTOR OF THE FEDERAL JUDICIAL CENTER—Section 627 of title 28, United States Code, is amended—

(1) in subsection (e), by inserting 'a congressional employee in the capacity of primary administrative assistant to a Member of Congress or in the capacity of staff director or chief counsel for the majority or the minority of a committee or subcommittee of the Senate or House of Representatives,' after 'Congress,';

(2) in subsection (c)—

(A) by striking 'who has served at least fifteen years and' and inserting 'who has at least fifteen years of service and has'; and

(B) in the first undesignated paragraph, by striking 'who has served at least ten years,' and inserting 'who has at least ten years of service,'; and

(3) in subsection (d)—

(A) by striking 'served at least fifteen years,' and inserting 'at least fifteen years of service,'; and

(B) by striking 'served less than fifteen years,' and inserting 'less than fifteen years of service,'.

SEC. 302. APPLICABILITY OF LEAVE PROVISIONS TO EMPLOYEES OF THE SENTENCING COMMISSION.

(a) IN GENERAL—Section 996(b) of title 28, United States Code, is amended by striking all after 'title 5,' and inserting 'except the following: chapters 45 (Incentive Awards), 63 (Leave), 81 (Compensation for Work Injuries), 83 (Retirement), 85 (Unemployment Compensation), 87 (Life Insurance), and 89 (Health Insurance), and subchapter VI of chapter 55 (Payment for accumulated and accrued leave).'.

(b) SAVINGS PROVISION—Any leave that an individual accrued or accumulated (or that otherwise became available to such individual) under the leave system of the United States Sentencing Commission and that remains unused as of the date of the enactment of this Act shall, on and after such date, be treated as leave accrued or accumulated (or that otherwise became available to such individual) under chapter 63 of title 5, United States Code.

SEC. 303. PAYMENTS TO MILITARY SURVIVORS BENEFITS PLAN.

Section 371(e) of title 28, United States Code, is amended by inserting after 'such retired or retainer pay' the following: ', except such pay as is deductible from the retired or retainer pay as a result of participation in any survivor's benefits plan in connection with the retired pay,'.

SEC. 304. CREATION OF CERTIFYING OFFICERS IN THE JUDICIAL BRANCH.

(a) APPOINTMENT OF DISBURSING AND CERTIFYING OFFICERS—Chapter 41 of title 28, United States Code, is amended by adding at the end the following:

'Sec. 613. Disbursing and certifying officers

'(a) DISBURSING OFFICERS—The Director may designate in writing officers and employees of the judicial branch of the Government, including the courts as defined in section 610 other than the Supreme Court, to be disbursing officers in such numbers and locations as the Director considers necessary. Such disbursing officers shall—

'(1) disburse moneys appropriated to the judicial branch and other funds only in strict accordance with payment requests certified by the Director or in accordance with subsection (b);

'(2) examine payment requests as necessary to ascertain whether they are in proper form, certified, and approved; and

'(3) be held accountable for their actions as provided by law, except that such a disbursing officer shall not be held accountable or responsible for any illegal, improper, or incorrect payment resulting from any false, inaccurate, or misleading certificate for which a certifying officer is responsible under subsection (b).

'(b) CERTIFYING OFFICERS—

'(1) IN GENERAL—The Director may designate in writing officers and employees of the judicial branch of the Government, including the courts as defined in section 610 other than the Supreme Court, to certify payment requests payable from appropriations and funds. Such certifying officers shall be responsible and accountable for—

'(A) the existence and correctness of the facts recited in the certificate or other request for payment or its supporting papers;

'(B) the legality of the proposed payment under the appropriation or fund involved; and

'(C) the correctness of the computations of certified payment requests.

'(2) LIABILITY—The liability of a certifying officer shall be enforced in the same manner and to the same extent as provided by law with respect to the enforcement of the liability of disbursing and other accountable officers. A certifying officer shall be required to make restitution to the United States for the amount of any illegal, improper, or incorrect payment resulting from any false, inaccurate, or misleading certificates made by the certifying officer, as well as for any payment prohibited by law or which did not represent a legal obligation under the appropriation or fund involved.

'(c) RIGHTS—A certifying or disbursing officer—

'(1) has the right to apply for and obtain a decision by the Comptroller General on any question of law involved in a payment request presented for certification; and '(2) is entitled to relief from liability arising under this section in accordance with title 31.

'(d) OTHER AUTHORITY NOT AFFECTED—Nothing in this section affects the authority of the courts with respect to moneys deposited with the courts under chapter 129 of this title.'.

(b) CONFORMING AMENDMENT- The table of sections for chapter 41 of title 28, United States Code, is amended by adding at the end the following:

'613. Disbursing and certifying officers.'.

(c) RULE OF CONSTRUCTION—The amendment made by subsection (a) shall not be construed to authorize the hiring of any Federal officer or employee.

(d) DUTIES OF DIRECTOR—Section 604(a)(8) of title 28, United States Code, is amended to read as follows:

'(8) Disburse appropriations and other funds for the maintenance and operation of the courts;'.

SEC. 305. AMENDMENT TO THE JURY SELECTION PROCESS.

Section 1865 of title 28, United States Code, is amended—

(1) in subsection (a) by inserting 'or the clerk under supervision of the court if the court's jury selection plan so authorizes,' after 'jury commission,'; and

(2) in subsection (b) by inserting 'or the clerk if the court's jury selection plan so provides,' after 'may provide,'.

SEC. 306. AUTHORIZATION OF A CIRCUIT EXECUTIVE FOR THE FEDERAL CIRCUIT.

Section 332 of title 28, United States Code, is amended by adding at the end the following:

'(h)(1) The United States Court of Appeals for the Federal Circuit may appoint a circuit executive, who shall serve at the pleasure of the court. In appointing a circuit executive, the court shall take into account experience in administrative and executive positions, familiarity with court procedures, and special training. The circuit executive shall exercise such administrative powers and perform such duties as may be delegated by the court. The duties delegated to the circuit executive may include the duties specified in subsection (e) of this section, insofar as such duties are applicable to the Court of Appeals for the Federal Circuit.

'(2) The circuit executive shall be paid the salary for circuit executives established under subsection (f) of this section.

'(3) The circuit executive may appoint, with the approval of the court, necessary employees in such number as may be approved by the Director of the Administrative Office of the United States Courts.

'(4) The circuit executive and staff shall be deemed to be officers and employees of the United States within the meaning of the statutes specified in subsection (f)(4).

'(5) The court may appoint either a circuit executive under this subsection or a clerk under section 711 of this title, but not both, or may appoint a combined circuit executive/clerk who shall be paid the salary of a circuit executive.'.

SEC. 307. RESIDENCE OF RETIRED JUDGES.

Section 175 of title 28, United States Code, is amended by adding at the end the following:

'(c) Retired judges of the Court of Federal Claims are not subject to restrictions as to residence. The place where a retired judge maintains the actual abode in which such judge customarily lives shall be deemed to be the judge's official duty station for the purposes of section 456 of this title.'.

SEC. 308. RECALL OF JUDGES ON DISABILITY STATUS.

Section 797(a) of title 28, United States Code, is amended—

(1) by inserting '(1)' after '(a)'; and
(2) by adding at the end the following:

'(2) Any judge of the Court of Federal Claims receiving an annuity under section 178(c) of this title (pertaining to disability) who, in the estimation of the chief judge, has recovered sufficiently to render judicial service, shall be known and designated as a senior judge and may perform duties as a judge when recalled under subsection (b) of this section.'.

SEC. 309. PERSONNEL APPLICATION AND INSURANCE PROGRAMS RELATING TO JUDGES OF THE COURT OF FEDERAL CLAIMS.

(a) IN GENERAL—Chapter 7 of title 28, United States Code, is amended by inserting after section 178 the following:

'Sec. 179. Personnel application and insurance programs

'(a) For purposes of construing and applying title 5, a judge of the United States Court of Federal Claims shall be deemed to be an 'officer' under section 2104(a) of such title.

'(b)(1)(A) For purposes of construing and applying chapter 89 of title 5, a judge of the United States Court of Federal Claims who—

'(i) is retired under subsection (b) of section 178 of this title, and

'(ii) at the time of becoming such a retired judge—

'(I) was enrolled in a health benefits plan under chapter 89 of title 5, but

'(II) did not satisfy the requirements of section 8905(b)(1) of title 5 (relating to eligibility to continue enrollment as an annuitant), shall be deemed to be an annuitant meeting the requirements of section 8905(b)(1) of title 5, in accordance with the succeeding provisions of this paragraph, if the judge gives timely written notification to the chief judge of the court that the judge is willing to be called upon to perform judicial duties under section 178(d) of this title during the period of continued eligibility for enrollment, as described in subparagraph (B)(ii) or (C)(ii) (whichever applies).

'(B) Except as provided in subparagraph (C)—

'(i) in order to be eligible for continued enrollment under this paragraph, notification under subparagraph (A) shall be made before the first day of the open enrollment period preceding the calendar year referred to in clause (ii)(II); and

'(ii) if such notification is timely made, the retired judge shall be eligible for continued enrollment under this paragraph for the period—

'(I) beginning on the date on which eligibility would otherwise cease, and

'(II) ending on the last day of the calendar year next beginning after the end of the open enrollment period referred to in clause (i).

'(C) For purposes of applying this paragraph for the first time in the case of any particular judge—

'(i) subparagraph (B)(i) shall be applied by substituting 'the expiration of the term of office of the judge' for the matter following 'before'; and

'(ii)(I) if the term of office of such judge expires before the first day of the open enrollment period referred to in subparagraph (B)(i), the period of continued eligibility for enrollment shall be as described in subparagraph (B)(ii); but

'(II) if the term of office of such judge expires on or after the first day of the open enrollment period referred to in subparagraph (B)(i), the period of continued eligibility shall not end until the last day of the calendar year next beginning after the end of the next full open enrollment period beginning after the date on which the term expires.

'(2) In the event that a retired judge remains enrolled under chapter 89 of title 5 for a period of 5 consecutive years by virtue of paragraph (1) (taking into account only periods of coverage as an active judge immediately before retirement and as a retired judge pursuant to paragraph (1)), then, effective as of the day following the last day of that 5-year period—

'(A) the provisions of chapter 89 of title 5 shall be applied as if such judge had satisfied the requirements of section 8905(b)(1) on the last day of such period; and

'(B) the provisions of paragraph (1) shall cease to apply.

'(3) For purposes of this subsection, the term 'open enrollment period' refers to a period described in section 8905(g)(1) of title 5.

'(c) For purposes of construing and applying chapter 87 of title 5, including any adjustment of insurance rates by regulation or otherwise, a judge of the United States Court of Federal Claims in regular active service or who is retired under section 178 of this title shall be deemed to be a judge of the United States described under section 8701(a)(5) of title 5.'.

(b) TECHNICAL AND CONFORMING AMENDMENT—The table of sections for chapter 7 of title 28, United States Code, is amended by striking the item relating to section 179 and inserting the following:

'179. Personnel application and insurance programs.'.

SEC. 310. LUMP-SUM PAYMENT FOR ACCUMULATED AND ACCRUED LEAVE ON SEPARATION.

Section 5551(a) of title 5, United States Code, is amended in the first sentence by striking 'or elects' and inserting ', is transferred to a position described under section 6301(2)(B)(xiii) of this title, or elects'.

SEC. 311. EMPLOYMENT OF PERSONAL ASSISTANTS FOR HANDI-CAPPED EMPLOYEES.

Section 3102(a)(1) of title 5, United States Code, is amended—

(1) in subparagraph (A) by striking 'and';

(2) in subparagraph (B) by adding 'and' after the semicolon; and

(3) by adding at the end the following:

'(C) an office, agency, or other establishment in the judicial branch;'.

SEC. 312. MANDATORY RETIREMENT AGE FOR DIRECTOR OF THE FEDERAL JUDICIAL CENTER.

(a) IN GENERAL—Section 627 of title 28, United States Code, is amended—

(1) by striking subsection (a); and

(2) by redesignating subsections (b) through (f) as subsections (a) through (e), respectively.

(b) TECHNICAL AND CONFORMING AMENDMENTS—Section 376 of title 28, United States Code, is amended—

(1) in paragraph (1)(D) by striking 'subsection (b)' and inserting 'subsection (a)'; and

(2) in paragraph (2)(D) by striking 'subsection (c) or (d)' and inserting 'subsection (b) or (c)'.

SEC. 313. REAUTHORIZATION OF CERTAIN SUPREME COURT PO-LICE AUTHORITY.

Section 9(c) of the Act entitled 'An Act relating to the policing of the building and grounds of the Supreme Court of the United States', approved August 18, 1949 (40 U.S.C. 13n(c)) is amended in the first sentence by striking '2000' and inserting '2004'

TITLE IV—FEDERAL PUBLIC DEFENDERS

SEC. 401. TORT CLAIMS ACT AMENDMENT RELATING TO LIABILITY OF FEDERAL PUBLIC DEFENDERS.

Section 2671 of title 28, United States Code, is amended in the second undesignated paragraph—

(1) by inserting '(1)' after 'includes' and

(2) by striking the period at the end and inserting the following: ', and (2) any officer or employee of a Federal public defender organization, except when such officer or employee performs professional services in the course of providing representation under section 3006A of title 18.'.

TITLE V—MISCELLANEOUS PROVISIONS

SEC. 501. EXTENSIONS RELATING TO BANKRUPTCY ADMINISTRA-TOR PROGRAM.

Section 302(d)(3) of the Bankruptcy Judges, United States Trustees, and Family Farmer Bankruptcy Act of 1986 (28 U.S.C. 581 note) is amended—

(1) in subparagraph (A), in the matter following clause (ii), by striking 'or October 1, 2002, whichever occurs first,'; and

(2) in subparagraph (F)—

(A) in clause (i)—

(i) in subclause (II), by striking 'or October 1, 2002, whichever occurs first' and

(ii) in the matter following subclause (II) —

(I) by striking 'October 1, 2003, or' and

(II) by striking ', whichever occurs first' and

(B) in clause (ii), in the matter following subclause (II)—

(i) by striking 'October 1, 2003, or' and

(ii) by striking ', whichever occurs first'

SEC. 502. ADDITIONAL PLACE OF HOLDING COURT IN THE DISTRICT OF OREGON.

Section 117 of title 28, United States Code, is amended by striking 'Eugene' and inserting 'Eugene or Springfield'

Speaker of the House of Representatives.
Vice President of the United States and
President of the Senate.

Source: Public Law 106-518 (2000)

68. An Act Relating to Civil Unions, 2000

Introduction

On December 20, 1999, the Vermont Supreme Court ruled in *Baker v. Vermont* that same-sex couples were entitled under the Vermont Constitution to obtain the same benefits and protections afforded by Vermont law to married opposite-sex couples. The Court did not rule on whether Vermont was required to grant marriage licenses to same-sex couples but suggested that the legislature could enact a parallel licensing scheme affording the same substantial benefits as marriage to same-sex couples. The legislature acted, and a civil unions act went into effect on July 1, 2000. Vermont thus became the third U.S. state to offer legal status to same-sex couples (after Hawaii and California) but the first to offer a civil union status encompassing the same legal rights and responsibilities of marriage. Finally, on September 1, 2009, Vermont became the first state to approve same-sex marriage.

Primary Source

(H.847)

It is hereby enacted by the General Assembly of the State of Vermont:

Sec. 1. LEGISLATIVE FINDINGS

The General Assembly finds that:

(1) Civil marriage under Vermont's marriage statutes consists of a union between a man and a woman. This interpretation of the state's marriage laws was upheld by the Supreme Court in Baker v. State.

(2) Vermont's history as an independent republic and as a state is one of equal treatment and respect for all Vermonters. This tradition is embodied in the Common Benefits Clause of the Vermont Constitution, Chapter I, Article 7th.

(3) The state's interest in civil marriage is to encourage close and caring families, and to protect all family members from the economic and social consequences of abandonment and divorce, focusing on those who have been especially at risk.

(4) Legal recognition of civil marriage by the state is the primary and, in a number of instances, the exclusive source of numerous benefits, responsibilities and protections under the laws of the state for married persons and their children.

(5) Based on the state's tradition of equality under the law and strong families, for at least 25 years, Vermont Probate Courts have qualified gay and lesbian individuals as adoptive parents.

(6) Vermont was one of the first states to adopt comprehensive legislation prohibiting discrimination on the basis of sexual orientation (Act No. 135 of 1992).

(7) The state has a strong interest in promoting stable and lasting families, including families based upon a same-sex couple.

(8) Without the legal protections, benefits and responsibilities associated with civil marriage, same-sex couples suffer numerous obstacles and hardships.

(9) Despite longstanding social and economic discrimination, many gay and lesbian Vermonters have formed lasting, committed, caring and faithful relationships with persons of their same sex. These couples live together, participate in their communities together, and some raise children and care for family members together, just as do couples who are married under Vermont law.

(10) While a system of civil unions does not bestow the status of civil marriage, it does satisfy the requirements of the Common Benefits Clause. Changes in the way

significant legal relationships are established under the constitution should be approached carefully, combining respect for the community and cultural institutions most affected with a commitment to the constitutional rights involved. Granting benefits and protections to same-sex couples through a system of civil unions will provide due respect for tradition and long-standing social institutions, and will permit adjustment as unanticipated consequences or unmet needs arise.

(11) The constitutional principle of equality embodied in the Common Benefits Clause is compatible with the freedom of religious belief and worship guaranteed in Chapter I, Article 3rd of the state constitution. Extending the benefits and protections of marriage to same-sex couples through a system of civil unions preserves the fundamental constitutional right of each of the multitude of religious faiths in Vermont to choose freely and without state interference to whom to grant the religious status, sacrament or blessing of marriage under the rules, practices or traditions of such faith.

Sec. 2. PURPOSE

(a) The purpose of this act is to respond to the constitutional violation found by the Vermont Supreme Court in Baker v. State, and to provide eligible same sex couples the opportunity to "obtain the same benefits and protections afforded by Vermont law to married opposite-sex couples" as required by Chapter I, Article 7th of the Vermont Constitution.

(b) This act also provides eligible blood-relatives and relatives related by adoption the opportunity to establish a reciprocal beneficiaries relationship so they may receive certain benefits and protections and be subject to certain responsibilities that are granted to spouses.

Sec. 3. 15 V.S.A. chapter 23 is added to read:

CHAPTER 23. CIVIL UNIONS

§ 1201. DEFINITIONS

As used in this chapter:

(1) "Certificate of civil union" means a document that certifies that the persons named on the certificate have established a civil union in this state in compliance with this chapter and 18 V.S.A. chapter 106.

(2) "Civil union" means that two eligible persons have established a relationship pursuant to this chapter, and may receive the benefits and protections and be subject to the responsibilities of spouses.

(3) "Commissioner" means the commissioner of health.

(4) "Marriage" means the legally recognized union of one man and one woman.

(5) "Party to a civil union" means a person who has established a civil union pursuant to this chapter and 18 V.S.A. chapter 106.

§ 1202. REQUISITES OF A VALID CIVIL UNION

For a civil union to be established in Vermont, it shall be necessary that the parties to a civil union satisfy all of the following criteria:

(1) Not be a party to another civil union or a marriage.

(2) Be of the same sex and therefore excluded from the marriage laws of this state.

(3) Meet the criteria and obligations set forth in 18 V.S.A. chapter 106.

§ 1203. PERSON SHALL NOT ENTER A CIVIL UNION WITH A RELATIVE

(a) A woman shall not enter a civil union with her mother, grandmother, daughter, granddaughter, sister, brother's daughter, sister's daughter, father's sister or mother's sister.

(b) A man shall not enter a civil union with his father, grandfather, son, grandson, brother, brother's son, sister's son, father's brother or mother's brother.

(c) A civil union between persons prohibited from entering a civil union in subsection (a) or (b) of this section is void.

§ 1204. BENEFITS, PROTECTIONS AND RESPONSIBILITIES OF PARTIES TO A CIVIL UNION

(a) Parties to a civil union shall have all the same benefits, protections and responsibilities under law, whether they derive from statute, administrative or court rule, policy, common law or any other source of civil law, as are granted to spouses in a marriage.

(b) A party to a civil union shall be included in any definition or use of the terms "spouse," "family," "immediate family," "dependent," "next of kin," and other terms that denote the spousal relationship, as those terms are used throughout the law.

(c) Parties to a civil union shall be responsible for the support of one another to the same degree and in the same manner as prescribed under law for married persons.

(d) The law of domestic relations, including annulment, separation and divorce, child custody and support, and property division and maintenance shall apply to parties to a civil union.

(e) The following is a nonexclusive list of legal benefits, protections and responsibilities of spouses, which shall apply in like manner to parties to a civil union:

(1) laws relating to title, tenure, descent and distribution, intestate succession, waiver of will, survivorship, or other incidents of the acquisition, ownership, or transfer, inter vivos or at death, of real or personal property, including eligibility to hold real and personal property as tenants by the entirety (parties to a civil union meet the common law unity of person qualification for purposes of a tenancy by the entirety);

(2) causes of action related to or dependent upon spousal status, including an action for wrongful death, emotional distress, loss of consortium, dramshop, or other torts or actions under contracts reciting, related to, or dependent upon spousal status;

(3) probate law and procedure, including nonprobate transfer;

(4) adoption law and procedure;

(5) group insurance for state employees under 3 V.S.A. § 631, and continuing care contracts under 8 V.S.A. § 8005;

(6) spouse abuse programs under 3 V.S.A. § 18;

(7) prohibitions against discrimination based upon marital status;

(8) victim's compensation rights under 13 V.S.A. § 5351;

(9) workers' compensation benefits;

(10) laws relating to emergency and nonemergency medical care and treatment, hospital visitation and notification, including the Patient's Bill of Rights under 18 V.S.A. chapter 42 and the Nursing Home Residents' Bill of Rights under 33 V.S.A. chapter 73;

(11) terminal care documents under 18 V.S.A. chapter 111, and durable power of attorney for health care execution and revocation under 14 V.S.A. chapter 121;

(12) family leave benefits under 21 V.S.A. chapter 5, subchapter 4A;

(13) public assistance benefits under state law;

(14) laws relating to taxes imposed by the state or a municipality other than estate taxes;

(15) laws relating to immunity from compelled testimony and the marital communication privilege;

(16) the homestead rights of a surviving spouse under 27 V.S.A. § 105 and homestead property tax allowance under 32 V.S.A. § 6062;

(17) laws relating to loans to veterans under 8 V.S.A. § 1849;

(18) the definition of family farmer under 10 V.S.A. § 272;

(19) laws relating to the making, revoking and objecting to anatomical gifts by others under 18 V.S.A. § 5240;

(20) state pay for military service under 20 V.S.A. § 1544;

(21) application for absentee ballot under 17 V.S.A. § 2532;

(22) family landowner rights to fish and hunt under 10 V.S.A. § 4253;

(23) legal requirements for assignment of wages under 8 V.S.A. § 2235; and

(24) affirmance of relationship under 15 V.S.A. § 7.

(f) The rights of parties to a civil union, with respect to a child of whom either becomes the natural parent during the term of the civil union, shall be the same as those of a married couple, with respect to a child of whom either spouse becomes the natural parent during the marriage.

§ 1205. MODIFICATION OF CIVIL UNION TERMS

Parties to a civil union may modify the terms, conditions, or effects of their civil union in the same manner and to the same extent as married persons who execute an antenuptial agreement or other agreement recognized and enforceable under the law, setting forth particular understandings with respect to their union.

§ 1206. DISSOLUTION OF CIVIL UNIONS

The family court shall have jurisdiction over all proceedings relating to the dissolution of civil unions. The dissolution of civil unions shall follow the same procedures and be subject to the same substantive rights and obligations that are involved in the dissolution of marriage in accordance with chapter 11 of this title, including any residency requirements.

§ 1207. COMMISSIONER OF HEALTH; DUTIES

(a) The commissioner shall provide civil union license and certificate forms to all town and county clerks.

(b) The commissioner shall keep a record of all civil unions.

Sec. 4. 4 V.S.A. § 454 is amended to read:

§ 454. JURISDICTION

Notwithstanding any other provision of law to the contrary, the family court shall have exclusive jurisdiction to hear and dispose of the following proceedings filed or pending on or after October 1, 1990. The family court shall also have exclusive jurisdiction to hear and dispose of any requests to modify or enforce any orders issued by the district or superior court relating to the following proceedings:

* * *

(17) All proceedings relating to the dissolution of a civil union.

Sec. 5. 18 V.S.A. chapter 106 is added to read:

CHAPTER 106. CIVIL UNION; RECORDS AND LICENSES

§ 5160. ISSUANCE OF CIVIL UNION LICENSE; CERTIFICATION; RETURN OF CIVIL UNION CERTIFICATE

(a) Upon application in a form prescribed by the department, a town clerk shall issue a civil union license in the form prescribed by the department, and shall enter thereon the names of the parties to the proposed civil union, fill out the form as far as practicable and retain a copy in the clerk's office. At least one party to the proposed civil union shall sign the application attesting to the accuracy of the facts stated. The license shall be issued by the clerk of the town where either party resides or, if neither is a resident of the state, by any town clerk in the state.

(b) A civil union license shall be delivered by one of the parties to a proposed civil union, within 60 days from the date of issue, to a person authorized to certify civil unions by section 5164 of this title. If the proposed civil union is not certified within 60 days from the date of issue, the license shall become void. After a person has certified the civil union, he or she shall fill out that part of the form on the license provided for such use, sign and certify the civil union. Thereafter, the document shall be known as a civil union certificate.

(c) Within ten days of the certification, the person performing the certification shall return the civil union certificate to the office of the town clerk from which the license was issued. The town clerk shall retain and file the original according to sections 5007 and 5008 of this title.

(d) A town clerk who knowingly issues a civil union license upon application of a person residing in another town in the state, or a county clerk who knowingly issues a civil union license upon application of a person other than as provided in section 5005 of this title, or a clerk who issues such a license without first requiring the applicant to fill out, sign and make oath to the declaration contained therein as provided in section 5160 of this title, shall be fined not more than $50.00 nor less than $20.00.

(e) A person making application to a clerk for a civil union license who makes a material misrepresentation in the declaration of intention shall be deemed guilty of perjury.

(f) A town clerk shall provide a person who applies for a civil union license with information prepared by the secretary of state that advises such person of the benefits, protections and responsibilities of a civil union and that Vermont residency may be required for dissolution of a civil union in Vermont.

§ 5161. ISSUANCE OF LICENSE

(a) A town clerk shall issue a civil union license to all applicants who have complied with the provisions of section 5160 of this title, and who are otherwise qualified under the laws of the state to apply for a civil union license.

(b) An assistant town clerk may perform the duties of a town clerk under this chapter.

§ 5162. PROOF OF LEGAL QUALIFICATIONS OF PARTIES TO A CIVIL UNION; PENALTY

(a) Before issuing a civil union license to an applicant, the town clerk shall be confident, through presentation of affidavits or other proof, that each party to the intended civil union meets the criteria set forth to enter into a civil union.

(b) Affidavits shall be in a form prescribed by the board, and shall be attached to and filed with the civil union certificate in the office of the clerk of the town wherein the license was issued.

(c) A clerk who fails to comply with the provisions of this section, or who issues a civil union license with knowledge that either or both of the parties to a civil union have failed to comply with the requirements of the laws of this state, or a person who, having authority and having such knowledge, certifies such a civil union, shall be fined not more than $100.00.

§ 5163. RESTRICTIONS AS TO MINORS AND INCOMPETENT PERSONS

(a) A clerk shall not issue a civil union license when either party to the intended civil union is:

(1) under 18 years of age;

(2) non compos mentis;

(3) under guardianship, without the written consent of such guardian.

(b) A clerk who knowingly violates subsection (a) of this section shall be fined not more than $20.00. A person who aids in procuring a civil union license by falsely pretending to be the guardian having authority to give consent to the civil union shall be fined not more than $500.00.

§ 5164. PERSONS AUTHORIZED TO CERTIFY CIVIL UNIONS

Civil unions may be certified by a supreme court justice, a superior court judge, a district judge, a judge of probate, an assistant judge, a justice of the peace or by a member of the clergy residing in this state and ordained or licensed, or otherwise regularly authorized by the published laws or discipline of the general conference, convention or other authority of his or her faith or denomination or by such a clergy person residing in an adjoining state or country, whose parish, church, temple, mosque or other religious organization lies wholly or in part in this state, or by a member of the clergy residing in some other state of the United States or in the Dominion of Canada, provided he or she has first secured from the probate court of the district within which the civil union is to be certified, a special authorization, authorizing him or her to certify the civil union if such probate judge determines that the circumstances make the special authorization desirable. Civil unions among the Friends or Quakers, the Christadelphian Ecclesia and the Baha'i Faith may be certified in the manner used in such societies.

§ 5165. CIVIL UNION LICENSE REQUIRED FOR CERTIFICATION; FAILURE TO RETURN

(a) Persons authorized by section 5164 of this title to certify civil unions shall require a civil union license of the parties before certifying the civil union. The license shall afford full immunity to the person who certifies the civil union.

(b) A person who certifies a civil union shall be fined not less than $10.00, if such person:

(1) certifies a civil union without first obtaining the license; or

(2) fails to properly fill out the license and, within ten days from the date of the certification, return the license and certificate of civil union to the clerk's office from which it was issued.

§ 5166. CERTIFICATION BY UNAUTHORIZED PERSON; PENALTY; VALIDITY OF CIVIL UNIONS

(a) An unauthorized person who knowingly undertakes to join others in a civil union shall be imprisoned not more than six months or fined not more than $300.00 nor less than $100.00, or both.

(b) A civil union certified before a person falsely professing to be a justice or a member of the clergy shall be valid, provided that the civil union is in other respects lawful, and that either of the parties to a civil union believed that he or she was lawfully joined in a civil union.

§ 5167. EVIDENCE OF CIVIL UNION

A copy of the record of the civil union received from the town or county clerk, the commissioner of health or the director of public records shall be presumptive evidence of the civil union in all courts.

§ 5168. CORRECTION OF CIVIL UNION CERTIFICATE

(a) Within six months after a civil union is certified, the town clerk may correct or complete a civil union certificate, upon application by a party to a civil union or by the person who certified the civil union. The town clerk shall certify that such correction or completion was made pursuant to this section and note the date. The town clerk may refuse an application for correction or completion; in which case, the applicant may petition the probate court for such correction or completion.

(b) After six months from the date a civil union is certified, a civil union certificate may only be corrected or amended pursuant to decree of the probate court in the district where the original certificate is filed.

(c) The probate court shall set a time for a hearing and, if the court deems necessary, give notice of the time and place by posting such information in the probate court office. After a hearing, the court shall make findings with respect to the correction of the civil union certificate as are supported by the evidence. The court shall issue a decree setting forth the facts as found, and transmit a certified copy of the decree to the supervisor of vital records registration. The supervisor of vital records registration shall transmit the same to the appropriate town clerk to amend the original or issue a new certificate. The words "Court Amended" shall be typed, written or stamped at the top of the new or amended certificate with the date of the decree and the name of the issuing court.

§ 5169. DELAYED CERTIFICATES OF CIVIL UNION

(a) Persons who were parties to a certified civil union ceremony in this state for whom no certificate of civil union was filed, as required by law, may petition the probate court of the district in which the civil union license was obtained to determine the facts, and to order the issuance of a delayed certificate of civil union.

(b) The probate court shall set a time for hearing on the petition and, if the court deems necessary, give notice of the time and place by posting such information in the probate court office. After hearing proper and relevant evidence as may be presented, the court shall make findings with respect to the civil union as are supported by the evidence.

(c) The court shall issue a decree setting forth the facts as found, and transmit a certified copy of said facts to the supervisor of vital records registration.

(d) Where a delayed certificate is to be issued, the supervisor of vital records registration shall prepare a delayed certificate of civil union, and transmit it, with the decree, to the clerk of the town where the civil union license was issued. This delayed certificate shall have the word "Delayed" printed at the top, and shall certify that the certificate was ordered by a court pursuant to this chapter, with the date of the decree. The town clerk shall file the delayed certificate and, in accordance with the provisions of section 5010 of this title, furnish a copy to the department of health.

(e) Town clerks receiving new certificates in accordance with this section shall file and index them in the most recent book of civil unions, and also index them with civil unions occurring at the same time.

Sec. 6. 18 V.S.A. § 5001 is amended to read:

§ 5001. VITAL RECORDS; FORMS OF CERTIFICATES

Certificates of birth, marriage, civil union, divorce, death and fetal death shall be in form prescribed by the commissioner of health and distributed by the health department.

Sec. 7. 18 V.S.A. § 5002 is amended to read:

§ 5002. RETURNS; TABLES

The health commissioner shall prepare from the returns of births, marriages, civil unions, deaths, fetal deaths and divorces required by law to be transmitted to him the commissioner such tables and append thereto such recommendations as he or she deems proper, and during the month of July in each even year, shall cause the same to be published as directed by the board. He The commissioner shall file and preserve all such returns. The commissioner shall periodically transmit the original returns or photostatic or photographic copies to the director of public records who shall keep the returns, or photostatic or photographic copies of the returns, on file for use by the public. The commissioner and the director of public records shall each, independently of the other, have power to issue certified copies of such records.

Sec. 8. 18 V.S.A. § 5004 is amended to read:

§ 5004. COUNTY FAMILY COURT CLERKS; DIVORCE RETURNS

The county family court clerk shall send to the commissioner, before the tenth day of each month, a report of the number of divorces which became absolute during the preceding month, showing as to each the names of the parties, date of marriage or civil union, number of children, grounds for divorce and such other statistical information available from the ~~county~~ family court clerk's file as may be required by the commissioner.

Sec. 9. 18 V.S.A. § 5005 is amended to read:

§ 5005. UNORGANIZED TOWNS AND GORES

(a) The county clerk of a county wherein is situated an unorganized town or gore shall perform the same duties and be subject to the same penalties as town clerks in respect to licenses, certificates, records and returns of parties, both of whom reside in an unorganized town or gore in such county or where ~~the groom~~ one party to a marriage or a civil union so resides and the ~~bride~~ other party resides in an unorganized town or gore in another county or without the state ~~or where the bride resides in an unorganized town or gore in such county and the groom resides without the state~~. The cost of binding such certificates shall be paid by the state.

* * *

Sec. 10. 18 V.S.A. § 5006 is amended to read:

§ 5006. VITAL RECORDS PUBLISHED IN TOWN REPORTS

Town clerks annually may compile and the auditors may publish in the annual town report a transcript of the record of births, marriages, civil unions and deaths recorded during the preceding calendar year.

Sec. 11. 18 V.S.A. § 5007 is amended to read:

§ 5007. PRESERVATION OF DATA

A town clerk shall receive, number and file for record certificates of births, marriages, civil unions and deaths, and shall preserve such certificates together with the burial-transit and removal permits returned to ~~him~~ the clerk, in a fireproof vault or safe, as provided by section 1178 of Title 24.

Sec. 12. 18 V.S.A. § 5008 is amended to read:

§ 5008. TOWN CLERK; RECORDING AND INDEXING PROCEDURES

A town clerk shall file for record and index in volumes all certificates and permits received in a manner prescribed by the public records director. Each volume or series shall contain an alphabetical index. Marriage certificates shall be filed for record in one volume or series, civil unions in another, birth certificates in another, and death certificates and burial-transit and removal permits in another. However, in a town having less than ~~five hundred~~ 500 inhabitants, the town clerk may cause marriage, civil union, birth and death certificates, and burial-transit and removal permits to be filed for record in one volume, provided that none of such volumes shall contain more than ~~two hundred and fifty~~ 250 certificates and permits. All volumes shall be maintained in the town clerk's office as permanent records.

Sec. 13. 18 V.S.A. § 5009 is amended to read:

§ 5009. NONRESIDENTS; CERTIFIED COPIES

On the first day of each month, ~~he~~ the town clerk shall make a certified copy of each original or corrected certificate of birth, marriage, civil union and death filed in ~~his~~ the clerk's office during the preceding month, whenever the parents of a child born were, or a ~~bride or a groom~~ party to a marriage or a civil union or a deceased person was, a resident in any other Vermont town at the time of such birth, marriage, civil union or death, and shall transmit such certified copy to the clerk of such other Vermont town, who shall file the same.

Sec. 14. 18 V.S.A. § 5010 is amended to read:

§ 5010. REPORT OF STATISTICS

The clerk in each town of over 5,000 population or in a town where a general hospital as defined in section 1902(a)(1) of this title, is located, shall each week transmit to the supervisor of vital records registration copies, duly certified, of each birth, death ~~and~~, marriage and civil union certificate filed in the town in the preceding week. In all other towns, the clerk shall transmit such copies of birth, death ~~and~~, marriage and civil union certificates received during the preceding month on or before the tenth day of each succeeding month.

Sec. 15. 18 V.S.A. § 5011 is amended to read:

§ 5011. PENALTY

A town clerk who fails to transmit such copies of birth, marriage, civil union and death certificates as provided in section 5010 of this title shall be fined not more than $100.00.

Sec. 16. 18 V.S.A. § 5012 is amended to read:

§ 5012. TOWN CLERK TO PROVIDE GENERAL INDEX; MARRIAGES AND CIVIL UNIONS

Except as provided by section 1153 of Title 24, town and county clerks shall prepare and keep a general index to the marriage and civil union records, in alphabetical order and in the following ~~form~~ forms, respectively:

Book 1	Page 1	Groom to Bride A. to B.	Date	Book 1	Page 1	Bride to Groom B. to A.	Date

Book 1	Page 1	Party to Party A. to B.	Date	Book 1	Page 1	Party to Party B. to A.	Date

Sec. 17. 8 V.S.A. § 4724(7)(E) is added to read:

(E) Making or permitting unfair discrimination between married couples and parties to a civil union as defined under 15 V.S.A. § 1201, with regard to the offering of insurance benefits to a couple, a spouse, a party to a civil union, or their family. The commissioner shall adopt rules necessary to carry out the purposes of this subdivision. The rules shall ensure that insurance contracts and policies offered to married couples, spouses, and families are also made available to parties to a civil union and their families. The commissioner may adopt by order standards and a process to bring the forms currently on file and approved by the department into compliance with Vermont law. The standards and process may differ from the provisions contained in chapter 101, subchapter 6 and sections 4062, 4201, 4515a, 4587, 4685, 4687, 4688, 4985, 5104 and 8005 of this title where, in the commissioner's opinion, the provisions regarding filing and approval of forms are not desirable or necessary to effectuate the purposes of this section.

Sec. 18. 8 V.S.A. § 4063a is added to read:

§ 4063a. COVERAGE FOR CIVIL UNIONS

(a) As used in this section:

(1) "Dependent coverage" means family coverage or coverage for one or more persons.

(2) "Party to a civil union" is defined for purposes of this section as under 15 V.S.A. § 1201.

(3) "Insurer" shall mean a health insurer as defined in 18 V.S.A. § 9402(7).

(b) Notwithstanding any law to the contrary, insurers shall provide dependent coverage to parties to a civil union that is equivalent to that provided to married insureds. An individual or group health insurance policy which provides coverage for a spouse or family member of the insured shall also provide the equivalent coverage for a party to a civil union.

Sec. 19. 32 V.S.A. § 1712 is amended to read:

§ 1712. TOWN CLERKS

Town clerks shall receive the following fees in the matter of vital registration:

(1) For issuing and recording a marriage or civil union license, $20.00 to be paid by the applicant, $5.00 of which sum shall be retained by the town clerk as a fee and $15.00 of which sum shall be paid by the town clerk to the state treasurer in a return filed quarterly upon forms furnished by the state treasurer and specifying all fees received by him or her during the quarter. Such quarterly period shall be as of the first day of January, April, July and October.

(2) $1.00 for other copies made under the provisions of section 5009 of Title 18 to be paid by the town;

(3) $2.00 for each birth certificate completed or corrected under the provisions of sections 449 and 816 of Title 15 and sections 5073, 5075-5078 of Title 18, for the correction of each marriage certificate under the provisions of section 816 of Title 15, and section 5150 of Title 18, for the correction or completion of each civil union certificate under the provisions of section 5168 of Title 18, and for each death certificate corrected under the provisions of section 5202a of Title 18, to be paid by the town;

(4) $1.00 for each certificate of facts relating to births, deaths, civil unions and marriages, transmitted to the commissioner of health in accordance with the provisions of section 5010 of Title 18. Such sum, together with the cost of binding the certificate shall be paid by the town;

(5) $7.00 for each certified copy of birth, death, civil union or marriage certificate.

Sec. 20. 32 V.S.A. § 3001 is amended to read:

§ 3001. ~~PERSON CONSTRUED~~ DEFINITIONS

(a) ~~The word "person"~~ "Person" as used in Parts 2, 4 and 5 of this subtitle shall include a partnership, association, corporation or limited liability company.

(b) "Party to a civil union" is defined for purposes of Title 32 as under subdivision 1201(4) of Title 15.

(c) "Laws of the United States", "federal tax laws" and other references to United States tax law (other than federal estate and gift tax law) shall mean United States tax law applied as if federal law recognized a civil union in the same manner as Vermont law.

Sec. 21. 32 V.S.A. § 5812 is added to read:

§ 5812. INCOME TAXATION OF PARTIES TO A CIVIL UNION

This chapter shall apply to parties to a civil union and surviving parties to a civil union as if federal income tax law recognized a civil union in the same manner as Vermont law.

Sec. 22. 32 V.S.A. § 7401(a) is amended to read:

(a) This chapter is intended to conform the Vermont ~~inheritance~~ estate tax laws with the estate and gift tax provisions of the United States Internal Revenue Code, except as otherwise expressly provided, in order to simplify the taxpayer's filing of returns, reduce the taxpayer's accounting burdens, and facilitate the collection and administration of these taxes. Because federal estate and gift tax law does not recognize a civil union in the same manner as Vermont law, and because a reduction in the Vermont estate tax liability for parties to a civil union based upon the federal marital deduction would not reduce the total estate tax liability, estates of parties to a civil union shall be subject to tax based on their actual federal estate tax liability and the federal credit for state death taxes, as provided under this chapter.

Sec. 23. 32 V.S.A. § 3802(11) is amended to read:

(11)(A) Real and personal property to the extent of $10,000.00 of appraisal value, except any part used for business or rental, occupied as the established residence of and owned in fee simple by a veteran of any war or a veteran who has received an

American Expeditionary Medal, his or her spouse, widow, widower or child, or jointly by any combination of them, if one or more of them are receiving disability compensation for at least ~~fifty~~ 50 percent disability, death compensation, dependence and indemnity compensation, or pension for disability paid through any military department or the veterans administration if, before May 1 of each year, there is filed with the listers:

~~(A)~~(i) a written application therefor; and

~~(B)~~(ii) a written statement from the military department or the veterans administration showing that the compensation or pension is being paid. Only one exemption may be allowed on a property.

(B) The terms used in this subdivision shall have the same definitions as in Title 38, U.S. Code § 101, except that:

(i) the definitions shall apply as if federal law recognized a civil union in the same manner as Vermont law;

(ii) such definitions shall not be construed to deny eligibility for exemption in the case where such exemption is based on retirement for disability and retirement pay is received from a federal agency other than the veterans administration~~,~~ ; and

(iii) the age and marital status limits in section 101(4)(A) shall not apply.

An unremarried widow or widower of a previously qualified veteran shall be entitled to the exemption provided in this subdivision whether or not he or she is receiving government compensation or pension. By majority vote of those present and voting at an annual or special meeting warned for the purpose, a town may increase the veterans' exemption under this subsection to up to $20,000.00 of appraisal value. Any increase in exemption shall take effect for the taxable year in which it was voted, and shall remain in effect for future taxable years until amended or repealed by a similar vote.

Sec. 24. 15 V.S.A. § 4 is amended to read:

§ 4. MARRIAGE CONTRACTED WHILE ONE IN FORCE

Marriages contracted while either party has ~~another wife or husband~~ a living spouse or a living party to a civil union shall be void.

Sec. 25. 15 V.S.A. § 8 is added to read:

§ 8. MARRIAGE DEFINITION

Marriage is the legally recognized union of one man and one woman.

Sec. 26. 18 V.S.A. § 5131 is amended to read:

§ 5131. ISSUANCE OF MARRIAGE LICENSE; SOLEMNIZATION; RETURN OF MARRIAGE CERTIFICATE

(a) Upon application in a form prescribed by the department, a town clerk shall issue to a person a marriage license in the form prescribed by the department and shall enter thereon the names of the parties to the proposed marriage, fill out the form as far as practicable and retain in his the clerk's office a copy thereof. At least one party to the proposed marriage shall sign the certifying application to the accuracy of the facts so stated. The license shall be issued by the clerk of the town where either the bride or groom resides or, if neither is a resident of the state, by a any town clerk in the county where the marriage is to be solemnized state.

* * *

Sec. 27. 18 V.S.A. § 5137 is amended to read:

§ 5137. ISSUANCE OF LICENSE

(a) A town clerk shall issue a marriage license to all applicants who have complied with the provisions of section 5131 of this title and who are otherwise qualified under the laws of the state to apply for a license to marry and to contract for such marriage.

(b) An assistant town clerk may perform the duties of a town clerk under this chapter.

Sec. 28. 18 V.S.A. § 5144 is amended to read:

§ 5144. PERSONS AUTHORIZED TO SOLEMNIZE MARRIAGE

Marriages may be solemnized by a supreme court justice, a superior court judge, a district judge, a judge of probate, an assistant judge or a justice of the peace or by a minister of the gospel member of the clergy residing in this state and ordained or licensed, or otherwise regularly authorized thereunto by the published laws or discipline of the general conference or, convention or other authority of his or her faith or denomination or by such a minister clergy person residing in an adjoining

state or country, whose parish, church, temple, mosque or other religious organization lies wholly or in part in this state, or by a ~~minister of the gospel~~ member of the
clergy residing in some other state of the United States or in the Dominion of
Canada ~~who is ordained or licensed, or otherwise regularly authorized thereunto
by the published laws or discipline of the general conference or convention of his
denomination~~, provided he or she has first secured from the probate court of the
district within which ~~said~~ the marriage is to be solemnized a special authorization
~~to said nonresident minister~~, authorizing him or her to certify ~~said~~ the marriage if
~~it appear to said~~ such probate judge determines that the circumstances ~~seem to~~
make ~~such~~ the special authorization desirable. Marriage among the Friends or
Quakers, the Christadelphian Ecclesia and the Baha'i Faith may be solemnized in
the manner heretofore used in such societies.

Sec. 29. 15 V.S.A. chapter 25 is added to read:

CHAPTER 25. RECIPROCAL BENEFICIARIES

§ 1301. PURPOSE

(a) The purpose of this chapter is to provide two persons who are blood-relatives
or related by adoption the opportunity to establish a consensual reciprocal beneficiaries relationship so they may receive the benefits and protections and be subject
to the responsibilities that are granted to spouses in the following specific areas:

(1) Hospital visitation and medical decision-making under 18 V.S.A. § 1853;

(2) Decision-making relating to anatomical gifts under 18 V.S.A. § 5240;

(3) Decision-making relating to disposition of remains under 18 V.S.A. § 5220;

(4) Durable power of attorney for health care under 14 V.S.A. § 3456 and terminal
care documents under 18 V.S.A. § 5254;

(5) Patient's bill of rights under 18 V.S.A. chapter 42;

(6) Nursing home patient's bill of rights under 33 V.S.A. chapter 73;

(7) Abuse prevention under 15 V.S.A. chapter 21.

(b) This chapter shall not be construed to create any spousal benefits, protections
or responsibilities for reciprocal beneficiaries not specifically enumerated herein.

§ 1302. DEFINITIONS

As used in this chapter:

(1) "Commissioner" means the commissioner of health.

(2) "Reciprocal beneficiary" means a person who has established a reciprocal beneficiaries relationship pursuant to this chapter.

(3) A "reciprocal beneficiaries relationship" means that two eligible persons have established such a relationship under this chapter, and may receive the benefits and protections and be subject to the responsibilities that are granted to spouses in specifically enumerated areas of law.

§ 1303. REQUISITES OF A VALID RECIPROCAL BENEFICIARIES RELATIONSHIP

For a reciprocal beneficiaries relationship to be established in Vermont, it shall be necessary that the parties satisfy all of the following criteria:

(1) Be at least 18 years of age and competent to enter into a contract.

(2) Not be a party to another reciprocal beneficiaries relationship, a civil union or a marriage.

(3) Be related by blood or by adoption and prohibited from establishing a civil union or marriage with the other party to the proposed reciprocal beneficiaries relationship.

(4) Consent to the reciprocal beneficiaries relationship without force, fraud or duress.

§ 1304. ESTABLISHING A RECIPROCAL BENEFICIARIES RELATIONSHIP

Two persons who meet the criteria set forth in section 1303 of this title may establish a reciprocal beneficiaries relationship by presenting a signed, notarized declaration of a reciprocal beneficiaries relationship to the commissioner and paying a filing fee of $10.00. The commissioner shall file the declaration and give the parties a certificate of reciprocal beneficiaries relationship showing that the declaration was filed in the names of the parties.

§ 1305. DISSOLUTION OF A RECIPROCAL BENEFICIARIES RELATIONSHIP

(a) Either party to a reciprocal beneficiaries relationship may terminate the relationship by filing a signed notarized declaration with the commissioner.

(b) Within 60 days of the filing of the declaration and payment of a filing fee of $10.00 by a party to a reciprocal beneficiaries relationship, the commissioner shall file the declaration and issue a certificate of termination of a reciprocal beneficiaries relationship to each party of the former relationship.

(c) If a party to a reciprocal beneficiaries relationship enters into a valid civil union or a marriage, the reciprocal beneficiaries relationship shall terminate and the parties shall no longer be entitled to the benefits, protections and responsibilities of the reciprocal beneficiaries relationship.

§ 1306. COMMISSIONER OF HEALTH; DUTIES

(a) The commissioner shall provide forms for a declaration of a reciprocal beneficiaries relationship and a declaration of termination of a reciprocal beneficiaries relationship.

(b) The commissioner shall keep a record of all declarations of a reciprocal beneficiaries relationship and declarations of termination of a reciprocal beneficiaries relationship.

(c) The commissioner shall prepare an informative circular or pamphlet that explains how a reciprocal beneficiaries relationship may be established and terminated, and the benefits, protections and responsibilities that are associated with the reciprocal beneficiaries relationship.

Sec. 30. 18 V.S.A. § 1853 is added to read:

§ 1853. HOSPITAL VISITATION POLICY; RECIPROCAL BENEFICIARY

A patient's reciprocal beneficiary, as defined in section 1302 of Title 15, shall have the same rights as a spouse with respect to visitation and making health care decisions for the patient.

Sec. 31. 18 V.S.A. § 5240 is amended to read:

§ 5240. MAKING, REVOKING AND OBJECTING TO ANATOMICAL GIFTS, BY OTHERS

(a) Any member of the following classes of individuals, in the order of priority listed, may make an anatomical gift of all or a part of the decedent's body for an authorized purpose, unless the decedent has made an unrevoked refusal to make that anatomical gift:

(1) The spouse of the decedent.

(2) The reciprocal beneficiary of the decedent.

(2)(3) An adult son or daughter of the decedent.

(3)(4) Either parent of the decedent.

(4)(5) An adult brother or sister of the decedent.

(5)(6) A grandparent of the decedent.

(6)(7) An individual possessing a durable power of attorney.

(7)(8) A guardian of the person of the decedent at the time of death.

(8)(9) Any other individual authorized or under obligation to dispose of the body.

* * *

Sec. 32. 18 V.S.A. § 5220 is added to read:

§ 5220. DECISION-MAKING REGARDING REMAINS; RECIPROCAL BENEFICIARY

A decedent's reciprocal beneficiary, as defined in section 1302 of Title 15, shall have the same rights as a spouse with respect to matters related to this chapter.

Sec. 33. 14 V.S.A. § 3456 is amended to read:

§ 3456. EXECUTION AND WITNESSES

The durable power of attorney for health care shall be signed by the principal in the presence of at least two or more subscribing witnesses, neither of whom shall, at the time of execution, be the agent, the principal's health or residential care provider or the provider's employee, the principal's spouse, heir, or reciprocal beneficiary, a person entitled to any part of the estate of the principal upon the death of the principal under a will or deed in existence or by operation of law or any other person who has, at the time of execution, any claims against the estate of the principal.

The witnesses shall affirm that the principal appeared to be of sound mind and free from duress at the time the durable power of attorney for health care was signed and that the principal affirmed that he or she was aware of the nature of the documents and signed it freely and voluntarily. If the principal is physically unable to sign, the durable power of attorney for health care may be signed by the principal's name written by some other person in the principal's presence and at the principal's express direction.

Sec. 34. 18 V.S.A. § 5254 is amended to read:

§ 5254. EXECUTION AND WITNESSES

The document set forth in section 5253 of this title shall be executed by the person making the same in the presence of two or more subscribing witnesses, none of whom shall be the person's spouse, heir, reciprocal beneficiary, attending physician or person acting under the direction or control of the attending physician or any other person who has at the time of the witnessing thereof any claims against the estate of the person.

Sec. 35. 18 V.S.A. § 1852 is amended to read:

§ 1852. PATIENTS' BILL OF RIGHTS; ADOPTION

(a) The general assembly hereby adopts the "Bill of Rights for Hospital Patients" as follows:

* * *

(3) The patient has the right to obtain, from the physician coordinating his or her care, complete and current information concerning diagnosis, treatment, and any known prognosis in terms the patient can reasonably be expected to understand. If the patient consents or if the patient is incompetent or unable to understand, immediate family members, a reciprocal beneficiary or a guardian may also obtain this information. When it is not medically advisable to give such information to the patient, the information shall be made available to immediate family members, a reciprocal beneficiary or a guardian. The patient has the right to know by name the attending physician primarily responsible for coordinating his or her care.

* * *

(14) Whenever possible, guardians or parents have the right to stay with their children 24 hours per day. Whenever possible, guardians, reciprocal beneficiaries or

immediate family members have the right to stay with terminally ill patients 24 hours a day.

* * *

Sec. 36. 33 V.S.A. § 7301 is amended to read:

§ 7301. NURSING HOME RESIDENTS' BILL OF RIGHTS

The general assembly hereby adopts the Nursing Home Residents' Bill of Rights as follows:

The governing body of the facility shall establish written policies regarding the rights and responsibilities of residents and, through the administrator, is responsible for development of, and adherence to, procedures implementing such policies. These policies and procedures shall be made available to residents, to any guardians, next of kin, reciprocal beneficiaries, sponsoring agency, or representative payees selected pursuant to section 205(j) of the Social Security Act, and Subpart Q of 20 CFR Part 404, and to the public. The staff of the facility shall ensure that, at least, each person admitted to the facility:

* * *

(14) if married or in a reciprocal beneficiaries relationship, is assured privacy for visits by his or her spouse or reciprocal beneficiary; if both are residents of the facility, they are permitted to share a room;

* * *

(20) residents and their families, including a reciprocal beneficiary, shall have the right to organize, maintain, and participate in either resident or family councils or both. The facility shall provide space and, if requested, assistance for meetings. Council meetings shall be afforded privacy, with staff or visitors attending only at the council's invitation. The facility shall respond in writing to written requests from council meetings. Resident councils and family councils shall be encouraged to make recommendations regarding facility policies;

(21) residents and their families, including a reciprocal beneficiary, shall have the right to review current and past state and federal survey and inspection reports of the facility, and upon request, to receive from the facility a copy of any report. Copies of reports shall be available for review at any time at one station in the facility. The facility may charge a reasonable amount for more than one copy per resident.

Sec. 37. 33 V.S.A. § 7306 is amended to read:

§ 7306. RESIDENT'S REPRESENTATIVE

(a) The rights and obligations established under this chapter shall devolve to a resident's reciprocal beneficiary, guardian, next of kin, sponsoring agency or representative payee (except when the facility itself is a representative payee) if the resident:

(1) has been adjudicated incompetent;

(2) has been found by his or her physician to be medically incapable of understanding or exercising the rights granted under this chapter; or

(3) exhibits a communication barrier.

* * *

Sec. 38. 15 V.S.A. § 1101(6) is added to read:

(6) "Family" shall include a reciprocal beneficiary.

Sec. 39. CONSTRUCTION

(a) This act shall be construed broadly in order to secure to eligible same-sex couples the option of a legal status with the benefits and protections of civil marriage, in accordance with the requirements of the Common Benefits Clause of the Vermont Constitution. Parties to a civil union shall have all of the same benefits, protections and responsibilities under state law, whether derived from statute, administrative or court rule, policy, common law or any other source of civil law, as are granted to spouses in a marriage. Treating the benefits, protections and responsibilities of civil marriage differently from the benefits, protections and responsibilities of civil unions is permissible only when clearly necessary because the gender-based text of a statute, rule or judicial precedent would otherwise produce an unjust, unwarranted, or confusing result, and different treatment would promote or enhance, and would not diminish, the common benefits and protections that flow from marriage under Vermont law.

(b) This act is intended to extend to parties to a civil union the benefits, protections and responsibilities that flow from marriage under Vermont law. Many of the laws of this state are intertwined with federal law, and the general assembly recognizes that it does not have the jurisdiction to control federal laws or the benefits, protections and responsibilities related to them.

(c) This act shall not be construed in a manner which violates the free exercise of religion of any person, religious or denominational institution or organization, or any organization operated for charitable or educational purposes which is operated, supervised, or controlled by or in connection with a religious organization, as guaranteed by the First Amendment to the Constitution of the United States or by Chapter I, Article 3rd, of the Constitution of the State of Vermont.

Sec. 40. VERMONT CIVIL UNION REVIEW COMMISSION

(a) The Vermont Civil Union Review Commission is established for a term of two years, commencing on the effective date of this act. The commission shall be comprised of 11 members, consisting of two members of the House designated by the Speaker of the House, who shall be of different political party affiliations; two members of the Senate designated by the Senate Committee on Committees, who shall be of different political party affiliations; four members appointed by the Governor representing the public, one of whom shall be an attorney familiar with Vermont family law; one member appointed by the Chief Justice of the Vermont Supreme Court; the chair of the Human Rights Commission or his or her designee; and the Attorney General or his or her designee.

(b) The commission members shall be appointed for a full term of two years; members who were members of the House of Representatives or the Senate at the time of their appointment shall continue as members of the commission, notwithstanding a change in their status as elected officials. A member who resigns, dies or takes up residency in another state or country shall be replaced in the same manner as the member was first selected.

(c) Upon passage of this act, the commission shall prepare and implement a plan to inform members of the public, state agencies, and private and public sector businesses and organizations about the act.

(d) The commission shall:

(1) collect information about the implementation, operation, and effect of this act, from members of the public, state agencies, and private and public sector businesses and organizations;

(2) collect information about the recognition and treatment of Vermont civil unions by other states and jurisdictions, including procedures for dissolution;

(3) evaluate the impact and effectiveness of this act, with particular attention to Secs. 1, 2 and 39;

(4) explore and propose methods and techniques, including existing and emerging forms of alternative dispute resolution, to complement the judicial system for the appropriate resolution of questions or disputes that may arise concerning the interpretation, implementation and enforcement of this act; and

(5) examine reciprocal beneficiaries relationships and evaluate whether non-related persons over 62 years of age should be permitted to establish a reciprocal beneficiaries relationship and whether the legal benefits, protections and responsibilities of a reciprocal beneficiaries relationship should be expanded.

(e) The commission shall report its findings, conclusions and recommendations to the general assembly, periodically as deemed necessary by the commission; however, the commission shall report to the general assembly and governor, at least annually, by January 15 of the years 2001 and 2002.

(f) The commission shall elect a chair and vice-chair, shall conduct its meetings pursuant to Robert's Rules of Order, and shall be subject to the public meeting laws pursuant to subchapter 2 of chapter 5 of Title 1.

(g) The commission may request and shall receive the assistance of any agency of the state of Vermont, and may solicit written comments from members of the public, civic organizations, businesses and others. The commission may hold public hearings throughout the state.

(h) The members of the commission shall have the assistance of the staff of legislative council and the joint fiscal office.

Sec. 41. SEVERABILITY

The provisions of this act are severable. If any provision of this act is invalid, or if any application thereof to any person or circumstance is invalid, the invalidity shall not affect other provisions or applications which can be given effect without the invalid provision or application.

Sec. 42. EFFECTIVE DATES

(a) This section and Secs. 1, 2 and 40 shall be effective upon passage.

(b) Secs. 17 and 18 (insurance) of this act shall become effective on January 1, 2001.

(c) Secs. 20 (tax definitions) and 21 (income taxation of parties to parties to a civil union) of this act shall apply to taxable years beginning on and after January 1, 2001.

(d) Sec. 23 of this act (veterans' property tax exemption) shall apply to grand lists for 2001 and after.

(e) All other sections of this act shall become effective on July 1, 2000.

Approved: April 26, 2000

> *Source: An Act Relating to Civil Unions*, Vermont Legislature, No. 91 (2000)

69. USA PATRIOT Act, 2001

Introduction

The USA PATRIOT Act was passed in October 2001 in the wake of the World Trade Center and Pentagon attacks, under the guidance of the George W. Bush administration and Attorney General John Ashcroft in particular. "USA PATRIOT Act" is an acronym for the bill's official title: Uniting and Strengthening America by Providing Appropriate Tools Required to Intercept and Obstruct Terrorism. As its name indicates, the act was created to deter terrorism domestically and abroad and to give law enforcement agencies tools to aid in the investigation and prevention of terrorism.

Primary Source

TITLE I—ENHANCING DOMESTIC SECURITY AGAINST TERRORISM

SEC. 101. COUNTERTERRORISM FUND.

(a) ESTABLISHMENT; AVAILABILITY.—There is hereby established in the Treasury of the United States a separate fund to be known as the "Counterterrorism Fund", amounts in which shall remain available without fiscal year limitation—

(1) to reimburse any Department of Justice component for any costs incurred in connection with—

(A) reestablishing the operational capability of an office or facility that has been damaged or destroyed as the result of any domestic or international terrorism incident;

(B) providing support to counter, investigate, or prosecute domestic or international terrorism, including, without limitation, paying rewards in connection with these activities; and

(C) conducting terrorism threat assessments of Federal agencies and their facilities; and

(2) to reimburse any department or agency of the Federal Government for any costs incurred in connection with detaining in foreign countries individuals accused of acts of terrorism that violate the laws of the United States.

(b) NO EFFECT ON PRIOR APPROPRIATIONS.—Subsection (a) shall not be construed to affect the amount or availability of any appropriation to the Counterterrorism Fund made before the date of the enactment of this Act. . . .

SEC. 105. EXPANSION OF NATIONAL ELECTRONIC CRIME TASK FORCE INITIATIVE.

The Director of the United States Secret Service shall take appropriate actions to develop a national network of electronic crime task forces, based on the New York Electronic Crimes Task Force model, throughout the United States, for the purpose of preventing, detecting, and investigating various forms of electronic crimes, including potential terrorist attacks against critical infrastructure and financial payment systems.

TITLE II—ENHANCED SURVEILLANCE PROCEDURES

SEC. 203. AUTHORITY TO SHARE CRIMINAL INVESTIGATIVE INFORMATION.

(a) AUTHORITY TO SHARE GRAND JURY INFORMATION.—

(1) IN GENERAL.—Rule 6(e)(3)(C) of the Federal Rules of Criminal Procedure is amended to read as follows:

"(C)(i) Disclosure otherwise prohibited by this rule of matters occurring before the grand jury may also be made—

"(I) when so directed by a court preliminarily to or in connection with a judicial proceeding;

"(II) when permitted by a court at the request of the defendant, upon a showing that grounds may exist for a motion to dismiss the indictment because of matters occurring before the grand jury;

"(III) when the disclosure is made by an attorney for the government to another Federal grand jury;

"(IV) when permitted by a court at the request of an attorney for the government, upon a showing that such matters may disclose a violation of State criminal law, to an appropriate official of a State or subdivision of a State for the purpose of enforcing such law; or

"(V) when the matters involve foreign intelligence or counterintelligence (as defined in section 3 of the National Security Act of 1947 (50 U.S.C. 401a)), or foreign intelligence information (as defined in clause (iv) of this subparagraph), to any Federal law enforcement, intelligence, protective, immigration, national defense, or national security official in order to assist the official receiving that information in the performance of his official duties.

"(ii) If the court orders disclosure of matters occurring before the grand jury, the disclosure shall be made in such manner, at such time, and under such conditions as the court may direct.

"(iii) Any Federal official to whom information is disclosed pursuant to clause (i)(V) of this subparagraph may use that information only as necessary in the conduct of that person's official duties subject to any limitations on the unauthorized disclosure of such information. Within a reasonable time after such disclosure, an attorney for the government shall file under seal a notice with the court stating the fact that such information was disclosed and the departments, agencies, or entities to which the disclosure was made.

"(iv) In clause (i)(V) of this subparagraph, the term 'foreign intelligence information' means—

"(I) information, whether or not concerning a United States person, that relates to the ability of the United States to protect against—

"(aa) actual or potential attack or other grave hostile acts of a foreign power or an agent of a foreign power;

"(bb) sabotage or international terrorism by a foreign power or an agent of a foreign power; or

"(cc) clandestine intelligence activities by an intelligence service or network of a foreign power or by an agent of foreign power; or

"(II) information, whether or not concerning a United States person, with respect to a foreign power or foreign territory that relates to—

"(aa) the national defense or the security of the United States; or

"(bb) the conduct of the foreign affairs of the United States.".

(b) AUTHORITY TO SHARE ELECTRONIC, WIRE, AND ORAL INTERCEP-
TION INFORMATION.—

(1) LAW ENFORCEMENT.—Section 2517 of title 18, United States Code, is
amended by inserting at the end the following:

"(6) Any investigative or law enforcement officer, or attorney for the Government,
who by any means authorized by this chapter, has obtained knowledge of the contents of any wire, oral, or electronic communication, or evidence derived therefrom, may disclose such contents to any other Federal law enforcement, intelligence,
protective, immigration, national defense, or national security official to the extent
that such contents include foreign intelligence or counterintelligence (as defined
in section 3 of the National Security Act of 1947 (50 U.S.C. 401a)), or foreign
intelligence information (as defined in subsection (19) of section 2510 of this
title), to assist the official who is to receive that information in the performance of
his official duties. Any Federal official who receives information pursuant to this
provision may use that information only as necessary in the conduct of that person's official duties subject to any limitations on the unauthorized disclosure of
such information.".

(2) DEFINITION.—Section 2510 of title 18, United States Code, is amended by—

(C) by inserting at the end the following:

"(19) 'foreign intelligence information' means—

"(A) information, whether or not concerning a United States person, that relates to
the ability of the United States to protect against—

"(i) actual or potential attack or other grave hostile acts of a foreign power or an
agent of a foreign power;

"(ii) sabotage or international terrorism by a foreign power or an agent of a foreign
power; or

"(iii) clandestine intelligence activities by an intelligence service or network of a
foreign power or by an agent of a foreign power; or

"(B) information, whether or not concerning a United States person, with respect
to a foreign power or foreign territory that relates to—

"(i) the national defense or the security of the United States; or "(ii) the conduct of the foreign affairs of the United States."

(c) PROCEDURES.—The Attorney General shall establish procedures for the disclosure of information pursuant to section 2517(6) and Rule 6(e)(3)(C)(i)(V) of the Federal Rules of Criminal Procedure that identifies a United States person, as defined in section 101 of the Foreign Intelligence Surveillance Act of 1978 (50 U.S.C. 1801)).

(d) FOREIGN INTELLIGENCE INFORMATION.—

(1) IN GENERAL.—Notwithstanding any other provision of law, it shall be lawful for foreign intelligence or counterintelligence (as defined in section 3 of the National Security Act of 1947 (50 U.S.C. 401a)) or foreign intelligence information obtained as part of a criminal investigation to be disclosed to any Federal law enforcement, intelligence, protective, immigration, national defense, or national security official in order to assist the official receiving that information in the performance of his official duties. Any Federal official who receives information pursuant to this provision may use that information only as necessary in the conduct of that person's official duties subject to any limitations on the unauthorized disclosure of such information.

(2) DEFINITION.—In this subsection, the term "foreign intelligence information" means—

(A) information, whether or not concerning a United States person, that relates to the ability of the United States to protect against—

(i) actual or potential attack or other grave hostile acts of a foreign power or an agent of a foreign power;

(ii) sabotage or international terrorism by a foreign power or an agent of a foreign power; or

(iii) clandestine intelligence activities by an intelligence service or network of a foreign power or by an agent of a foreign power; or

(B) information, whether or not concerning a United States person, with respect to a foreign power or foreign territory that relates to—

(i) the national defense or the security of the United States; or

(ii) the conduct of the foreign affairs of the United States.

SEC. 213. AUTHORITY FOR DELAYING NOTICE OF THE EXECUTION OF A WARRANT.

Section 3103a of title 18, United States Code, is amended—

(1) by inserting "(a) IN GENERAL.—" before "In addition"; and

(2) by adding at the end the following:

"(b) DELAY.—With respect to the issuance of any warrant or court order under this section, or any other rule of law, to search for and seize any property or material that constitutes evidence of a criminal offense in violation of the laws of the United States, any notice required, or that may be required, to be given may be delayed if—

"(1) the court finds reasonable cause to believe that providing immediate notification of the execution of the warrant may have an adverse result (as defined in section 2705);

"(2) the warrant prohibits the seizure of any tangible property, any wire or electronic communication (as defined in section 2510), or, except as expressly provided in chapter 121, any stored wire or electronic information, except where the court finds reasonable necessity for the seizure; and

"(3) the warrant provides for the giving of such notice within a reasonable period of its execution, which period may thereafter be extended by the court for good cause shown.".

SEC. 215. ACCESS TO RECORDS AND OTHER ITEMS UNDER THE FOREIGN INTELLIGENCE SURVEILLANCE ACT.

Title V of the Foreign Intelligence Surveillance Act of 1978 (50 U.S.C. 1861 et seq.) is amended by striking sections 501 through 503 and inserting the following:

"SEC. 501. ACCESS TO CERTAIN BUSINESS RECORDS FOR FOREIGN INTELLIGENCE AND INTERNATIONAL TERRORISM INVESTIGATIONS.

"(a)(1) The Director of the Federal Bureau of Investigation or a designee of the Director (whose rank shall be no lower than Assistant Special Agent in Charge) may make an application for an order requiring the production of any tangible things (including books, records, papers, documents, and other items) for an investigation to protect against international terrorism or clandestine intelligence activities, provided that such investigation of a United States person is not conducted solely upon the basis of activities protected by the first amendment to the Constitution.

"(2) An investigation conducted under this section shall—

"(A) be conducted under guidelines approved by the Attorney General under Executive Order 12333 (or a successor order); and

"(B) not be conducted of a United States person solely upon the basis of activities protected by the first amendment to the Constitution of the United States.

"(b) Each application under this section—

"(1) shall be made to—

"(A) a judge of the court established by section 103(a); or

"(B) a United States Magistrate Judge under chapter 43 of title 28, United States Code, who is publicly designated by the Chief Justice of the United States to have the power to hear applications and grant orders for the production of tangible things under this section on behalf of a judge of that court; and

"(2) shall specify that the records concerned are sought for an authorized investigation conducted in accordance with subsection (a)(2) to obtain foreign intelligence information not concerning a United States person or to protect against international terrorism or clandestine intelligence activities.

"(c)(1) Upon an application made pursuant to this section, the judge shall enter an ex parte order as requested, or as modified, approving the release of records if the judge finds that the application meets the requirements of this section.

"(2) An order under this subsection shall not disclose that it is issued for purposes of an investigation described in subsection (a).

"(d) No person shall disclose to any other person (other than those persons necessary to produce the tangible things under this section) that the Federal Bureau of Investigation has sought or obtained tangible things under this section.

"(e) A person who, in good faith, produces tangible things under an order pursuant to this section shall not be liable to any other person for such production. Such production shall not be deemed to constitute a waiver of any privilege in any other proceeding or context.

"SEC. 502. CONGRESSIONAL OVERSIGHT.

"(a) On a semiannual basis, the Attorney General shall fully inform the Permanent Select Committee on Intelligence of the House of Representatives and the Select Committee on Intelligence of the Senate concerning all requests for the production of tangible things under section 402.

"(b) On a semiannual basis, the Attorney General shall provide to the Committees on the Judiciary of the House of Representatives and the Senate a report setting forth with respect to the preceding 6-month period—

"(1) the total number of applications made for orders approving requests for the production of tangible things under section 402; and

"(2) the total number of such orders either granted, modified, or denied.".

SEC. 217. INTERCEPTION OF COMPUTER TRESPASSER COMMUNICATIONS.

Chapter 119 of title 18, United States Code, is amended—

(1) in section 2510—

(C) by inserting after paragraph (19) the following:

"(20) 'protected computer' has the meaning set forth in section 1030; and

"(21) 'computer trespasser'—

"(A) means a person who accesses a protected computer without authorization and thus has no reasonable expectation of privacy in any communication transmitted to, through, or from the protected computer; and

"(B) does not include a person known by the owner or operator of the protected computer to have an existing contractual relationship with the owner or operator of the protected computer for access to all or part of the protected computer."; and

(2) in section 2511(2), by inserting at the end the following:

"(i) It shall not be unlawful under this chapter for a person acting under color of law to intercept the wire or electronic communications of a computer trespasser transmitted to, through, or from the protected computer, if—

"(I) the owner or operator of the protected computer authorizes the interception of the computer trespasser's communications on the protected computer;

"(II) the person acting under color of law is lawfully engaged in an investigation;

"(III) the person acting under color of law has reasonable grounds to believe that the contents of the computer trespasser's communications will be relevant to the investigation; and

"(IV) such interception does not acquire communications other than those transmitted to or from the computer trespasser.".

TITLE III—INTERNATIONAL MONEY LAUNDERING ABATEMENT AND ANTITERRORIST FINANCING ACT OF 2001

Subtitle A—International Counter Money Laundering and Related Measures

SEC. 316. ANTI-TERRORIST FORFEITURE PROTECTION.

(a) RIGHT TO CONTEST.—An owner of property that is confiscated under any provision of law relating to the confiscation of assets of suspected international terrorists, may contest that confiscation by filing a claim in the manner set forth in the Federal Rules of Civil Procedure (Supplemental Rules for Certain Admiralty and Maritime Claims), and asserting as an affirmative defense that—

(1) the property is not subject to confiscation under such provision of law; or

(2) the innocent owner provisions of section 983(d) of title 18, United States Code, apply to the case.

(b) EVIDENCE.—In considering a claim filed under this section, a court may admit evidence that is otherwise inadmissible under the Federal Rules of Evidence, if the court determines that the evidence is reliable, and that compliance with the Federal Rules of Evidence may jeopardize the national security interests of the United States.

(c) CLARIFICATIONS.—

(1) PROTECTION OF RIGHTS.—The exclusion of certain provisions of Federal law from the definition of the term "civil forfeiture statute" in section 983(i) of title 18, United States Code, shall not be construed to deny an owner of property the right to contest the confiscation of assets of suspected international terrorists under—

(A) subsection (a) of this section;

(B) the Constitution; or

(C) subchapter II of chapter 5 of title 5, United States Code (commonly known as the "Administrative Procedure Act").

(2) SAVINGS CLAUSE.—Nothing in this section shall limit or otherwise affect any other remedies that may be available to an owner of property under section 983 of title 18, United States Code, or any other provision of law.

(d) TECHNICAL CORRECTION.—Section 983(i)(2)(D) of title 18, United States Code, is amended by inserting "or the International Emergency Economic Powers Act (IEEPA) (50 U.S.C. 1701 et seq.)" before the semicolon.

TITLE IV—PROTECTING THE BORDER

Subtitle A—Protecting the Northern Border

SEC. 403. ACCESS BY THE DEPARTMENT OF STATE AND THE INS TO CERTAIN IDENTIFYING INFORMATION IN THE CRIMINAL HISTORY RE-CORDS OF VISA APPLICANTS AND APPLICANTS FOR ADMISSION TO THE UNITED STATES.

(a) AMENDMENT OF THE IMMIGRATION AND NATIONALITY ACT.—
Section 105 of the Immigration and Nationality Act (8 U.S.C. 1105) is amended—

(4) by adding at the end the following:

"(b)(1) The Attorney General and the Director of the Federal Bureau of Investigation shall provide the Department of State and the Service access to the criminal history record information contained in the National Crime Information Center's Interstate Identification Index (NCIC-III), Wanted Persons File, and to any other files maintained by the National Crime Information Center that may be mutually agreed upon by the Attorney General and the agency receiving the access, for the purpose of determining whether or not a visa applicant or applicant for admission has a criminal history record indexed in any such file.

"(2) Such access shall be provided by means of extracts of the records for placement in the automated visa lookout or other appropriate database, and shall be provided without any fee or charge.

"(3) The Federal Bureau of Investigation shall provide periodic updates of the extracts at intervals mutually agreed upon with the agency receiving the access. Upon receipt of such updated extracts, the receiving agency shall make corresponding updates to its database and destroy previously provided extracts.

"(4) Access to an extract does not entitle the Department of State to obtain the full content of the corresponding automated criminal history record. To obtain the full content of a criminal history record, the Department of State shall submit the applicant's fingerprints and any appropriate fingerprint processing fee authorized by law to the Criminal Justice Information Services Division of the Federal Bureau of Investigation.

"(c) The provision of the extracts described in subsection (b) may be reconsidered by the Attorney General and the receiving agency upon the development and deployment of a more cost-effective and efficient means of sharing the information.

"(d) For purposes of administering this section, the Department of State shall, prior to receiving access to NCIC data but not later than 4 months after the date of enactment of this subsection, promulgate final regulations—

"(1) to implement procedures for the taking of fingerprints;

"(2) to establish the conditions for the use of the information received from the Federal Bureau of Investigation, in order—

"(A) to limit the redissemination of such information;

"(B) to ensure that such information is used solely to determine whether or not to issue a visa to an alien or to admit an alien to the United States;

"(C) to ensure the security, confidentiality, and destruction of such information; and

"(D) to protect any privacy rights of individuals who are subjects of such information.".

(b) REPORTING REQUIREMENT.—Not later than 2 years after the date of enactment of this Act, the Attorney General and the Secretary of State jointly shall report to Congress on the implementation of the amendments made by this section.

(c) TECHNOLOGY STANDARD TO CONFIRM IDENTITY.—

(1) IN GENERAL.—The Attorney General and the Secretary of State jointly, through the National Institute of Standards and Technology (NIST), and in consultation with the Secretary of the Treasury and other Federal law enforcement and intelligence agencies the Attorney General or Secretary of State deems appropriate and in consultation with Congress, shall within 2 years after the date of the enactment of this section, develop and certify a technology standard that can be used to verify the identity of persons applying for a United States visa or such persons seeking to enter the United States pursuant to a visa for the purposes of conducting background checks, confirming identity, and ensuring that a person has not received a visa under a different name or such person seeking to enter the United States pursuant to a visa.

(2) INTEGRATED.—The technology standard developed pursuant to paragraph (1), shall be the technological basis for a cross-agency, cross-platform electronic system that is a cost-effective, efficient, fully integrated means to share law enforcement and intelligence information necessary to confirm the identity of such persons applying for a United States visa or such person seeking to enter the United States pursuant to a visa.

(3) ACCESSIBLE.—The electronic system described in paragraph

(2), once implemented, shall be readily and easily accessible to—

(A) all consular officers responsible for the issuance of visas;

(B) all Federal inspection agents at all United States border inspection points; and

(C) all law enforcement and intelligence officers as determined by regulation to be responsible for investigation or identification of aliens admitted to the United States pursuant to a visa.

(4) REPORT.—Not later than 18 months after the date of the enactment of this Act, and every 2 years thereafter, the Attorney General and the Secretary of State shall jointly, in consultation with the Secretary of Treasury, report to Congress describing the development, implementation, efficacy, and privacy implications of the technology standard and electronic database system described in this subsection.

(5) FUNDING.—There is authorized to be appropriated to the Secretary of State, the Attorney General, and the Director of the National Institute of Standards and Technology such sums as may be necessary to carry out the provisions of this subsection.

(d) STATUTORY CONSTRUCTION.—Nothing in this section, or in any other law, shall be construed to limit the authority of the Attorney General or the Director of the Federal Bureau of Investigation to provide access to the criminal history record information contained in the National Crime Information Center's (NCIC) Interstate Identification Index (NCIC-III), or to any other information maintained by the NCIC, to any Federal agency or officer authorized to enforce or administer the immigration laws of the United States, for the purpose of such enforcement or administration, upon terms that are consistent with the National Crime Prevention and Privacy Compact Act of 1998 (subtitle A of title II of Public Law 105–251; 42 U.S.C. 14611–16) and section 552a of title 5, United States Code.

Subtitle B—Enhanced Immigration Provisions

SEC. 411. DEFINITIONS RELATING TO TERRORISM.

(a) GROUNDS OF INADMISSIBILITY.—Section 212(a)(3) of the Immigration and Nationality Act (8 U.S.C. 1182(a)(3)) is amended—

(1) in subparagraph (B)—

(A) in clause (i)—

(i) by amending subclause (IV) to read as follows:

"(IV) is a representative (as defined in clause (v)) of—

"(aa) a foreign terrorist organization, as designated by the Secretary of State under section 219, or

"(bb) a political, social or other similar group whose public endorsement of acts of terrorist activity the Secretary of State has determined undermines United States efforts to reduce or eliminate terrorist activities,";

(ii) in subclause (V), by inserting "or" after "section 219,"; and

(iii) by adding at the end the following new subclauses:

"(VI) has used the alien's position of prominence within any country to endorse or espouse terrorist activity, or to persuade others to support terrorist activity or a terrorist organization, in a way that the Secretary of State has determined undermines United States efforts to reduce or eliminate terrorist activities, or

"(VII) is the spouse or child of an alien who is inadmissible under this section, if the activity causing the alien to be found inadmissible occurred within the last 5 years,";

(B) by redesignating clauses (ii), (iii), and (iv) as clauses (iii), (iv), and (v), respectively;

(C) in clause (i)(II), by striking "clause (iii)" and inserting "clause (iv)";

(D) by inserting after clause (i) the following:

"(ii) EXCEPTION.—Subclause (VII) of clause (i) does not apply to a spouse or child—

"(I) who did not know or should not reasonably have known of the activity causing the alien to be found inadmissible under this section; or

"(II) whom the consular officer or Attorney General has reasonable grounds to believe has renounced the activity causing the alien to be found inadmissible under this section.";

(E) in clause (iii) (as redesignated by subparagraph (B))—

(i) by inserting "it had been" before "committed in the United States"; and

(ii) in subclause (V)(b), by striking "or firearm" and inserting ", firearm, or other weapon or dangerous device";

(F) by amending clause (iv) (as redesignated by subparagraph (B)) to read as follows:

"(iv) ENGAGE IN TERRORIST ACTIVITY DEFINED.— As used in this chapter, the term 'engage in terrorist activity' means, in an individual capacity or as a member of an organization—

"(I) to commit or to incite to commit, under circumstances indicating an intention to cause death or serious bodily injury, a terrorist activity;

"(II) to prepare or plan a terrorist activity;

"(III) to gather information on potential targets for terrorist activity;

"(IV) to solicit funds or other things of value for—

"(aa) a terrorist activity;

"(bb) a terrorist organization described in clause (vi)(I) or (vi)(II); or

"(cc) a terrorist organization described in clause (vi)(III), unless the solicitor can demonstrate that he did not know, and should not reasonably have known, that the solicitation would further the organization's terrorist activity;

"(V) to solicit any individual—

"(aa) to engage in conduct otherwise described in this clause;

"(bb) for membership in a terrorist organization described in clause (vi)(I) or (vi)(II); or

"(cc) for membership in a terrorist organization described in clause (vi)(III), unless the solicitor can demonstrate that he did not know, and should not reasonably have known, that the solicitation would further the organization's terrorist activity; or

"(VI) to commit an act that the actor knows, or reasonably should know, affords material support, including a safe house, transportation, communications, funds, transfer of funds or other material financial benefit, false documentation or identification, weapons (including chemical, biological, or radiological weapons), explosives, or training—

"(aa) for the commission of a terrorist activity;

"(bb) to any individual who the actor knows, or reasonably should know, has committed or plans to commit a terrorist activity;

"(cc) to a terrorist organization described in clause (vi)(I) or (vi)(II); or

"(dd) to a terrorist organization described in clause (vi)(III), unless the actor can demonstrate that he did not know, and should not reasonably have known, that the act would further the organization's terrorist activity.

This clause shall not apply to any material support the alien afforded to an organization or individual that has committed terrorist activity, if the Secretary of State, after consultation with the Attorney General, or the Attorney General, after consultation with the Secretary of State, concludes in his sole unreviewable discretion, that this clause should not apply."; and

(G) by adding at the end the following new clause:

"(vi) TERRORIST ORGANIZATION DEFINED.—As used in clause (i)(VI) and clause (iv), the term 'terrorist organization' means an organization—

"(I) designated under section 219;

"(II) otherwise designated, upon publication in the Federal Register, by the Secretary of State in consultation with or upon the request of the Attorney General, as a terrorist organization, after finding that the organization engages in the activities described in subclause (I), (II), or (III) of clause (iv), or that the organization provides material support to further terrorist activity; or

"(III) that is a group of two or more individuals, whether organized or not, which engages in the activities described in subclause (I), (II), or (III) of clause (iv)."; and

(2) by adding at the end the following new subparagraph:

"(F) ASSOCIATION WITH TERRORIST ORGANIZATIONS.— Any alien who the Secretary of State, after consultation with the Attorney General, or the Attorney General, after consultation with the Secretary of State, determines has been associated with a terrorist organization and intends while in the United States to engage solely, principally, or incidentally in activities that could endanger the welfare, safety, or security of the United States is inadmissible.".

(c) RETROACTIVE APPLICATION OF AMENDMENTS.—

(1) IN GENERAL.—Except as otherwise provided in this subsection, the amendments made by this section shall take effect on the date of the enactment of this Act and shall apply to—

(A) actions taken by an alien before, on, or after such date; and

(B) all aliens, without regard to the date of entry or attempted entry into the United States—

(i) in removal proceedings on or after such date (except for proceedings in which there has been a final administrative decision before such date); or

(ii) seeking admission to the United States on or after such date.

(2) SPECIAL RULE FOR ALIENS IN EXCLUSION OR DEPORTATION PRO-CEEDINGS.—Notwithstanding any other provision of law, sections 212(a)(3)(B) and 237(a)(4)(B) of the Immigration and Nationality Act, as amended by this Act, shall apply to all aliens in exclusion or deportation proceedings on or after the date of the enactment of this Act (except for proceedings in which there has been a final administrative decision before such date) as if such proceedings were removal proceedings.

(3) SPECIAL RULE FOR SECTION 219 ORGANIZATIONS AND ORGANI-ZATIONS DESIGNATED UNDER SECTION 212(a)(3)(B)(vi)(II).—

(A) IN GENERAL.—Notwithstanding paragraphs (1) and (2), no alien shall be considered inadmissible under section 212(a)(3) of the Immigration and National-ity Act (8 U.S.C. 1182(a)(3)), or deportable under section 237(a)(4)(B) of such Act (8 U.S.C. 1227(a)(4)(B)), by reason of the amendments made by subsection (a), on the ground that the alien engaged in a terrorist activity described in subclause (IV) (bb), (V)(bb), or (VI)(cc) of section 212(a)(3)(B)(iv) of such Act (as so amended) with respect to a group at any time when the group was not a terrorist organization designated by the Secretary of State under section 219 of such Act (8 U.S.C. 1189) or otherwise designated under section 212(a)(3)(B)(vi)(II) of such Act (as so amended).

(B) STATUTORY CONSTRUCTION.—Subparagraph (A) shall not be construed to prevent an alien from being considered inadmissible or deportable for having engaged in a terrorist activity—

(i) described in subclause (IV)(bb), (V)(bb), or (VI)(cc) of section 212(a)(3)(B)(iv) of such Act (as so amended) with respect to a terrorist organization at any time when such organization was designated by the Secretary of State under section 219 of such Act or otherwise designated under section 212(a)(3)(B)(vi)(II) of such Act (as so amended); or

(ii) described in subclause (IV)(cc), (V)(cc), or (VI)(dd) of section 212(a)(3)(B) (iv) of such Act (as so amended) with respect to a terrorist organization described in section 212(a)(3)(B)(vi)(III) of such Act (as so amended).

(4) EXCEPTION.—The Secretary of State, in consultation with the Attorney General, may determine that the amendments made by this section shall not apply with respect to actions by an alien taken outside the United States before the date of the enactment of this Act upon the recommendation of a consular officer who

has concluded that there is not reasonable ground to believe that the alien knew or reasonably should have known that the actions would further a terrorist activity.

(c) DESIGNATION OF FOREIGN TERRORIST ORGANIZATIONS.—Section 219(a) of the Immigration and Nationality Act (8 U.S.C. 1189(a)) is amended—

(1) in paragraph (1)(B), by inserting "or terrorism (as defined in section 140(d)(2) of the Foreign Relations Authorization Act, Fiscal Years 1988 and 1989 (22 U.S.C. 2656f(d)(2)), or retains the capability and intent to engage in terrorist activity or terrorism" after "212(a)(3)(B)";

(2) in paragraph (1)(C), by inserting "or terrorism" after "terrorist activity";

(3) by amending paragraph (2)(A) to read as follows:

"(A) NOTICE.—

"(i) TO CONGRESSIONAL LEADERS.—Seven days before making a designation under this subsection, the Secretary shall, by classified communication, notify the Speaker and Minority Leader of the House of Representatives, the President pro tempore, Majority Leader, and Minority Leader of the Senate, and the members of the relevant committees of the House of Representatives and the Senate, in writing, of the intent to designate an organization under this subsection, together with the findings made under paragraph (1) with respect to that organization, and the factual basis therefor.

"(ii) PUBLICATION IN FEDERAL REGISTER.—The Secretary shall publish the designation in the Federal Register seven days after providing the notification under clause (i).";

SEC. 412. MANDATORY DETENTION OF SUSPECTED TERRORISTS; HABEAS CORPUS; JUDICIAL REVIEW.

(a) IN GENERAL.—The Immigration and Nationality Act (8 U.S.C. 1101 et seq.) is amended by inserting after section 236 the following:

"MANDATORY DETENTION OF SUSPECTED TERRORISTS; HABEAS CORPUS; JUDICIAL REVIEW

"SEC. 236A. (a) DETENTION OF TERRORIST ALIENS.—

"(1) CUSTODY.—The Attorney General shall take into custody any alien who is certified under paragraph (3).

"(2) RELEASE.—Except as provided in paragraphs (5) and (6), the Attorney General shall maintain custody of such an alien until the alien is removed from the United States. Except as provided in paragraph (6), such custody shall be maintained irrespective of any relief from removal for which the alien may be eligible, or any relief from removal granted the alien, until the Attorney General determines that the alien is no longer an alien who may be certified under paragraph (3). If the alien is finally determined not to be removable, detention pursuant to this subsection shall terminate.

"(3) CERTIFICATION.—The Attorney General may certify an alien under this paragraph if the Attorney General has reasonable grounds to believe that the alien—

"(A) is described in section 212(a)(3)(A)(i), 212(a)(3)(A)(iii), 212(a)(3)(B), 237(a)(4)(A)(i), 237(a)(4)(A)(iii), or 237(a)(4)(B); or

"(B) is engaged in any other activity that endangers the national security of the United States.

"(4) NONDELEGATION.—The Attorney General may delegate the authority provided under paragraph (3) only to the Deputy Attorney General. The Deputy Attorney General may not delegate such authority.

"(5) COMMENCEMENT OF PROCEEDINGS.—The Attorney General shall place an alien detained under paragraph (1) in removal proceedings, or shall charge the alien with a criminal offense, not later than 7 days after the commencement of such detention. If the requirement of the preceding sentence is not satisfied, the Attorney General shall release the alien.

"(6) LIMITATION ON INDEFINITE DETENTION.—An alien detained solely under paragraph (1) who has not been removed under section 241(a)(1)(A), and whose removal is unlikely in the reasonably foreseeable future, may be detained for additional periods of up to six months only if the release of the alien will threaten the national security of the United States or the safety of the community or any person.

"(7) REVIEW OF CERTIFICATION.—The Attorney General shall review the certification made under paragraph (3) every 6 months. If the Attorney General determines, in the Attorney General's discretion, that the certification should be revoked, the alien may be released on such conditions as the Attorney General deems appropriate, unless such release is otherwise prohibited by law. The alien may request each 6 months in writing that the Attorney General reconsider the certification and may submit documents or other evidence in support of that request.

"(b) HABEAS CORPUS AND JUDICIAL REVIEW.—

"(1) IN GENERAL.—Judicial review of any action or decision relating to this section (including judicial review of the merits of a determination made under subsection (a)(3) or (a)(6)) is available exclusively in habeas corpus proceedings consistent with this subsection. Except as provided in the preceding sentence, no court shall have jurisdiction to review, by habeas corpus petition or otherwise, any such action or decision.

"(2) APPLICATION.—

"(A) IN GENERAL.—Notwithstanding any other provision of law, including section 2241(a) of title 28, United States Code, habeas corpus proceedings described in paragraph

(1) may be initiated only by an application filed with—

"(i) the Supreme Court;

"(ii) any justice of the Supreme Court;

"(iii) any circuit judge of the United States Court of Appeals for the District of Columbia Circuit; or

"(iv) any district court otherwise having jurisdiction to entertain it.

"(B) APPLICATION TRANSFER.—Section 2241(b) of title 28, United States Code, shall apply to an application for a writ of habeas corpus described in subparagraph (A).

"(3) APPEALS.—Notwithstanding any other provision of law, including section 2253 of title 28, in habeas corpus proceedings described in paragraph (1) before a circuit or district judge, the final order shall be subject to review, on appeal, by the United States Court of Appeals for the District of Columbia Circuit. There shall be no right of appeal in such proceedings to any other circuit court of appeals.

"(4) RULE OF DECISION.—The law applied by the Supreme Court and the United States Court of Appeals for the District of Columbia Circuit shall be regarded as the rule of decision in habeas corpus proceedings described in paragraph (1).

"(c) STATUTORY CONSTRUCTION.—The provisions of this section shall not be applicable to any other provision of this Act.".

(b) CLERICAL AMENDMENT.—The table of contents of the Immigration and Nationality Act is amended by inserting after the item relating to section 236 the following:

"Sec. 236A. Mandatory detention of suspected terrorist; habeas corpus; judicial review.".

(c) REPORTS.—Not later than 6 months after the date of the enactment of this Act, and every 6 months thereafter, the Attorney General shall submit a report to the Committee on the Judiciary of the House of Representatives and the Committee on the Judiciary of the Senate, with respect to the reporting period, on—

(1) the number of aliens certified under section 236A(a)(3) of the Immigration and Nationality Act, as added by subsection (a);

(2) the grounds for such certifications;

(3) the nationalities of the aliens so certified;

(4) the length of the detention for each alien so certified; and

(5) the number of aliens so certified who—

(A) were granted any form of relief from removal;

(B) were removed;

(C) the Attorney General has determined are no longer aliens who may be so certified; or

(D) were released from detention.

SEC. 414. VISA INTEGRITY AND SECURITY.

(a) SENSE OF CONGRESS REGARDING THE NEED TO EXPEDITE IMPLEMENTATION OF INTEGRATED ENTRY AND EXIT DATA SYSTEM.—

(1) SENSE OF CONGRESS.—In light of the terrorist attacks perpetrated against the United States on September 11, 2001, it is the sense of the Congress that—

(A) the Attorney General, in consultation with the Secretary of State, should fully implement the integrated entry and exit data system for airports, seaports, and land border ports of entry, as specified in section 110 of the Illegal Immigration Reform and Immigrant Responsibility Act of 1996 (8 U.S.C. 1365a), with all deliberate speed and as expeditiously as practicable; and

(B) the Attorney General, in consultation with the Secretary of State, the Secretary of Commerce, the Secretary of the Treasury, and the Office of Homeland Security, should immediately begin establishing the Integrated Entry and Exit Data System Task Force, as described in section 3 of the Immigration and Naturalization Service Data Management Improvement Act of 2000 (Public Law 106–215).

(2) AUTHORIZATION OF APPROPRIATIONS.—There is authorized to be appropriated such sums as may be necessary to fully implement the system described in paragraph (1)(A).

(b) DEVELOPMENT OF THE SYSTEM.—In the development of the integrated entry and exit data system under section 110 of the Illegal Immigration Reform and Immigrant Responsibility Act of 1996 (8 U.S.C. 1365a), the Attorney General and the Secretary of State shall particularly focus on—

(1) the utilization of biometric technology; and

(2) the development of tamper-resistant documents readable at ports of entry.

(c) INTERFACE WITH LAW ENFORCEMENT DATABASES.—The entry and exit data system described in this section shall be able to interface with law enforcement databases for use by Federal law enforcement to identify and detain individuals who pose a threat to the national security of the United States.

(d) REPORT ON SCREENING INFORMATION.—Not later than 12 months after the date of enactment of this Act, the Office of Homeland Security shall submit a report to Congress on the information that is needed from any United States agency to effectively screen visa applicants and applicants for admission to the United States to identify those affiliated with terrorist organizations or those that pose any threat to the safety or security of the United States, including the type of information currently received by United States agencies and the regularity with which such information is transmitted to the Secretary of State and the Attorney General.

TITLE V—REMOVING OBSTACLES TO INVESTIGATING TERRORISM

SEC. 504. COORDINATION WITH LAW ENFORCEMENT.

(a) INFORMATION ACQUIRED FROM AN ELECTRONIC SURVEILLANCE.—
Section 106 of the Foreign Intelligence Surveillance Act of 1978 (50 U.S.C. 1806),
is amended by adding at the end the following:

"(k)(1) Federal officers who conduct electronic surveillance to acquire foreign intelligence information under this title may consult with Federal law enforcement
officers to coordinate efforts to investigate or protect against—

"(A) actual or potential attack or other grave hostile acts of a foreign power or an
agent of a foreign power;

"(B) sabotage or international terrorism by a foreign power or an agent of a foreign
power; or

"(C) clandestine intelligence activities by an intelligence service or network of a
foreign power or by an agent of a foreign power.

"(2) Coordination authorized under paragraph (1) shall not preclude the certification required by section 104(a)(7)(B) or the entry of an order under section 105.".

(b) INFORMATION ACQUIRED FROM A PHYSICAL SEARCH.—Section 305
of the Foreign Intelligence Surveillance Act of 1978 (50 U.S.C. 1825) is amended
by adding at the end the following:

"(k)(1) Federal officers who conduct physical searches to acquire foreign intelligence information under this title may consult with Federal law enforcement officers to coordinate efforts to investigate or protect against—

"(A) actual or potential attack or other grave hostile acts of a foreign power or an
agent of a foreign power;

"(B) sabotage or international terrorism by a foreign power or an agent of a foreign
power; or

"(C) clandestine intelligence activities by an intelligence service or network of a
foreign power or by an agent of a foreign power.

"(2) Coordination authorized under paragraph (1) shall not preclude the certification required by section 303(a)(7) or the entry of an order under section 304.".

TITLE VI—PROVIDING FOR VICTIMS OF TERRORISM, PUBLIC SAFETY
OFFICERS, AND THEIR FAMILIES

Subtitle A—Aid to Families of Public Safety Officers

SEC. 611. EXPEDITED PAYMENT FOR PUBLIC SAFETY OFFICERS INVOLVED IN THE PREVENTION, INVESTIGATION, RESCUE, OR RECOVERY EFFORTS RELATED TO A TERRORIST ATTACK.

(a) IN GENERAL.—Notwithstanding the limitations of subsection (b) of section 1201 or the provisions of subsections (c), (d), and (e) of such section or section 1202 of title I of the Omnibus Crime Control and Safe Streets Act of 1968 (42 U.S.C. 3796, 3796a), upon certification (containing identification of all eligible payees of benefits pursuant to section 1201 of such Act) by a public agency that a public safety officer employed by such agency was killed or suffered a catastrophic injury producing permanent and total disability as a direct and proximate result of a personal injury sustained in the line of duty as described in section 1201 of such Act in connection with prevention, investigation, rescue, or recovery efforts related to a terrorist attack, the Director of the Bureau of Justice Assistance shall authorize payment to qualified beneficiaries, said payment to be made not later than 30 days after receipt of such certification, benefits described under subpart 1 of part L of such Act (42 U.S.C. 3796 et seq.).

(b) DEFINITIONS.—For purposes of this section, the terms "catastrophic injury", "public agency", and "public safety officer" have the same meanings given such terms in section 1204 of title I of the Omnibus Crime Control and Safe Streets Act of 1968 (42 U.S.C. 3796b).

TITLE VIII—STRENGTHENING THE CRIMINAL LAWS AGAINST TERRORISM

SEC. 802. DEFINITION OF DOMESTIC TERRORISM.

(a) DOMESTIC TERRORISM DEFINED.—Section 2331 of title 18, United States Code, is amended—

(1) in paragraph (1)(B)(iii), by striking "by assassination or kidnapping" and inserting "by mass destruction, assassination, or kidnapping";

(2) in paragraph (3), by striking "and";

(3) in paragraph (4), by striking the period at the end and inserting "; and"; and

(4) by adding at the end the following:

"(5) the term 'domestic terrorism' means activities that—

"(A) involve acts dangerous to human life that are a violation of the criminal laws of the United States or of any State;

"(B) appear to be intended—

"(i) to intimidate or coerce a civilian population;

"(ii) to influence the policy of a government by intimidation or coercion; or

"(iii) to affect the conduct of a government by mass destruction, assassination, or kidnapping; and

"(C) occur primarily within the territorial jurisdiction of the United States.".

(b) CONFORMING AMENDMENT.—Section 3077(1) of title 18, United States Code, is amended to read as follows:

"(1) 'act of terrorism' means an act of domestic or international terrorism as defined in section 2331;".

SEC. 810. ALTERNATE MAXIMUM PENALTIES FOR TERRORISM OFFENSES.

(a) ARSON.—Section 81 of title 18, United States Code, is amended in the second undesignated paragraph by striking "not more than twenty years" and inserting "for any term of years or for life".

(b) DESTRUCTION OF AN ENERGY FACILITY.—Section 1366 of title 18, United States Code, is amended—

(1) in subsection (a), by striking "ten" and inserting "20"; and

(2) by adding at the end the following:

"(d) Whoever is convicted of a violation of subsection (a) or (b) that has resulted in the death of any person shall be subject to imprisonment for any term of years or life.".

(c) MATERIAL SUPPORT TO TERRORISTS.—Section 2339A(a) of title 18, United States Code, is amended—

(1) by striking "10" and inserting "15"; and

(2) by striking the period and inserting ", and, if the death of any person results, shall be imprisoned for any term of years or for life.".

(d) MATERIAL SUPPORT TO DESIGNATED FOREIGN TERRORIST ORGA-NIZATIONS.—Section 2339B(a)(1) of title 18, United States Code, is amended—

(1) by striking "10" and inserting "15"; and

(2) by striking the period after "or both" and inserting ", and, if the death of any person results, shall be imprisoned for any term of years or for life.".

(e) DESTRUCTION OF NATIONAL-DEFENSE MATERIALS.—Section 2155(a) of title 18, United States Code, is amended—

(1) by striking "ten" and inserting "20"; and

(2) by striking the period at the end and inserting ", and, if death results to any person, shall be imprisoned for any term of years or for life.".

(f) SABOTAGE OF NUCLEAR FACILITIES OR FUEL.—Section 236 of the Atomic Energy Act of 1954 (42 U.S.C. 2284), is amended—

(1) by striking "ten" each place it appears and inserting "20";

(2) in subsection (a), by striking the period at the end and inserting ", and, if death results to any person, shall be imprisoned for any term of years or for life."; and

(3) in subsection (b), by striking the period at the end and inserting ", and, if death results to any person, shall be imprisoned for any term of years or for life.".

(g) SPECIAL AIRCRAFT JURISDICTION OF THE UNITED STATES.—Section 46505(c) of title 49, United States Code, is amended—

(1) by striking "15" and inserting "20"; and

(2) by striking the period at the end and inserting ", and, if death results to any person, shall be imprisoned for any term of years or for life.".

(h) DAMAGING OR DESTROYING AN INTERSTATE GAS OR HAZARDOUS LIQUID PIPELINE FACILITY.—Section 60123(b) of title 49, United States Code, is amended—

(1) by striking "15" and inserting "20"; and

(2) by striking the period at the end and inserting ", and, if death results to any person, shall be imprisoned for any term of years or for life.".

SEC. 816. DEVELOPMENT AND SUPPORT OF CYBERSECURITY FORENSIC CAPABILITIES.

(a) IN GENERAL.—The Attorney General shall establish such regional computer forensic laboratories as the Attorney General considers appropriate, and provide support to existing computer forensic laboratories, in order that all such computer forensic laboratories have the capability—

(1) to provide forensic examinations with respect to seized or intercepted computer evidence relating to criminal activity (including cyberterrorism);

(2) to provide training and education for Federal, State, and local law enforcement personnel and prosecutors regarding investigations, forensic analyses, and prosecutions of computer-related crime (including cyberterrorism);

(3) to assist Federal, State, and local law enforcement in enforcing Federal, State, and local criminal laws relating to computer-related crime;

(4) to facilitate and promote the sharing of Federal law enforcement expertise and information about the investigation, analysis, and prosecution of computer-related crime with State and local law enforcement personnel and prosecutors, including the use of multijurisdictional task forces; and

(5) to carry out such other activities as the Attorney General considers appropriate.

(b) AUTHORIZATION OF APPROPRIATIONS.—

(1) AUTHORIZATION.—There is hereby authorized to be appropriated in each fiscal year $50,000,000 for purposes of carrying out this section.

(2) AVAILABILITY.—Amounts appropriated pursuant to the authorization of appropriations in paragraph (1) shall remain available until expended.

TITLE IX—IMPROVED INTELLIGENCE

SEC. 904. TEMPORARY AUTHORITY TO DEFER SUBMITTAL TO CONGRESS OF REPORTS ON INTELLIGENCE AND INTELLIGENCE- RELATED MATTERS.

(a) AUTHORITY TO DEFER.—The Secretary of Defense, Attorney General, and Director of Central Intelligence each may, during the effective period of this section, defer the date of submittal to Congress of any covered intelligence report under the jurisdiction of such official until February 1, 2002.

(b) COVERED INTELLIGENCE REPORT.—Except as provided in subsection (c), for purposes of subsection (a), a covered intelligence report is as follows:

(1) Any report on intelligence or intelligence-related activities of the United States Government that is required to be submitted to Congress by an element of the intelligence community during the effective period of this section.

(2) Any report or other matter that is required to be submitted to the Select Committee on Intelligence of the Senate and Permanent Select Committee on Intelligence of the House of Representatives by the Department of Defense or the Department of Justice during the effective period of this section.

(c) EXCEPTION FOR CERTAIN REPORTS.—For purposes of subsection (a), any report required by section 502 or 503 of the National Security Act of 1947 (50 U.S.C. 413a, 413b) is not a covered intelligence report.

(d) NOTICE TO CONGRESS.—Upon deferring the date of submittal to Congress of a covered intelligence report under subsection (a), the official deferring the date of submittal of the covered intelligence report shall submit to Congress notice of the deferral. Notice of deferral of a report shall specify the provision of law, if any, under which the report would otherwise be submitted to Congress.

(e) EXTENSION OF DEFERRAL.—(1) Each official specified in subsection (a) may defer the date of submittal to Congress of a covered intelligence report under the jurisdiction of such official to a date after February 1, 2002, if such official submits to the committees of Congress specified in subsection (b)(2) before February 1, 2002, a certification that preparation and submittal of the covered intelligence report on February 1, 2002, will impede the work of officers or employees who are engaged in counterterrorism activities.

(2) A certification under paragraph (1) with respect to a covered intelligence report shall specify the date on which the covered intelligence report will be submitted to Congress.

(f) EFFECTIVE PERIOD.—The effective period of this section is the period beginning on the date of the enactment of this Act and ending on February 1, 2002.

(g) ELEMENT OF THE INTELLIGENCE COMMUNITY DEFINED.—In this section, the term "element of the intelligence community" means any element of the intelligence community specified or designated under section 3(4) of the National Security Act of 1947 (50 U.S.C. 401a(4)).

SEC. 905. DISCLOSURE TO DIRECTOR OF CENTRAL INTELLIGENCE OF FOREIGN INTELLIGENCE-RELATED INFORMATION WITH RESPECT TO CRIMINAL INVESTIGATIONS.

(a) IN GENERAL.—Title I of the National Security Act of 1947 (50 U.S.C. 402 et seq.) is amended—

(1) by redesignating subsection 105B as section 105C; and

(2) by inserting after section 105A the following new section 105B:

"DISCLOSURE OF FOREIGN INTELLIGENCE ACQUIRED IN CRIMINAL INVESTIGATIONS; NOTICE OF CRIMINAL INVESTIGATIONS OF FOREIGN INTELLIGENCE SOURCES

"SEC. 105B. (a) DISCLOSURE OF FOREIGN INTELLIGENCE.—(1) Except as otherwise provided by law and subject to paragraph (2), the Attorney General, or the head of any other department or agency of the Federal Government with law enforcement responsibilities, shall expeditiously disclose to the Director of Central Intelligence, pursuant to guidelines developed by the Attorney General in consultation with the Director, foreign intelligence acquired by an element of the Department of Justice or an element of such department or agency, as the case may be, in the course of a criminal investigation.

"(2) The Attorney General by regulation and in consultation with the Director of Central Intelligence may provide for exceptions to the applicability of paragraph (1) for one or more classes of foreign intelligence, or foreign intelligence with respect to one or more targets or matters, if the Attorney General determines that disclosure of such foreign intelligence under that paragraph would jeopardize an ongoing law enforcement investigation or impair other significant law enforcement interests.

"(b) PROCEDURES FOR NOTICE OF CRIMINAL INVESTIGATIONS.—Not later than 180 days after the date of enactment of this section, the Attorney General, in consultation with the Director of Central Intelligence, shall develop guidelines to ensure that after receipt of a report from an element of the intelligence community of activity of a foreign intelligence source or potential foreign intelligence source that may warrant investigation as criminal activity, the Attorney General provides notice to the Director of Central Intelligence, within a reasonable period of time, of his intention to commence, or decline to commence, a criminal investigation of such activity.

"(c) PROCEDURES.—The Attorney General shall develop procedures for the administration of this section, including the disclosure of foreign intelligence by elements of the Department of Justice, and elements of other departments and agencies of the Federal Government, under subsection (a) and the provision of notice with respect to criminal investigations under subsection (b).".

(b) CLERICAL AMENDMENT.—The table of contents in the first
   section of that Act is amended by striking the item relating to section 105B and inserting the following new items:

"Sec. 105B. Disclosure of foreign intelligence acquired in criminal investigations; notice of criminal investigations of foreign intelligence sources.

"Sec. 105C. Protection of the operational files of the National Imagery and Mapping Agency.".

TITLE X—MISCELLANEOUS

SEC. 1005. FIRST RESPONDERS ASSISTANCE ACT.

(a) GRANT AUTHORIZATION.—The Attorney General shall make grants described in subsections (b) and (c) to States and units of local government to improve the ability of State and local law enforcement, fire department and first responders to respond to and prevent acts of terrorism.

(b) TERRORISM PREVENTION GRANTS.—Terrorism prevention grants under this subsection may be used for programs, projects, and other activities to—

(1) hire additional law enforcement personnel dedicated to intelligence gathering and analysis functions, including the formation of full-time intelligence and analysis units;

(2) purchase technology and equipment for intelligence gathering and analysis functions, including wire-tap, pen links, cameras, and computer hardware and software;

(3) purchase equipment for responding to a critical incident, including protective equipment for patrol officers such as quick masks;

(4) purchase equipment for managing a critical incident, such as communications equipment for improved interoperability among surrounding jurisdictions and mobile command posts for overall scene management; and

(5) fund technical assistance programs that emphasize coordination among neighboring law enforcement agencies for sharing resources, and resources coordination among law enforcement agencies for combining intelligence gathering and analysis functions, and the development of policy, procedures, memorandums of understanding, and other best practices.

(c) ANTITERRORISM TRAINING GRANTS.—Antiterrorism training grants under this subsection may be used for programs, projects, and other activities to address—

(1) intelligence gathering and analysis techniques;

(2) community engagement and outreach;

(3) critical incident management for all forms of terrorist attack;

(4) threat assessment capabilities;

(5) conducting followup investigations; and

(6) stabilizing a community after a terrorist incident.

(d) APPLICATION.—

(1) IN GENERAL.—Each eligible entity that desires to receive a grant under this section shall submit an application to the Attorney General, at such time, in such manner, and accompanied by such additional information as the Attorney General may reasonably require.

(2) CONTENTS.—Each application submitted pursuant to paragraph (1) shall—

(A) describe the activities for which assistance under this section is sought; and

(B) provide such additional assurances as the Attorney General determines to be essential to ensure compliance with the requirements of this section.

(e) MINIMUM AMOUNT.—If all applications submitted by a State or units of local government within that State have not been funded under this section in any fiscal year, that State, if it qualifies, and the units of local government within that

State, shall receive in that fiscal year not less than 0.5 percent of the total amount appropriated in that fiscal year for grants under this section.

(f) AUTHORIZATION OF APPROPRIATIONS.—There are authorized to be appropriated $25,000,000 for each of the fiscal years 2003 through 2007.

SEC. 1013. EXPRESSING THE SENSE OF THE SENATE CONCERNING THE PROVISION OF FUNDING FOR BIOTERRORISM PREPAREDNESS AND RESPONSE.

(a) FINDINGS.—The Senate finds the following:

(1) Additional steps must be taken to better prepare the United States to respond to potential bioterrorism attacks.

(2) The threat of a bioterrorist attack is still remote, but is increasing for a variety of reasons, including—

(A) public pronouncements by Osama bin Laden that it is his religious duty to acquire weapons of mass destruction, including chemical and biological weapons;

(B) the callous disregard for innocent human life as demonstrated by the terrorists' attacks of September 11, 2001;

(C) the resources and motivation of known terrorists and their sponsors and supporters to use biological warfare;

(D) recent scientific and technological advances in agent delivery technology such as aerosolization that have made weaponization of certain germs much easier; and

(E) the increasing access to the technologies and expertise necessary to construct and deploy chemical and biological weapons of mass destruction.

(3) Coordination of Federal, State, and local terrorism research, preparedness, and response programs must be improved.

(4) States, local areas, and public health officials must have enhanced resources and expertise in order to respond to a potential bioterrorist attack.

(5) National, State, and local communication capacities must be enhanced to combat the spread of chemical and biological illness.

(6) Greater resources must be provided to increase the capacity of hospitals and local health care workers to respond to public health threats.

(7) Health care professionals must be better trained to recognize, diagnose, and treat illnesses arising from biochemical attacks.

(8) Additional supplies may be essential to increase the readiness of the United States to respond to a bio-attack.

(9) Improvements must be made in assuring the safety of the food supply.

(10) New vaccines and treatments are needed to assure that we have an adequate response to a biochemical attack.

(11) Government research, preparedness, and response programs need to utilize private sector expertise and resources.

(12) Now is the time to strengthen our public health system and ensure that the United States is adequately prepared to respond to potential bioterrorist attacks, natural infectious disease outbreaks, and other challenges and potential threats to the public health.

(b) SENSE OF THE SENATE.—It is the sense of the Senate that the United States should make a substantial new investment this year toward the following:

(1) Improving State and local preparedness capabilities by upgrading State and local surveillance epidemiology, assisting in the development of response plans, assuring adequate staffing and training of health professionals to diagnose and care for victims of bioterrorism, extending the electronics communications networks and training personnel, and improving public health laboratories.

(2) Improving hospital response capabilities by assisting hospitals in developing plans for a bioterrorist attack and improving the surge capacity of hospitals.

(3) Upgrading the bioterrorism capabilities of the Centers for Disease Control and Prevention through improving rapid identification and health early warning systems.

(4) Improving disaster response medical systems, such as the National Disaster Medical System and the Metropolitan Medical Response System and Epidemic Intelligence Service.

(5) Targeting research to assist with the development of appropriate therapeutics and vaccines for likely bioterrorist agents and assisting with expedited drug and device review through the Food and Drug Administration.

(6) Improving the National Pharmaceutical Stockpile program by increasing the amount of necessary therapies (including smallpox vaccines and other post-exposure vaccines) and ensuring the appropriate deployment of stockpiles.

(7) Targeting activities to increase food safety at the Food and Drug Administration.

(8) Increasing international cooperation to secure dangerous biological agents, increase surveillance, and retrain biological warfare specialists.

SEC. 1016. CRITICAL INFRASTRUCTURES PROTECTION.

(a) SHORT TITLE.—This section may be cited as the "Critical Infrastructures Protection Act of 2001".

(b) FINDINGS.—Congress makes the following findings:

(1) The information revolution has transformed the conduct of business and the operations of government as well as the infrastructure relied upon for the defense and national security of the United States.

(2) Private business, government, and the national security apparatus increasingly depend on an interdependent network of critical physical and information infrastructures, including telecommunications, energy, financial services, water, and transportation sectors.

(3) A continuous national effort is required to ensure the reliable provision of cyber and physical infrastructure services critical to maintaining the national defense, continuity of government, economic prosperity, and quality of life in the United States.

(4) This national effort requires extensive modeling and analytic capabilities for purposes of evaluating appropriate mechanisms to ensure the stability of these complex and interdependent systems, and to underpin policy recommendations, so as to achieve the continuous viability and adequate protection of the critical infrastructure of the Nation.

(c) POLICY OF THE UNITED STATES.—It is the policy of the United States—

(1) that any physical or virtual disruption of the operation of the critical infrastructures of the United States be rare, brief, geographically limited in effect, manageable, and minimally detrimental to the economy, human and government services, and national security of the United States;

(2) that actions necessary to achieve the policy stated in paragraph (1) be carried out in a public-private partnership involving corporate and non-governmental organizations; and

(3) to have in place a comprehensive and effective program to ensure the continuity of essential Federal Government functions under all circumstances.

(d) ESTABLISHMENT OF NATIONAL COMPETENCE FOR CRITICAL INFRASTRUCTURE PROTECTION.—

(1) SUPPORT OF CRITICAL INFRASTRUCTURE PROTECTION AND CONTINUITY BY NATIONAL INFRASTRUCTURE SIMULATION AND ANALYSIS CENTER.—There shall be established the National Infrastructure Simulation and Analysis Center (NISAC) to serve as a source of national competence to address critical infrastructure protection and continuity through support for activities related to counterterrorism, threat assessment, and risk mitigation.

(2) PARTICULAR SUPPORT.—The support provided under paragraph (1) shall include the following:

(A) Modeling, simulation, and analysis of the systems comprising critical infrastructures, including cyber infrastructure, telecommunications infrastructure, and physical infrastructure, in order to enhance understanding of the large-scale complexity of such systems and to facilitate modification of such systems to mitigate the threats to such systems and to critical infrastructures generally.

(B) Acquisition from State and local governments and the private sector of data necessary to create and maintain models of such systems and of critical infrastructures generally.

(C) Utilization of modeling, simulation, and analysis under subparagraph (A) to provide education and training to policymakers on matters relating to—

(i) the analysis conducted under that subparagraph;

(ii) the implications of unintended or unintentional disturbances to critical infrastructures; and

(iii) responses to incidents or crises involving critical infrastructures, including the continuity of government and private sector activities through and after such incidents or crises.

(D) Utilization of modeling, simulation, and analysis under subparagraph (A) to provide recommendations to policymakers, and to departments and agencies of the Federal Government and private sector persons and entities upon request, regarding means of enhancing the stability of, and preserving, critical infrastructures.

(3) RECIPIENT OF CERTAIN SUPPORT.—Modeling, simulation, and analysis provided under this subsection shall be provided, in particular, to relevant Federal, State, and local entities responsible for critical infrastructure protection and policy.

(e) CRITICAL INFRASTRUCTURE DEFINED.—In this section, the term "critical infrastructure" means systems and assets, whether physical or virtual, so vital to the United States that the incapacity or destruction of such systems and assets would have a debilitating impact on security, national economic security, national public health or safety, or any combination of those matters.

(f) AUTHORIZATION OF APPROPRIATIONS.—There is hereby authorized for the Department of Defense for fiscal year 2002, $20,000,000 for the Defense Threat Reduction Agency for activities of the National Infrastructure Simulation and Analysis Center under this section in that fiscal year.

Approved October 26, 2001.

Source: Public Law 107-56 (2001)

Glossary of Common Legal Terms

acquittal A jury verdict that a criminal defendant is not guilty (i.e., beyond a reasonable doubt) or the finding of a judge that the evidence is insufficient to support a conviction.

activism (judicial) The willingness of a judge to inject into a case his or her own personal values about what is good and bad public policy. Activism is usually contrasted with judicial restraint or self-restraint.

actus reus The material element of the crime—that is, the guilty act—that may be manifested as the commission of a forbidden action (e.g., robbery) or as the failure to perform a required action (e.g., to stop and render aid to an accident victim).

admissible Evidence that may be properly considered by a jury or a judge in civil and criminal cases.

adversary process or proceeding The process used in courtrooms whereby the trial is seen as a battle between two opposing sides and the role of the judge is to act as a sort of passive referee. The adversary process or proceeding is contrasted with an inquisitorial method.

advisory opinion A decision on an abstract or hypothetical question, something that most American courts do not traditionally allow or admit.

affidavit A written or printed statement of facts or other testimony made under oath before a notary or officer having authority to administer oaths.

affirmed In a court of appeals, the formal conclusion that the lower court decision is correct and will stand as rendered by the lower court.

alternate juror A juror selected in the same manner as a regular juror who hears all the evidence but does not help decide the case unless called on to replace a regular juror.

alternative dispute resolution (ADR) A procedure for settling a dispute outside the courtroom, often with the help of neutral third parties, without a trial. Mediation and arbitration are two well-known ADR techniques.

amicus brief A brief filed on an advisory basis by a person, organization, or group who is not a party to the litigation. The term "amicus brief" is derived from the Latin term "amicus curiae," or "friend of the court."

amicus curiae Latin for "friend of the court." Amicus curiae is advice formally offered to the court in a brief filed by an entity interested in but not a party to the case.

answer The formal written statement by a defendant responding to a civil complaint and setting forth the grounds for his or her defense.

appeal A request made to a higher court after a trial by a party that has lost on one or more issues in which the higher court reviews the decision to determine if it was correct. The party who appeals is called the appellant; the other party is the appellee.

appellant The party who appeals a court's decision, usually seeking reversal of that decision.

appellate Concerned with appeals; an appellate court has the power to review the judgment of a lower court or tribunal.

appellate jurisdiction The authority of a higher court to review the decision of a lower court.

appellee The party who opposes an appellant's appeal.

arraignment A proceeding in which an individual who is accused of committing a crime is brought into court, told of the charges, and asked to plead guilty or not guilty.

Article III judge A federal judge who is appointed for life, during good behavior, under Article III of the Constitution. Article III judges are nominated by the president and confirmed by the Senate.

bail The amount of bond money or other security given for the release of a criminal defendant or witness from legal custody to secure his or her appearance on the day and time set by the court.

bankruptcy A legal process by which persons or businesses that cannot pay their debts can seek the assistance of the court to discharge the debts, usually by paying a portion of each debt.

bench trial A trial without a jury in which the judge serves as the fact finder and thus decides which party prevails.

bill of attainder A law that makes conduct illegal for one person (or class of persons) but not for the population in general. This sort of enactment is forbidden by the U.S. Constitution.

brief	A written statement submitted by each party in a trial or appellate proceeding that explains why the court should decide the case, or particular issues in a case, in that party's favor.
burden of proof	The duty to prove disputed facts. In civil cases, a plaintiff generally has the burden of proving his or her case. In criminal cases, the government has the burden of proving the defendant's guilt beyond a reasonable doubt (which is referred to as the standard of proof).
capital offense	A crime punishable by death.
case file	A complete collection of every document filed in court in a case.
case law	The law as established in previous written decisions of courts.
caseload	The number of cases handled by a judge or a court.
cause of action	A legal claim that is the basis of a lawsuit.
certiorari	The process by which a party to a case requests that the case be accepted for review by the U.S. Supreme Court.
chambers	The offices of a judge and his or her staff.
chief judge	In multiple-judge jurisdictions, the judge who has primary responsibility for the administration of a court; chief judgeships are typically determined by seniority.
civil law	The body of law that pertains to the relationship between one private citizen (or corporation) and another. Also, the term "civil law" may refer to the traditional European system of jurisprudence, originally largely inherited from the Roman system of law.
claim	A plaintiff's assertion in a civil complaint.
class action	A lawsuit in which one or more members of a large group, or class, of individuals or other entities sue on behalf of the entire class.
clerk of court	The court officer who oversees institutional functions, especially managing the flow of cases through the court, maintaining court records, handling financial and personnel matters, and providing other administrative support to the court.
collateral	Property that is promised as security for the satisfaction of a debt.
collegial courts	Courts having more than one judge and especially appellate courts that rely on panels of judges.
common law	The legal system that originated in English feudal traditions that was based on judicial precedents. Courts in the United

States, Canada, and Australia follow many of the principles of common law.

community service
An alternative to punishment. Usually a special condition the court imposes that requires an individual to donate work to a civic or nonprofit organization.

complaint
A written statement filed by the plaintiff that initiates a civil case stating the wrongs allegedly committed by the defendant and requesting relief from the court.

concurrent jurisdiction
A situation in which two courts have a legal right to hear the same case.

concurrent sentence
Prison terms for two or more offenses to be served at the same time rather than one after the other.

concurring opinion
An opinion by a member of a court that agrees with the result reached in a case but offers its own rationale for the decision.

consecutive sentence
Prison terms for two or more offenses to be served one after the other.

contract
An agreement between two or more persons that creates an obligation to do or not to do a particular thing for the exchange of something of value (i.e., an act in consideration of the exchange).

conviction
A judgment of guilt against a criminal defendant.

counsel
A term that may refer to the lawyers in a case or to their actual legal advice.

count
An allegation in an indictment or information charging a defendant with a crime.

court
A government entity authorized to resolve legal disputes.

court of appeals
A court that is higher than an ordinary trial court and has the function of reviewing or correcting the decisions of trial judges.

court-martial
A military trial conducted by military officers who serve as both judge and jury.

court reporter
A person who makes a record of what is said in court generally by using a stenographic machine, shorthand, or audio recording and who may then produce a transcript of the proceedings.

courtroom workgroup
The regular participants in the activities of a court. This group usually includes judges, prosecutors, and defense attorneys.

crime
An offense against the state punishable by fine, imprisonment, or death.

criminal law	The law that pertains to offenses against the state itself, actions that may be directed against a person but are deemed to be offensive to society as a whole.
cross-examination	The questions posed to a witness who has been called to the stand by the opposing attorney during a trial.
damages	Money that a defendant pays a plaintiff in a civil case if the plaintiff has won. Damages may be compensatory (for loss or injury) or punitive (to punish and deter future misconduct).
declaratory judgment	A judge's statement about someone's rights under a particular statute or constitutional provision.
de facto	Latin term meaning "in fact" or "actually" that refers to something that exists in fact but not as a matter of law.
default judgment	A judgment awarding a plaintiff the relief sought in the complaint because the defendant has failed to appear in court or otherwise respond to the complaint.
defendant	In a civil case, the person or organization against whom the plaintiff brings suit. In a criminal case, the person accused of the crime.
de jure	Latin for "in law." Something that exists by operation of law.
de novo	Latin, meaning "anew." A trial de novo is a completely new trial. When applied to an appellate review, de novo implies the appellate judges will give no deference to the trial judge's ruling.
deposition	An oral statement made before an officer authorized by law to administer oaths. Such statements are often taken to examine potential witnesses, to obtain discovery, or to be used later in trial.
discovery	Procedures used to obtain exchange or other disclosure of evidence before trial. Typical tools of discovery include depositions, interrogatories, and requests for documents.
dismissal with prejudice	Court action that prevents an identical lawsuit from being filed later.
dismissal without prejudice	Court action that allows a later refiling of a case.
dissenting opinion	An opinion by a member of a court that disagrees with the result reached in the case by the court.
diversity jurisdiction	The jurisdiction exercised by a federal court over cases involving parties from different states.

diversity of citizenship suit
A civil legal proceeding brought by a citizen of one state against a citizen of another state.

docket
A schedule of upcoming cases in a particular court or a log containing the history of each case that has been conducted.

due process
In criminal law, the constitutional guarantee that a defendant will receive a fair and impartial trial. In civil law, the legal rights of someone in an adverse action threatening liberty or property.

en banc
French term meaning "in the bench" or "as a full bench" that refers to court sessions with the entire membership of a court participating rather than the usual number of a hearing panel. U.S. circuit courts of appeal usually sit in panels of three judges, for example, but all the judges in the court may decide certain matters together at the request of one of the parties.

equity or equitable
Pertaining to civil suits in equity rather than in law (i.e., under common law). Federal courts have both legal and equitable power, but the distinction remains important since under equity rules, a judge is able to issue a remedy (such as an injunction) that will either prevent or cure a wrong.

evidence
Information presented in testimony or in documents that is used to persuade the fact finder (judge or jury) to decide the case in favor of one side or the other.

exclusionary rule
Legal doctrine rooted in the due process protections found in the Fourth and Fifth Amendments that holds that evidence obtained in violation of a criminal defendant's constitutional or statutory rights is not admissible at trial.

exculpatory evidence
Evidence indicating that a defendant did not commit the crime charged in the indictment.

ex parte
A legal proceeding brought before a court by one party only, without notice to or challenge by the other side.

ex post facto law
A law that declares conduct to be illegal after the conduct takes place. This sort of enactment is forbidden by the U.S. Constitution.

federal question
A legal complaint or case that involves a federal law or officials, the U.S. Constitution, or a treaty.

federal question jurisdiction
Jurisdiction given to federal courts in cases involving the interpretation and application of the U.S. Constitution, acts of Congress, federal officials, and treaties.

felony	A serious crime usually punishable by at least one year of imprisonment and usually in a penitentiary.
file	To place a paper in the official custody of the clerk of court to enter into the records of a case.
grand jury	A body of between 16 and 23 citizens who listen to evidence of criminal allegations, which is presented by the prosecutors, and determine whether there is probable cause to believe that an individual committed an offense.
habeas corpus	Latin phrase meaning "you have the body." A writ of habeas corpus generally is a judicial order forcing law enforcement authorities to produce a prisoner they are holding and to justify the prisoner's continued confinement.
hearsay	Evidence presented by a witness who did not see or hear the incident in question but learned about events from someone else. With some exceptions, hearsay generally is not admissible as evidence at trial.
home confinement	A special condition that the court imposes that requires an individual to remain at home, frequently while being electronically or otherwise monitored, except for certain approved activities such as work and medical appointments.
impeachment	The process of calling a witness's testimony into doubt during cross-examination. Alternately, impeachment is the constitutional process whereby the House of Representatives may impeach (accuse of misconduct) high officers of the federal government, who are then tried by the Senate; for example, this is the only way in which a federal judge may be removed from office.
in camera	Latin phrase meaning "in a chamber," that is, the judge's offices. Often used to refer to meetings conducted outside the presence of a jury and the public.
inculpatory evidence	Evidence indicating that a defendant did commit the crime.
indictment	The formal charge issued by a grand jury stating that there is enough evidence that the defendant committed the crime to justify having a trial.
in forma pauperis	Latin for "in the manner of a pauper," in forma pauperis is permitted by the court to a person to file a case without payment of the required court fees because the person cannot pay them.

information	A formal accusation by a government attorney that the defendant committed a misdemeanor. Also known as a bill of information, this is used in states that do not employ a grand jury.
injunction	A court order preventing one or more named parties from taking some action or compelling them to perform a specific act. A preliminary injunction often is issued to allow fact finding so that a judge can determine whether a permanent injunction is justified.
inquisitorial method	The procedure used in most European and Latin American courtrooms in which the judge and jury take an active role in the trial and the attorneys act only to aid and supplement the judicial inquiry. The inquisitorial method is contrasted with the adversarial process.
interrogatories	A form of discovery consisting of written questions to be answered in writing and under oath.
joint administration	A court-approved mechanism under which two or more cases can be administered together.
judge	An official of the judicial branch with authority to decide lawsuits brought before courts.
judgeship	The seat or employed position of judge. By statute, the U.S. Congress authorizes the number of federal judgeships for each district and appellate court.
judgment	The official decision of a court finally resolving the dispute between the parties to the lawsuit.
Judicial Conference of the United States	The policy-making entity for the federal court system. The nominal presiding officer is the chief justice of the United States.
judicial review	The traditionally accepted power of members of the judicial branch to declare acts of the executive and legislative branches unconstitutional.
jurisdiction	The legal authority of a court to hear and decide a certain type of case. The term "jurisdiction" is also used for venue, that is, the geographic area over which the court has territorial jurisdiction to decide cases.
jurisprudence	The study of legal philosophy and theory as well as the study of the legal system.
jury (trial)	The group of persons selected to hear the evidence in a trial and render a verdict on matters of fact.

jury instructions	A judge's directions to the jury before it begins deliberations regarding the factual questions that it must answer and the legal rules that it must apply.
justiciable or justiciability	A question of whether or not a judge ought to hear or refrain from hearing certain types of cases, often resting on whether the judge will be able to affect any change in the case or condition of the parties. The terms "justiciable" and "justiciability" differ from the term "jurisdiction," which pertains to the technical right of a judge to hear a case.
lawsuit	A legal action started by a plaintiff against a defendant.
litigation	A case, controversy, or lawsuit. Plaintiffs and defendants in lawsuits are called litigants.
magistrate	In many jurisdictions, including the federal courts, a magistrate is a judicial official to whom the accused is brought after the arrest. A magistrate often has the obligation during the first appearance of informing the accused of the charges against him or her and of his or her legal rights.
magistrate judge (U.S.)	A judicial officer of a federal district court who conducts initial proceedings in criminal cases, decides criminal misdemeanor cases, conducts many pretrial civil and criminal matters on behalf of district judges, and decides civil cases with the consent of the parties.
mandatory sentencing laws	Refers to statutes that require automatic jail time for a conviction for a particular crime, usually for a minimum period of time.
mens rea	The necessary mental element of a crime—the guilty mind—that indicated that the defendant intended to commit or was aware that he or she was committing a crime.
merit selection	A method of selecting judges in many states that requires the governor to make the appointment from a short list of names submitted by a special commission established for that purpose. After serving for a short period of time, the judge must run in a retention election.
misdemeanor	An offense punishable by one year of imprisonment or less, often in a city or county jail rather than a prison.
mistrial	An invalid trial, caused by fundamental error. When a mistrial is declared, the trial must start again with the selection of a new jury.

moot   Not subject to a court ruling because the controversy has not actually arisen or has ended.

motion   A request by a litigant to a judge for a decision on an issue relating to the case.

motion in limine   A pretrial motion requesting the court to prohibit the other side from presenting or even referring to evidence on matters said to be so highly prejudicial that no steps taken by the judge can prevent the jury from being unduly influenced.

nolo contendere   A Latin term meaning "no contest," nolo contendere is a plea by a criminal defendant in which he or she does not deny the facts of the case but claims that he or she has not committed any crime.

opinion   A judge's written explanation of the decision of the court. In appellate cases, only the majority opinion can serve as binding precedent in future cases.

oral argument   An opportunity for lawyers to summarize their position before the court and also to answer questions posed by the assembled judges.

original jurisdiction   The court that by law must be the first to hear a particular type of case.

overcharging   The process whereby a prosecutor charges a criminal defendant with crimes more serious than the facts warrant or multiple counts of a crime in order to obtain a more favorable plea bargain from the defendant's attorney.

oyez   A Norman French term meaning "hear ye," in some jurisdictions oyez call is still used to call a court session to order.

panel   In appellate cases, a panel is a group of judges (usually three) assigned to decide the case. Alternatively, in the jury selection process a panel is the group of potential jurors. Finally, a panel might refer to a list of attorneys who are both available and qualified to serve as court-appointed counsel for criminal defendants who cannot afford their own counsel.

parole   The release of an inmate after completing part of her or his sentence. When the parolee is released to the community, he or she is placed under the supervision of a probation officer. In the federal system, the Sentencing Reform Act of 1984 abolished parole in favor of a determinate (i.e., fixed) sentencing system in which the sentence is set by sentencing guidelines.

party   One of the litigants.

per curiam	Latin meaning "for the court," per curiam in appellate courts often refers to an unsigned opinion.
peremptory challenge	A district court may grant each side in a civil or criminal trial the right to exclude a certain number of prospective jurors without cause or giving a reason. The number of such challenges is limited by law.
petit jury (or trial jury)	A group of citizens who hear the evidence presented by both sides at trial and determine the facts in dispute. Federal criminal juries consist of 12 persons. Federal civil juries consist of at least 6 persons. Most states follow the federal example and rely on smaller juries in civil trials.
petty offense	A federal misdemeanor punishable by six months or less in prison.
plaintiff	A person or business that files a formal complaint with the court in a civil lawsuit.
plea	In a criminal case, the defendant's statement pleading guilty, not guilty, or nolo contendere in answer to the charges.
plea bargain	A bargain or deal that has been struck between the prosecutor and the defendant's attorney through which some form of leniency is offered in exchange for a guilty plea.
pleadings	Written statements filed with the court that describe a party's legal or factual assertions about the case.
precedent	A binding court decision in an earlier case with facts and legal issues similar to a dispute currently before a court. A judge will disregard precedent if a party can show that the earlier case was wrongly decided or that it differed in some significant way from the current case (known as distinguishing a case from the precedent).
presentence report	A report prepared by a court's probation officer, after a person has been convicted of an offense, summarizing for the court the background information needed to determine the appropriate sentence.
pretrial conference	A meeting of the judge and lawyers to plan the steps of a trial, to discuss which matters should be presented to the jury, to review proposed evidence and witnesses, and to set a trial schedule. Typically, the judge and the parties also discuss the possibility of settlement of the case.
private law	Law or legal processes that deal with the rights and obligations that private individuals or institutions owe to one another.

probation A sentencing alternative to imprisonment in which the court, instead of sending an individual to prison, may release the person to the community, ordering her or him to abide by certain conditions and to complete a period of supervision monitored by a probation officer.

probation officer Probation officer duties include conducting presentence investigations, preparing presentence reports on convicted defendants, and supervising released defendants.

pro bono publico A Latin meaning "for the public good," pro bono publico usually refers to legal representation undertaken without fee for some charitable or public purpose.

procedure The rules for conducting a lawsuit or criminal trial. For example, there are rules of civil procedure, criminal procedure, evidence, bankruptcy, and appellate procedure.

pro se A Latin term meaning "on one's own behalf," pro se refers to persons who present their own cases in trials, that is, without lawyers.

prosecute To charge someone with a crime and then try that person on the charge or charges.

public law The relationships that individuals have with the state, that is, with the government or fellow citizens as a collective body; for example, public law includes criminal laws that keep the public or social order.

record A written account of the proceedings in a case, including all pleadings, evidence, and exhibits submitted in the course of the case.

remand The act of an appellate court sending a case back to a lower court for further proceedings. The lower court then issues a new decision that conforms to the higher court's ruling.

reverse The act of an appellate court setting aside the decision of a trial court. A reversal is often accompanied by a remand to the lower court for further proceedings.

reversible error An error committed at the trial court level that is so serious that it requires the appellate court to reverse the decision of the trial judge.

Rule of 80 This refers to the practice of the federal courts that allow judges (who serve for life) to retire. When the sum of a federal judge's age and number of years on the bench is 80 years, the U.S. Congress permits the individual to retire with full pay and benefits.

Rule of Four	This refers to the practice of the U.S. Supreme Court that requires that at least four justices agree to take a case before the Court as a whole will consider it.
sanction	A penalty or other type of enforcement used to bring about compliance with the law or with rules and regulations.
self-restraint (judicial)	The reluctance of a judge to inject into a case his or her own personal ideas of what is good or bad public policy. This is often contrasted with judicial activism.
senior judge	A federal judge who after attaining the requisite age and length of judicial experience takes senior status, thus creating a vacancy among a court's active judges but maintaining a reduced schedule.
sentence	The punishment ordered by a court for a defendant convicted of a crime.
sentencing guidelines	A set of rules and principles established by the U.S. Sentencing Commission that federal trial judges use to determine the sentence for a convicted defendant.
sequester	The separation of juries from outside influences during their deliberations. In very important or notorious cases, the jury may be kept away from the press and the public by the judge.
service of process	The delivery of writs or summonses to the appropriate party.
settlement	The agreement by parties to a lawsuit who resolve their dispute without having a trial. Settlements often involve payment of compensation by one party in at least partial satisfaction of the other party's claims but usually do not include the admission of fault.
socialization (judicial)	The process by which a new judge is formally and informally trained to perform the specific tasks of the judgeship.
standard of proof	The degree of proof required in a particular variety of case. In criminal cases, prosecutors must prove a defendant's guilt beyond a reasonable doubt. The majority of civil lawsuits require proof by a preponderance of the evidence, but in some the standard is higher and requires clear and convincing proof.
standing	The status of someone who wishes to bring a lawsuit. To have standing, the person must have suffered (or be immediately about to suffer) a direct and significant injury.
stare decisis	A Latin term meaning to "stand by what has been decided," stare decisis is a legal doctrine that requires lower courts to

follow the precedents set by previous courts. In effect, stare decisis is the tradition of honoring and following previous decisions of the courts and established points of law.

statute of limitations
The time within which a lawsuit must be filed or a criminal prosecution begun. If the deadline passes, the statute of limitations has run, or tolled, and the party may be prohibited from bringing a lawsuit.

statutory law or statute
The type of law enacted by a legislative body, such as the U.S. Congress, a state legislature, or a city council. Statutory law is contrasted with regulations and also judge-made law observed under common law through judicial decisions.

sua sponte
A Latin term meaning "of its own will," sua sponte often refers to a court taking an action in a case without being asked to do so by either side.

subject matter jurisdiction
The jurisdiction of a court over the facts of a given case.

subpoena
A command, issued under a court's authority, to a witness to appear and give testimony.

subpoena duces tecum
A command to a witness to appear and produce documents.

summary judgment
A decision made on the basis of statements and evidence presented for the record without a trial.

supervised release
An alternative to imprisonment, meaning a term of supervision served after a person is released from prison. Unlike parole, supervised release does not replace a portion of the sentence of imprisonment but is in addition to the time spent in prison.

supplemental jurisdiction
The jurisdiction exercised by a federal court over a state-law case to help resolve all issues between the parties in one forum. This is also known as ancillary jurisdiction or pendent jurisdiction.

temporary restraining order
A judge's short-term order forbidding certain actions until a full hearing can be conducted and often referred to as a TRO. This differs from an injunction in that a TRO may be granted immediately without notice to the opposing party and without a hearing.

testimony
Evidence presented orally by witnesses during trials or before grand juries.

three-judge district courts
With some types of important cases, the U.S. Congress formerly mandated that the case cannot be heard by a federal district judge acting alone but instead has to be decided by a

panel of three judges, one of whom must be a circuit court judge. This is now reserved for certain voting rights cases.

three-judge panels (of appellate courts)	Refers to the fact that most decisions of the U.S. courts of appeal are not made by the entire court sitting together but instead by three judges, often selected at random, to hear any given case.
tort	A civil wrong, that is, an act that causes an injury but does not constitute a criminal act. Tort refers to a negligent or intentional injury against a person or property, with the exception of breach of contract.
transcript	A written word-for-word record of what was said, either in a proceeding such as a trial or during some other formal conversation such as a hearing or an oral deposition.
trustee	In a bankruptcy case, a person appointed to represent the interests of the bankruptcy estate and the unsecured creditors.
uphold	The affirmation or agreement by an appellate court with the lower court decision that allows the decision to stand.
U.S. attorney	A lawyer appointed by the president in each judicial district to prosecute and defend cases for the federal government. The U.S. attorney employs a staff of assistant U.S. attorneys who appear as the government's attorneys in individual cases.
venue	The geographic area in which a court has jurisdiction. A change of venue is a change or transfer of a case from one judicial district to another.
verdict	The decision of a trial jury or a judge that determines the guilt or innocence of a criminal defendant or that determines the final outcome of a civil case.
voir dire	A French phrase meaning "to speak the truth," voir dire is the process by which judges and lawyers select a trial jury from among those eligible to serve by questioning them to make certain that they would fairly decide the case.
warrant	A written order authorizing official action by law enforcement officials, usually directing them to arrest the individual named in the warrant. Also, a search warrant ordering that a specific location be searched for items that, if found, can be used in court as evidence.
witness	A person called upon by either side in a lawsuit to give testimony before the court or jury.

writ   A formal written command or order, issued by a court, requir-
                      ing the performance of a specific act.

writ of   An order issued by the U.S. Supreme Court directing the lower
certiorari   court to transmit records for a case that the Court will hear on
                      appeal.

writ of   A court order compelling a public official to perform his or her
mandamus   duty.

General Bibliography

Books and Articles

Adams, Willi Paul. *The First American Constitutions: Republican Ideology and the Making of the State Constitutions in the Revolutionary Era.* Lanham, MD: Rowman and Littlefield, 2001.

Amar, Akhil Reed. *America's Constitution: A Biography.* New York: Random House, 2005.

Bator, Paul M., Daniel J. Meltzer, Paul J. Mishkin, and David L. Shapiro. *Hart & Wechsler's The Federal Courts and the Federal System.* 3rd ed. Westbury, NY: Foundation Press, 1988.

Baum, Lawrence. *American Courts: Process and Policy.* 6th ed. Florence, KY: Wadsworth, 2007.

Belknap, Michal R. *Federal Law and the Southern Order: Racial Violence and the Constitutional Conflict in the Post-Brown South.* Athens: University of Georgia Press, 1995.

Calvi, James, and Susan Coleman. *American Law and Legal Systems.* 6th ed. Upper Saddle River, NJ: Prentice Hall, 2007.

Canon, Bradley C., and Charles A. Johnson. *Judicial Policies: Implementation and Impact.* 2nd ed. Washington, DC: CQ Press, 1998.

Carp, Robert A., Ronald Stidham, and Kenneth L. Manning. *Judicial Process in America.* 6th ed. Washington, DC: CQ Press, 2004.

Cooper, Phillip J. *Hard Judicial Choices: Federal District Court Judges and State and Local Officials.* New York: Oxford University Press, 1988.

Diascro, Jennifer Segal, and Gregg Ivers, eds. *Inside the Judicial Process: A Contemporary Reader in Law, Politics, and the Courts.* Florence, KY: Wadsworth, 2005.

DiIulio, John J., Jr., ed. *Courts, Corrections, and the Constitution: The Impact of Judicial Intervention on Prisons and Jails.* New York: Oxford University Press, 1990.

Doernberg, Donald L., C. Keith Wingate, and Donald H. Zeigler, eds. *Federal Courts, Federalism and Separation of Powers: Cases and Materials.* Eagan, MN: West Group, 2004.

Farhang, Sean. *The Litigation State: Public Regulation and Private Lawsuits in the United States.* Princeton, NJ: Princeton University Press, 2010.

Feeley, Malcolm M., and Edward L. Rubin. *Judicial Policy Making and the Modern State: How the Courts Reformed America's Prisons.* Cambridge: Cambridge University Press, 1998.

Friedman, Lawrence M. *American Law in the 20th Century.* New Haven, CT: Yale University Press, 2004.

Friedman, Lawrence M. *A History of American Law.* 3rd ed. New York: Touchstone, 2005.

Friedman, Lawrence M. *Crime and Punishment in American History.* New York: Basic Books, 1993.

Fuller, John Randolph. *Criminal Justice: Mainstream and Crosscurrents.* Upper Saddle River, NJ: Prentice Hall, 2005.

Geyh, Charles Gardner. *When Courts and Congress Collide: The Struggle for Control of America's Judicial System.* Ann Arbor: University of Michigan Press, 2006.

Hoffer, Peter Charles. *Law and People in Colonial America.* Rev. ed. Baltimore: Johns Hopkins University Press, 1998.

Hoffer, Peter Charles. *The Law's Conscience: Equitable Constitutionalism in America.* Chapel Hill: University of North Carolina Press, 1990.

Holmes, Oliver Wendell, Jr. *The Common Law.* 1881; reprint, New York: Dover, 1991.

Kruman, Marc W. *Between Authority and Liberty: State Constitution Making in Revolutionary America.* Chapel Hill: University of North Carolina Press, 1997.

Mezey, Susan Gluck. *In Pursuit of Equality: Women, Public Policy, and the Federal Courts.* New York: St. Martin's, 1992.

Monk, Linda R. *The Bill of Rights: A User's Guide.* 3rd ed. Alexandria, VA: Close Up, 2000.

Monk, Linda R. *The Words We Live By: Your Annotated Guide to the Constitution.* New York: Hyperion, 2003.

Neubauer, David W., and Henry F. Fradella. *America's Courts and the Criminal Justice System.* 10th ed. Florence, KY: Wadsworth, 2010.

Neubauer, David W., and Stephen Meinhold. *Judicial Process: Law, Courts, and Politics in the United States.* 4th ed. Florence, KY: Wadsworth, 2007.

O'Brien, David M. *Judges on Judging: Views from the Bench.* 3rd ed. Washington, DC: CQ Press, 2008.

Patterson, Dennis M. *Philosophy of Law and Legal Theory.* Oxford: Blackwell, 2002.

Patterson, James T. *Brown v. Board of Education: A Civil Rights Milestone and Its Troubled Legacy.* New York: Oxford University Press, 2001.

Posner, Richard A. *Frontiers of Legal Theory.* Cambridge: Harvard University Press, 2001.

Posner, Richard A. *How Judges Think.* Cambridge: Harvard University Press, 2008.

Posner, Richard A. *The Problems of Jurisprudence.* Cambridge: Harvard University Press, 1990.

Rachal, Patricia. *Federal Narcotics Enforcement: Reorganization and Reform.* Boston: Auburn House, 1982.

Rakove, Jack N. *Original Meanings: Politics and Ideas in the Making of the Constitution.* New York: Vintage Books, 1997.

Rosenberg, Gerald N. *The Hollow Hope: Can Courts Bring about Social Change?* 2nd ed. Chicago: University of Chicago Press, 2008.

Saari, David J. *American Court Management: Theories and Practices.* Westport, CT: Quorum Books, 1982.

Scheb, John M., and John M. Scheb II. *Introduction to the American Legal System.* 2nd ed. Frederick, MD: Aspen Publishers, 2009.

Scheingold, Stuart, and Austin Sarat. *Something to Believe In: Politics, Professionalism, and Cause Lawyering.* Palo Alto, CA: Stanford University Press, 2004.

Sinclair, Barbara. *Unorthodox Lawmaking: New Legislative Processes in the U.S. Congress.* Washington, DC: CQ Press, 2000.

Subrin, Stephen N., Martha L. Minow, Mark S. Brodin, and Thomas O. Main. *Civil Procedure: Doctrine, Practice, and Context.* Frederick, MD: Aspen Publishers, 2004.

Tocqueville, Alexis de. *Democracy in America.* Edited by Phillips Bradley. 2 vols. New York: Vintage Books, 1990.

Tushnet, Mark. *The NAACP's Strategy against Segregated Education 1925–1950.* Chapel Hill: University of North Carolina Press, 1987.

Walker, Samuel. *Popular Justice: A History of American Criminal Justice.* New York: Oxford University Press, 1980.

Wheeler, Russell, and Cynthia Harrison. *Creating the Federal Judicial System.* 3rd ed. Washington, DC: Federal Judicial Center, 2005.

Yeazell, Stephen. *Civil Procedure*. 7th ed. Frederick, MD: Aspen Publishers 2008.

Internet-Based Resources

American Bar Association, National Conference of Specialized Court Judges, Judicial Division. www.abanet.org/jd/ncscj/home.html.

American Bar Association, Women and the Law. http://www.americanbar.org/groups/women/events_cle.html.

American Law Sources On-line. http://www.lawsource.com/also/usa.cgi?us1.

Avalon Project, Documents of Law, History, and Diplomacy (Yale Law School). http://avalon.law.yale.edu/.

Crime and Criminal Law. http://law.jrank.org/collection/46/Crime-Criminal-Law.html.

Environmental Law Institute. http://www.eli.org/.

The Founders Constitution. (Anthology of sources on the ratification of the U.S. Constitution, edited by Philip B. Kurland and Ralph Lerner). http://press-pubs.uchicago.edu/founders/.

Federal Judicial Center. www.fjc.gov/.

FindLaw. www.findlaw.com/.

FindLaw for Legal Professionals. http://www.findlaw.com/casecode/constitution/.

Great American Court Cases. http://law.jrank.org/collection/192/Great-American-Court-Cases.html.

"History of the Federal Judiciary." Federal Judicial Center, http://www.fjc.gov/history/home.nsf.

Legal Information Institute (Cornell University Law School). http://topics.law.cornell.edu/wex/.

National Archives, Bill of Rights. http://www.archives.gov/exhibits/charters/bill_of_rights_transcript.html.

National Center for State Courts. www.ncsconline.org.

National Judicial College. www.judges.org.

Perspectives on Criminal Justice. http://www.360degrees.org/.

U.S. Courts (District and Circuit Links). www.uscourts.gov/links.html.

U.S. Department of Justice. http://www.justice.gov/.

U.S. Department of Justice, Bureau of Justice Statistics. http://bjs.ojp.usdoj.gov/.

U.S. Department of Justice, Federal Bureau of Investigation. http://www.fbi.gov/.

U.S. Department of Justice, Office of Juvenile Justice and Delinquency Prevention. http://www.ojjdp.gov/.

U.S. Government Printing Office, Analysis and Interpretation of the U.S. Constitution. http://www.gpoaccess.gov/constitution/index.html.

U.S. Supreme Court of the United States. www.supremecourtus.gov/.

U.S. Supreme Court Arguments and More, The OYEZ Project. www.oyez.org/oyez/frontpage.

Editor and Contributors

Editor

Steven Harmon Wilson is associate dean of liberal arts at Tulsa Community College's Metro Campus. From 2003 to 2006 he was associate professor of history at Prairie View A&M University in Texas. Wilson received his MA and PhD in history from Rice University, where he focused on American legal and constitutional history. He previously earned a BS in electrical engineering at Rice and, before becoming a historian, worked at the National Security Agency and at NASA.

Dr. Wilson is the author of *The Rise of Judicial Management in the U.S. District Court, Southern District of Texas, 1955–2000* (University of Georgia, 2003); "Some Are Born White, Some Achieve Whiteness, and Some Have Whiteness Thrust Upon Them: Mexican Americans and the Politics of Racial Classification in the Federal Judicial Bureaucracy, Twenty-Five Years after *Hernández v. Texas,*" in *"Colored Men and Hombres Aqui": Hernández v. Texas and the Emergence of Mexican American Lawyering,* edited by Michael A. Olivas (Arte Publico, 2006); and "Brown over 'Other White': Mexican Americans' Legal Arguments and Litigation Strategy in Desegregation Litigation" (*Law & History Review,* March 2003).

Contributors

Cassie Adams-Walls
West Central Technical College
Carrollton, Georgia

David Belden
Purdue University Calumet
Hammond, Indiana

Roberta Sue Alexander
University of Dayton
Dayton, Ohio

Sara Benesh
University of Wisconsin–Milwaukee
Milwaukee, Wisconsin

Ryan K. Baggett
Eastern Kentucky University
Richmond, Kentucky

Danton Asher Berube
Yale University
New Haven, Connecticut

Robert M. Bohm
University of Central Florida
Orlando, Florida

Martin Carcieri
University of Tennessee
Knoxville, Tennessee

Chaya Chandrasekaran
University of Tennessee
Knoxville, Tennessee

Kelly K. Chaves
University of New Brunswick
Fredericton, New Brunswick, Canada

Jason A. Checque
Erie, Pennsylvania

Keith A. Clark
University of North Carolina at
    Wilmington
Wilmington, North Carolina

Tom Clark
Princeton University
Princeton, New Jersey

Keith Clement
University of West Florida
Penasacola, Florida

Charles D. Cole
Samford University
Birmingham, Alabama

Pamela A. Collins
Eastern Kentucky University
Richmond, Kentucky

Amanda Harmon Cooley
South Texas College of Law
Houston, Texas

James V. Cornehls
University of Texas–Arlington
Arlington, Texas

Nancy Cornwell
Linfield College
McMinnville, Oregon

Dennis J. Coyle
Catholic University of America
Washington, D.C.

Malori Dahmen
Attorney at Law
Oklahoma City, Oklahoma

Mathieu Deflem
University of South Carolina
Columbia, South Carolina

Timothy Dixon
Nova Southeastern University
Fort Lauderdale, Florida

Rachael Drenovsky
Michigan Supreme Court
Lansing, Michigan

Darius V. Echeverría
Rutgers University
Piscataway, New Jersey

Jeff Ewen
Warren County Community
    College
Washington, New Jersey

Giuseppe Fazari
Superior Court of New Jersey–Essex
    Vicinage
Newark, New Jersey

R. Fernández-Calienes
St. Thomas University School of Law
Miami Gardens, Florida

James A. Gardner
Western New England College
Springfield, Massachusetts

Richard Glenn
Millersville University
Millersville, Pennsylvania

Sheldon Goldman
University of Massachusetts
Amherst, Massachusetts

Lino A. Graglia
University of Texas School of Law
Austin, Texas

Jo-Ann Della Giustina
John Jay College
New York, New York

Kenneth Einar Himma
Seattle Pacific University
Seattle, Washington

Alyssa Honnette
Rice University
Houston, Texas

Ronald J. Hrebenar
University of Utah
Salt Lake City, Utah

Kyle Irwin
University of South Carolina
Columbia, South Carolina

Katariina Rosenblatt Juliao
Nova Southeastern University
Fort Lauderdale, Florida

Peter T. Kelly
St. Thomas University
Miami Gardens, Florida

George Kiser
Illinois State University
Normal, Illinois

Helen J. Knowles
State University of New York at Oswego
Oswego, New York

David Lawson
Attorney at Law
Tulsa, Oklahoma

William Lyons
University of Tennessee
Knoxville, Tennessee

Thomas Maxwell-Long
California State University, San
    Bernardino
San Bernardino, California

Susan Gluck Mezey
Loyola University
Chicago, Illinois

Chris Miller
Attorney at Law
Tulsa, Oklahoma

Patit Paban Mishra
Sambalpur University
Sambalpur, India

Sarah Miller
University of Toledo
Toledo, Ohio

Matthew Muraskin
Long Island, New York

Roslyn Muraskin
C. W. Post Campus, Long Island
    University
Brookville, New York

Lorraine P. Nertney
Florida Court of Appeal, Second
    District
Tampa, Florida

Steve Russell
Indiana University
Bloomington, Indiana

Kathryn E. Scarborough
Eastern Kentucky University
Richmond, Kentucky

Honarable John M. Scheb
Florida Court of Appeal, Second
    District (Ret.)
Sarasota, Florida

John M. Scheb II
University of Tennessee
Knoxville, Tennessee

Julia Selman-Ayetey
Anglia Ruskin University
Cambridge, United Kingdom

Michael Shally-Jensen
Amherst, Massachusetts

Matthew Shannon
Temple University
Philadelphia, Pennsylvania

Melissa Stallings
ABC-CLIO
Santa Barbara, California

Jack Stark
Fitchburg, Wisconsin

Glenn L. Starks
Defense Logistics Agency
Richmond, Virginia

Otis H. Stephens Jr.
University of Tennessee
Knoxville, Tennessee

Dwight L. Teeter Jr.
University of Tennessee
Knoxville, Tennessee

Theodore M. Vestal
Oklahoma State University
Stillwater, Oklahoma

John R. Vile
Middle Tennessee State University
Murfreesboro, Tennessee

Andrew J. Waskey
Dalton State University
Dalton, Georgia

William Whyte
East Stroudsburg University
Nazareth, Pennsylvania

Charles L. Zelden
Nova Southeastern University
Fort Lauderdale, Florida

Index

Abington School District v. Schemp, 681, 682

Abolitionists, 842

Abortion, 439–442, 451, 630, 644, 650, 653, 668, 1058

Abortion law, 668–669

Abortion rights, 171

Abourezk, James, 411

Abrams v. United States, 550

Absolute immunity, 554

Accomodationists, 518

An Act for the Gradual Abolition of Slavery, March 1, 1780, 770–775

An Act Relating to Civil Unions, 2000, 1145–1173

Activism. *See* judicial activism

Activist court, 452

Activist judges, 295, 495

Actual damages, 261

Adams, John, 13, 15–16, 18, 20, 21–22, 23, 26, 33, 64, 91, 583, 612, 797, 800

Adams, Samuel, 15, 22, 33, 419

Adarand Constructors, Inc. v. Peña, 403, 696

Adequacy, 249

Adjudication, 389

Adjudicatory hearing, 591

Adjunct tribunals, 107

Adler v. Board of Education, 1023

Administrative and bureaucratic support for the federal judiciary, 107–109; Administrative Office of the U.S. Courts, 109; Federal Judicial Center (FJC), 109; Judicial Conference of the United States, 108–109

Administrative bureaucracy, 198

Administrative judges, 121

Administrative law, additional sources of: appellate court decisions, 205; executive orders and proclamations, 204; legislative intent, 204–205; United States Statutes at Large *and* United States Code, 204; U.S. Constitution, 204

Administrative law, bureaucracies, and regulatory enforcement: about, 191–193; administrative law judge (ALJ), 205–211; Administrative Procedure Act, 197–205; federal bureaucracy, 193–197; oversight, reform, and reduction of the bureaucracy, 215–223; state administrative law, 211–215

Administrative law cases, 200

Administrative law judges (ALJ), 150, 192; about, 389; administrative law judges and the administrative procedure act, 390; appealing an adjudication, 208–210; federal agencies with administrative law judges, 210–211; limitations, 206–207; professional organizations, 207; role of the administrative law judge, 205–207; selection and retention, 390–391

Administrative law process and procedure projct, 222

Administrative Office of the United States Courts, 391–395, 947

Administrative Office of the United States Courts, Office of the Director, 395–396

Administrative Office of the U.S. Courts establishment, 1939, 947–952

Administrative Procedure Act (APA), 192, 201, 202, 207, 390, 391; about, 197–198; additional sources of administrative law, 204–205; amendments, 217;

Administrative Procedure Act (*Cont.*) enforcement of federal rules and regulations, 201–202; publication of administrative rules and regulations, 202–203; purposes of, 199; rule making versus adjudication, 199–202; Section 10, 207

Administrative Rules Review Committee, 213

Admiralty and maritime law, 396–399. *See also* U.S. district courts

Admiralty cases, 74

Admiralty law, 106

Adoption, 643–644

Adventures of Huckleberry Finn (Twain), 437

Adversary system, 399–400. *See also* jury systems

Adverse litigants, 400–401. *See also* adversary system; equity

Advertising campaigns, 571

Advisory opinions, 65, 173, 400, 401–402. *See also* checks and balances

Affirm (action), 96

Affirmative action, 274, 402–403, 445, 446, 573, 575. *See also* civil liberties; civil rights; constitutional interpretation; disparate impact

African Americans: affirmative action scrutiny, 575; citizenship, 92, 450; civil rights, 598; civil rights legislation, 984; equal protection clause, 575; federal protection of equal access, 280; harassment of, 279; Jim Crow laws, 515, 856; juvenile justice system, 593; newly freed, 859; Paxton case, 13; racial segregation, 268; racially restrictive covenants, 685; restoration of housing covenants, 445; rights and privileged of social contact, 866; school children, 270–271; school segregation, 980; segregated education, 164; segregation, 856; Supreme Court justice, 270; union segregation, 724; voter registration, 1025; voters, 445; voting rights, 548, 727

Agencies: enabling statute, 209; legal guidance, 204

Agency (definition), 199

Agricultural Adjustment Act of 1938, 577

Aikman, A. B., 431

Alexander, James, 12, 743

Alexander v. Holmes, 445

Alien Act (1798), 797

Alien and Sedition Acts (1798), 797–799

Alien Enemies Act (1798), 797

Allgeyer v. Louisiana, 915

Almeida-Sanchez v. United States, 427

Alternative dispute resolution (ADR), 222, 225; about, 263–264; arbitration, 264–265; mediation, 264; minitrial, 265; neutral fact finding, 265; private judging, 265–266; summary jury trial, 265

Amendment process, 170, 404–405. *See also* bill of rights

Amendment ratification, 31

Amendments, 50

Amerasia (journal), 616

American Association of Retired Persons (AARP), 572

American Bar Association (ABA), 70, 587

American Civil Liberties Union (ACLU), 99, 597–598, 638, 682

American Civil War (Holmes), 549

American Common law vs. English common law, 117

American Communist Party, 495

American Federation of Labor-Congress of Industrial Unions (AFL/CIO), 725

American G.I. Forum, 538

American Indian Movement (AIM), 598

American Indians, 142, 715–719; courts of the federal territories and tribal governments of the United States, 143–144; federal government policies towards, 903; judicial branch of the Navajo Nation, 143–144; land allocation, 877; Navajo common law, 144; sovereignty, 718; tribal authority, 877

American Insurance Company v. Canter, 106–107

American Law Institute (ALL), 119, 212

American Law Review, 550

American legal system vs. British legal system, 151–152

American Legislative Exchange Council, 219

American Medical Association (AMA), 290–291

American Scripture: Making the Declaration of Independence, (Maier), 17

American State Government: about, 114–115; Americanization of common law, 117–118; codification of state laws, 118–119; executive branch, 115; judicial branch, 115–117; legislative branch, 115

An American Tragedy (Dreiser), 635

American United for Separation of Church and State, 682

American veterans (AMVETS), 405–406. *See also* interest groups and lobbying

"America's Vanishing Wilderness" (*Ladies Home Journal*), 496

Amicus curiae, 68, 93, 100, 269, 698

Amount-in controversy standard, 75

Analytical positivism, 160

Ancillary powers of courts: case-flow management, 182; power over process, 183; referees, magistrates, and masters, 182–183

Annapolis Convention, 25

Annual Report of the Director of the Administrative Office of the United States Courts, 282

Anslinger, Harry, 499

Answer: affirmative defense, 238; amendments during and after trial, 240; counterclaim, 238–239; cross-claim, 239; demurrer, 237–238; impleader, 239–240

Anthony, Susan B., 864

Anti-Arab discrimination, 411

Anti-Drug Abuse Act of 1986, 503

Anti-Federalists, 32, 33

Antigovernment speech, 436

Anti-Muslim discrimination, 411

Anti-Okie Law, 577

Antiriot Act, 596

Antiterrorism and Effective Death Penalty Act of 1996, 106, 542

Antitrust laws, 887, 907

Anti-war movement, 529

Anti-war speech, 435

Apodaca v. Oregon, 124

Appealing an adjudication: chevron doctrine, 209–210; judicial review under the administrative procedure act, 208; jurisdiction, exhaustion, ripeness, and mootness, 208–209; standard of judicial review, 209

Appellant, 86, 407

Appellate courts, 116, 406–411, 862, jury system; federal, 408–409; state, 409–411. *See also* judicial review

Appellate jurisdiction, 30, 74, 89, 916

Appellate process: about, 183–184; limitations on judicial power, 185–187; standards of appellate review, 184–185

Appellee, 86

Applicant, 249

Apportionment, 506

Arab-American Anti-Discrimination Committee (ADC), 411–412. *See also* civil liberties; civil rights

Arbitrary and capricious test, 184, 209, 407

Arcara v. Cloud Books, Inc., 638

Argesinger v. Hamlin, 657, 557

Arizona v. Evans, 535

Armed Services Committee, 45

Army-McCarthy hearings, 617

Arrest warrants: apprehensions, wants, and alarms, 331; arrests without a warrant, 330–331; misdemeanor arrests, 331–332

Arrests: about, 329–330; arrest warrants, 330–336; interrogation procedures, 332–333; *Miranda* exceptions, 334; *Miranda* triggers, 333–334; police discretion, 332

Arthur, Chester A., 873

Article I courts, 73, 77, 96, 97

Article I courts of specific jurisdiction: U.S. Alien Terrorist Removal Court (ATRC), 106; U.S. Bankruptcy Courts, 104–105; U.S. Court of Appeals for the Armed Forces (CAAF), 103–104; U.S. Court of Appeals for Veterans Claims (CAVC), 102; U.S. Court of Federal Claims (CFC), 101–102; U.S. Tax Court, 105

Article I judges, 107, 206, 608

Article I legislative courts, 77

Article I tribunals, 107

Article III constitutional courts, 77

Article III courts, 73, 77, 96, 107, 777

Article III courts of specific or limited jurisdiction: U.S. Court of Appeals for the Federal Circuit (CAFC), 98–99; U.S. Court of International Trade (CIT), 96–98; U.S. Foreign Intelligence Surveillance Court (FISC), 99–100; U.S. Foreign Intelligence Surveillance Court of Review (FISCR), 100–101
Article III judges, 80, 90, 107, 206, 207, 389, 608
Article III of the Constitution of the United States of America (1787), 777–789
Article III power, 107
Article III tribunals, 107
Articles of Confederation, 8, 19, 20, 25, 34, 62, 404, 438, 762–770
Articles of War, 720, 721
Arver v. United States, 961
Ashcroft, John, 1173
Ashcroft v. Free Speech Coalition, 640
Assistant majority leader (whip), 44
Atkins v. Virginia, 465, 475
Atomic secrets, 617
Attainders, bills of. *See* bills of attainder
Austin, Benjamin, 557, 656
Austin, John, 160
Automatic stay provision, 287

Bailey, Francis Lee, Jr., 413–415. *See also* adversary system; jury systems
Baker v. Carr, 186, 415–418
Baker v. State, 1146, 1147
Baker v. Vermont, 1145
Bankruptcy Act of 1898, 104
Bankruptcy Act of 1978, 104
Bankruptcy Amendments and Federal Judgeship Act of 1984, 105
Bankruptcy Code: Chapter 7, 104; Chapter 11, 104
Bankruptcy court, 74
Bankruptcy judges, 66
Bankruptcy Reform Act of 1978, 1075
Banks, Dennis, 598
Barker v. Wingo, 690
Barnes v. Glen Theatre, Inc., 637, 648
Barristers, 424
Barrows v. Jackson, 1023

Beecher v. Wetherby, 904
Bell v. Hood, 423
Bell v. Ohio, 473
Bellotti v. Baird, 441, 644
Bench trial, 80, 177, 178
Benefit of clergy, 16
Bentham, Jeremy, 162, 666, 703
Bentley, Elizabeth, 616
Benton v. Maryland, 492, 493
Berea College v. Kentucky, 548
Berger v. New York, 508
Berman v. Parker, 707
Berry, Jeffrey, 572
Betts v. Brady, 657
Between Authority and Liberty: State Constitution Making in Revolutionary America (Kruman), 24
"Beyond the Wall" (Neem), 523
Bicameral legislature, 23, 115
Bicameralism, 221
Big Tucker Act (1887), 101
Bill designation system, 49
Bill of Rights, 33, 42, 62, 78, 155, 180, 273, 404, 418–420, 427, 495, 618, 634, 647, 652, 706. *See also* common law; cruel and unusual punishment; double jeopardy; search warrants; separation of church and state; speedy trial, right to
The Bill of Rights (Hand), 546
Bills of attainder, 28, 420–422. *See also* cruel and unusual punishment
Bi-Metallic Investment Co. v. State Board of Equalization, 200
Binding precedent, 150
Bivens v. Six Unknown Named Federal Narcotics Agents, 422–423, 428
Black, Hugo, 181, 274, 495, 513, 518, 523, 577, 651, 677, 681
Black Codes of Mississippi, 1865, 856–859
Black market, 565
BlackBerry, 560, 561
Black-letter law, 483
Blacklists, 617
Blackmun, Harry, 496, 508–509, 643, 650, 669, 670, 671, 695, 1058
Black's Law Dictionary, 561, 562, 563, 565

Blackstone, William, 11, 423–426, 454, 493, 630, 647. *See also* admiralty and maritime law
Blakely v. Washington, 124
Board of Education v. Barnette, 1024
Board of General Appraisers, 97
Board of Trustees v. Garrett, 581
Board of Veterans' Appeals, 102
Boggs Amendment, 502
Bolling v. Sharpe, 271, 515
Bolshevik Revolution, 662
Bolshevism, 663, 664
Boos v. Barry, 714
Bordenkircher v. Hayes, 646
Border searches, 427–429. *See also* drugs and controlled substances; search warrants; war on drugs
Boreman, Linda, 605–606
Bork, Robert, 596, 737
Boroughs, 117
Boston Massacre, 15, 16
Boston strangler, 413
Boston Tea Party, 16
Bowdoin, James, 22
Bowers v. Hardwick, 581, 601, 602, 603, 648, 653, 698
Boyd v. United States, 1024, 1061
Braden v. 30th Judicial Circuit Court of Kentucky, 544
Bradford, William, 469
Bradley, Richard, 743
Bradley v. State, 491
Bradwell, Myra, 864
Bradwell v. Illinois, 864
Branch Dividians, 530
Brandeis, Louis D., 163–164, 494, 507, 508, 649, 912
Brandeis brief, 164
Brandenburg v. Ohio, 546
Brattle, William, 16
Breard v. Alexandria, 1024
Brecht v. Abrahamson, 542
Brennan, William J., Jr., 416, 423, 451, 513, 635, 669, 682, 692, 708, 711, 714
British legal system vs. American legal system, 151–152
Brooks v. United States, 957

Brown, H. Rap, 598
Brown, Linda, 269, 270
Brown, Nicole, 492
Brown v. Board of Education (1954), 4, 5, 164, 180, 226, 268, 269–270, 271, 272, 275–276, 278, 285, 290, 294, 296, 402, 418, 445, 452, 515, 577, 650, 686, 973–977, 980
Brown v. Board of Education II (1955), 180, 270, 977–979
Brutus (pen name), 33
Bulger, James, 704
Bureau of Alcohol, Tobacco, Firearms and Explosives, 60
Bureau of Drug Abuse, 502
Bureau of Investigation, 663, 665
Bureau of Narcotics, 502
Bureau of Narcotics and Dangerous Drugs (BNDD), 502
Bureaucratic expansion, 193
Burger, Warren E., 446, 512, 513, 515, 602, 643, 669, 672, 692
Burger court, 637
Burlington Northern v. U.S., 698
Burnett v. Coronado Oil Co., 649
Burnside, Ambrose, 627
Burr, Aaron, 579
Burstyn v. Wilson, 635
Bush, George H. W., 218, 692
Bush, George W., 41, 99, 216–217, 219, 492, 1119
Bush v. Gore, 516, 1119–1127
Bush v. Palm Beach County Canvassing Board, 1119
Business necessity, 478
Butler, John, 519
Butterfield, Alexander, 632, 688, 736, 737
Butz v. Economou, 207, 391

Cabinet, 53, 58
Cabinet departments, 58–59
Cabinet members, 58–59
Cabinet rank positions, 59
Cable Television Consumer Protection and Competition Act of 1992, 639
Calder v. Bull, 524–525
Calhoun, John C., 840

California Criminal Syndicalism Act, 740

Campaign Against Marijuana Production (CAMP), 500

Canadian-U.S. Free Trade Agreement (1988), 97

Capital murder, 473. *See also* murder

Capital punishment, 124, 130–131, 465–466, 469, 471, 474, 476

Cardozo, Benjamin, 165, 536

Carmichael, Stokely, 598

Carriage of Goods by Sea Act (COGSA), 397

Carrington, Paul D., 454

Carrington v. Rash, 1112

Carson, Rachel, 496

Carter, Jimmy, 217, 500, 501, 539

Case flow, 430

Case in chief, 259

Case law, 150; on agency activity, 205; nomenclature, 227

Case loads, 90

Case method, 161

Case-flow management, 430–435; management challenges, 432–434; management strategies, 431–432. *See also* jury systems

Caseload crisis, 446

Cases of first impression, 129, 410

Casey, P., 431

Categories of crime: consensual crimes, 304–305; conventional crimes, 303–304; economic crimes, 304; organized crime, 304; political crimes, 304

Catholic Archdiocese of Portland, 277–278

Cato's Letters (Gordon), 743

Cause challenges, 585

Cause lawyering and the public interest: about, 287–288; public interest groups, 288–292; public interest law firms, 293–294

Cellular telephones, 509

Censorship, 435–438, 635, 637, 639; of broadcasting, 436; wartime, 437. *See also* obscenity; pornography

Census, 41

Central Intelligence Agency, 56, 195

Central panel agency, 213

Certiorai petition, 130, 512. *See also* grant certiorari (or grant cert); writ of certiorari

Chadha, Jagdish Rai, 220–221

Chadha Decision, 221

Chain of custody, 487

Chambers, Whittaker, 616

Chambers Handbook for Judges' Law Clerks and Secretaries (FLC), 532

Chancery court, 153, 517

Changing Times in Trial Courts (Mahoney, Aikman, Casey, Flango, Gallas, Henderson, Ito, Steelman and Weller), 431

Chapter XV, 392, 948–952

Charles River Bridge v. Warren Bridge, 695

Chase, Samuel, 69

Chavez, Caesar, 725

Chayes, Abram, 268, 295

Checkerboarding, 717

Checks and balances, 22, 33, 42, 296, 438–439, 451, 568. *See also* Bill of Rights; judicial review

Cherokee Nation v. Georgia, 904

Cherokee Nation v. Hitchcock, 906

Chevron doctrine, 210

Chevron two-step test, 210

Chevron U.S.A., Inc. v. Natural Resources Defense Council, Inc., 209

Chicago, Burlington and Quincy Railway v. Chicago, 706

Chicago Seven, 598

Chicano Movement, 539

Chief judge, 66, 121

Chief justice, 29

Chief justice of court of last resort (COLR), 117

Child labor, 550

Child Online Protection Act (1998), 640

Child pornography, 636, 639

Child Pornography Prevention Act of 1996, 640

Children's Internet Protection Act of 2000, 640

China, 613, 614, 617

Chinese Exclusion Act of 1882, 873–877

Chinese Exclusion Act of 1888, 609

Chinese immigrants, 873

Chisholm v. Georgia, 64, 90, 91
Choctaw Nation v. United States, 906
Church, William C., 627
Church and state, 519
Church and state, separation of. *See* separation of church and state
Cicero, 630
Circuit court for California, 847
Circuit Court for California establishment, 1855, 847–850
Circuit courts, 120, 916
Circuit courts of appeals, 923
Circuit judges, 88, 108, 408, 609, 802, 803, 810, 815, 854, 862, 863. *See also* Judiciary Act of 1869 (Circuit Judges Act)
Citizens United v. Federal Election Commission, 571
Citizenship jurisdiction, 481
Citizenship of businesses, 481
City of Akron v. Akron Center for Reproductive Health, 439–443
City of Cleburne v. Cleburne Living Center, Inc., 662
City of Los Angeles v. Lyons, 282
City of Renton v. Playtime Theatres, Inc, 637
Civil action (lawsuit), 229, 233
Civil appellate review, 130
Civil cases, 226
Civil Discovery Act, 230, 250
Civil disobedience, 443–444. *See also* natural law and natural rights
Civil Disobedience (Thoreau), 443
Civil justice system and civil procedure in the united states, 225–266; about, 225–227; alternative dispute resolution, 263–266; pretrial procedures, 232–253; rules of civil procedure, 227–232; trial proceedings, 253–263
Civil law tradition, 118
Civil law vs. criminal law, 150
Civil lawsuits, 79–80
Civil liberties, 171, 186, 486, 495, 552, 615, 665
Civil liberties organizations, 100
Civil proceedings vs. criminal proceedings, 226

Civil rights, 171, 181, 186, 445, 537
Civil Rights Act of 1866, 280, 609, 859–861
Civil Rights Act of 1871, 280, 423, 554
Civil Rights Act of 1875 [Excerpt], 866–867
Civil Rights Act of 1964, 279, 294, 402, 403, 475, 686, 984–1021; commission on civil rights, 995–1000; desegregation of public education, 992–995; desegregation of public facilities, 991–992; equal employment opportunity, 1001–1017; injunctive relief against discrimination in places of public accommodation, 986–991; nondiscrimination in federally assisted programs, 1000–1001; registration and voting statistics, 1018–1021; Title IV, 271; Title VI, 271–272; Title VII, 274, 293; voting rights, 984–986
Civil Rights Act of 1991, 475
Civil rights and civil liberties, 444–446. *See also* affirmative action; civil disobedience; interest groups and lobbying; judicial activism
Civil Rights Attorney's Fees Awards Act of 1976, 262, 293
Civil rights cases, 280, 446, 548
Civil rights cases against state officials: Section 1983 actions, 280–282; sovereign immunity and damages, 284–285; sovereign immunity and *ex parte Young*, 282–284; Three-Judge Court Act, 285
Civil rights claims, 122
Civil unions, 1145
Civil War, 43, 51, 60, 71, 179, 547, 850
Civilian detentions, 179
Claimant, 227
Claims, court of. *See* court of claims
Clark, Tom, 199, 416, 417, 508, 534, 621
Clark, William, 580
Clarke v. Deckebach, 966
Class Action Fairness Act of 2005, 249, 262, 276, 278
Class actions, 232, 268, 270
Class certification, 276, 277
Class-action litigation, 122, 155

Classifications, 661, 696, 697
Clay, Henry, 840
Clean Air Act, 191, 209
Clean Water Act, 191
Clear and present danger, 495
Cleared for the Approach (Bailey), 414
Clearly erroneous standard, 407, 408
Cleland, John, 636
Clerk of the court, 122, 129
Clinton, Bill, 218, 219, 500, 539, 692
Clinton, Hillary Rodham, 692
Clinton v. City of New York, 54
Closed-circuit television (CCTV), 701
Code of Civil Procedure, 156
Code of Federal Regulations, 202–203
Code of Hammurabi, 666
Code pleading, 233
Coercion, 621, 623
Coercive Acts, 16
Coffee, Linda, 669
Cohen, Felix, 165
Coke, Edward, 160
Coker v. Georgia, 465, 473
Coker v. Georgia and Eberheart v. Georgia, 473
Colegrove v. Green, 416, 417
Colonial charters, 9
Colson, Charles, 689
Com. v. Hamilton Mfg. Co., 914
Comity, 273, 279, 740
Commander-in-chief, 53
Commentaries on American Law (Kent), 550
Commentaries on Bills of Exchange (Story), 695
Commentaries on Equity (Story), 695
Commentaries on the Constitution of the United States (Cooley), 454
Commentaries on the Constitution (Story), 679, 695
Commentaries on the Law of Bailments (Story), 695
Commentaries on the Laws of England (Blackstone), 11, 423–424, 426, 493, 540, 647
Commentaries on the Laws of England (Cooley), 454
Commerce clause, 405

Commission on Law Enforcement and Administration of Justice, 589
Committee on Homeland Security, 45
Committee on the Judiciary, 45
Committee to Re-Elect the President (CRP), 631, 734
Committee v. Beatty, 914
Commodity Futures Trading Commission v. Schor, 107
Common Cause, 288
Common equity tool, 153
Common law, 16, 447–448, 516. *See also* appellate courts; Blackstone, William
The Common Law (Holmes), 161, 550
Common law writ pleading, 233
Common Sense (Paine), 17
Commonality, 249
Communications Decency Act of 1996, 639
Communism, 614, 615
Communist Revolution, 613
Communist threat, 529
Communists, 613, 617
Compassionate Use Act (CUA), 501
Compelling a witness to testify: *Dickerson v. United States*, 322–323; *Miranda v. Arizona*, 320–322
Compensation, 122
Complaint: case information statement, 234; causes of action, 233–234
Complete-diversity rule, 75
Comprehensive Crime Control Act of 1984, 499
Comprehensive Drug Abuse Prevention and Control Act of 1970, 503
Compromise of 1850, 840–842
Compulsory Education Act of 1922 (Oregon), 642
Comstock Law, 435
Comte, Auguste, 159
Conant v. Walters, 501
The Concept of Law (Hart), 160
Concurring opinion, 95, 96
Confederates, 850
Confederation Congress, 19, 32
Conference committees, 46
Conference of Senior Circuit Judges, 918

Conference of Senior Circuit Judges establishment, 1922, 918–922
Confidentiality, 486
Conformity Act, 229
Congressional Budget Office (CBO), 193, 220
Congressional Committees on the Judiciary: about, 46–47; House of Representatives Committees, 48–49; Joint and Select Committees, 49–51; Senate Committees, 47–48; Standing Committees, 48–49
Congressional elections, 505
Congressional oversight and control of agency rule making: appropriations riders, 220; Chadha Decision and the fate of the legislative veto, 220–221; committee hearings, 220; Congressional Review Act of 1996, 221–222; legislative veto in the states, 221
Congressional power to tax (and spend), 556
Congressional Record, 204, 512
Connecticut, 10, 21
Consensual crimes, 304–305
Consent judgment, 261
Constitution: implied powers of. *See* implied powers of U.S. Constitution ratification, 31, 33
Constitutional construction, 167
Constitutional Context: Women and Rights Discourse in Nineteenth-Century America (Sullivan), 698
Constitutional Convention, 25, 26, 579
Constitutional interpretation, 85, 449–452, 453, 682, 1063. *See also* equal protection clause
Constitutional rights warning, 445
Construction, 167
Construction vs. amendment process, 170
Consumer Product Safety Commission, 195
Contempt of Congress, 46
Continuances, 433
Contraception, 602, 669
Contract, 565
Contract law, 267
Controlled substances, 503. *See also* equal protection clause

Controlled Substances Act (CSA), 499, 503
Conventional crimes, 303–304
Convicted prisoners' rights, 79
Cooley, Thomas McIntyre, 452–456. *See also* constitutional interpretation
Coolidge v. New Hampshire, 676
Copyright Act, 562
Copyright issues, 546
Copyright law, 561
Copyright protection, 562, 565
Corporation for Public Broadcasting (CPB), 196
Corpus Juris Civilis, 154
Cosby, William, 12, 742, 743, 755
Cost-benefit approach vs. personal Constitutional rights, 535
Council of Economic Advisers (CEA), 55, 56, 197
Council of Revision, 30
Counterclaim, 239
Counterterrorist activities, 531
Counties, 117
County governments, 117
County quorum court, 127
Coupon settlements, 278
Court administrators, 122
Court fragmentation, 119
Court jurisdictions, 128
Court of appeals, 889
Court of claims, 456–457. *See also* appellate courts; U.S. district courts
Court of Customs and Patent Appeals, 566
Court of Errors, 118
Court of Errors and Appeals, 118
Court of Federal Claims, U.S., 86, 96, 457, 1104. *See also* Court of Claims
Court of last resort (COLR), 116
Court of law vs. court of equity, 118
Court officers, 182
Court unification, 119
Court-packing, 552
Courts, 458
Courts of the District of Columbia: District of Columbia Court of Appeals, 144; Superior Court of the District of Columbia, 144–145

Courts of the federal territories and tribal governments of the United States: about, 142–143; courts of American Samoa, 146–147; courts of Puerto Rico, 146; courts of the Northern Mariana Islands, 145–146; courts of the Territories of the United States, 144; courts of the Territory of Guam, 145; courts of the U.S. Virgin Islands, 147; Native American tribal courts, 143–144; U.S. District Court for, 146

Courts on Trial (Jerome), 165

Courts-martial, 107, 458–459

Cover sheet, 234

Cox, Archibald, 632, 633, 737

Cozy triangle, 289

Craig, Curtis, 459

Craig v. Boren, 459–462

The Creation of the American Republic (Wood), 21

Crichfield, Ammon B., 627

Crime victims, rights of, 462–464. *See also* jury systems

Criminal appellate review, 130

Criminal due process protections under the Fourth and Fifth amendments: about, 312; Fifth Amendment, 318–323; Fourth Amendment, 313–318

Criminal information, 121

Criminal investigations: about, 323–324; arrests, 329–336; probable cause, 324–327; search warrants, 327–329

Criminal jurisdiction, 717

Criminal justice system in the United States: about, 299–300; criminal due process protections under the fourth and fifth amendments, 312–323; criminal investigations, 323–336; forms and functions of criminal law, 300–305; law enforcement organizations, 305–312; postarrest and pretrial procedures, 336–340

Criminal law: vs. civil law, 149, 150; procedure reform, 445

Criminal proceedings vs. civil proceedings, 226

Criminal trials, 610

Critical legal studies (CLS), 166

Crofton, Walter, 654

Cross-examinations, 584

Crow Dog, 716

Cruel and unusual punishment, 35, 78, 285, 450, 464–467, 475. *See also* bill of rights; bills of attainder; death penalty in the United States

Cumming v. County Board of Education, 975

Cummings, Homer, 198

Cummings v. Missouri, 421, 525

Curry, Thomas, 518, 519

Cushing, William, 33, 694

Custody, 624

Customs and Border Protection Service, 97

Customs Court Act of 1980, 96

Customs Courts Act of 1970, 97

Customs Service, 194

Danbury Baptists, 520, 522, 523, 680

Dane, Nathan, 32

Darrow, Clarence, 453

Dash, Samuel, 508

Daubert v. Merrell Dow Pharmaceuticals, Inc., 487

Davis, Angela, 598

Davis, Derek, 519

Davis v. Beason, 1117

Dawes, Henry, 877, 882

Dawes Act, 1887, 877–882

Day, William, 453, 534

Day v. Owen, 900

D.C. Circuit, 86

De jure segregation, 270, 272

De Lancey, James, 743–744

De novo review, 107, 209, 210, 244, 407, 408

De Republica (Cicero), 630

De Toqueville, Alex, 569

Dean, John, 632, 735

Death on High Seas Act (DOHSA), 398

Death penalty, 451–452, 472; mandatory, 472; racial discrimination and, 474

Death penalty in the United States, 468–477; degrees of murder, 469; future prospects, 475–477; hiding executions from the public, 469–470; key events, 469; legal decisions by the U.S.

Supreme Court, 471–472; limiting death-eligible crimes, 469; from local to state-authorized executions, 470–471; from mandatory to discretionary capital punishment statutes, 470; states abolish the death penalty, 471. *See also* cruel and unusual punishment

Debs, Eugene, 435

Declaration of Independence, 18, 159–160, 469, 578, 584, 629

Declaration of Rights, 23

Declaration of Rights and Grievances, 17

Declaration of Sentiments, 1848, 837–839

Declaratory judgments, 200, 263

Deed and record system, 10

Deep Throat (movie), 605

Defendants, 121, 227

The Defense Never Rests (Bailey), 414

Defense of Marriage Act, 1996, 1109–1111

Definitions of crimes: about, 301–302; misdemeanors vs. felonies, 302; state versus federal crimes, 302–303

Deinstitutionalization, 593

Delaware, 33

Delaware-chartered corporations, 153

Delay, 431, 432, 433, 434

Delinquents, 590

DeLovio v. Boit, 695

Democracy in America (de Tocqueville), 295

Dempsey, Jack, 688

Demurrer, 237, 242

Dennis, Eugene, 495

Dennis v. United States, 495, 577

Denver Area Educ. Telcom. Consortium v. FCC, 639

Department of Agriculture, 215

Department of Defense (DOD), 194, 215, 721, 722

Department of Education, 59, 215, 216–217

Department of Energy (DOE), 216

Department of Health and Human Services, 59, 193, 194, 215, 502

Department of Health, Education, and Welfare (HEW), 502

Department of Homeland Security (DHS), 59, 194, 195, 531

Department of Justice (DOJ), 59, 81, 193, 194, 201, 215, 275, 479

Department of Labor, 59

Department of the Interior, 390

Department of the Treasury, 392

Department of Treasury, 215

Department of Veterans Affairs (DVA), 194, 215, 405

Deportation, 525

Deregulation, 216

DeSalvo, Albert, 413

Desegregation, 445, 972

Design patents, 562

Designer drugs, 503

Detention centers, 591

Deterrents, 526

Detroit Bank v. United States, 965

Deviate sexual intercourse provision, 601

Dickerson v. United States, 322–323, 626

Dickinson, John, 26, 32, 762

Dickinson, Julia, 438

Dies, Martin, 615

Dies Committee, 616

Dies non juridicum, 236

Digital Millennium Copyright Act (DMCA), 562–563, 565

Discipline and Punish (Foucault), 702

Discovery, 80, 157, 225, 228, 237, 243; about, 250; Deposition, 251–252; interrogatories, 251; Production of Documents, 252; request for admissions, 252; Stipulations and the Final Pretrial Conference, 252–253

Discovery rules, 230, 232

Discrete and insular minorities (test), 661

Discretionary release, 654

Discretionary reviews, 129

Discrimination, 515, 952

Discriminatory motivation, 477

Disobedience, civil. *See* civil disobedience

Disparate impact, 186, 477–479. *See also* equal protection clause

Disposition, 430

Dissenting opinion, 95, 96

District attorney, 84, 479–480. *See also* adversary system; crime victims, rights of; jury systems; public defender system; U.S. attorneys

District Court of Guam, 145

District Court of the Virgin Islands, 147

District courts, 120, 480–484. *See also* U.S. district courts

District judges, 1042

District of Columbia v. Heller, 628

Diversity jurisdiction, 64, 481, 483

DNA dragnets, 486

DNA Fingerprint, Unsolved Crime and Innocence Protection Act, 488

DNA fingerprinting, 484, 485

DNA Identification Act of 1994, 486

DNA profiling, 485, 488, 489

DNA usage in criminal justice, 484–490; future prospects, 488–489; key events, 485–487; legal decisions, 487–488. *See also* district attorney; Federal Bureau of Investigation (FBI)

Docket, 67

Docket management, 83

Dockets, 182

Doe, Mary, 671

Doe v. Ashcroft, 510

Doe v. Bolton, 668, 671, 1059

Dolan, Florence, 709

Dolan v. City of Tigard, 709–710

Dombrowski v. Pfister, 181, 273

Domestic violence, 490–492

Double jeopardy, 34, 124, 715, 718

Double jeopardy, prohibition of, 492–495. *See also* bill of rights

Douglas, William O., 69, 417, 494–497, 513, 581, 652, 669, 672, 681, 707. *See also* constitutional interpretation; judicial review

Douglas v. California, 558, 657

Dow Chemical Company v. United States, 509

Doyle v. Ohio, 626

Dragnets, 486

Dred Scott case, 582

Dred Scott v. Sandford, 71, 92, 170, 400, 1069

Dreiser, Theodore, 635

Drinking age, 460–461

Drone, Eaton S., 561

Drug Abuse Control Amendments, 502

Drug courts, 497–499

Drug Enforcement Administration, 59–60, 215

Drug Enforcement Administration (DEA), 500

Drugs, war on, 446, 499–502, 730

Drugs and controlled substances, 502–503

DuBoc, Claude, 414

Due process clause, 76, 170, 180, 200, 201, 246, 262, 273, 450, 534, 602, 626, 643, 644, 648, 671, 684, 706, 912

Due process of law, 9, 34

Due process rights, 78–79

Duff, James C., 392

Duro, Albert, 717

Duro fix, 717, 718

Duro v. Reina, 717, 718

Dworkin, Angela, 606

Dworkin, Ronald, 160

The Eavesdroppers (Dash), 508

Eavesdropping, 701

Eberheart v. Georgia, 473

Economic crimes, 304

Economic Espionage Act, 565

Economic regulation, 907

Economic Stabilization Act of 1970, 98

Education Amendments of 1972, 272

Edwards v. Arizona, 624

Edwards v. California, 577

Ehrlich, Eugene, 163

Ehrlichman, John, 734, 736

Eighth Amendment, 35, 78, 156, 285, 464, 465, 466, 467, 471. *See also* death penalty

Eighth and Ninth Circuits establishment, 1837, 834–837

Eighth Circuit, 834, 854, 933

Eisenhower, Dwight D., 614, 617, 631, 980

Eisenstadt v. Baird, 642, 668–669, 1061

Elderly, George, 413

Election of judges: about, 132–133; nonpartisan election of justices, 134–136; partisan election of justices, 133–134

Elections, 505–507. *See also* Voting Rights Act of 1965
Electoral college, 28, 40, 51, 52
Electors, 52
Electronic Communications Privacy Act of 1986, 509
Electronic eavesdropping, 510. *See also* wiretapping
Electronic surveillance, 507–511. *See also* search warrants; surveillance, technological
Elements of the cause of action, 234
Eleventh Amendment, 64, 91, 283, 284
Eleventh Circuit, 1101
Eleventh Judicial Circuit establishment, 1980, 1101–1104
Ellis, Joseph, 577
Ellsberg, Daniel, 511–514, 632. *See also* censorship; civil rights and civil liberties; Nixon, Richard M.; surveillance, technological; Watergate scandal
Ellsworth, Oliver, 789
Emancipation Proclamation, 852
Emancipation Proclamation (1863), 852–853
Emergency Petroleum Allocation Act of 1973, 98
Emergency rule making, 202
Eminent domain, 34, 707. *See also* Fifth Amendment; takings clause
Encyclopedia of Associations, 569
Enemy aliens, 544
Energy Policy and Conservation Act, 98
Engel v. Vitale, 681
English Bill of Rights, 11, 13, 16, 419, 464
English common law, 9, 113, 117, 541, 646, 648
English language, 256
English language fluency, 585
English literacy tests, 1025–1026
"Enhanced Surveillance Procedures," 510
Entitlement disbursement, 200
Enumerated powers, 28, 42
Environmental activism, 496
Environmental movement, 446
Environmental Protection Agency (EPA), 191, 194, 202, 215, 216, 219

Equal Education Opportunities Act of 1974, 272
Equal Employment Opportunity Commission (EEOC), 478, 605
Equal Pay Act, 1963, 982–983
Equal protection clause, 170, 180, 186, 269, 271, 273, 283, 403, 416, 445, 450, 459, 506, 514–516, 596, 602–603, 661, 684, 685, 697, 706, 718, 1119. *See also* civil rights and civil liberties; constitutional interpretation; Fourteenth Amendment; judicial review
Equal protection guarantee, 257
Equitable doctrine, 155
Equitable injunction, 200, 268
Equitable remedies: about, 272–275; Class Action Fairness Act of 2005, 278; defendant and bilateral class actions, 277–278; equitable remedies and abstention in state criminal cases, 273–274; federal class actions, 276–277; government as institutional reformer, 275; limitations on the injunctive power, 274–275; mass actions, 278; state class actions, 277
Equity, 516–517. *See also* admiralty and maritime law; common law; U.S. district courts
Equity courts, 517
"Equity must come with clean hands" doctrine, 175
Equity pleading rules, 155
Equity rules, 276
Erie doctrine, 397
Erie Railroad Co. v. Tompkins, 397, 483
Ervin, Sam, 632, 688
Escobedo v. Illinois, 623
Espionage, 616, 618, 673
Espionage Act of 1917, 513, 546, 550, 663, 665
Established church, 14
Establishment clause, 518–524, 682. *See also* Bill of Rights; separation of church and state
Ethics, 486
Euclid v. Ambler Realty, 708
European civil law, 424
Evarts Act of 1891, 88, 889

Everson v. Board of Education, 518, 681
Ex parte Bollman, 541
Ex parte Crow Dog, 716
Ex parte Garland, 421
Ex Parte Garland, 525
Ex parte Merryman, 543
Ex parte Milligan, 543
Ex parte Quirin, 961, 962
Ex parte Yerger, 540
Ex parte Young, 283, 284
Ex post facto laws, 43, 524–526. *See also* bills of attainder
Examination before trial, 251
Exclusionary rule, 313–314, 533–536; about, 313–314; poisonous tree, 314. *See also* Fourth Amendment
Exclusionary rule exceptions: automobile search, 315–316; border search, 316; consent search, 317; emergency situation, 317; good faith, 314; inevitable discovery, 315; inventory search, 316; moving vehicle, 316; open fields, 317; plain view, 314–315; search by private individual, 317; search incidental to arrest (Chimel rule), 315
Executions, 468, 470, 471, 475, 673
Executive branch: organization of, 55–61; presidential powers, 53–55; terms and qualifications, 51–52
Executive branch oversight of federal agency rule making: about, 216–217; national performance review, 218; Regulatory Flexibility Act (RFA), 217–218; Small Business Regulatory Enforcement Fairness Act, 219
Executive Office of the President (EOP), 55, 197
Executive Order 8248, 197
Executive Order 8802, 402, 952–953
Executive Order 8972, 955
Executive Order 9066, 954–955, 958–961, 968–970
Executive Order 9981, 972–973
Executive Order 10214, 722
Executive Order 10730, 980–981
Executive Order 10925, 402, 1014
Executive Order 11246, 402
Executive Order 12333, 1179
Executive Order 12866, 218
Executive Order 13272, 219
Executive Order 91029, 958
Executive Order D0035, 1113, 1115
Executive orders, 204
Executive privilege, 54, 197, 632
Expert witnesses, 259
Extradition, international, 526–528
Extradition treaties, 526, 527

Fact pleading, 157, 233
Factions, 568–569
Facts vs. legal arguments, 87
Factual assessments, 183–184
Fair Housing Act, 75
False arrest, 281
Familial searching, 486
Family law, 234
Family law cases, 75
Fanny Hill: Memoirs of a Woman of Pleasure (Cleland), 636
Faubus, Orval, 980
Fay v. Noia, 285, 541
FCC v. Pacifica Foundation, 638
Federal agency, 198; limit of power, 200; responsibility to, 217
Federal Assault Weapons Ban (1994), 628
Federal Bureau of Investigation (FBI), 59, 61, 99, 194, 309–310, 529–531, 576, 599, 614, 616, 621, 674. *See also* Bill of Rights; civil rights and civil liberties; Red Scare
Federal Bureau of Narcotics, 194, 499, 502
Federal Bureau of Prisons, 60
Federal bureaucracy: about, 193–194; controlling the modern bureaucracy, 196–197
Federal circuit, 1104
Federal circuit establishment, 1982, 1104–1109
Federal civil cases, 75
Federal civil rights litigation and state institutions: civil rights cases against state officials, 279–285; prison reform litigation, 285–286; Prison Reform Litigation Act, 286–287
Federal Communications Commission (FCC), 195, 202, 436, 638

Federal courts. *See* Article I courts

Federal Courts Improvement Act of 1982, 98, 101

Federal Courts Improvement Act of 2000, 1127–1145

Federal courts of limited jurisdiction: Article I courts of specific jurisdiction, 101–106; Article III courts of specific or limited jurisdiction, 96–101; other Article I tribunals of special subject-matter jurisdiction, 106; Supreme Court rulings limiting the power of Article I tribunals, 106–107

Federal courts vs. state courts, 868

Federal criminal cases, 75

Federal criminal courts, 481

Federal Declaratory Judgment Act of 1934, 178

Federal Deposit Insurance Corporation, 196

Federal Emergency Management Agency, 195

Federal Energy Regulatory Commission, 195

Federal government employee levels, 215–216

Federal Highway Administration, 202

Federal judges, 40, 54, 65, 66, 69–70, 80–81, 82, 83, 109, 125, 131, 146, 154, 181, 183, 230, 273, 285, 286, 287, 295, 311, 336, 392, 447, 480, 483, 532, 560

Federal judgeships, 81, 480

Federal Judicial Center establishment, 1967, 1032–1041

Federal Judicial Center (FJC), 531–533, 1032. *See also* Administrative Office of the United States Courts

Federal judiciary, 194–195; about, 73–74; administrative and bureaucratic support for the federal judiciary, 107–109; federal courts of limited jurisdiction, 96–107; jurisdiction of the federal judiciary, 74–76; major courts of the federal judiciary, 77–96

Federal jurisdiction, 868

Federal law enforcement agencies: about, 308–309; Bureau of Alcohol, Tobacco, Firearms and Explosives, 310; Drug Enforcement Administration, 310; immigration and customs enforcement service, 311–312; secret service, 311; U.S. Marshals Service, 310–311. *See also* Federal Bureau of Investigation (FBI)

Federal law vs. state law, 75

Federal Magistrate Act of 1968, 607, 1042–1050

Federal Magistrate Act of 1976, 610

Federal Magistrate Act of 1979, 610

Federal magistrates, 183

Federal Magistrates Act of 1968, 610

Federal prisoners, 180

Federal Programs Branch, 202

Federal question jurisdiction, 481

Federal Register, 202–203, 204, 218

Federal Regulation of Lobbying Act, 289

Federal regulatory commission, 882

Federal Reserve Board, 195

Federal Rules of Appellate Procedure, 263

Federal Rules of Appellate Procedure, Rule 38, 242

Federal Rules of Civil Procedure (FRCP), 157, 183, 228, 230, 271; Rule 1, 229; Rule 2, 229; Rule 3, 233; Rule 4, 234, 235; Rule 7, 232; Rule 8, 238, 239; Rule 8(b), 238; Rule 8(c), 238; Rule 9(b), 233; Rule 11, 242; Rule 12, 237, 238, 253; Rule 12(b), 238, 242; Rule 12(c), 243; Rule 13, 239; Rule 13(g), 239; Rule 14, 239; Rule 15, 240, 247; Rule 16, 252; Rule 18, 247, 276; Rule 19, 242; Rule 20, 247, 276; Rule 22, 248; Rule 23, 249, 276; Rule 24(a), 249; Rule 24(b), 249; Rule 26, 250; Rule 29, 245; Rule 30, 251; Rule 32, 252; Rule 36, 252; Rule 38, 255; Rule 39, 255; Rule 41, 677; Rule 41(a), 242; Rule 41(b), 242; Rule 42, 248, 276; Rule 47, 257; Rule 48, 257, 260; Rule 49, 261; Rule 50, 245; Rule 51, 260; Rule 52, 256; Rule 55, 241; Rule 56, 244; Rule 57, 263; Rule 59, 246; Rule 60, 241, 246; Rule 64, 262; Rule 65, 262, 273

Federal Rules of Criminal Procedure, 5, 109, 328; Rule 2, 342; Rule 3, 330; Rule 7, 302; Rule 15, 252; Rule 29, 245; Rule 41, 677; Rule 52, 185, 408

Federal Rules of Decision (F.R.D.), 232
Federal Rules of Evidence, 97, 257
Federal Sunshine Act, 212
Federal Trade Commission, 195
Federalist Paper No. 45, 647
Federalist Paper No. 51, 438
Federalist Paper No. 78, 35, 420
Federalist Paper No. 84, 33, 524
Federalist Papers ("Publius"), 33, 35, 91, 267, 419, 420, 438, 568
Federalists, 32, 33
Felony complaint, 236
Female offenders, 593
Field, David Dudley, 118, 156, 229
Field, David Dudley, II, 156–157
Field, Stephen J., 118, 156
Field Code, 118, 156, 229
Fielding, Lewis, 734
Fifteenth Amendment, 42, 173
Fifteenth Amendment Section 2, 1025
Fifth Amendment, 34, 76, 78, 121, 123, 162, 165, 170, 201, 235, 252, 262, 458, 492, 495, 515, 518, 554, 620, 621, 623, 624, 626; compelling a witness to testify, 320–323; double jeopardy, 318–319; self-incrimination, 319; takings clause, 706–712. *See also* Bill of Rights
Fifth Amendment absolutists, 495
Fifth Circuit, 1101
Filibustering, 50
Filled Milk Act, 444
Final disposition, 200
Final judgment rule, 244
Finnis, John, 630
Fireside Chat on Reorganization of the Judiciary (1937), 936–946
First Amendment, 34, 100, 162, 169, 181, 273, 281, 435, 436, 451, 495, 501, 506, 510, 512, 513, 518, 519, 521, 546, 550, 634, 635, 637, 638, 640, 642, 652, 681, 706, 713, 740
First among Equals: The Supreme Court in American Life (Starr), 693
First Continental Congress, 16–17
First English Evangelical Lutheran Church of Glendale v. Los Angeles County, 708, 709
The First Freedoms (Curry), 518

First Nat. Bank v. Leonard, 913
Fiske, Robert B., 692
Flagiello v. Pennsylvania Hospital, 649
Flango, V. E., 431
Fletcher v. Peck, 525
Food and Drug Administration (FDA), 193
Ford, Gerald, 217, 497, 633, 738
Ford v. Wainwright, 465
Foreign case law, 152
Foreign Intelligence Surveillance Act (FISA) (1978): 2008 amendments, 100; warrants, 99
Foreign Relations Committee, 45
Formal adjudication, 200–201
Forms and functions of criminal law: categories of crime, 303–305; definitions of crimes, 301–303; necessary elements of a crime, 300–301
Forrestal, James, 722
Fort Wayne Books, Inc. v. Indiana, 638
Fortas, Abe, 69
Forum shopping, 278
Foster, Vince, 692
Foucault, Michel, 702, 703
The Founding Fathers (Lambert), 518
Four-fifths rule, 478
Fourteenth Amendment, 42, 71, 76, 92, 127, 129, 162, 163, 165, 170, 173, 180, 186, 200, 201, 227, 257, 262, 269, 271, 273, 283, 284, 403, 410, 417, 444, 445, 471, 475, 492, 495, 506, 514, 515, 534, 548, 554, 582, 596, 602, 604, 647, 669, 670, 671, 672, 683, 684, 695, 706, 713, 740, 859, 894, 1119
Fourth Amendment, 34, 78, 93, 162, 281, 427, 486, 507, 508, 510, 534, 535, 536, 542, 652, 676, 677. *See also* Bill of Rights; border searches; exclusionary rule; search warrants
Francis Fauquier, 578
Frank, Jerome, 165
Frank v. Mangum, 541
Frank v. Maryland, 1024
Frankfurter, Felix, 600, 649
Franklin, Benjamin, 18, 26, 579
Franklin v. Massachusetts, 199
Free speech, 435, 506
Freedom from Religion Foundation, 682

Freedom of expression, 714
Freedom of Information Act, 203
Freedom of movement, 955
Freedom of political expression, 634
Freedom of religion, 34, 775
Freedom of speech, 34, 550, 634, 713
Freedom of the press, 34, 634
Freedom Riders, 598
Freedom to peaceful assembly, 34
Friedman, Lawrence, 10
Friends of the Earth, 571
Frivolous lawsuits, 566
From Red Tape to Results: Creating a Government That Works Better and Costs Less (National Partnership for Reinventing Government), 218
Frontiero v. Richardson, 696–697
Frye v. United States, 487
Fugitive Slave Act of 1850, 609, 842–847
Fuhrman, Mark, 414
Fulbright, J. William, 512
Fulgrahm, v. State, 491
Fundamental Laws of the Dine, 144
Fundamental Principles of the Sociology of Law (Ehrlich), 163
Fundamental rights, 603
Furman, William Henry, 471
Furman v. Georgia, 465, 473, 474
Future conduct, 199

Gag order, 175
Gagnon v. Scarpelli, 654
Gallas, G., 431
Gangster era, 529
García, Hector P., 537–539. *See also* United Farm Workers of America
Garner, Tyron, 601
Gaustad, Edwin, 521
Gay marriages, 1109
Gayle v. Browder, 271
Gender inequality, 460
Gender-based mortality tables, 462
A General Abridgement of Law and Equity (Viner), 425
General Allotment Act, 877
The General Principles of Constitutional Law in the United States of America (Cooley), 454

General Services Administration (GSA), 203
Genessee Chief v. Fitzhugh, 397
Genocide, 606
George II, King of England, 12
George III, King of England, 7, 14, 15, 18, 579
Gerry, Elbridge, 32, 41, 419
Gerrymandering, 41, 506
Gibbons v. Ogden, 647
Giboney v. Empire Storage Co., 1023
Gideon v. Wainwright, 226, 399, 542, 557, 657, 659
Gilded Age, 60
Giles v. Harris, 548
Ginsburg, Douglas, 596
Ginsburg, Ruth, 643
Ginzburg v. United States, 636
Gitlow v. New York, 180, 273
Glorious Revolution of 1688-1689, 11, 15, 159
Goldman, Ronald, 414
Gong Lum v. Rice, 975
Gonzales v. Carhart, 442, 596
Gonzales v. Raich, 501, 596
Good-faith exception, 535
Gordon, Thomas, 743
Gordon v. Lance, 1112
Gore, Al, 218, 1119
Gore v. Harris, 1120, 1123
Gorin v. United States, 957
Government accountability, 281
Government Accountability Office (GAO), 195
Government agency management, 200
Grand Convention, 25
Grand jury, 78, 121, 257
Grand trials, 78
Granger Movement, 882
Granholm v. Heald, 698
Grant certiorari (or grant cert), 67, 68, 89, 93, 129, 131, 410
Grassroots lobbying, 570–571
Gratz v. Bollinger, 403
Gravel, Mike, 513
Gray, Horace, 600
Gray, L. Patrick, 736
Gray v. Sanders, 417, 1124

Great Compromise, 27
"Great Dissenter," 547, 550
The Great Writ, 179
Green v. Board of Education, 445
Green v. United States, 493
Greenfield, L. A., 717
Greg decision, 473
Gregg v. Georgia, 465, 472
Griggs v. Duke Power Co., 476
Griswold, Erwin, 512, 513
Griswold v. Connecticut, 162, 495–496,
    581, 602, 652, 668–669, 1021–1025,
    1058, 1061
Grotius, Hugo, 630
Grutter v. Bollinger, 403
Guilty plea, 644
Gun owners, 628

Habeas corpus, 9, 43; eligibility for, 544;
    federal habeas corpus jurisdiction over
    state prisoners, 541–542; origin and
    development of the writ, 540–541;
    suspension of habeas corpus, 542–544.
    See also writ of habeas corpus
Habeas Corpus Act of 1679, 541
Habeas corpus petitions, 268
Habeas review, 125
Habermas, Jürgen, 166
Hakim, Joy, 439
Haldeman, H.R., 633, 689, 735
Hale, Matthew, 491
*Half Pound Papers of Smoking Tobacco v.
    United States*, 902
Hamburger, Philip, 521, 522
Hamilton, Alexander, 12, 25, 26, 27, 33,
    35, 58, 419, 420, 524, 555, 556, 579,
    619, 743–744, 763
Hamilton, Andrew, 755
Hamilton v. Alabama, 558, 657
Hamilton v. Dillin, 960
Hammer v. Dagnehart, 550
Hancock, John, 33
Hand, Billings Learned, 545–547. *See also*
    constitutional interpretation; judicial
    review
Hanson, Ole, 664
Harlan, John Marshall, 513, 547–549, 621,
    622

Harlan, John Marshall, II, 418
Harlan, Marshall, 283
Harmelin, Ronald, 466
Harmelin v. Michigan, 466
Harper v. Virginia Bd. of Elections, 1112,
    1122
Harris, John, Jr., 740
Harris v. Nelson, 540
Harris v. New York, 625
Harrison Act, 502
Harry Potter (Rowling), 437
Hart, Edward J., 616
Hart, H. L. A., 160
Harvard Law School, 550
Hatch Act (1939), 196, 615
Hawaii Housing Authority v. Midkiff, 707
Hawaii v. Mankichi, 548
Hawaiian Organic Act (1900), 542–543
Hayden, Tom, 598
Hayes, Paul Lewis, 646
Health Insurance Association of America,
    571
Heard v. Railroad Co., 900
Hearing en blanc, 67, 87
*Heffron v. International Society for
    Krishna Consciousness*, 714
Helms, Jesse, 436, 466, 735
Helvering v. Hallock, 649
Hemings, Sally, 580
Henderson, T. A., 431
Henry, Patrick, 14, 26, 519
Henry III, King of England, 745
High Court of American Samoa, 146–147
Hill v. Texas, 965
Hirabayashi v. United States, 955–968, 970
Hiss, Alger, 616, 631
A History of American Law (Friedman), 10
"The History of the U.S. Decision-Making
    Process n Vietnam." *See Pentagon
    Papers* (Ellsberg)
Hobbes, Thomas, 159
Hoffer, Peter Charles, 10
Hoffman, Abbie, 598
Hoffman, Julius J., 598
Hogue v. CIO, 280
Holden v. Hardy, 908, 915
Holmes, Oliver Wendell, Jr., 161, 162,
    163–164, 170, 507, 549–551, 600. *See*

also civil rights and civil liberties; constitutional interpretation

Home rule, 117

Homeland Security Council, 194

Homestead Act, 1862, 850–852

Homosexuals, 602, 648, 1109

Hoover, J. Edgar, 529, 614, 665, 734, 736

Houck v. Railway Co., 900

House, Paul, 487

House Committee on Oversight and Government Reform, 45

House Committee on Ways and Means, 45

House Judiciary Committee, 45

House of Burgesses, 8, 9, 18

House of Representatives, 40; amendments, 404; Article I power, 40; election tie, 58; impeachment, 54, 693; leadership, 43–44; *Marbury v. Madison*, 579; seat allocation, 52; veto, 39, 221. *See also* U.S. Constitution, Article III

House Un-American Activities Committee (HUAC), 616, 631

Hughes, Charles Evans, 392, 551–553, 576. *See also* constitutional interpretation; judicial review

Human rights, 486, 528

Hunt, E. Howard, 632, 735

Hunter education courses, 628

Hunter v. Erickson, 1112

Hurtado v. California, 548

Huston, Tom Charles, 734

Hutson, James, 520–521

Huxley, Julian, 739

Hybrid election process, 133

Identification: about, 336–337; DNA typing, 338–339; photographic identification, 338; postindictment lineups, 338; preindictment lineups, 337–338; show-ups, 337

Illinois v. Gates, 677

Illinois v. Krull, 535

Immigrants, 665, 797, 873

Immigration and Naturalization Service (INS), 59, 194

Immigration and Naturalization Service v. Chadha, 220, 451

Immigration proceedings, 74

Immunity, Judicial, 554–555. *See also* checks and balances

Impeachment, 29, 42, 53, 54, 69, 99, 142, 497, 734, 737–738

Implied Powers of the U.S. Constitution, 555–556. *See also* constitutional interpretation

Implied powers of U.S. Constitution, 449, 618

in camera, 240

in camera encounters, 175

in personam jurisdiction, 482

in personam jurisdiction vs. in rem jurisdiction, 483

In re Gault, 590

In re Kent, 590

In Re Sealed Case, 100

in rem/res, 76

Incidental appellate jurisdiction, 120

Indecency, 436

Independence Day, 18

Indian Reorganization Act, 143

Indictments, 121, 236

Indigence, 559

Indigent defendant representation, 556–560; future prospects, 559–560; indigent defense services, 558–559; legal developments, 555–558. *See also* district attorney; Public Defender System

Indigent defendants, 656

Industrial unions, 724

Informal adjudication, 201

Infringement, 563–564

Injunctions, 80, 176, 180, 273, 281, 284, 517, 565

Injunctive judgments, 200

Injunctive relief, 560

Innocence Protection Act of 2004, 487

Inns of Court, 424

Inquisitorial system, 399

Insanity plea, 238

Instructing the jury, 177

Instrumentalism, 162

Insular cases, 548

Intake units, 591

Intellectual property, 74

Intellectual property rights, 560–568; consequences of piracy to business, 563–564; controversial aspects of, 566–567; copyright, 562–563; importance of, 561–562; international protection of, 564–565; legal relief: infringement causes of action, injunctions, and contracts, 565–566; patents, 562; trade secret, 563; trademark, 563. *See also* appellate courts; U.S. district courts

Interest groups, 571

Interest groups and lobbying, 568–573; Madison's warning, 568–569; money, 572; nature of, 569–571. *See also* civil rights and civil liberties

Interim U.S. attorneys, 84

Intermediate appellate courts (IAC), 116

Intermediate review, 696

Intermediate scrutiny, 573–575, 661, 662. *See also* equal protection clause

Internal Revenue Service (IRS), 105, 194, 712

International Judicial Relations Office (FLC), 531

International law, 448

International Trade Commission, 561

Internment of Japanese Americans, 968

Interpol, 529

Interracial relationships, 643

Interrogation procedures, 621

Interstate Commerce Act, 1887, 882–887

Interstate Commerce Commission (ICC), 193, 882

Intolerable Acts, 16

Iron triangle, 289

Irreparable injury, 181

Isbrandtsen- Moller Co. v. United States, 960

Ito, J. A., 431

Jackson, Andrew, 58, 196

Jackson, Robert Houghwout, 576–578, 676. *See also* constitutional interpretation; judicial review

Jacobellis v. Ohio, 636

James I, King of England, 8, 11

James II, King of England, 159

Japanese Americans: freedom of movement, 955; internment of, 102, 494, 968

Jaworski, Leon, 633, 737

Jay, John, 26, 33, 65, 91, 401, 419

Jefferson, Thomas, 18, 33, 58, 64, 159, 401, 519, 520–521, 522, 523, 555, 556, 578–581, 583, 584, 619, 679, 680, 681, 775, 799. *See also* Bill of Rights; separation of church and state

Jeffreys, Alec, 484, 485

Jenkins v. Georgia, 637

Jenkins v. Missouri, 272

Jim Crow laws, 296, 515, 856, 894

John, King of England, 745

John Doe v. Kamehameha, 698

John R. Brown Judicial Scholarship Foundation, 533

John Warner National Defense Authorization Act for Fiscal Year 2007, 723

John XXIII, Pope, 677

Johnson, Andrew, 859

Johnson, Lyndon B., 52, 402, 502, 538, 589, 1025

Johnson, Robert Underwood, 686

Johnson v. Eisentrager, 544

Johnson v. M'Intosh, 904

Johnson v. United States, 676

Johnson v. Zerbst, 557, 657

Joinder, 239

Joinder of claims, 247

Joinder of parties, 247

Joint Chiefs of Staff, 56

Joint committees, 46

Joint Economic Committee, 46

Joint resolutions, 49, 222

Jones, Paula Corbin, 693

Jones Act, 396, 398

Jones v. Bock, 287

Joyce, James, 635

Judge advocate general (JAG), 103

Judges' Bill, 92

The Judges' Bill, 1925, 923–932

Judges of the justice court, 127

Judgment: appeals, 263; Compensatory Relief (Damages), 261–262; Declaratory Relief, 262–263; Equitable Relief, 262

Judiciability, 65

Judicial action basis: beneficiaries cannot sue, 175; exhaustion of remedies, 174–175; jurisdiction, 172–173; justiciability, 173; ripeness and mootness, 174; standing, 173–174

Judicial activism, 546, 581–582. *See also* constitutional interpretation; precedent doctrine

Judicial adjuncts, 182

Judicial appointments, 51

Judicial branch: about, 61–62; appointment of federal judges and judicial independence, 69–70; creating the federal judiciary, 62–63; judicial review, 70–71; jurisdiction, 63–65; organization of the federal judiciary, 65–69

Judicial circuits, 861

The Judicial Code of 1911 [Excerpt], 916–917

Judicial Conference of the United States, 88, 105, 108, 393–394, 607, 608, 918, 1032, 1042

Judicial construction approaches, 167

Judicial council, 103

Judicial councils /conferences, 128, 129

Judicial discipline, 142

Judicial elections, 132–133

Judicial error, 555

Judicial exemption, 740

Judicial immunity. *See* immunity, judicial

Judicial Improvements Act, 608

Judicial independence, 29

Judicial minimalism, 171

Judicial misconduct, 555

Judicial nominees, 81

Judicial power exercised at trial: instructing the jury, 177–178; pretrial proceedings, 175–176; trial proceedings, 176–177

Judicial power to issue writs, decrees, orders, and injunctions: declaratory judgments, 178; equitable remedies, 180–181; equitable remedies in criminal cases, 181; limitation on the injunctive power, 181–182; writ of habeas corpus, 179–180; writ of mandamus, 179

Judicial powers, 35

Judicial procedure, power, and policy in America, 149–150; appellate process, 183–187; judicial process, 171–183; jurisprudence and judicial reasoning in the United States, 157–171; sources and methods of American law, 150–157

Judicial Procedures Reform Bill of 1937, 946

Judicial process: about, 171–172; ancillary powers of courts, 182–183; basis of judicial action, 172–175; exercise of judicial power at trial, 175–178; judicial power to issue writs, decrees, orders, and injunctions, 178–182

Judicial reasoning and interpretation: about, 166–167; judicial restraint, activism, and minimalism, 170–171; legislative intent, 169; living constitution, 170; originalism, 167–168; strict construction, 168–169; textualism and plain meaning, 168

Judicial Reform Act (1985), 143

Judicial Reorganization Bill of Rights, 392

Judicial restraint, 546, 581, 1063

Judicial review, 30, 149, 582–584, 815. *See also* constitutional interpretation; judicial activism

Judicial selection, 113, 136

Judicial self-restraint, 582

Judicial Writing Manual (FLC), 532

Judiciary Act of 1789, 30, 47, 59, 60, 62, 63, 64, 67, 73, 75, 77, 85, 90, 91, 153, 174, 178, 179, 181, 193, 274, 396, 475, 517, 541, 580, 583, 612, 695, 789–796, 800, 916

Judiciary Act of 1801, 799–815

Judiciary Act of 1802, 800, 815–822

Judiciary Act of 1869 (Circuit Judges Act), 862–863

Judiciary Act of 1925 (Judges' Bill), 92, 108

Judiciary acts, 173

Judiciary Improvement Act of 1990, 1042

Jurek v. Texas, 472

Jurimetrics (American Bar Association), 166

Juris predencia, 157

Jurisdiction, 277

The Jurisdiction and Removal Act of 1875, 868–873
Jurisdiction in personam, 76
Jurisdiction of the federal judiciary, 74–76
Jurisprudence: about, 158–159; contemporary schools of jurisprudence, 165–166; formalism, 160–162; legal realism, 164–165; positive law and natural law, 159–160; sociological jurisprudence, 162–164
Jurisprudence and judicial reasoning in the United States: judicial reasoning and interpretation, 166–171; jurisprudence, 158–166
Jurors, 79
Jury, 225; about, 255; in civil trial, 80; role, 177; selecting a jury pool, 256–257; sequestering the jury, 258; voir dire: selecting the jury members, 257
Jury discretion, 471
Jury nullification, 470, 585
Jury selection, 123–124
Jury size, 124, 257
Jury system management best practices, 586–587
Jury systems, 584–588. *See also* common law
Justice, William Wayne, 286
Justice Department, 529
Justice for All Act of 2004, 487
Justices of the peace, 127
Justiciable dispute, 400
Justinian's Code, 158–159
Juvenile justice and delinquency prevention act of 1974, 590
Juvenile justice system, 588–593; criticisms of the system, 592–593; current system, 590–592; historical background, 588–590. *See also* judicial review; police power; privacy

Kadic v. Karadzic, 606
Kadrmas v. Dickinson Public Schools, 1118
Kathleen Sullivan on Civil Liberties in a Time of National Crisis (Sullivan), 698
Katz v. United States, 508, 1061
Katzenbach v. Morgan, 1026

Kavanagh, Sandy, 471
Kendal, George, 468
Kennedy, Anthony McLeod, 451, 595–597, 601, 602, 603, 604, 639, 648, 650. *See also* constitutional interpretation; judicial review
Kennedy, John F., 52, 195, 402, 442, 511, 538, 632
Keokee Consol. Coke Co. v. Taylor, 965
Kimel v. Board of Regents, 581
King, Martin Luther, Jr., 529, 598
King, Rodney, 281, 714
Kirby, Ron, 599
Kissinger, Henry, 514
Kitchen Cabinet, 58
Klein, Herbert M., 497
Klopfer v. North Carolina, 691
Knock-and-announce requirement, 677–678
Korean War, 614
Korematsu v. United States, 460, 494, 577, 696, 968–972
Kotch v. Board of River Port Pilot Comm'rs for Port of New Orleans, 1117
Kovacs v. Cooper, 713
Kraemer v. Shelley, 683
Kruman, Marc W., 24
Ku Klux Klan (KKK) Act, 280, 281
Kunstler, William M, 597–599. *See also* civil rights and civil liberties; jury systems
Kyllo v. United States, 509

La Jeune Eugeine (Story), 695
Labor and bolshevism, 663–664
Labor laws, 912
Labor unions, 724–725
Ladies Home Journal, 496
Lady Chatterly's Lover (Lawrence), 635
Laissez-faire policy, 285–286
Lambert, Frank, 518
Land-use restrictions, 711
Langdell, Christopher Columbus (C. C.), 160, 161, 162
Lanham Act, 563
Lansdale, Edward, 511
Lanza v. New York, 1024
Lara, Billy Jo, 718

Lassiter v. Department of Social Services, 643

Latinos, 537–538

Lattimore, Owen, 614, 617

Law and constitution in early America: about, 7–8; Article III, 29–32; Articles of Confederation, 18–20; Bill of Rights, 34–36; Continental Congress and the Declaration of Independence, 16–18; creation of the federal constitution, 24–29; federal judiciary creation, 29–32; legal revolution, 11–16; origins of the American justice system, 8–11; ratification controversy, 32–34; state constitutions, 20–24

Law and People in Colonial America (Hoffer), 10

Law and the Modern Mind (Frank), 164

Law clerks, 92, 93, 121, 182, 600–601. *See also* appellate courts; judicial review

Law degrees, 120, 127, 129, 132

Law enforcement organizations: federal law enforcement agencies, 308–312; state and local law enforcement, 305–308

Law of prizes, 398

Law Revision Council, 204

Lawrence, D.H., 635

Lawrence, John Geddes, 601, 602

Lawrence v. Texas, 581, 596, 601–604, 648

Laws and Liberties, 10

Lay justices, 127

League of Women Voters, 288

Leary v. United States, 500

Leavenworth, L. & G. R. Co. v. United States, 904

Lee, Richard Henry, 17–18, 32

Lee v. Washington, 286

Legal arguments vs. facts, 87

Legal costs, 262

Legal Defense Fund, Inc. (LDF), 269, 289

Legal error standard, 185, 408

Legal executions, 468

Legal opinions, 205

Legal positivists, 159

Legal precedents, 294

Legal process jurisprudence, 165

Legal realism, 161

Legal remedy, 261

Legislative branch: about, 39–41; congressional committees, hearings, and oversight, 44–46; congressional committees on the judiciary, 46–49; congressional districts, 41–42; leadership in the House of Representatives, 43–44; leadership in the Senate, 44; legislative process, 49–51; powers of Congress, 42–43

Legislative tribunals, 206

Legislative veto by resolution, 221

Legislative veto provision, 221

Leoni, Raúl, 538

"Letter from the Birmingham Jail" (King), 444

"Letter to the Danbury Baptist Association" (Jefferson), 680

Levine, James, 704

Lewinsky, Monica, 693

Lewis, John L., 724

Lewis, Meriwether, 580

Libel, 743

The Libel Case of John Peter Zenger, 1735, 755–762

Liberty of establishment privileges, 522

Liberty to contract, 163

Licensing, 200

Liddy, G. Gordon, 632, 734, 735

Life tenure, 96, 99

Lifetime appointments, 132

Limitations on judicial power: burden of proof is on the petitioner, 185–186; judges do not rule on political questions, 186; laws are only overturned on the narrowest grounds, 187; no rulings are made on the wisdom of legislation, 186–187

Lincoln, Abraham, 51, 542, 852

Lincoln, Levi, 521

Lincoln Union v. Northwestern Co., 1023

Line-item veto, 53

Literal construction, 171

Literalists, 169

Litigating parties: class-action litigation, 248–249; compulsory joinder of parties, 247–248; interpleader, 248; intervention,

Litigating parties (*Cont.*)
249–250; permissive joinder of parties, 247
Litigation backlog, 432
Little Tucker Act (1887), 101
Living Constitution, 171, 449, 451, 452
Living law, 163
Livingston, Robert R., 18
Llewellyn, Karl, 165
Lobbyists, 49, 289, 569–570
Lochner v. New York, 546, 548, 582, 647, 907–911, 912, 914, 915, 916, 1023, 1071
Locke, John, 18, 21, 159, 629
Lockett v. Ohio, 473
Lockett v. Ohio and Bell v. Ohio, 473–474
Lockhart v. McCree, 474
Logical reasoning, 449, 451
Logwood v. Railroad Co., 900
Londoner v. City and County of Denver, 201
Lone Wolf, 903
Lone Wolf v. Hitchcock, 903–907
Long-arm statute, 482
Longoria, Felix, 538
Longshoremen's and Harbor Workers' Compensation Act (LHWCA), 398
Louisville, N. O. & T. Ry. Co. v. State, 899, 900
Loving v. Virginia, 1061
LSD, 502
Lucas, David H., 710
Lucas v. South Carolina Coastal Council, 710

MacKinnon, Catherine Alice, 605–607, 606. *See also* obscenity; pornography
Maconochie, Alexander, 654
Madison, James, 25, 26, 30, 33, 34, 404, 419, 420, 438, 568, 569, 579, 583, 611, 619, 647, 679, 694, 775
Magistrate Act in 1979, 607
Magistrate courts, 607–609. *See also* case-flow management; U.S. district courts
Magistrate judges, 608, 609–611, 1127. *See also* appellate courts; U.S. district courts
Magistrates, 125–126, 1042

Magna Carta (1215), 9, 13, 16, 464, 540, 745–755
Magruder, Jeb, 632, 734, 735
Mahoney, B., 431
Maier, Pauline, 17
Maintenance and cure principle, 398
Major courts of the federal judiciary: Supreme Court of the United States, 89–96; U.S. Courts of Appeal, 85–89; U.S. District Courts, 77–85
Major Crimes Act, 716, 717
Majoritarian animus, 603
Majority leader, 44
Majority opinion, 95
Malapportionment, 417
Malloy v. Hogan, 623
Management, case-flow. *See* case-flow management
Mandatory death penalty, 472
Mandatory jurisdiction, 90
Mandatory minimum sentences, 86, 500, 503
Mandatory release, 654
Mann Act (1912), 529
Manual for Complex Litigation (FLC), 532
Manual for Cooperation between State and Federal Court (FLC), 532
Manual on the Administrative Procedure Act, 199
Manufacturers Hanover Trust Co. v. United States, 462
Mao Zedong, 617
Mapp v. Ohio, 93, 285, 534, 535, 1024
Marbury, William, 64, 583
Marbury v. Madison, 30, 64, 71, 91, 179, 187, 449, 451, 583, 611–612, 800, 815, 825–831, 1065, 1067
Mardian Robert, 689
Marihuana: Assassin of Youth, 499
Marijuana, 509
Marijuana Tax Act, 499
Maritime law. *See* admiralty and maritime law
Marriage, 1109
Marshall, George C., 614
Marshall, John, 30, 64, 91, 106, 170, 183, 449, 451, 525, 556, 611, 619, 647, 694, 695, 825

Marshall, Thurgood, 269, 513, 669, 685, 696, 714

Marshall Court, 91

Martial law, 543

Martin v. Hunter's Lesee, 694

Martin v. Mott, 962

Marx, Karl, 166

Marxist jurisprudence, 166

Mary II, Queen of England, 11

Maryland, 10, 19

Mason, George, 26, 32, 419

Mason Co. v. Tax Comm'n., 960–961

Mass media, 172

Massachusetts, 33

Massachusetts Bay Colony, 9–10

Massachusetts Body of Liberties, 419

Massachusetts Constitution, 23

Massachusetts v. Laird, 581

The Masses (magazine), 544

Masses Publishing Co. v. Patten, 545

Maternity leave, 281

Mathias, Charles, 512

Maury, James, 14

McAllister, Matthew, 847

McCarran Act, 614, 617

McCarthy, Joseph Raymond, 613–615, 617. *See also* civil rights and civil liberties; McCarthyism; Red Scare

McCarthyism, 613, 615–618, 665. *See also* civil rights and civil liberties; Federal Bureau of Investigation (FBI); Red Scare; surveillance, technological

McCleskey, Warren, 474

McCleskey v. Kemp, 474–475

McCloskey, Paul, 512

McConnell, Edward C., 430

McCord, James, 688, 735–736

McCorlke, William, 414

McCormack Act, 615

McCorvey, Norma, 669

McCulloch, James, 619

McCulloch v. Maryland, 449, 556, 618–619, 965

McGhee family, 684

McGovern, George, 512

McGuinn v. Forbes, People v. King, 900

McKinley v. United States, 961

McLaurin v. Oklahoma State Regents, 686, 976

McNamara, Robert, 512

McPherson v. *Blacker*, 1122

McReynolds, James Clark, 643

Means, Russell, 598

Meany, George, 724

Medical cannabis laws, 501

Medina, Ernest, 413

Memoirs v. Massachusetts, 636

"A Memorial and Remonstrance" (Madison), 679

Mental/emotional abuse, 490

Merit selection, 610

Merit Systems Protection Board, 206

Meritor Savings Bank v. Vinson, 605

Mexican Americans, 537–538

Meyer v. Nebraska, 642, 1023, 1061

Michael, Musheno, 704

Michael v. Superior Court of Sonoma County, 461, 462

Michigan: A History of Governments (Cooley), 454

Michigan v. Mosley, 624

Military laws, 458. *See also* Uniform Code of Military Justice (UCMJ)

Military necessity, 955

Mill, Johns Stuart, 435, 491

Miller and Paris, 637

Miller v. California, 637, 640

Miller v. French, 287

Miller v. United States, 961

Milliken v. Bradley, 272

Milton, John, 526

Ministerial acts, 179

Minor, Virginia, 864

Minor v. Happersett, 1872, 864–866

Minority leader, 44

Minors, 126

Miranda, Ernesto, 621, 622

Miranda exceptions: attorney waivers, 335; booking procedures, 335; delayed warnings, 335; derivative evidence, 335; illegal search and seizure, 335; impeachment, 335; independent evidence, 335–336; jailhouse informers and surreptitious questioning, 335; private

Miranda exceptions (*Cont.*)
   security, 336; public safety, 336; purged taint, 336; resumed questioning, 336
Miranda requirements, 621
Miranda triggers: about, 333–334; confession, 334
Miranda v. Arizona, 285, 320–322, 558, 620–622, 626, 657
Miranda warnings, 622–626; background, 623–624; future prospects, 626; key legal cases, 624–626. *See also* Bill of Rights; constitutional interpretation
Mississippi University for Women v. Hogan, 574
Missouri, K. & Title R. Co. v. Roberts, 905
Missouri Compromise (1820), 92
Missouri Plan, 131, 136
Missouri v. Holland, 1064
Missouri v. Seibert, 625
Mistrial, 243, 261
Mitchell, John, 512, 632, 689, 734, 735
Mitigating circumstances, 473–474
M.L.B. v. S.L.J, 643
Model administrative civil penalty statute, 222
Model of public law litigation: Equitable Remedies, 272–275; Public Law Litigation and *Brown v. Board of Education*, 269–272
Model Penal Code, 119, 212
Model State Administrative Procedure Act (MSAPA), 192
Modern Uses of Logic in Law (American Bar Association), 166
Modified Missouri Plan, 137
Monell v. Department of Social Services of the City of New York, 281, 282, 285
Monetary damages, 153, 281
Money damages, 284
Monopolies, 546
Monroe Family, 279–280
Monroe v. Pape, 279–281, 282, 285, 1024
Montesquieu, 21, 22
Montoya de Hernandez, 428
Moore v. Ogilvie, 1124
Moragne v. States Marine Lines, 398
Moral opposition, 602

Moral principle, 629
Morality, 436
Morgan v. Virginia, 445
Morris, Governeur, 743
Morris, Lewis, 742–743
Morrissey v. Brewer, 655
Motion for default judgment, 241
Motion for judgment, 261
Motion for new trial, 261
Motion for relief from judgment, 261
Motion to amend, 234
Motion to dismiss, 237
Motion to make more definite, 240
Motion to quash, 240
Motion to strike, 240
Motions: posttrial motions, 244–246; pretrial motions, 240–244
Motorola, 561
Mott, Frank, 576
Mott, Lucretia, 837
Mount Vernn Conference, 24
Muir, John, 686
Muller v. Oregon, 163, 912–916
Multidistrict litigation, 249
Multiple establishment, 519
Municipal government, 117
Murder, 469, 473, 476
Murphy, Frank, 198, 536
Muskrat v. United States, 400
Musmanno, Michael, 649
Mutual Film Corporation v. Ohio Industrial Commission, 635
My Lai Massacre, 413

NAACP v. Alabama, 1023
NAACP v. Button, 1023
Napoleonic Code, 113, 118, 154, 399
Narcotics Act of 1914, 502
Narcotics Control Act of 1956, 502
National Aeronautics and Space Administration, 194, 215–216
National Archives and Research Administration, 204
National Association for the Advancement of Colored People (NAACP), 269, 289, 571
National Bankruptcy Review Commission, 105

National Center for State Courts (NCSC), 126, 430–431

National Childhood Vaccine Injury Act of 1986, 102

National Conference of Commissioners on Uniform State Laws (NCCUSL), 119, 192, 212

National defense, 513

National DNA Database (NDNAD), 485

National DNA Index System (NDIS), 486

National Endowment for the Arts, 436, 638

National Endowment for the Arts v. Finley, 638

National Industrial Recovery Act, 552

National judiciary, 20

National Labor Relations Board, 195

National Law Journal, 697

National Legal Aid and Defender Association, 557, 656

National Motor Vehicle Theft Act of 1919, 529

National Organization of Women, 571

National Probation Act, 653

National Railroad Passenger Corporation (Amtrak), 196

National Recovery Administration, 196–197

National Resources Defense Council, 210

National Rifle Association, 627–629. *See also* Bill of Rights

National Security Act of 1947, 722

National security adviser, 56

National Security Agency (NSA), 99

National security claim, 512

National Security Council (NSC), 55, 197

National sovereignty vs. state sovereignty, 619

National Voting Rights Act of 1965, 41

Native American tribal courts: courts of the federal territories and tribal governments of the United States, 143–144; judicial branch of the Navajo Nation, 143–144

Native American tribes, 142

Natural Gas Policy Act of 1978, 98

Natural law and natural rights, 629–631. *See also* common law; constitutional interpretation; equity

Natural law freedoms, 12

Natural law theory, 443, 549

Natural rights, 18

Naturalization Act (1798), 797

Navajo common law, 144

Navajo Nation Courts, 143

Navigation Acts, 11, 12

Nazi leaders, 577

Near v. Minnesota, 552

Necessary and proper clause, 42–43, 192, 405

Necessary elements of a crime: actus reus, 300–301; injury or result, 301; law defining the crime and the punishment, 300; mens rea, 301

Neem, Johann N., 523

Negligence, 234

New Deal, 171, 196, 198

New Federalist Papers: Essays in Defense of the Constitution (Sullivan), 698

New Jersey Plan, 27

New York, 10, 19, 33

New York Married Woman's Property Act, 1848, 839–840

New York Times, 511, 512, 513, 568, 734

New York Times Company v. the United States, 512

New York v. Ferber, 639

New York v. P.J. Video Inc., 637

New York v. Quarles, 625

New York Weekly Journal, 742, 755

Newton, Isaac, 438

Nicholson, Max, 739

Ninth Amendment, 35, 162, 495

Ninth Circuit, 834, 854, 933

Nix v. Williams, 535

Nixon, Richard M., 499, 512, 513, 616, 618, 631–633, 688, 689, 733, 734, 736, 737. *See also* censorship; checks and balances; electronic surveillance; Ellsberg, Daniel; judicial review; Sirica, John Joseph; Watergate scandal

Nixon v. Administrator of General Services, 421

NLRB v. Friedman-Harry Marks Clothing Co., 553

NLRB v. Jones & Laughlin Steel Corp., 553

No Child Left Behind law, 217

Nollan test, 709
Nollan v. California Coastal Commission, 708, 709
Nolle prosequi, 246
Nonpartisan election to 6-year terms, 134–135
Nonpartisan election to 8-year terms, 135–136
Nonpartisan election to 10-year terms, 136
North American Free Trade Agreement, 564
North Carolina v. Alford, 646
Northern Mariana Islands Superior Court, 145–146
Northern Mariana Islands Supreme Court, 145
Northern Pipeline Construction Co. v. Marathon Pipe Line Co., 104, 107
Northern Securities Company v. United States, 549
Not guilty verdict, 79, 86
Notice pleading, 157, 233
"The Notion of a Living Constitution" by William H. Rehnquist, 1976, 1063–1075
NTP Inc., 560
Nuclear bomb, 616
Numerosity, 249
Nuremburg Trials, 576

Obama, Barack H., 572, 699
Obiter dicta, 151, 447
Obscenity, 435, 436, 635, 636
Obscenity and pornography, 634–641; broadcast media and telephone communication, 638–639; defining obscenity, 635–636; more recent trends, 637–638; protecting children, 639–641; redefining obscenity, 637. *See also* MacKinnon, Catherine Alice; Warren, Earl
Occupational Safety and Health Administration (OSHA), 219
O'Connor, Sandra Day, 403, 441, 442, 451, 596, 602, 642, 650
October Revolution, 663
Of Mice and Men (Steinbeck), 437
Offender accountability, 463
Office of Advocacy, 217–218, 219

Office of Community Oriented Policing Services, 61
Office of Information and Regulatory Affairs (OIRA), 216
Office of Justice Programs, 61
Office of Management and Budget (OMB), 55, 56, 197
Office of National Drug Control Policy, 500
Office of Personnel Management (OPM), 195, 390
Office of Technology Assessment, 193
Office of the Vice President, 197
Oliphant, Mark David, 717
Oliphant v. Suquamish Indian Tribe, 717, 718
Olmstead, Tommy, 507
Olmstead v. United States, 507–508, 652, 1061
Olsen v. Nebraska, 1023
Omnibus Anti-Drug Abuse Act (1988), 503
Omnibus Crime Control and Safe Streets, 508
On Liberty (Mill), 435
One person, one vote principle, 451
Online agency information, 203
Opinion, advisory. *See* advisory opinions
Opp Cotton Mills v. Administrator, 967
Oral argument, 94, 184
Oral arguments, 240, 407
Order, 200
Order of succession, 52
Organization and functions of the modern federal bureaucracy: cabinet departments, 194; government corporations, 195–196; independent agencies, 194–195; independent regulatory commissions, 195
Organization and operation of state courts: about, 118–120; state appellate organization and jurisdiction, 128–131; state trial courts of general jurisdiction, 120–125; state trial courts of limited jurisdiction, 125–128
Organization of the executive branch: Cabinet, 57–59; Department of Justice, 59–60; Executive Office of the President, 55–57; Solicitor General, 60–61;

specialized divisions and offices, 61; U.S. Attorney General, 60

Organization of the Federal Judiciary: courts of limited jurisdiction and legislative courts, 69; Supreme Court of the United States, 67–69; U.S. Courts of Appeal, 67; U.S. District Courts, 65–67

Organized crime, 304, 599

Original intent, 449, 520

Original jurisdiction, 63, 64, 89, 120

Originalism, 450

Orleans v. Dukes, 1116

Osborne v. Ohio, 639

Otis, James, Jr., 12–13

"Our Federalism," 181, 274, 741

Oversight, Reform, and Reduction of the Bureaucracy: Administrative Conference of the United States, 222–223; congressional oversight and control of agency rule making, 219–222; executive branch oversight of federal agency rule making, 216–219

Paine, Thomas, 17

Palko v. Connecticut, 121, 165, 1061

Palm Beach Canvassing Bd. v. *Harris*, 1126

Palmer, A. Mitchell, 61, 665

Palmer Raids, 662, 665

Palmore v. Sidoti, 643

Palumbo, Dennis, 704

Panoptic surveillance, 703

Pardons, 53

Parens patriae, 589

Parens patriae doctrine, 642

Parental rights, 642–644; commitment of a child to a mental institution, 644; custody, 643–644; reproductive rights of minors, 644; right to be a parent, 642. *See also* juvenile justice system

Paris Adult Theatre v. Slaton, 637

Paris Convention, 564

Parishes, 117

Parkinson, Ken, 689

Parliament, 15

Parole, 654. *See also* probation and parole

Parson's Cause, 14

Partisan litigation, 295

Partisan politics, 132

Partisan reelection, 134

Party of the first part, 227

Party of the second part, 227

Parvin, Albert, 496

Parvin Foundation, 496

Patent claims, 146

Patent Cooperation Treaty, 564

Patents, 74, 560

Paterson, William, 27

Patriot Act Reauthorization Bill of 2005, 84

Patronage positions, 81, 132, 196

Paxton, James, 13

Paxton's case, 13

Payne v. Tennessee, 464

Pearl Harbor attack, 543, 631

Pen register, 508–509

Pendleton Act (1893), 196

Penn Central Transportation Company v. New York, 710

Pennsylvania Coal Company v. Mahon, 708

Penry v. Lynaugh, 466

Pentagon attacks (2001), 1173

Pentagon Papers (Ellsberg), 511, 513, 514, 734

People ex rel. Detroit & Howell Railroad v. Township of Salem, 454

People ex rel. Joseph Workman v. The Board of Education of Detroit, 454

People v. Castro, 487

People v. Defore, 536

Per curiam opinion, 87, 95, 96

Peremptory challenges, 257, 585

Permanent Court of Arbitration, 552

Permissive intervention, 249

Personal Constitutional rights vs. cost-benefit approach, 535

Petit (trial) jury, 78, 79, 121, 257, 608

Petitioner, 227

Pfizer, 566

Physical abuse, 491

Pierce v. Society of Sisters, 642, 1022, 1023, 1061

Pierson v. Ray, 554

Pinchot, Gifford, 687

Pinckney, Charles, 30

Piracy, 563–564, 567

Pitchfork, Colin, 484–485

Pitchfork Case, 484, 486

Plain meaning rule, 168, 169

Plaintiff, 227

Planned Parenthood League of Connecticut, 1021

Planned Parenthood of Central Missouri v. Danforth, 441, 644

Planned Parenthood v. Casey, 441, 442, 451, 596, 602, 603, 644, 650

Plant Patent Act of 1930, 562

Plea bargain, 121, 176

Plea bargaining, 644–646. *See also* district attorney; public defender system

Pleadings: about, 232–233; answer, 237–240; complaint, 233–234; summons, 234–237

Plenary power, 114, 716

Plenury jurisdiction, 173

Plessy, Homer, 894

Plessy v. Ferguson, 269, 271, 452, 515, 548, 650, 856, 894–903, 973, 974, 975, 977, 1111

Plumbers, 631, 734, 735

Pocket veto, 51

Poe v. Ullman, 1024

Police brutality, 281

Police discretion: trivial offenses, 332; victim also involved in misconduct, 332; victim will not seek prosecution, 332

Police power, 646–648, 715

Political action committees (PACs), 289

Political crimes, 304

Political parties, 506

Political speech, 181, 274

Pollock v. Farmer's Loan and Trust Company, 548

Pornography, 437, 605, 606, 636, 637. *See also* obscenity and pornography

Positivism, 159

Positivists, 159

Posner, Richard, 164, 561, 563

Postarrest, pretrial procedures: asset forfeiture, 339–340; bail, 338–339; identification, 336–339

Post-Marxist jurisprudence, 166

Posttrial motions: about, 244–245; judgment as a matter of law, 245; motion for a directed verdict, 245; motion for judgment *non obstante veredicto*, 245; motion for new trial, 246; motion for nolle prosequi, 246; motion to set aside judgment, 246; renewed judgment as a matter of law, 245–246

Potential party, 249

Pound, Roscoe, 119, 163

Powell, Adam C., Jr., 598

Powell, Lewis, 440–441, 442, 535, 595, 596, 669, 676, 690

Powell v. Alabama, 557, 657

Power of the purse, 35, 216

Power of the sword, 35

Pragmatism, 162

Preanswer motion, 237

Precedent doctrine, 95, 150–151, 171, 447, 448, 449, 450, 648–651. *See also* appellate courts; common law; judicial review

Preclusion, 239

Presentation of the case: closing arguments, 260; instructing the jury, 260; motion for directed verdict, 259; opening statements, 258; plaintiff's rebuttal, 259–260; presentation of the defendant's case, 259; presentation of the plaintiff's case, 258–259; verdict, 260–261

Presidential appointments, 53

Presidential election, 51, 52

Presidential powers, 53–55, 54–55

Presidential Succession Act, 52

Presiding judge, 121

Preston, Thomas, 15

Pretrial motions: default judgment, 241; defense to a claim, 242; involuntary dismissal, 242–243; motion for judgment on the pleadings, 243; motion for summary judgment, 243–244; motion in limine, 243; motion to compel, 243; motion to dismiss, 242; voluntary dismissal, 242

Pretrial procedures: discovery, 250–253; litigating parties, 247–250; motions, 240–246; pleadings, 232–240

Price controls, 550

Primary rules of conduct, 160

Primogeniture, 10

Prince of Wales, 425

Prince v. Massachusetts, 642, 1061
Prior restraint, 513
Prison Litigation Reform Act of 1996 (PLRA), 182, 274, 275, 287
Prison overcrowding, 286
Prisoners, 180, 268; civil rights litigation, 285, 286; conditions, 446; federal habeas corpus, 541
Privacy, 651–653. *See also* Bill of Rights
Privacy invasion, 699
Private action vs. state action, 685
Private law, 267
Private law vs. public law, 226
Privileges and immunities clauses, 684–685
Pro bono policy, 288
Pro se appearance, 232
Pro se petition, 601
Probable cause, 34, 427, 508; admitted ownership, 325; association with known criminals, 326; failure to protest, 325; false or improbable answers, 326; flight or evasion, 325; furtive movements, 325; indirect sources of probable cause, 326–327; observation, 325; past criminal conduct, 326; presence at a crime scene or presence in high-crime areas, 325; reasonable suspicion, 324
Probate cases, 75
Probate process, 74
Probation and parole, 653–655. *See also* Bill of Rights; district attorney; jury systems
Problem-solving courts, 125
Procedural rights, 78–79
Process Act of 1789, 183
Process Act of 1792, 183, 228
Process serving, 233, 235
Proffitt v. Florida, 472
Progressives, 161–163
Property law, 150
Property rights, 24, 35, 583
Property rights, intellectual. *See* intellectual property rights
Proposed legislation, 49
Proposition 8, 693
Proposition 69, 488, 489
Proposition 215, 501

Proposition 220, 127
Proposition P, 499
Prosecutorial immunity, 554
Prostitution, 606
Protect America Act (2007), 100, 101
Protection of Children Against Sexual Exploitation Act of 1977, 639
Public Citizen, 288
Public decency statute, 637
Public defender system, 656–660; indigent defense services, 657–659; legal developments, 657; stresses in the system, 659. *See also* indigent defendant representation
Public defenders, 557, 558, 559
Public interest groups: amicus curiae, 290; goals and objectives of interest groups, 288–289; litigation by interest groups, 289–290; prominent public interest groups, 291–292
Public knowledge/awareness, 172
Public Law 280, 716, 717
Public law litigation and public interest law in the United States: about, 267–269; cause lawyering and the public interest, 287–294; federal civil rights litigation and state institutions, 278–287; judicial policy making and public law litigation, 294–296; model of public law litigation, 269–278
Public law vs. private law, 226
Public Papers of the President, 204
Public Utilities Comm'n v. Pollak, 1024
Publication of administrative rules and regulations: *Code of Federal Regulations*, 203; *Federal Register*, 203; *Notice of Proposed Rule Making*, 202–203
Publius. *See Federalist Papers* ("Publius")
Pulley v. Harris, 474
Pulley v. Harris In Pulley v. Harris, 474
Punishment. *See* cruel and unusual punishment
Punitive damages, 261–262
Pure Food and Drug Act of 1906, 193
Putnam, Samuel, 694

Qualified immunity doctrine, 284, 554
Quartering troops, 34

Quayle, Dan, 218
Quilloin v. Walcott, 643

R. v. Butler, 606
Race questions, 488
Race-based segregation, 269
Racial discrimination, 477, 686, 894;
    death penalty and, 474; in voting, 506
Racial DNA profiling, 488
Racial integration, 270
Racial minorities, 445
Racial preference, 575
Racial quotas, 403
Racial segregation, 180–181, 227, 268,
    272, 515, 650, 856, 978
Racially restrictive covenant, 684, 685
Racketeer Influenced and Corrupt Organi-
    zations Act (RICO Act), 275
Radio frequency identification device
    (RFID), 701
Railroad Co. v. Benson, 900
Railroad Co. v. Wells, 900
Railroad v. Miles, 900
Railway Co. v. Williams, 900
Railway Express Agency, Inc. v. New York,
    460, 1116
Ranbaxy Laboratories Ltd, 566
RAND Corporation, 511
Randolph, A. Philip, 402
Randolph, Edmund, 26, 27, 32, 555, 556
Rasul v. Bush, 544
Rational Basis Scrutiny, 661–662. *See also*
    equal protection clause
Rational basis scrutiny, 574
Rational basis test, 459–460, 696, 697
Ravin v. State, 500
Reagan, Nancy, 500
Reagan, Ronald, 216, 500, 539, 595, 668,
    692
Reapportionment, 186, 415–416, 445
Reapportionment Act of 1929, 40
Recall by election, 142
Recidivism, 466, 497, 593, 655
Reconstruction, 60, 856, 862
Reconstruction amendments, 42, 173
Reconstruction program, 548
Red Scare, 662–665. *See also* civil rights
    and civil liberties; Federal Bureau of

Investigation (FBI); McCarthyism;
    Rosenberg, Julius and Ethel
Red tape, 216
Redistricting, 41
Reed, Stanley, 713
Reed v. Reed, 460, 461, 515
Reefer Madness (movie), 499
Reformatories, 589
*Regents of the University of California v.
    Bakke*, 403
Regina v. Hicklin, 635
Regulatory Council, 217
Regulatory enforcement, 200
Regulatory takings, 707–709, 711
Rehnquist, William H., 427, 441, 442,
    603, 651, 671, 672, 677, 682, 708, 709,
    714, 1063
Rehnquist court, 542, 637, 639, 640
Reitman v. Mulkey, 1112
"Religion, Government, and Power in the
    New American Nation" (Wilson, J. F.),
    522
Religion and the Continental Congress
    (Davis), 519
Remedies, 153, 517
Removal power, 174
Reno, Janet, 692
Reno v. American Civil Liberties Union, 640
Reno v. Flores, 643
Renton v. Playtime Theatres, Inc., 714–715
Reorganization Act of 1939, 197
Reorganization of the Judicial Circuits,
    1866, 861–862
The Reorganization of the Judiciary (Field,
    David), 156
Reorganization Plan 1, 197
Reorganization Plan 2, 197
Representation, indigent defendant. *See*
    indigent defendant representation
Republic vs. democracy, 569
Res indicata, 263
Res judicata, 492
Research in Motion Ltd. (RIM), 560–561
Reservation law enforcement, 717
Respondent, 86, 227
Restitution, 463, 666–667. *See also* crime
    victims, rights of
Restraining order, 262

Retention elections, 134
Retirement plans, 142
Return of service, 236
Reuther, Walter, 724
Reverse (action), 96
Review, 129
Reynolds v. Sims, 41, 417, 516, 1112, 1122
Reynolds v. United States, 680
Rhode Island, 21
Richardson, Elliot, 633, 736, 737
Ridde, Mildred, 496
Riders, 50
Right of appeals, 923
Right of personal choice, 670
Right of privacy, 581, 1058
Right to a public trial, 644
Right to a speedy trial, 35, 644, 690–691.
   See also Bill of Rights
Right to an attorney, 445, 557, 558, 621,
   625
Right to bear arms, 34
Right to die, 630
Right to due process of law, 555
Right to freedom of assembly, 797
Right to freedom of the press, 797
Right to jury trial, 34, 206, 389, 585
Right to privacy, 282, 495–496, 672
Right to public trial, 78
Right to restitution, 667
Right to speedy trial, 35, 78, 690–691
Right to travel, 672
Right to trial by jury, 9, 30, 35
Rights. *See* natural law and natural rights;
   parental rights; speedy trial, right to
*The Rights of the Colonies Asserted and
   Proved* (Otis), 13
Riparian rights, 152, 448
Ritchie v. People, 914
Robbins v. Lower Merion School District,
   282
Roberts, John, 650, 651
Roberts v. Louisiana, 472
Robinson v. California, 465
Rochin v. California, 428
Rockefeller Drug Laws, 499
Roe v. Wade, 171, 439, 440, 441, 442,
   451, 496, 581, 650, 651, 653, 668–673,
   1058–1063

Role of the administrative law judge:
   appointment of administrative law
   judges, 207; independence of adminis-
   trative law judges, 206–207; professional
   organizations for administrative law
   judges, 207
"The Role of the Judge in Public Law
   Litigation" (Chayes), 295
Roman law, 399, 424
Romer v. Evans, 596, 603, 1111–1118
*Romero v. International Terminal Operat-
   ing Co.*, 396
Roosevelt, Franklin D., 52, 55, 196, 197,
   198, 392, 402, 494, 530, 576, 577, 615,
   631, 936, 946, 952–953, 968
Roosevelt, Theodore, 529, 887
Roper v. Simmons, 475
Rosenberg, Julius and Ethel, 617, 673–675.
   See also civil rights and civil liberties;
   Federal Bureau of Investigation (FBI);
   McCarthyism; Red Scare
Roth v. United States, 635
Rowling, J. K., 437
Rubin, Jerry, 598
Ruby Ridge events, 530
Ruckelhaus, William, 633, 737
Ruiz v. Estelle, 286
Rule making procedures, 212
Rule making vs. adjudication: adjudica-
   tion, 200–201; rule making, 199–200
Rule of 80, 66, 82
Rule of Four, 93
Rule of reason theory, 549
Rule-making process, 202
Rules Enabling Act (1934), 229
Rules of abstention, 274
Rules of civil procedure, 225, 226;
   about, 227–228; chapters and cate-
   gories of the Federal Rules of Civil
   Procedure, 231–232; Federal Rules
   of Civil Procedure and state rules,
   228–230
Rules of evidence, 445
Rummel, William James, 466
Rummel v. Estelle, 466
Rush, Benjamin, 469
Russo, Anthony, 512
Rust v. Sullivan, 698

Rutledge, John, 26
Rutledge, Wiley, 642

Sable Communications of California, Inc. v. FCC, 638–639
Saffell, Genevieve, 428
Saffell v. Crews, 429
Same-sex couples, 1145
Same-sex marriage, 604, 1145
San Diego Gas and Electric Company v. City of San Diego, 708, 710
Sanctions, 176
Santobello v. New York, 646
Santosky v. Kramer, 643
Saturday Night Massacre, 632, 737
Saving to suitors clause, 397
Savings and loan scandals, 216
Scalia, Antonin, 582, 603, 604, 648, 709
Schechter Poultry Corporation v. United States, 552
Schenck v. United States, 550
Schlup v. Delo, 487
School desegregation, 269
Schware v. Board of Bar Examiners, 1024
Scott v. Sandford, 450
Search and seizure, 34
Search and seizure restrictions, 93
Search warrants, 78, 676–678, 730; exceptions, 535; no-knock warrants, 328; particularity of search warrants, 327–328; stop and frisk, 329; surveillance warrants, 328–329. *See also* border searches
Searches, border. *See* border searches
Second Amendment, 34, 627, 628, 629
Second Continental Congress, 17, 18, 578, 762
Second Red Scare, 614, 617, 665
Second Treatise on Government (Hobbes), 159
Secondary rules of conduct, 160
Secondat, Charles-Louis de. *See* Montesquieu
Secrets (Bailey), 414
Section 2241, 180
Section 2255, 180
Securities and Exchange Commission, 195
Sedition Act (1798), 797

Sedition Act of 1918, 663, 665
Segregated public buses, 445
Segregation, 445, 973, 984; de jure segregation, 270, 272; desegregation of public education, 992–995; desegregation of public facilities, 991–992; race-based segregation, 269; school segregation, 980; segregation, 856; state segregation laws, 973; union segregation, 724; of U.S. military, 972. *See also* racial segregation
Segura v. United States, 535
Seizure of evidence, 78
Select Committee on Presidential Campaign Activities, 734
Select committees, 44–45
Selection to 6-year terms, 137–138
Selection to 8-year terms, 138–139
Selection to 10-year terms, 139–140
Selection to 12-year terms, 140
Selection to life terms, 140–141
Self-defense, 238
Self-incrimination, 34, 621, 623
Self-incrimination clause, 623
Senate, 40; administrative nominations, 55, 58; amendments, 404; electoral college, 52; impeachment, 69, 90, 131, 693; judicial confirmation, 51, 54, 61, 66, 70, 80, 83, 84, 90, 98, 99, 102, 103, 104, 131, 141, 146, 207, 344, 346, 390, 479, 550, 552, 576, 596; treaty ratification, 51, 552. *See also* McCarthyism; Watergate scandal
Senate Committee on Homeland Security and Government Affairs, 45
Senate Committee on the Judiciary, 47
Senate committees: joint committees, 48; select committees, 48; standing committees, 47–48
Senate Judiciary Committee, 70, 946–947
Senate Watergate Committee, 631, 688, 734
Seneca Falls Convention, 837, 839
Senior judges, 66
Seniority rule, 82
Sentencing, 124
Sentencing Reform Act of 1984, 503, 655
Separate but equal doctrine, 973, 977

Separate sovereign doctrine, 715, 718

Separation of church and state, 451, 678–683. *See also* Warren, Earl

Separation of Church and State (Hamburger), 521

Separation of powers, 451

Separationists, 518

September 11 attacks, 544, 595, 699, 1173

Service delivery, 658

Servicemembers Civil Relief Act, 104

Settlement, 176

Seventeenth Amendment, 40, 505

Seventh Amendment, 35, 80, 156, 177, 206, 246, 255, 389, 584

Seventh Circuit, 832

Seventh Circuit establishment, 1807, 832–834

Sewall, Samuel, 694

Sex discrimination, 605, 982

Sexual abuse, 491

Sexual harassment, 605

Sexual Harassment of Working Women: A Case of Sex Discrimination (MacKinnon), 605

Sexual orientation, 596, 601, 603, 1111

Sexual privacy, 445

Shafer Commission, 500

Shapiro, Robert, 414

Shaw v. Reno, 42

Shays, Daniel, 25

Shays' Rebellion, 25

Sheehan, Neil, 512

Sheldon v. Metro-Goldwyn Pictures, 546

Shelley v. Kraemer, 445, 683–686

Shelly family, 684

Shepard, Sam, 413

Sherman, John, 887

Sherman, Roger, 18, 27, 31, 419

Sherman Anti-Trust Act (1890), 193, 195, 546

Sherman Antitrust Act, 1890, 887–888

Sierra Club, 686–687. *See also* interest groups and lobbying

Sierra Club v. Morton, 496

Silent Spring (Carson), 496

Simpson, C. J., 414

Simpson, O. J., 492

Sipes v. McGhee, 683–685

Sirica, John Joseph, 687–690, 735–736, 737. *See also* checks and balances; Nixon, Richard M.; Watergate scandal

Sixth Amendment, 35, 78, 80, 226, 235, 255, 399, 557, 584, 644, 656, 690

Skinner v. Oklahoma, 1024, 1061

Slaughterhouse Cases, 514

Slavery, 18, 24, 31, 32, 43, 695, 770, 840, 842, 852

Slip laws, 204

Small, William, 578

Small Business Administration, 217

Smith, S. K., 717

Smith, William French, 692

Smith Act of 1940, 495

Smith v. Allwright, 445

Smith v. Hooey, 690

Smith v. Maryland, 508

Snyder v. Massachusetts, 647

Social Security Administration, 73, 196, 208, 215

Sociological jurisprudence, 163

Socratic method, 161

Sodomy, 602, 653

Solem v. Helm, 466

Solicitors, 424

Sotomayor, Sonja, 699

Sources and methods of American Law: civil law tradition, 154–155; codification movement, 155–156; common law, 150–152; contemporary court procedure, 156–157; equity, 152–154

Souter, David H., 442, 451, 596, 650, 692, 699

South Carolina v. Katzenbach, 1026

Southern Pacific Co. v. Jensen, 397

Sovereign immunity, 64, 90, 98, 282, 283

Soviet Union, 613

Spalding v. Chandler, 905

Speaker of the House, 43–44

Special prosecutor, 631–632

Special scrutiny, 186

Special verdicts, 261

Speedy disposition, 432

Speedy Trial Act of 1974, 691

Speedy trial, right to. *See* right to a speedy trial

The Spirit of Liberty (Hand), 546

The Spirit of the Laws (Montesquieu), 21
Spiritual abuse, 491
Spoils system, 196
Spotted Tail, 716
Stamp Act Congress, 15
Stamp Act of 1765, 14, 15
Standard of proof, 260
Standard Oil Company v. United States, 549
Standards of appellate review: arbitrary
   and capricious, 184–185; clearly
   erroneous standards, 185; review de
   novo, 185
Standards of review, 407
Standing, 65
Stanford v. Kentucky, 465
Stanford v. Texas, 677
Stanley v. Georgia, 636, 639, 1061
Stanley v. Illinois, 643
Stanton, Elizabeth Cady, 837
Stare decisis doctrine, 9, 95, 113, 151, 153,
   171, 447, 450, 626, 649, 651. *See also*
   precedent doctrine
Starr, Kenneth Winston, 692–693. *See also*
   checks and balances
State action vs. private action, 685
State administrative law: state administra-
   tive law judges, 213–215; state adminis-
   trative procedure acts, 212–213
State administrative law judges: about,
   213–214; state departments and agencies
   with ALJs, 214–215
State administrative procedure acts: 1946
   Model State Administrative Procedure
   Act, 212; 1961 Model State Administrative Procedure Act, 212–213; 1981
   Model State Administrative Procedure
   Act, 213
State and local law enforcement: federal
   support of state and local law enforcement, 307–308; history of American
   police departments, 305–306; municipal
   police, 306; oversight of police department operations, 307; state and county
   police, 306
State appellate organization and jurisdiction: about, 128–129; intermediate
   appellate courts, 129–130; state courts
   of last resort, 130–131

State citizenship, 481
State constitution(s), 1, 2, 8, 20–24, 26–27,
   29, 32, 70, 114–115, 117, 128, 130, 131,
   139, 150, 172, 186, 187, 211, 212, 221,
   226, 228, 241, 299, 327, 355, 368, 409,
   420, 463, 541, 603, 706–707, 713, 911
State court administrator, 430
State court inadequacy, 281
State courts, 74, 116, 118
State courts vs. federal courts, 868
State electoral practices, 505
State judges, 81
State judicial selection and service: about,
   131–132; election of judges, 132–136;
   gubernatorial appointment and legislative appointment, 141–142; merit
   selection, 136–141
State judiciary, 113–147; about, 113–147;
   American state government, 114–119;
   courts of the federal territories and
   tribal governments of the united states,
   142–147; organization and operation of
   state courts, 119–131; removal of state
   judges, 142; state judicial selection and
   service, 131–142
State law: vs. federal law, 75; origins, 448
State of the Union message, 53
State prison systems, 446
State religion, 34
State segregation laws, 548
State sovereign immunity, 581
State sovereignty, 114
State sovereignty vs. national sovereignty,
   619
State supreme court nomenclature, 131
State trial courts of general jurisdiction:
   about, 120–121; administrative staff,
   122; civil cases, 121–125; criminal
   cases, 121; state jury, 123–124; state
   sentencing, 124; state sentencing and
   habeas corpus, 124–125
State trial courts of limited jurisdiction:
   about, 125–126; justice of the peace
   courts, 127; juvenile courts, 126; state
   trial court administration, 128; unified
   courts, 127–128
State v. Buchanan, 914
State v. Judge, 900

States' rights, 980

Statute of limitations, 238, 242

Statutory construction, 167

Statutory criminal offense, 565

Statutory invalidation, 186

Staying proceedings, 274

Steelman, D. C., 431

Steinham, Gloria, 606

Stennis, John C., 737

Stephen, Viña, 428

Stephens v. Choctaw Nation, 906

Stern, Howard, 436

Stevens, John P., 501, 575, 650, 711

Stewart, Potter, 417, 471, 513, 636, 669, 670, 677

Stewart, Roy Allen, 621

Stewart v. Kahn, 961

Stipulations, 252

Stone, Harlan Fiske, 444–445, 460, 576, 577, 661

Stone v. Powell, 542

Story, Joseph, 483, 679, 694–696. *See also* common law; constitutional interpretation; equity; judicial review

Strachan, Gordon, 689

Strauder v. West Virginia, 898

Strict construction scrutiny, 574

Strict scrutiny, 661. *See also* intermediate scrutiny; rational basis scrutiny

Strikes, 664, 665

Structural cases, 295

Structural reform, 290

Structure and function of the federal government: executive branch, 51–61; judicial branch, 61–71; legislative branch, 39–51

Stuart, et al. v. School District No. 1 of the Village of Kalamazoo, et al., 454

Stump v. Sparkman, 555

"The Subjection of Women" (Mill), 491

Subject-matter jurisdiction, 120; concurrent jurisdiction, 76; diversity jurisdiction, 75; federal question jurisdiction, 75; personal jurisdiction, 76; supplemental jurisdiction, 76; territorial jurisdiction, 76

Subpoena duces tecum, 252

Subpoenas, 632

Substantial evidence test, 209

Substituted service, 235

Suffrage. *See* women's suffrage

Suggestions, 240

Suits in common law, 177

Sullivan, Kathleen Marie, 697–699. *See also* Bill of Rights; civil rights and civil liberties; constitutional interpretation

Summa Theologica (Thomas Aquinas), 630

Summary adjudication, 244

Summations, 260

Summons, 482; about, 234–235; criminal complaints, 236–237; service of process, 235–236

Sumner, Charles, 866

Sunset acts, 211

Sunset rules, 221

Sunshine Act, 203

Superior courts, 116, 120

Supermajority, 50

Supremacy clause, 31, 116, 410

Supreme Court of Guam, 145

Supreme Court of Puerto Rico, 146

Supreme Court of the United States (SCOTUS), 29; about, 89–90; Administrative Office of the United States Courts, 395–396; ALJ's, 206–207; annual term, 68; appeal process, 407–410; appellate review, 92, 102; Article VI, 204; briefs, 93; composition and jurisdiction, 90; conference, 94–95; death penalty in the United States, 471–472; federal courts of limited jurisdiction, 106–107; granting cert and the Rule of Four, 92–93; jurisdiction, 2; major courts of the federal judiciary, 89–96; membership, 67–68; membership size, 799–800, 832, 834, 861, 862, 946; opinions, 96; opinions of the Supreme Court, 95–96; oral arguments, 93–94; organization of the federal judiciary, 67–69; origin of judicial review by the U.S. Supreme Court, 90–92; origins, 62–63; review process, 573; on rights to appeal, 129; Roosevelt reorganization plans, 936, 946; Rules Enabling Act (1934), 229; sessions, 94. *See also* amicus curiae; Burger court; comity;

Supreme Court of the United States (*Cont.*) constitutional interpretation; de novo review; habeas corpus; judicial activism; judicial review; Judiciary Act of 1789; living Constitution; originalism; precedent doctrine; Rehnquist court; stare decisis doctrine; Warren court

Supreme courts of sovereign nations, 143

Surveillance, technological, 699–705; background, 700–701; theories and research over time, 702–704; types of, 701–702. *See also* electronic surveillance; search warrants

Sutherland, George, 453

Swann v. Charlotte-Mecklenburg Board of Education, 445

Swayne & Hoyt, Ltd. v. United States, 960

Sweatt v. Painter, 445, 686, 975, 976

Swift v. Tyson, 483

Taft, William H., 108, 507, 600, 918

Takings clause, 706–712. *See also* Bill of Rights

Taney, Roger B., 450

Tax court, 712–713. *See also* appellate courts; district courts; magistrate courts

Taxation, 578

Taylor, John, 619

Tea Party, 571

Teamsters Union, 725

Technological surveillance, 700

Telecommunications Act of 1996, 639

Temporary restraining order (TRO), 153, 262, 517

Tennessee Valley Authority (TVA), 196

Tenth Amendment, 35, 114, 449, 619. *See also* implied powers of U.S. Constitution

Tenth Circuit, 847, 854, 933

Tenth Circuit establishment, 1863, 854–856

Tenth Judicial Circuit establishment, 1929, 933–936

Term limits, 52, 88

Terminicello, Arthur, 495

Terminicello v. Chicago, 495

Terrett v. Taylor, 695

Terrorism, 1173

Terry v. Ohio, 1061

Texas prisons, 286

Textual interpretation, 449–450

Third Amendment, 34, 162, 495, 652

Thirteenth Amendment, 42, 173, 852, 894

Thomas, Clarence, 603

Thomas Aquinas, 630

The Thomas Jefferson, 396

"Thomas Jefferson, Danbury Baptists, and 'Eternal Hostility'" (Gaustad), 521

"Thomas Jefferson's Letter to the Danbury Baptists" (Hutson), 520

Thomas v. Gay, 905

Thompson v. Keohane, 624

Thoreau, David, 443

Thornburgh v. American College of Obstetricians and Gynecologists, 442

"Those seeking equity must do equity" doctrine, 175

Thoughts on Government, (Adams), 21, 22, 23

Three-fifths clause, 40

Three-fifths compromise, 32

Tiaco v. Forbes, 960

Tileston v. Ullman, 1022

Time (magazine), 688

Time, place, and manner restrictions, 713–715. *See also* Bill of Rights

Tinker v. Des Moines, 281

Tocqueville, Alexis de, 295

Tort law, 150, 267

Townshend Acts, 13

Trap-and-trace devices, 509–510

Treason, 30

Treasury Department, 194

Treasury Employees Union v. Von Raab, 500

A Treatise on the Constitutional Limitations Which Rest upon the Legislative Power of the States of the American Union (Cooley), 453, 454, 455

A Treatise on the Law of Property in Intellectual Productions (Drone), 561

A Treatise on the Law of Taxation Including the Law of Arise Independent of Contract (Cooley), 454–455

Treaty of Paris of 1783, 24, 694

Treaty ratification, 51

Trenchard, John, 743

Trial by jury. *See* right to trial by jury

Trial courts, 889

Trial de novo, 120, 126

Trial proceedings: change of venue, 254; forum non conveniens (FNC), 254–255; judgment, 261–263; jury, 255–258; presentation of the case, 258–261; venue, 253–254

Tribal court criminal jurisdiction, 715–719; background, 716; future prospects, 718–719; key legal cases, 716–717. *See also* appellate courts; jury systems

Tribal sovereignty, 718

Tribe, Lawrence H., 697

Trimester approach, 670

Trop, Albert, 465

Trop v. Dulles, 285, 465

Troxel v. Granville, 642

Truax v. Corrigan, 550

Truax v. Raich, 1022

Truman, Harry, 54, 198, 402, 405, 577, 614, 616, 617, 722, 972–973

Trust busting, 887

Tucker Act (1887), 98, 101, 146

Twain, Mark, 437

Twelfth Amendment, 52

Twenty-Fifth amendment, 52

Twenty-Second amendment, 52

Twenty-Third amendment, 52

Two Penny Act, 14

Two Treatises of Government (Locke), 18, 21

Tydings, Millard, 612, 617

Tydings Committee, 614

Tyson & Brothers v. Banton, 550

Udall v. Federal Power Commission, 496

Underground railroad, 842

Unger, Roberto, 166

Unicameral legislature, 115

Uniform Code of Military Justice (UCMJ), 103, 458, 459, 621, 720–724. *See also* courts-martial

Uniform Commercial Code, 119, 212

Uniform Declaratory Judgments Act (1922), 178

Uniform Jury Selection and Service Act, 123, 256

Union Pacific R. Co. v. Botsford, 1060

United Auto Workers (UAW), 724–725. *See also* interest groups and lobbying

United Farm Workers of America, 725–726. *See also* civil rights and civil liberties; interest groups and lobbying

United States Bankruptcy Courts, 1075

United States Code (U.S.C.), 75, 204; Section 1981, 281; Section 1983, 281, 282, 285, 286, 287, 293; Section 2201, 283; Section 2202, 284; Section 2241, 180; Section 2255, 180; Section 2283, 284; Title 5, 208; Title 10, 720; Title 11, 1075; Title 28, 208; Title 42, 281

United States Court of Federal Claims, 457

United States Government Manual, 193

United States Manual for Courts-Martial (MCM), 720

United States Railroad Retirement Bd. v. Fritz, 1117

United States Reports, 5

United States Statutes at Large, 204

United States v. Associated Press, 546

United States v. Calandra, 535

United States v. Carolene Products Co, 460, 661

United States v. Cook, 904

United States v. Harris, 548

United States v. Heinszen & Co., 960

United States v. John Mitchell, et al., 633

United States v. Kagama, 905

United States v. Leon, 535

United States v. Libellants and Claimants of the Schooner Amistad, 695

United States v. Local 560, International Brotherhood of Teamsters, 275

United States v. Lopez, 596, 647

United States v. MacDonald, 691

United States v. Macintosh, 961–962

United States v. Montoya de Hernandez, 428

United States v. Nixon, 633

United States v. Oakland Cannabis Buyers Cooperative, 501

United States v. One Book called "Ulysses," 635

United States v. Playboy, Inc., 639

United States v. Ramsey, 427

United States v. Thirty-seven Photographs, 427

United States v. United States District Court, 508, 676

United States v. Wade, 558, 657

United States Virgin Islands Superior Court, 147

Unreasonable search and seizure, 281, 534

Unseaworthiness, 398

U.S. Alien Tort Statute, 606

U.S. Attorney General, 193

U.S. attorneys, 66, 84, 479

U.S. bankruptcy, 66

U.S. Bankruptcy Courts establishment [Excerpt], 1978, 1075–1101

U.S. circuit courts, 868, 916

U.S. Circuit Courts of Appeals establishment (Evarts Act 1891), 889–894

U.S. Claims Court, 457

U.S. Congress: American Indian relationship, 143; apportionment, 415; Article III interpretation, 62, 274, 396; courts established by, 144, 147; vs. executive branch, 55; federal crimes, 343; federal judisdiction, 2; habeas corpus, 382; independent regulatory commissions, 195; judiciary acts, 173; legislative powers, 39, 204; *Marbury v. Madison*, 420; Speedy Trial Act of 1974, 352; tribunals, 144. *See also* House of Representatives; Senate

U.S. Constitution: Article I, 29, 39, 42, 43, 53, 73, 74, 104, 144, 179, 420, 449, 450, 458, 505, 524, 555, 608, 619, 720; Article II, 29, 51, 53, 54, 55, 73, 458, 505, 1119; Article III, 61, 62, 63, 64, 69, 74, 75, 82, 89, 91, 106, 131, 144, 152, 173, 206, 228, 274, 282, 295, 389, 396, 400, 401, 516, 612, 777; Article IV, 31, 42, 114, 192, 527, 679, 842; Article V, 31, 42, 168, 611, 825; Article VI, 31, 116, 204. *See also* implied powers of U.S. Constitution; state constitution(s); *specific amendment*

U.S. Court of Appeals for the District of Columbia Circuit, 86

U.S. Court of Claims, 1104

U.S. Court of Customs and Patent Appeals, 1104

U.S. Court of Federal Claims, 1104. *See also* court of claims

U.S. Court of Military Appeals (CMA), 103

U.S. courts of appeal, 65, 73, 566; about, 85–86; review by, 86–88

U.S. Customs Court, 97

U.S. Department of Justice (DOJ), 41

U.S. District Court for the District of Puerto Rico, 146

U.S. District Court for the Northern Mariana Islands, 146

U.S. district court judicial personnel: appointment of U.S. district judges, 80–82; chief judges of U.S. district courts, 82; senior judges, 82; U.S. magistrate judges, 82–83

U.S. district courts, 73, 75; chief judge of a U.S. court of appeals, 88–89; civil cases in, 79–80; clerk of court, 83; criminal cases in, 78–79; law clerks, 83–84; supporting personnel in, 83–85; U.S. attorneys, 84; U.S. district court judicial personnel, 80–83; U.S. marshals, 84–85

U.S. Export-Import Bank, 196

U.S. magistrate judges, 82–83, 183

U.S. marshal, 66, 84

U.S. Marshals Service, 60

U.S. military desegregation, 972

U.S. Patent and Trademark Office, 561, 563, 566

U.S. Postal Service (USPS), 215

U.S. territories, 40, 107

U.S. v. American Library Association, Inc., 640

U.S. v. Carolene Products, 444

U.S. v. John Mitchell, et al., 689

U.S. v. John N. Mitchell, et al., 735

U.S. v. Kagama, 716

U.S. v. Lara, 718

U.S. v. X-Citement Video, Inc., 639

U.S. Veteran Administration, 538

U.S. Virgin Islands Supreme Court, 147

USA PATRIOT Act (2001), 100, 510, 531, 1173–1208

Utilitarianism, 162
Utility patents, 562
Uylsses (Joyce), 635

Vacate (action), 96
Van Dam, Rip, 742
Vanderbilt, Arthur, 430
Venire, 585
Venona Project, 674
Verbal abuse, 490
Vermont Constitution, 114
Veterans Administration. *See* Department of Veterans Affairs (DVA)
Veterans' Judicial Review Act (1988), 102
Veterans' Programs Enhancement Act of 1998, 102
Veto, 51
Veto override, 51
Veto power, 53
Vetting, 81
Vice admiralty courts, 14
Vice president, 44, 52, 54
Victim impact statements, 464
Victims' rights, 727. *See also* crime victims, rights of
Vietnam, 511, 514
Vignera, Michael, 621
The Vindication of the Rights of Woman (Wollstonecraft), 491
Vindictive revenge, 476
Viner, Charles, 425
Vinson, F. M., 495, 683
Violence, domestic, 727. *See also* domestic violence
Violence Against Women Act (VAWA), 492
Virginia, 10, 19, 20, 33
Virginia Plan, 27, 29
Virginia Statute for Religious Freedom (1786), 775–777
Virtual representation, 155
Voice mail, 510
Voir dire, 123–124, 585, 608
Voter eligibility, 505
Voting, racial discrimination in, 506
Voting rights, 984
Voting Rights Act amendments (1982), 728

Voting Rights Act of 1965, 78, 275, 506, 727–729, 1025–1031. *See also* elections
Voting rights standard, 186

Waco, Texas events, 530
Wagner Act, 553, 724
Waite, Morrison, 864
Waivable defenses, 254
Waiver of service, 236
Walker, Leone, 494
Wall of separation, 518, 520, 521, 522, 523
Wallace v. Jaffree, 682
War of 1812, 580
War on drugs. *See* drugs, war on
War power, 42
Ward v. Race Horse, 905
Warrant requirements, 427
Warrantless searches, 509, 676
Warrants, search. *See* search warrants
Warren, Earl, 269, 279, 418, 445, 452, 465, 495, 577, 620, 730–733, 1032. *See also* appellate courts; constitutional interpretation; judicial activism; judicial review
Warren court, 285–286, 418, 452, 496, 636, 637, 680, 682
Washington, George, 24, 26, 57, 65, 91, 193, 401, 556, 579, 619, 842
Washington Conference on the Limitation of Armaments, 552
Washington Post, 512, 513, 568, 734, 736
Washington v. Davis, 515
Washington v. Glucksberg, 604
Washington v. Seattle School Dist. No. 1, 1112
Water courts, 125–126
Watergate scandal, 688, 733–738
Watergate Special Prosecution Force, 631
Watergate special prosecutor, 689
Wayman v. Southard, 183
Webster, Daniel, 840
Webster v. Reproductive Health Services, 442
Weddington, Sarah, 669
Weekly Compilation of Presidential Documents, 204
Weeks v. United States, 533–534, 535
Weems, Paul A., 465

Weems v. United State, 465, 466
Weller, S., 431
Wenham v. State, 914
West Coast Hotel Co. v. Parrish, 553, 907, 1023
West Virginia Board of Education v. Barnette, 577
Westover, Carl Calvin, 621
Whip, 44
White, Byron, 441, 513, 621, 622, 672
White House Office (WHO), 55, 56, 57
White House Special Investigation Unit (Plumbers), 631
Whitewater Affair, 692
Whittaker, Charles, 416
Wickard v. Filburn, 576
Wickersham, George W., 61
Wilder, Douglas, 728
William III, King of England, 11
Williams, Roger, 522
Williams, Wayne, 599
Williams v. Florida, 124
Williams v. Rhodes, 1112
Williamson v. Lee Optical Co., 460, 1023, 1116
Wills, Frank, 735
Wilson, James, 31
Wilson, John F., 522
Wilson, Woodrow, 663
Wilson v. Arkansas, 677
Wingate, George, 627
Winstar cases, 101
Wiretapping, 507–508, 701, 733
Wisconsin v. Yoder, 290, 643
Witness Security Program, 85
Witnesses, 584
Wolf v. Colorado, 534, 536
Wollstonecraft, Mary, 491
Women, working hours of, 912
Women's rights, 285, 492
Women's rights and issues, 839

Women's suffrage, 837, 864
Women's suffrage movement, 837
Wood, Gordon S., 21
Woods, Rose Mary, 737
Woodson v. North Carolina, 472
Woodson v. North Carolina and Gregg v. Georgia, 472–473
Worcester v. Georgia, 904
Works Progress Administration, 196
The World Faiths (Butler), 519
World Intellectual Property Organization Geneva, 565
World Intellectual Property Organization (WIPO), 562
World Trade Center attacks (2001), 1173
World Trade Center bombing (1993), 599
World War II, 615
World Wildlife Fund, 738–739. *See also* interest groups and lobbying
Worthy, William, 598
Wounded Knee, South Dakota, 598
Writ of certiorari, 63, 68, 89, 179, 923
Writ of habeas corpus, 79, 124, 178, 179–180, 283
Writ of mandamus, 64, 179, 612
Writ of prohibition, 179
Writ writing, 155
Wrongful death, 398
Wrythe, George, 578

Yick Wo v. Hopkins, 901, 965
The Yosemite (Muir), 686
Young, Edward, 283
Younger, Evelle J., 740
Younger v. Harris, 181, 274, 740–741
Yu Cong Eng v. Trinidad, 965

Zenger, John Peter, 12, 742–744. *See also* civil rights and civil liberties
Zoning laws, 637
Zorach v. Clauson, 681